16 YEARS

JEE MAIN

ONLINE 2020

PHASE I & II Solved Papers

Corporate Office

DISHA PUBLICATION

45, 2nd Floor, Maharishi Dayanand Marg,
Corner Market, Malviya Nagar, New Delhi - 110017
Tel : 49842349 / 49842350

Typeset by Disha DTP Team

www.dishapublication.com
Books &
ebooks for
School &
Competitive
Exams

www.mylearninggraph.com
Etests
for
Competitive
Exams

Write to us at **feedback_disha@aiets.co.in**

CONTENTS

TREND ANALYSIS OF JEE MAIN 2020 PHASE-1 & II

JEE MAIN 2020 – Phase-I

JEE MAIN 2020 – Phase-II

TREND ANALYSIS JEE MAIN 2020 PHASE-1 (PHYSICS)							
Chap. No.	Chapter Name	Exam Date And Shift (Morning/Evening)					
		7 JAN(M)	7 JAN(E)	8 JAN(M)	8 JAN(E)	9 JAN(M)	9 JAN(E)
1	Physical World, Units and Measurements	0	1	1	1	2	1
2	Motion in a Straight Line	0	0	0	1	1	0
3	Motion in a Plane	0	1	0	1	0	1
4	Laws of Motion	0	1	1	0	0	0
5	Work, Energy and Power	2	1	2	1	3	1
6	System of Particles and Rotational Motion	3	2	3	2	2	3
7	Gravitation	1	1	0	1	0	1
8	Mechanical Properties of Solids	0	0	0	0	1	1
9	Mechanical Properties of Fluids	0	1	1	1	1	1
10	Thermal Properties of Matter	1	1	1	1	0	0
11	Thermodynamics	2	1	1	1	1	1
12	Kinetic Theory	1	1	1	1	1	1
13	Oscillations	0	0	0	0	0	0
14	Waves	1	1	2	1	1	1
15	Electric Charges and Fields	1	1	1	1	2	1
16	Electrostatic Potential and Capacitance	1	1	1	2	0	0
17	Current Electricity	1	2	2	1	1	1
18	Moving Charges and Magnetism	0	0	1	2	2	2
19	Magnetism and Matter	0	1	0	0	0	0
20	Electromagnetic Induction	3	1	1	0	1	0
21	Alternating Current	1	1	0	1	0	1
22	Electromagnetic Waves	1	1	0	1	1	1
23	Ray Optics and Optical Instruments	1	1	3	1	1	1
24	Wave Optics	2	1	0	1	1	1
25	Dual Nature of Radiation and Matter	1	1	1	1	2	1
26	Atoms	1	0	1	1	0	1
27	Nuclei	0	1	0	0	0	0
28	Semiconductor Electronics : Materials, Devices and Simple Circuits	1	1	1	1	1	3
29	Communication Systems	0	0	0	0	0	0
	Total	25	25	25	25	25	25

TREND ANALYSIS JEE MAIN 2020 PHASE-1 (CHEMISTRY)							
Chap. No.	Chapter Name	Exam Date And Shift (Morning/Evening)					
		7 JAN(M)	7 JAN(E)	8 JAN(M)	8 JAN(E)	9 JAN(M)	9 JAN(E)
1	Some Basic Concepts of Chemistry	1	1	1	1	0	1
2	Structure of Atom	1	0	1	1	1	0

Chap. No.	Chapter Name	7 JAN(M)	7 JAN(E)	8 JAN(M)	8 JAN(E)	9 JAN(M)	9 JAN(E)
3	Classification of Elements and Periodicity in Properties	1	1	1	1	2	0
4	Chemical Bonding and Molecular Structure	2	1	0	0	1	0
5	States of Matter	1	1	1	0	0	0
6	Thermodynamics	1	1	1	1	1	1
7	Equilibrium	1	1	1	1	1	2
8	Redox Reactions	1	1	0	0	1	0
9	Hydrogen	1	1	0	1	1	1
10	The s-Block Elements	0	0	1	1	0	2
11	The p-Block Elements (gp - 13 & 14)	0	0	0	0	0	1
12	Organic Chemistry-Some Basic Principles and Techniques	0	1	0	0	1	2
13	Hydrocarbons	0	0	2	3	1	0
14	Environmental Chemistry	0	0	1	0	0	1
15	The Solid State	0	0	0	1	1	0
16	Solutions	1	1	1	0	2	1
17	Electrochemistry	1	1	1	1	1	0
18	Chemical Kinetics	1	2	1	1	1	1
19	Surface Chemistry	0	1	1	0	0	1
20	General Principles and Processes of Isolation of Elements	1	1	0	1	1	0
21	The p-Block Elements (gp - 15, 16, 17 & 18)	1	1	1	2	0	0
22	The d and f-Block Elements	1	1	1	1	1	2
23	Coordination Compounds	1	2	2	3	2	2
24	Haloalkanes and Haloarenes	2	2	0	0	1	1
25	Alcohols, Phenols and Ethers	0	0	2	1	1	1
26	Aldehydes, Ketones and Carboxylic Acids	1	0	1	1	1	1
27	Amines	1	1	0	0	1	2
28	Biomolecules	1	1	1	1	1	0
29	Polymers	0	0	0	1	0	1
30	Chemistry in Everyday Life	1	1	1	0	1	0
31	Analytical Chemistry	2	1	2	1	0	1
	Total	**25**	**25**	**25**	**25**	**25**	**25**

TREND ANALYSIS JEE MAIN 2020 PHASE-1 (MATHEMATICS)

Chap. No.	Chapter Name	Exam Date And Shift (Morning/Evening)					
		7 JAN(M)	7 JAN(E)	8 JAN(M)	8 JAN(E)	9 JAN(M)	9 JAN(E)
1	Sets	0	1	0	0	0	1
2	Relation and Function-I	0	0	0	1	0	0
3	Trigonometry Functions	1	0	0	1	2	1
4	Principle of Mathematical Induction	0	0	0	0	0	0
5	Complex Number and Quadratic Equations	2	2	2	2	2	2
6	Linear Inequalities	0	0	0	0	0	0
7	Permutations and Combinations	1	1	2	1	1	0
8	Binomial Theorem	0	1	0	1	1	2

9	Sequence and Series	2	2	2	2	1	2
10	Straight Lines and Pair of Straight Lines	2	1	0	0	1	0
11	Conic Sections	1	2	2	1	2	3
12	Introduction to 3-Dimensional Geometry	0	0	0	0	0	0
13	Limits and Derivatives	0	0	1	1	0	0
14	Mathematical Reasoning	1	1	1	1	1	1
15	Statistics	1	1	1	1	1	0
16	Probability-I	0	0	0	1	0	0
17	Relations and Functions-II	1	0	1	0	0	0
18	Inverse Trigonometric Functions	0	0	0	0	0	0
19	Matrices	0	0	1	1	0	0
20	Determinants	2	2	2	1	2	2
21	Continuity and Differentiability	3	3	2	1	1	3
22	Application of Derivatives	2	1	2	4	2	0
23	Integrals	1	2	1	1	3	2
24	Application of Integrals	1	1	1	1	0	1
25	Differential Equations	1	1	1	1	2	1
26	Vector Algebra	1	1	1	1	2	1
27	3-Dimensional Geometry	1	1	1	1	0	1
28	Linear Programming	0	0	0	0	0	0
29	Probability-II	1	1	1	0	1	2
	Total	**25**	**25**	**25**	**25**	**25**	**25**

TREND ANALYSIS JEE MAIN 2020 PHASE-2 (PHYSICS)

Chap. No.	Chapter Name	Exam Date And Shift (Morning/Evening)									
		2 Sep(M)	2 Sep(E)	3 Sep(M)	3 Sep(E)	4 Sep(M)	4 Sep(E)	5 Sep(M)	5 Sep(E)	6 Sep(M)	6 Sep(E)
1	Physical World, Units and Measurements	2	1	1	1	1	1	1	1	2	1
2	Motion in a Straight Line	1	0	0	0	1	1	1	1	0	0
3	Motion in a Plane	0	0	0	0	1	0	2	0	1	1
4	Laws of Motion	0	0	0	1	0	1	0	1	1	1
5	Work, Energy and Power	2	1	1	2	1	1	0	1	1	1
6	System of Particles and Rotational Motion	4	2	3	2	2	2	1	1	2	2
7	Gravitation	1	1	1	1	1	1	1	1	1	1
8	Mechanical Properties of Solids	0	0	0	0	0	1	0	0	1	0
9	Mechanical Properties of Fluids	0	1	2	0	1	1	1	1	0	1
10	Thermal Properties of Matter	0	1	1	2	1	0	1	1	0	1
11	Thermodynamics	1	1	1	1	0	1	1	1	0	1
12	Kinetic Theory	1	1	1	1	2	1	1	1	2	1
13	Oscillations	0	1	0	1	0	0	0	0	1	1
14	Waves	1	1	1	0	1	1	2	1	1	0
15	Electric Charges and Fields	1	1	0	0	1	1	0	0	1	2
16	Electrostatic Potential and Capacitance	1	2	2	2	1	1	2	3	1	0

17	Current Electricity	1	2	1	2	1	2	1	1	0	2
18	Moving Charges and Magnetism	1	2	2	1	1	0	2	1	2	2
19	Magnetism and Matter	1	0	0	1	1	2	0	2	0	0
20	Electromagnetic Induction	1	0	1	1	1	0	1	1	0	0
21	Alternating Current	0	1	1	0	0	1	0	0	3	1
22	Electromagnetic Waves	1	1	1	1	1	1	1	1	0	1
23	Ray Optics and Optical Instruments	1	1	1	1	1	1	2	1	1	1
24	Wave Optics	1	1	1	1	1	1	0	1	1	1
25	Dual Nature of Radiation and Matter	1	1	1	1	2	1	1	1	1	1
26	Atoms	0	1	0	0	1	0	1	0	0	0
27	Nuclei	1	0	1	1	0	1	1	1	1	1
28	Semiconductor Electronics : Materials, Devices and Simple Circuits	0	1	1	1	1	1	1	1	1	1
29	Communication Systems	1	0	0	0	0	0	0	0	0	0
	Total	**25**	**25**	**25**	**25**	**25**	**25**	**25**	**25**	**25**	**25**

TREND ANALYSIS JEE MAIN 2020 PHASE-2 (CHEMISTRY)

Chap. No.	Chapter Name	Exam Date And Shift (Morning/Evening)									
		2 Sep(M)	2 Sep(E)	3 Sep(M)	3 Sep(E)	4 Sep(M)	4 Sep(E)	5 Sep(M)	5 Sep(E)	6 Sep(M)	6 Sep(E)
1	Some Basic Concepts of Chemistry	0	1	1	2	2	1	1	1	1	1
2	Structure of Atom	1	2	0	1	1	1	2	1	0	0
3	Classification of Elements and Periodicity in Properties	1	1	1	2	2	1	0	1	1	1
4	Chemical Bonding and Molecular Structure	1	2	1	0	0	1	2	1	0	0
5	States of Matter	1	1	0	1	0	0	0	0	1	0
6	Thermodynamics	1	1	0	0	2	1	0	2	0	0
7	Equilibrium	1	0	1	1	1	1	2	1	3	2
8	Redox Reactions	1	1	0	0	0	1	0	0	0	0
9	Hydrogen	0	0	1	1	0	0	1	2	0	1
10	The s-Block Elements	1	1	0	0	1	1	0	0	1	1
11	The p-Block Elements (gp - 13 & 14)	0	0	0	0	0	0	0	0	0	0
12	Organic Chemistry-Some Basic Principles and Techniques	1	0	2	0	1	0	0	0	1	1
13	Hydrocarbons	1	0	1	0	0	0	0	2	3	1
14	Environmental Chemistry	1	0	1	1	0	1	1	0	1	0
15	The Solid State	0	0	1	0	0	0	1	1	0	1
16	Solutions	1	0	1	1	1	1	0	0	1	1
17	Electrochemistry	1	1	2	1	1	1	1	1	1	1
18	Chemical Kinetics	0	1	1	1	1	1	1	1	1	1
19	Surface Chemistry	2	2	1	1	1	1	1	1	1	1
20	General Principles and Processes of Isolation of Elements	0	1	0	0	1	0	1	1	1	2
21	The p-Block Elements (gp - 15, 16, 17 & 18)	1	0	3	0	1	1	0	1	2	2
22	The d and f-Block Elements	0	0	0	1	0	1	1	0	1	1
23	Coordination Compounds	2	2	2	2	2	2	2	2	1	1

Chap. No.	Chapter Name	2 Sep(M)	2 Sep(E)	3 Sep(M)	3 Sep(E)	4 Sep(M)	4 Sep(E)	5 Sep(M)	5 Sep(E)	6 Sep(M)	6 Sep(E)
24	Haloalkanes and Haloarenes	1	2	2	2	1	2	0	0	0	0
25	Alcohols, Phenols and Ethers	1	2	0	1	2	1	0	2	0	1
26	Aldehydes, Ketones and Carboxylic Acids	1	1	1	3	2	2	3	0	1	1
27	Amines	0	0	0	1	0	1	2	1	1	1
28	Biomolecules	1	1	0	1	2	1	2	1	0	1
29	Polymers	0	0	0	0	0	0	0	1	1	1
30	Chemistry in Everyday Life	1	0	1	1	0	1	1	1	0	0
31	Analytical Chemistry	2	2	1	0	0	0	0	0	1	1
	Total	**25**	**25**	**25**	**25**	**25**	**25**	**25**	**25**	**25**	**25**

TREND ANALYSIS JEE MAIN 2020 PHASE-2 (MATHEMATICS)

Chap. No.	Chapter Name	Exam Date And Shift (Morning/Evening)									
		2 Sep(M)	2 Sep(E)	3 Sep(M)	3 Sep(E)	4 Sep(M)	4 Sep(E)	5 Sep(M)	5 Sep(E)	6 Sep(M)	6 Sep(E)
1	Sets	0	0	0	0	1	1	1	0	1	0
2	Relation and Function-I	1	1	0	1	1	0	0	0	0	0
3	Trigonometry Functions	0	2	0	0	0	0	0	1	0	0
4	Principle of Mathematical Induction	0	0	0	0	0	0	0	0	0	0
5	Complex Number and Quadratic Equations	2	1	2	2	1	2	2	2	1	2
6	Linear Inequalities	0	0	1	0	0	0	0	0	1	0
7	Permutations and Combinations	1	1	1	1	0	1	1	1	1	1
8	Binomial Theorem	1	1	1	1	2	1	1	1	1	1
9	Sequence and Series	2	3	2	2	2	1	2	2	2	2
10	Straight Lines and Pair of Straight Lines	0	0	0	1	1	1	1	0	1	1
11	Conic Sections	3	2	3	2	2	3	3	2	2	2
12	Limits and Derivatives	1	1	2	1	0	0	1	1	0	0
13	Mathematical Reasoning	1	1	1	1	1	1	1	1	1	1
14	Statistics	1	1	1	1	1	2	1	1	1	1
15	Probability-I	0	0	0	0	0	0	0	0	0	1
16	Relations and Functions-II	0	0	0	0	0	0	0	1	1	1
17	Inverse Trigonometric Functions	0	0	1	0	0	0	1	0	0	0
18	Matrices	1	1	1	0	1	0	0	0	0	0
19	Determinants	2	1	1	2	1	2	2	2	1	2
20	Continuity and Differentiability	1	1	1	0	3	1	2	1	0	2
21	Application of Derivatives	3	2	1	3	0	1	0	3	3	2
22	Integrals	1	1	1	2	3	2	2	1	2	1
23	Application of Integrals	0	1	1	0	0	0	0	1	1	1
24	Differential Equations	1	1	1	1	1	2	1	1	1	1
25	Vector Algebra	1	1	1	1	1	1	1	1	1	1
26	3-Dimensional Geometry	1	1	2	2	1	1	1	1	1	1
27	Probability-II	1	1	1	1	1	1	1	1	0	0
28	Properties of Triangle	1	0	0	0	1	1	1	0	2	1
	Total	**25**	**25**	**25**	**25**	**25**	**25**	**25**	**25**	**25**	**25**

JEE MAIN 2020
(Held on 07-01-2020 Morning Shift)

PHYSICS

1. A litre of dry air at STP expands adiabatically to a volume of 3 litres. If $\gamma = 1.40$, the work done by air is: $(3^{1.4} = 4.6555)$ [Take air to be an ideal gas]

(1) 60.7 J
(2) 90.5 J
(3) 100.8 J
(4) 48 J

2. A 60 HP electric motor lifts an elevator having a maximum total load capacity of 2000 kg. If the frictional force on the elevator is 4000 N, the speed of the elevator at full load is close to: (1 HP = 746 W, g = 10 ms^{-2})

(1) 1.7 ms^{-1}
(2) 1.9 ms^{-1}
(3) 1.5 ms^{-1}
(4) 2.0 ms^{-1}

3. As shown in the figure, a bob of mass m is tied by a massless string whose other end portion is wound on a fly wheel (disc) of radius r and mass m. When released from rest the bob starts falling vertically. When it has covered a distance of h, the angular speed of the wheel will be:

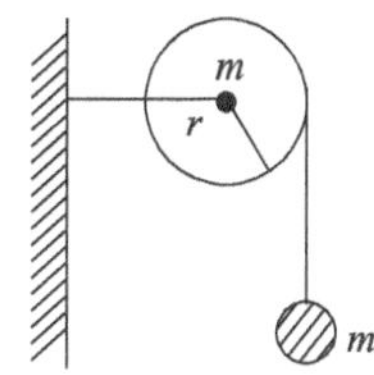

(1) $\dfrac{1}{r}\sqrt{\dfrac{4gh}{3}}$
(2) $r\sqrt{\dfrac{3}{2gh}}$
(3) $\dfrac{1}{r}\sqrt{\dfrac{2gh}{3}}$
(4) $r\sqrt{\dfrac{3}{4gh}}$

4. Which of the following gives a reversible operation?

(1) 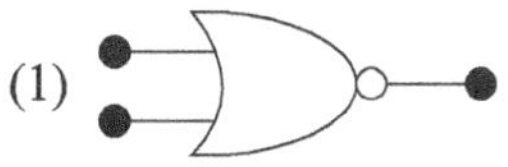

(2) 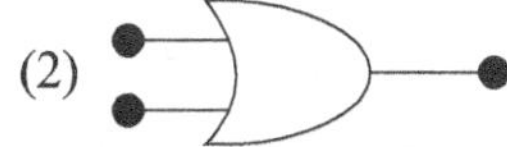

(3) 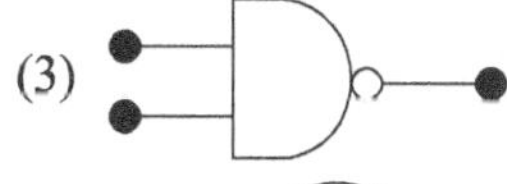

(4) 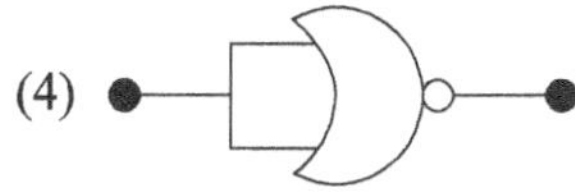

5. Consider a circular coil of wire carrying constant current I, forming a magnetic dipole. The magnetic flux through an infinite plane that contains the circular coil and excluding the circular coil area is given by ϕ_i. The magnetic flux through the area of the circular coil area is given by ϕ_0. Which of the following option is correct?

(1) $\phi_i = \phi_0$
(2) $\phi_i > \phi_0$
(3) $\phi_i < \phi_0$
(4) $\phi_i = -\phi_0$

6. A polarizer - analyser set is adjusted such that the intensity of light coming out of the analyser is just 10% of the original intensity. Assuming that the polarizer - analyser set does not absorb any light, the angle by which the analyser need to be rotated further to reduce the output intensity to be zero, is:

(1) 71.6°
(2) 18.4°
(3) 90°
(4) 45°

7. A LCR circuit behaves like a damped harmonic oscillator. Comparing it with a physical spring-mass damped oscillator having damping constant 'b', the correct equivalence would be:

(1) $L \leftrightarrow m, C \leftrightarrow k, R \leftrightarrow b$

(2) $L \leftrightarrow \dfrac{1}{b}, C \leftrightarrow \dfrac{1}{m}, R \leftrightarrow \dfrac{1}{k}$

(3) $L \leftrightarrow k, C \leftrightarrow b, R \leftrightarrow m$

(4) $L \leftrightarrow m, C \leftrightarrow \dfrac{1}{k}, R \leftrightarrow b$

8. A satellite of mass m is launched vertically upwards with an initial speed u from the surface of the earth. After it reaches height R (R = radius of the earth), it ejects a rocket of mass $\dfrac{m}{10}$ so that subsequently the satellite moves in a circular orbit. The kinetic energy of the rocket is (G is the gravitational constant; M is the mass of the earth):

(1) $\dfrac{m}{20}\left(u^2 + \dfrac{113}{200}\dfrac{GM}{R}\right)$

(2) $5m\left(u^2 - \dfrac{119}{200}\dfrac{GM}{R}\right)$

(3) $\dfrac{3m}{8}\left(u + \sqrt{\dfrac{5GM}{6R}}\right)^2$

(4) $\dfrac{m}{20}\left(u - \sqrt{\dfrac{2GM}{3R}}\right)^2$

9. A long solenoid of radius R carries a time (t) - dependent current $I(t) = I_0 t(1 - t)$. A ring of radius $2R$ is placed coaxially near its middle. During the time interval $0 \le t \le 1$, the induced current (I_R) and the induced $EMF(V_R)$ in the ring change as:

(1) Direction of I_R remains unchanged and V_R is maximum at $t = 0.5$

(2) At $t = 0.25$ direction of I_R reverses and V_R is maximum

(3) Direction of I_R remains unchanged and V_R is zero at $t = 0.25$

(4) At $t = 0.5$ direction of I_R reverses and V_R is zero

10. Speed of a transverse wave on a straight wire (mass 6.0 g, length 60 cm and area of cross-section 1.0 mm^2) is 90 ms^{-1}. If the Young's modulus of wire is 16×10^{11} Nm^{-2} the extension of wire over its natural length is:

(1) 0.03 mm (2) 0.02 mm
(3) 0.04 mm (4) 0.01 mm

11. Two moles of an ideal gas with $\dfrac{C_p}{C_V} = \dfrac{5}{3}$ are mixed with 3 moles of another ideal gas with $\dfrac{C_p}{C_V} = \dfrac{4}{3}$. The value of $\dfrac{C_p}{C_V}$ for the mixture is:

(1) 1. 45 (2) 1.50
(3) 1.47 (4) 1.42

12. If we need a magnification of 375 from a compound microscope of tube length 150 mm and an objective of focal length 5 mm, the focal length of the eye-piece, should be close to:

(1) 22 mm (2) 12 mm
(3) 2 mm (4) 33 mm

13. The time period of revolution of electron in its ground state orbit in a hydrogen atom is 1.6×10^{-16} s. The frequency of revolution of the electron in its first excited state (in s^{-1}) is:

(1) 1.6×10^{14} (2) 7.8×10^{14}
(3) 6.2×10^{15} (4) 5.6×10^{12}

14. A parallel plate capacitor has plates of area A separated by distance 'd' between them. It is filled with a dielectric which has a dielectric constant that varies as $k(x) = K(1 + \alpha x)$ where 'x' is the distance measured from one of the plates. If $(\alpha d) \ll 1$, the total capacitance of the system is best given by the expression:

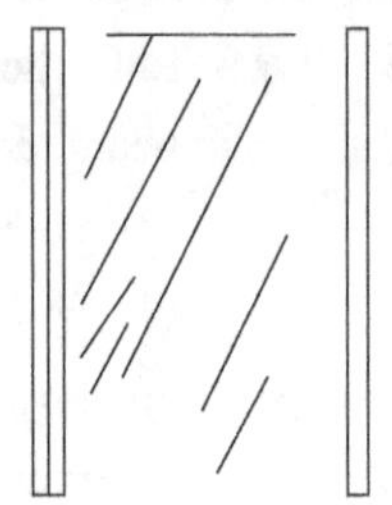

(1) $\dfrac{AK \in_0}{d}\left(1 + \dfrac{\alpha d}{2}\right)$

(2) $\dfrac{A \in_0 K}{d}\left(1 + \left(\dfrac{\alpha d}{2}\right)^2\right)$

(3) $\dfrac{A \in_0 K}{d}\left(1 + \dfrac{\alpha^2 d^2}{2}\right)$

(4) $\dfrac{AK \in_0}{d}(1 + \alpha d)$

15. The current I_1 (in A) flowing through 1 Ω resistor in the following circuit is:

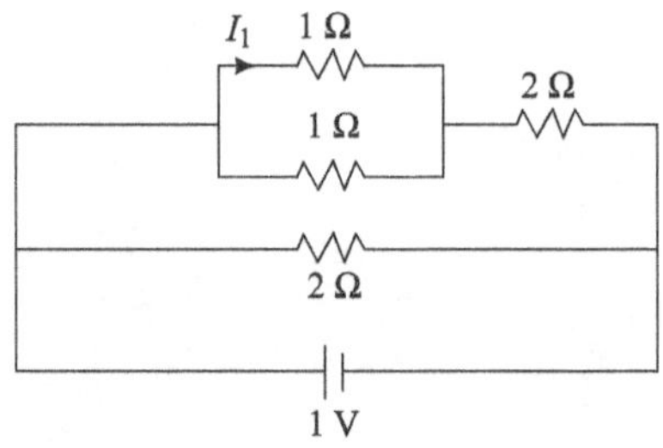

(1) 0.4 (2) 0.5
(3) 0.2 (4) 0.25

16. Visible light of wavelength 6000×10^{-8} cm falls normally on a single slit and produces a diffraction pattern. It is found that the second diffraction minimum is at 60° from the central maximum. If the first minimum is produced at θ_1, then θ_1 is close to:

(1) 20° (2) 30°
(3) 25° (4) 45°

17. Three point particles of masses 1.0 kg, 1.5 kg and 2.5 kg are placed at three corners of a right angle triangle of sides 4.0 cm, 3.0 cm and 5.0 cm as shown in the figure. The center of mass of the system is at a point:

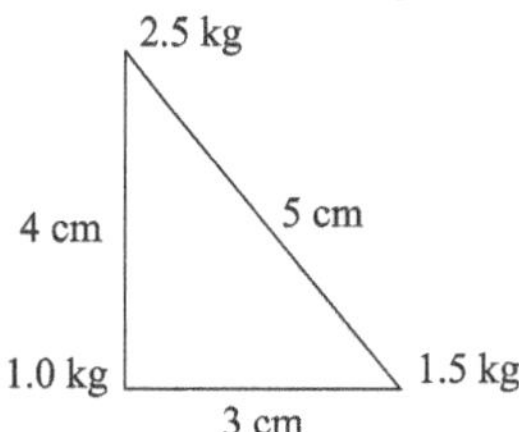

(1) 0.6 cm right and 2.0 cm above 1 kg mass
(2) 1.5 cm right and 1.2 cm above 1 kg mass
(3) 2.0 cm right and 0.9 cm above 1 kg mass
(4) 0.9 cm right and 2.0 cm above 1 kg mass

18. Two infinite planes each with uniform surface charge density $+\sigma$ are kept in such a way that the angle between them is 30°. The electric field in the region shown between them is given by:

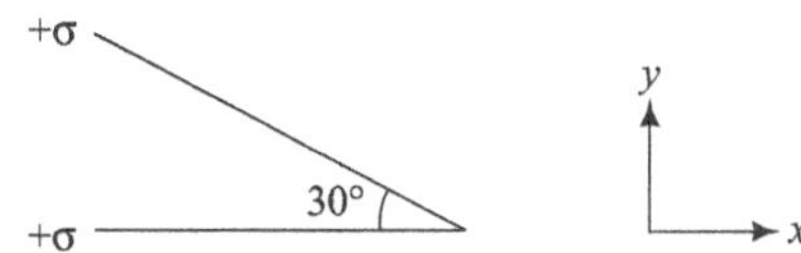

(1) $\dfrac{\sigma}{2\epsilon_0}\left[(1+\sqrt{3})\hat{y}-\dfrac{\hat{x}}{2}\right]$

(2) $\dfrac{\sigma}{\epsilon_0}\left[\left(1+\dfrac{\sqrt{3}}{2}\right)\hat{y}+\dfrac{\hat{x}}{2}\right]$

(3) $\dfrac{\sigma}{2\epsilon_0}\left[(1+\sqrt{3})\hat{y}+\dfrac{\hat{x}}{2}\right]$

(4) $\dfrac{\sigma}{2\epsilon_0}\left[\left(1-\dfrac{\sqrt{3}}{2}\right)\hat{y}-\dfrac{\hat{x}}{2}\right]$

19. If the magnetic field in a plane electromagnetic wave is given by $\vec{B} = 3 \times 10^{-8} \sin(1.6 \times 10^3 x + 48 \times 10^{10} t)\,\hat{j}$ T, then what will be expression for electric field?

(1) $\vec{E} = (60 \sin(1.6 \times 10^3 x + 48 \times 10^{10} t)\,\hat{k}$ v/m)

(2) $\vec{E} = (9 \sin(1.6 \times 10^3 x + 48 \times 10^{10} t)\,\hat{k}$ v/m)

(3) $\vec{E} = (3 \times 10^{-8} \sin(1.6 \times 10^3 x + 48 \times 10^{10} t)\,\hat{j}$ v/m)

(4) $\vec{E} = (3 \times 10^{-8}\sin(1.6 \times 10^3 x + 48 \times 10^{10} t)\,\hat{i}$ v/m)

20. The radius of gyration of a uniform rod of length l, about an axis passing through a point $\dfrac{l}{4}$ away from the centre of the rod, and perpendicular to it, is:

(1) $\dfrac{1}{4}l$

(2) $\dfrac{1}{8}l$

(3) $\sqrt{\dfrac{7}{48}}l$

(4) $\sqrt{\dfrac{3}{8}}l$

21. A Carnot engine operates between two reservoirs of temperatures 900 K and 300 K. The engine performs 1200 J of work per cycle. The heat energy (in J) delivered by the engine to the low temperature reservoir, in a cycle, is __________ .

22. A non-isotropic solid metal cube has coefficients of linear expansion as: $5 \times 10^{-5}/°C$ along the x-axis and $5 \times 10^{-6}/°C$ along the y and the z-axis. If the coefficient of volume expansion of the solid is $C \times 10^{-6}/°C$ then the value of C is ________ .

23. A loop ABCDEFA of straight edges has six corner points $A(0, 0, 0)$, $B\{5, 0, 0)$, $C(5, 5, 0)$, $D(0, 5, 0)$, $E(0, 5, 5)$ and $F(0, 0, 5)$. The magnetic field in this region is $\vec{B} = (3\hat{i} + 4\hat{k})$T. The quantity of flux through the loop ABCDEFA (in Wb) is ________ .

24. A particle ($m = 1$ kg) slides down a frictionless track (AOC) starting from rest at a point A (height 2 m). After reaching C, the particle continues to move freely in air as a projectile. When it reaching its highest point P (height 1 m), the kinetic energy of the particle (in J) is: (Figure drawn is schematic and not to scale; take $g = 10$ ms^{-2}) ________ .

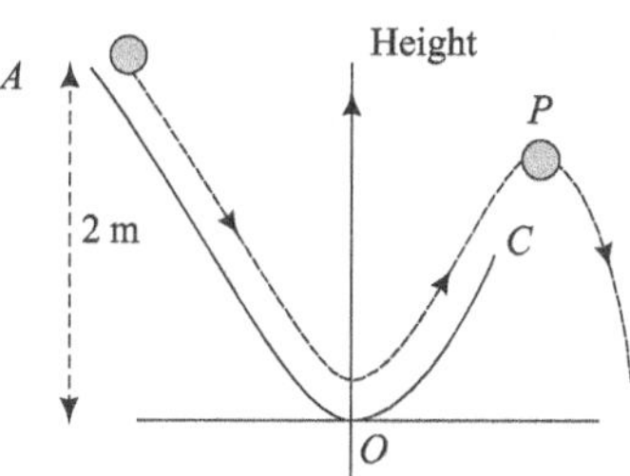

25. A beam of electromagnetic radiation of intensity 6.4×10^{-5} W/cm^2 is comprised of wavelength, $\lambda = 310$ nm. It falls normally on a metal (work function $\varphi = 2$eV) of surface area of 1 cm^2. If one in 10^3 photons ejects an electron, total number of electrons ejected in 1 s is 10^x. ($hc = 1240$ eVnm, 1 eV $= 1.6 \times 10^{-19}$ J), then x is ________ .

CHEMISTRY

26. The number of orbitals associated with quantum numbers $n = 5$, $m_s = +\frac{1}{2}$ is:

(1) 11   (2) 25

(3) 50   (4) 15

27. Given that the standard potentials (E^0) of Cu^{2+}/Cu and Cu^+/Cu are 0.34 V and 0.522 V respectively, the E^0 of Cu^{2+}/Cu^+ is:

(1) $+ 0.182$ V   (2) $+ 0.158$ V

(3) $- 0.182$ V   (4) $- 0.158$ V

28. In comparison to the zeolite process for the removal of permanent hardness, the synthetic resins method is:

(1) less efficient as it exchanges only anions

(2) more efficient as it can exchange both cations as well as anions

(3) less efficient as the resins cannot be regenerated

(4) more efficient as it can exchange only cations

29. Match the following:

(i) Riboflavin   (a) Beriberi

(ii) Thiamine   (b) Scurvy

(iii) Pyridoxine   (c) Cheilosis

(iv) Ascorbic acid   (d) Convulsions

(1) (i) – (a), (ii) – (d), (iii) – (c), (iv) – (b)

(2) (i) – (c), (ii) – (d), (iii) – (a), (iv) – (b)

(3) (i) – (c), (ii) – (a), (iii) – (d), (iv) – (b)

(4) (i) – (d), (ii) – (b), (iii) – (a), (iv) – (c)

30. At 35 °C, the vapour pressure of CS_2 is 512 mm Hg and that of acetone is 344 mm Hg. A solution of CS_2 in acetone has a total vapour pressure of 600 mm Hg. The false statement amongst the following is:

(1) Raoult's law is not obeyed by this system

(2) a mixture of 100 mL CS_2 and 100 mL acetone has a volume < 200 mL

(3) CS_2 and acetone are less attracted to each other than to themselves

(4) heat must be absorbed in order to produce the solution at 35 °C

31. A solution of m-chloroaniline, m-chlorophenol and m-chlorobenzoic acid in ethyl acetate was extracted initially with a saturated solution of $NaHCO_3$ to give fraction A. The left over organic phase was extracted with dilute NaOH solution to give fraction B. The final organic layer was labelled as fraction C. Fractions A, B and C, contain respectively:

(1) m-chlorobenzoic acid, m-chloroaniline and m-chlorophenol

(2) m-chlorobenzoic acid, m-chlorophenol and m-chloroaniline

(3) m-chlorophenol, m-chlorobenzoic acid and m-chloroaniline

(4) m-chloroaniline, m-chlorobenzoic acid and m-chlorophenol

32. What is the product of following reaction?

Hex-3-ynal

(i) $\xrightarrow{\text{NaBH}_4}$?

(ii) PBr_3

(iii) Mg/ether

(iv) CO_2/H_3O^+

(1) 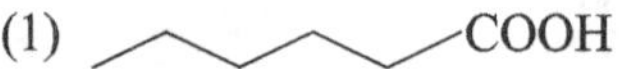 COOH

(2) 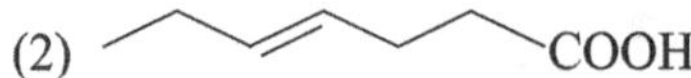 COOH

(3) /=\ COOH

(4) —≡— COOH

33. Amongst the following statements, that which was not proposed by Dalton was:

(1) Chemical reactions involve reorganization of atoms. These are neither created nor destroyed in a chemical reaction.

(2) All the atoms of a given element have identical properties including identical mass. Atoms of different elements differ in mass.

(3) When gases combine or reproduced in a chemical reaction they do so in a simple ratio by volume provided all gases are at the same T & P.

(4) Matter consists of indivisible atoms.

34. The dipole moments of CCl_4, $CHCl_3$ and CH_4 are in the order:

(1) $CHCl_3 < CH_4 = CCl_4$

(2) $CCl_4 < CH_4 < CHCl_3$

(3) $CH_4 < CCl_4 < CHCl_3$

(4) $CH_4 = CCl_4 < CHCl_3$

35. The IUPAC name of the complex $[Pt(NH_3)_2Cl(NH_2CH_3)]Cl$ is:

(1) Diamminechlorido (methanamine) platinum (II) chloride

(2) Diammine (methanamine) chlorido platinum (II) chloride

(3) Diamminechlorido (aminomethane) platinum (II) chloride

(4) Bisammine (methanamine) chlorido platinum (II) chloride

36. The purest form of commercial iron is:

(1) pig iron

(2) wrought iron

(3) cast iron

(4) scrap iron and pig iron

37. The electron gain enthalpy (in kj/mol) of fluorine, chlorine, bromine and iodine, respectively, are:

(1) –296, –325, –333 and –349

(2) –349, –333, –325 and –296

(3) –333, –349, –325 and –296

(4) –333, –325, –349 and –296

38. 1-methyl ethylene oxide when treated with an excess of HBr produces:

(1) 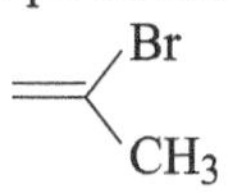

(2) 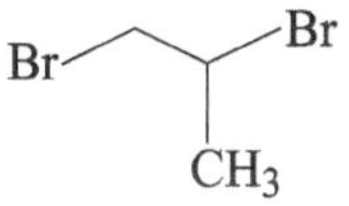

(3) 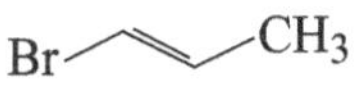

(4) 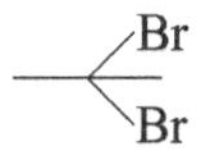

39. The increasing order of pK_b for the following compounds will be:

$NH_2-CH=NH$,

(A)

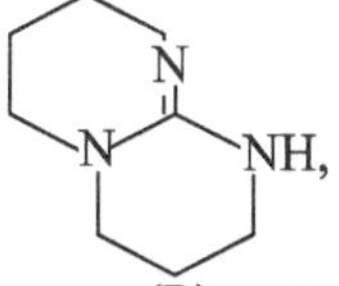

(B)

CH_3NHCH_3

(C)

(1) (B) < (C) < (A) (2) (A) < (B) < (C)

(3) (C) < (A) < (B) (4) (B) < (A) < (C)

40. Oxidation number of potassium in K_2O, K_2O_2 and KO_2, respectively, is:

(1) +2, +1 and $+\frac{1}{2}$

(2) +1, +1 and +1

(3) +1, +4 and +2

(4) +1, +2 and +4

41. Consider the following reaction:

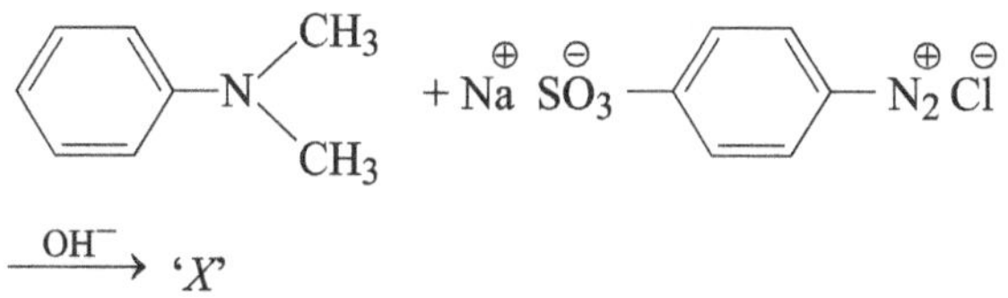

The product '*X*' is used:

(1) in protein estimation as an alternative to ninhydrin

(2) in acid base titration as an indicator

(3) as food grade colourant

(4) in laboratory test for phenols

42. The atomic radius of Ag is closest to:

(1) Au (2) Ni

(3) Cu (4) Hg

43. The theory that can completely/properly explain the nature of bonding in $[Ni(CO)_4]$ is:

(1) Werner's theory

(2) Molecular orbital theory

(3) Crystal field theory

(4) Valence bond theory

44. Consider the following reactions:

(a) $(CH_3)_3CCH(OH)CH_3 \xrightarrow{conc.H_2SO_4}$

(b) $(CH_3)_2CHCH(Br)CH_3 \xrightarrow{alc.KOH}$

(c) $(CH_3)_2CHCH(Br)CH_3 \xrightarrow{(CH_3)_3O^-K^\oplus}$

(d) $(CH_3)_2C(OH)-CH_2-CHO \xrightarrow{\Delta}$

Which of these reaction(s) will not produce Saytzeff product?

(1) (a), (c) and (d)

(2) (d) only

(3) (c) only

(4) (b) and (d)

45. The relative strength of interionic/ intermolecular forces in decreasing order is:

(1) dipole-dipole > ion-dipole > ion-ion

(2) ion-dipole > ion-ion > dipole-dipole

(3) ion-dipole > dipole-dipole > ion-ion

(4) ion-ion > ion-dipole > dipole-dipole

46. Chlorine reacts with hot and concentrated NaOH and produces compounds (X) and (Y). Compound (X) gives white precipitate with silver nitrate solution. The average bond order between Cl and O atoms in (Y) is ________.

47. The number of chiral carbons in chloramphenicol is ________

48. During the nuclear explosion, one of the products is ^{90}Sr with half life of 6.93 years. If 1 μg of ^{90}Sr was absorbed in the bones of a newly born baby in place of Ca, how much time, in years, is required to reduce it by 90% if it is not lost metabolically ________.

49. For the reaction ;
$A(l) \rightarrow 2B(g)$
$\Delta U = 2.1$ kcal, $\Delta S = 20$ cal K^{-1} at 300 K.
Hence ΔG in kcal is ________.

50. Two solutions, A and B, each of 100 L was made by dissolving 4g of NaOH and 9.8 g of H_2SO_4 in water, respectively. The pH of the resultant solution obtained from mixing 40 L of solution A and 10 L of solution. B is ________.

MATHEMATICS

51. If $y(\alpha) = \sqrt{2\left(\dfrac{\tan\alpha + \cot\alpha}{1 + \tan^2\alpha}\right) + \dfrac{1}{\sin^2\alpha}}, \alpha \in \left(\dfrac{3\pi}{4}, \pi\right),$

then $\dfrac{dy}{d\alpha}$ at $\alpha = \dfrac{5\pi}{6}$ is:

(1) 4   (2) $\dfrac{4}{3}$

(3) −4   (4) $-\dfrac{1}{4}$

52. Five numbers are in A.P., whose sum is 25 and product is 2520. If one of these five numbers is $-\dfrac{1}{2}$, then the greatest number amongst them is:

(1) 27   (2) 7

(3) $\dfrac{21}{2}$ (4) 16

53. If $g(x) = x^2 + x - 1$ and $(g \circ f)(x) = 4x^2 - 10x + 5$, then $f\left(\dfrac{5}{4}\right)$ is equal to:

(1) $\dfrac{3}{2}$ (2) $-\dfrac{1}{2}$

(3) $\dfrac{1}{2}$ (4) $-\dfrac{3}{2}$

54. Total number of 6-digit numbers in which only and all the five digits 1, 3, 5, 7 and 9 appear, is:

(1) $\dfrac{1}{2}(6!)$ (2) 6!

(3) 5^6 (4) $\dfrac{5}{2}(6!)$

55. A vector $\vec{a} = \alpha\hat{i} + 2\hat{j} + \beta\hat{k}$ ($\alpha, \beta \in \mathbf{R}$) lies in the plane of the vectors, $\vec{b} = \hat{i} + \hat{j}$ and $\vec{c} = \hat{i} - \hat{j} + 4\hat{k}$. If $\vec{a}$ bisects the angle between $\vec{b}$ and $\vec{c}$, then:

(1) $\vec{a} \cdot \hat{i} + 3 = 0$ (2) $\vec{a} \cdot \hat{i} + 1 = 0$

(3) $\vec{a} \cdot \hat{k} + 2 = 0$ (4) $\vec{a} \cdot \hat{k} + 4 = 0$

56. Let $x^k + y^k = a^k$, $(a, k > 0)$ and $\dfrac{dy}{dx} + \left(\dfrac{y}{x}\right)^{\frac{1}{3}} = 0$, then k is:

(1) $\dfrac{3}{2}$ (2) $\dfrac{4}{3}$

(3) $\dfrac{2}{3}$ (4) $\dfrac{1}{3}$

57. Let α and β be two real roots of the equation $(k + 1)\tan^2 x - \sqrt{2} \cdot \lambda\tan x = (1 - k)$, where $k(\neq -1)$ and λ are real numbers. If $\tan^2(\alpha + \beta) = 50$, then a value of λ is:

(1) $10\sqrt{2}$ (2) 10

(3) 5   (4) $5\sqrt{2}$

58. If $f(a + b + 1 - x) = f(x)$, for all x, where a and b are fixed positive real numbers,

then $\dfrac{1}{a+b}\displaystyle\int_a^b x(f(x) + f(x+1))dx$ is equal to:

(1) $\displaystyle\int_{a+1}^{b+1} f(x)dx$ (2) $\displaystyle\int_{a-1}^{b-1} f(x)dx$

(3) $\displaystyle\int_{a-1}^{b-1} f(x+1)dx$ (4) $\displaystyle\int_{a+1}^{b+1} f(x+1)dx$

59. The area of the region, enclosed by the circle $x^2 + y^2 = 2$ which is not common to the region bounded by the parabola $y^2 = x$ and the straight line $y = x$, is:

(1) $\dfrac{1}{6}(24\pi - 1)$

(2) $\dfrac{1}{3}(6\pi - 1)$

(3) $\dfrac{1}{3}(12\pi - 1)$

(4) $\dfrac{1}{6}(12\pi - 1)$

60. If the system of linear equations

$2x + 2ay + az = 0$

$2x + 3by + bz = 0$

$2x + 4cy + cz = 0,$

where $a, b, c \in R$ are non-zero and distinct; has a non-zero solution, then:

(1) $\dfrac{1}{a}, \dfrac{1}{b}, \dfrac{1}{c}$ are in A.P.

(2) a, b, c are in G.P.

(3) $a + b + c = 0$

(4) a, b, c are in A.P.

61. Let P be a plane passing through the points $(2, 1, 0)$, $(4, 1, 1)$ and $(5, 0, 1)$ and R be any point $(2, 1, 6)$. Then the image of R in the plane P is:

(1) $(6, 5, 2)$ (2) $(6, 5, -2)$

(3) $(4, 3, 2)$ (4) $(3, 4, -2)$

62. The logical statement

$(p \Rightarrow q) \wedge (q \Rightarrow \sim p)$ is equivalent to:

(1) p (2) q

(3) $\sim P$ (4) $\sim q$

63. If the distance between the foci of an ellipse is 6 and the distance between its directrices is 12, then the length of its latus rectum is:

(1) $\sqrt{3}$ (2) $3\sqrt{2}$

(3) $\dfrac{3}{\sqrt{2}}$ (4) $2\sqrt{3}$

64. An unbiased coin is tossed 5 times. Suppose that a variable X is assigned the value k when k consecutive heads are obtained for $k = 3, 4, 5$, otherwise X takes the value -1.

Then the expected value of X, is:

(1) $\dfrac{3}{16}$ (2) $\dfrac{1}{8}$

(3) $-\dfrac{3}{16}$ (4) $-\dfrac{1}{8}$

65. If $y = mx + 4$ is a tangent to both the parabolas, $y^2 = 4x$ and $x^2 = 2by$, then b is equal to:

(1) -32 (2) -64

(3) -128 (4) 128

66. The greatest positive integer k, for which $49^k + 1$ is a factor of the sum $49^{125} + 49^{124} + \dots + 49^2 + 49 + 1$, is:

(1) 32 (2) 63

(3) 60 (4) 65

67. If $\text{Re}\left(\dfrac{z-1}{2z+i}\right) = 1$, where $z = x + iy$, then the point (x, y) lies on a:

(1) circle whose centre is at $\left(-\dfrac{1}{2}, -\dfrac{3}{2}\right)$.

(2) straight line whose slope is $-\dfrac{2}{3}$.

(3) straight line whose slope is $\dfrac{3}{2}$.

(4) circle whose diameter is $\dfrac{\sqrt{5}}{2}$.

68. Let α be a root of the equation $x^2 + x + 1 = 0$ and the matrix $A = \dfrac{1}{\sqrt{3}}\begin{bmatrix} 1 & 1 & 1 \\ 1 & \alpha & \alpha^2 \\ 1 & \alpha^2 & \alpha^4 \end{bmatrix}$,

then the matrix A^{31} is equal to:

(1) A (2) I_3

(3) A^2 (4) A^3

69. If $y = y(x)$ is the solution of the differential equation,

$e^y\left(\dfrac{dy}{dx} - 1\right) = e^x$ such that $y(0) = 0$, then $y(1)$ is equal to:

(1) $1 + \log_e 2$

(2) $2 + \log_e 2$

(3) $2e$

(4) $\log_e 2$

70. Let the function, $f: [-7, 0] \to R$ be continuous on $[-7, 0]$ and differentiable on $(-7, 0)$. If $f(-7) = -3$ and $f'(x) \le 2$, for all $x \in (-7, 0)$, then for all such functions f, $f'(-1) + f(0)$ lies in the interval:

(1) $(-\infty, 20]$

(2) $[-3, 11]$

(3) $(-\infty, 11]$

(4) $[-6, 20]$

71. $\lim\limits_{x \to 2} \dfrac{3^x + 3^{3-x} - 12}{3^{-x/2} - 3^{1-x}}$ is equal to ———.

72. If the sum of the coefficients of all even powers of x in the product
$$(1 + x + x^2 + \ldots + x^{2n})(1 - x + x^2 - x^3 + \ldots + x^{2n})$$ is 61, then n is equal to ———.

73. Let S be the set of points where the function, $f(x) = |2 - |x - 3||, x \in R$, is not differentiable. Then $\sum\limits_{x \in S} f(f(x))$ is equal to ———.

74. If the variance of the first n natural numbers is 10 and the variance of the first m even natural numbers is 16, then $m + n$ is equal to ———.

75. Let $A(1, 0)$, $B(6, 2)$ and $C\left(\dfrac{3}{2}, 6\right)$ be the vertices of a triangle ABC. If P is a point inside the triangle ABC such that the triangles APC, APB and BPC have equal areas, then the length of the line segment PQ, where Q is the point $\left(-\dfrac{7}{6}, -\dfrac{1}{3}\right)$, is ———.

PHYSICS

1. A mass of 10 kg is suspended by a rope of length 4 m, from the ceiling. A force F is applied horizontally at the mid-point of the rope such that the top half of the rope makes an angle of 45° with the vertical. Then F equals: (Take $g = 10$ ms^{-2} and the rope to be massless)

(1) 100 N

(2) 90 N

(3) 70 N

(4) 75 N

2. A particle of mass m and charge q has an initial velocity $\vec{v} = v_0\hat{j}$. If an electric field $\vec{E} = E_0\hat{i}$ and magnetic field $\vec{B} = B_0\hat{i}$ act on the particle, its speed will double after a time:

(1) $\dfrac{2mv_0}{qE_0}$

(2) $\dfrac{3mv_0}{qE_0}$

(3) $\dfrac{\sqrt{3}mv_0}{qE_0}$

(4) $\dfrac{\sqrt{2}mv_0}{qE_0}$

3. In a building there are 15 bulbs of 45 W, 15 bulbs of 100 W, 15 small fans of 10 W and 2 heaters of 1 kW. The voltage of electric main is 220 V. The minimum fuse capacity (rated value) of the building will be:

(1) 10 A

(2) 25 A

(3) 15 A

(4) 20 A

4. An ideal fluid flows (laminar flow) through a pipe of non-uniform diameter. The maximum and minimum diameters of the pipes are 6.4 cm and 4.8 cm, respectively. The ratio of the minimum and the maximum velocities of fluid in this pipe is:

(1) $\dfrac{9}{16}$

(2) $\dfrac{\sqrt{3}}{2}$

(3) $\dfrac{3}{4}$

(4) $\dfrac{81}{256}$

5. The dimensions of $\dfrac{B^2}{2\mu_0}$, where B is magnetic field and μ_0 is the magnetic permeability of vacuum, is:

(1) MLT^{-2}

(2) ML^2T^{-1}

(3) ML^2T^{-2}

(4) $ML^{-1}T^{-2}$

6. The electric field of a plane electromagnetic wave is given by

$$\vec{E} = E_0\frac{\hat{i}+\hat{j}}{\sqrt{2}}\cos(kz+\omega t)$$

At $t = 0$, a positively charged particle is at the point $(x, y, z) = \left(0, 0, \dfrac{\pi}{k}\right)$. If its instantaneous velocity at $(t = 0)$ is $v_0\hat{k}$, the force acting on it due to the wave is:

(1) parallel to $\dfrac{\hat{i}+\hat{j}}{\sqrt{2}}$

(2) zero

(3) antiparallel to $\dfrac{\hat{i}+\hat{j}}{\sqrt{2}}$

(4) parallel to $\hat{k}$

7. An elevator in a building can carry a maximum of 10 persons, with the average mass of each person being 68 kg. The mass of the elevator itself is 920 kg and it moves with a constant speed of 3 m/s. The frictional force opposing the motion is 6000 N. If the elevator is moving up with its full capacity, the power delivered by the motor to the elevator ($g = 10$ m/s^2) must be at least:

(1) 56300 W

(2) 62360 W

(3) 48000 W

(4) 66000 W

8. A stationary observer receives sound from two identical tuning forks, one of which approaches and the other one recedes with the same speed (much less than the speed of sound). The observer hears 2 beats/sec. The oscillation frequency of each tuning fork is $v_0 = 1400$ Hz and the velocity of sound in air is 350 m/s. The speed of each tuning fork is close to:

(1) $\dfrac{1}{2}$ m/s

(2) 1 m/s

(3) $\dfrac{1}{4}$ m/s

(4) $\dfrac{1}{8}$ m/s

9. An emf of 20 V is applied at time $t = 0$ to a circuit containing in series 10 mH inductor and 5 Ω resistor. The ratio of the currents at time $t = \infty$ and at $t = 40$ s is close to: (Take $e^2 = 7.389$)

(1) 1.06 (2) 1.15
(3) 1.46 (4) 0.84

10. A thin lens made of glass (refractive index = 1.5) of focal length $f = 16$ cm is immersed in a liquid of refractive index 1.42. If its focal length in liquid is f_l, then the ratio f_l/f is closest to the integer:

(1) 1 (2) 9
(3) 5 (4) 17

11. An electron (of mass m) and a photon have the same energy E in the range of a few eV. The ratio of the de-Broglie wavelength associated with the electron and the wavelength of the photon is (c = speed of light in vacuum)

(1) $\dfrac{1}{c}\left(\dfrac{2E}{m}\right)^{1/2}$ (2) $c(2mE)^{1/2}$

(3) $\dfrac{1}{c}\left(\dfrac{E}{2m}\right)^{1/2}$ (4) $\left(\dfrac{E}{2m}\right)^{1/2}$

12. A planar loop of wire rotates in a uniform magnetic field. Initially, at $t = 0$, the plane of the loop is perpendicular to the magnetic field. If it rotates with a period of 10 s about an axis in its plane then the magnitude of induced emf will be maximum and minimum, respectively at:

(1) 2.5 s and 7.5 s (2) 2.5 s and 5.0 s
(3) 5.0 s and 7.5 s (4) 5.0 s and 10.0 s

13. In the figure, potential difference between A and B is:

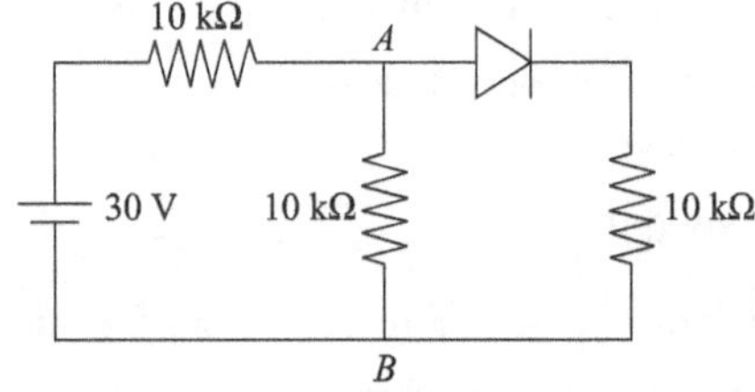

(1) 10 V (2) 5 V
(3) 15 V (4) zero

14. In a Young's double slit experiment, the separation between the slits is 0.15 mm. In the experiment, a source of light of wavelength 589 nm is used and the interference pattern is observed on a screen kept 1.5 m away. The separation between the successive bright fringes on the screen is:

(1) 6.9 mm (2) 3.9 mm
(3) 5.9 mm (4) 4.9 mm

15. The activity of a radioactive sample falls from 700 s^{-1} to 500 s^{-1} in 30 minutes. Its half life is close to:

(1) 72 min (2) 62 min
(3) 66 min (4) 52 min

16. A box weighs 196 N on a spring balance at the north pole. Its weight recorded on the same balance if it is shifted to the equator is close to (Take $g = 10$ ms^{-2} at the north pole and the radius of the earth = 6400 km):

(1) 195.66 N (2) 194.32 N
(3) 194.66 N (4) 195.32 N

17. Mass per unit area of a circular disc of radius a depends on the distance r from its centre as $\sigma(r) = A + Br$. The moment of inertia of the disc about the axis, perpendicular to the plane and passing through its centre is:

(1) $2\pi a^4\left(\dfrac{A}{4}+\dfrac{aB}{5}\right)$ (2) $2\pi a^4\left(\dfrac{aA}{4}+\dfrac{B}{5}\right)$

(3) $\pi a^4\left(\dfrac{A}{4}+\dfrac{aB}{5}\right)$ (4) $2\pi a^4\left(\dfrac{A}{4}+\dfrac{B}{5}\right)$

18.

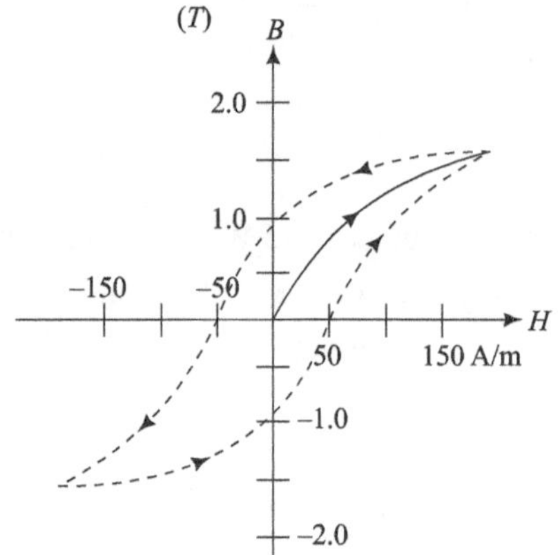

The figure gives experimentally measured B vs. H variation in a ferromagnetic material. The retentivity, co-ercivity and saturation, respectively, of the material are:

(1) 1.5 T, 50 A/m and 1.0 T
(2) 1.5 T, 50 A/m and 1.0 T
(3) 150 A/m, 1.0 T and 1.5 T
(4) 1.0 T, 50 A/m and 1.5 T

19. Under an adiabatic process, the volume of an ideal gas gets doubled. Consequently the mean collision time between the gas molecule changes from τ_1 to τ_2. If $\dfrac{C_p}{C_v} = \gamma$ for this gas then a good estimate for $\dfrac{\tau_2}{\tau_1}$ is given by:

(1) 2

(2) $\dfrac{1}{2}$

(3) $\left(\dfrac{1}{2}\right)^{\gamma}$

(4) $\left(\dfrac{1}{2}\right)^{\frac{\gamma+1}{2}}$

20. Two ideal Carnot engines operate in cascade (all heat given up by one engine is used by the other engine to produce work) between temperatures, T_1 and T_2. The temperature of the hot reservoir of the first engine is T_1 and the temperature of the cold reservoir of the second engine is T_2. T is temperature of the sink of first engine which is also the source for the second engine. How is T related to T_1 and T_2, if both the engines perform equal amount of work ?

(1) $T = \dfrac{2T_1 T_2}{T_1 + T_2}$

(2) $T = \dfrac{T_1 + T_2}{2}$

(3) $T = \sqrt{T_1 T_2}$

(4) $T = 0$

21. The sum of two forces $\vec{P}$ and $\vec{Q}$ is $\vec{R}$ such that $|\vec{R}| = |\vec{P}|$. The angle θ (in degrees) that the resultant of $2\vec{P}$ and $\vec{Q}$ will make with $\vec{Q}$ is __________.

22. A 60 pF capacitor is fully charged by a 20 V supply. It is then disconnected from the supply and is connected to another uncharged 60 pF capacitor in parallel. The electrostatic energy that is lost in this process by the time the charge is redistributed between them is (in nJ)

23.

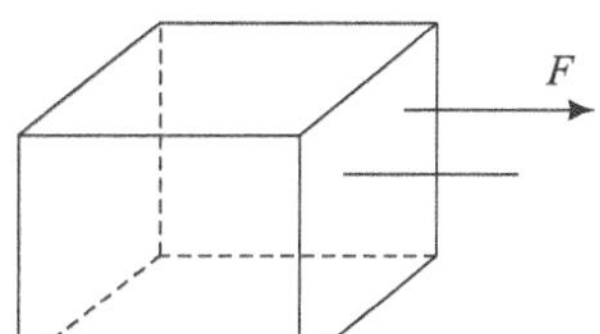

Consider a uniform cubical box of side a on a rough floor that is to be moved by applying minimum possible force F at a point b above its centre of mass (see figure). If the coefficient of friction is $\mu = 0.4$, the maximum possible value of $100 \times \dfrac{b}{a}$ for box not to topple before moving is __________.

24. The balancing length for a cell is 560 cm in a potentiometer experiment. When an external resistance of 10 Ω is connected in parallel to the cell, the balancing length changes by 60 cm. If the internal resistance of the cell is $\dfrac{N}{10}$ Ω, where N is an integer then value of N is __________.

25. M grams of steam at 100°C is mixed with 200 g of ice at its melting point in a thermally insulated container. If it produces liquid water at 40°C [heat of vaporization of water is 540 cal/ g and heat of fusion of ice is 80 cal/g], the value of M is __________.

CHEMISTRY

26. The redox reaction among the following is:

(1) formation of ozone from atmospheric oxygen in the presence of sunlight

(2) reaction of $[Co(H_2O)_6]Cl_3$ with $AgNO_3$

(3) reaction of H_2SO_4 with NaOH

(4) combination of dinitrogen with dioxygen at 2000 K

27. Among statements (A)-(D), the correct ones are:

(A) Decomposition of hydrogen peroxide gives dioxygen.

(B) Like hydrogen peroxide, compounds, such as $KClO_3$, $Pb(NO_3)_2$ and $NaNO_3$ when heated liberate dioxygen.

(C) 2-Ethylanthraquinone is useful for the industrial preparation of hydrogen peroxide.

(D) Hydrogen peroxide is used for the manufacture of sodium perborate.

(1) (A) (B), (C) and (D)

(2) (A), (B) and (C) only

(3) (A), (C) and (D) only

(4) (A) and (C) only

28. In the following reactions, products (A) and (B), respectively, are:

$NaOH + Cl_2 \rightarrow$ (A) + side products (hot and conc.)

$Ca(OH)_2 + Cl_2 \rightarrow$ (B) + side products (dry)

(1) $NaClO_3$, and $Ca(OCl)_2$

(2) $NaClO_3$ and $Ca(ClO_3)_2$

(3) $NaOCl$ and $Ca(OCl)_2$

(4) $NaOCl$ and $Ca(ClO_3)_2$

29. For the following reactions

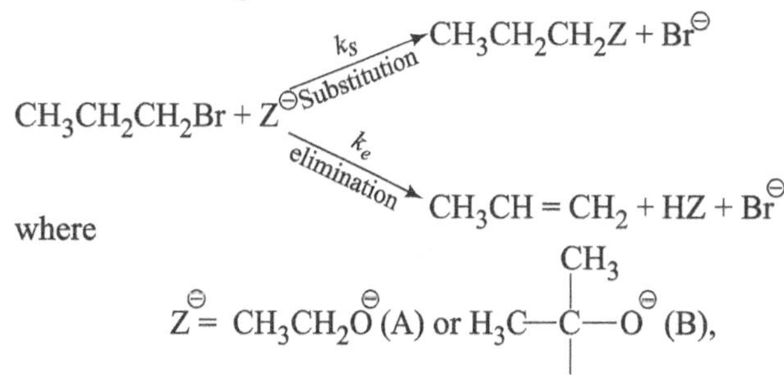

where

$$Z^{\ominus} = CH_3CH_2\overset{\ominus}{O} \text{ (A) or } H_3C-\overset{\overset{\textstyle CH_3}{|}}{\underset{\underset{\textstyle CH_3}{|}}{C}}-\overset{\ominus}{O} \text{ (B),}$$

k_s and k_e, are, respectively, the rate constants for substitution and elimination, and $\mu = \dfrac{k_s}{k_e}$, the correct option is ________ .

(1) $\mu_B > \mu_A$ and $k_e(A) > k_e(B)$

(2) $\mu_A > \mu_B$ and $k_e(B) > k_e(A)$

(3) $\mu_B > \mu_A$ and $k_e(B) > k_e(A)$

(4) $\mu_A > \mu_B$ and $k_e(A) > k_e(B)$

30. The correct order of stability for the following alkoxides is:

(A)   (B)   (C)

(1) (B) > (A) > (C)
(2) (C) > (B) > (A)
(3) (C) > (A) > (B)
(4) (B) > (C) > (A)

31. The number of possible optical isomers for the complexes MA_2B_2 with sp^3 and dsp^2 hybridized metal atom, respectively, is:

Note: A and B are unidentate neutral and unidentate monoanionic ligands, respectively.

(1) 0 and 2   (2) 2 and 2
(3) 0 and 0   (4) 0 and 1

32. A chromatography column, packed with silica gel as stationary phase, was used to separate a mixture of compounds consisting of (A) benzanilide (B) aniline and (C) acetophenone. When the column is eluted with a mixture of solvents, hexane: ethyl acetate (20:80), the sequence of obtained compounds is:

(1) (B), (C) and (A)
(2) (B), (A) and (C)
(3) (C), (A) and (B)
(4) (A), (B) and (C)

33. Among the statements (A)-(D), the incorrect ones are:

(A) Octahedral Co(III) complexes with strong field ligands have very high magnetic moments.

(B) When $\Delta_0 < P$, the d-electron configuration of Co(III) in an octahedral complex is $t_{2g}^4 e_g^2$.

(C) Wavelength of light absorbed by $[Co(en)_3]^{3+}$ is lower than that of $[CoF_6]^{3-}$.

(D) If the Δ_0 for an octahedral complex of Co(III) is 18,000 cm^{-1}, the Δ_t for its tetrahedral complex with the same ligand will be 16,000 cm^{-1}.

(1) (A) and (D) only
(2) (C) and (D) only
(3) (A) and (B) only
(4) (B) and (C) only

34. Consider the following reactions:

(A)

(B)

(C)

(D)

Which of these reactions are possible ?

(1) (A) and (B)
(2) (A) and (D)
(3) (B), (C) and (D)
(4) (B) and (D)

35. The equation that is incorrect is:

(1) $\left(\Lambda_m^0\right)_{NaBr} - \left(\Lambda_m^0\right)_{NaCl} = \left(\Lambda_m^0\right)_{KBr} - \left(\Lambda_m^0\right)_{KCl}$

(2) $\left(\Lambda_m^0\right)_{KCl} - \left(\Lambda_m^0\right)_{NaCl} = \left(\Lambda_m^0\right)_{KBr} - \left(\Lambda_m^0\right)_{NaBr}$

(3) $\left(\Lambda_m^0\right)_{H_2O} = \left(\Lambda_m^0\right)_{HCl} + \left(\Lambda_m^0\right)_{NaOH} - \left(\Lambda_m^0\right)_{NaCl}$

(4) $\left(\Lambda_m^0\right)_{NaBr} - \left(\Lambda_m^0\right)_{NaI} = \left(\Lambda_m^0\right)_{KBr} - \left(\Lambda_m^0\right)_{NaBr}$

36. In the following reaction sequence, structures of A and B, respectively will be:

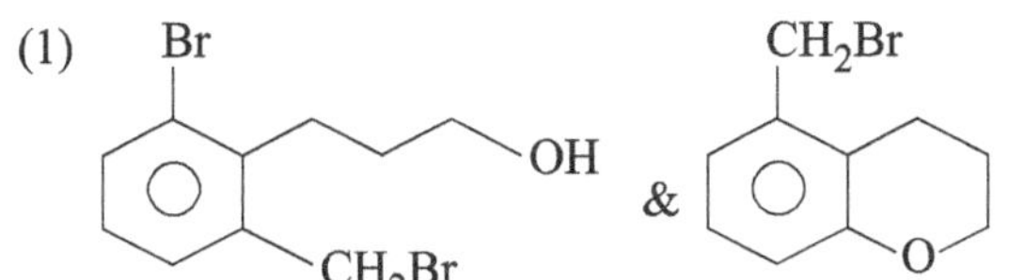

$$\xrightarrow[\Delta]{\text{HBr}} A \xrightarrow[\text{Ether}]{\text{Na}} \text{(Intramolecular Product) B}$$

(1)

Br ... OH & CH$_2$Br ... O

(2)

OH ... Br & OH ...

(3)

OH ... Br & OH ...

(4)

Br ... OH & Br ... O

37. In the following reaction sequence,

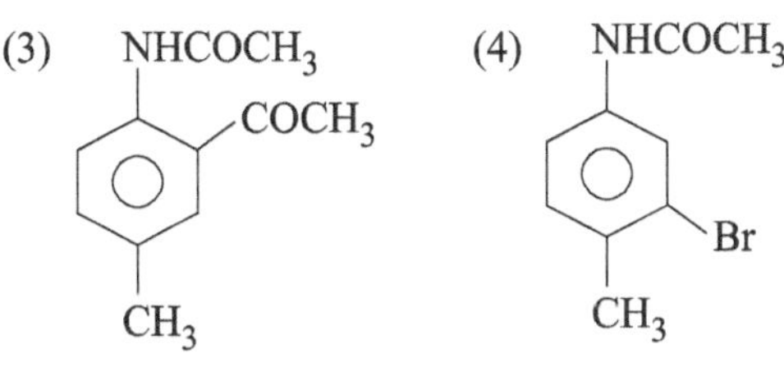

$$\xrightarrow{\text{Ac}_2\text{O}} A \xrightarrow[\text{AcOH}]{\text{Br}_2} B$$

the major product B is:

(1) NHCOCH$_3$, Br, CH$_3$

(2) NHCOCH$_3$, Br, CH$_2$Br

(3) NHCOCH$_3$, COCH$_3$, CH$_3$

(4) NHCOCH$_3$, Br, CH$_3$

38. Identify the correct labels of A, B and C in the following graph from the options given below:

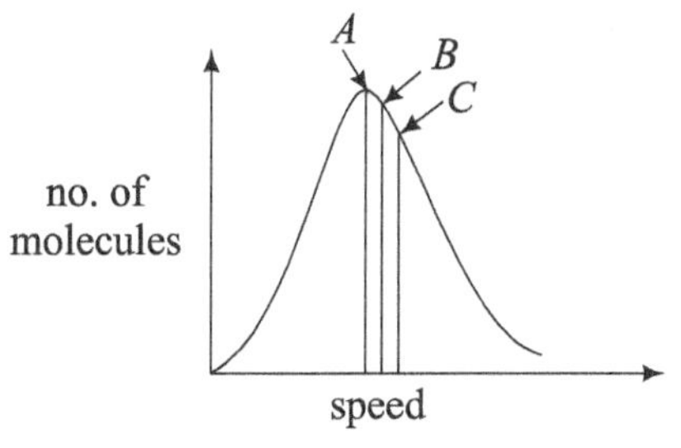

Root mean square speed (V$_{rms}$); most probable speed (V$_{mp}$); average speed (V$_{av}$)

(1) A – V$_{mp}$; B – V$_{rms}$; C – V$_{av}$
(2) A – V$_{av}$; B – V$_{rms}$; C – V$_{mp}$
(3) A – V$_{rms}$; B – V$_{mp}$; C – V$_{av}$
(4) A – V$_{mp}$; B – V$_{av}$; C – V$_{rms}$

39. The refining method used when the metal and the impurities have low and high melting temperatures, respectively, is:

(1) liquation   (2) vapour phase refining
(3) zone refining   (4) distillation

40. The ammonia (NH$_3$) released on quantitative reaction of 0.6 g urea (NH$_2$CONH$_2$) with sodium hydroxide (NaOH) can be neutralized by:

(1) 200 mL of 0.4 N HCl
(2) 200 mL of 0.2 N HCl
(3) 100 mL of 0.2 N HCl
(4) 100 mL of 0.1 N HCl

41. Within each pair of elements F & Cl, S & Se, and Li & Na, respectively, the elements that release more energy upon an electron gain are:

(1) Cl, Se and Na   (2) Cl, S and Li
(3) F, S and Li   (4) F, Se and Na

42. The bond order and the magnetic characteristics of CN$^-$ are:

(1) $2\frac{1}{2}$, diamagnetic
(2) 3, diamagnetic
(3) 3, paramagnetic
(4) $2\frac{1}{2}$, paramagnetic

43. For the reaction
$2H_2(g) + 2NO(g) \rightarrow N_2(g) + 2H_2O(g)$ the observed rate expression is, rate = $k_f[NO]^2 [H_2]$. The rate expression for the reverse reaction is:

(1) $k_b[N_2][H_2O]^2$
(2) $k_b[N_2][H_2O]^2/[NO]$
(3) $k_b[N_2][H_2O]$
(4) $k_b[N_2][H_2O]^2/[H_2]$

44. Which of the following statements is correct ?

(1) Gluconic acid can form cyclic (acetal/hemiacetal) structure

(2) Gluconic acid is a dicarboxylic acid

(3) Gluconic acid is a partial oxidation product of glucose

(4) Gluconic acid is obtained by oxidation of glucose with HNO_3

45. Two open beakers one containing a solvent and the other containing a mixture of that solvent with a non volatile solute are together sealed in a container. Over time:

(1) the volume of the solution increases and the volume of the solvent decreases

(2) the volume of the solution decreases and the volume of the solvent increases

(3) the volume of the solution and the solvent does not change

(4) the volume of the solution does not change and the volume of the solvent decreases

46. Consider the following reactions:

$NaCl + K_2Cr_2O_7 + H_2SO_4 \rightarrow$ (A) + Side products (Conc.)

(A) + NaOH $\rightarrow$ (B) + Side products

(B) + H_2SO_4 + $H_2O_2 \rightarrow$ (C) + Side products (dilute)

The sum of the total number of atoms in one molecule each of (A), (B) and (C) is _________.

47. The number of sp^2 hybridised carbons present in "Aspartame" is _________.

48. The standard heat of formation ($\Delta_f H^0_{298}$) of ethane (in kJ/mol), if the heat of combustion of ethane, hydrogen and graphite are -1560, -393.5 and -286 kJ/mol, respectively is _________.

49. The flocculation value of HCl for arsenic sulphide sol. is 30 m mol L^{-1}. If H_2SO_4 is used for the flocculation of arsenic sulphide, the amount, in grams, of H_2SO_4 in 250 mL required for the above purpose is _________.

(molecular mass of $H_2SO_4 = 98$ g/mol)

50. 3 g of acetic acid is added to 250 mL of 0.1 M HCl and the solution made up to 500 mL. To 20 mL of this solution $\dfrac{1}{2}$ mL of 5 M NaOH is added. The pH of the solution is _________.

[Given: pKa of acetic acid = 4.75, molar mass of acetic acid = 60 g/mol, log 3 = 0.4771]

Neglect any changes in volume.

MATHEMATICS

51. Let $\vec{a}$, $\vec{b}$ and $\vec{c}$ be three unit vectors such that $\vec{a}+\vec{b}+\vec{c}=\vec{0}$. if

$\lambda = \vec{a}\cdot\vec{b}+\vec{b}\cdot\vec{c}+\vec{c}\cdot\vec{a}$ and

$\vec{d} = \vec{a}\times\vec{b}+\vec{b}\times\vec{c}+\vec{c}\times\vec{a}$, then

the ordered pair, $\left(\lambda,\vec{d}\right)$ is equal to:

(1) $\left(\dfrac{3}{2},3\vec{a}\times\vec{c}\right)$

(2) $\left(-\dfrac{3}{2},3\vec{c}\times\vec{b}\right)$

(3) $\left(\dfrac{3}{2},3\vec{b}\times\vec{c}\right)$

(4) $\left(-\dfrac{3}{2},3\vec{a}\times\vec{b}\right)$

52. The locus of the mid-points of the perpendiculars drawn from points on the line, $x = 2y$ to the line $x = y$ is:

(1) $2x - 3y = 0$

(2) $5x - 7y = 0$

(3) $3x - 2y = 0$

(4) $7x - 5y = 0$

53. Let $a_1, a_2, a_3, \ldots$ be a G. P. such that $a_1 < 0$, $a_1 + a_2 = 4$ and $a_3 + a_4 = 16$. If $\displaystyle\sum_{i=1}^{9} a_i = 4\lambda$, then λ is equal to:

(1) -513

(2) -171

(3) 171

(4) $\dfrac{511}{3}$

54. The value of c in the Lagrange's mean value theorem for the function $f(x) = x^3 - 4x^2 + 8x + 11$, when $x \in [0,1]$ is:

(1) $\dfrac{4-\sqrt{5}}{3}$

(2) $\dfrac{4-\sqrt{7}}{3}$

(3) $\dfrac{2}{3}$

(4) $\dfrac{\sqrt{7}-2}{3}$

55. The coefficient of x^7 in the expression $(1+x)^{10} + x(1+x)^9 + x^2(1+x)^8 + \ldots + x^{10}$ is:

(1) 210

(2) 330

(3) 120

(4) 420

56. The area (in sq. units) of the region $\{(x, y) \in R^2 | 4x^2 \le y \le 8x + 12\}$ is:

(1) $\dfrac{125}{3}$

(2) $\dfrac{128}{3}$

(3) $\dfrac{124}{3}$

(4) $\dfrac{127}{3}$

57. In a workshop, there are five machines and the probability of any one of them to be out of service on a day is $\dfrac{1}{4}$. If the probability that at most two machines will be out of service on the same day is $\left(\dfrac{3}{4}\right)^3 k$, then k is equal to:

(1) $\dfrac{17}{8}$

(2) $\dfrac{17}{4}$

(3) $\dfrac{17}{2}$

(4) 4

58. Let $f(x)$ be a polynomial of degree 5 such that $x = \pm 1$ are its critical points. If $\displaystyle\lim_{x \to 0}\left(2 + \dfrac{f(x)}{x^3}\right) = 4$, then which one of the following is not true ?

(1) f is an odd function.

(2) $f(1) - 4f(-1) = 4$.

(3) $x = 1$ is a point of maxima and $x = -1$ is a point of minima of f.

(4) $x = 1$ is a point of minima and $x = -1$ is a point of maxima of f.

59. If $3x + 4y = 12\sqrt{2}$ is a tangent to the ellipse $\dfrac{x^2}{a^2} + \dfrac{y^2}{9} = 1$ for some $a \in R$, then the distance between the foci of the ellipse is:

(1) $2\sqrt{7}$

(2) 4

(3) $2\sqrt{5}$

(4) $2\sqrt{2}$

60. If $\dfrac{3 + i\sin\theta}{4 - i\cos\theta}$, $\theta \in [0, 2\pi]$, is a real number, then an argument of $\sin\theta + i\cos\theta$ is:

(1) $\pi - \tan^{-1}\left(\dfrac{4}{3}\right)$

(2) $\pi - \tan^{-1}\left(\dfrac{3}{4}\right)$

(3) $-\tan^{-1}\left(\dfrac{3}{4}\right)$

(4) $\tan^{-1}\left(\dfrac{4}{3}\right)$

61. Let $y = y(x)$ be the solution curve of the differential equation, $(y^2 - x)\dfrac{dy}{dx} = 1$, satisfying $y(0) = 1$. This curve intersects the x-axis at a point whose abscissa is:

(1) $2 - e$

(2) $-e$

(3) 2

(4) $2 + e$

62. Let A, B, C and D be four non-empty sets. The contrapositive statement of "If $A \subseteq B$ and $B \subseteq D$, then $A \subseteq C$" is:

(1) If $A \not\subseteq C$, then $A \subseteq B$ and $B \subseteq D$

(2) If $A \subseteq C$, then $B \subset A$ or $D \subset B$

(3) If $A \not\subseteq C$, then $A \not\subseteq B$ and $B \subseteq D$

(4) If $A \not\subseteq C$, then $A \not\subseteq B$ or $B \not\subseteq D$

63. Let the tangents drawn from the origin to the circle, $x^2 + y^2 - 8x - 4y + 16 = 0$ touch it at the points A and B. The $(AB)^2$ is equal to:

(1) $\dfrac{52}{5}$

(2) $\dfrac{56}{5}$

(3) $\dfrac{64}{5}$

(4) $\dfrac{32}{5}$

64. Let α and β be the roots of the equation $x^2 - x - 1 = 0$. If $p_k = (\alpha)^k + (\beta)^k$, $k \geq 1$, then which one of the following statements is not true ?

(1) $p_3 = p_5 - p_4$

(2) $P_5 = 11$

(3) $(p_1 + p_2 + p_3 + p_4 + p_5) = 26$

(4) $p_5 = p_2 \cdot p_3$

65. The value of α for which $4\alpha \displaystyle\int_{-1}^{2} e^{-\alpha|x|}dx = 5$, is :

(1) $\log_e 2$

(2) $\log_e\left(\dfrac{3}{2}\right)$

(3) $\log_e \sqrt{2}$

(4) $\log_e\left(\dfrac{4}{3}\right)$

66. The number of ordered pairs (r, k) for which $6.^{35}C_r = (k^2 - 3).^{36}C_{r+1}$, where k is an integer, is:

(1) 3

(2) 2

(3) 6

(4) 4

67. If the sum of the first 40 terms of the series, $3 + 4 + 8 + 9 + 13 + 14 + 18 + 19 + ...$ is $(102)m$, then m is equal to:

(1) 20

(2) 25

(3) 5

(4) 10

68. Let $y = y(x)$ be a function of x satisfying $y\sqrt{1 - x^2} = k - x\sqrt{1 - y^2}$ where k is a constant and $y\left(\dfrac{1}{2}\right) = -\dfrac{1}{4}$. Then $\dfrac{dy}{dx}$ at $x = \dfrac{1}{2}$, is equal to:

(1) $-\dfrac{\sqrt{5}}{4}$

(2) $-\dfrac{\sqrt{5}}{2}$

(3) $\dfrac{2}{\sqrt{5}}$

(4) $\dfrac{\sqrt{5}}{2}$

69. If θ_1 and θ_2 be respectively the smallest and the largest values of θ in $(0, 2\pi) - \{\pi\}$ which satisfy the equation,

$$2\cot^2\theta - \frac{5}{\sin\theta} + 4 = 0 \text{, then } \int_{\theta_1}^{\theta_2} \cos^2 3\theta \, d\theta \text{ is equal to:}$$

(1) $\dfrac{\pi}{3}$ (2) $\dfrac{2\pi}{3}$

(3) $\dfrac{\pi}{3} + \dfrac{1}{6}$ (4) $\dfrac{\pi}{9}$

70. Let $A = [a_{ij}]$ and $B = [b_{ij}]$ be two 3×3 real matrices such that $b_{ij} = (3)^{(i+j-2)} a_{ij}$, where $i, j = 1, 2, 3$. If the determinant of B is 81, then the determinant of A is:

(1) $1/3$ (2) 3

(3) $1/81$ (4) $1/9$

71. If the mean and variance of eight numbers 3, 7, 9, 12, 13, 20, x and y be 10 and 25 respectively, then $x \cdot y$ is equal to __________.

72. If the foot of the perpendicular drawn from the point $(1, 0, 3)$ on a line passing through $(\alpha, 7, 1)$ is $\left(\dfrac{5}{3}, \dfrac{7}{3}, \dfrac{17}{3}\right)$, then α is equal to __________.

73. Let $X = \{n \in N : 1 \le n \le 50\}$. If

$A = \{n \in X : n$ is a multiple of 2$\}$ and

$B = \{n \in X : n$ is a multiple of 7$\}$, then the number of elements in the smallest subset of X containing both A and B is __________.

74. If the system of linear equations,

$x + y + z = 6$

$x + 2y + 3z = 10$

$3x + 2y + \lambda z = \mu$

has more than two solutions, then $\mu - \lambda^2$ is equal to __________.

75. If the function f defined on $\left(-\dfrac{1}{3}, \dfrac{1}{3}\right)$ by

$$f(x) = \begin{cases} \dfrac{1}{x}\log_e\left(\dfrac{1+3x}{1-2x}\right), & \text{when } x \ne 0 \\ k, & \text{when } x = 0 \end{cases}$$

is continuous, then k is equal to __________.

PHYSICS

1. The critical angle of a medium for a specific wavelength, if the medium has relative permittivity 3 and relative permeability $\frac{4}{3}$ for this wavelength, will be:

(1) 15° (2) 30°

(3) 45° (4) 60°

2. Effective capacitance of parallel combination of two capacitors C_1 and C_2 is 10 µF. When these capacitors are individually connected to a voltage source of 1 V, the energy stored in the capacitor C_2 is 4 times that of C_1. If these capacitors are connected in series, their effective capacitance will be:

(1) 4.2 µF (2) 3.2 µF

(3) 1.6 µF (4) 8.4 µF

3. The coordinates of centre of mass of a uniform flag shaped lamina (thin flat plale) of mass 4 kg. (The coordinates of the same are shown in figure) are:

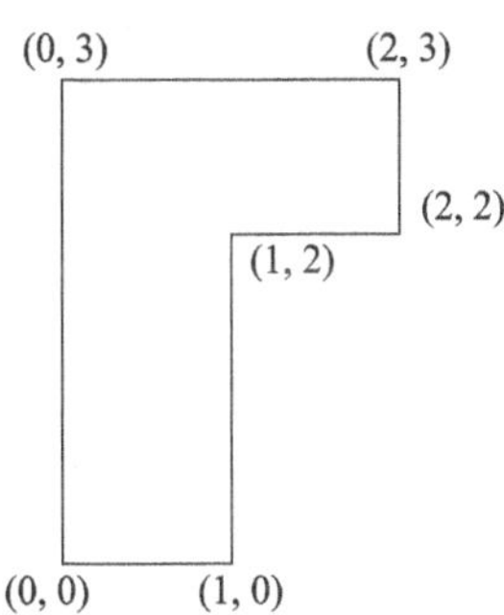

(1) (1.25 m, 1.50 m) (2) (0.75 m, 1.75 m)

(3) (0.75 m, 0.75 m) (4) (1 m, 1.75 m)

4. A particle of mass m is fixed to one end of a light spring having force constant k and unstretched length l. The other end is fixed. The system is given an angular speed ω about the fixed end of the spring such that it rotates in a circle in gravity free space. Then the stretch in the spring is:

(1) $\dfrac{ml\omega^2}{k-\omega m}$ (2) $\dfrac{ml\omega^2}{k-m\omega^2}$

(3) $\dfrac{ml\omega^2}{k+m\omega^2}$ (4) $\dfrac{ml\omega^2}{k+m\omega}$

5. A thermodynamic cycle $xyzx$ is shown on a V-T diagram.

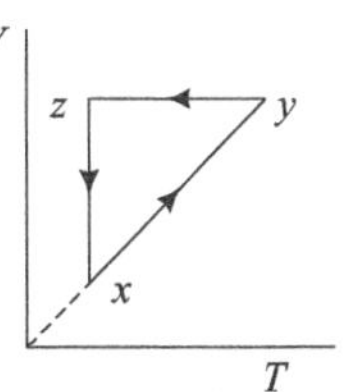

The P-V diagram that best describes this cycle is: (Diagrams are schematic and not to scale)

(1) 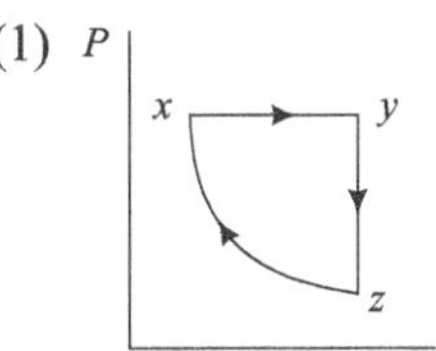 (2) 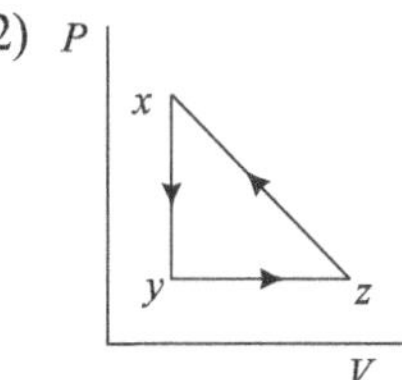

(3) 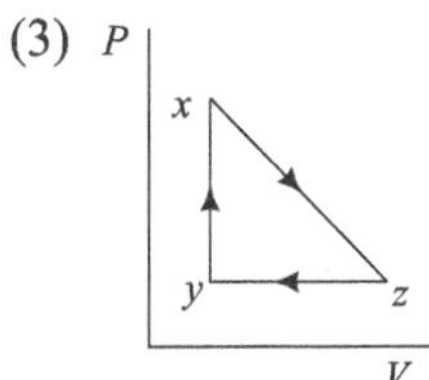 (4) 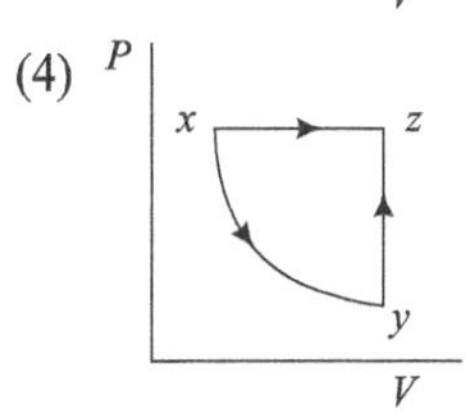

6. A leak proof cylinder of length 1 m, made of a metal which has very low coefficient of expansion is floating vertically in water at 0°C such that its height above the water surface is 20 cm. When the temperature of water is increased to 4°C, the height of the cylinder above the water surface becomes 21 cm. The density of water at $T = 4$°C, relative to the density at $T = 0$°C is close to:

(1) 1.26 (2) 1.04

(3) 1.01 (4) 1.03

7. Three charged particles A, B and C with charges $-4q$, $2q$ and $-2q$ are present on the circumference of a circle of radius d. The charged particles A, C and centre O of the circle formed an equilateral triangle as shown in figure. Electric field at O along x-direction is:

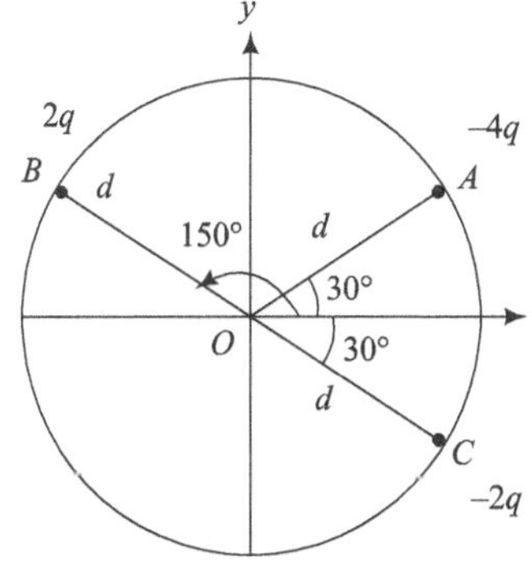

(1) $\dfrac{\sqrt{3}q}{\pi \in_0 d^2}$

(2) $\dfrac{2\sqrt{3}q}{\pi \in_0 d^2}$

(3) $\dfrac{\sqrt{3}q}{4\pi \in_0 d^2}$

(4) $\dfrac{3\sqrt{3}q}{4\pi \in_0 d^2}$

8. Consider two solid spheres of radii $R_1 = 1m$, $R_2 = 2m$ and masses M_1 and M_2, respectively. The gravitational field due to sphere ① and ② are shown. The value of $\dfrac{m_1}{m_2}$ is:

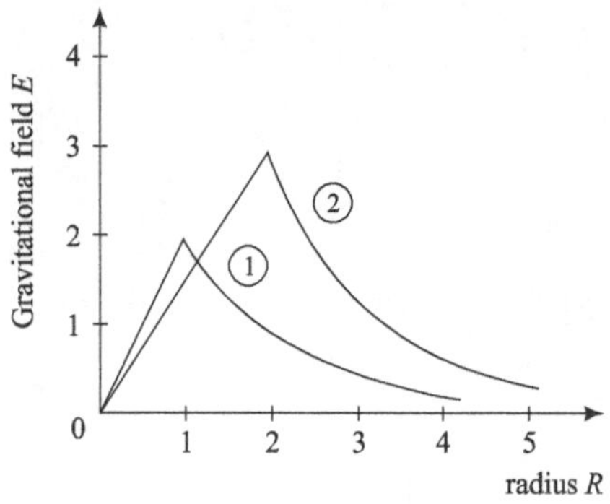

(1) $\dfrac{2}{3}$

(2) $\dfrac{1}{6}$

(3) $\dfrac{1}{2}$

(4) $\dfrac{1}{3}$

9. Consider a uniform rod of mass $M = 4m$ and length l pivoted about its centre. A mass m moving with velocity v making angle $\theta = \dfrac{\pi}{4}$ to the rod's long axis collides with one end of the rod and sticks to it. The angular speed of the rod-mass system just after the collision is:

(1) $\dfrac{3}{7\sqrt{2}}\dfrac{v}{l}$

(2) $\dfrac{3}{7}\dfrac{v}{l}$

(3) $\dfrac{3\sqrt{2}}{7}\dfrac{v}{l}$

(4) $\dfrac{4}{7}\dfrac{v}{l}$

10. The dimension of stopping potential V_0 in photoelectric effect in units of Planck's constant 'h', speed of light 'c' and Gravitational constant 'G' and ampere A is:

(1) $h^{1/3}G^{2/3}c^{1/3}A^{-1}$

(2) $h^{2/3}c^{5/3}G^{1/3}A^{-1}$

(3) $h^{-2/3}e^{-1/3}G^{4/3}A^{-1}$

(4) $h^2G^{3/2}C^{1/3}A^{-1}$

11. Boolean relation at the output stage-Y for the following circuit is:

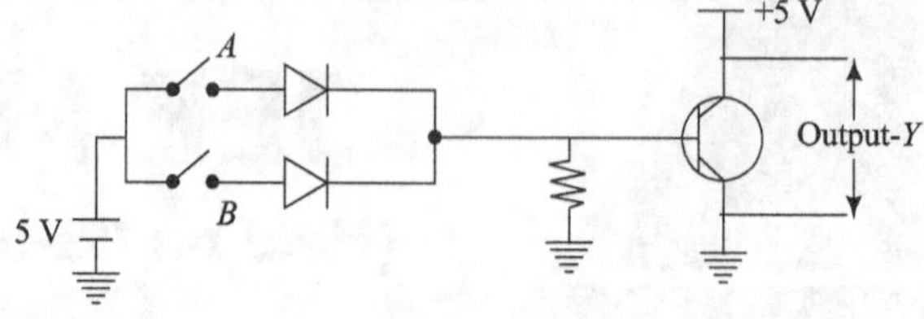

(1) $\overline{A} + \overline{B}$

(2) $A + B$

(3) $A.B$

(4) $\overline{A}.\overline{B}$

12. The plot that depicts the behavior of the mean free time τ (time between two successive collisions) for the molecules of an ideal gas, as a function of temperature (T), qualitatively, is: (Graphs are schematic and not drawn to scale)

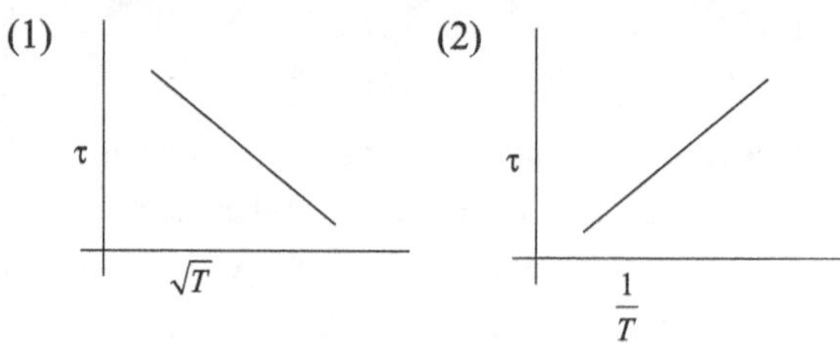

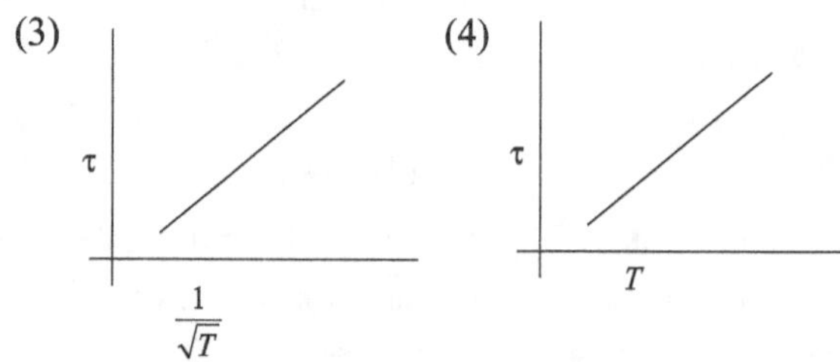

13. When photon of energy 4.0 eV strikes the surface of a metal A, the ejected photoelectrons have maximum kinetic energy T_A eV and de-Broglie wavelength λ_A. The maximum kinetic energy of photoelectrons liberated from another metal B by photon of energy 4.50 eV is $T_B = (T_A - 1.5)$eV. If the de-Broglie wavelength of these photoelectrons $\lambda_B = 2\lambda_A$, then the work function of metal B is:

(1) 4 eV

(2) 2 eV

(3) 1.5 eV

(4) 3 eV

14. The magnifying power of a telescope with tube length 60 cm is 5. What is the focal length of its eye piece?

(1) 20 cm

(2) 40 cm

(3) 30 cm

(4) 10 cm

15. The graph which depicts the results of Rutherford gold foil experiment with

α-particles is:

θ: Scattering angle

Y: Number of scattered α-particles detected

(Plots are schematic and not to scale)

(1) 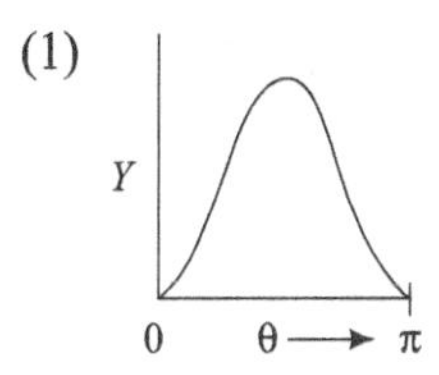

(2) 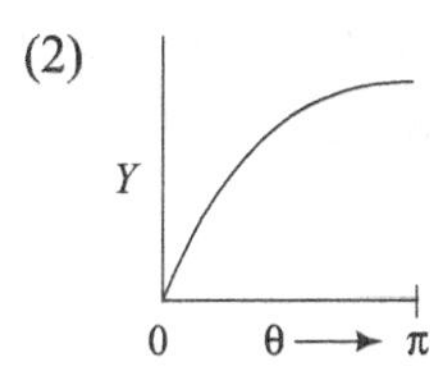

(3) 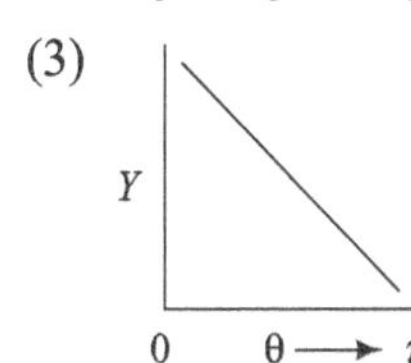

(4) 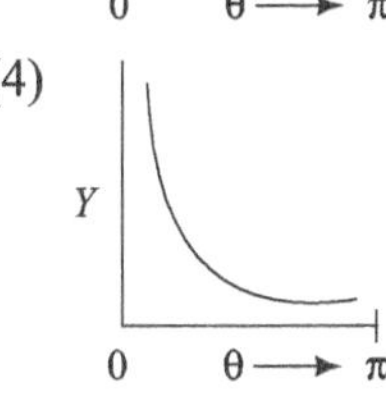

16. At time $t = 0$ magnetic field of 1000 Gauss is passing perpendicularly through the area defined by the closed loop shown in the figure. If the magnetic field reduces linearly to 500 Gauss, in the next 5 s, then induced EMF in the loop is:

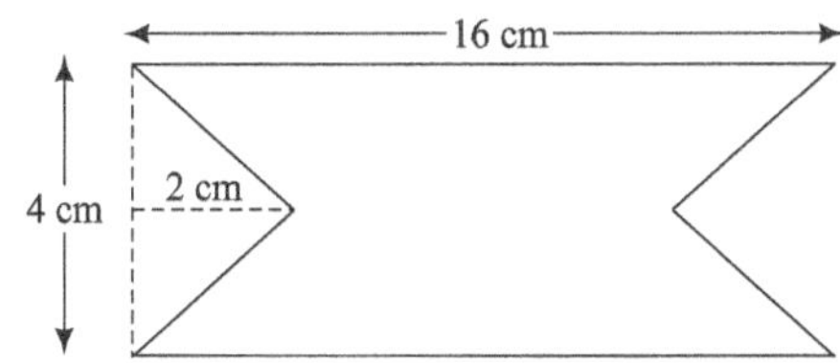

(1) 56 μV

(2) 28 μV

(3) 48 μV

(4) 36 μV

17. In finding the electric field using Gauss law the formula $|\vec{E}| = \dfrac{q_{enc}}{\epsilon_0 |A|}$ is applicable. In the formula ϵ_0 is permittivity of free space, A is the area of Gaussian surface and q_{enc} is charge enclosed by the Gaussian surface. This equation can be used in which of the following situation?

(1) Only when the Gaussian surface is an equipotential surface.

Only when the Gaussian surface is an

(2) equipotential surface and $|\vec{E}|$ is constant on the surface.

(3) Only when $|\vec{E}|$ = constant on the surface.

(4) For any choice of Gaussian surface.

18. The length of a potentiometer wire is 1200 cm and it carries a current of 60 mA. For a cell of emf 5 V and internal resistance of 20 Ω, the null point on it is found to be at 1000 cm. The resistance of whole wire is:

(1) 80 Ω

(2) 120 Ω

(3) 60 Ω

(4) 100 Ω

19. Proton with kinetic energy of 1 MeV moves from south to north. It gets an acceleration of 10^{12} m/s^2 by an applied magnetic field (west to east). The value of magnetic field: (Rest mass of proton is 1.6×10^{-27} kg)

(1) 0.71 mT

(2) 7.1 mT

(3) 0.071 mT

(4) 71 mT

20. Consider a solid sphere of radius R and mass density $\rho(r) = \rho_0\left(1 - \dfrac{r^2}{R^2}\right)$, $0 < r \le R$. The minimum density of a liquid in which it will float is:

(1) $\dfrac{\rho_0}{3}$

(2) $\dfrac{\rho_0}{5}$

(3) $\dfrac{2\rho_0}{5}$

(4) $\dfrac{2\rho_0}{3}$

21. A particle is moving along the x-axis with its coordinate with time 't' given by $x(t) = 10 + 8t - 3t^2$. Another particle is moving along the y-axis with its coordinate as a function of time given by $y(t) = 5 - 8t^3$. At $t = 1$ s, the speed of the second particle as measured in the frame of the first particle is given as $\sqrt{v}$. Then v (in m/s) is________

22. Four resistances of 15 Ω, 12 Ω, 4 Ω and 10 Ω respectively in cyclic order to form Wheatstone's network. The resistance that is to be connected in parallel with the resistance of 10 Ω to balance the network is ______ Ω.

23. A point object in air is in front of the curved surface of a *plano-convex* lens. The radius of curvature of the curved surface is 30 cm and the refractive index of the lens material is 1.5, then the focal length of the lens (in cm) is__________.

24. A body A, of mass $m = 0.1$ kg has an initial velocity of $3\hat{i}$ ms^{-1}. It collides elastically with another body, B of the same mass which has an initial velocity of $5\hat{j}$ ms^{-1}. After collision, A moves with a velocity $\vec{v} = 4\left(\hat{i} + \hat{j}\right)$. The energy of B after collision is written as $\dfrac{x}{10}$ J. The value of x is ________.

25. A one metre long (both ends open) organ pipe is kept in a gas that has double the density of air at STP. Assuming the speed of sound in air at STP is 300 m/s, the frequency difference between the fundamental and second harmonic of this pipe is ______ Hz.

CHEMISTRY

26. Among the gases (a)–(e), the gases that cause greenhouse effect are:

(a) CO_2 (b) H_2O

(c) CFCs   (d) O_2

(e) O_3

(1) (a), (b), (c) and (d)

(2) (a), (b), (c) and (e)

(3) (a) and (d)

(4) (a), (c), (d) and (e)

27. A graph of vapour pressure and temperature for three different liquids X, Y, and Z is shown below:

The following inferences are made:

(A) X has higher intermolecular interactions compared to Y.

(B) X has lower intermolecular interactions compared to Y.

(C) Z has lower intermolecular interactions compared to Y.

The correct inference(s) is/are:

(1) (A) and (C)   (2) (A)

(3) (B)   (4) (C)

28. The major product of the following reaction is:

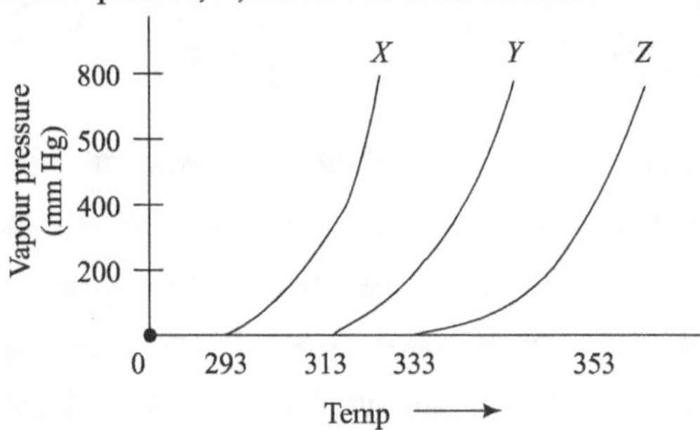

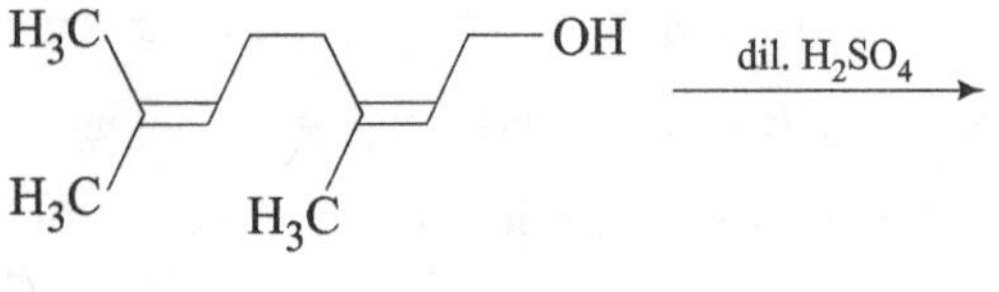

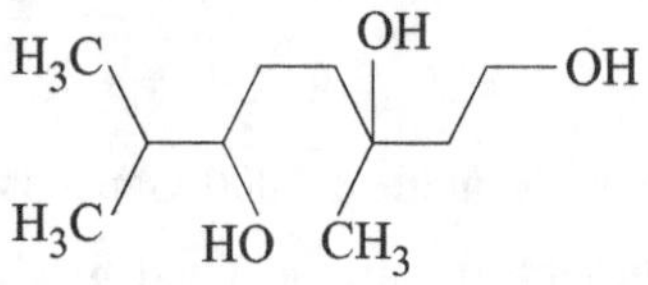

29. The strength of an aqueous NaOH solution is *most accurately* determined by titrating: (Note: consider that an appropriate indicator is used)

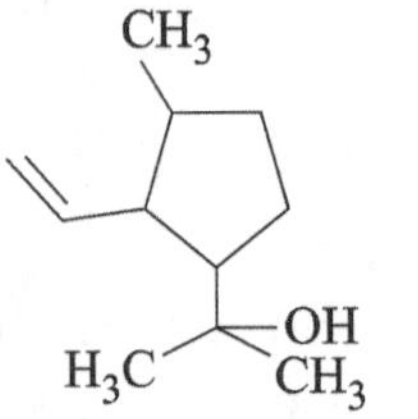

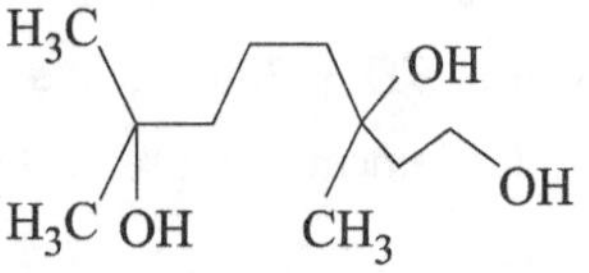

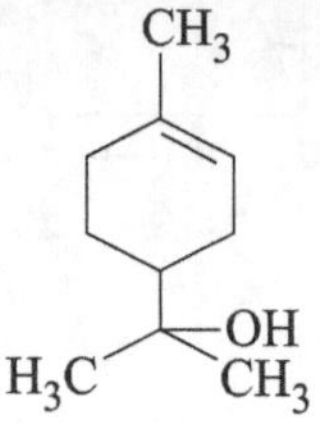

(1) Aq. NaOH in a pipette and aqueous oxalic acid in a burette

(2) Aq. NaOH in a burette and aqueous oxalic acid in a conical flask

(3) Aq. NaOH in a burette and concentrated H_2SO_4 in a conical flask

(4) Aq. NaOH in a volumetric flask and concentrated H_2SO_4 in a conical flask

30. The rate of a certain biochemical reaction at physiological temperature (T) occurs 10^6 times faster with enzyme than without. The change in the activation energy upon adding enzyme is:

(1) $-6(2.303)RT$ (2) $-6RT$

(3) $+6(2.303)RT$ (4) $+6RT$

31. The first ionization energy (in kJ/mol) of Na, Mg, Al and Si respectively, are:

(1) 496, 737, 577,786   (2) 496, 577,737, 786

(3) 786,737,577,496   (4) 496, 577,786, 737

32. The complex that can show *fac-* and *mer-* isomers is:

(1) $[Co(NH_3)_4Cl_2]^+$ (2) $[Pt(NH_3)_2Cl_2]$

(3) $[CoCl_2(en)_2]$ (4) $[Co(NH_3)_3(NO_2)_3]$

33. The decreasing order of reactivity towards dehydrohalogenation (E_1) reaction of the following compounds is:

(A) 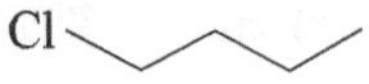 Cl⌒⌒⌒   (B) 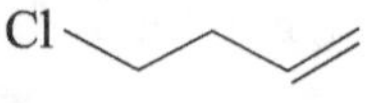 Cl⌒⌒⌒

(C) 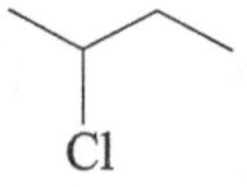   (D)

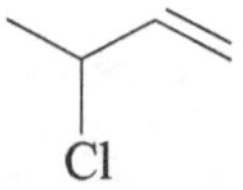

(1) D > B > C > A   (2) B > D > A > C

(3) B > D > C > A   (4) B > A > D > C

34. The major products A and B in the following reactions are:

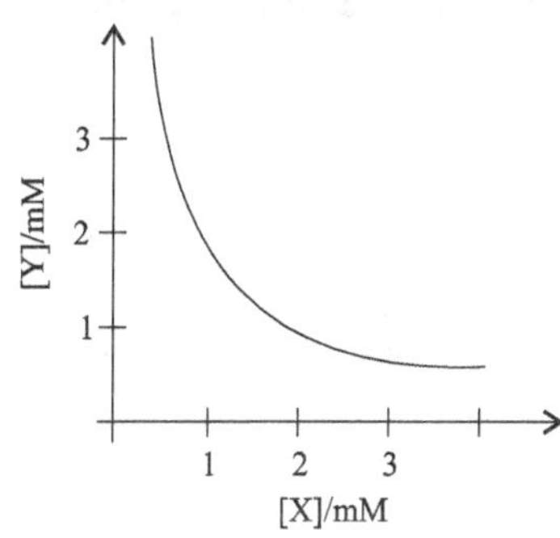

35. The predominant intermolecular forces present in ethyl acetate, a liquid, are:
(1) London dispersion and dipole-dipole
(2) hydrogen bonding and London dispersion
(3) Dipole-dipole and hydrogen bonding
(4) London dispersion, dipole-dipole and hydrogen bonding

36. The stoichiometry and solubility product of a salt with the solubility curve given below is, respectively:

(1) X_2Y, $2 \times 10^{-9}\,M^3$
(2) XY_2, $4 \times 10^{-9}\,M^3$
(3) XY_2, $1 \times 10^{-9}\,M^3$
(4) XY, $2 \times 10^{-6}\,M^3$

37. The most suitable reagent for the given conversion is:

(1) B_2H_6
(2) $NaBH_4$
(3) $LiAlH_4$
(4) H_2/Pd

38. Arrange the following compounds in increasing order of C – OH bond length: methanol, phenol, p-ethoxyphenol
(1) methanol $<$ p-ethoxyphenol $<$ phenol
(2) phenol $<$ methanol $<$ p-ethoxyphenol
(3) phenol $<$ p-ethoxyphenol $<$ methanol
(4) methanol $<$ phenol $<$ p-ethoxyphenol

39. When gypsum is heated to 393 K, it forms:
(1) Anhydrous $CaSO_4$
(2) $CaSO_4 \cdot 5\,H_2O$
(3) $CaSO_4 \cdot 0.5\,H_2O$
(4) Dead burnt plaster

40. A flask contains a mixture of isohexane and 3-methylpentane. One of the liquids boils at 63 °C while the other boils at 60 °C. What is the best way to separate the two liquids and which one will be distilled out first?
(1) fractional distillation, isohexane
(2) simple distillation, 3-methylpentane
(3) simple distillation, isohexane
(4) fractional distillation, 3-methylpentane

41. Which of the following statement is not true for glucose?
(1) Glucose exists in two crystalline forms α and β
(2) Glucose gives Schiff's test for aldehyde
(3) Glucose reacts with hydroxylamine to form oxime
The pentaacetate of glucose does not
(4) react with hydroxylamine to give oxime

42. The number of bonds between sulphur and oxygen atoms in $S_2O_8^{2-}$ and the number of bonds between sulphur and sulphur atoms in rhombic sulphur, respectively, are:
(1) 4 and 6
(2) 8 and 8
(3) 8 and 6
(4) 4 and 8

43. The third ionization enthalpy is minimum for:
(1) Co
(2) Fe
(3) Ni
(4) Mn

44. For the Balmer series in the spectrum of H atom,
$$\bar{v} = R_H \left\{ \frac{1}{n_1^2} - \frac{1}{n_2^2} \right\},$$ the correct statements among (I) to (IV) are:
(I) As wavelength decreases, the lines in the series converge
(II) The integer n_1 is equal to 2
(III) The lines of longest wavelength corresponds to $n_2 = 3$
(IV) The ionization energy of hydrogen can be calculated from wave number of these lines
(1) (I), (III), (IV)
(2) (I), (II), (III)
(3) (I), (II), (IV)
(4) (II), (III), (IV)

45. As per Hardy-Schulze formulation, the flocculation values of the following for ferric hydroxide sol are in the order:

(1) $K_3[Fe(CN)_6] < K_2CrO_4 < KBr = KNO_3 = AlCl_3$

(2) $K_3[Fe(CN)_6] < K_2CrO_4 < AlCl_3 < KBr < KNO_3$

(3) $AlCl_3 > K_3[Fe(CN)_6] > K_2CrO_4 > KBr = KNO_3$

(4) $K_3[Fe(CN)_6] > AlCl_3 > K_2CrO_4 > KBr > KNO_3$

46. What would be the electrode potential for the given half cell reaction at pH=5?

__________ .

$2H_2O \rightarrow O_2 + 4H^\oplus + 4e^-; \; E^0_{red} = 1.23V$

(R = 8.314 J mol^{-1} K^{-1}; Temp = 298 K; oxygen under std. atm. pressure of 1 bar)

47. The magnitude of work done by a gas that undergoes a reversible expansion along the path ABC shown in the figure is __________

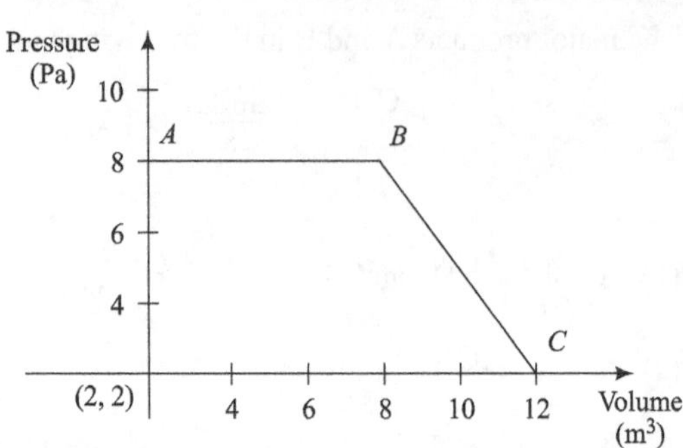

48. Ferrous sulphate heptahydrate is used to fortify foods with iron. The amount (in grams) of the salt required to achieve 10 ppm of iron in 100 kg of wheat is ______ .Atomic weight: Fe = 55.85; S = 32.00; O = 16.00

49. The volume (in mL) of 0.125 M $AgNO_3$ required to quantitatively precipitate chloride ions in 0.3 g of $[Co(NH_3)_6]Cl_3$ is _______ .

$M_{[Co(NH_3)_6]Cl_3} = 267.46$ g/mol

$M_{AgNO_3} = 169.87$ g/mol

50. The number of chiral centres in penicillin is _______ .

MATHEMATICS

51. The shortest distance between the lines

$$\frac{x-3}{3} = \frac{y-8}{-1} = \frac{z-3}{1} \text{ and}$$

$$\frac{x+3}{-3} = \frac{y+7}{2} = \frac{z-6}{4} \text{ is:}$$

(1) $2\sqrt{30}$ (2) $\frac{7}{2}\sqrt{30}$

(3) $3\sqrt{30}$ (4) 3

52. The mean and the standard deviation (s.d.) of 10 observations are 20 and 2 respectively. Each of these 10 observations is multiplied by p and then reduced by q, where $p \neq 0$ and $q \neq 0$. If the new mean and new s.d. become half of their original values, then q is equal to:

(1) –5   (2) 10

(3) –20   (4) –10

53. $\displaystyle\lim_{x\to 0}\left(\frac{3x^2+2}{7x^2+2}\right)^{1/x^2}$ is equal to:

(1) $\dfrac{1}{e}$ (2) $\dfrac{1}{e^2}$

(3) e^2 (4) e

54. Let two points be $A(1, -1)$ and $B(0, 2)$. If a point $P(x', y')$ be such that the area of $\Delta PAB = 5$ sq. units and it lies on the line, $3x + y - 4\lambda = 0$, then a value of λ is:

(1) 4   (2) 3

(3) 1   (4) –3

55. If c is a point at which Rolle's theorem holds for the function, $f(x) = \log_e\left(\dfrac{x^2+a}{7x}\right)$ in the interval $[3, 4]$, where $\alpha \in R$, then $f''(c)$ is equal to:

(1) $-\dfrac{1}{12}$ (2) $\dfrac{1}{12}$

(3) $-\dfrac{1}{24}$ (4) $\dfrac{\sqrt{3}}{7}$

56. Let $f(x) = x\cos^{-1}(-\sin|x|), x \in \left[-\dfrac{\pi}{2}, \dfrac{\pi}{2}\right]$, then which of the following is true?

(1) f' is increasing in $\left(-\dfrac{\pi}{2}, 0\right)$ and decreasing in $\left(0, \dfrac{\pi}{2}\right)$

(2) $f'(0) = -\dfrac{\pi}{2}$

(3) f' is not differentiable at $x=0$

(4) f' is decreasing in $\left(-\dfrac{\pi}{2}, 0\right)$ and increasing in $\left(0, \dfrac{\pi}{2}\right)$

57. Which one of the following is a tautology?

(1) $(p \wedge (p \rightarrow q)) \rightarrow q$ (2) $q \rightarrow (p \wedge (p \rightarrow q))$

(3) $p \wedge (p \vee q)$ (4) $p \vee (p \wedge q)$

58. Let the line $y = mx$ and the ellipse $2x^2 + y^2 = 1$ intersect at a point P in the first quadrant. If the normal to this ellipse at P meets the co-ordinate axes at $\left(-\dfrac{1}{3\sqrt{2}}, 0\right)$ and $(0, \beta)$, then β is equal to:

(1) $\dfrac{2\sqrt{2}}{3}$

(2) $\dfrac{2}{\sqrt{3}}$

(3) $\dfrac{2}{3}$

(4) $\dfrac{\sqrt{2}}{3}$

59. The locus of a point which divides the line segment joining the point $(0, -1)$ and a point on the parabola, $x^2 = 4y$, internally in the ratio $1 : 2$, is:

(1) $9x^2 - 12y = 8$

(2) $9x^2 - 3y = 2$

(3) $x^2 - 3y = 2$

(4) $4x^2 - 3y = 2$

60. Let A and B be two independent events such that $P(A) = \dfrac{1}{3}$ and $P(B) = \dfrac{1}{6}$. Then, which of the following is TRUE ?

(1) $P(A/B) = \dfrac{2}{3}$

(2) $P(A/B') = \dfrac{1}{3}$

(3) $P(A'/B') = \dfrac{1}{3}$

(4) $P(A/(A \cup B)) = \dfrac{1}{4}$

61. Let the volume of a parallelopiped whose coterminous edges are given by $\vec{u} = \hat{i} + \hat{j} + \lambda\hat{k}, \vec{v} = \hat{i} + \hat{j} + 3\hat{k}$ and $\vec{w} = 2\hat{i} + \hat{j} + \hat{k}$ be 1 cu. unit. If θ be the angle between the edges $\vec{u}$ and $\vec{w}$, then $\cos\theta$ can be:

(1) $\dfrac{7}{6\sqrt{6}}$

(2) $\dfrac{7}{6\sqrt{3}}$

(3) $\dfrac{5}{7}$

(4) $\dfrac{5}{3\sqrt{3}}$

62. If $\displaystyle\int \dfrac{\cos x\, dx}{\sin^3 x(1 + \sin^6 x)^{2/3}} = f(x)(1 + \sin^6 x)^{1/\lambda} + c$ where c is a constant of integration, then $\lambda f\left(\dfrac{\pi}{3}\right)$ is equal to:

(1) $-\dfrac{9}{8}$

(2) 2

(3) $\dfrac{9}{8}$

(4) -2

63. If the equation, $x^2 + bx + 45 = 0$ $(b \in R)$ has conjugate complex roots and they satisfy $|z + 1| = 2\sqrt{10}$, then:

(1) $b^2 - b = 30$

(2) $b^2 + b = 72$

(3) $b^2 - b = 42$

(4) $b^2 + b = 12$

64. Let $f: R \to R$ be such that for all $x \in R$, $(2^{1+x} + 2^{1-x})$, $f(x)$ and $(3^x + 3^{-x})$ are in A.P., then the minimum value of $f(x)$ is:

(1) 2

(2) 3

(3) 0

(4) 4

65. For $a > 0$, let the curves $C_1 : y^2 = ax$ and $C_2 : x^2 = ay$ intersect at origin O and a point P. Let the line $x = b$ $(0 < b < a)$ intersect the chord OP and the x-axis at points Q and R, respectively. If the line $x = b$ bisects the area bounded by the curves, C_1 and C_2, and the area of $\Delta OQR = \dfrac{1}{2}$, then '$a$' satisfies the equation:

(1) $x^6 - 6x^3 + 4 = 0$

(2) $x^6 - 12x^3 + 4 = 0$

(3) $x^6 + 6x^3 - 4 = 0$

(4) $x^6 - 12x^3 - 4 = 0$

66. The inverse function of $f(x) = \dfrac{8^{2x} - 8^{-2x}}{8^{2x} + 8^{-2x}}, x \in (-1, 1)$, is __________.

(1) $\dfrac{1}{4}\log_e\left(\dfrac{1+x}{1-x}\right)$

(2) $\dfrac{1}{4}(\log_8 e)\log_e\left(\dfrac{1-x}{1+x}\right)$

(3) $\dfrac{1}{4}\log_e\left(\dfrac{1-x}{1+x}\right)$

(4) $\dfrac{1}{4}(\log_8 e)\log_e\left(\dfrac{1+x}{1-x}\right)$

67. For which of the following ordered pairs (μ, δ), the system of linear equations

$x + 2y + 3z = 1$

$3x + 4y + 5z = \mu$

$4x + 4y + 4z = \delta$

is inconsistent?

(1) $(4, 3)$

(2) $(4, 6)$

(3) $(1, 0)$

(4) $(3, 4)$

68. If a, b and c are the greatest values of $^{19}C_p$, $^{20}C_q$ and $^{21}C_r$ respectively, then:

(1) $\dfrac{a}{11} = \dfrac{b}{22} = \dfrac{c}{21}$

(2) $\dfrac{a}{10} = \dfrac{b}{11} = \dfrac{c}{21}$

(3) $\dfrac{a}{11} = \dfrac{b}{22} = \dfrac{c}{42}$

(4) $\dfrac{a}{10} = \dfrac{b}{11} = \dfrac{c}{42}$

69. Let $f(x) = (\sin(\tan^{-1} x) + \sin(\cot^{-1} x))^2 - 1$, $|x| > 1$. If $\dfrac{dy}{dx} = \dfrac{1}{2}\dfrac{d}{dx}(\sin^{-1}(f(x)))$ and $y(\sqrt{3}) = \dfrac{\pi}{6}$, then $y(-\sqrt{3})$ is equal to:

  (1) $\dfrac{2\pi}{3}$ (2) $-\dfrac{\pi}{6}$

  (3) $\dfrac{5\pi}{6}$ (4) $\dfrac{\pi}{3}$

70. Let $y = y(x)$ be a solution of the differential equation,

$$\sqrt{1-x^2}\,\dfrac{dy}{dx} + \sqrt{1-y^2} = 0, |x| < 1.$$

If $y\left(\dfrac{1}{2}\right) = \dfrac{\sqrt{3}}{2}$, then $y\left(\dfrac{-1}{\sqrt{2}}\right)$ is equal to:

  (1) $\dfrac{\sqrt{3}}{2}$ (2) $-\dfrac{1}{\sqrt{2}}$

  (3) $\dfrac{1}{\sqrt{2}}$ (4) $-\dfrac{\sqrt{3}}{2}$

71. The sum $\displaystyle\sum_{k=1}^{20}(1+2+3+\ldots+k)$ is __________.

72. The number of all 3×3 matrices A, with enteries from the set $\{-1, 0, 1\}$ such that the sum of the diagonal elements of AA^T is 3, is __________.

73. Let the normal at a point P on the curve $y^2 - 3x^2 + y + 10 = 0$ intersect the y-axis at $\left(0, \dfrac{3}{2}\right)$. If m is the slope of the tangent at P to the curve, then $|m|$ is equal to __________.

74. An urn contains 5 red marbles, 4 black marbles and 3 white marbles. Then the number of ways in which 4 marbles can be drawn so that at the most three of them are red is __________.

75. The least positive value of 'a' for which the equation, $2x^2 + (a - 10)x + \dfrac{33}{2} = 2a$ has real roots is __________.

JEE MAIN 2020

(Held on 08-01-2020 Evening Shift)

PHYSICS

1. A uniform sphere of mass 500 g rolls without slipping on a plane horizontal surface with its centre moving at a speed of 5.00 cm/s. Its kinetic energy is:

(1) 8.75×10^{-4} J   (2) 8.75×10^{-3} J

(3) 6.25×10^{-4} J   (4) 1.13×10^{-3} J

2. An object is gradually moving away from the focal point of a concave mirror along the axis of the mirror. The graphical representation of the magnitude of linear magnification (m) versus distance of the object from the mirror (x) is correctly given by

(Graphs are drawn schematically and are not to scale)

(1)

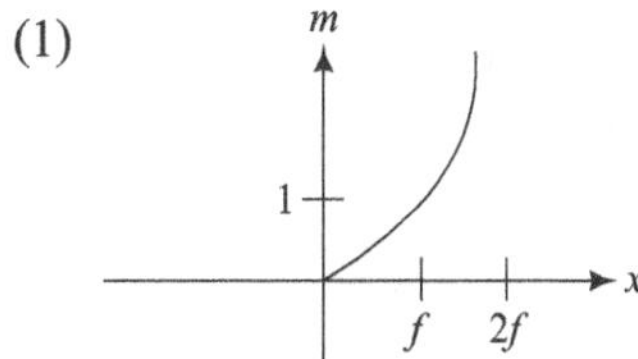

(2)

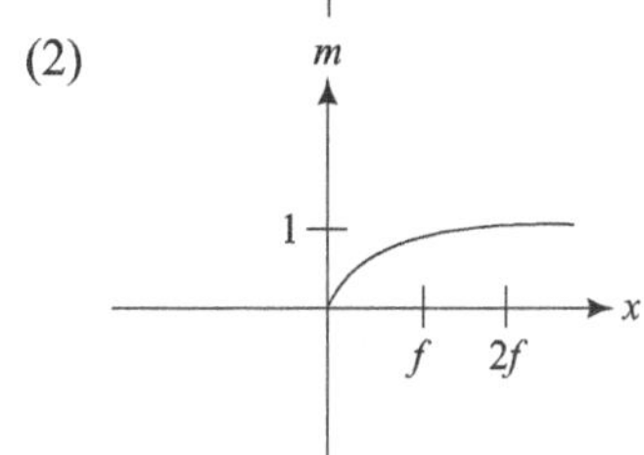

(3)

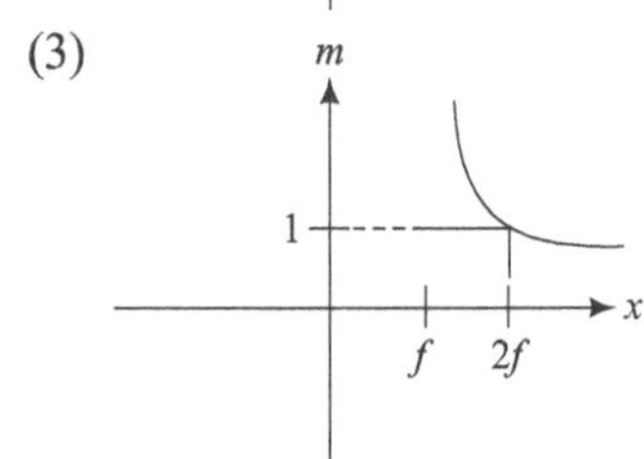

(4)

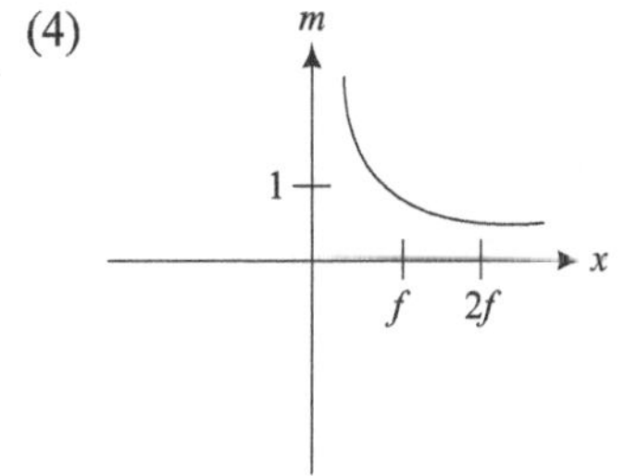

3. A transverse wave travels on a taut steel wire with a velocity of v when tension in it is 2.06×10^4 N. When the tension is changed to T, the velocity changed to $v/2$. The value of T is close to:

(1) 2.50×10^4 N   (2) 5.15×10^3 N

(3) 30.5×10^4 N   (4) 10.2×10^2 N

4. Consider a mixture of n moles of helium gas and $2n$ moles of oxygen gas (molecules taken to be rigid) as an ideal gas. Its C_P/C_V value will be:

(1) 19/13   (2) 67/45

(3) 40/27   (4) 23/15

5. As shown in fig. when a spherical cavity (centred at O) of radius 1 is cut out of a uniform sphere of radius R (centred at C), the centre of mass of remaining (shaded) part of sphere is at G, i.e on the surface of the cavity. R can be determined by the equation:

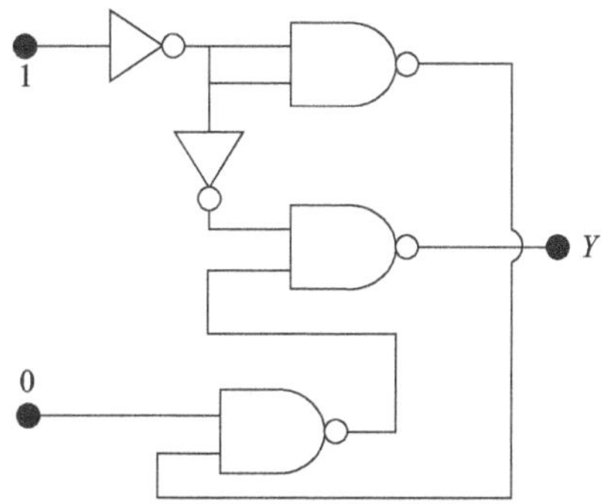

(1) $(R^2 + R + 1)(2 - R) = 1$

(2) $(R^2 - R - 1)(2 - R) = 1$

(3) $(R^2 - R + 1)(2 - R) = 1$

(4) $(R^2 + R - 1)(2 - R) = 1$

6. In the given circuit, value of Y is:

(1) 0

(2) toggles between 0 and 1

(3) will not execute

(4) 1

7. A Carnot engine having an efficiency of $\dfrac{1}{10}$ is being used as a refrigerator. If the work done on the refrigerator is 10 J, the amount of heat absorbed from the reservoir at lower temperature is:

(1) 99 J   (2) 100 J

(3) 1 J   (4) 90 J

8. In a double-slit experiment, at a certain point on the screen the path difference between the two interfering waves is $\dfrac{1}{8}$ th of a wavelength. The ratio of the intensity of light at that point to that at the centre of a bright fringe is:

(1) 0.853   (2) 0.672

(3) 0.568   (4) 0.760

9. A very long wire $ABDMNDC$ is shown in figure carrying current I. AB and BC parts are straight, long and at right angle. At D wire forms a circular turn $DMND$ of radius R. AB, BC parts are tangential to circular turn at N and D. Magnetic field at the centre of circle is:

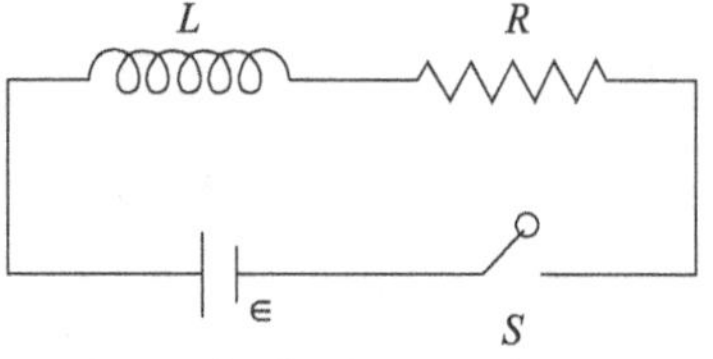

(1) $\dfrac{\mu_0 I}{2\pi R}\left(\pi + \dfrac{1}{\sqrt{2}}\right)$

(2) $\dfrac{\mu_0 I}{2\pi R}\left(\pi - \dfrac{1}{\sqrt{2}}\right)$

(3) $\dfrac{\mu_0 I}{2\pi R}(\pi + 1)$

(4) $\dfrac{\mu_0 I}{2R}$

10. A particle of mass m is dropped from a height h above the ground. At the same time another particle of the same mass is thrown vertically upwards from the ground with a speed of $\sqrt{2gh}$. If they collide head-on completely inelastically, the time taken for the combined mass to reach the ground, in units of $\sqrt{\dfrac{h}{g}}$ is:

(1) $\sqrt{\dfrac{1}{2}}$ 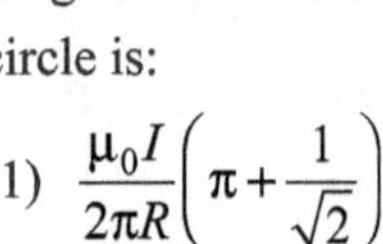 (2) $\sqrt{\dfrac{3}{4}}$

(3) $\dfrac{1}{2}$ 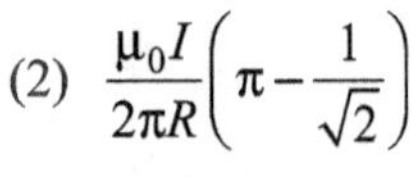 (4) $\sqrt{\dfrac{3}{2}}$

11. A plane electromagnetic wave of frequency 25 GHz is propagating in vacuum along the z-direction. At a particular point in space and time, the magnetic field is given by $\vec{B} = 5\times10^{-8}\,\hat{j}\ T$. The corresponding electric field $\vec{E}$ is (speed of light $c = 3 \times 10^8$ ms^{-1})

(1) $1.66 \times 10^{-16}\,\hat{i}$ V/m   (2) $-1.66 \times 10^{-16}\,\hat{i}$ V/m

(3) $-15\,\hat{i}$ V/m   (4) $15\,\hat{i}$ V/m

12. An electron (mass m) with initial velocity $\vec{v} = v_0\hat{i} + v_0\hat{j}$ is in an electric field $\vec{E} = -E_0\hat{k}$. If λ_0 is initial de-Broglie wavelength of electron, its de-Broglie wave length at time t is given by:

(1) $\dfrac{\lambda_0 \sqrt{2}}{\sqrt{1 + \dfrac{e^2 E^2 t^2}{m^2 v_0^2}}}$ (2) $\dfrac{\lambda_0}{\sqrt{1 + \dfrac{e^2 E_0^2 t^2}{m^2 v_0^2}}}$

(3) $\dfrac{\lambda_0}{\sqrt{1 + \dfrac{e^2 E^2 t^2}{2m^2 v_0^2}}}$ (4) $\dfrac{\lambda_0}{\sqrt{2 + \dfrac{e^2 E^2 t^2}{m^2 v_0^2}}}$

13. A simple pendulum is being used to determine the value of gravitational acceleration g at a certain place. The length of the pendulum is 25.0 cm and a stop watch with 1 s resolution measures the time taken for 40 oscillations to be 50 s. The accuracy in g is:

(1) 5 40%   (2) 3.40%

(3) 4.40%   (4) 2.40%

14.

As shown in the figure, a battery of emf $\in$ is connected to an inductor L and resistance R in series. The switch is closed at $t = 0$. The total charge that flows from the battery, between $t = 0$ and $t = t_c$ (t_c is the time constant of the circuit) is:

(1) $\dfrac{\in}{eL}$ (2) $\dfrac{\in L}{R^2}\left(1 - \dfrac{1}{e}\right)$

(3) $\dfrac{\in L}{R^2}$ (4) $\dfrac{\in R}{eL^2}$

15. Consider two charged metallic spheres S_1 and S_2 of radii R_1 and R_2, respectively. The electric fields E_1 (on S_1) and E_2 (on S_2) on their surfaces are such that $E_1/E_2 = R_1/R_2$. Then the ratio V_1(on S_1)/V_2(on S_2) of the electrostatic potentials on each sphere is:

(1) R_1/R_2 (2) $(R_1/R_2)^2$

(3) (R_2/R_1) (4) $\left(\dfrac{R_1}{R_2}\right)^3$

16. A particle moves such that its position vector $\vec{r}\,(t)$ = $\cos \omega t\;\hat{i}$ + $\sin \omega t\;\hat{j}$ where ω is a constant and t is time. Then which of the following statements is true for the velocity $\vec{v}\,(t)$ and acceleration $\vec{a}\,(t)$ of the particle:

(1) $\vec{v}$ is perpendicular to $\vec{r}$ and $\vec{a}$ is directed away from the origin

(2) $\vec{v}$ and $\vec{a}$ both are perpendicular to $\vec{r}$

(3) $\vec{v}$ and $\vec{a}$ both are parallel to $\vec{r}$

(4) $\vec{v}$ is perpendicular to $\vec{r}$ and $\vec{a}$ is directed towards the origin

17. A capacitor is made of two square plates each of side 'a' making a very small angle a between them, as shown in figure. The capacitance will be close to:

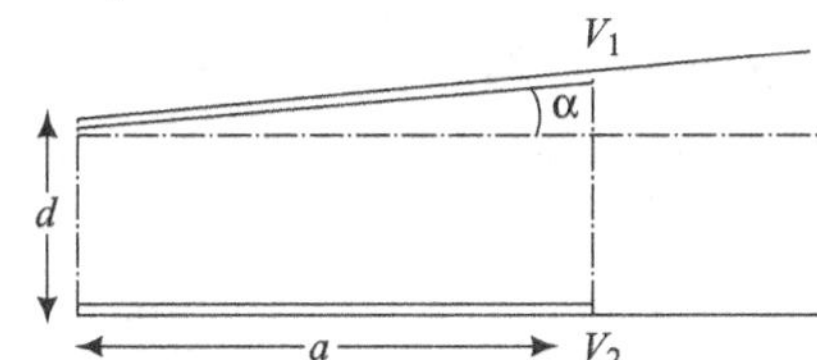

(1) $\dfrac{\epsilon_0\,a^2}{d}\left(1-\dfrac{\alpha a}{2d}\right)$

(2) $\dfrac{\epsilon_0\,a^2}{d}\left(1-\dfrac{\alpha a}{4d}\right)$

(3) $\dfrac{\epsilon_0\,a^2}{d}\left(1+\dfrac{\alpha a}{d}\right)$

(4) $\dfrac{\epsilon_0\,a^2}{d}\left(1-\dfrac{3\alpha a}{2d}\right)$

18. A particle of mass m and charge q is released from rest in a uniform electric field. If there is no other force on the particle, the dependence of its speed v on the distance x travelled by it is correctly given by (graphs are schematic and not drawn to scale)

(1)
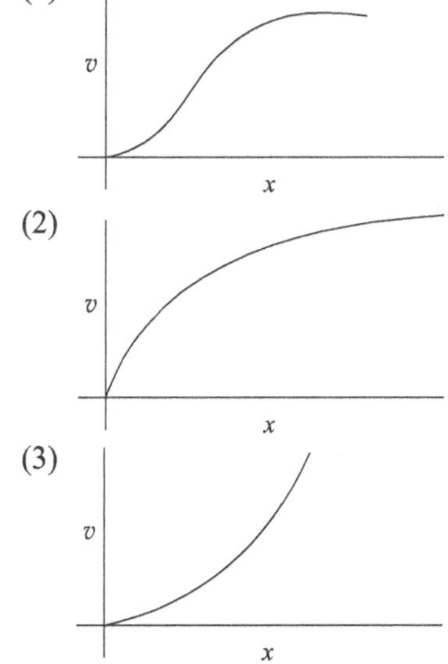

(2)

(3)

(4)
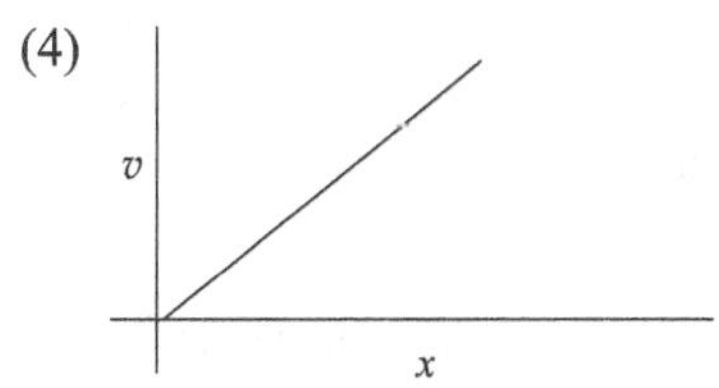

19. A galvanometer having a coil resistance 100 Ω gives a full scale deflection when a current of 1 mA is passed through it. What is the value of the resistance which can convert this galvanometer into a voltmeter giving full scale deflection for a potential difference of 10 V?

(1) 10 kΩ (2) 8.9 kΩ

(3) 7.9 kΩ (4) 9.9 kΩ

20.

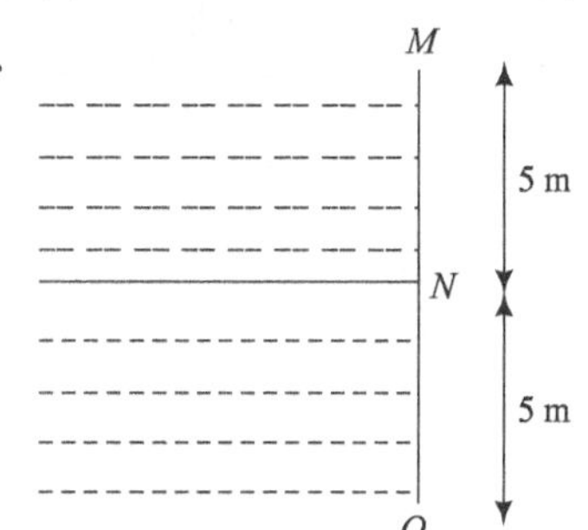

Two liquids of densities ρ_1 and $\rho_2 (\rho_2 = 2\rho_1)$ are filled up behind a square wall of side 10 m as shown in figure. Each liquid has a height of 5 m. The ratio of the forces due to these liquids exerted on upper part MN to that at the lower part NO is (Assume that the liquids are not mixing):

(1) 1/3   (2) 2/3

(3) 1/2   (4) 1/4

21. A ball is dropped from the top of a 100 m high tower on a planet. In the last $\dfrac{1}{2}$ s before hitting the ground, it covers a distance of 19 m. Acceleration due to gravity (in ms^{-2}) near the surface on that planet is _______.

22. The first member of the Balmer series of hydrogen atom has a wavelength of 6561 Å. The wavelength of the second member of the Balmer series (in nm) is _______.

23. The series combination of two batteries, both of the same emf 10 V, but different internal resistance of 20 Ω and 5 Ω, is connected to the parallel combination of two resistors 30 Ω and R Ω. The voltage difference across the battery of internal resistance 20 Ω is zero, the value of R (in Ω) is _______.

24. Three containers C_1, C_2 and C_3 have water at different temperatures. The table below shows the final temperature T when different amounts of water (given in liters) are taken from each container and mixed (assume no loss of heat during the process)

C_1	C_2	C_3	T
$1l$	$2l$	--	60°C
–	$1l$	$2l$	30°C
$2l$	--	$1l$	60°C
$1l$	$1l$	$1l$	θ

The value of θ (in °C to the nearest integer) is______.

25. An asteroid is moving directly towards the centre of the earth. When at a distance of $10\,R$ (R is the radius of the earth) from the earths centre, it has a speed of 12 km/s. Neglecting the effect of earths atmosphere, what will be the speed of the asteroid when it hits the surface of the earth (escape velocity from the earth is 11.2 km/ s)? Give your answer to the nearest integer in kilometer/s _____.

CHEMISTRY

26. The major product in the following reaction is:

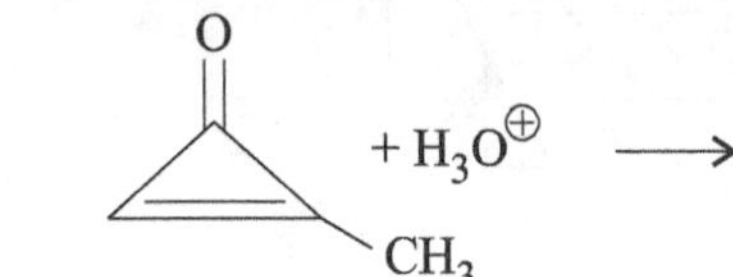

(1)

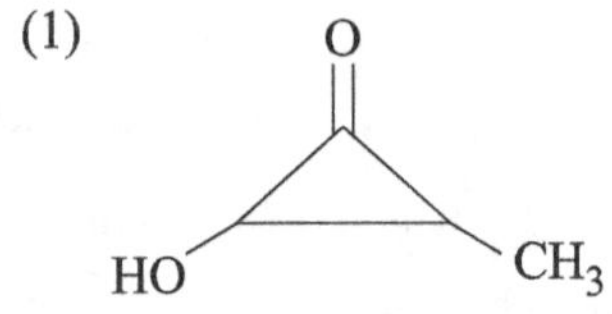

(2)

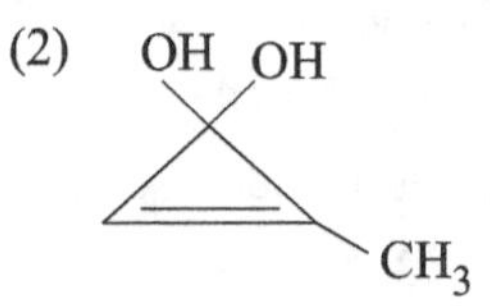

(3)

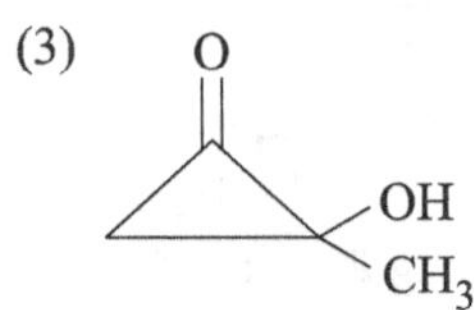

(4)

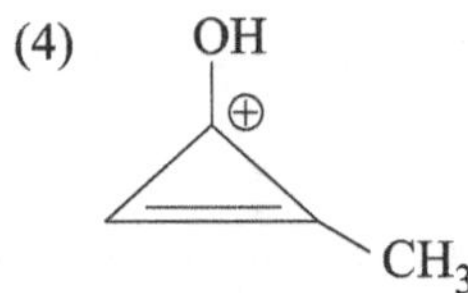

27. Among the reactions (a) - (d), the reaction(s) that does/do not occur in the blast furnace during the extraction of iron is/are:

(a) $CaO + SiO_2 \rightarrow CaSiO_3$

(b) $3Fe_2O_3 + CO \rightarrow 2Fe_3O_4 + CO_2$

(c) $FeO + SiO_2 \rightarrow FeSiO_3$

(d) $FeO \rightarrow Fe + \dfrac{1}{2}\,O_2$

(1) (a)   (2) (a) and (d)

(3) (c) and (d)   (4) (d)

28. Hydrogen has three isotopes (A), (B) and (C). If the number of neutron(s) in (A), (B) and (C) respectively, are (x), (y) and (z), the sum of (x), (y) and (z) is:

(1) 3   (2) 2

(3) 4   (4) 1

29. For the following Assertion and Reason, the correct option is:

Assertion: For hydrogenation reactions, the catalytic activity increases from Group 5 to Group 11 metals with maximum activity shown by Group 7-9 elements.

Reason: The reactants are most strongly adsorbed on group 7-9 elements.

(1) The assertion is true, but the reason is false.

(2) Both assertion and reason are false.

(3) Both assertion and reason are true and the reason is the correct explanation for the assertion.

(4) Both assertion and reason are true but the reason is not the correct explanation for the assertion.

30. Two monomers in maltose are:

(1) α-D-glucose and β-D-glucose

(2) α-D-glucose and α-D-galactose

(3) α-D-glucose and α-D-fructose

(4) α-D-glucose and α-D-glucose

31. Preparation of Bakelite proceeds via reactions:

(1) Electrophilic addition and dehydration

(2) Condensation and elimination

(3) Electrophilic substitution and dehydration

(4) Nucleophilic addition and dehydration

32. The radius of the second Bohr orbit, in terms of the Bohr radius, a_0, in Li^{2+} is:

(1) $\dfrac{2a_0}{3}$ (2) $\dfrac{4a_0}{9}$

(3) $\dfrac{4a_0}{3}$ (4) $\dfrac{2a_0}{9}$

33. A metal (A) on heating in nitrogen gas gives compound B. B on treatment with H_2O gives a colourless gas which when passed through $CuSO_4$ solution gives a dark blue-violet coloured solution. A and B respectively, are:

(1) Na and $NaNO_3$ (2) Na and Na_3N

(3) Mg and Mg_3N_2 (4) Mg and $Mg(NO_3)_2$

34. Among (a) - (d), the complexes that can display geometrical isomerism are:

(a) $[Pt(NH_3)_3Cl]^+$ (b) $[Pt(NH_3)Cl_5]^-$
(c) $[Pt(NH_3)_2Cl(NO_2)]$ (d) $[Pt(NH_3)_4ClBr]^{2+}$
(1) (b) and (c)   (2) (d) and (a)
(3) (c) and (d)   (4) (a) and (b)

35. Consider the following plots of rate constant versus $\dfrac{1}{T}$ for four different reactions. Which of the following orders is correct for the activation energies of these reactions?

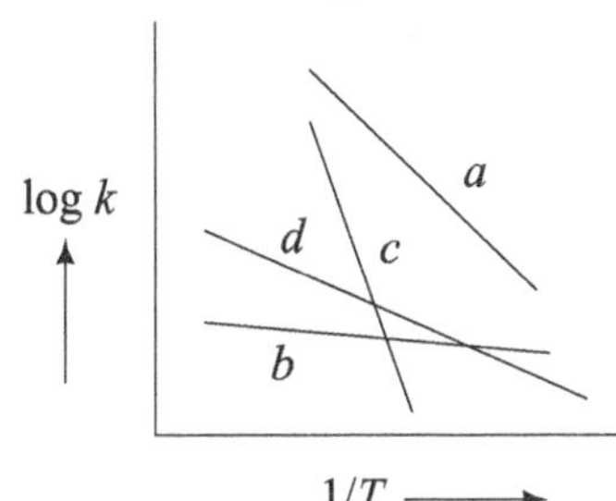

(1) $E_b > E_a > E_d > E_c$ (2) $E_a > E_c > E_d > E_b$
(3) $E_c > E_a > E_d > E_b$ (4) $E_b > E_d > E_c > E_a$

36. The major product [B] in the following sequence of reactions is:

$$CH_3 - C = CH - CH_2CH_3 \xrightarrow[\text{(ii) } H_2O_2,\ OH^\ominus]{\text{(i) } B_2H_6} [A]$$
$$\underset{CH(CH_3)_2}{|}$$

$$\xrightarrow[\Delta]{\text{dil. } H_2SO_4} [B]$$

(1) $CH_2 = \underset{\underset{CH(CH_3)_2}{|}}{C} - CH_2CH_2CH_3$

(2) $CH_3 - \underset{\underset{\underset{H_3C \quad CH_3}{}}{C}}{\overset{\parallel}{C}} - CH_2CH_2CH_3$

(3) $CH_3 - C = CH - CH_2CH_3$
         $\underset{CH(CH_3)_2}{|}$

(4) $CH_3 - CH - CH = CH - CH_3$
         $\underset{CH(CH_3)_2}{|}$

37. The correct order of the calculated spin-only magnetic moments of complexes (A) to (D) is:

(A) $Ni(CO)_4$ (B) $[Ni(H_2O)_6]Cl_2$
(C) $Na_2[Ni(CN)_4]$ (D) $PdCl_2(PPh_3)_2$
(1) $(A) \approx (C) < (B) \approx (D)$ (2) $(C) < (D) < (B) < (A)$
(3) $(C) \approx (D) < (B) < (A)$ (4) $(A) \approx (C) \approx (D) < (B)$

38. Arrange the following bonds according to their average bond energies in descending order: $C-Cl, C-Br, C-F, C-I$

(1) $C-F > C-Cl > C-Br > C-I$
(2) $C-Br > C-I > C-Cl > C-F$
(3) $C-I > C-Br > C-Cl > C-F$
(4) $C-Cl > C-Br > C-I > C-F$

39. Kjeldahl's method cannot be used to estimate nitrogen for which of the following compounds?

(1) $C_6H_5NH_2$ (2) $CH_3CH_2 - C \equiv N$

(3) $C_6H_5NO_2$ (4) $NH_2 - \overset{\overset{\textstyle O}{\parallel}}{C} - NH_2$

40. Among the compounds A and B with molecular formula $C_9H_{18}O_3$, A is having higher boiling point the B. The possible structures of A and B are:

(1) $A = $ HO⟋⟍OH, HO (cyclohexane with three CH$_2$OH)

$B = $ H$_3$CO⟋⟍OCH$_3$, OCH$_3$ (cyclohexane with three OCH$_3$)

(2) $A = $ H$_3$CO⟋⟍OCH$_3$, OCH$_3$ (cyclohexane with three OCH$_3$)

$B = $ HO⟋⟍OH, HO (cyclohexane with three CH$_2$OH)

(3) $A = $ HO⟋⟍OH, HO (cyclohexane with three CH$_2$OH)

$B = $ HO⟍⟋OH, OH (cyclohexane)

(4) $A = $ H$_3$CO⟍⟋OCH$_3$, OCH$_3$ (cyclohexane with three OCH$_3$)

$B = $ HO⟍⟋OH, OH (cyclohexane)

41. For the following Assertion and Reason, the correct option is:

Assertion: The pH of water increases with increase in temperature.

Reason: The dissociation of water into H^+ and OH^- is an exothermic reaction.

(1) Both assertion and reason are true, and the reason is the correct explanation for the assertion.

(2) Both assertion and reason are false.

(3) Both assertion and reason are true, but the reason is not the correct explanation for the assertion.

(4) Assertion is not true, but reason is true.

42. Which of the following compounds is likely to show both Frenkel and Schottky defects in its crystalline form?

  (1) AgBr   (2) CsCl

  (3) KBr   (4) ZnS

43. White phosphorus on reaction with concentrated NaOH solution in an inert atmosphere of CO_2 gives phosphine and compound (X). (X) on acidification with HCl gives compound (Y). The basicity of compound (Y) is:

  (1) 2   (2) 1

  (3) 4   (4) 3

44. An unsaturated hydrocarbon X absorbs two hydrogen molecules on catalytic hydrogenation, and also gives following reaction:

$$X \xrightarrow[\text{Zn/H}_2\text{O}]{\text{O}_3} A \xrightarrow{[\text{Ag(NH}_3)_2]^+}$$

B(3-oxo-hexanedicarboxylic acid)

(1) 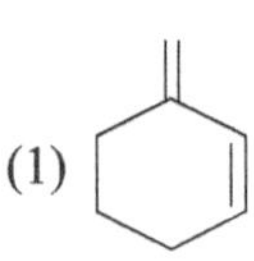

(2) 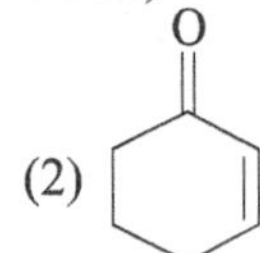

(3) 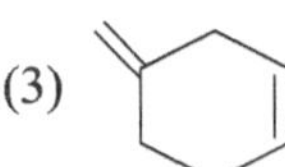

(4) 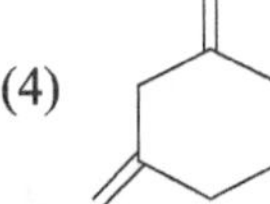

45. The increasing order of the atomic radii of the following elements is:

  (a) C   (b) O

  (c) F   (d) Cl

  (e) Br

  (1) (b) < (c) < (d) < (a) < (e)

  (2) (d) < (c) < (b) < (a) < (e)

  (3) (c) < (b) < (a) < (d) < (e)

  (4) (a) < (b) < (c) < (d) < (e)

46. In the following sequence of reactions the maximum number of atoms present in molecule 'C' in one plane is ________ .

$$A \xrightarrow[\text{Cutube}]{\text{Red hot}} B \xrightarrow[\text{Anhydrous AlCl}_3]{\text{CH}_3\text{Cl(1.eq.)}}$$

(A is a lowest molecular weight alkyne)

47. For an electrochemical cell

$Sn(s)|Sn^{2+}$ $(aq, 1M) \| Pb^{2+}$ $(aq, 1M)|Pb(s)$ the ratio $\dfrac{[Sn^{2+}]}{[Pb^{2+}]}$ when this cell attains equilibrium is ________ .

$\left(\text{Given: } E^0_{Sn^{2+}|Sn} = -0.14V, \right.$

$\left. E_{Pb|Pb} = -0.13 \text{ V}, \dfrac{2.303 \, RT}{} = 0.06 \right)$

48. At constant volume, 4 mol of an ideal gas when heated from 300 K to 500 K changes its internal energy by 5000 J. The molar heat capacity at constant volume is ________ .

49. Complexes (ML_5) of metals Ni and Fe have ideal square pyramidal and trigonal bipyramidal geometries, respectively. The sum of the 90°, 120° and 180° L-M-Langles in the two complexes is ________ .

50. $NaClO_3$ is used, even in spacecrafts, to produce O_2. The daily consumption of pure O_2 by a person is 492 L at 1 atm, 300 K. How much amount of $NaClO_3$, in grams, is required to produce O_2 for the daily consumption of a person at 1 atm, 300 K? ________ .

$NaClO_3(s) + Fe(s) \rightarrow O_2(g) + NaCl(s) + FeO(s)$ R = 0.082 Latm mol^{-1} K^{-1}

MATHEMATICS

51. $\displaystyle\lim_{x \to 0} \int_0^x \dfrac{t\sin(10t)dt}{x}$ is equal to:

  (1) 0   (2) $\dfrac{1}{10}$

  (3) $-\dfrac{1}{5}$ (4) $-\dfrac{1}{10}$

52. The length of the perpendicular from the origin, on the normal to the curve, $x^2 + 2xy - 3y^2 = 0$ at the point (2, 2) is:

  (1) $\sqrt{2}$ (2) $4\sqrt{2}$

  (3) 2   (4) $2\sqrt{2}$

53. Let $a = \hat{i} - \hat{j} + \hat{k}$ and $\vec{b} = \hat{i} - \hat{j} + \hat{k}$ be two vectors. If $\vec{c}$ is a vector such that $\vec{b} \times \vec{c} = \vec{b} \times \vec{a}$ and $\vec{c} \cdot \vec{a} = 0$, then $\vec{c} \cdot \vec{b}$ is equal to:

  (1) $-\dfrac{3}{2}$ (2) $\dfrac{1}{2}$

  (3) $-\dfrac{1}{2}$ (4) -1

54. The area (in sq. units) of the region
$\{(x, y) \in R^2 : x^2 \le y \le |3 - 2x|\}$, is:

(1) $\dfrac{32}{3}$ (2) $\dfrac{34}{3}$

(3) $\dfrac{29}{3}$ (4) $\dfrac{31}{3}$

55. If $A = \begin{pmatrix} 2 & 2 \\ 9 & 4 \end{pmatrix}$ and $I = \begin{pmatrix} 1 & 0 \\ 0 & 1 \end{pmatrix}$, then $10A^{-1}$ is equal to:

(1) $A - 4I$ (2) $6I - A$

(3) $A - 6I$ (4) $4I - A$

56. The mean and variance of 20 observations are found to be 10 and 4, respectively. On rechecking, it was found that an observation 9 was incorrect and the correct observation was 11. Then the correct variance is:

(1) 3.99   (2) 4.01

(3) 4.02   (4) 3.98

57. The differential equation of the family of curves, $x^2 = 4b\,(y + b)$, $b \in R$, is:

(1) $x(y')^2 = x + 2yy'$ (2) $x(y')^2 = 2yy' - x$

(3) $xy'' = y'$ (4) $x(y')^2 = x - 2yy'$

58. If a hyperbola passes through the point $P(10,16)$ and it has vertices at $(\pm 6, 0)$, then the equation of the normal to it at P is:

(1) $3x + 4y = 94$

(2) $2x + 5y = 100$

(3) $x + 2y = 42$

(4) $x + 3y = 58$

59. Which of the following statements is a tautology?

(1) $p \vee (\sim q) \rightarrow p \wedge q$

(2) $\sim(p \wedge \sim q) \rightarrow p \vee q$

(3) $\sim(p \vee \sim q) \rightarrow P \wedge q$

(4) $\sim(P \vee \sim q) \rightarrow p \vee q$

60. If the 10th term of an A.P. is $\dfrac{1}{20}$ and its 20th term is $\dfrac{1}{10}$, then the sum of its first 200 terms is:

(1) 50   (2) $50\dfrac{1}{4}$

(3) 100   (4) $100\dfrac{1}{2}$

61. Let $\alpha = \dfrac{-1 + i\sqrt{3}}{2}$. If $a = (1 + \alpha)\sum\limits_{k=0}^{100} \alpha^{2k}$ and $b = \sum\limits_{k=0}^{100} \alpha^{3k}$, then a and b are the roots of the quadratic equation:

(1) $x^2 + 101x + 100 = 0$ (2) $x^2 - 102\,x + 101 = 0$

(3) $x^2 - 101x + 100 = 0$ (4) $x^2 + 102x + 101 = 0$

62. Let S be the set of all functions $f : [0,1] \rightarrow R$, which are continuous on $[0, 1]$ and differentiable on $(0,1)$. Then for every f in S, there exists a $c \in (0,1)$, depending on f, such that:

(1) $|f(c) - f(1)| < (1 - c)|f'(c)|$

(2) $\dfrac{f(1) - f(c)}{1 - c} = f'(c)$

(3) $|f(c) + f(1)| < (1 + c)\,|f'(c)|$

(4) $|f(c) - f(1)| < |f'(c)|$

63. Let A and B be two events such that the probability that exactly one of them occurs is $\dfrac{2}{5}$ and the probability that A or B occurs is $\dfrac{1}{2}$, then the probability of both of them occur together is:

(1) 0.02   (2) 0.20

(3) 0.01   (4) 0.10

64. If $I = \int\limits_{1}^{2} \dfrac{dx}{\sqrt{2x^3 - 9x^2 + 12x + 4}}$, then:

(1) $\dfrac{1}{8} < I^2 < \dfrac{1}{4}$ (2) $\dfrac{1}{9} < I^2 < \dfrac{1}{8}$

(3) $\dfrac{1}{16} < I^2 < \dfrac{1}{9}$ (4) $\dfrac{1}{6} < I^2 < \dfrac{1}{2}$

65. Let $f(1, 3) \rightarrow R$ be a function defined by $f(x) = \dfrac{x[x]}{1 + x^2}$, where $[x]$ denotes the greatest integer $\le x$. Then the range of f is:

(1) $\left(\dfrac{2}{5}, \dfrac{3}{5}\right) \cup \left(\dfrac{3}{4}, \dfrac{4}{5}\right)$ (2) $\left(\dfrac{2}{5}, \dfrac{1}{2}\right) \cup \left(\dfrac{3}{5}, \dfrac{4}{5}\right)$

(3) $\left(\dfrac{2}{5}, \dfrac{4}{5}\right)$ (4) $\left(\dfrac{3}{5}, \dfrac{4}{5}\right)$

66. The mirror image of the point $(1, 2, 3)$ in a plane is $\left(-\dfrac{7}{3}, -\dfrac{4}{3}, -\dfrac{1}{3}\right)$. Which of the following points lies on this plane?

(1) $(1, 1, 1)$ (2) $(1, -1, 1)$

(3) $(-1, -1, 1)$ (4) $(-1, -1, -1)$

67. The system of linear equations
$\lambda x + 2y + 2z = 5$
$2\lambda x + 3y + 5z = 8$
$4x + \lambda y + 6z = 10$ has:

(1) no solution when $\lambda = 8$

(2) a unique solution when $\lambda = -8$

(3) no solution when $\lambda = 2$

(4) infinitely many solutions when $\lambda = 2$

68. Let S be the set of all real roots of the equation,
$3^x(3^x - 1) + 2 = |3^x - 1| + |3^x - 2|$. Then S:

(1) contains exactly two elements.

(2) is a singleton.

(3) is an empty set.

(4) contains at least four elements.

69. If α and β be the coefficients of x^4 and x^2 respectively in the expansion of

$$\left(x + \sqrt{x^2 - 1}\right)^6 + \left(x - \sqrt{x^2 - 1}\right)^6, \text{ then:}$$

(1) $\alpha + \beta = 60$

(2) $\alpha + \beta = -30$

(3) $\alpha - \beta = 60$

(4) $\alpha - \beta = -132$

70. If a line, $y = mx + c$ is a tangent to the circle, $(x - 3)^2 + y^2 = 1$ and it is perpendicular to a line L_1, where L_1 is the tangent to the circle, $x^2 + y^2 = 1$ at the point $\left(\dfrac{1}{\sqrt{2}}, \dfrac{1}{\sqrt{2}}\right)$; then:

(1) $c^2 - 7c + 6 = 0$　　　　(2) $c^2 + 7c + 6 = 0$

(3) $c^2 + 6c + 7 = 0$　　　　(4) $c^2 - 6c + 7 = 0$

71. Let a line $y = mx$ ($m > 0$) intersect the parabola, $y^2 = x$ at a point P, other than the origin. Let the tangent to it at P meet the x-axis at the point Q, If area $(\Delta OPQ) = 4$ sq. units, then m is equal to _______.

72. The number of 4 letter words (with or without meaning) that can be formed from the eleven letters of the word 'EXAMINATION' is _________.

73. The sum, $\displaystyle\sum_{n=1}^{7} \dfrac{n(n+1)(2n+1)}{4}$ is equal to _________.

74. Let $f(x)$ be a polynomial of degree 3 such that $f(-1) = 10$, $f(1) = -6$, $f(x)$ has a critical point at $x = -1$ and $f'(x)$ has a critical point at $x = 1$. Then $f(x)$ has a local minima at $x =$ _______.

75. If $\dfrac{\sqrt{2}\sin\alpha}{\sqrt{1 + \cos 2\alpha}} = \dfrac{1}{7}$ and $\sqrt{\dfrac{1 - \cos 2\beta}{2}} = \dfrac{1}{\sqrt{10}}$,

$\alpha, \beta \in \left(0, \dfrac{\pi}{2}\right)$, then $\tan(\alpha + 2\beta)$ is equal to _____.

JEE MAIN 2020
(Held on 09-01-2020 Morning Shift)

PHYSICS

1. Radiation, with wavelength 6561 Å falls on a metal surface to produce photoelectrons. The electrons are made to enter a uniform magnetic field of 3×10^{-4} T. If the radius of the largest circular path followed by the electrons is 10 mm, the work function of the metal is close to:

(1) 1.1 ev (2) 0.8 ev
(3) 1.6 ev (4) 1.8 ev

2. A quantity f is given by $f = \sqrt{\dfrac{hc^5}{G}}$ where c is speed of light, G universal gravitational constant and h is the Planck's constant. Dimension of f is that of :

(1) area (2) energy
(3) momentum (4) volume

3. Consider a force $\vec{F} = -x\hat{i} + y\hat{j}$. The work done by this force in moving a particle from point A(1, 0) to B(0, 1) along the line segment is: (all quantities are in SI units)

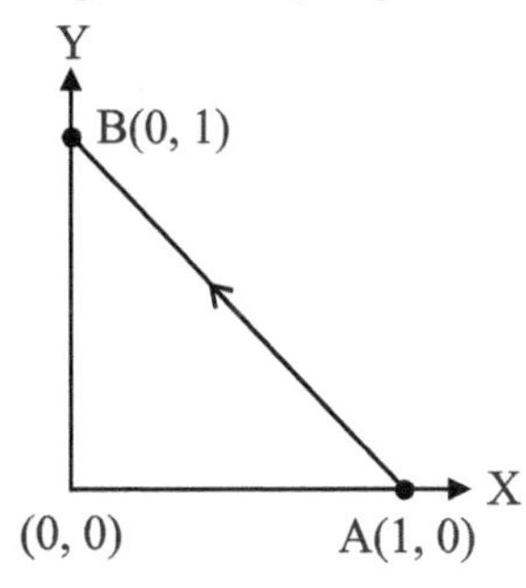

(1) 2 (2) $\dfrac{1}{2}$

(3) 1 (4) $\dfrac{3}{2}$

4. Water flows in a horizontal tube (see figure). The pressure of water changes by 700 Nm^{-2} between A and B where the area of cross section are 40 cm^2 and 20 cm^2, respectively. Find the rate of flow of water through the tube. (density of water = 1000 kgm^{-3})

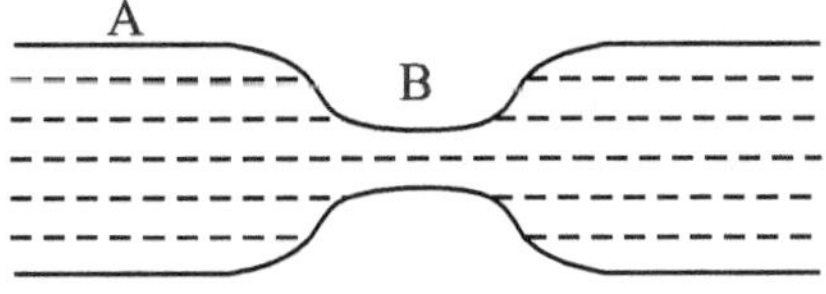

(1) 3020 cm^3/s (2) 2720 cm^3/s
(3) 2420 cm^3/s (4) 1810 cm^3/s

5. A long, straight wire of radius a carries a current distributed uniformly over its cross-section. The ratio of the magnetic fields due to the wire at distance $\dfrac{a}{3}$ and 2a, respectively from the axis of the wire is:

(1) $\dfrac{2}{3}$ (2) 2

(3) $\dfrac{1}{2}$ (4) $\dfrac{3}{2}$

6. The electric fields of two plane electromagnetic plane waves in vacuum are given by
$\vec{E}_1 = E_0 \hat{j} \cos(\omega t - kx)$ and $\vec{E}_2 = E_0 \hat{k} \cos(\omega t - ky)$.
At $t = 0$, a particle of charge q is at origin with a velocity $\vec{v} = 0.8 c\hat{j}$ (c is the speed of light in vacuum). The instantaneous force experienced by the particle is:

(1) $E_0 q(0.8\hat{i} - \hat{j} + 0.4\hat{k})$ (2) $E_0 q(0.4\hat{i} - 3\hat{j} + 0.8\hat{k})$

(3) $E_0 q(-0.8\hat{i} + \hat{j} + \hat{k})$ (4) $E_0 q(0.8\hat{i} + \hat{j} + 0.2\hat{k})$

7. Consider a sphere of radius R which carries a uniform charge density ρ. If a sphere of radius $\dfrac{R}{2}$ is carved out of it, as shown, the ratio $\dfrac{\left|\vec{E}_A\right|}{\left|\vec{E}_B\right|}$ of magnitude of electric field $\vec{E}_A$ and $\vec{E}_B$, respectively, at points A and B due to the remaining portion is:

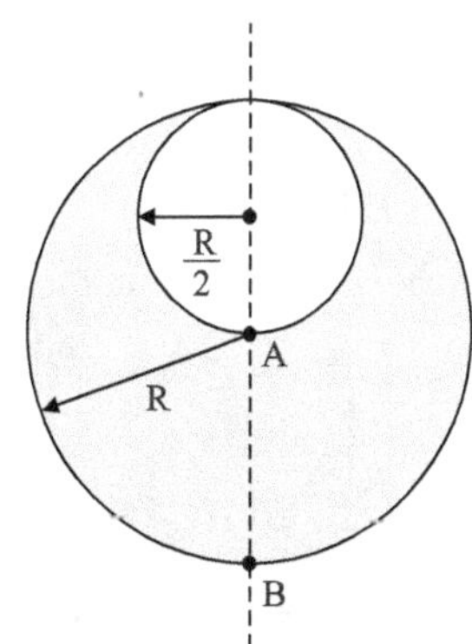

(1) $\dfrac{21}{34}$ (2) $\dfrac{18}{34}$

(3) $\dfrac{17}{54}$ (4) $\dfrac{18}{54}$

8. There harmonic waves having equal frequency ν and same intensity I_0, have phase angles 0, $\dfrac{\pi}{4}$ and $-\dfrac{\pi}{4}$ respectively. When they are superimposed the intensity of the resultant wave is close to:

(1) $5.8\,I_0$ (2) $0.2\,I_0$

(3) $3\,I_0$ (4) I_0

9. An electric dipole of moment $\vec{p} = (\hat{i} - 3\hat{j} + 2\hat{k}) \times 10^{-29}$ C.m is at the origin $(0, 0, 0)$. The electric field due to this dipole at $\vec{r} = +\hat{i} + 3\hat{j} + 5\hat{k}$

(note that $\vec{r} \cdot \vec{p} = 0$) is parallel to:

(1) $(+\hat{i} - 3\hat{j} - 2\hat{k})$ (2) $(-\hat{i} + 3\hat{j} - 2\hat{k})$

(3) $(+\hat{i} + 3\hat{j} - 2\hat{k})$ (4) $(-\hat{i} - 3\hat{j} + 2\hat{k})$

10. Consider two ideal diatomic gases A and B at some temperature T. Molecules of the gas A are rigid, and have a mass m. Molecules of the gas B have an additional vibrational mode, and have a mass $\dfrac{m}{4}$. The ratio of the specific heats $(C_V^A \text{ and } C_V^B)$ of gas A and B, respectively is:

(1) $7:9$ (2) $5:9$

(3) $3:5$ (4) $5:7$

11. A particle moving with kinetic energy E has de Broglie wavelength λ. If energy ΔE is added to its energy, the wavelength become $\dfrac{\lambda}{2}$. Value of ΔE, is:

(1) E   (2) 4E

(3) 3E   (4) 2E

12. Which of the following is an equivalent cyclic process corresponding to the thermodynamic cyclic given in the figure?

where, $1 \rightarrow 2$ is adiabatic.

(Graphs are schematic and are not to scale)

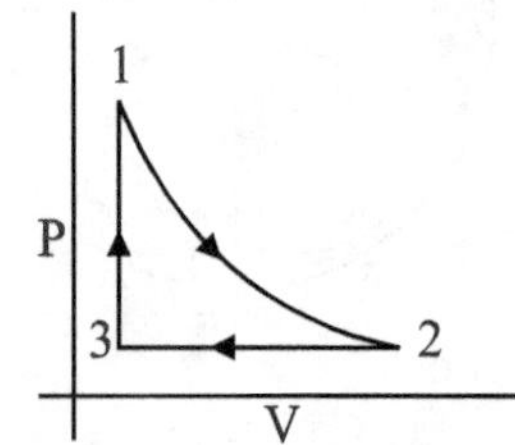

13. Two particles of equal mass m have respective initial velocities $u\hat{i}$ and $u\left(\dfrac{\hat{i} + \hat{j}}{2}\right)$. They collide completely inelastically. The energy lost in the process is:

(1) $\dfrac{1}{3}\,mu^2$ (2) $\dfrac{1}{8}\,mu^2$

(3) $\dfrac{3}{4}\,mu^2$ (4) $\sqrt{\dfrac{2}{3}}\,mu^2$

14. In the given circuit diagram, a wire is joining points B and D. The current in this wire is:

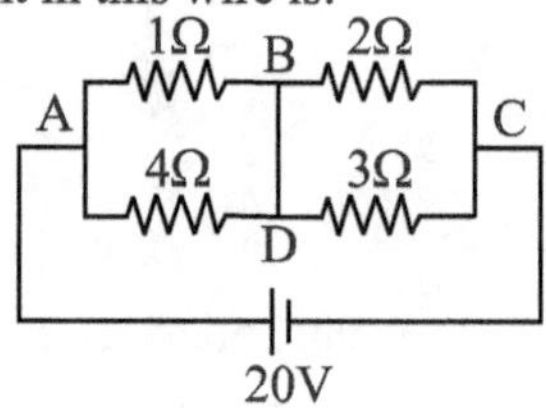

(1) 0.4A   (2) 2A

(3) 4A   (4) zero

15. The aperture diameter of aelescope is 5m. The separation between the moon and the earth is 4×10^5 km. With light of wavelength of 5500 Å, the minimum separation between objects on the surface of moon, so that they are just resolved, is close to:

(1) 60 m   (2) 20 m

(3) 200 m   (4) 600 m

(1) 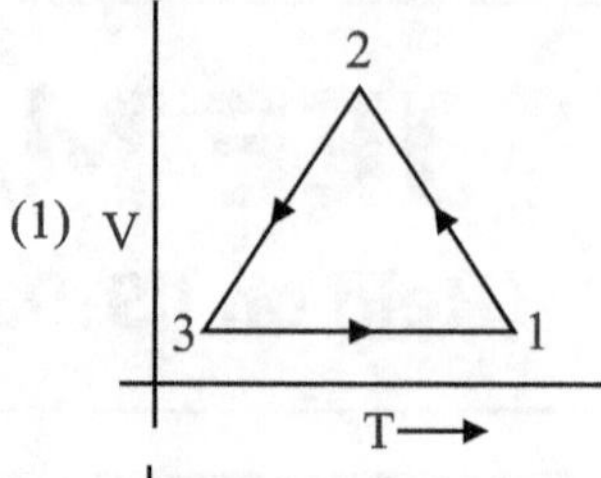

(2) 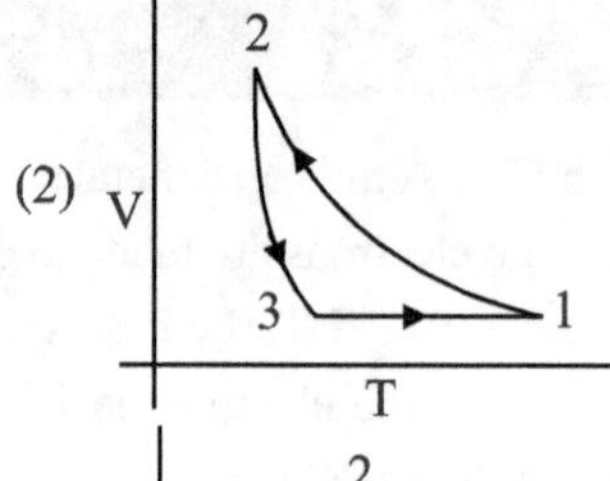

(3) 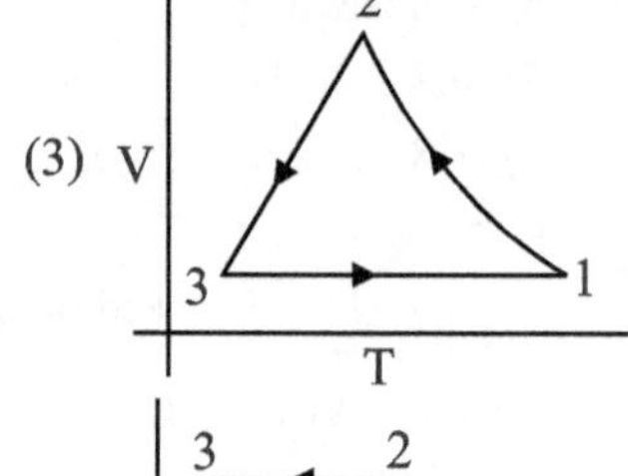

(4) 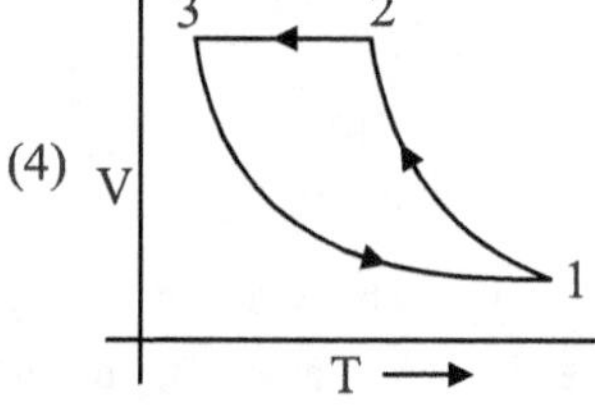

16. If the screw on a screw-gauge is given six rotations, it moves by 3 mm on the main scale. If there are 50 divisions on the circular scale the least count of the screw gauge is:

(1) 0.001 cm   (2) 0.02 mm

(3) 0.01 cm   (4) 0.001 mm

17. A charged particle of mass 'm' and charge 'q' moving under the influence of uniform electric field $E\hat{i}$ and a uniform magnetic field $B\vec{k}$ follows a trajectory from point P to Q as shown in figure. The velocities at P and Q are respectively, $v\vec{i}$ and $-2v\vec{j}$. Then which of the following statements (A, B, C, D) are the correct? (Trajectory shown is schematic and not to scale)

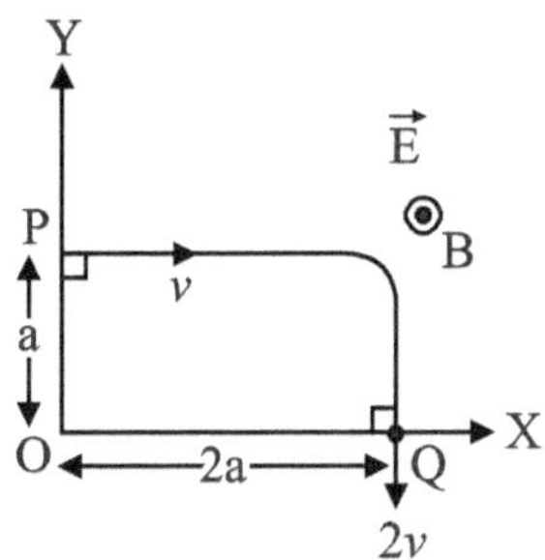

(A) $E = \dfrac{3}{4}\left(\dfrac{mv^2}{qa}\right)$

(B) Rate of work done by the electric field at P is $\dfrac{3}{4}\left(\dfrac{mv^2}{a}\right)$

(C) Rate of work done by both the fields at Q is zero

(D) The difference between the magnitude of angular momentum of the particle at P and Q is 2 ma$v$.

(1) (A), (C), (D)   (2) (B), (C), (D)

(3) (A), (B), (C)   (4) (A), (B), (C) , (D)

18. Three solid spheres each of mass m and diameter d are stuck together such that the lines connecting the centres form an equilateral triangle of side of length d. The ratio $\dfrac{I_0}{I_A}$ of moment of inertia I_0 of the system about an axis passing the centroid and about center of any of the spheres I_A and perpendicular to the plane of the triangle is:

(1) $\dfrac{13}{23}$ (2) $\dfrac{15}{13}$

(3) $\dfrac{23}{13}$ (4) $\dfrac{13}{15}$

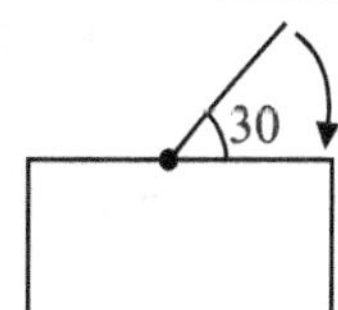

19. A vessel of depth 2h is half filled with a liquid of refractive index $2\sqrt{2}$ and the upper half with another liquid of refractive index $\sqrt{2}$. The liquids are immiscible. The apparent depth of the inner surface of the bottom of vessel will be:

(1) $\dfrac{h}{\sqrt{2}}$ (2) $\dfrac{h}{2(\sqrt{2}+1)}$

(3) $\dfrac{h}{3\sqrt{2}}$ (4) $\dfrac{3}{4}h\sqrt{2}$

20. A body A of mass m is moving in a circular orbit of radius R about a planet. Another body B of mass $\dfrac{m}{2}$ collides with A with a velocity which is half $\left(\dfrac{\vec{v}}{2}\right)$ the instantaneous velocity $\vec{v}$ or A. The collision is completely inelastic. Then, the combined body:

(1) continues to move in a circular orbit

(2) Escapes from the Planet's Gravitational field

(3) Falls vertically downwards towards the planet

(4) starts moving in an elliptical orbit around the planet

21. Both the diodes used in the circuit shown are assumed to be ideal and have negligible resistance when these are forward biased. Built in potential in each diode is 0.7 V. For the input voltages shown in the figure, the voltage (in Volts) at point A is _________ .

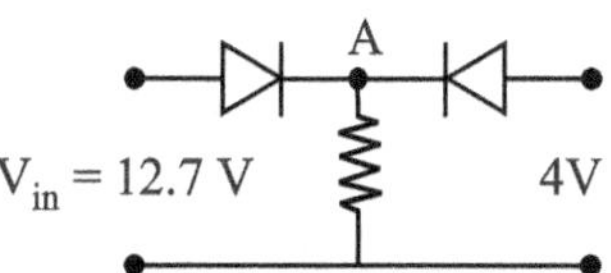

22. In a fluorescent lamp choke (a small transformer) 100 V of reverse voltage is produced when the choke current changes uniformly from 0.25 A to 0 in a duration of 0.025 ms. The self-inductance of the choke (in mH) is estimated to be _______ .

23. The distance x covered by a particle in one dimensional motion varies with time t as $x^2 = at^2 + 2bt + c$. If the acceleration of the particle depends on x as x^{-n}, where n is an integer, the value of n is _______ .

24. A body of mass m = 10 kg is attached to one end of a wire of length 0.3 m. The maximum angular speed (in rad s^{-1}) with which it can be rotated about its other end in space station is (Breaking stress of wire = 4.8×10^7 Nm^{-2} and area of cross-section of the wire = 10^{-2} cm^2) is _______ .

25. One end of a straight uniform 1 m long bar is pivoted on horizontal table. It is released from rest when it makes an angle 30° from the horizontal (see figure). Its angular speed when it hits the table is given as $\sqrt{n}s^{-1}$, where n is an integer. The value of n is _________ .

CHEMISTRY

26. The K_{sp} for the following dissociation is 1.6×10^{-5}

$$PbCl_{2(s)} \rightleftharpoons Pb^{2+}_{(aq)} + 2Cl^{-}_{(aq)}$$

Which of the following choices is correct for a mixture of 300 mL 0.134 M $Pb(NO_3)_2$ and 100 mL 0.4 M NaCl?

(1) Not enough data provided

(2) $Q < K_{sp}$

(3) $Q > K_{sp}$

(4) $Q = K_{sp}$

27. The correct order of heat of combustion for following alkadienes is:

(A) 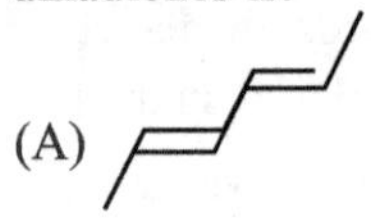

(B) 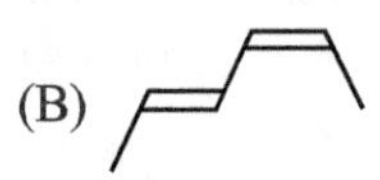

(C) 

(1) $(A) < (B) < (C)$ (2) $(A) < (C) < (B)$

(3) $(C) < (B) < (A)$ (4) $(B) < (C) < (A)$

28. According to the following diagram, A reduces BO_2 when the temperature is:

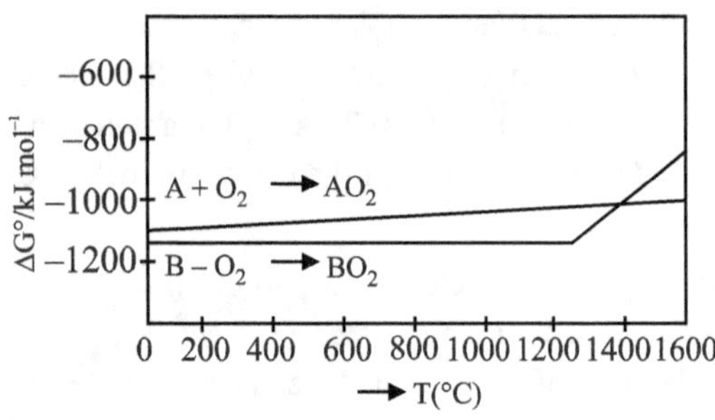

(1) $< 1400\ ^{\circ}C$

(2) $> 1400\ ^{\circ}C$

(3) $> 1200\ ^{\circ}C$ but $< 1400\ ^{\circ}C$

(4) $< 1200\ ^{\circ}C$

29. B has a smaller first ionization enthalpy than Be. Consider the following statements:

(I) it is easier to remove $2p$ electron than $2s$ electron

(II) $2p$ electron of B is more shielded from the nucleus by the inner core of electrons than the $2s$ electrons of Be

(III) $2s$ electron has more penetration power than $2p$ electron

(IV) atomic radius of B is more than Be
(atomic number B = 5, Be = 4)

The correct statements are:

(1) (I), (II) and (IV)

(2) (II), (III) and (IV)

(3) (I), (II) and (III)

(4) (I), (III) and (IV)

30. If the magnetic moment of a dioxygen species is 1.73 B.M, it may be:

(1) O_2^- or O_2^+ (2) O_2 or O_2^+

(3) O_2 or O_2^- (4) O_2, O_2^- or O_2^+

31. The de Broglie wavelength of an electron in the 4th Bohr orbit is:

(1) $2\pi a_0$ (2) $4\pi a_0$

(3) $6\pi a_0$ (4) $8\pi a_0$

32. 'X' melts at low temperature and is a bad conductor of electricity in both liquid and solid state. X is:

(1) Zinc sulphide

(2) Mercury

(3) Silicon carbide

(4) Carbon tetrachloride

33. The major product Z obtained in the following reaction scheme is:

(1)

(2)

(3)

(4)

34. Complex X of composition $Cr(H_2O)_6Cl_n$ has a spin only magnetic moment of 3.83 BM. It reacts with $AgNO_3$ and shows geometrical isomerism. The IUPAC nomenclature of X is:

(1) Hexaaqua chromium (III) chloride

(2) Tetraaquadichlorido chromium (IV) chloride dihydrate

(3) Dichloridotetraaqua chromium (IV) chloride dihydrate

(4) Tetraaquadichlorido chromium (III) chloride dihydrate

35. A chemist has 4 samples of artificial sweetener A, B, C and D. To identify these samples, he performed certain experiments and noted the following observations:

(I) A and D both form blue-biolet colour with ninhydrin.

(II) Lassaigne extract of C gives positive $AgNO_3$ test and negative $Fe_4[Fe(CN)_6]_3$ test.

(III) Lassaigne extract of B and D gives positive sodium nitroprusside test.

Based on these observations which option is correct?

(1) A : Aspartame;　　B : Saccharin;
　　C : Sucralose;　　D : Alitame

(2) A : Alitame;　　B : Saccharin;
　　C : Aspartame;　　D : Sucralose

(3) A : Saccharin;　　B : Alitame;
　　C : Sucralose;　　D : Aspartame

(4) A : Aspartame;　　B : Alitame;
　　C : Saccharin;　　D : Sucralose

36. The acidic, basic and amphoteric oxides, respectively, are:

(1) Na_2O, SO_3, Al_2O_3

(2) Cl_2O, CaO, P_4O_{10}

(3) N_2O_3, Li_2O, Al_2O_3

(4) MgO, Cl_2O, Al_2O_3

37. If enthalpy of atomisation for $Br_2(l)$ is x kJ/mol and bond enthalpy for Br_2 is y kJ/mol, the relation between them:

(1) is $x = y$　　　　(2) does not exist

(3) is $x > y$　　　　(4) is $x < y$

38. The electronic configurations of bivalent europium and trivalent cerium are:

(atomic number : Xe = 54, Ce = 58, Eu = 63)

(1) $[Xe]\,4f^2$ and $[Xe]\,4f^7$

(2) $[Xe]\,4f^7$ and $[Xe]\,4f^1$

(3) $[Xe]\,4f^7\,6s^2$ and $[Xe]\,4f^2\,6s^2$

(4) $[Xe]\,4f^4$ and $[Xe]\,4f^9$

39. For following reactions:

$$A \xrightarrow{700\,K} Product$$

$$A \xrightarrow[catalyst]{500\,K} Product$$

it was found that the E_a is decrease by 30 kJ/mol in the presence of catalyst. If the rate remains unchanged, the activation energy for catalysed reaction is (Assume pre exponential factor is same):

(1) 75 kJ/mol　　　　(2) 105 kJ/mol

(3) 135 kJ/mol　　　　(4) 198 kJ/mol

40. The increasing order of basic it for the following intermediates is (from weak to strong)

$$H_3C-\overset{CH_3}{\underset{CH_3}{\overset{|}{\underset{|}{C}}}}{}^{\ominus} \qquad H_3C=CH-\overset{\ominus}{C}H_2$$
(i)　　　　　　　　(ii)

$$HC\equiv\overset{\ominus}{C} \qquad \overset{\ominus}{C}H_3 \qquad \overset{\ominus}{C}N$$
(iii)　　(iv)　　(v)

(1) (iii) < (i) < (ii) < (iv) < (v)

(2) (v) < (i) < (iv) < (ii) < (iii)

(3) (v) < (iii) < (ii) < (iv) < (i)

(4) (iii) < (iv) < (ii) < (i) < (v)

41. The major product (Y) in the following reactions is:

$$CH_3-\overset{CH_3}{\overset{|}{CH}}-C\equiv CH \xrightarrow[H_2O]{HgSO_4,\ H_2SO_4}$$

$$\xrightarrow[(ii)\ Conc.\ H_2SO_4/\Delta]{(i)\ C_2H_5MgBr,\ H_2O}$$

(1) $CH_3-\overset{CH_3}{\overset{|}{CH}}-\underset{\underset{CH_3}{|}}{C}=CH-CH_3$

(2) $H_3C-\overset{\overset{CH_2}{\|}}{C}-\underset{\underset{C_2H_5}{|}}{CH}-CH_3$

(3) $CH_3-\overset{CH_3}{\overset{|}{CH}}-\underset{\underset{CH_2CH_3}{|}}{C}=CH_2$

(4) $CH_3-\overset{CH_3}{\overset{|}{C}}=\underset{\underset{CH_2CH_3}{|}}{C}-CH_3$

42. Which of these will produce the highest yield in Friedel Crafts reaction?

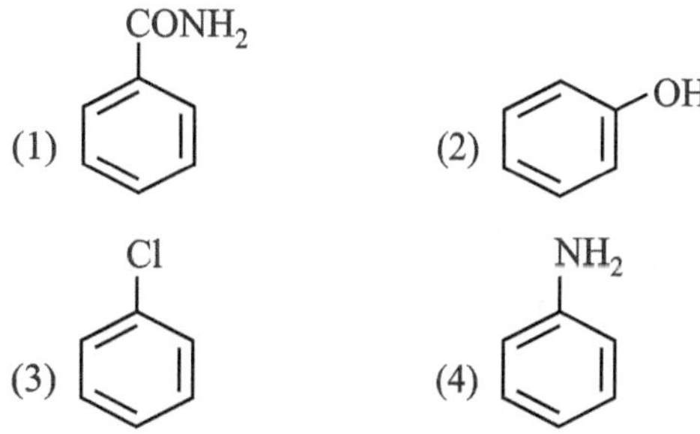

43. The compound that cannot act both as oxidising and reducing agent is:

(1) H_3PO_4

(2) HNO_2

(3) H_2SO_3

(4) H_2O_2

44. $[Pd(F)(Cl)(Br)(I)]^{2-}$ has n number of geometrical isomers. Then, the spin-only magnetic moment and crystal field stabilisation energy [CFSE] of $[Fe(CN)_6]^{n-6}$, respectively, are:

[**Note :** Ignore the pairing energy]

(1) 2.84 BM and $-1.6\,\Delta_0$

(2) 5.92 BM and 0

(3) 1.73 BM and $-2.0\,\Delta_0$

(4) 0 BM and $-2.4\,\Delta_0$

45. Identify (A) in the following reaction sequence:

(A) Gives positive idoform test $\xrightarrow[\text{(ii) } H^+, H_2O]{\text{(i) } CH_3MgBr}$ (B) $\xrightarrow{O_3/Zn,\ H_2O}$

(ii) Conc. H_2SO_4/Δ

46. The molarity of HNO_3 in a sample which has density 1.4 g/mL and mass percentage of 63% is ______ . (Molecular Weight of $HNO_3 = 63$)

47. The hardness of a water sample containing 10^{-3} M $MgSO_4$ expressed as $CaCO_3$ equivalents (in ppm) is ______ . (molar mass of $MgSO_4$ is 120.37 g/mol)

48. How much amount of NaCl should be added to 600 g of water (ρ = 1.00 g/mL) to decrease the freezing point of water to $-0.2°C$? ______ . (The freezing point depression constant for water = 2 K kg mol^{-1})

49. 108 g of silver (molar mass 108 g mol^{-1}) is deposited at cathode from $AgNO_3$(aq) solution by a certain quantity of electricity. The volume (in L) of oxygen gas produced at 273 K and 1 bar pressure from water by the same quantity of electricity is ______ .

50. The mass percentage of nitrogen in histamine is ______ .

MATHEMATICS

51. Let f be any function continuous on $[a,\ b]$ and twice differentiable on $(a,\ b)$. If for all $x \in (a,\ b), f'(x) > 0$ and $f''(x) < 0$, then for any $c \in (a,\ b)$, $\dfrac{f(c)-f(a)}{f(b)-f(c)}$ is greater than:

(1) $\dfrac{b+a}{b-a}$

(2) 1

(3) $\dfrac{b-c}{c-a}$

(4) $\dfrac{c-a}{b-c}$

52. If for all real triplets (a, b, c), $f(x) = a + bx + cx^2$; then $\displaystyle\int_0^1 f(x)\,dx$ is equal to:

(1) $2\left\{3f(1)+2f\left(\dfrac{1}{2}\right)\right\}$

(2) $\dfrac{1}{2}\left\{f(1)+3f\left(\dfrac{1}{2}\right)\right\}$

(3) $\dfrac{1}{3}\left\{f(0)+f\left(\dfrac{1}{2}\right)\right\}$

(4) $\dfrac{1}{6}\left\{f(0)+f(1)+4f\left(\dfrac{1}{2}\right)\right\}$

53. Let z be a complex number such that $\left|\dfrac{z-i}{z+2i}\right|=1$ and $|z|=\dfrac{5}{2}$. Then the value of $|z+3i|$ is :

(1) $\sqrt{10}$

(2) $\dfrac{7}{2}$

(3) $\dfrac{15}{4}$

(4) $2\sqrt{3}$

54. If for some α and β in **R**, the intersection of the following three planes

$x + 4y - 2z = 1$

$x + 7y - 5z = \beta$

$x + 5y + \alpha z = 5$

is a line in R^3, then $\alpha + \beta$ is equal to:

(1) 0   (2) 10

(3) 2   (4) −10

55. The number of real roots of the equation,

$e^{4x} + e^{3x} - 4e^{2x} + e^x + 1 = 0$ is:

(1) 1   (2) 3

(3) 2   (4) 4

56. The value of $\displaystyle\int_0^{2\pi} \frac{x\sin^8 x}{\sin^8 x + \cos^8 x}\,dx$ is equal to:

(1) 2π (2) $2\pi^2$

(3) π^2 (4) 4π

57. If $f(x) = \begin{cases} \dfrac{\sin(a+2)x + \sin x}{x} & ;\ x < 0 \\[2mm] b & ;\ x = 0 \\[2mm] \dfrac{(x+3x^2)^{1/3} - x^{1/3}}{x^{4/3}} & ;\ x > 0 \end{cases}$

is continuous at $x = 0$, then $a + 2b$ is equal to:

(1) 1   (2) −1

(3) 0   (4) −2

58. In a box, there are 20 cards, out of which 10 are labelled as A and the remaining 10 are labelled as B. Cards are drawn at random, one after the other and with replacement, till a second A-card is obtained. The probability that the second A-card appears before the third B-card is :

(1) $\dfrac{9}{16}$ (2) $\dfrac{11}{16}$

(3) $\dfrac{13}{16}$ (4) $\dfrac{15}{16}$

59. If the number of five digit numbers with distinct digits and 2 at the 10th place is 336 k, then k is equal to:

(1) 4   (2) 6

(3) 7   (4) 8

60. If e_1 and e_2 are the eccentricities of the ellipse, $\dfrac{x^2}{18} + \dfrac{y^2}{4} = 1$ and the hyperbola, $\dfrac{x^2}{9} - \dfrac{y^2}{4} = 1$ respectively and (e_1, e_2) is a point on the ellipse, $15x^2 + 3y^2 = k$, then k is equal to

(1) 16   (2) 17

(3) 15   (4) 14

61. A spherical iron ball of 10 cm radius is coated with a layer of ice of uniform thickness that melts at a rate of 50 cm^3/min. When the thickness of ice is 5 cm, then the rate (in cm/min.) at which of the thickness of ice decreases, is:

(1) $\dfrac{5}{6\pi}$ (2) $\dfrac{1}{54\pi}$

(3) $\dfrac{1}{36\pi}$ (4) $\dfrac{1}{18\pi}$

62. Let the observations $x_i (1 \le i \le 10)$ satisfy the equations, $\displaystyle\sum_{i=1}^{10}(x_i - 5) = 10$ and $\displaystyle\sum_{i=1}^{10}(x_i - 5)^2 = 40$. If μ and λ are the mean and the variance of the observations, $x_1 - 3, x_2 - 3, ...,$ $x_{10} - 3$, then the ordered pair (μ, λ) is equal to:

(1) $(3, 3)$ (2) $(6, 3)$

(3) $(6, 6)$ (4) $(3, 6)$

63. Negation of the statement:

$\sqrt{5}$ is an integer of 5 is irrational is:

(1) $\sqrt{5}$ is not an integer or 5 is not irrational

(2) $\sqrt{5}$ is not an integer and 5 is not irrational

(3) $\sqrt{5}$ is irrational or 5 is an integer.

(4) $\sqrt{5}$ is an integer and 5 is irrational

64. A circle touches the y-axis at the point $(0, 4)$ and passes through the point $(2, 0)$. Which of the following lines is not a tangent to this circle?

(1) $4x - 3y + 17 = 0$ (2) $3x - 4y - 24 = 0$

(3) $3x + 4y - 6 = 0$ (4) $4x + 3y - 8 = 0$

65. If the matrices $A = \begin{bmatrix} 1 & 1 & 2 \\ 1 & 3 & 4 \\ 1 & -1 & 3 \end{bmatrix}$, $B = \text{adj } A$

and $C = 3A$, then $\dfrac{|\text{adj } B|}{|C|}$ is equal to :

(1) 8   (2) 16

(3) 72   (4) 2

66. If $f'(x) = \tan^{-1}(\sec x + \tan x)$, $-\dfrac{\pi}{2} < x < \dfrac{\pi}{2}$, and $f(0) = 0$, then $f(1)$ is equal to:

(1) $\dfrac{\pi+1}{4}$ (2) $\dfrac{1}{4}$

(3) $\dfrac{\pi-1}{4}$ (4) $\dfrac{\pi+2}{4}$

67. The value of $\cos^3\left(\dfrac{\pi}{8}\right)\cdot\cos\left(\dfrac{3\pi}{8}\right) + \sin^3\left(\dfrac{\pi}{8}\right)\cdot\sin\left(\dfrac{3\pi}{8}\right)$ is

(1) $\dfrac{1}{\sqrt{2}}$ (2) $\dfrac{1}{2\sqrt{2}}$

(3) $\dfrac{1}{2}$ (4) $\dfrac{1}{4}$

68. Let C be the centroid of the triangle with vertices $(3, -1)$, $(1, 3)$ and $(2, 4)$. Let P be the point of intersection of the lines $x + 3y - 1 = 0$ and $3x - y + 1 = 0$. Then the line passing through the points C and P also passes through the point:

(1) $(-9, -6)$ (2) $(9, 7)$

(3) $(7, 6)$ (4) $(-9, -7)$

69. The integral $\displaystyle\int \frac{dx}{(x+4)^{8/7}(x-3)^{6/7}}$ is equal to:

(where C is a constant of integration)

(1) $\left(\dfrac{x-3}{x+4}\right)^{1/7} + C$

(2) $-\left(\dfrac{x-3}{x+4}\right)^{-1/7} + C$

(3) $\dfrac{1}{2}\left(\dfrac{x-3}{x+4}\right)^{3/7} + C$

(4) $-\dfrac{1}{13}\left(\dfrac{x-3}{x+4}\right)^{-13/7} + C$

70. The product $2^{\frac{1}{4}} \cdot 4^{\frac{1}{16}} \cdot 8^{\frac{1}{48}} \cdot 16^{\frac{1}{128}} \ldots$ to ∞ is equal to:

(1) $2^{\frac{1}{2}}$ (2) $2^{\frac{1}{4}}$

(3) 1 (4) 2

71. The projection of the line segment joining the points $(1, -1, 3)$ and $(2, -4, 11)$ on the line joining the points $(-1, 2, 3)$ and $(3, -2, 10)$ is _______ .

72. If the vectors, $\vec{p} = (a+1)\hat{i} + a\hat{j} + a\hat{k}$, $\vec{q} = a\hat{i} + (a+1)\hat{j} + a\hat{k}$ and $\vec{r} = a\hat{i} + a\hat{j} + (a+1)\hat{k}$ $(a \in R)$ are complanar and $3(\vec{p}.\vec{q})^2 - \lambda\,|\vec{r} \times \vec{q}|^2 = 0$, then the value of λ is _____ .

73. The coefficient of x^4 in the expansion of $(1 + x + x^2)^{10}$ is _______ .

74. The number of distinct solutions of the equation, $\log_{1/2}|\sin x| = 2 - \log_{1/2}|\cos x|$ in the interval $[0, 2\pi]$, is _____ .

75. If for $x \geq 0$, $y = y(x)$ is the solution of the differential equation,
$(x + 1)dy = ((x + 1)^2 + y - 3)dx,\ y(2) = 0$,
then $y(3)$ is equal to _____ .

JEE MAIN 2020

(Held on 09-01-2020 Evening Shift)

PHYSICS

1. The current i in the network is:

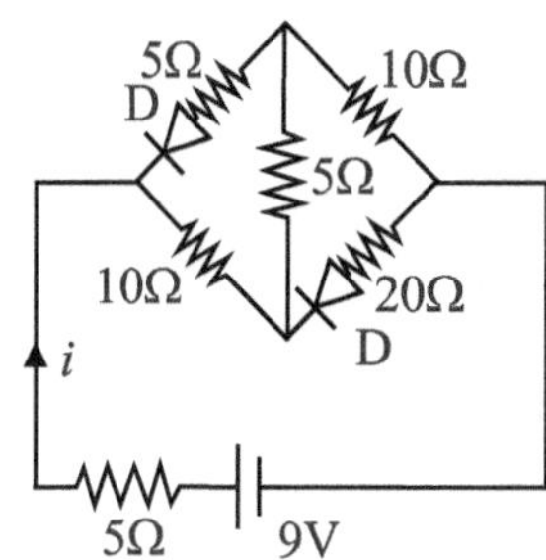

(1) 0.2 A

(2) 0.6 A

(3) 0.3 A

(4) 0 A

2. A wire of length L and mass per unit length 6.0×10^{-3} kgm^{-1} is put under tension of 540 N. Two consecutive frequencies that it resonates at are: 420 Hz and 490 Hz. Then L in meters is:

(1) 2.1 m

(2) 1.1 m

(3) 8.1 m

(4) 5.1 m

3. An electron of mass m and magnitude of charge $|e|$ initially at rest gets accelerated by a constant electric field E. The rate of change of de-Broglie wavelength of this electron at time t ignoring relativistic effects is:

(1) $-\dfrac{h}{|e|E\sqrt{t}}$

(2) $\dfrac{|e|Et}{h}$

(3) $-\dfrac{h}{|e|Et}$

(4) $\dfrac{-h}{|e|Et^2}$

4. In LC circuit the inductance L = 40 mH and capacitance C = 100 μF. If a voltage $V(t) = 10 \sin(314\,t)$ is applied to the circuit, the current in the circuit is given as:

(1) 0.52 cos 314 t

(2) 10 cos 314 t

(3) 5.2 cos 314 t

(4) 0.52 sin 314 t

5. A small circular loop of conducting wire has radius a and carries current I. It is placed in a uniform magnetic field B perpendicular to its plane such that when rotated slightly about its diameter and released, it starts performing simple harmonic motion of time period T. If the mass of the loop is m then :

(1) $T = \sqrt{\dfrac{2\,m}{IB}}$

(2) $T = \sqrt{\dfrac{\pi\,m}{2\,IB}}$

(3) $T = \sqrt{\dfrac{2\pi\,m}{IB}}$

(4) $T = \sqrt{\dfrac{\pi\,m}{IB}}$

6. Two identical capacitors A and B, charged to the same potential 5V are connected in two different circuits as shown below at time $t = 0$. If the charge on capacitors A and B at time $t = $ CR is Q_A and Q_B respectively, then (Here e is the base of natural logarithm)

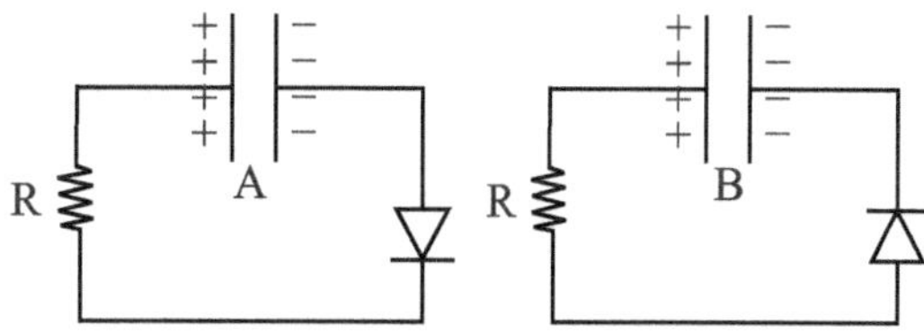

(1) $Q_A = \dfrac{VC}{e}, Q_B = \dfrac{CV}{2}$

(2) $Q_A = VC, Q_B = CV$

(3) $Q_A = VC, Q_B = \dfrac{VC}{e}$

(4) $Q_A = \dfrac{CV}{2}, Q_B = \dfrac{VC}{e}$

7. A uniformly thick wheel with moment of inertia I and radius R is free to rotate about its centre of mass (see fig). A massless string is wrapped over its rim and two blocks of masses m_1 and m_2 ($m_1 > m_2$) are attached to the ends of the string. The system is released from rest. The angular speed of the wheel when m_1 descents by a distance h is:

(1) $\left[\dfrac{2(m_1 - m_2)gh}{(m_1 + m_2)R^2 + 1}\right]^{1/2}$

(2) $\left[\dfrac{2(m_1 + m_2)gh}{(m_1 + m_2)R^2 + 1}\right]^{1/2}$

(3) $\left[\dfrac{(m_1 - m_2)}{(m_1 + m_2)R^2 + 1}\right]^{1/2} gh$

(4) $\left[\dfrac{m_1 + m_2}{(m_1 + m_2)R^2 + 1}\right]^{1/2} gh$

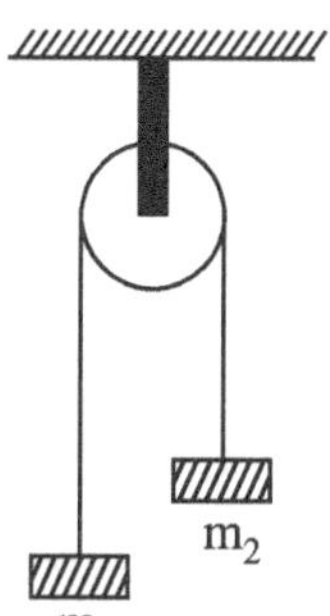

8. There is a small source of light at some depth below the surface of water (refractive index $= \dfrac{4}{3}$) in a tank of large cross sectional surface area. Neglecting any reflection from the bottom and absorption by water, percentage of light that emerges out of surface is (nearly):

[Use the fact that surface area of a spherical cap of height h and radius of curvature r is $2\pi rh$]

(1) 21% (2) 34%

(3) 17% (4) 50%

9. A spring mass system (mass m, spring constant k and natural length l) rests in equilibrium on a horizontal disc. The free end of the spring is fixed at the centre of the disc. If the disc together with spring mass system, rotates about it's axis with an angular velocity ω, $(k \gg m\omega^2)$ the relative change in the length of the spring is best given by the option:

(1) $\sqrt{\dfrac{2}{3}}\left(\dfrac{m\omega^2}{k}\right)$ (2) $\dfrac{2m\omega^2}{k}$

(3) $\dfrac{m\omega^2}{k}$ (4) $\dfrac{m\omega^2}{3k}$

10. A small spherical droplet of density d is floating exactly half immersed in a liquid of density ρ and surface tension T. The radius of the droplet is (take note that the surface tension applies an upward force on the droplet):

(1) $r = \sqrt{\dfrac{2T}{3(d+\rho)g}}$ (2) $r = \sqrt{\dfrac{T}{(d-\rho)g}}$

(3) $r = \sqrt{\dfrac{T}{(d+\rho)g}}$ (4) $r = \sqrt{\dfrac{3T}{(2d-\rho)g}}$

11. Planet A has mass M and radius R. Planet B has half the mass and half the radius of Planet A. If the escape velocities from the Planets A and B are v_A and v_B, respectively, then $\dfrac{v_A}{v_B} = \dfrac{n}{4}$. The value of n is :

(1) 4 (2) 1

(3) 2 (4) 3

12. A rod of length L has non-uniform linear mass density given by $\rho(x) = a + b\left(\dfrac{x}{L}\right)^2$, where a and b are constants and $0 \le x \le L$. The value of x for the centre of mass of the rod is at:

(1) $\dfrac{3}{2}\left(\dfrac{a+b}{2a+b}\right)L$ (2) $\dfrac{3}{4}\left(\dfrac{2a+b}{3a+b}\right)L$

(3) $\dfrac{4}{3}\left(\dfrac{a+b}{2a+3b}\right)L$ (4) $\dfrac{3}{2}\left(\dfrac{2a+b}{3a+b}\right)L$

13. For the four sets of three measured physical quantities as given below. Which of the following options is correct?

(A) $A_1 = 24.36$, $B_1 = 0.0724$, $C_1 = 256.2$

(B) $A_2 = 24.44$, $B_2 = 16.082$, $C_2 = 240.2$

(C) $A_3 = 25.2$, $B_3 = 19.2812$, $C_3 = 236.183$

(D) $A_4 = 25$, $B_4 = 236.191$, $C_4 = 19.5$

(1) $A_4 + B_4 + C_4 < A_1 + B_1 + C_1 < A_3 + B_3 + C_3 < A_2 + B_2 + C_2$

(2) $A_1 + B_1 + C_1 = A_2 + B_2 + C_2 = A_3 + B_3 + C_3 = A_4 + B_4 + C_4$

(3) $A_4 + B_4 + C_4 < A_1 + B_1 + C_1 = A_2 + B_2 + C_2 = A_3 + B_3 + C_3$

(4) $A_1 + B_1 + C_1 < A_3 + B_3 + C_3 < A_2 + B_2 + C_2 < A_4 + B_4 + C_4$

14. Two gases-argon (atomic radius 0.07 nm, atomic weight 40) and xenon (atomic radius 0.1 nm, atomic weight 140) have the same number density and are at the same temperature. The ratio of their respective mean free times is closest to:

(1) 3.67 (2) 1.83

(3) 2.3 (4) 4.67

15. Two steel wires having same length are suspended from a ceiling under the same load. If the ratio of their energy stored per unit volume is 1 : 4, the ratio of their diameters is:

(1) $\sqrt{2} : 1$ (2) $1 : 2$

(3) $2 : 1$ (4) $1 : \sqrt{2}$

16. The energy required to ionise a hydrogen like ion in its ground state is 9 Rydbergs. What is the wavelength of the radiation emitted when the electron in this ion jumps from the second excited state to the ground state?

(1) 24.2 nm (2) 11.4 nm

(3) 35.8 nm (4) 8.6 nm

17. A particle of mass m is projected with a speed u from the ground at an angle $\theta = \dfrac{\pi}{3}$ w.r.t. horizontal (x-axis). When it has reached its maximum height, it collides completely inelastically with another particle of the same mass and velocity $u\hat{i}$. The horizontal distance covered by the combined mass before reaching the ground is:

(1) $\dfrac{3\sqrt{3}}{8}\dfrac{u^2}{g}$

(2) $\dfrac{3\sqrt{2}}{4}\dfrac{u^2}{g}$

(3) $\dfrac{5}{8}\dfrac{u^2}{g}$

(4) $2\sqrt{2}\dfrac{u^2}{g}$

18. An electron gun is placed inside a long solenoid of radius R on its axis. The solenoid has n turns/length and carries a current I. The electron gun shoots an electron along the radius of the solenoid with speed v. If the electron does not hit the surface of the solenoid, maximum possible value of v is (all symbols have their standard meaning):

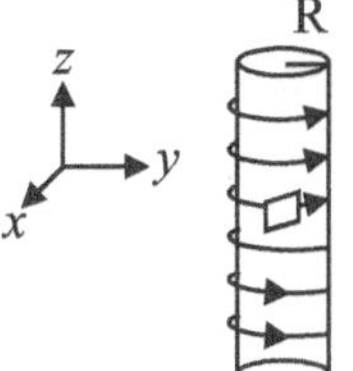

(1) $\dfrac{e\mu_0 n I R}{m}$

(2) $\dfrac{e\mu_0 n I R}{2m}$

(3) $\dfrac{e\mu_0 n I R}{4m}$

(4) $\dfrac{2e\mu_0 n I R}{m}$

19. A particle starts from the origin at $t = 0$ with an initial velocity of $3.0\hat{i}$ m/s and moves in the x-y plane with a constant acceleration $(6.0\hat{i} + 4.0\hat{j})$ m/s^2. The x-coordinate of the particle at the instant when its y-coordinate is 32 m is D meters. The value of D is:

(1) 32
(2) 50
(3) 60
(4) 40

20. A plane electromagnetic wave is propagating along the direction $\dfrac{\hat{i}+\hat{j}}{\sqrt{2}}$, with its polarization along the direction $\hat{k}$. The correct form of the magnetic field of the wave would be (here B_0 is an appropriate constant):

(1) $B_0\dfrac{\hat{i}-\hat{j}}{\sqrt{2}}\cos\left(\omega t - k\dfrac{\hat{i}+\hat{j}}{\sqrt{2}}\right)$

(2) $B_0\dfrac{\hat{j}-\hat{i}}{\sqrt{2}}\cos\left(\omega t + k\dfrac{\hat{i}+\hat{j}}{\sqrt{2}}\right)$

(3) $B_0\hat{k}\cos\left(\omega t - k\dfrac{\hat{i}+\hat{j}}{\sqrt{2}}\right)$

(4) $B_0\dfrac{\hat{i}+\hat{j}}{\sqrt{2}}\cos\left(\omega t - k\dfrac{\hat{i}+\hat{j}}{\sqrt{2}}\right)$

21. Starting at temperature 300 K, one mole of an ideal diatomic gas ($\gamma = 1.4$) is first compressed adiabatically from volume V_1 to $V_2 = \dfrac{V_1}{16}$. It is then allowed to expand isobarically to volume $2V_2$. If all the processes are the quasi-static then the final temperature of the gas (in °K) is (to the nearest integer) _______.

22. An electric field $\vec{E} = 4x\hat{i} - (y^2+1)\hat{j}$ N/C passes through the box shown in figure. The flux of the electric field through surfaces ABCD and BCGF are marked as ϕ_1 and ϕ_{11} respectively. The difference between $(\phi_1 - \phi_{11})$ is (in Nm^2/C) _______.

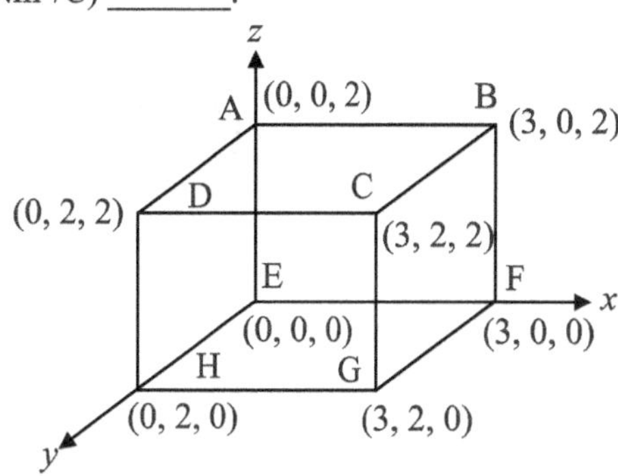

23. In a meter bridge experiment S is a standard resistance. R is a resistance wire. It is found that balancing length is $l = 25$ cm. If R is replaced by a wire of half length and half diameter that of R of same material, then the balancing distance l' (in cm) will now be _____.

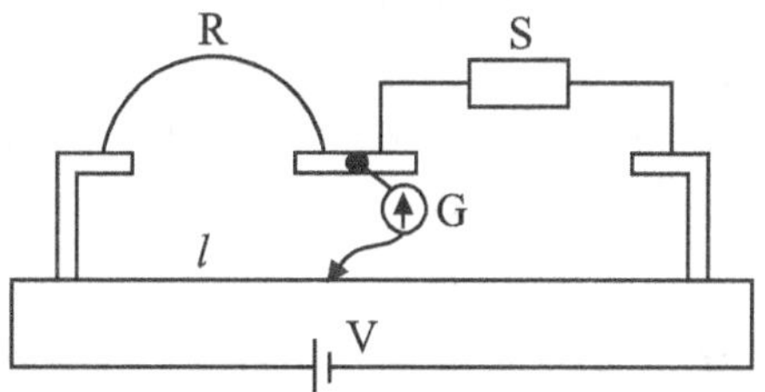

24. The circuit shown below is working as a 8 V dc regulated voltage source. When 12 V is used as input, the power dissipated (in mW) in each diode is; (considering both zener diodes are identical) _____.

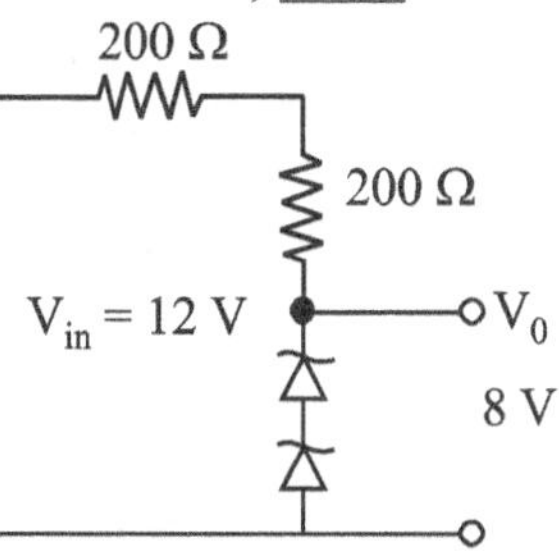

25. In a Young's double slit experiment 15 fringes are observed on a small portion of the screen when light of wavelength 500 nm is used. Ten fringes are observed on the same section of the screen when another light source of wavelength λ is used. Then the value of λ is (in nm) _______.

CHEMISTRY

26. Consider the following reactions,

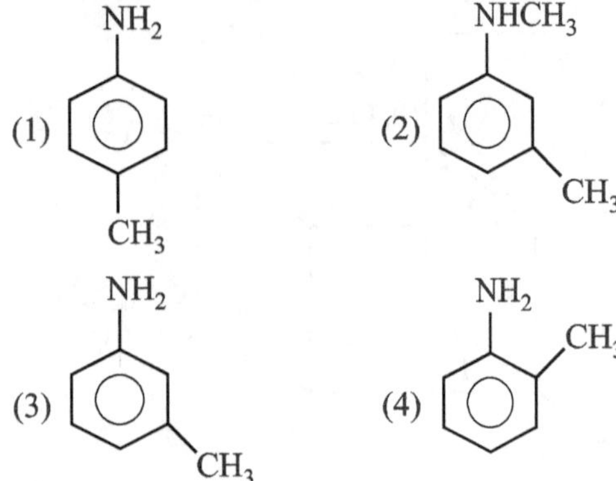

The compound [P] is:

(1) p-toluidine (NH₂ with CH₃ para)
(2) 3-methyl-N-methylaniline
(3) 3-methylaniline
(4) 2-methylaniline

27. Among the statements (A)–(D), the correct ones are:
(A) Lithium has the highest hydration enthalpy among the alkali metals.
(B) Lithium chloride is insoluble in pyridine.
(C) Lithium cannot form ethynide upon its reaction with ethyne.
(D) Both lithium and magnesium react slowly with H_2O.
(1) (A), (B) and (D) only
(2) (A), (C) and (D) only
(3) (B) and (D) only
(4) (A) and (D) only

28. The solubility product of $Cr(OH)_3$ at 298 K is 6.0×10^{-31}. The concentration of hydroxide ions in a saturated solution of $Cr(OH)_3$ will be:
(1) $(2.22 \times 10^{-31})^{1/4}$
(2) $(18 \times 10^{-31})^{1/4}$
(3) $(18 \times 10^{-31})^{1/2}$
(4) $(4.86 \times 10^{-29})^{1/4}$

29. Which of the following has the shortest C–Cl bond?
(1) $Cl–CH=CH_2$
(2) $Cl–CH=CH–NO_2$
(3) $Cl–CH=CH–CH_3$
(4) $Cl–CH=CH–OCH_3$

30. The reaction of $H_3N_3B_3Cl_3$(A) with $LiBH_4$ in tetrahydrofuran gives inorganic benzene (B). Further, the reaction of (A) with (C) leads to $H_3N_3B_3(Me)_3$. Compounds (B) and (C) respectively, are:

(1) Borazine and MeBr
(2) Diborane and MeMgBr
(3) Boron nitride and MeBr
(4) Borazine and MeMgBr

31. The first and second ionisation enthalpies of a metal are 496 and 4560 kJ mol⁻¹, respectively. How many moles of HCl and H_2SO_4, respectively, will be needed to react completely with 1 mole of the metal hydroxide?
(1) 1 and 1
(2) 2 and 0.5
(3) 1 and 2
(4) 1 and 0.5

32. The decreasing order of basicity of the following amines is:

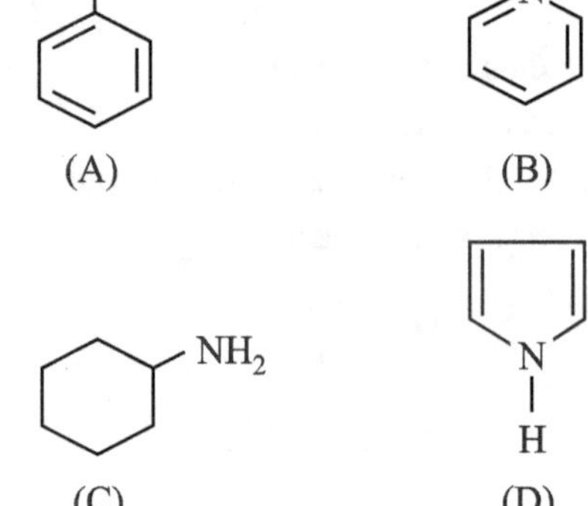

(1) (A) > (C) > (D) > (B)
(2) (C) > (A) > (B) > (D)
(3) (B) > (C) > (D) > (A)
(4) (C) > (B) > (A) > (D)

33. In the following reaction A is:

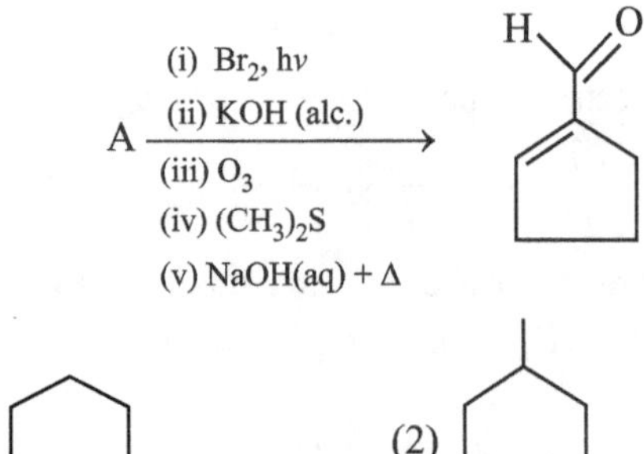

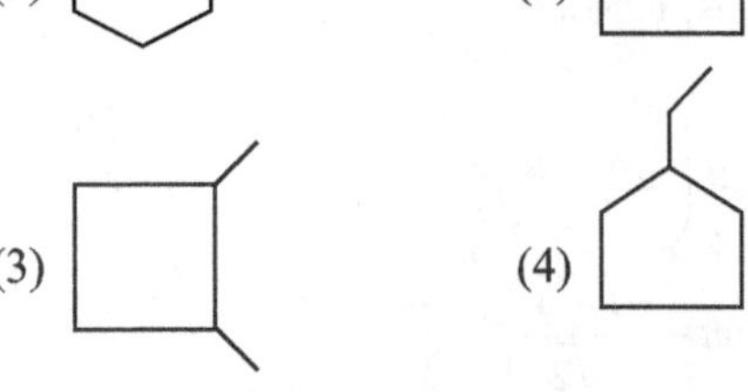

34. The correct order of the spin-only magnetic moments of the following complexes is:

(A) $[Cr(H_2O)_6]Br_2$

(B) $Na_4[Fe(CN)_6]$

(C) $Na_3[Fe(C_2O_4)_3]$ $(\Delta_0 > P)$

(D) $(Et_4N)_2[CoCl_4]$

(1) (C) > (A) > (D) > (B)

(2) (C) > (A) > (B) > (D)

(3) (A) > (D) > (C) > (B)

(4) (B) ≈ (A) > (D) > (C)

35. 5 g of zinc is treated separately with an excess of

(A) dilute hydrochloric acid and

(B) aqueous sodium hydroxide.

The ratio of the volumes of H_2 evolved in these two reactions is:

(1) 1 : 2 　　　　(2) 1 : 1

(3) 1 : 4 　　　　(4) 2 : 1

36. In the figure shown below reactant A (represented by square) is in equilibrium with product B (represented by circle). The equilibrium constant is:

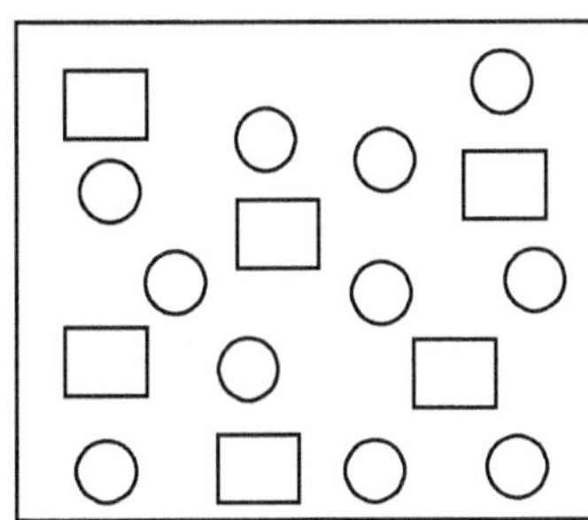

(1) 4 　　　　(2) 8

(3) 1 　　　　(4) 2

37. A mixture of gases O_2, H_2 and CO are taken in a closed vessel containing charcoal. The graph that represents the correct behaviour of pressure with time is:

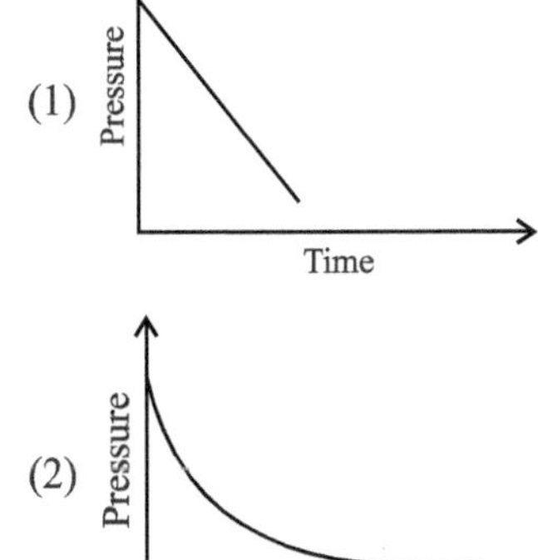

(3)

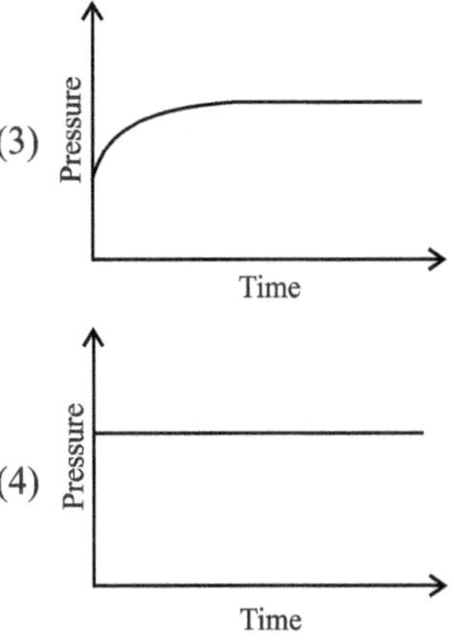

(4)

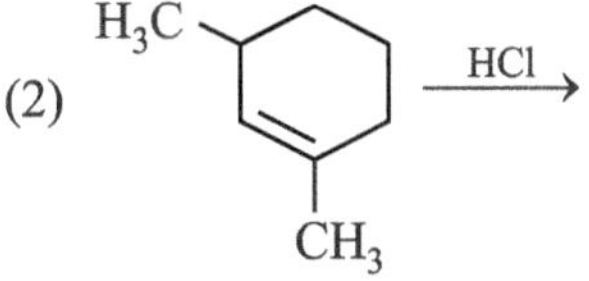

38. Which of the following reactions will not produce a racemic product?

(1) $CH_3-\overset{\overset{O}{\|}}{C}\,CH_2\,CH_3 \xrightarrow{HCN}$

(2)

(3) $CH_3CH_2CH{=}CH_2 \xrightarrow{HBr}$

(4) $CH_3-\overset{\overset{\displaystyle CH_3}{|}}{\underset{\underset{\displaystyle H}{|}}{C}}-CH{=}CH_2 \xrightarrow{HCl}$

39. Which polymer has 'chiral' monomer(s)?

(1) Neoprene 　　　　(2) Buna-N

(3) Nylon 6, 6 　　　　(4) PHBV

40. The number of sp^2 hybrid orbitals in a molecule of benzene is:

(1) 24 　　　　(2) 6

(3) 18 　　　　(4) 12

41. Amongst the following, the form of water with the lowest ionic conductance at 298 K is :

(1) distilled water

(2) saline water used for intravenous injection

(3) water from a well

(4) sea water

42. A, B and C are three biomolecules. The results of the tests performed on them are given below:

	Molisch's Test	Barfoed Test	Biuret Test
A	Positive	Negative	Negative
B	Positive	Positive	Negative
C	Negative	Negative	Positive

A, B and C are respectively:

(1) A = Glucose, B = Fructose, C = Albumin

(2) A = Lactose, B = Glucose, C = Albumin

(3) A = Lactose, B = Glucose, C = Alanine

(4) A = Lactose, B = Fructose, C = Alanine

43. The true statement amongst the following is :

(1) Both ΔS and S are functions of temperature.

(2) Both S and ΔS are not functions of temperature.

(3) S is not a function of temperature but ΔS is a function of temperature.

(4) S is a function of temperature but ΔS is not a function of temperature.

44. Biochemical Oxygen Demand (BOD) is the amount of oxygen required (in ppm):

(1) for sustaining life in a water body.

(2) by bacteria to break-down organic waste in a certain volume of a water sample.

(3) for the photochemical breakdown of waste present in 1 m^3 volume of a water body.

(4) by anaerobic bacteria to breakdown inorganic waste present in a water body.

45. The isomer(s) of $[Co(NH_3)_4Cl_2]$ that has/have a Cl–Co–Cl angle of 90°, is/are :

(1) meridional and *trans*

(2) *cis* and *trans*

(3) *trans* only

(4) *cis* only

46. 10.30 mg of O_2 is dissolved into a liter of sea water of density 1.03 g/mL. The concentration of O_2 in ppm is _____.

47. Consider the following reactions

$$A \xrightarrow[\text{(ii)}\,H_3O^+]{\text{(i)}\,CH_3MgBr} B \xrightarrow[573\ K]{Cu} \text{2-methyl-2-butene}$$

The mass percentage of carbon in A is _____.

48. A sample of milk splits after 60 min. at 300 K and after 40 min. at 400 K when the population of *lactobacillus acidophilus* in it doubles. The activation energy (in kJ/mol) for this process is closest to _____.

(Given, R = 8.3 J mol^{-1} K^{-1}, $\ln\left(\dfrac{2}{3}\right) = 0.4$, $e^{-3} = 4.0$)

49. A cylinder containing an ideal gas (0.1 mol of 1.0 dm^3) is in thermal equilibrium with a large volume of 0.5 molal aqueous solution of ethylene glycol at its freezing point. If the stoppers S_1 and S_2 (as shown in the figure) are suddenly withdrawn, the volume of the gas in litres after equilibrium is achieved will be _____.

(Given, K_f (water) = 2.0 K kg mol^{-1}, R = 0.08 dm^3 atm K^{-1} mol^{-1})

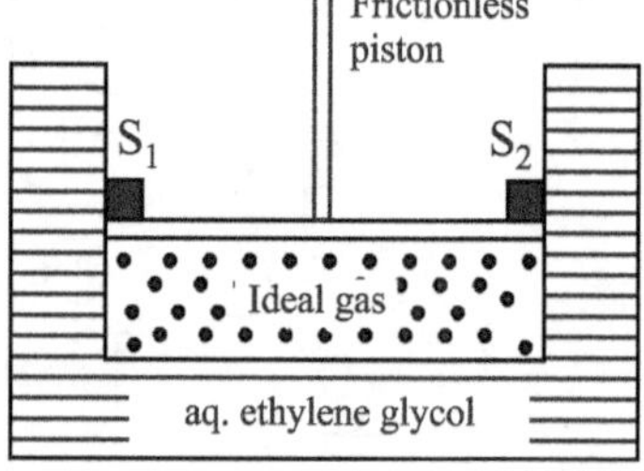

50. The sum of the total number of bonds between chromium and oxygen atoms in chromate and dichromate ions is _____.

MATHEMATICS

51. The following system of linear equations

$7x + 6y - 2z = 0$

$3x + 4y + 2z = 0$

$x - 2y - 6z = 0$, has

(1) infinitely many solutions, (x, y, z) satisfying $y = 2z$.

(2) no solution.

(3) infinitely many solutions, (x, y, z) satisfying $x = 2z$.

(4) only the trivial solution.

52. If 10 different balls are to be placed in 4 distinct boxes at random, then the probability that two of these boxes contain exactly 2 and 3 balls is :

(1) $\dfrac{965}{2^{11}}$

(2) $\dfrac{965}{2^{10}}$

(3) $\dfrac{945}{2^{10}}$

(4) $\dfrac{945}{2^{11}}$

53. Let f and g be differentiable functions on $\mathbf{R}$ such that fog is the identity function. If for some $a, b \in \mathbf{R}$, $g'(a) = 5$ and $g(a) = b$, then $f'(b)$ is equal to:

(1) $\dfrac{1}{5}$

(2) 1

(3) 5

(4) $\dfrac{2}{5}$

54. Let a function $f : [0, 5] \to \mathbf{R}$ be continuous, $f(1) = 3$ and F be defined as:

$$F(x) = \int_1^x t^2 g(t)\,dt, \quad \text{where } g(t) = \int_1^x f(u)\,du$$

Then for the function F, the point $x = 1$ is :

(1) a point of local minima.

(2) not a critical point.

(3) a point of local maxima.

(4) a point of inflection.

55. Let a_n be the nth term of a G.P. of positive terms.

If $\displaystyle\sum_{n=1}^{100} a_{2n+1} = 200$ and

$\displaystyle\sum_{n=1}^{100} a_{2n} = 100$, then $\displaystyle\sum_{n=1}^{200} a_n$ is equal to :

(1) 300

(2) 225

(3) 175

(4) 150

56. Let $[t]$ denote the greatest integer $\leq t$ and $\displaystyle\lim_{x \to 0} x\left[\dfrac{4}{x}\right] = A$.

Then the function, $f(x) = [x^2]\sin(\pi x)$ is discontinuous, when x is equal to :

(1) $\sqrt{A+1}$

(2) $\sqrt{A+5}$

(3) $\sqrt{A+21}$

(4) $\sqrt{A}$

57. If z be a complex number satisfying $|\text{Re}(z)| + |\text{Im}(z)| = 4$, then $|z|$ cannot be:

(1) $\sqrt{\dfrac{17}{2}}$

(2) $\sqrt{10}$

(3) $\sqrt{7}$

(4) $\sqrt{8}$

58. If $x = \displaystyle\sum_{n=0}^{\infty} (-1)^n \tan^{2n}\theta$ and $y = \displaystyle\sum_{n=0}^{\infty} \cos^{2n}\theta$, for $0 < \theta < \dfrac{\pi}{4}$, then :

(1) $x(1+y) = 1$

(2) $y(1-x) = 1$

(3) $y(1+x) = 1$

(4) $x(1-y) = 1$

59. If $x = 2\sin\theta - \sin 2\theta$ and $y = 2\cos\theta - \cos 2\theta$, $\theta \in [0, 2\pi]$, then $\dfrac{d^2 y}{dx^2}$ at $\theta = \pi$ is :

(1) $\dfrac{3}{4}$

(2) $-\dfrac{3}{8}$

(3) $\dfrac{3}{2}$

(4) $-\dfrac{3}{4}$

60. Given: $f(x) = \begin{cases} x & , \quad 0 \leq x < \dfrac{1}{2} \\ \dfrac{1}{2} & , \quad x = \dfrac{1}{2} \\ 1 - x & , \quad \dfrac{1}{2} < x \leq 1 \end{cases}$

and $g(x) = \left(x - \dfrac{1}{2}\right)^2$, $x \in \mathbf{R}$. Then the area (in sq. units) of the region bounded by the curves, $y = f(x)$ and $y = g(x)$ between the lines, $2x = 1$ and $2x = \sqrt{3}$, is :

(1) $\dfrac{1}{3} + \dfrac{\sqrt{3}}{4}$

(2) $\dfrac{\sqrt{3}}{4} - \dfrac{1}{3}$

(3) $\dfrac{1}{2} - \dfrac{\sqrt{3}}{4}$

(4) $\dfrac{1}{2} + \dfrac{\sqrt{3}}{4}$

61. The length of the minor axis (along y-axis) of an ellipse in the standard form is $\dfrac{4}{\sqrt{3}}$. If this ellipse touches the line, $x + 6y = 8$; then its eccentricity is:

(1) $\dfrac{1}{2}\sqrt{\dfrac{11}{3}}$

(2) $\sqrt{\dfrac{5}{6}}$

(3) $\dfrac{1}{2}\sqrt{\dfrac{5}{3}}$

(4) $\dfrac{1}{3}\sqrt{\dfrac{11}{3}}$

62. Let $a, b \in \mathbf{R}$, $a \neq 0$ be such that the equation, $ax^2 - 2bx + 5 = 0$ has a repeated root α, which is also a root of the equation, $x^2 - 2bx - 10 = 0$. If β is the other root of this equation, then $\alpha^2 + \beta^2$ is equal to :

(1) 25

(2) 26

(3) 28

(4) 24

63. If one end of a focal chord AB of the parabola $y^2 = 8x$ is at $A\left(\dfrac{1}{2}, -2\right)$, then the equation of the tangent to it at B is:

(1) $2x + y - 24 = 0$

(2) $x - 2y + 8 = 0$

(3) $x + 2y + 8 = 0$

(4) $2x - y - 24 = 0$

64. If $\dfrac{dy}{dx} = \dfrac{xy}{x^2 + y^2}$; $y(1) = 1$; then a value of x satisfying $y(x) = e$ is:

(1) $\dfrac{1}{2}\sqrt{3}\,e$

(2) $\dfrac{e}{\sqrt{2}}$

(3) $\sqrt{2}\,e$

(4) $\sqrt{3}\,e$

65. Let $a - 2b + c = 1$.

If $f(x) = \begin{vmatrix} x+a & x+2 & x+1 \\ x+b & x+3 & x+2 \\ x+c & x+4 & x+3 \end{vmatrix}$, then :

(1) $f(-50) = 501$ (2) $f(-50) = -1$

(3) $f(50) = -501$ (4) $f(50) = 1$

66. If $A = \{x \in R : |x| < 2\}$ and

$B = \{x \in R : |x - 2| \ge 3\}$; then :

(1) $A \cap B = (-2, -1)$

(2) $B - A = R - (-2, 5)$

(3) $A \cup B = R - (2, 5)$

(4) $A - B = [-1, 2)$

67. In the expansion of $\left(\dfrac{x}{\cos\theta} + \dfrac{1}{x\sin\theta} \right)^{16}$, if l_1 is the least value of the term independent of x when $\dfrac{\pi}{8} \le \theta \le \dfrac{\pi}{4}$ and l_2 is the least value of the term independent of x when $\dfrac{\pi}{16} \le \theta \le \dfrac{\pi}{8}$, then the ratio $l_2 : l_1$ is equal to :

(1) $1 : 8$ (2) $16 : 1$

(3) $8 : 1$ (4) $1 : 16$

68. A random variable X has the following probability distribution:

X	:	1	2	3	4	5
P(X)	:	K^2	$2K$	K	$2K$	$5K^2$

Then, $P(X > 2)$ is equal to:

(1) $\dfrac{7}{12}$ (2) $\dfrac{1}{36}$

(3) $\dfrac{1}{6}$ (4) $\dfrac{23}{36}$

69. If $p \to (p \wedge \sim q)$ is false, then the truth values of p and q are respectively:

(1) F, F   (2) T, F

(3) T, T   (4) F, T

70. If $\displaystyle\int \dfrac{d\theta}{\cos^2\theta(\tan 2\theta + \sec 2\theta)} = \lambda\tan\theta + 2\log_e|f(\theta)| + C$ where C is a constant of integration, then the ordered pair $(\lambda, f(\theta))$ is equal to:

(1) $(1, 1 - \tan\theta)$ (2) $(-1, 1 - \tan\theta)$

(3) $(-1, 1 + \tan\theta)$ (4) $(1, 1 + \tan\theta)$

71. If $C_r \equiv {}^{25}C_r$ and $C_0 + 5 \cdot C_1 + 9 \cdot C_2 + ... + (101) \cdot C_{25} = 2^{25} \cdot k$, then k is equal to _________.

72. The number of terms common to the two A.P.'s 3, 7, 11, ..., 407 and 2, 9, 16, ..., 709 is _____.

73. Let $\vec{b}$, $\vec{b}$ and $\vec{c}$ be three vectors such that $|\vec{a}| = \sqrt{3}$, $|\vec{b}| = 5$, $\vec{b} \cdot \vec{c} = 10$ and the angle between $\vec{b}$ and $\vec{c}$ is $\dfrac{\pi}{3}$. If $\vec{b}$ is perpendicular to the vector $\vec{b} \times \vec{c}$, then $|\vec{a} \times (\vec{b} \times \vec{c})|$ is equal to _____.

74. If the distance between the plane, $23x - 10y - 2z + 48 = 0$ and the plane containing the lines

$$\dfrac{x+1}{2} = \dfrac{y-3}{4} = \dfrac{z+1}{3}$$

and $$\dfrac{x+3}{2} = \dfrac{y+2}{6} = \dfrac{z-1}{\lambda} \quad (\lambda \in R)$$

is equal to $\dfrac{k}{\sqrt{633}}$, then k is equal to _____.

75. If the curves, $x^2 - 6x + y^2 + 8 = 0$ and $x^2 - 8y + y^2 + 16 - k = 0$, $(k > 0)$ touch each other at a point, then the largest value of k is _____.

JEE Main 2020 (07-01-2020) Morning Shift

PHYSICS

1. **(2)** Given, $V_1 = 1$ litre, $P_1 = 1$ atm
$V_2 = 3$ litre, $\gamma = 1.40$,

Using, $PV^r = $ constant $\Rightarrow P_1 V_1^\gamma = P_2 V_2^\gamma$

$$\Rightarrow P_2 = P_1 \times \left(\frac{1}{3}\right)^{1.4} = \frac{1}{4.6555}\ atm$$

$\therefore$ Work done, $W = \dfrac{P_1 V_1 - P_2 V_2}{\gamma - 1}$

$$= \frac{\left(1\times 1 - \dfrac{1}{4.6555}\times 3\right)1.01325\times 10^5 \times 10^{-3}}{0.4} = 90.1\ J$$

Closest value of $W = 90.5\ J$

2. **(2)** Total force required to lift maximum load capacity against frictional force $= 400\ N$
$F_{total} = Mg + $ friction
$= 2000 \times 10 + 4000$
$= 20{,}000 + 4000 = 24000\ N$
Using power, $P = F \times v$
$60 \times 746 = 24000 \times v$
$\Rightarrow v = 1.86$ m/s $\approx 1.9\ m/s$
Hence speed of the elevator at full load is close to 1.9 ms^{-1}

3. **(1)** When the bob covered a distance 'h'

Using $mgh = \dfrac{1}{2}mv^2 + \dfrac{1}{2}I\omega^2$

$$= \frac{1}{2}\text{m}(\omega r)^2 + \frac{1}{2}\times \frac{mr^2}{2}\times \omega^2 \ (\because v = \omega r\ no\ slipping)$$

$$\Rightarrow \quad mgh = \frac{3}{4}m\omega^2 r^2$$

$$\Rightarrow \omega = \sqrt{\frac{4gh}{3r^2}} = \frac{1}{r}\sqrt{\frac{4gh}{3}}$$

4. **(4)** A logic gate is reversible if we can recover input data from the output. Hence NOT gate.

5. **(4)** As magnetic field lines form close loop, hence every magnetic field line creating magnetic flux through the inner region (ϕ_i) must be passing through the outer region. Since flux in two regions are in opposite region.

$\therefore \phi_i = -\phi_0$

6. **(2)** According to question, the intensity of light coming out of the analyser is just 10% of the original intensity (I_0)

Using, $I = I_0 \cos^2\theta$

$$\Rightarrow \frac{I_0}{10} = I_0 \cos^2\theta \quad \Rightarrow \frac{1}{10} = \cos^2\theta$$

$$\Rightarrow \cos\theta = \frac{1}{\sqrt{10}} = 0.316 \Rightarrow \theta \approx 71.6°$$

Therefore, the angle by which the analyser need to be rotated further to reduced the output intensity to be zero
$\phi = 90° - \theta = 90° - 71.6° = 18.4°$

7. **(4)** In damped harmonic oscillation,

$$\frac{md^2 x}{dt^2} = -kx - bv$$

$$\Rightarrow \frac{md^2 x}{dt^2} + b\frac{dx}{dt} + kx = 0 \quad ....(i)$$

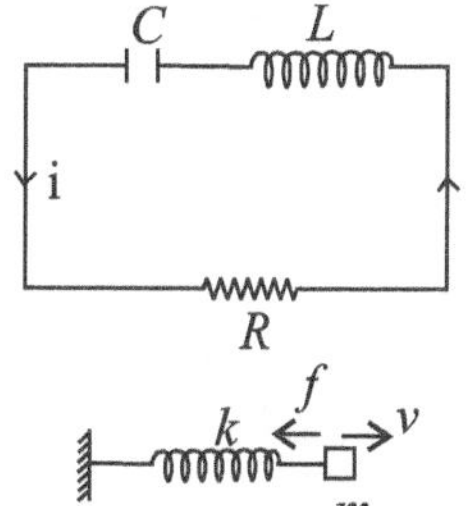

In LCR circuit, $\dfrac{-q}{C} - iR - \dfrac{Ldi}{dt} = 0$

$$L\frac{d^2}{dt^2} + R\frac{dq}{dt} + \frac{q}{C} = 0 \ ...(ii)$$

Comparing equations (i) & (ii)

$$L \leftrightarrow m,\ C \leftrightarrow \frac{1}{k},\ R \leftrightarrow b$$

8. **(2)**

$$\frac{1}{2}mu^2 + \frac{-GMm}{R} = \frac{1}{2}mv^2 + \frac{-GMm}{2R}$$

$$\Rightarrow \frac{1}{2}m(v^2 - u^2) = \frac{-GMm}{2R}$$

$$\Rightarrow V = \sqrt{V = u^2 - \frac{GM}{R}} \qquad ...(i)$$

$$v_0 = \sqrt{\frac{GM}{2R}} \quad \therefore v_{rad} = \frac{m\times v}{\left(\dfrac{m}{10}\right)} = 10\ v$$

Ejecting a rocket of mass $\dfrac{m}{10}$

$$\therefore \dfrac{9m}{10} \times \sqrt{\dfrac{GM}{2R}} = \dfrac{m}{10} \times v_\tau \Rightarrow V_\tau^2 = 81\dfrac{GM}{2R}$$

Kinetic energy of rocket,

$$KE_{rocket} = \dfrac{1}{2}\dfrac{M}{10}\left(V_T^2 + V_r^2\right) = \dfrac{1}{2} \times \dfrac{m}{10} \times \left((u^2 - \dfrac{GM}{R})100 + 81\dfrac{GM}{R}\right)$$

$$= \dfrac{m}{20} \times 100\left(u^2 - \dfrac{GM}{R} + \dfrac{81}{200}\dfrac{GM}{R}\right)$$

$$= 5m\left(u^2 - \dfrac{119}{200}\dfrac{GM}{R}\right)$$

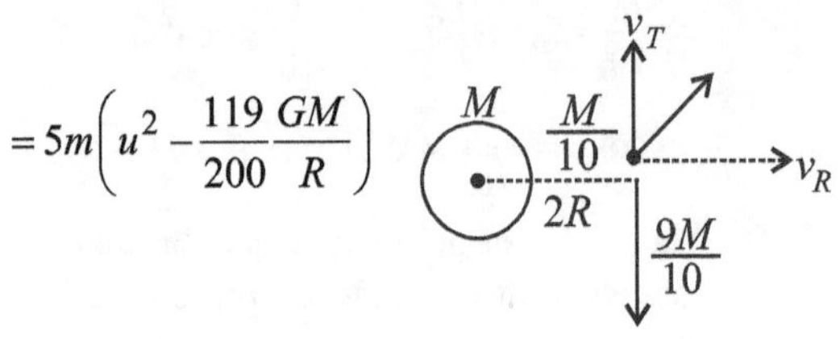

9. (4) According to question, $I(t) = I_0 t(1 - t)$

$$\therefore I = I_0 t - I_0 t^2$$

$$\phi = B.A$$

$$\phi = (\mu_0 nI) \times (\pi R^2)$$

$$(\because B = \mu_0 nI \text{ and } A = \pi R^2)$$

$$V_R = \dfrac{-d\phi}{dt}$$

$$V_R = \mu_0 n\pi R^2 (I_0 - 2I_0 t)$$

$$\Rightarrow V_R = 0 \text{ at } t = \dfrac{1}{2}s$$

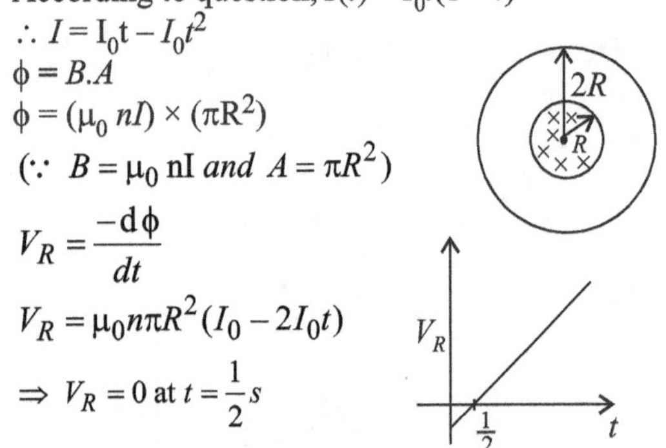

10. (1) Given, $l = 60$ cm, $m = 6$ g, $A = 1$ mm^2, $v = 90$ m/s and $Y = 16 \times 10^{11}$ Nm^{-2}

Using, $v = \sqrt{\dfrac{T}{m} \times l} \Rightarrow T = \dfrac{mv^2}{l}$

Again from, $Y = \dfrac{T}{A}\Delta L / L_0$

$$\Delta L = \dfrac{Tl}{YA} = \dfrac{mv^2 \times l}{l(YA)}$$

$$= \dfrac{6 \times 10^{-3} \times 90^2}{16 \times 10^{11} \times 10^{-6}} = 3 \times 10^{-4}\,m$$

$$= 0.03 \text{ mm}$$

11. (4) Using, $\gamma_{mixture} = \dfrac{n_1 C_{p_1} + n_2 C_{p_2}}{n_1 C_{v_1} + n_2 C_{v_2}}$

$$\Rightarrow \dfrac{n_1}{\gamma_1 - 1} + \dfrac{n_2}{\gamma_2 - 1} = \dfrac{n_1 + n_2}{\gamma_m - 1}$$

$$\Rightarrow \dfrac{3}{\dfrac{4}{3} - 1} + \dfrac{2}{\dfrac{5}{3} - 1} = \dfrac{5}{\gamma_m - 1}$$

$$\Rightarrow \dfrac{9}{1} + \dfrac{2 \times 3}{2} = \dfrac{5}{\gamma_m - 1}$$

$$\Rightarrow \gamma_m - 1 = \dfrac{5}{12}$$

$$\Rightarrow \gamma_m = \dfrac{17}{12} = 1.42$$

12. (1) According question, $M = 375$
$L = 150$ mm, $f_0 = 5$ mm and $f_e = ?$

Using, magnification, $M \approx \dfrac{L}{f_0}\left(1 + \dfrac{D}{f_e}\right)$

$$\Rightarrow 375 = \dfrac{150}{5}\left(1 + \dfrac{250}{f_e}\right) \qquad (\because D = 25 \text{ cm} = 250 \text{ mm})$$

$$\Rightarrow 12.5 = 1 + \dfrac{250}{f_e}$$

$$\Rightarrow f_e = \dfrac{250}{11.5} = 21.7 \approx 22\,mm$$

13. (2) For first excited state $n' = 3$

Time period $T \propto \dfrac{n^3}{z^2}$

$$\Rightarrow \dfrac{T_2}{T_1} = \dfrac{n'^3}{n^3}$$

$$\therefore T_2 = 8T_1 = 8 \times 1.6 \times 10^{-16}s$$

$$\therefore \text{Frequency, } v = \dfrac{1}{T_2} = \dfrac{1}{8 \times 1.6 \times 10^{-16}}$$

$$\approx 7.8 \times 10^{14}\,Hz$$

14. (1) Given, $K(x) = K(1 + \alpha x)$

Capacitance of element, $C_{el} = \dfrac{K\varepsilon_0 A}{dx}$

$$\Rightarrow C_{el} = \dfrac{\varepsilon_0 K(1 + \alpha x)A}{dx}$$

$$\therefore \int d\left(\dfrac{1}{C}\right) = \dfrac{1}{C_{el}} = \int_0^d \left(\dfrac{dx}{\varepsilon_0 KA(1 + \alpha x)}\right)$$

$$\Rightarrow \dfrac{1}{C} = \dfrac{1}{\varepsilon_0 KA\alpha}[ln(1 + \alpha x)]_0^d$$

$$\Rightarrow \dfrac{1}{C} = \dfrac{1}{\varepsilon_0 KA\alpha}ln(1 + \alpha d)[\alpha d << 1]$$

$$= \dfrac{1}{\varepsilon_0 KA\alpha}\left[\alpha d - \dfrac{\alpha^2 d^2}{2}\right]$$

$$= \dfrac{1}{\varepsilon_0 KA}\left[1 - \dfrac{\alpha d}{2}\right]$$

$$\therefore C = \frac{\varepsilon_0 KA}{d\left(1-\frac{\alpha d}{2}\right)} \Rightarrow C = \frac{\varepsilon_0 KA}{d}\left(1+\frac{\alpha d}{2}\right)$$

15. (3)

16. (3) Given, $\lambda = 6000 \times 10^{-8}$ cm

Second diffraction minimum at $60°$ i.e., $\theta_2 = 60°$

Using, $d\sin\theta = n\lambda$

$d\sin\theta_2 = 2\lambda$ (for 2nd minima)

$\Rightarrow d\sin 60° = 2\lambda$

$$\Rightarrow d\times\left(\frac{\sqrt{3}}{2}\right) = 2\lambda \qquad\qquad ...(i)$$

$$\Rightarrow \frac{\lambda}{d} = \frac{\sqrt{3}}{4}$$

For first minima,

$d\sin\theta_1 = \lambda$

$$\Rightarrow \sin\theta_1 = \frac{\lambda}{d} = \frac{\sqrt{3}}{4} = 0.43 \Rightarrow \theta_1 < 30°$$

Hence closest option, $\theta_1 \approx 25°$

17. (4)

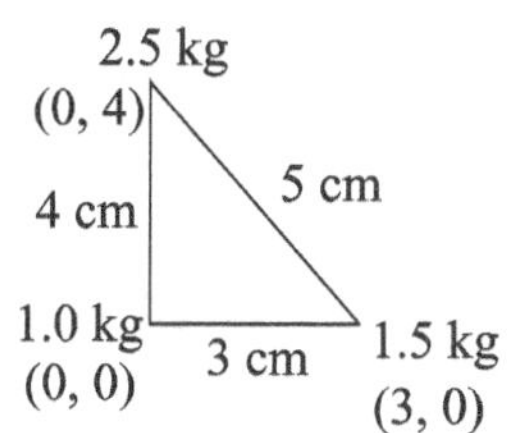

$$X_{cm} = \frac{m_1 x_1 + m_2 x_2 + m_3 x_3}{m_1 + m_2 + m_3}$$

$$X_{cm} = \frac{1\times 0 + 1.5\times 3 + 2.5\times 0}{1+1.5+2.5} = \frac{1.5\times 3}{5} = 0.9 cm$$

$$Y_{cm} = \frac{m_1 y_1 + m_2 y_2 + m_3 y_3}{m_1 + m_2 + m_3}$$

$$Y_{cm} = \frac{1\times 0 + 1.5\times 0 + 2.5\times 4}{1+1.5+2.5} = \frac{2.5\times 4}{5} = 2 cm$$

Hence, centre of mass of system is at point (0.9, 2)

18. (4)

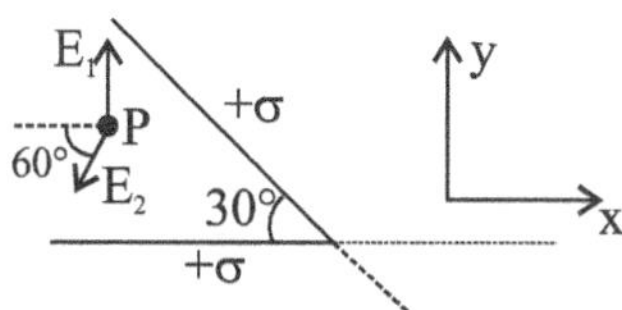

From figure,

$$\vec{E}_1 = \frac{\sigma}{2\varepsilon_0}\hat{y} \text{ and } \vec{E}_2 = \frac{\sigma}{2\varepsilon_0}(-\cos 60°\hat{x} - \sin 60°\hat{y})$$

$$= \frac{\sigma}{2\varepsilon_0}\left(-\frac{1}{2}\hat{x} - \frac{\sqrt{3}}{2}\hat{y}\right)$$

Electric field in the region shown in figure (P)

$$\vec{E}_P = \vec{E}_1 + \vec{E}_2 = \frac{\sigma}{2\varepsilon_0}\left[-\frac{1}{2}\hat{x} + \left(1-\frac{\sqrt{3}}{2}\right)\hat{y}\right]$$

$$\text{or, } \vec{E}_P = \frac{\sigma}{2\varepsilon_0}\left[\left(1-\frac{\sqrt{3}}{2}\right)\hat{y} - \frac{\hat{x}}{2}\right]$$

19. (2) Given, $\vec{B} = 3\times 10^{-8}\sin(1.6\times 10^3 x + 48\times 10^{10} t)\ \hat{j}\ T$

Using, $E_0 = B_0 \times C = 3\times 10^{-8} \times 3\times 10^8 = 9\ V/m$

$\therefore$ Electric field, $\vec{E} = 9\sin(1.6\times 10^3 x + 48\times 10^{10} t)\hat{k}\ V/m$

20. (3) Moment inertia of the rod passing through a point — away from the centre of the rod

$$I = Ig + m\ell^2$$

$$\Rightarrow I = \frac{MI^2}{12} + M\times\left(\frac{I^2}{16}\right) = \frac{7MI^2}{48}$$

Using $I = MK^2 = \frac{7MI^2}{48}$ (K = radius of gyration)

$$\Rightarrow K = \sqrt{\frac{7}{48}}I$$

21. (600.00) Given; $T_1 = 900\ K$, $T_2 = 300K$, $W = 1200\ J$

Using, $1-\frac{T_2}{T_1} = \frac{W}{Q_1}$

$$\Rightarrow 1 - \frac{300}{900} = \frac{1200}{Q_1}$$

$$\Rightarrow \frac{2}{3} = \frac{1200}{Q_1} \Rightarrow Q_1 = 1800$$

Therefore heat energy delivered by the engine to the low temperature reservoir, $Q_2 = Q_1 - W = 1800 - 1200 = 600.00\ J$

22. (60.00) Volume, $V = Ibh$

$$\therefore \gamma = \frac{\Delta V}{V} = \frac{\Delta\ell}{\ell} + \frac{\Delta b}{b} + \frac{\Delta h}{h}$$

(γ = coefficient of volume expansion)

$$\Rightarrow \gamma = 5\times 10^{-5} + 5\times 10^{-6} + 5\times 10^{-6}$$

$$= 60\times 10^{-6}/°C$$

$\therefore$ Value of $C = 60.00$

23. (175.00)

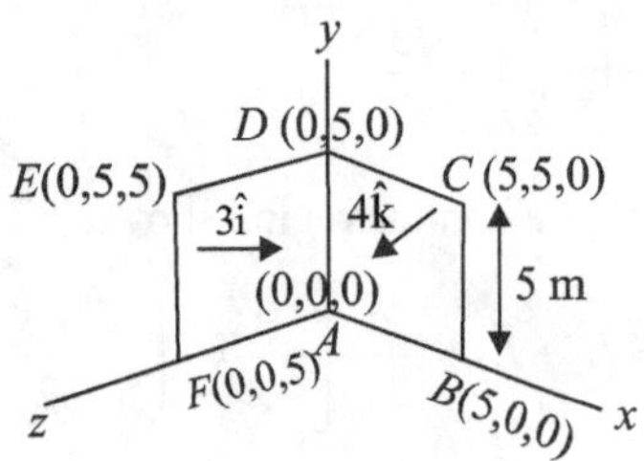

Flux through the loop ABCDEFA,

$$\phi = \vec{B}.\vec{A} = (3\hat{i} + 4\hat{k}).(25\hat{i} + 25\hat{k})$$

$$\Rightarrow \phi = (3 \times 25) + (4 \times 25) = 175 \text{ weber}$$

24. (10.00)

Kinetic energy = change in potential energy of the particle,

$$KE = mg\Delta h$$

Given, $m = 1$ kg,

$$\Delta h = h_2 - h_1 = 2 - 1 = 1 m$$

$$\therefore KE = 1 \times 10 \times 1 = 10 \, J$$

25. (11.00)   Energy of proton

$$E = \frac{hc}{\lambda} = \frac{1240}{310} = 4eV > 2eV \; [= \phi]$$

(so emission of photoelectron will take place)

$$= 4 \times 1.6 \times 10^{-19} = 6.4 \times 10^{-19} \text{ joule}$$

$$N = \frac{6.4 \times 10^{-5} \times 1}{4 \times 6.4 \times 10^{-19}} = 10^{14}$$

No. of photoelectrons emitted per second

$$= \frac{10^{14}}{10^3} = 10^{11} \; (\because 1 \text{ in } 10^3 \text{ photons ejects an electron})$$

$$\therefore \text{ Value of } X = 11.00$$

CHEMISTRY

26. (2)   The possible number of orbitals in a shell in term of 'n' is n^2

$$\therefore n = 5 \; ; n^2 = 25$$

27. (2) $Cu^{2+} + 2e^- \longrightarrow Cu, \; \Delta G_1^\circ = -2F(0.34) \dots(i)$

$Cu^+ + e^- \longrightarrow Cu, \; \Delta G_2^\circ = -F(0.522) \dots(ii)$

Subtract (ii) from (i)

$Cu^{2+} + e^- \longrightarrow Cu^+, \quad \Delta G_3^\circ = -F(E^0)$

$\therefore \Delta G_1^\circ - \Delta G_2^\circ = G_3^\circ$

$\Rightarrow -FE^\circ = -2F(0.34) + F(0.522)$

$\Rightarrow E^\circ = 0.68 - 0.522 = 0.158$ V

28. (2)   Synthetic resin method is more efficient than zeolite process as it can exchange both cations as well as anions.

29. (3)

Vitamins	Deficiency Diseases
Vitamin B$_1$ (thiamine)	Beri Beri
Vitamin B$_2$ (riboflavin)	Cheilosis
Vitamin B$_6$ (pyridoxine)	Convulsions
Vitamin C (ascorbic acid)	Scurvy

30. (2)   Mixture of carbon disulphide and acetone will show positive deviation from Raoult's Law.

The dipolar interaction between solute (CS_2) solvent (acetone) molecules in solution are weaker. So the vapour pressure of solution will be greater than the individual vapoure pressure of pure components.

31. (2)

32. (4)

33. **(3)** Except (3) all postulates was given by the Dalton.

34. **(4)** $\mu_{CCl_4} = \mu_{CH_4} = 0$ due to symmetrical structure but $\mu_{CHCl_3} \neq 0$. So dipole moment order is :

$$CHCl_3 > CH_4 = CCl_4$$

35. **(1)** $[Pt(NH_3)_2Cl(NH_2CH_3)]Cl$
Diamine chlorido (methanamine) platinum (II) chloride

36. **(2)** Wrought iron is purest form of commercial iron.

37. **(3)** Chlorine has highest electron gain enthalpy (most negative) among the given elements, the electron gain enthalpy decreases down the group i.e., moves to least negative.

38. **(2)**

1-Methylethylene oxide

39. **(4)** Conjugate acid of guanadine(B) is resonance stabilised and have 2 resonance structure.
Similarly conjugate acid of (A) is also resonance stabilised and have one resonance structure. (C) does not exhibit resonance structure.
therefore the basic order is, k_b : (B) > (A) > (C)
∴ pk_b : (B) < (A) < (C)

40. **(2)** $K_2O : 2x - 2 = 0 \Rightarrow x = +1$
$K_2O_2 : 2x - 2 = 0 \Rightarrow x = +1$
$KO_2 : x - 1 = 0 \Rightarrow x = +1$
Thus, potassium shows +1 state in all its oxides, superoxides and peroxides.

41. **(2)**

Methyl orange

Methyl orange is used as an indicator in acid base titrations.

42. **(1)** Atomic size of elements of $4d$ and $5d$ transition series are nearly same due to lanthanide contraction.

43. **(2)** The covalant character of the bonding (M – C σ and M – C π bonding) which exists between the metal and the carbon atom of the CO can only be explained by the molecular orbital theory.

44. **(3)** (A) $(CH_3)_2CCH(OH)CH_3 \xrightarrow{\text{conc.}H_2SO_4}$

$$CH_3-\underset{\underset{CH_3}{|}}{\overset{\overset{CH_3}{|}}{C}}-CH=CH_2$$

(B) $(CH_3)_2CHCH(Br)CH_3 \xrightarrow{\text{alc.KOH}}$

$$CH_3-\underset{}{\overset{\overset{CH_3}{|}}{C}}=CH-CH_3$$

(C) $(CH_3)_2CHCH(Br)CH_3 \xrightarrow{t\text{-BuO}^-K^+}$

$$CH_3-\underset{\underset{CH_3}{|}}{CH}-CH=CH_2$$

Due to bulky nature of tertiary butoxide, the least hindered hydrogen is eliminated. Therefore, Hoffman product is formed.

(D) $(CH_3)_2\underset{\underset{OH}{|}}{C}-CH_2-CHO \xrightarrow{\Delta}$

$$CH_3-\underset{\underset{CH_3}{|}}{C}=CH-CHO$$

45. **(4)** Among given intermolecular forces, ionic interactions are stronger as compared to van der Waal interaction Thus, correct order is ion-ion > ion-dipole > dipole-dipole

46. **(1.67)**

$$3Cl_2 + 6NaOH \longrightarrow 5\underset{(X)}{NaCl} + \underset{(Y)}{NaClO_3} + 3H_2O$$
$$\text{Hot \& conc.}$$

$$\underset{(X)}{NaCl} + AgNO_3 \longrightarrow \underset{(white\ ppt.)}{AgCl} + NaNO_3$$

Average bond order between Cl and O atom in

$$NaClO_3 = \frac{5}{3} = 1.67$$

47. **(2.00)**

48. **(23.03)** $t_{1/2} = 6.93$ years,
$a = 10^{-6}$ g

$$t_{1/2} = \frac{0.693}{K}$$

$$\Rightarrow \quad K = \frac{0.693}{t_{1/2}} = \frac{0.693}{6.93} = 0.1$$

For Ist order reaction,

$$K = \frac{2.303}{t}\log\frac{a}{a-x}$$

$$t = \frac{2.303}{K}\log\frac{a}{a-x}$$

$$= \frac{2.303}{0.1}\log\frac{10^{-6}}{10^{-7}}$$

$$= \frac{2.303}{0.1} = 23.03 \text{ years}$$

49. **(–2.70)**

$$\Delta U = 2.1 \text{ kcal} = 2.1 \times 10^3 \text{ cal}$$

$$\Delta n_g = 2$$

$$\begin{aligned}\Delta H &= \Delta U + \Delta n_g RT \\ &= 2.1 \times 10^3 + 2 \times 2 \times 300 \\ &= 2100 + 1200 \\ &= 3300 \text{ cal}\end{aligned}$$

$$\begin{aligned}\Delta G &= \Delta H - T\Delta S \\ &= 3300 - 300 \times 20 \\ &= 3300 - 6000 \\ &= -2700 \text{ cals} \\ &= -2.7 \text{ kcal}\end{aligned}$$

50. **(10.60)** $M_{H_2SO_4} = \dfrac{9.8}{98 \times 100} = 10^{-3}$ M

$$M_{NaOH} = \frac{4}{40 \times 100} = 10^{-3} \text{ M}$$

After neutralisation $[OH^-]$ can be calculated as

$$[OH^-] = \frac{\left(40 \times 10^{-3}\right) - \left(2 \times 10^{-3} \times 10\right)}{50}$$

$$= \frac{20}{50} \times 10^{-3}$$

$$[OH^-] = \frac{2}{5} \times 10^{-3}$$

$$pOH = 3.397$$

$$\begin{aligned}pH &= 14 - pOH \\ &= 14 - 3.397 = 10.603\end{aligned}$$

MATHEMATICS

51. **(1)** $\quad y(\alpha) = \sqrt{\dfrac{\dfrac{2\sin\alpha}{\cos\alpha} + \dfrac{\cos\alpha}{\sin\alpha}}{\sec^2\alpha}} = \sqrt{\dfrac{2\cos^2\alpha}{\sin\alpha\cos\alpha} + \dfrac{1}{\sin^2\alpha}}$

$$= \sqrt{2\cot\alpha + \operatorname{cosec}^2\alpha} = \sqrt{2\cot\alpha + 1 + \cot^2\alpha}$$

$$= |1 + \cot\alpha| = -1 - \cot\alpha \qquad \left[\because \alpha \in \left(\frac{3\pi}{4}, \pi\right)\right]$$

$$\frac{dy}{d\alpha} = \operatorname{cosec}^2\alpha \implies \left(\frac{dy}{d\alpha}\right)_{\alpha = \frac{5\pi}{6}} = 4$$

52. **(4)** Let 5 terms of A.P. be

$a - 2d, a - d, a, a + d, a + 2d.$

Sum $= 25 \implies 5a = 25 \implies a = 5$

Product $= 2520$

$$(5 - 2d)(5 - d)\,5\,(5 + d)(5 + 2d) = 2520$$

$$\implies (25 - 4d^2)(25 - d^2) = 504$$

$$\implies 625 - 100d^2 - 25d^2 + 4d^4 = 504$$

$$\implies 4d^4 - 125d^2 + 625 - 504 = 0$$

$$\implies 4d^4 - 125d^2 + 121 = 0$$

$$\implies 4d^4 - 121d^2 - 4d^2 + 121 = 0$$

$$\implies (d^2 - 1)(4d^2 - 121) = 0$$

$$\implies d = \pm 1, \; d = \pm \frac{11}{2}$$

$d = \pm 1$ and $d = -\dfrac{11}{2}$, does not give $\dfrac{-1}{2}$ as a term

$$\therefore \quad d = \frac{11}{2}$$

$$\therefore \quad \text{Largest term} = 5 + 2d = 5 + 11 = 16$$

53. **(2)** $(g\!of)(x) = g(f(x)) = f^2(x) + f(x) - 1$

$$g\left(f\left(\frac{5}{4}\right)\right) = 4\left(\frac{5}{4}\right)^2 - 10 \cdot \frac{5}{4} + 5 = -\frac{5}{4}$$

$$[\because g(f(x)) = 4x^2 - 10x + 5]$$

$$g\left(f\left(\frac{5}{4}\right)\right) = f^2\left(\frac{5}{4}\right) + f\left(\frac{5}{4}\right) - 1$$

$$-\frac{5}{4} = f^2\left(\frac{5}{4}\right) + f\left(\frac{5}{4}\right) - 1$$

$$f^2\left(\frac{5}{4}\right) + f\left(\frac{5}{4}\right) + \frac{1}{4} = 0$$

$$\left(f\left(\frac{5}{4}\right) + \frac{1}{2}\right)^2 = 0$$

$$t\left(\frac{5}{4}\right) = -\frac{1}{2}$$

54. **(4)** Five digits numbers be 1, 3, 5, 7, 9

For selection of one digit, we have $^5C_1$ choice.

And six digits can be arrange in $\dfrac{6!}{2!}$ ways.

Hence, total such numbers $= \dfrac{5 \cdot 6!}{2!} = \dfrac{5}{2} \cdot 6!$

55. **(3)** Angle bisector between $\vec{b}$ and $\vec{c}$ can be

$$\vec{a} = \lambda(\hat{b} + \hat{c}) \quad \text{or} \quad \vec{a} = \mu(\hat{b} - \hat{c})$$

$$\text{If } \vec{a} = \lambda\left(\frac{\hat{i} + \hat{j}}{\sqrt{2}} + \frac{\hat{i} - \hat{j} + 4\hat{k}}{3\sqrt{2}}\right)$$

$$= \frac{\lambda}{3\sqrt{2}}[3\hat{i} + 3\hat{j} + \hat{i} - \hat{j} + 4\hat{k}]$$

$$= \frac{\lambda}{3\sqrt{2}}[4\hat{i} + 2\hat{j} + 4\hat{k}]$$

Compare with $\vec{a} = \alpha\hat{i} + 2\hat{j} + \beta\hat{k}$

$$\frac{2\lambda}{3\sqrt{2}} = 2 \quad \Rightarrow \quad \lambda = 3\sqrt{2}$$

$$\vec{a} = 4\hat{i} + 2\hat{j} + 4\hat{k}$$

Not satisfy any option

Now consider $\vec{a} = \mu\left(\dfrac{\hat{i}+\hat{j}}{\sqrt{2}} - \dfrac{\hat{i}-\hat{j}+4\hat{k}}{3\sqrt{2}}\right)$

$$\vec{a} = \frac{\mu}{3\sqrt{2}}(3\hat{i} + 3\hat{j} - \hat{i} + \hat{j} - 4\hat{k})$$

$$= \frac{\mu}{3\sqrt{2}}(2\hat{i} + 4\hat{j} - 4\hat{k})$$

Compare with $\vec{a} = \alpha\hat{i} + 2\hat{j} + \beta\hat{k}$

$$\frac{4\mu}{3\sqrt{2}} = 2 \quad \Rightarrow \quad \mu = \frac{3\sqrt{2}}{2}$$

$$\vec{a} = \hat{i} + 2\hat{j} - 2\hat{k}$$

$$\therefore \quad \vec{a}.\vec{k} + 2 = 0$$

$$-2 + 2 = 0$$

56. (3) $\quad k.x^{k-1} + k.y^{k-1}\dfrac{dy}{dx} = 0$

$$\Rightarrow \quad \frac{dy}{dx} = -\left(\frac{x}{y}\right)^{k-1}$$

$$\Rightarrow \quad \frac{dy}{dx} + \left(\frac{x}{y}\right)^{k-1} = 0$$

$$\Rightarrow \quad k - 1 = -\frac{1}{3}$$

$$\Rightarrow \quad k = 1 - \frac{1}{3} = \frac{2}{3}$$

57. (2) $\quad (k+1)\tan^2 x - \sqrt{2}\lambda\tan x + (k-1) = 0$

$$\tan\alpha + \tan\beta = \frac{\sqrt{2}\lambda}{k+1} \qquad \text{[Sum of roots]}$$

$$\tan\alpha \cdot \tan\beta = \frac{k-1}{k+1} \qquad \text{[Product of roots]}$$

$$\therefore \quad \tan(\alpha+\beta) = \frac{\dfrac{\sqrt{2}\lambda}{k+1}}{1 - \dfrac{k-1}{k+1}} = \frac{\sqrt{2}\lambda}{2} = \frac{\lambda}{\sqrt{2}}$$

$$\tan^2(\alpha+\beta) = \frac{\lambda^2}{2} = 50$$

$$\lambda = 10.$$

58. (3) $\quad I = \dfrac{1}{(a+b)}\displaystyle\int_a^b x[f(x) + f(x+1)]dx \qquad \text{...(i)}$

$$x \rightarrow a + b - x$$

$$I = \frac{1}{(a+b)}\int_a^b (a+b-x)[f(a+b-x) + f(a+b+1-x)]dx$$

$$I = \frac{1}{(a+b)}\int_a^b (a+b-x)[f(x+1) + f(x)]dx \qquad \text{...(ii)}$$

$$[\because \text{ put } x \rightarrow x+1 \text{ in } f(a+b+1-x) = f(x)]$$

Add (i) and (ii)

$$2I = \int_a^b [f(x+1) + f(x)]dx$$

$$2I = \int_a^b f(x+1)dx + \int_a^b f(x)dx$$

$$= \int_a^b f(a+b+1-x)dx + \int_a^b f(x)dx$$

$$2I = 2\int_a^b f(x)dx$$

$$\therefore \quad \int_{a-1}^{b-1} f(x+1)dx \qquad [\because \text{ Put } x \rightarrow x+1]$$

59. (4) Total area − enclosed area between line and parabola

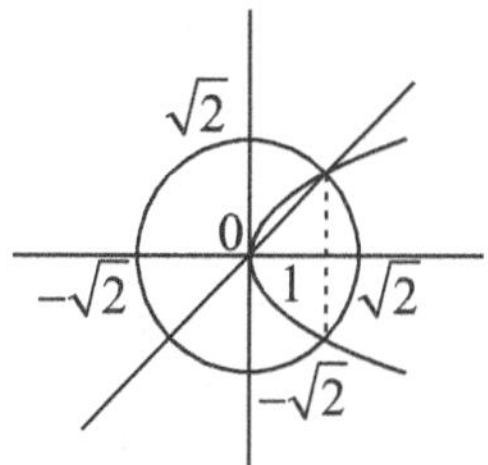

$$= 2\pi - \int_0^1 \sqrt{x} - x\,dx$$

$$= 2\pi - \left(\frac{2x^{3/2}}{3} - \frac{x^2}{2}\right)_0^1$$

$$= 2\pi - \left(\frac{2}{3} - \frac{1}{2}\right) = 2\pi - \left(\frac{1}{6}\right) = \frac{12\pi - 1}{6}$$

60. (1) For non-zero solution

$$\begin{vmatrix} 2 & 2a & a \\ 2 & 3b & b \\ 2 & 4c & c \end{vmatrix} = 0$$

$$\Rightarrow \begin{vmatrix} 1 & 2a & a \\ 1 & 3b & b \\ 1 & 4c & c \end{vmatrix} = 0$$

$$\Rightarrow \quad (3bc - 4bc) - (2ac - 4ac) + (2ab - 3ab) = 0$$

$$\Rightarrow \quad -bc + 2ac - ab = 0$$

$$\Rightarrow \quad ab + bc + 2ac$$

$$\Rightarrow \quad \frac{2}{b} = \frac{1}{a} + \frac{1}{c}$$

$$\Rightarrow \quad \frac{1}{a}, \frac{1}{b}, \frac{1}{c} \text{ in A.P.}$$

61. **(2)** Equation of plane is $x + y - 2z = 3$

$$\Rightarrow \quad \frac{x-2}{1} = \frac{y-1}{1} = \frac{z-6}{-2} = \frac{-2(2+1-12-3)}{6}$$

$$\Rightarrow \quad (x, y, z) = (6, 5, -2)$$

62. **(3)**

p	q	$p \Rightarrow q$	$\sim p$	$q \Rightarrow \sim p$	$(p \Rightarrow q) \wedge (p \Rightarrow \sim q)$
T	T	T	F	F	F
T	F	F	F	T	F
F	T	T	T	T	T
F	F	T	T	T	T

Clearly $(p \Rightarrow q) \wedge (q \Rightarrow \sim p)$ is equivalent to $\sim p$

63. **(2)** $2ae = 6$ and $\dfrac{2a}{e} = 12$

$$\Rightarrow \quad ae = 3 \qquad \qquad \qquad \text{...(i)}$$

and $\dfrac{a}{e} = 6 \Rightarrow e = \dfrac{a}{6} \qquad \text{...(ii)}$

$$\Rightarrow \quad a^2 = 18 \qquad \text{[From (i) and (ii)]}$$
$$\Rightarrow \quad b^2 = a^2 - a^2 e^2 = 18 - 9 = 9$$

$$\therefore \quad \text{Latus rectum} = \frac{2b^2}{a} = \frac{2 \times 9}{3\sqrt{2}} = 3\sqrt{2}$$

64. **(2)**

k	0	1	2	3	4	5
$P(k)$	$\dfrac{1}{32}$	$\dfrac{12}{32}$	$\dfrac{11}{32}$	$\dfrac{5}{32}$	$\dfrac{2}{32}$	$\dfrac{1}{32}$

$k = $ No. of times head occur consecutively
Now expectation

$$= \sum xP(k) = (-1) \times \frac{1}{32} + (-1) \times \frac{12}{32} + (-1) \times \frac{11}{32}$$

$$+ 3 \times \frac{5}{32} + 4 \times \frac{2}{32} + 5 \times \frac{1}{32} = \frac{1}{8}$$

65. **(3)** $y = mx + 4 \qquad \qquad \text{...(i)}$
Tangent of $y^2 = 4x$ is

$$\Rightarrow \quad y = mx + \frac{1}{m} \qquad \qquad \text{...(ii)}$$

$\left[\because \text{ Equation of tangent of } y^2 = 4\,ax \text{ is } y = mx + \dfrac{a}{m} \right]$

From (i) and (ii)

$$4 = \frac{1}{m} \Rightarrow m = \frac{1}{4}$$

So, line $y = \dfrac{1}{4}x + 4$ is also tangent to parabola

$x^2 = 2by$, so solve both equations.

$$x^2 = 2b\left(\frac{x+16}{4}\right)$$

$$\Rightarrow \quad 2x^2 - bx - 16b = 0$$
$$\Rightarrow \quad D = 0 \qquad \text{[For tangent]}$$
$$\Rightarrow \quad b^2 - 4 \times 2 \times (-16b) = 0$$
$$\Rightarrow \quad b^2 + 32 \times 4b = 0$$
$$b = -128, \ b = 0 \ (\text{not possible})$$

66. **(2)** $\dfrac{(49)^{126} - 1}{48} = \dfrac{((49)^{63} + 1)(49^{63} - 1)}{48} \left[\because S_n = \dfrac{a(r^n - 1)}{r - 1} \right]$

$$\therefore \ K = 63$$

67. **(4)** $\because \quad z = x + iy$

$$\left(\frac{z-1}{2z+i} \right) = \frac{(x-1) + iy}{2(x+iy) + i}$$

$$= \frac{(x-1) + iy}{2x + (2y+1)i} \times \frac{2x - (2y+1)i}{2x - (2y+1)i}$$

$$\text{Re}\left(\frac{z+1}{2z+i} \right) = \frac{2x(x-1) + y(2y+1)}{(2x)^2 + (2y+1)^2} = 1$$

$$\Rightarrow \quad \left(x + \frac{1}{2} \right)^2 + \left(y + \frac{3}{4} \right)^2 = \left(\frac{\sqrt{5}}{4} \right)^2.$$

68. **(4)** Solution of $x^2 + x + 1 = 0$ is ω, ω^2
So, $\alpha = \omega$ and
$\omega^4 = \omega^3 . \omega = 1 . \omega = \omega$

$$A^2 = \frac{1}{3} \begin{bmatrix} 1 & 1 & 1 \\ 1 & \omega & \omega^2 \\ 1 & \omega^2 & \omega \end{bmatrix} \begin{bmatrix} 1 & 1 & 1 \\ 1 & \omega & \omega^2 \\ 1 & \omega^2 & \omega \end{bmatrix} = \begin{bmatrix} 1 & 0 & 0 \\ 0 & 0 & 1 \\ 0 & 1 & 0 \end{bmatrix}$$

$$\Rightarrow \quad A^4 = I$$
$$\Rightarrow \quad A^{30} = A^{28} \times A^3 = A^3$$

69. **(1)** Let $e^y = t$

$$e^y \frac{dy}{dx} = \frac{dt}{dx}$$

$$\therefore \quad \frac{dt}{dx} - t = e^x \qquad \left[\because \ e^y \frac{dy}{dx} - e^y = e^x \right]$$

$$\text{I.F.} = e^{\int -1.dx} = e^{-x}$$

$$t(e^{-x}) = \int e^x . e^{-x} dx \Rightarrow e^{y-x} = x + c$$

Put $x = 0, y = 0$, then we get $c = 1$
$e^{y-x} = x + 1$
$y = x + \log_e(x+1)$
Put $x = 1 \quad \therefore \quad y = 1 + \log_e 2$

70. **(1)** From, LMVT for $x \in [-7, -1]$

$$\frac{f(-1) - f(-7)}{(-1+7)} \leq 2 \Rightarrow \frac{f(-1) + 3}{6} \leq 2 \Rightarrow f(-1) \leq 9$$

From, LMVT for $x \in [-7, 0]$

$$\frac{f(0) - f(-7)}{(0+7)} \leq 2$$

$$\frac{f(0) + 3}{7} \leq 2 \Rightarrow f(0) \leq 11$$

$$\therefore \quad f(0) + f(-1) \leq 20$$

71. **(36)** Let $3^x = t^2$

$$\lim_{t \to 3} \frac{t^2 + \dfrac{27}{t^2} - 12}{\dfrac{1}{t} - \dfrac{3}{t^2}}$$

$$= \lim_{t \to 3} \frac{t^4 - 12t^2 + 27}{t - 3}$$

$$= \lim_{t \to 3} \frac{(t^2 - 3)(t + 3)(t - 3)}{t - 3}$$

$$= (3^2 - 3)\,(3 + 3) = 36.$$

72. **(30)** Let $(1 - x + x^2 \dots x^{2n})\,(1 + x + x^2 \dots x^{2n})$

$$= a_0 + a_1 x + a_2 x^2 + \dots$$

put $x = 1$

$$1(2n + 1) = a_0 + a_1 + a_2 + \dots a_{2n} \qquad \dots(i)$$

put $x = -1$

$$(2n + 1) \times 1 = a_0 - a_1 + a_2 + \dots a_{2n} \qquad \dots(ii)$$

Adding (i) and (ii), we get,

$$4n + 2 = 2(a_0 + a_2 + \dots) = 2 \times 61$$
$$\Rightarrow \quad 2n + 1 = 61 \quad \Rightarrow \quad n = 30.$$

73. **(3)** $\because$ $f(x)$ is non differentiable at $x = 1, 3, 5$

$$[\because |x - 3| \text{ is not differentiable at } x = 3]$$

$$\Sigma\, f(f(x)) = f(f(1)) + f(f(3)) + f(f(5))$$
$$= 1 + 1 + 1 = 3$$

74. **(18)** Var $(1, 2, \dots, n) = 10$

$$\Rightarrow \quad \frac{1^2 + 2^2 + \dots + n^2}{n} - \left(\frac{1 + 2 + \dots + n}{n}\right)^2 = 10$$

$$\Rightarrow \quad \frac{(n+1)(2n+1)}{6} - \left(\frac{n+1}{2}\right)^2 = 10$$

$$\Rightarrow \quad n^2 - 1 = 120 \quad \Rightarrow \quad n = 11$$

Var $(2, 4, 6, \dots, 2m) = 16 \Rightarrow$ Var $(1, 2, \dots, m) = 4$

$$\Rightarrow \quad m^2 - 1 = 48 \Rightarrow m = 7$$
$$\Rightarrow \quad m + n = 18$$

75. **(5)** P will be centroid of $\triangle ABC$

$$P\left(\frac{17}{6}, \frac{8}{3}\right) \quad \Rightarrow \quad PQ = \sqrt{(4)^2 + (3)^2} = 5$$

PHYSICS

1. (1) From the free body diagram

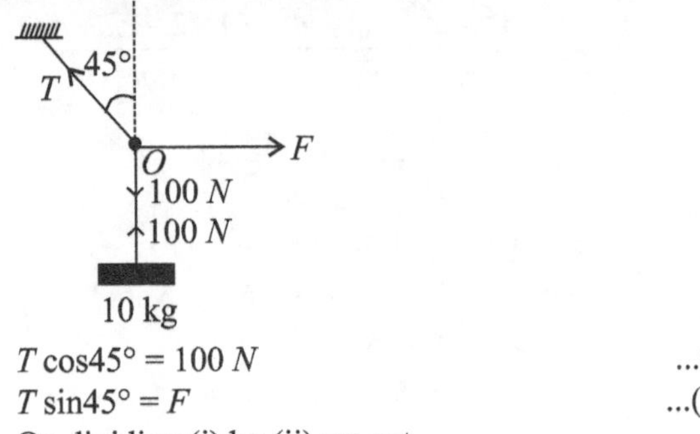

$$T\cos45° = 100\ N \qquad \qquad \text{...(i)}$$
$$T\sin45° = F \qquad \qquad \text{...(ii)}$$

On dividing (i) by (ii) we get

$$\frac{T\cos45°}{T\sin45°} = \frac{100}{F}$$

$$\Rightarrow \quad F = 100\ \text{N}$$

2. (3) In the x direction

$$F_x = qE$$
$$\Rightarrow \quad ma_x = qE$$
$$\Rightarrow \quad a_x = \frac{E_0 q}{m}$$

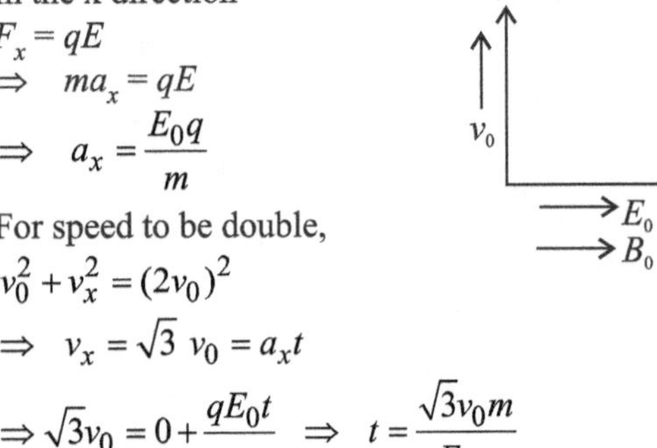

For speed to be double,

$$v_0^2 + v_x^2 = (2v_0)^2$$
$$\Rightarrow \quad v_x = \sqrt{3}\,v_0 = a_x t$$
$$\Rightarrow \sqrt{3}v_0 = 0 + \frac{qE_0 t}{m} \quad \Rightarrow \quad t = \frac{\sqrt{3}v_0 m}{E_0 q}$$

3. (4) Net Power, P

$$= 15 \times 45 + 15 \times 100 + 15 \times 10 + 2 \times 1000$$
$$= 15 \times 155 + 2000\ \text{W}$$

Power, $P = VI$

$$\Rightarrow \quad I = \frac{P}{V}$$

$$\therefore \quad I_{\text{main}} = \frac{15 \times 155 + 2000}{220} = 19.66\ A \approx 20A$$

4. (1) From the equation of continuity

$$A_1 v_1 = A_2 v_2$$

Here, v_1 and v_2 are the velocities at two ends of pipe. A_1 and A_2 are the area of pipe at two ends

$$\Rightarrow \quad \frac{v_1}{v_2} = \frac{A_2}{A_1} = \frac{\pi(4.8)^2}{\pi(6.4)^2} = \frac{9}{16}$$

5. (4) The quantity $\dfrac{B^2}{2\mu_0}$ is the energy density of magnetic field.

$$\Rightarrow \quad \left[\frac{B^2}{2\mu_0}\right] = \frac{\text{Energy}}{\text{Volume}} = \frac{\text{Force} \times \text{displacement}}{(\text{displacement})^3}$$

$$= \left[\frac{ML^2 T^{-2}}{L^3}\right] = ML^{-1}T^{-2}$$

6. (3) At $t = 0$, $z = \dfrac{\pi}{k}$

$$\therefore \quad \vec{E} = \frac{E_0}{\sqrt{2}}(\hat{i} + \hat{j})\cos[\pi] = -\frac{E_0}{\sqrt{2}}(\hat{i} + \hat{j})$$
$$\vec{F}_E = q\vec{E}$$

Force due to electric field will be in the direction $\dfrac{-(\hat{i} + \hat{j})}{\sqrt{2}}$

Force due to magnetic field is in direction

$q(\vec{v} \times \vec{B})$ and $\vec{v} \parallel \vec{k}$. Therefore, it is parallel to $\vec{E}$.

$$\Rightarrow \quad \vec{F}_{\text{net}} = \vec{F}_E + \vec{F}_B \text{ is antiparallel to } \frac{\hat{i} + \hat{j}}{\sqrt{2}}$$

7. (4) Net force on the elevator = force on elevator + frictional force

$$\Rightarrow \quad F = (10\,m + M)g + f$$

where, m = mass of person, M = mass of elevator, f = frictional force

$$\Rightarrow \quad F = (10 \times 68 + 920) \times 9.8 + 600$$
$$\Rightarrow \quad F = 22000\ N$$
$$\Rightarrow \quad P = FV = 22000 \times 3 = 66000\ W$$

8. (3) From Doppler's effect, frequency of sound heard (f_1) when source is approaching

$$f_1 = f_0 \frac{c}{c - v}$$

Here, c = velocity of sound
v = velocity of source

Frequency of sound heard (f_2) when source is receding

$$f_2 = f_0 \frac{c}{c + v}$$

Beat frequency $= f_1 - f_2$

$$\Rightarrow \quad 2 = f_1 - f_2 = f_0 c\left[\frac{1}{c - v} - \frac{1}{c + v}\right]$$

$$= f_0 c \frac{2v}{c^2\left[1 - \dfrac{v^2}{c^2}\right]}$$

For $c \gg v$

$$\Rightarrow \quad v = \frac{2c}{2f_0} = \frac{c}{f_0} = \frac{350}{1400} = \frac{1}{4}\ \text{m/s}$$

9. (1) The current (I) in LR series circuit is given by

$$I = \frac{V}{R}\left(1 - e^{-\frac{tR}{L}}\right)$$

At $t = \infty$,

$$I_\infty = \frac{20}{5}\left(I - e^{\frac{-\infty}{L/R}}\right) = 4 \qquad \ldots(i)$$

At $t = 40$s,

$$I_{40} = \frac{20}{5}\left(1 - e^{\frac{-40 \times 5}{10 \times 10^{-3}}}\right) = 4(1 - e^{-20,000}) \qquad \ldots(ii)$$

Dividing (i) by (ii) we get

$$\Rightarrow \quad \frac{I_\infty}{I_{40}} = \frac{1}{1 - e^{-20,000}},$$

which is slightly greater than $1 \Rightarrow (1.06)$

10. (2) Using lens maker's formula

$$\frac{1}{f} = \left(\frac{\mu_g}{\mu_a} - 1\right)\left[\frac{1}{R_1} - \frac{1}{R_2}\right]$$

Here, μ_g and μ_a are the refractive index of glass and air respectively

$$\Rightarrow \quad \frac{1}{f} = (1.5 - 1)\left(\frac{1}{R_1} - \frac{1}{R_2}\right) \qquad \ldots(i)$$

When immersed in liquid

$$\frac{1}{f_l} = \left(\frac{\mu_g}{\mu_l} - 1\right)\left(\frac{1}{R_1} - \frac{1}{R_2}\right)$$

[Here, μ_l = refractive index of liquid]

$$\Rightarrow \quad \frac{1}{f_l} = \left(\frac{1.5}{1.42} - 1\right)\left(\frac{1}{R_1} - \frac{1}{R_2}\right) \qquad \ldots(ii)$$

Dividing (i) by (ii)

$$\Rightarrow \quad \frac{f_l}{f} = \frac{(1.5 - 1)1.42}{0.08} = \frac{1.42}{0.16} = \frac{142}{16} \approx 9$$

11. (3) De-Broglie wavelength of electron (λ_e) is given by

$$\lambda_e = \frac{h}{p_e} = \frac{h}{\sqrt{2mE}} \qquad \ldots(i) \qquad \left(\because p = \sqrt{2mE}\right)$$

Energy of photon (E) is given by

$$E = \frac{hc}{\lambda_P} \qquad \text{(Here } \lambda \text{ p = wavelength of Photon)}$$

$$\Rightarrow \quad \lambda_P = \frac{hc}{E} \qquad \ldots(ii)$$

On dividing (i) by (ii) we get

$$\Rightarrow \quad \frac{\lambda_e}{\lambda_P} = \frac{h}{\sqrt{2mE}}\frac{E}{hc} = \sqrt{\frac{E}{2m}}\cdot\frac{1}{c}$$

12. (4) We have given, time period, $T = 10$s

$$\therefore \quad \text{Angular velocity, } \omega = \frac{2\pi}{10} = \frac{\pi}{5}$$

Magnetic flux, $\phi(t) = BA \cos \omega t$

Emf induced, $E = \frac{-d\phi}{dt} = BA\omega \sin \omega t = BA\omega \sin(\omega t)$

Induced emf, $|\varepsilon|$ is maximum when $\omega t = \frac{\pi}{2}$

$$\Rightarrow \quad t = \frac{\frac{\pi}{2}}{\frac{\pi}{5}} = 2.5 \text{ s}$$

For induced emf to be minimum i.e zero

$$\omega t = \pi \quad \Rightarrow \quad t = \frac{\pi}{\frac{\pi}{5}} = 5 \, s$$

$\therefore$ Induced emf is zero at t = 5 s

13. (1) The given circuit has two $10k\Omega$ resistances in parallel, so we can reduce this parallel combination to a single equivalent resistance of $5k\Omega$.

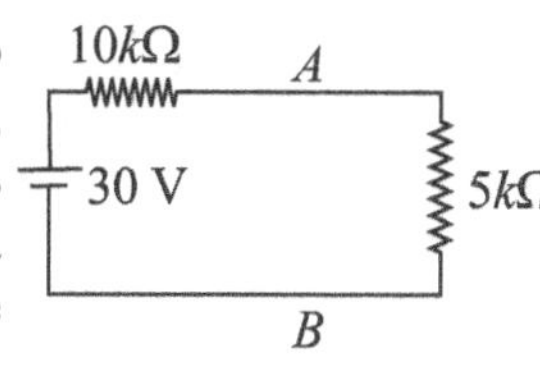

Diode is in forward bias. So it will behave like a conducting wire.

$$V_A - V_B = \frac{30}{5 + 10} \times 5 = 10 \, V$$

14. (3) Given, distance between screen and slits, $D = 1.5$ m
Seperation between slits, d = 0.15 mm
Wavelength of source of light, $\lambda = 589$ nm

$$\text{Fringe-width, } w = \frac{D}{d}\lambda = \frac{1.5}{0.15 \times 10^{-3}} \times 589 \times 10^{-9}\, m$$

$$= 589 \times 10^{-2} \text{ mm} = 5.89 \text{ mm} \approx 5.9 \text{ mm}$$

15. (2) We know that

Activity, $A = A_0 e^{-\lambda t}$

$$A = A_0 e^{-t In2/T_{1/2}} \left(\because \lambda = \frac{In2}{T_{1/2}}\right)$$

$$\Rightarrow \quad 500 = 700 \, e^{-t In2/T_{1/2}}$$

$$\Rightarrow \quad In\frac{7}{5} = \frac{30 In2}{T_{1/2}} \qquad (\because t = 30 \text{ minute})$$

$$\Rightarrow \quad T_{1/2} = 30\frac{In \, 2}{In \, 1.4} = 61.8 \text{ minute}$$

$$(\because \ln 2 = 0.693 \text{ and } \ln. 1.4 = 0.336)$$

$$\Rightarrow \quad T_{1/2} \approx 62 \text{ minute}$$

16. (4) Weight at pole, $w = mg = 196 \, N$

$$\Rightarrow \quad m = 19.6 \text{ kg}$$

Weight at equator, $w' = mg' = m(g - \omega^2 R)$

$$= 19.6\left[10 - \left(\frac{2\pi}{24 \times 3600}\right)^2 \times 6400 \times 10^3\right] N$$

$$\left(\because \omega = \frac{2\pi}{T}\right)$$

$$= 19.6 \, [10 - 0.034] = 195.33 \, N$$

17. (1) Given,

mass per unit area of circular disc, $\sigma = A + Br$

Area of the ring $= 2\pi r dr$

Mass of the ring, $dm = \sigma 2\pi r dr$

Moment of inertia,

$$I = \int dm r^2 = \int \sigma 2\pi r dr . r^2$$

$$\Rightarrow \quad I = 2\pi \int_0^a (A + Br) r^3 dr = 2\pi \left[\frac{Aa^4}{4} + \frac{Ba^5}{5} \right]$$

$$\Rightarrow \quad I = 2\pi a^4 \left[\frac{A}{4} + \frac{Ba}{5} \right]$$

18. (4)

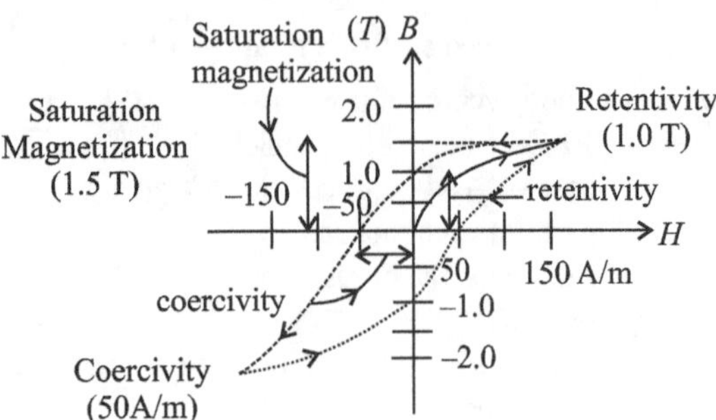

19. (Bonus) We know that Relaxation time,

$$T \propto \frac{V}{\sqrt{T}} \qquad \qquad \dots\text{(i)}$$

Equation of adiabatic process is

$TV^{\gamma-1} = $ constant

$$\Rightarrow \quad T \propto \frac{1}{V^{\gamma-1}}$$

$$\Rightarrow \quad T \propto V^{1 + \frac{\gamma-1}{2}} \qquad \qquad \text{using (i)}$$

$$\Rightarrow \quad T \propto V^{\frac{1+\gamma}{2}}$$

$$\Rightarrow \quad \frac{T_f}{T_i} = \left(\frac{2V}{V} \right)^{\frac{1+\gamma}{2}} = (2)^{\frac{1+\gamma}{2}}$$

20. (2) Let $Q_H = $ Heat taken by first engine

$Q_L = $ Heat rejected by first engine

$Q_2 = $ Heat rejected by second engine

Work done by 1st engine = work done by 2nd engine

$W = Q_H - Q_L = Q_L - Q_2 \Rightarrow 2Q_L = Q_H + Q_2$

$$2 = \frac{\theta_H}{\theta_L} + \frac{\theta_2}{\theta_L}$$

Let T be the temperature of cold reservoir of first engine. Then in carnot engine.

$$\frac{Q_H}{Q_L} = \frac{T_1}{T} \quad \text{and} \quad \frac{Q_L}{Q_2} = \frac{T}{T_2}$$

$$\Rightarrow \quad 2 = \frac{T_1}{T} + \frac{T_2}{T} \qquad \qquad \text{using (i)}$$

$$\Rightarrow \quad 2T = T_1 + T_2 \quad \Rightarrow \quad T = \frac{T_1 + T_2}{2}$$

21. (90) Given,

$$\left| \vec{R} \right| = \left| \vec{P} \right| \quad \Rightarrow \quad \left| \vec{P} + \vec{Q} \right| = \left| \vec{P} \right|$$

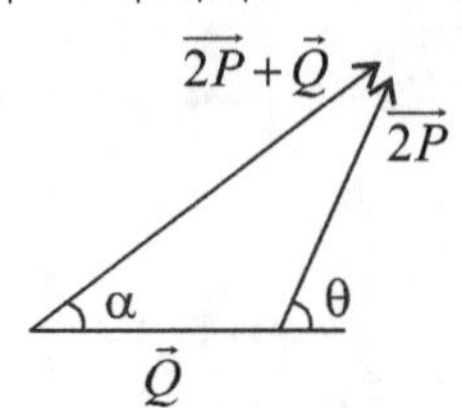

$P^2 + Q^2 + 2PQ. \cos\theta = P^2$

$\Rightarrow \quad Q + 2P\cos\theta = 0$

$$\Rightarrow \quad \cos\theta = -\frac{Q}{2P} \qquad \qquad \dots\text{(i)}$$

$$\tan\alpha = \frac{2P\sin\theta}{Q + 2P\cos\theta} = \infty \quad (\because 2P\cos\theta + Q = 0)$$

$\Rightarrow \quad \alpha = 90°$

22. (6) In the first condition, electrostatic energy is

$$U_i = \frac{1}{2} CV_0^2 = \frac{1}{2} \times 60 \times 10^{-12} \times 400 = 12 \times 10^{-9} J$$

In the second condition $U_F = \frac{1}{2} C'V'^2$

$$U_f = \frac{1}{2} 2C . \left(\frac{V_0}{2} \right)^2 \qquad \left(\because C' = 2C, V' = \frac{V_0}{2} \right)$$

$$= \frac{1}{4} \times 60 \times 10^{-12} \times (20)^2 = 6 \times 10^{-9} J$$

Energy lost $= U_i - U_f = 12 \times 10^{-9} J - 6 \times 10^{-9} J = 6 \, nJ$

23. (50) For the box to be slide

$F = \mu mg = 0.4 \, mg$

For no toppling

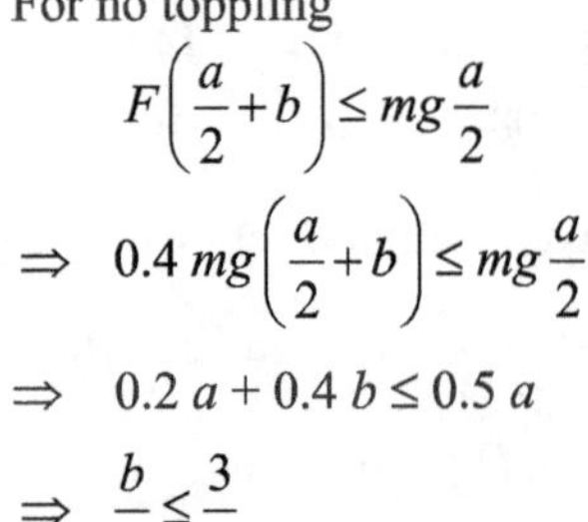

$$F \left(\frac{a}{2} + b \right) \le mg \frac{a}{2}$$

$$\Rightarrow \quad 0.4 \, mg \left(\frac{a}{2} + b \right) \le mg \frac{a}{2}$$

$$\Rightarrow \quad 0.2 \, a + 0.4 \, b \le 0.5 \, a$$

$$\Rightarrow \quad \frac{b}{a} \le \frac{3}{4}$$

i.e. $b \le 0.75 \, a$ but this is not possible.

As the maximum value of b can be equal to $0.5a$.

$$\Rightarrow \quad \frac{100b}{a} = 50$$

24. (12) We know that

$E \propto \ell$ where l is the balancing length

$$\therefore \quad E = k (560) \qquad \qquad \dots\text{(i)}$$

When the balancing length changes by 60 cm

$$\frac{E}{r + 10} 10 = k (500) \qquad \qquad \dots\text{(ii)}$$

Dividing (i) by (ii) we get

$$\Rightarrow \quad \frac{r+10}{10} = \frac{56}{50}$$

$$\Rightarrow \quad 50\,r + 500 = 560$$

$$\Rightarrow \quad r = \frac{6}{5}\,\Omega = \frac{N}{10}\,\Omega$$

$$\Rightarrow \quad N = 12$$

25. **(40)** Using the principal of calorimetry

$$M_{ice}\,L_f + m_{ice}\,(40-0)\,C_w$$
$$= m_{stream}\,L_v + m_{stream}\,(100-40)\,C_w$$
$$\Rightarrow \quad M\,(540) + M \times 1 \times (100-40)$$
$$\qquad = 200 \times 80 + 200 \times 1 \times 40$$
$$\Rightarrow \quad 600\,M = 24000$$
$$\Rightarrow \quad M = 40g$$

CHEMISTRY

26. **(4)** $N_2 + O_2 \rightarrow 2NO$ (Redox reaction)

$3O_2 \rightarrow 2O_3$ (Photochemical reaction)

$2NaOH + H_2SO_4 \rightarrow Na_2SO_4 + 2H_2O$
(Neutralisation reaction)

$[Co(H_2O)_6]Cl_3 + 3AgNO_3 \rightarrow [CO(H_2O)_6](NO_3)_3$
$\qquad\qquad\qquad\qquad\qquad\qquad + 3AgCl$
(Neutralisation reaction)

27. **(1)** All the statements are correct.

28. **(1)** $6NaOH + 3Cl_2 \rightarrow 5NaCl + NaClO_3 + 3H_2O$

$2Ca(OH)_2 + Cl_2 \rightarrow Ca(OCl)_2 + CaCl_2 + H_2O$

29. **(2)** Among the given bases (A) and (B), *t*-butoxide being bulky base favours elimination reaction and ethoxide favours substitution reaction.

$\therefore$ when $Z\ominus = CH_3CH_2O^-$, substitution reaction favoured

and when $Z\ominus = CH_3-\underset{\underset{CH_3}{|}}{\overset{\overset{CH_3}{|}}{C}}-O^-$, elimination reaction favoured

Hence, $\mu_A > \mu_B$ and $k_e(B) > k_e(A)$

30. **(2)** Electron withdrawing group like (NO_2) increase stability of alkoxide ion by dispersal of negative charge. In (B) and (C) structures negative charge is in conjugation with double bond and also stabilised by electron withdrawing effect of nitro group.

31. **(3)** $[MA_2B_2]$ will not exhibit optical isomerism in both conditions.

32. **(3)** Compounds which are able to form strong H-bond with the stationary phase (silica gel) will come last with the mobile phase.

H-bonding order :

aniline > benzanilide > acetophenone
   B   >   A   >   C

$\therefore$ Sequence of obtained compounds is (C, A , B)

33. **(1)** Co^{3+} with strong field ligand forms complex of low magnetic moment.

$$\Delta_t = \left(\frac{4}{9}\right)\Delta_0$$

$$\Rightarrow \quad \Delta_t = \frac{4}{9} \times 18000 = 8000 \text{ cm}^{-1}$$

34. **(4)** Vinyl halides and aryl halides are unreactive towards Friedel Craft's reaction.

Therefore reactions (A) and (C) are not possible.

35. **(4)** $(\Lambda^0_m)_{NaBr} - (\Lambda^0_m)_{NaI}$

$$= \Lambda^0_m Na^+ + \Lambda^0_m Br^- - (\Lambda^0_m Na^+ + \Lambda^0_m I^-)$$
$$= \Lambda^0_m Na^+ + \Lambda^0_m Br^- - \Lambda^0_m Na^+ - \Lambda^0_m I$$
$$= \Lambda^0_m Br^- + \Lambda^0_m I^-$$

$(\Lambda^0_m)_{KBr} - (\Lambda^0_m)_{NaBr}$

$$= \Lambda^0_m K^+ + \Lambda^0_m Br^- - (\Lambda^0_m Na^+ + \Lambda^0_m Br^-)$$
$$= \Lambda^0_m K^+ + \Lambda^0_m Br^- - \Lambda^0_m Na^+ - \Lambda^0_m Br^-$$
$$= \Lambda^0_m K^+ + \Lambda^0_m Na^+$$

$\therefore (\Lambda^0_m)_{NaBr} - (\Lambda^0_m)_{NaI} \neq (\Lambda^0_m)_{KBr} - (\Lambda^0_m)_{NaBr}$

36. **(3)**

37. **(1)**

38. **(4)** $V_{rms} > V_{average} > V_{mps}$

$$\sqrt{\frac{3RT}{M}} > \sqrt{\frac{8RT}{\pi M}} > \sqrt{\frac{2RT}{M}}$$

39. **(1)** Liquation method is used for purification of metals having low melting point.

40. **(3)** 1 mol of urea = 2 mol of NH_3
60 g of urea = 2 mol of NH_3

$$0.6 \text{ g of urea} = \frac{2}{60} \times 0.6 \text{ mol} = 0.02 \text{ mol of } NH_3$$

mol of NH_3 = mol of HCl

$\therefore$ mol of HCl = 0.02 mol
$\Rightarrow$ Normality of HCl = 0.2 N
Volume of HCl = 100 mL

41. **(2)** Generally, electron affinity decreases on moving down a group. Chlorine has more electron affinity than F because of very small size of fluorine. Therefore chlorine, sulphur and Li has higher electron affinity among given groups.

42. **(2)** Total number of electrons in $CN^- = 6 + 7 + 1 = 14$
$\therefore$ Molecular orbital distribution

$$\sigma 1s^2 \, \sigma^* 1s^2 \, \sigma 2s^2 \, \sigma^* 2s^2 \begin{bmatrix} \pi 2px^2 \\ \pi 2py^2 \end{bmatrix} \sigma 2p_z^2$$

$\therefore$ Bond order $= \dfrac{10-4}{2} = 3$

CN^- is diamagnetic because all electrons are paired.

43. **(4)** Rate of forward reaction $= k_f [NO]^2 [H_2]^2$

Observed rate $= k_f [NO]^2 [H_2]$

$$\text{Observed rate} = \frac{\text{Rate of forward reaction}}{[H_2]}$$

$\therefore$ Rate of backward reaction $= \dfrac{k_b [N_2][H_2O]^2}{[H_2]}$

44. **(3)** Gluconic acid is obtained by partial oxidation of glucose by mild oxidising agent e.g. Tollen's reagent, Fehling solution, Br_2 water.

$$\begin{array}{c} \text{CHO} \\ | \\ (\text{CHOH})_4 \\ | \\ CH_2OH \\ \text{Glucose} \end{array} \xrightarrow{Br_2 \text{ water}} \begin{array}{c} \text{COOH} \\ | \\ (\text{CHOH})_4 \\ | \\ CH_2OH \\ \text{Gluconic acid} \end{array}$$

Gluconic acid can not form hemiacetal or acetal.

45. **(1)** There will be lowering in vapour pressure in second beaker.

46. **(18.00)**

$$4NaCl + K_2Cr_2O_4 + 3H_2SO_4 \longrightarrow 2CrO_2Cl_2 + K_2SO_4$$
$$\hspace{3.5cm} \text{(Conc.)} \hspace{2.2cm} \text{(A)}$$
$$+ 2NaSO_4 + 3H_2O$$

$$\underset{\text{(A)}}{CrO_2Cl_2} + NaOH \longrightarrow \underset{\text{(B)}}{Na_2CrO_4} + H_2O + NaCl$$

$$\underset{B}{Na_2CrO_4} + H_2SO_4 + \underset{\text{(dilute)}}{H_2O_2} \longrightarrow \underset{\text{(C)}}{CrO_5} + Na_2SO_4 + H_2O$$

47. **(9.00)**

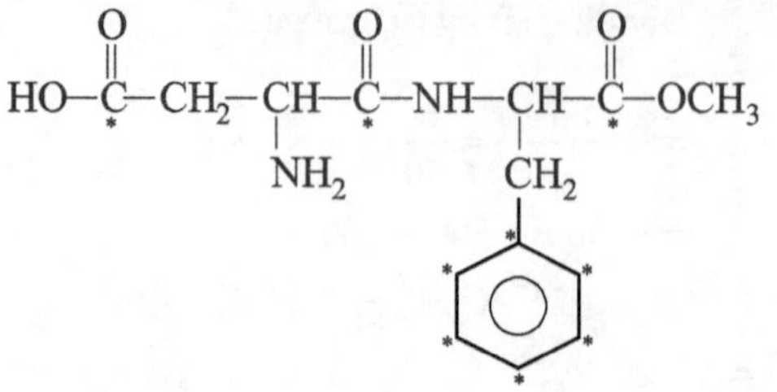

$$HO-\overset{O}{\overset{\|}{C}}-CH_2-\underset{\underset{NH_2}{|}}{CH}-\overset{O}{\overset{\|}{C}}-NH-\underset{\underset{CH_2}{|}}{CH}-\overset{O}{\overset{\|}{C}}-OCH_3$$

Structure of aspartame is shown above. It is a methyl ester of dipeptide formed from aspartic acid and phenylalanine. sp^2 hybridised carbon atoms are shown by the star mark in the structure.

48. **(−192.5)**

$$C + O_2 \rightarrow CO_2 \ ; \Delta_C H^0 = -286.0 \text{ kJ/mol} \hspace{1cm} ...(i)$$

$$H_2 + \frac{1}{2}O_2 \rightarrow H_2O \ ; \Delta_C H^0 = -393.5 \text{ kJ/mol} \hspace{0.5cm} ...(ii)$$

$$C_2H_6 + \frac{7}{2}O_2 \rightarrow 2CO_2 + 3H_2O \ ; \Delta_C H^0 = -1560 \text{ kJ/mol} \hspace{1cm} ...(iii)$$

$\Delta_f H^0$ of $C_2H_6(g) =$

$2 \times \Delta_C^0 H[C_{graphite}] + 3 \times \Delta_C H^0[H_2(g)] - \Delta_C H^0[C_2H_6(g)]$

$\hspace{1cm} = 2 \times (-286.0) + 3(-393.5) - (-1560)$

$\hspace{1cm} = -192.5 \text{ kJ/mol}$

49. **(0.37)**

For 1 L sol 30 m mol of HCl is required
$\therefore$ For 1 L sol 15 m mol H_2SO_4 is required
For 250 mL of sol, H_2SO_4 required

$$= \frac{15}{1000} \times 250 \text{ m mol } H_2SO_4$$

$$= 3.75 \text{ m mol of } H_2SO_4$$

1 mol H_2SO_4 = 98 g
3.75 m mol of H_2SO_4

$$= 3.75 \times 98 \times 10^{-3}$$
$$= 0.3675 \text{ g } H_2SO_4$$

50. **(5.22)**

$$\text{No. of moles} = \frac{\text{Mass}}{\text{Molar Mass}}$$

$$3g \ CH_3COOH = \frac{3}{60} = 0.5 \text{ mol} = 50 \text{ m mol}$$

No. of millimoles = Molarity × Volume in m_L

250 mL of 0.1 MHCl = 250 × 0.1 = 25 m mol

500 mL solution = 50 m mol CH_3COOH

$$20 \text{ mL solution} = \frac{50}{500} \times 20 = 2 \text{ m mol } CH_3COOH$$

500 mL solution contains = 25 m mol HCl

$$20 \text{ mL solution contains} = \frac{25}{500} \times 20 = 1 \text{ m mol HCl}$$

$\dfrac{1}{2}$ mL of 5M NaOH $= \dfrac{1}{2} \times 5 = 2.5$ m mol NaOH

$$\text{HCl} + \text{NaOH} \longrightarrow \text{NaCl} + \text{H}_2\text{O}$$

$$1 \qquad 2.5 \qquad 1$$

Remaining NaOH $= 2.5 - 1 = 1.5$ m mol

$$\text{CH}_3\text{COOH} + \text{NaOH (remaining)} \rightarrow \text{CH}_3\text{COONa} + \text{Water}$$

| 2 | 1.5 | 0 | 0 |
| 0.5 | 0 | 1.5 | – |

$$\text{pH} = \text{pK}_a + \log \dfrac{1.5}{2} = 4.74 + \log \dfrac{3/2}{2}$$

$$= 4.74 + \log 3 = 4.74 + 0.48 = 5.22$$

MATHEMATICS

51. (4) $\left|\vec{a} + \vec{b} + \vec{c}\right|^2 = 0$

$$3 + 2(\vec{a}.\vec{b} + \vec{b}.\vec{c} + \vec{c}.\vec{a}) = 0$$

$$(\vec{a}.\vec{b} + \vec{b}.\vec{c} + \vec{c}.\vec{a}) = \dfrac{-3}{2} \quad \Rightarrow \quad \lambda = \dfrac{-3}{2}$$

$$\vec{d} = \vec{a} \times \vec{b} + \vec{b} \times (-\vec{a} - \vec{b}) + (-\vec{a} - \vec{b}) \times \vec{a} \quad [\because \vec{c} = -\vec{a} - \vec{b}]$$

$$= \vec{a} \times \vec{b} + \vec{a} \times \vec{b} + \vec{a} \times \vec{b}$$

$$\vec{d} = 3(\vec{a} \times \vec{b})$$

52. (2)

Since, slope of $PQ = \dfrac{k - \alpha}{h - 2\alpha} = -1$

$$\Rightarrow \quad k - \alpha = -h + 2\alpha$$

$$\Rightarrow \quad \alpha = \dfrac{h + k}{3} \qquad \qquad \text{...(i)}$$

Also, $2h = 2\alpha + \beta$ and

$$2k = \alpha + \beta$$

$$\Rightarrow \quad 2h = \alpha + 2k$$

$$\Rightarrow \quad \alpha = 2h - 2k \qquad \qquad \text{...(ii)}$$

From (i) and (ii), we have

$$\dfrac{h + k}{3} = 2(h - k)$$

So, locus is $6x - 6y = x + y$

$$\Rightarrow \quad 5x = 7y \quad \Rightarrow \quad 5x - 7y = 0$$

53. (2) Since, $a_1 + a_2 = 4 \Rightarrow a_1 + a_1 r = 4 \qquad \text{...(i)}$

$$a_3 + a_4 = 16 \Rightarrow a_1 r^2 + a_1 r^3 = 16 \qquad \text{...(ii)}$$

From eqn. (i), $a_1 = \dfrac{4}{1 + r}$ and substituting the value of

a_1, in eqn (ii),

$$\left(\dfrac{4}{1 + r}\right) r^2 + \left(\dfrac{4}{1 + r}\right) r^3 = 16$$

$$\Rightarrow \quad 4r^2 (1 + r) = 16(1 + r)$$

$$\Rightarrow \quad r^2 = 4 \quad \therefore \quad r = \pm 2$$

$$r = 2, a_1(1 + 2) = 4 \quad \Rightarrow \quad a_1 = \dfrac{4}{3}$$

$$r = -2, a_1(1 - 2) = 4 \quad \Rightarrow \quad a_1 = -4$$

$$\sum_{i=1}^{a} a_i = \dfrac{a_1(r^q - 1)}{r - 1} = \dfrac{(-4)((-2)^9 - 1)}{-2 - 1}$$

$$= \dfrac{4}{3}(-513) = 4\lambda \quad \Rightarrow \quad \lambda = -171$$

54. (2) Since, $f(x)$ is a polynomial function.

$\therefore$ It is continuous and differentiable in $[0, 1]$

Here, $f(0) = 11, f(1) = 1 - 4 + 8 + 11 = 16$

$$f'(x) = 3x^2 - 8x + 8$$

$$\therefore \quad f'(c) = \dfrac{f(1) - f(0)}{1 - 0} = \dfrac{16 - 11}{1}$$

$$= 3c^2 - 8c + 8$$

$$\Rightarrow \quad 3c^2 - 8c + 3 = 0$$

$$\Rightarrow \quad c = \dfrac{8 \pm 2\sqrt{7}}{6} = \dfrac{4 \pm \sqrt{7}}{3}$$

$$\therefore \quad c = \dfrac{4 - \sqrt{7}}{3} \in (0, 1)$$

55. (2) The given series is in G.P. then

$$S_n = \dfrac{a(1 - r^n)}{1 - r}$$

$$\dfrac{(1 + x)^{10}\left[1 - \left(\dfrac{x}{1 + x}\right)^{11}\right]}{\left(1 - \dfrac{x}{1 + x}\right)}$$

$$\Rightarrow \quad \dfrac{(1 + x)^{10}\left[(1 + x)^{11} - x^{11}\right]}{(1 + x)^{11} \times \dfrac{1}{(1 + x)}} = (1 + x)^{11} - x^{11}$$

$\therefore$ Coefficient of x^7 is $^{11}C_7 = {}^{11}C_{11-7} = {}^{11}C_4 = 330$

56. (2)

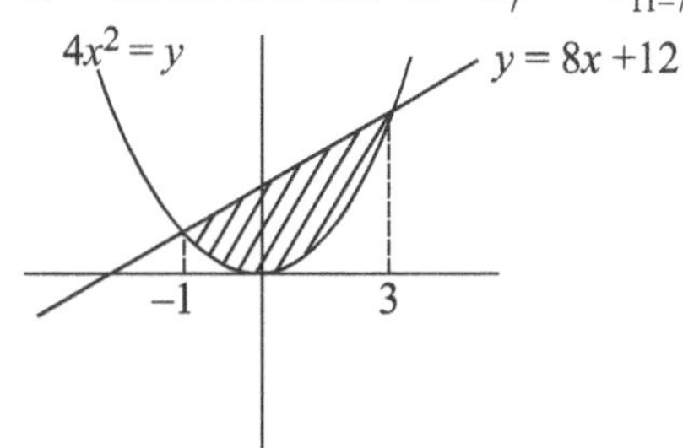

Given curves are

$$4x^2 = y \qquad \qquad \text{...(i)}$$

$y = 8x + 12$ ...(ii)

From eqns. (i) and (ii),

$4x^2 = 8x + 12$

$\Rightarrow \quad x^2 - x - 3 = 0$

$\Rightarrow \quad x^2 - 2x - 3 = 0$

$\Rightarrow \quad x^2 - 3x + x - 3 = 0$

$\Rightarrow \quad (x + 1)(x - 3) = 0$

$\Rightarrow \quad x = -1, 3$

Required area bounded by curves is given by

$$A = \int_{-1}^{3} (8x + 12 - 4x^2)\,dx$$

$$A = \left. \frac{8x^2}{2} + 12x - \frac{4x^3}{3} \right|_{-1}^{3}$$

$$= (4(9) + 36 - 36) - \left(4 - 12 + \frac{4}{3}\right)$$

$$= 36 + 8 - \frac{4}{3} = 44 - \frac{4}{3} = \frac{132 - 4}{3} = \frac{128}{3}$$

57. (1) Required probability = when no machine has fault + when only one machine has fault + when only two machines have fault.

$$= {}^5C_0 \left(\frac{3}{4}\right)^5 + {}^5C_1 \left(\frac{1}{4}\right)\left(\frac{3}{4}\right)^4 + {}^5C_2 \left(\frac{1}{4}\right)^2\left(\frac{3}{4}\right)^3$$

$$= \frac{243}{1024} + \frac{405}{1024} + \frac{270}{1024} = \frac{918}{1024} = \frac{459}{512} = \frac{27 \times 17}{64 \times 8}$$

$$= \left(\frac{3}{4}\right)^3 \times k = \left(\frac{3}{4}\right)^3 \times \frac{17}{8}$$

$$\therefore \quad k = \frac{17}{8}$$

58. (4) $f(x) = ax^5 + bx^4 + cx^3$

$$\lim_{x \to 0} \left(2 + \frac{ax^5 + bx^4 + cx^3}{x^3}\right) = 4$$

$$\Rightarrow \quad 2 + c = 4 \quad \Rightarrow \quad c = 2$$

$$f'(x) = 5ax^4 + 4bx^3 + 6x^2$$

$$= x^2(5ax^2 + 4bx + 6)$$

Since, $x = \pm 1$ are the critical points,

$\therefore \quad f'(1) = 0 \quad \Rightarrow \quad 5a + 4b + 6 = 0$ ...(i)

$\quad\quad f'(-1) = 0 \quad \Rightarrow \quad 5a - 4b + 6 = 0$ ...(ii)

From eqns. (i) and (ii),

$$b = 0 \text{ and } a = -\frac{6}{5}$$

$$f(x) = \frac{-6}{5}x^5 + 2x^3$$

$$f'(x) = -6x^4 + 6x^2 = 6x^2 (-x^2 + 1)$$

$$= -6x^2 (x + 1)(x - 1)$$

－   ＋   ＋   －
——＋————————＋——
-1 1

$\therefore \quad f(x)$ has minima at $x = -1$ and maxima at $x = 1$

59. (1) $3x + 4y = 12\sqrt{2}$

$$\Rightarrow \quad 4y = -3x + 12\sqrt{2}$$

$$\Rightarrow \quad y = -\frac{3}{4}x + 3\sqrt{2}$$

Now, condition of tangency, $c^2 = a^2m^2 + b^2$

$$\therefore \quad 18 = a^2 \cdot \frac{9}{16} + 9 \quad \Rightarrow \quad a^2 \cdot \frac{9}{16} = 9$$

$$\Rightarrow \quad a^2 = 16 \quad \Rightarrow \quad a = 4$$

Eccentricity $e = \sqrt{1 - \frac{b^2}{a^2}} = \sqrt{1 - \frac{9}{16}} = \frac{\sqrt{7}}{4}$

$$\therefore \quad ae = \frac{\sqrt{7}}{4} \cdot 4 = \sqrt{7}$$

$\therefore \quad$ Focus are $(\pm\sqrt{7}, 0)$

$\therefore \quad$ Distance between foci of ellipse $= 2\sqrt{7}$

60. (2) Let $z = \dfrac{3 + i\sin\theta}{4 - i\cos\theta}$, after rationalising

$$z = \frac{(3 + i\sin\theta)}{(4 - i\cos\theta)} \times \frac{(4 + i\cos\theta)}{(4 + i\cos\theta)}$$

As z is purely real

$$\Rightarrow \quad 3\cos\theta + 4\sin\theta = 0 \quad \Rightarrow \quad \tan\theta = -\frac{3}{4}$$

$$arg(\sin\theta + i\cos\theta) = \pi + \tan^{-1}\left(\frac{\cos\theta}{\sin\theta}\right)$$

$$= \pi + \tan^{-1}\left(-\frac{4}{3}\right) = \pi - \tan^{-1}\left(\frac{4}{3}\right)$$

61. (1) The given differential equation is $\dfrac{dx}{dy} + x = y^2$

Comparing with $\dfrac{dx}{dy} + Px = Q$, where $P = 1, Q = y^2$

Now, I.F. $= e^{\int 1.dy} = e^y$

$$x.e^y = \int (y^2)e^y \cdot dy = y^2.e^y - \int 2y.e^y.dy$$

$$= y^2 e^y - 2(y.e^y - e^y) + C$$

$$\Rightarrow \quad x.e^y = y^2 e^y - 2ye^y + 2e^y + C$$

$$\Rightarrow \quad x = y^2 - 2y + 2 + C.e^{-y} \quad\quad ...(i)$$

As $y(0) = 1$, satisfying the given differential eqn,

$\therefore \quad$ put $x = 0, y = 1$ in eqn. (i)

$$0 = 1 - 2 + 2 + \frac{C}{e}$$

$$C = -e$$

$$y = 0, x = 0 - 0 + 2 + (-e)(e^{-0})$$

$$x = 2 - e$$

62. (4) Let $P = A \subseteq B, Q = B \subseteq D, R = A \subseteq C$

Contrapositive of $(P \wedge Q) \to R$ is $\sim R \to \sim (P \wedge Q)$

$$\sim R \to \sim P \vee \sim Q$$

63. (3) $L = \sqrt{S_1} = \sqrt{16} = 4$

$$R = \sqrt{16 + 4 - 16} = 2$$

Length of chord of contact

$$= \frac{2LR}{\sqrt{L^2 + R^2}} = \frac{2 \times 4 \times 2}{\sqrt{16 + 4}} = \frac{16}{\sqrt{20}}$$

Square of length of chord of contact $= \dfrac{64}{5}$

64. (4) $\alpha^5 = 5\alpha + 3$

$\beta^5 = 5\beta + 3$

$p_5 = 5(\alpha + \beta) + 6 = 5(1) + 6$

$$\left[\because \text{ from } x^2 - x - 1 = 0, \ \alpha + \beta = \frac{-b}{a} = 1 \right]$$

$p_5 = 11$ and $p_5 = \alpha^2 + \beta^2 = \alpha + 1 + \beta + 1$

$p_2 = 3$ and $p_3 = \alpha^3 + \beta^3 = 2\alpha + 1 + 2\beta + 1$

$\quad = 2(1) + 2 = 4$

$p_2 \times p_3 = 12$ and $p_5 = 11 \ \Rightarrow \ p_5 \neq p_2 \times p_3$

65. (1) $4\alpha \left\{ \displaystyle\int_{-1}^{0} e^{\alpha x} dx + \int_{0}^{2} e^{-\alpha x} dx \right\} = 5$

$$\Rightarrow \ 4\alpha \left\{ \frac{e^{\alpha x}}{\alpha} \bigg|_{-1}^{0} + \frac{e^{-\alpha x}}{-\alpha} \bigg|_{0}^{2} \right\} = 5$$

$$\Rightarrow \ 4\alpha \left\{ \left(\frac{1 - e^{-\alpha}}{\alpha} \right) - \left(\frac{e^{-2\alpha} - 1}{\alpha} \right) \right\} = 5$$

$$\Rightarrow \ 4(2 - e^{-\alpha} - e^{-2\alpha}) = 5$$

Put $e^{-\alpha} = t$

$\Rightarrow \ 4t^2 + 4t - 3 = 0 \qquad \Rightarrow \ (2t + 3)(2t - 1) = 0$

$\Rightarrow \ e^{-\alpha} = \dfrac{1}{2} \ \Rightarrow \ \alpha = \log_e 2$

66. (4) $\dfrac{36}{r+1} \times {}^{35}C_r (k^2 - 3) = {}^{35}C_r \cdot 6$

$$\Rightarrow \ k^2 - 3 = \frac{r+1}{6}$$

$$\Rightarrow \ k^2 = 3 + \frac{r+1}{6}$$

r can be 5, 35 for $k \in I$

$\quad r = 5, k = \pm 2$

$\quad r = 35, k = \pm 3$

Hence, number of ordered pairs = 4.

67. (1) $S = \underline{3+4} + \underline{8+9} + \underline{13+14} + \underline{18+19}.....40 \text{ terms}$

$S = 7 + 17 + 27 + 37 + 47 + ... \ 20 \text{ terms}$

$$S_{40} = \frac{20}{2}[2 \times 7 + (19)10] = 10[14 + 190]$$

$\quad = 10[2040] = (102)(20)$

$\Rightarrow \ m = 20$

68. (2) Given, $x = \dfrac{1}{2}, y = \dfrac{-1}{4} \ \Rightarrow \ xy = \dfrac{-1}{8}$

$$y \cdot \frac{1 \cdot (-2x)}{2\sqrt{1 - x^2}} + y'\sqrt{1 - x^2}$$

$$= -\left\{ 1 \cdot \sqrt{1 - y^2} + \frac{x \cdot (-2y)}{2\sqrt{1 - y^2}} y' \right\}$$

$$\Rightarrow \ -\frac{xy}{\sqrt{1 - x^2}} + y'\sqrt{1 - x^2} = -\sqrt{1 - y^2} + \frac{xy \cdot y'}{\sqrt{1 - y^2}}$$

$$\Rightarrow \ y'\left(\sqrt{1 - x^2} - \frac{xy}{\sqrt{1 - y^2}} \right) = \frac{xy}{\sqrt{1 - x^2}} - \sqrt{1 - y^2}$$

$$\Rightarrow \ y'\left(\frac{\sqrt{3}}{2} + \frac{1}{8 \cdot \frac{\sqrt{15}}{4}} \right) = \frac{-1}{8 \cdot \sqrt{\frac{3}{2}}} - \frac{\sqrt{15}}{4}$$

$$\Rightarrow \ y'\left(\frac{\sqrt{45} + 1}{2\sqrt{15}} \right) = -\frac{(1 + \sqrt{45})}{4\sqrt{3}}$$

$$\therefore \ y' = -\frac{\sqrt{5}}{2}$$

69. (1) $2\cot^2 \theta - \dfrac{5}{\sin \theta} + 4 = 0$

$$\frac{2\cos^2 \theta}{\sin^2 \theta} - \frac{5}{\sin \theta} + 4 = 0$$

$\Rightarrow \ 2\cos^2\theta - 5\sin\theta + 4\sin^2\theta = 0, \sin\theta \neq 0$

$\Rightarrow \ 2\sin^2\theta - 5\sin\theta + 2 = 0$

$\Rightarrow \ (2\sin\theta - 1)(\sin\theta - 2) = 0$

$\therefore \ \sin\theta = \dfrac{1}{2} \ \Rightarrow \ \theta = \dfrac{\pi}{6}, \dfrac{5\pi}{6}$

$$\therefore \ \int_{\pi/6}^{5\pi/6} \cos^2 3\theta \, d\theta = \int_{\pi/6}^{5\pi/6} \frac{1 + \cos 6\theta}{2} d\theta$$

$$= \frac{1}{2}\left[\theta + \frac{\sin 6\theta}{6} \right]_{\pi/6}^{5\pi/6} = \frac{1}{2}\left[\frac{5\pi}{6} - \frac{\pi}{6} + \frac{1}{6}(0 - 0) \right]$$

$$= \frac{1}{2} \cdot \frac{4\pi}{6} = \frac{\pi}{3}$$

70. (4) It is given that $|B| = 81$

$$\therefore \ |B| = \begin{vmatrix} b_{11} & b_{12} & b_{13} \\ b_{21} & b_{22} & b_{23} \\ b_{31} & b_{32} & b_{33} \end{vmatrix} = \begin{vmatrix} 3^0 a_{11} & 3^1 a_{12} & 3^2 a_{13} \\ 3^1 a_{21} & 3^2 a_{22} & 3^3 a_{23} \\ 3^2 a_{31} & 3^3 a_{32} & 3^4 a_{33} \end{vmatrix}$$

$\Rightarrow \ 81 = 3^3 \cdot 3^2 \cdot 3^1 |A|$

$\Rightarrow \ 3^4 = 3^6 |A| \ \Rightarrow \ |A| = \dfrac{1}{9}$

71. (52) Mean $= \bar{x} = \dfrac{3 + 7 + 9 + 12 + 13 + 20 + x + y}{8} = 10$

$\Rightarrow \ x + y = 16 \hspace{3cm} ...(i)$

Variance $= \sigma^2 = \dfrac{\Sigma(x_i)^2}{8} - (\bar{x})^2 = 25$

$$\sigma^2 = \frac{9 + 49 + 81 + 144 + 169 + 400 + x^2 + y^2}{8} - 100 = 25$$

$\Rightarrow \quad x^2 + y^2 = 148$ ...(ii)

From eqn. (i), $(x + y)^2 = (16)^2$

$\Rightarrow \quad x^2 + y^2 + 2xy = 256$

Using eqn. (ii), $148 + 2xy = 256$

$\Rightarrow \quad xy = 52$

72. **(4)** Since, PQ is perpendicular to L

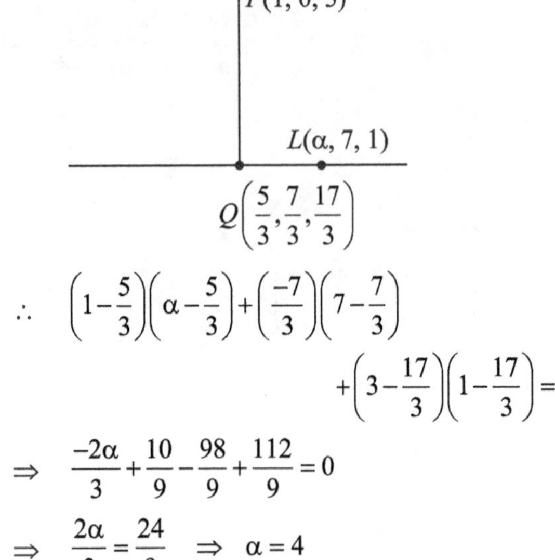

$$\therefore \quad \left(1 - \frac{5}{3}\right)\left(\alpha - \frac{5}{3}\right) + \left(\frac{-7}{3}\right)\left(7 - \frac{7}{3}\right)$$

$$+ \left(3 - \frac{17}{3}\right)\left(1 - \frac{17}{3}\right) = 0$$

$$\Rightarrow \quad \frac{-2\alpha}{3} + \frac{10}{9} - \frac{98}{9} + \frac{112}{9} = 0$$

$$\Rightarrow \quad \frac{2\alpha}{3} = \frac{24}{9} \quad \Rightarrow \quad \alpha = 4$$

73. **(29)** From the given conditions,

$n(A) = 25$, $n(B) = 7$ and $n(A \cap B) = 3$

$n(A \cup B) = n(A) + n(B) - n(A \cap B)$

$\qquad = 25 + 7 - 3 = 29$

74. **(13)** $x + y + z = 6$ ...(i)

$x + 2y + 3z = 10$ ...(ii)

$3x + 2y + \lambda z = \mu$ ...(iii)

From (i) and (ii),

If $z = 0 \Rightarrow x + y = 6$ and $x + 2y = 10$

$\Rightarrow \quad y = 4, x = 2$

$\qquad (2, 4, 0)$

If $y = 0 \Rightarrow x + z = 6$ and $x + 3z = 10$

$\Rightarrow \quad z = 2$ and $x = 4$

$\qquad (4, 0, 2)$

So, $3x + 2y + \lambda z = \mu$, must pass through $(2, 4, 0)$ and $(4, 0, 2)$

So, $6 + 8 = \mu \quad \Rightarrow \quad \mu = 14$

and $12 + 2\lambda = \mu$

$12 + 2\lambda = 14 \quad \Rightarrow \quad \lambda = 1$

So, $\mu - \lambda^2 = 14 - 1 = 13$

75. **(5)** $\displaystyle \lim_{x \to 0} f(x) = \lim_{x \to 0}\left(\frac{1}{x}\ln\left(\frac{1+3x}{1-2x}\right)\right)$

$$= \lim_{x \to 0}\left(\frac{\ln(1+3x)}{x} - \frac{\ln(1-2x)}{x}\right)$$

$$= \lim_{x \to 0}\left(\frac{3\ln(1+3x)}{3x} - \frac{2\ln(1-2x)}{-2x}\right)$$

$\qquad = 3 + 2 = 5$

$\because \quad f(x)$ will be continuous

$\therefore \quad \mathrm{k} = f(0) = \displaystyle\lim_{x \to 0} f(x) = 5$

PHYSICS

1. **(2)** Here, from question, relative permittivity

$$\varepsilon_r = \frac{\varepsilon}{\varepsilon_0} = 3 \Rightarrow \varepsilon = 3\varepsilon_0$$

Relative permeability $\mu_r = \frac{\mu}{\mu_0} = \frac{4}{3} \Rightarrow \mu = \frac{4}{3}\mu_0$

$\therefore \mu\varepsilon = 4\mu_0\varepsilon_0$

$$\sqrt{\frac{\mu_0\varepsilon_0}{\mu\varepsilon}} = \frac{v}{c} = \frac{1}{2}\left(\because c = \frac{1}{\sqrt{\mu_0\varepsilon_0}}\right)$$

$$n = \sqrt{\mu_r \varepsilon_r} = \sqrt{\frac{4}{3} \times 3} = 2$$

And $n = \dfrac{1}{\sin\theta_c}$

$$\Rightarrow \sin\theta_c = \frac{1}{n} = \frac{1}{2}$$

$\therefore$ Critical angle, $\theta_c = 30°$

2. **(3)** In parallel combination, $C_{eq} = C_1 + C_2 = 10\ \mu F$
When connected across $1\ V$ battery, then

$$\frac{U_1}{U_2} = \frac{\left(\frac{1}{2}C_1 V^2\right)}{\left(\frac{1}{2}C_2 V^2\right)} = \frac{1}{4} \Rightarrow \frac{C_1}{C_2} = \frac{1}{4}$$

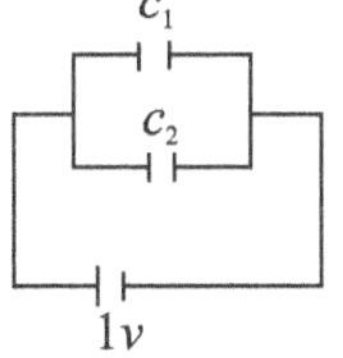

$\therefore C_2 = 8\ \mu F$ and $C_1 = 2\ \mu F$

Now C_1 and C_2 are connected in series combination,

$$\therefore C_{equivalent} = \frac{C_1 C_2}{C_1 + C_2} = \frac{2 \times 8}{2+8} = \frac{16}{10} = 1.6\mu F$$

3. **(2)**

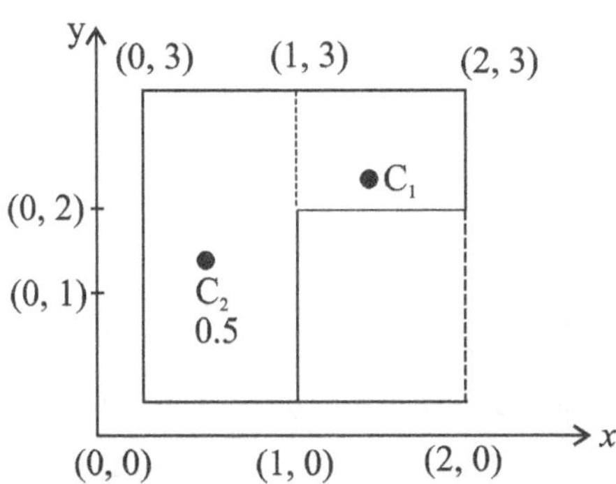

For given Lamina

$\qquad\qquad x \quad y$
$m_1 = 1,\ C_1 = (1.5, 2.5)$
$m_2 = 3,\ C_2 = (0.5, 1.5)$

$$X_{cm} = \frac{m_1 x_1 + m_2 x_2}{m_1 + m_2} = \frac{1.5 + 1.5}{4} = 0.75$$

$$Y_{cm} = \frac{m_1 y_1 + m_2 y_2}{m_1 + m_2} = \frac{2.5 + 4.5}{4} = 1.75$$

$\therefore$ Coordinate of centre of mass of flag shaped lamina $(0.75, 1.75)$

4. **(2)** At elongated position (x),

$$F_{radial} = \frac{mv^2}{r} = mr\omega^2$$

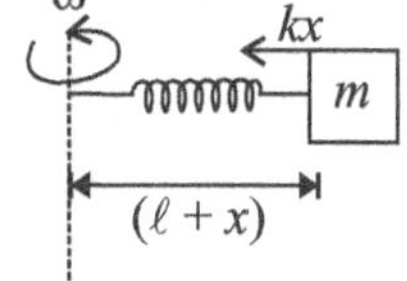

$\therefore kx = m(\ell + x)\omega^2$

$(\because r = \ell + x$ here$)$

$kx = m\ell\omega^2 + mx\omega^2$

$$\therefore x = \frac{m\ell\omega^2}{k - m\omega^2}$$

5. **(1)** From the corresponding V-T graph given in question,
Process $xy \to$ Isobaric expansion,
Process $yz \to$ Isochoric (Pressure decreases)
Process $zx \to$ Isothermal compression
Therefore, corresponding PV graph is as shown in figure

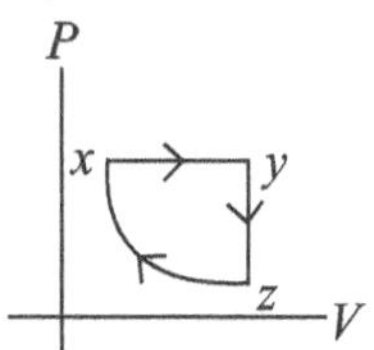

6. **(3)** When cylinder is floating in water at $0°C$
Net thrust $= A(h_2 - h_1)\rho_{0°c} g$

$$= A(100 - 80)\rho_{0°c} g$$

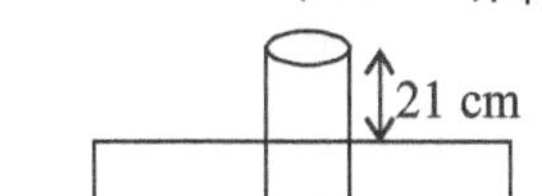

When cylinder is floating in water at $4°\ C$

Net thrust $= A(h_2 - h_1)\rho_{4°c} g$

$$= A(100 - 21)\rho_{4°c} g$$

$$\therefore \frac{\rho_{4°c}}{\rho_{0°c}} = \frac{80}{79} = 1.01$$

7. **(1)**

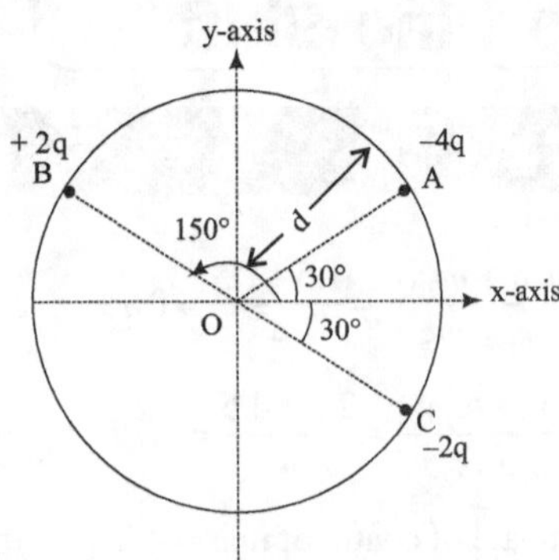

Electric field due to charge $+2q$ at centre O

$$\vec{E}_1 = \frac{1}{4\pi\varepsilon_0} \times \frac{2q}{d^2}\left[\frac{\sqrt{3}\hat{i} - \hat{j}}{2}\right]$$

Electric field due to charge $-2q$ at centre O

$$\vec{E}_2 = \frac{1}{4\pi\varepsilon_0} \times \frac{2q}{d^2}\left[\frac{\sqrt{3}\hat{i} - \hat{j}}{2}\right]$$

Electric field due to charge $-4q$ at centre O

$$\vec{E}_3 = \frac{1}{4\pi\varepsilon_0} \times \frac{4q}{d^2}\left[\frac{\sqrt{3}\hat{i} + \hat{j}}{2}\right]$$

$\therefore$ Net electric field at point O

$$\vec{E}_0 = \vec{E}_1 + \vec{E}_2 + \vec{E}_3 = \frac{\sqrt{3}\,q}{\pi\varepsilon_0 d^2}\hat{i}$$

8. **(2)** Gravitation field at the surface

$$E = \frac{Gm}{r^2}$$

$$\therefore E_1 = \frac{Gm_1}{r_1^2} \text{ and } E_2 = \frac{Gm_2}{r_2^2}$$

From the diagram given in question,

$$\frac{E_1}{E_2} = \frac{2}{3}\ (r_1 = 1\text{m}, R_2 = 2m \text{ given})$$

$$\therefore \frac{E_1}{E_2} = \left(\frac{r_2}{r_1}\right)^2\left(\frac{m_1}{m_2}\right) \Rightarrow \frac{2}{3} = \left(\frac{2}{1}\right)^2\left(\frac{m_1}{m_2}\right)$$

$$\Rightarrow \left(\frac{m_1}{m_2}\right) = \frac{1}{6}$$

9. **(3)**

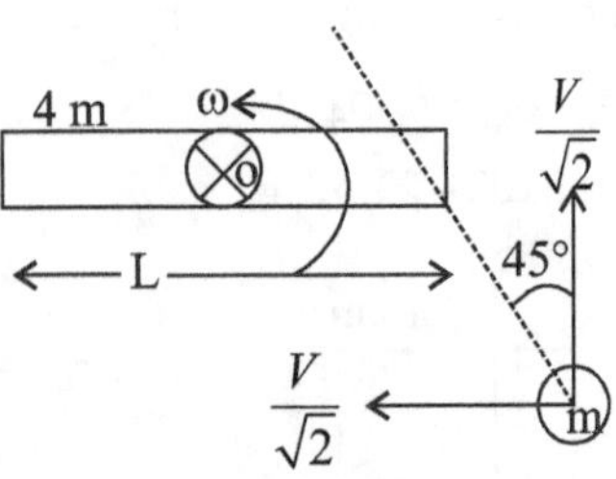

About point O angular momentum
$L_{\text{initial}} = L_{\text{final}}$

$$\Rightarrow \frac{mV}{\sqrt{2}} \times \frac{1}{2} = \left[\frac{4mL^2}{12} + \frac{mL^2}{4}\right] \times \omega$$

$$\therefore \omega = \frac{6V}{7\sqrt{2}L} = \frac{3\sqrt{2}V}{7L}$$

10. **(No option is correct)**

Stopping potential $(V_0) \propto h^x I^y G^z C^r$

Here, h = Planck's constant $= \left[ML^2T^{-1}\right]$

I = current $= [A]$

G = Gravitational constant $= [M^{-1}L^3T^{-2}]$

and c = speed of light $= [LT^{-1}]$

V_0 = potential $= [ML^2T^{-3}A^{-1}]$

$\therefore [ML^2T^{-3}A^{-1}] = [ML^2T^{-1}]^x [A]^y [M^{-1}L^3T^{-2}]^z [LT^{-1}]^r$

$M^{x-z}; L^{2x+3z+r}; T^{-x-2z-r}; A^y$

Comparing dimension of M, L, T, A, we get

$y = -1, x = 0, z = -1, r = 5$

$\therefore V_0 \propto h^0 I^{-1} G^{-1} C^5$

11. **(4)**

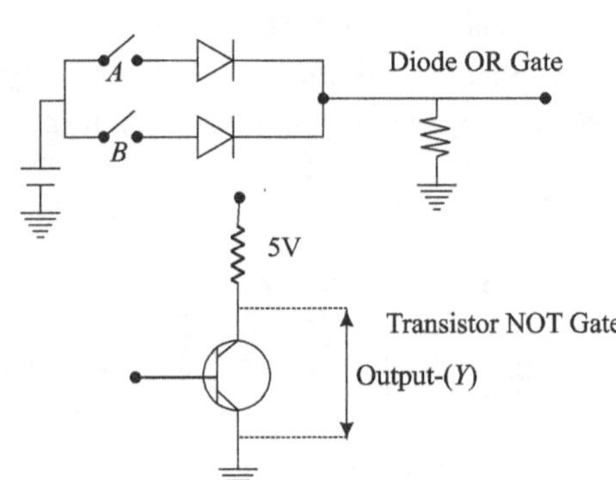

OR + NOT $\rightarrow$ NOR Gate

Hence Boolean relation at the output stage $- Y$ for the circuit,

$$Y = \overline{A + B} = \overline{A}.\overline{B}$$

12. **(3)** Relaxation time $(\tau) \propto \dfrac{\text{mean free path}}{\text{speed}} \Rightarrow \tau \propto \dfrac{1}{v}$

and, $v \propto \sqrt{T}$

$$\therefore \tau \propto \frac{1}{\sqrt{T}}$$

Hence graph between τ v/s $\dfrac{1}{\sqrt{T}}$ is a straight line which is correctly depicted by graph shown in option (3).

13. **(1)** de-Broglie wavelength (λ),

Momentum, $mv = \dfrac{h}{\lambda} = p = \sqrt{2m(KE)}$

$$\therefore \lambda = \frac{h}{\sqrt{2mKE}} \Rightarrow \lambda \propto \frac{1}{\sqrt{KE}}$$

$$\therefore \frac{\lambda_A}{\lambda_B} = \sqrt{\frac{K_B}{K_A}} = \sqrt{\frac{T_A - 1.5}{T_A}} \text{ (as given)}$$

Also, $\frac{\lambda_A}{\lambda_B} = \frac{1}{2}$

On solving we get, $T_A = 2\ eV$

$\therefore KE_B = T_A - 1.5 = 2 - 1.5 = 0.5\ eV$

$\therefore$ Work function of metal B is

$\phi_B = E_B - KE_B = 4.5 - 0.5 = 4\ eV$

14. (4) For telescope
Tube length (L) $= f_o + f_e = 60$

and magnification $(m) = \dfrac{f_o}{f_e} = 5 \Rightarrow f_0 = 5f_e$

$\therefore f_0 = 50$ cm and $f_e = 10$ cm
Hence focal length of eye-piece, $f_e = 10$ cm

15. (4) As per Rutherford α-particle scattering experiment, number of α-particles scattered (N) related with deflection angle θ as

$$N \propto \frac{1}{\sin^4 \dfrac{\theta}{2}} \text{ i.e. } Y \propto \frac{1}{\sin^4 \left(\dfrac{\theta}{2}\right)}$$

$\therefore$ Corresponding $Y_{versus}\theta$ graph is as shown below.

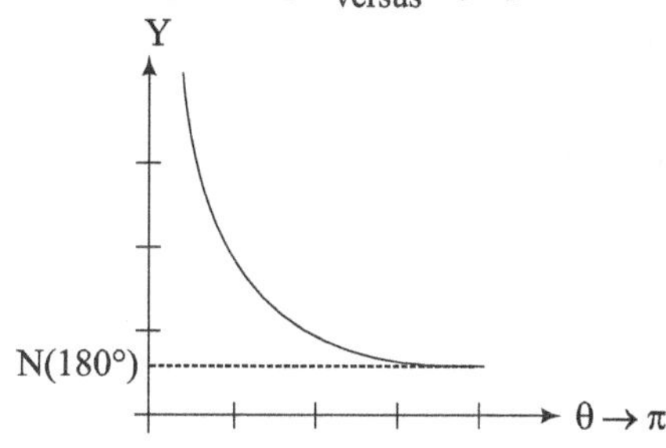

16. (1) According to question, $dB = 1000 - 500 = 500$ gauss
$= 500 \times 10^{-4} T$
Time $dt = 5$ s
Using faraday law

Induced EMF, $e = \left| -\dfrac{d\phi}{dt} \right| = \left| A\dfrac{dB}{dt} \right|$

$$\frac{dB}{dt} = \frac{1000 - 500}{5} \times 10^{-4} = 10^{-2} \text{ T/sec}$$

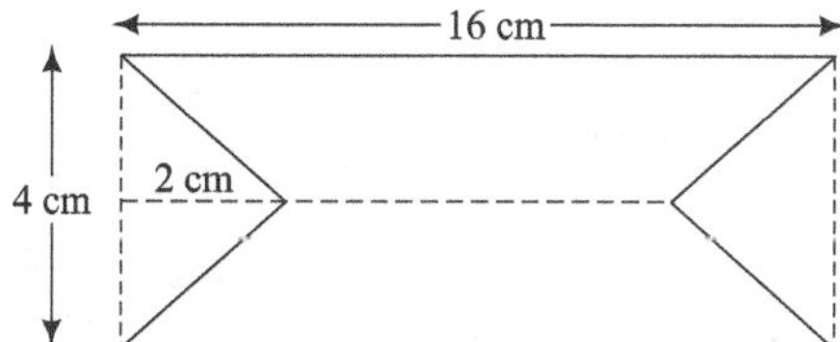

Area, $A =$ ar of $\square$ -2 ar of $\triangle = (16 \times 4 - 2 \times$ Area of triangle$)$ cm^2

$$= \left(64 - 2 \times \frac{1}{2} \times 2 \times 4\right) \text{cm}^2$$

$$= 56 \times 10^{-4} \text{ m}^2$$

$$\therefore \varepsilon_{induced} = \left| A\frac{dB}{dt} \right| = 56 \times 10^{-4} \times 10^{-2} = 56 \times 10^{-6} V = 56 \mu V$$

17. (1)

18. (4)

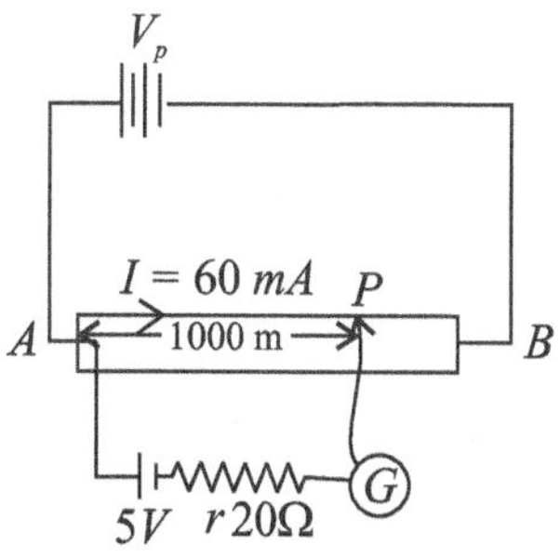

Let R be the resistance of the whole wire
Potential gradient for the potentiometer wire

$$'AB' = -\frac{dV}{d\ell} = \frac{I \times R}{\ell} = \left[\frac{60 \times R}{\ell_{AB}}\right] mv/m$$

$$V_{AP} = \left(\frac{dV}{d\ell_{AB}}\right)\ell_{AP} = \frac{60 \times R}{1200} \times 1000\ mV$$

$\Rightarrow V_{AP} = 50$ R mV
Also, $V_{AP} = 5\ V$ (for balance point at P)

$$\therefore R = \frac{V_{AP}}{50 \times 10^{-3}} = \frac{5}{50 \times 10^{-3}} = 100\Omega$$

19. (1)

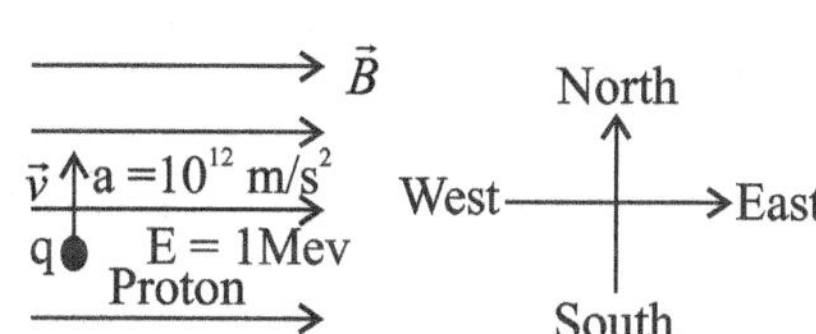

As we know, magnetic force $F = qvB = ma$

$\therefore \vec{a} = \left(\dfrac{qvB}{m}\right)$ perpendicular to velocity.

$$\therefore \text{Also } v = \sqrt{\frac{2KE}{m}} = \sqrt{\frac{2 \times e \times 10^6}{m}}$$

$$\therefore a = \frac{qvB}{m} = \frac{eB}{m}\sqrt{\frac{2 \times e \times 10^6}{m}}$$

$$\therefore 10^{12} = \left(\frac{1.6 \times 10^{-19}}{1.67 \times 10^{-27}}\right)^{\frac{3}{2}} \cdot \sqrt{2} \times 10^3 B$$

$$\therefore B \simeq \frac{1}{\sqrt{2}} \times 10^{-3} T = 0.71 \text{ mT (approx)}$$

20. (3) For minimum density of liquid, solid sphere has to float (completely immersed) in the liquid.
$mg = F_B$ (also $V_{immersed} = V_{total}$)

$$\text{or} \int \rho dV = \frac{4}{3}\pi R^3 \rho_\ell$$

$$\left[\rho(r) = \rho_0\left(1 - \frac{r^2}{R^2}\right) 0 < r \le R \ \text{given} \right]$$

$$\Rightarrow \int_0^R \rho_0 4\pi\left(1 - \frac{r^2}{R^2}\right) \cdot r^2 dr = \frac{4}{3}\pi R^3 \rho_\ell$$

$$\Rightarrow 4\pi\rho_0 \left[\frac{r^3}{3} - \frac{r^5}{5R^2}\right]_0^R = \frac{4}{3}\pi R^3 \rho_\ell$$

$$\frac{4\pi\rho_0 R^3}{3} \times \frac{2}{5} = \frac{4}{3}\pi R^3 \rho_\ell$$

$$\therefore \rho_\ell = \frac{2\rho_0}{5}$$

21. (580)

For pariticle 'A'	For particle 'B'

$X_A = -3t^2 + 8t + 10$ $Y_B = 5 - 8t^3$

$\vec{V}_A = (8 - 6t)\hat{i}$ $\vec{V}_B = -24t^2\hat{j}$

$\vec{a}_A = -6\hat{i}$ $\vec{a}_B = -48t\hat{j}$

At $t = 1$ sec

$$\vec{V}_A = (8 - 6t)\hat{i} = 2\hat{i} \ \text{and} \ \vec{v}_B = -24\hat{j}$$

$$\therefore \vec{V}_{B/A} = -\vec{v}_A + \vec{v}_B = -2\hat{i} - 24\hat{j}$$

$$\therefore \ \text{Speed of } B \text{ w.r.t. } A, \ \sqrt{v} = \sqrt{2^2 + 24^2}$$

$$= \sqrt{4 + 576} = \sqrt{580}$$

$$\therefore v = 580 \ (\text{m/s})$$

22. (10)

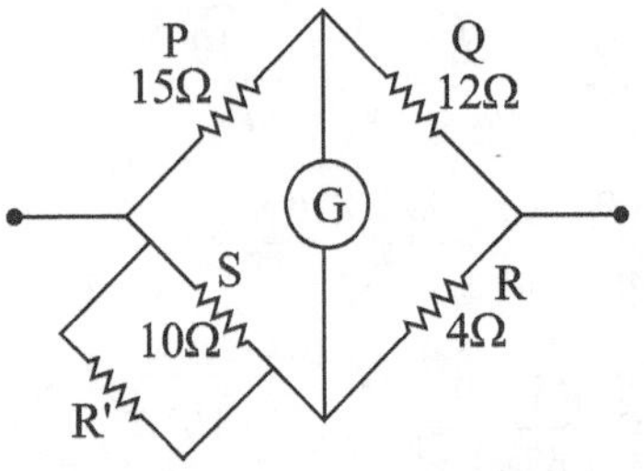

P   15Ω   Q   12Ω

G

S   10Ω   R   4Ω

R'

As per Wheatstone bridge balance condition $\dfrac{P}{Q} = \dfrac{S}{R}$

Let resistance R' is connected in parallel with resistance S of 10Ω

$$\therefore \frac{15}{12} = \frac{10R'}{\dfrac{10 + R'}{4}} \Rightarrow 5 = \frac{10R'}{10 + R'}$$

$$\Rightarrow 50 + 5R' = 10R'$$

$$\therefore R' = \frac{50}{5} = 10\Omega$$

23. (60) Given : $\mu = 1.5$; $R_{\text{curved}} = 30$ cm

Using, Lens-maker formula

$$\frac{1}{f} = (\mu - 1)\left(\frac{1}{R_1} - \frac{1}{R_2}\right)$$

For plano-convex lens

$R_1 \to \infty$ then $R_2 = -R$

$$\therefore f = \frac{R}{\mu - 1} = \frac{30}{1.5 - 1} = 60 \ \text{cm}$$

24. (1) For elastic collision $KE_i = KE_f$

$$\frac{1}{2}m \times 25 + \frac{1}{2} \times m \times 9 = \frac{1}{2}m \times 32 + \frac{1}{2}mv_B^2$$

$$34 = 32 + V_B^2 \Rightarrow V_B = \sqrt{2}$$

$$KE_B = \frac{1}{2}mv_B^2 = \frac{1}{2} \times 0.1 \times 2 = 0.1 J = \frac{1}{10}J$$

$$\therefore x = 1$$

25. (106) Given : $V_{\text{air}} = 300$ m/s, $\rho_{\text{gas}} = 2 \rho$ air

Using, $V = \sqrt{\dfrac{B}{\rho}}$

$$\frac{V_{\text{gas}}}{V_{\text{air}}} = \frac{\sqrt{\dfrac{B}{2\rho_{\text{air}}}}}{\sqrt{\dfrac{B}{\rho_{\text{air}}}}}$$

$$\Rightarrow V_{\text{gas}} = \frac{V_{\text{air}}}{\sqrt{2}} = \frac{300}{\sqrt{2}} = 150\sqrt{2}\text{m/s}$$

And f_{nth} harmonic $= \dfrac{nv}{2L}$ (in open organ pipe)

(L = 1 metre given)

$$\therefore f_{\text{2nd}} \text{ harmonic} - f_{\text{fundamental}} = \frac{2v}{2 \times 1} - \frac{v}{2 \times 1} = \frac{v}{2}$$

$$\therefore f_{\text{2n}} \text{ harmonic} - f_{\text{fundamental}} = \frac{150\sqrt{2}}{2} = \frac{150}{\sqrt{2}} \approx 106 \ Hz$$

CHEMISTRY

26. (2) CO_2, O_3, H_2O vapours and CFC's are the gases that cause green house effect.

27. (3) At a particular temperature as intermolecular force of attraction increases vapour pressure decreases.

Thus, intermolecular forces are inversely proportional to vapour pressure and directly proportional to temperature.

Therefore X has lower intermolecular interactions compared to Y.

28. (3)

29. (2) Oxalic acid is a primary standard solution whereas H_2SO_4 is a secondary standard solution. So it does not matter whether oxalic acid is taken in a burette or in a conical flask. Therefore accurate measurement of concentration by titration depends on the nature of the solution.

30. (1) The rate constant of a reaction is given by

$$k = Ae^{-E_a/RT}$$

The rate constant in tpresence of catalyst is given by

$$k' = Ae^{-E_a'/RT}$$

$$\frac{k'}{k} = e^{-(E_a'-E_a)/RT}$$

$$10^6 = e^{-(E_a'-E_a)/RT}$$

$$\ln 10^6 = -\frac{(E_a'-E_a)}{RT}$$

$$E_a' - E_a = -6(2.303)RT$$

31. (1) All given elements belongs to period III and generally their ionisation energy will increase along the period but Mg will show higher ionisation potential compared to Al due to its stable configuration. Thus correct order of ionisation energy will be : Na < Al < Mg < Si.

Ionisation energy (kJ/mol) of the given metals are Na : 496; Al : 577; Mg : 737; Si : 786

32. (4) $[Ma_3b_3]$ type complex shows facial and meridional isomerism.

So, the complex $[CO(NH_3)_3 (NO_2)_3]$ will shows fac- and mer-isomers.

33. (1) E_1 reaction proceeds via carbocation formation, therefore greater the stability of carbocation, faster will be the E_1 reaction.

Thus correct decreasing order of the given halides towards dehydrohalogenation by E_1 is

$$D > B > C > A$$

34. (4)

(A) is more stable radical and undergoes Markovnikov addition to form (B).

35. (1) Ethyl acetate is polar molecule so dipole-dipole interaction and London dispersion will be present in its liquid state.

36. (2) From the given curve,
if [X] = 1 mM then [Y] = 2 mM

∴ Salt is XY_2

$K_{sp} = [X][Y]^2 = (10^{-3}) (2 \times 10^{-3})^2 = 4 \times 10^{-9}$ M^3

37. (1) B_2H_6 is a very selective reducing agent and usually used to reduce acid to alcohol.

38. (3) Order of C–OH bond length:

Resonance is a deciding factor to determine the order of bond length in given compounds. Phenol exhibits least C–OH bond length due to resonance whereas methanol will show maximum bond length due to lack of resonance and p-ethoxyphenol will have some intermediate value of bond length.

39. (3) Gypsum on heating to 393 K forms plaster of Paris.

$$CaSO_4 \cdot 2H_2O \xrightarrow{393K} CaSO_4 \cdot 0.5H_2O + 1.5H_2O$$

40. (1) Liquid having lower boiling point comes out first in fractional distillation. Simple distillation can't be used as boiling point difference is very small.

3-Methylpantane will show greater boiling point (63°C) comparatives to isohexane due to symmetrical structure. Therefore isohexane distilled out first.

41. (2) Glucose exists in cyclic form in which aldehyde group is not free, therefore it does not give Schiff's test.

42. (2) $S_2O_8^{2-}$

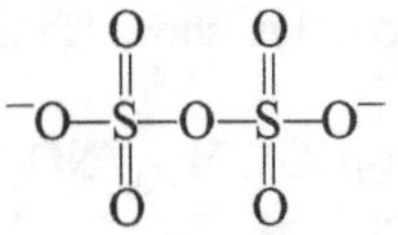

$$\overset{\displaystyle O}{\underset{\displaystyle O}{\underset{\|}{\overset{\|}{S}}}} \text{—O—} \overset{\displaystyle O}{\underset{\displaystyle O}{\underset{\|}{\overset{\|}{S}}}} \text{—O}^-$$

S_8

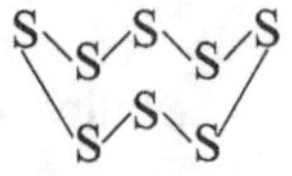

43. (2) $_{26}Fe = [Ar]\ 3d^6 4s^2$. Third ionisation results into stable d^5 configuration.

44 (2) In the Balmer series of H–atom the transition takes place from the higher oribtal to n = 2. Therefore the longest wave length corresponds to $n_1 = 2$ and $n_2 = 3$. As the wave length decreases, the lines in the series converges. Hence, statement I, II, III are the correct statements among the given options.

45. (1) According to Hardy-Schulte,

Coagulation value or fluocculation value

$$\propto \frac{1}{\text{Coagulation power}}$$

order of coagulation power:

$K_3[Fe(CN)_6] > K_2CrO_4 > KBr = KNO_3 = AlCl_3$

∴   order of flocculation value :

$K_3[Fe(CN)_6] < K_2CrO_4 < KBr = KNO_3 = AlCl_3$

46. (1.52)

$$E = 1.23 - \frac{0.0591}{4}\ \log[H^+]^4$$

$$= 1.23 + 0.0591 \times pH$$

$$= 1.23 + 0.0591 \times 5$$

$$= 1.23 + 0.2955$$

$$= 1.52\ V$$

47. (48.00)

Work done is given by the area under the trapezium.

$$\therefore\ |w| = \frac{1}{2}(6 + 10) \times 6 = 48\ J$$

48. (4.96)

$$10 = \frac{\text{Mass of Fe (in g)}}{100 \times 1000} \times 10^6$$

$\Rightarrow$ Mass of Fe = 1 g

Molar mass of $FeSO_4.7H_2O = 278$

56 g of iron present in 1 mole of $FeSO_4.7H_2O$

1 g of Fe present in $\dfrac{278}{56}$ g of salt = 4.96 g

49. (26.92)

$$[ML_6]Cl_3 + 3AgNO_3 \longrightarrow 3AgCl$$

$$0.3\ g \qquad\quad V\ mL,\ 0.125\ M$$

Number of moles of the complex $= \dfrac{0.3}{267.46}$

Number of moles of $AgNO_3 = 0.125 \times V \times 10^{-3}$

$$\frac{0.3}{267.46} \times 3 = 0.125 \times V \times 10^{-3}$$

Or, $V = \dfrac{0.3 \times 3 \times 1000}{267.46 \times 0.125} = 26.92\ mL$

50. (3.00)

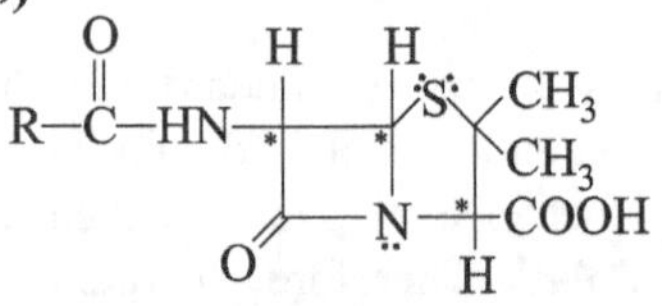

There are three chiral centres in penicillin.

MATHEMATICS

51. (3) $\overrightarrow{AB} = 6\hat{i} + 15\hat{j} + 3\hat{k}$

$$\vec{p} = \hat{i} + 4\hat{j} + 22\hat{k}$$

$$\vec{q} = \hat{i} + \hat{j} + 7\hat{k}$$

$$\vec{p} \times \vec{q} = \begin{vmatrix} i & j & k \\ 1 & 4 & 22 \\ 1 & 1 & 7 \end{vmatrix} = 6\hat{i} + 15\hat{j} - 3\hat{k}$$

Shortest distance between the lines is

$$= \frac{|\overrightarrow{AB}.(\vec{p} \times \vec{q})|}{|\vec{p} \times \vec{q}|} = \frac{|36 + 225 + 9|}{\sqrt{36 + 225 + 9}} = 3\sqrt{30}$$

52. (3) Let $\bar{x}$ and σ be the mean and standard deviations of given observations.

If each observation is multiplied with p and then q is subtracted.

New mean $(\bar{x}_1) = p\bar{x} - q$

$\Rightarrow\ 10 = p(20) - q$ ...(i)

and new standard deviations $\sigma_1 = |p|\ \sigma$

$\Rightarrow\ 1 = |p|\ (2)\ \Rightarrow\ |p| = \dfrac{1}{2}\ \Rightarrow\ p = \pm \dfrac{1}{2}$

If $p = \dfrac{1}{2}$, then $q = 0$ (from equation (i))

If $p = -\dfrac{1}{2}$, then $q = -20$

53. (2) Let $R = \displaystyle\lim_{x \to 0} \left(\frac{3x^2 + 2}{7x^2 + 2} \right)^{\frac{1}{x^2}} = e^{\displaystyle\lim_{x \to 0} \frac{1}{x^2}\left\{ \frac{3x^2 + 2}{7x^2 + 2} - 1 \right\}}$

$$= e^{\displaystyle\lim_{x \to 0} \frac{1}{x^2}\left\{ \frac{-4x^2}{7x^2 + 2} \right\}} = e^{\frac{-4}{2}} = e^{-2} = \frac{1}{e^2}$$

54. (2) $D = \dfrac{1}{2}\begin{vmatrix} 0 & 2 & 1 \\ 1 & -1 & 1 \\ x' & y' & 1 \end{vmatrix} = 5$

$\Rightarrow -2(1 - x') + (y' + x') = \pm 10$
$\Rightarrow -2 + 2x' + y' + x' = \pm 10$
$\Rightarrow 3x' + y' = 12 \quad \text{or} \quad 3x' + y' = -8$
$\therefore \quad \lambda = 3, -2$

55. (2) Since, Rolle's theorem is applicable
$\therefore \quad f(a) = f(b)$
$f(3) = f(4) \Rightarrow \alpha = 12$
$f'(x) = \dfrac{x^2 - 12}{x(x^2 + 12)}$

As $f'(c) = 0$ (by Rolle's theorem)
$x = \pm\sqrt{12}, \quad \therefore \quad c = \sqrt{12}, \therefore \quad f''(c) = \dfrac{1}{12}$

56. (4) $f'(x) = x\,(\pi - \cos^{-1}(\sin|x|))$

$= x\left(\pi - \left(\dfrac{\pi}{2} - \sin^{-1}(\sin|x|)\right)\right) = x\left(\dfrac{\pi}{2} + |x|\right)$

$f(x) = \begin{cases} x\left(\dfrac{\pi}{2} + x\right), & x \geq 0 \\ x\left(\dfrac{\pi}{2} - x\right), & x < 0 \end{cases}$

$f'(x) = \begin{cases} \dfrac{\pi}{2} + 2x, & x \geq 0 \\ \dfrac{\pi}{2} - 2x, & x < 0 \end{cases}$

Hence, $f'(x)$ is increasing in $\left(0, \dfrac{\pi}{2}\right)$ and decreasing in $\left(\dfrac{-\pi}{2}, 0\right)$.

57. (1)

p	q	$p \to q$	$p \wedge (p \to q)$	$(p \wedge (p \to q)) \to q$	$q \to p \wedge (p \to q)$	$p \wedge q$	$p \vee (p \wedge q)$	$p \vee q$	$p \wedge (p \vee q)$
T	T	T	T	T	T	T	T	T	T
T	F	F	F	T	T	F	T	T	T
F	T	T	F	T	F	F	F	T	F
F	F	T	F	T	T	F	F	F	F

58. (4) Let P be (x_1, y_1).
So, equation of normal at P is

$\dfrac{x}{2x_1} - \dfrac{y}{y_1} = -\dfrac{1}{2}$

It passes through $\left(-\dfrac{1}{3\sqrt{2}}, 0\right)$

$\Rightarrow \dfrac{-1}{6\sqrt{2}x_1} = -\dfrac{1}{2} \Rightarrow x_1 = \dfrac{1}{3\sqrt{2}}$

So, $y_1 = \dfrac{2\sqrt{2}}{3}$ (as P lies in Ist quadrant)

So, $\beta = \dfrac{y_1}{2} = \dfrac{\sqrt{2}}{3}$

59. (1) Let point P be $(2t, t^2)$ and Q be (h, k)
Using section formula,

$h = \dfrac{2t}{3}, k = \dfrac{-2 + t^2}{3}$

Hence, locus is $3k + 2 = \left(\dfrac{3h}{2}\right)^2$

$\Rightarrow 9x^2 = 12y + 8$

60. (2) A and B are independent events.

So, $P\left(\dfrac{A}{B'}\right) = \dfrac{P(A \cap B')}{P(B')} = \dfrac{\dfrac{1}{3} - \dfrac{1}{3}\cdot\dfrac{1}{6}}{\dfrac{1}{6}} = \dfrac{1}{3}$

61. (2) It is given that $\vec{u} = \hat{i} + \hat{j} + \lambda\hat{k}$, $\vec{v} = \hat{i} + \hat{j} + 3\hat{k}$ and $w = 2\hat{i} + \hat{j} + \hat{k}$

Volume of parallelopiped $= [\vec{u} \cdot \vec{v} \cdot \vec{w}]$

$\Rightarrow \pm 1 = \begin{vmatrix} 1 & 1 & \lambda \\ 1 & 1 & 3 \\ 2 & 1 & 1 \end{vmatrix} \Rightarrow -\lambda + 3 = \pm 1 \Rightarrow \lambda = 2 \text{ or } \lambda = 4$

For $\lambda = 2$

$\cos\theta = \dfrac{2 + 1 + 2}{\sqrt{6}\sqrt{6}} = \dfrac{5}{6}$

For $\lambda = 4$

$\cos\theta = \dfrac{2 + 1 + 4}{\sqrt{6}\sqrt{18}} = \dfrac{7}{6\sqrt{3}}$

62. (4) Let $I = \int \dfrac{\cos x\, dx}{\sin^3 x (1 + \sin^6 x)^{2/3}}$

$= f(x)\,(1 + \sin^6 x)^{1/\lambda} + c$ ...(i)

If $\sin x = t$
then, $\cos x\, dx = dt$

$I = \int \dfrac{dt}{t^3\left(1 + t^6\right)^{\frac{2}{3}}} = \int \dfrac{dt}{t^7\left(1 + \dfrac{1}{t^6}\right)^{\frac{2}{3}}}$

Put $1 + \dfrac{1}{t^6} = r^3 \Rightarrow \dfrac{dt}{t^7} = \dfrac{-1}{2}r^2 dr$

$$-\frac{1}{2}\int\frac{r^2\,dr}{r^2}=-\frac{1}{2}r+c$$

$$=-\frac{1}{2}\left(\frac{\sin^6 x+1}{\sin^6 x}\right)^{\frac{1}{3}}+c$$

$$=-\frac{1}{2\sin^2 x}(1+\sin^6 x)^{\frac{1}{3}}+c$$

$$f(x)=-\frac{1}{2}\ \mathrm{cosec}^2 x \text{ and } \lambda=3 \qquad \text{[from eqn. (i)]}$$

$$\therefore\ \lambda f\!\left(\frac{\pi}{3}\right)=-2$$

63. (1) Let $z=\alpha\pm i\beta$ be the complex roots of the equation
So, sum of roots $=2\alpha=-b$ and
Product of roots $=\alpha^2+\beta^2=45$
$(\alpha+1)^2+\beta^2=40$
Given, $|z+1|=2\sqrt{10}$
$\Rightarrow\ (\alpha+1)^2-\alpha^2=-5 \qquad [\because \beta^2=45-\alpha^2]$
$\Rightarrow\ 2\alpha+1=-5\ \Rightarrow\ 2\alpha=-6$
Hence, $b=6$ and $b^2-b=30$

64. (2) If $2^{1-x}+2^{1+x}, f(x), 3^x+3^{-x}$ are in A.P., then

$$f(x)=\left(\frac{2^{1+x}+2^{1-x}+3^x+3^{-x}}{2}\right)$$

$$2f(x)=2\left(2^x+\frac{1}{2^x}\right)+\left(3^x+\frac{1}{3^x}\right)$$

Using AM $\geq$ GM
$f(x)\geq 3$

65. (2) Given eqns. are, $x^2=ay$ and $y^2=ax$

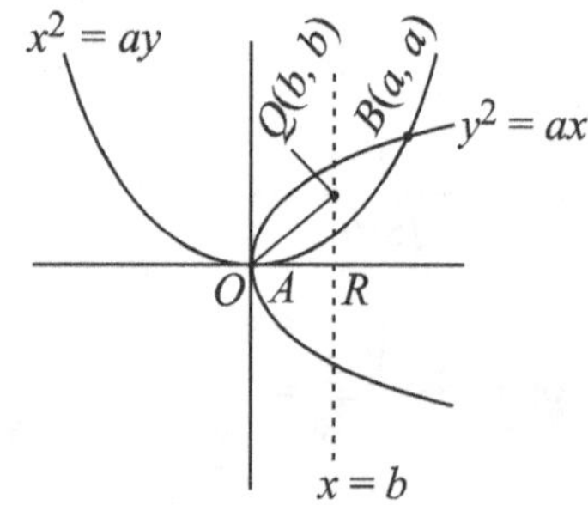

After solving, we get $x=a, y=a$
Now, coordinates of B is (a,a) and A is $(0,0)$
Now, coordinates of Q is (b,b)

$$\therefore\ \frac{1}{2}b^2=\frac{1}{2}\ \Rightarrow\ b=1$$

Area bounded by curves and $x=1$ is

$$\int_0^1\left(\sqrt{a}\,x^{1/2}-\frac{x^2}{a}\right)dx=\frac{1}{2}\int_0^a\left(\sqrt{a}\,x^{1/2}-\frac{x^2}{a}\right)dx$$

$$\Rightarrow\ \frac{2}{3}\sqrt{a}-\frac{1}{3a}=\frac{a^2}{6}$$

$$\Rightarrow\ 4a\sqrt{a}-2=a^3$$

$$\Rightarrow\ a^6+4a^3+4=16a^3$$
$$\Rightarrow\ a^6-12a^3+4=0$$

66. (1) $y=\dfrac{8^{2x}-8^{-2x}}{8^{2x}+8^{-2x}}$

$$\frac{1+y}{1-y}=\frac{8^{2x}}{8^{-2x}}\ \Rightarrow\ 8^{4x}=\frac{1+y}{1-y}$$

$$\Rightarrow\ 4x=\log_8\!\left(\frac{1+y}{1-y}\right)$$

$$\Rightarrow\ x=\frac{1}{4}\log_8\!\left(\frac{1+y}{1-y}\right)$$

$$\therefore\ f^{-1}(x)=\frac{1}{4}\log_8\!\left(\frac{1+x}{1-x}\right)$$

67. (1) From the given linear equation, we get

$$D=\begin{vmatrix}1 & 2 & 3\\ 3 & 4 & 5\\ 4 & 4 & 4\end{vmatrix}(R_3\to R_3-2R_2+3R_3)$$

$$=\begin{vmatrix}1 & 2 & 3\\ 3 & 4 & 5\\ 0 & 0 & 0\end{vmatrix}=0$$

Now, let $P_3=4x+4y+4z-\delta=0$. If the system has solutions it will have infinite solution.
So, $P_3\equiv\alpha P_1+\beta P_2$
Hence, $3\alpha+\beta=4$ and $4\alpha+2\beta=4$
$\Rightarrow\ \alpha=2$ and $\beta=-2$
So, for infinite solution $2\mu-2=\delta$
$\Rightarrow\ $ For $2\mu\neq\delta+2$ system is inconsistent

68. (3) We know ^nC_r is greatest at middle term.
So, $a=(^{19}C_p)_{\max}=\,^{19}C_{10}=\,^{19}C_9$
$b=(^{20}C_q)_{\max}=\,^{20}C_{10}$
$c=(^{21}C_6)_{\max}=\,^{21}C_{10}=\,^{21}C_{11}$

Now, $\dfrac{a}{^{19}C_9}=\dfrac{b}{\dfrac{20}{10}\cdot\,^{19}C_9}=\dfrac{c}{\dfrac{21}{11}\cdot\dfrac{20}{10}\,^{19}C_9}$

$$\Rightarrow\ \frac{a}{1}=\frac{b}{2}=\frac{c}{42/11}\qquad\therefore\ \frac{a}{11}=\frac{b}{22}=\frac{c}{42}$$

69. (2) $\dfrac{dy}{dx}=\dfrac{1}{2}\dfrac{d}{dx}\!\left(\sin^{-1}f(x)\right)$

$$2y=\sin^{-1}f(x)+C=\sin^{-1}(\sin(2\tan^{-1}x))+C$$

$$\Rightarrow 2\left(\frac{\pi}{6}\right)=\sin^{-1}\!\left(\sin\!\left(\frac{2\pi}{3}\right)\right)+C$$

$$\frac{\pi}{3}=\frac{\pi}{3}+C\quad\therefore\quad C=0$$

for $x=-\sqrt{3}$, $2y=\sin^{-1}\!\left(\sin\!\left(\dfrac{-2\pi}{6}\right)\right)+0$

$$\Rightarrow 2y=\frac{-\pi}{3}\Rightarrow y=\frac{-\pi}{6}$$

70. **(3)** The given differential eqn. is

$$\frac{dy}{\sqrt{1-y^2}} + \frac{dx}{\sqrt{1-x^2}} = 0 \quad \Rightarrow \quad \sin^{-1}y + \sin^{-1}x = c$$

At $\quad x = \frac{1}{2}, y = \frac{\sqrt{3}}{2} \quad \Rightarrow \quad c = \frac{\pi}{2}$

$$\Rightarrow \quad \sin^{-1}y = \cos^{-1}x$$

Hence, $y\left(-\frac{1}{\sqrt{2}}\right) = \sin\left(\cos^{-1}\left(-\frac{1}{\sqrt{2}}\right)\right)$

$$= \sin\left(\pi - \cos^{-1}\left(\frac{1}{\sqrt{2}}\right)\right) = \frac{1}{\sqrt{2}}$$

71. **(1540)** Given series can be written as

$$\sum_{k=1}^{20} \frac{k(k+1)}{2} = \frac{1}{2} \sum_{k=1}^{20} (k^2 + k)$$

$$= \frac{1}{2}\left[\frac{20(21)(41)}{6} + \frac{20(21)}{2}\right]$$

$$= \frac{1}{2}\left[\frac{420 \times 41}{6} + \frac{20 \times 21}{2}\right] = \frac{1}{2}[2870 + 210] = 1540$$

72. **(672)** Let $A = [a_{ii}]_{3 \times 3}$

It is given that sum of diagonal elements of AA^T is 3
i.e., $\text{tr}(AA^T) = 3$

$$a_{11}^2 + a_{12}^2 + a_{13}^2 + a_{21}^2 + \ldots + a_{33}^2 = 3$$

Possible cases are

$$\left.\begin{array}{ll} 0, 0, 0, 0, 0, 0, 1, 1, 1 & \to 1 \\ 0, 0, 0, 0, 0, 0, -1, -1, -1 & \to 1 \\ 0, 0, 0, 0, 0, 0, 1, 1, -1 & \to 3 \\ 0, 0, 0, 0, 0, 0, -1, 1, -1 & \to 3 \end{array}\right\} \,{}^{9}C_6 \times 8 = 84 \times 8 = 672$$

73. **(4)** $P \equiv (x_1, y_1)$

$$2yy' - 6x + y' = 0$$

$$\Rightarrow \quad y' = \left(\frac{6x_1}{1 + 2y_1}\right)$$

$$\left(\frac{\frac{3}{2} - y_1}{-x_1}\right) = -\left(\frac{1 + 2y_1}{6x_1}\right)$$

[By point slope form, $y - y_1 = m(x - x_1)$]

$$\Rightarrow \quad 9 - 6y_1 = 1 + 2y_1$$
$$\Rightarrow \quad y_1 = 1$$
$$\therefore \quad x_1 = \pm 2$$

$$\therefore \quad \text{Slope of tangent } (m) = \left(\frac{\pm 12}{3}\right) = \pm 4$$

$$\therefore \quad |m| = 4$$

74. **(3)** 0 Red, 1 Red, 2 Red, 3 Red
Number of ways of selecting atmost three red balls
$$= {}^{7}C_4 + {}^{5}C_1 \cdot {}^{7}C_3 + {}^{5}C_2 \cdot {}^{7}C_2 + {}^{5}C_3 \cdot {}^{7}C_1$$
$$= 35 + 175 + 210 + 70 = 490$$

75. **(8)** Since, $2x^2 + (a - 10)x + \frac{33}{2} = 2a$ has real roots,

$$\therefore \quad D \geq 0$$

$$\Rightarrow \quad (a-10)^2 - 4(2)\left(\frac{33}{2} - 2a\right) \geq 0$$

$$\Rightarrow \quad (a-10)^2 - 4(33 - 4a) \geq 0$$

$$\Rightarrow \quad a^2 - 4a - 32 \geq 0$$

$$\Rightarrow \quad (a - 8)(a + 4) \geq 0$$

$$\Rightarrow \quad a \leq -4 \cup a \geq 8$$

$$\Rightarrow \quad a \in (-\infty, -4] \cup [8, \infty)$$

PHYSICS

1. (1) $K.E$ of the sphere = translational $K.E$ + rotational $K.E$

$$= \frac{1}{2}mv^2 + \frac{1}{2}I\omega^2$$

Where, I = moment of inertia,
ω = Angular, velocity of rotation
m = mass of the sphere
v = linear velocity of centre of mass of sphere

$\because$ Moment of inertia of sphere $I = \frac{2}{5}mR^2$

$\therefore K.E = \frac{1}{2}mv^2 + \frac{1}{2} \times \frac{2}{5}mR^2 \times \omega^2$

$$\Rightarrow K.E = \frac{1}{2}mv^2 + \frac{1}{2} \times \frac{2}{5}mR^2 \times \left(\frac{v}{R}\right)^2 \left(\because \omega = \frac{v}{R}\right)$$

$$\Rightarrow KE = \frac{1}{2}\left(\frac{2}{5}mR^2 + mR^2\right)\left(\frac{v}{R}\right)^2$$

$$\Rightarrow KE = \frac{1}{2}mR^2 \times \frac{7}{5} \times \frac{v^2}{R^2} = \frac{7}{10} \times \frac{1}{2} \times \frac{25}{10^4}$$

$$\Rightarrow KE = \frac{35}{4} \times 10^{-4} \text{ joule}$$

$$\Rightarrow KE = 8.75 \times 10^{-4} \text{ joule}$$

2. (3) Using mirror formula, magnification is given by

$$m = \frac{f}{u - f} = \frac{-1}{1 - \frac{u}{f}}$$

At focus magnification is ∞
And at $u = 2f$, magnification is 1.
Hence graph (4) correctly depicts 'm' versus distance of object 'x' graph.

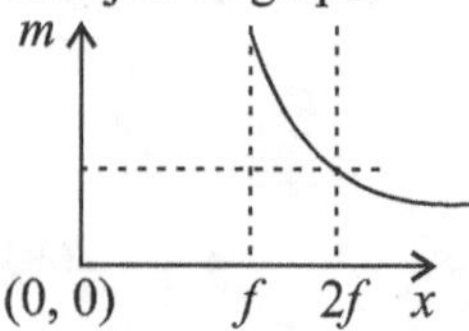

3. (2) The velocity of a transverse wave in a stretched wire is given by

$$v = \sqrt{\frac{T}{\mu}}$$

Where,
T = Tension in the wire
μ = linear density of wire

$$\left(\because V \propto T\right)$$

$$\therefore \frac{v_1}{v_2} = \sqrt{\frac{T_1}{T_2}}$$

$$\Rightarrow \frac{v}{v} \times 2 = \sqrt{\frac{2.06 \times 10^4}{T_2}}$$

$$\Rightarrow T_2 = \frac{2.06 \times 10^4}{4} = 0.515 \times 10^4 \, N$$

$$\Rightarrow T_2 = 5.15 \times 10^3 \, N$$

4. (1) Helium is a monoatomic gas and Oxygen is a diatomic gas.

For helium, $C_{V_1} = \frac{3}{2}R$ and $C_{P_1} = \frac{5}{2}R$

For oxygen, $C_{V_2} = \frac{5}{2}R$ and $C_{P_2} = \frac{7}{2}R$

$$\gamma = \frac{N_1 C_{P_1} + N_2 C_{P_2}}{N_1 C_{V_1} + N_2 C_{V_2}}$$

$$\Rightarrow \gamma = \frac{n.\frac{5}{2}R + 2n.\frac{7}{2}R}{n.\frac{3}{2}R + 2n.\frac{5}{2}R} = \frac{19nR \times 2}{2(13nR)}$$

$$\therefore \left(\frac{C_P}{C_V}\right)_{mixture} = \frac{19}{13}$$

5. (1) Mass of sphere = volume of sphere x density of sphere

$$= \frac{4}{3}\pi R^3 \rho$$

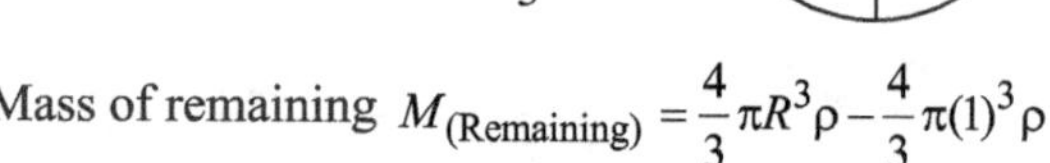

Mass of cavity $M_{\text{cavity}} = \frac{4}{3}\pi (1)^3 \rho$

Mass of remaining $M_{(\text{Remaining})} = \frac{4}{3}\pi R^3 \rho - \frac{4}{3}\pi (1)^3 \rho$

Centre of mass of remaining part,

$$X_{\text{COM}} = \frac{M_1 r_1 + M_2 r_2}{M_1 + M_2}$$

$$\Rightarrow -(2 - R) = \frac{\left[\frac{4}{3}\pi R^3 \rho\right]0 + \left[\frac{4}{3}\pi(1)^3(-\rho)\right][R-1]}{\frac{4}{3}\pi R^3 \rho + \frac{4}{3}\pi(1)^3(-\rho)}$$

$$\Rightarrow \frac{(R-1)}{(R^3 - 1)} = 2 - R$$

$$\Rightarrow \frac{(R-1)}{(R-1)(R^2 + R + 1)} = 2 - R$$

$$\Rightarrow (R^2 + R + 1)(2 - R) = 1$$

6. (1)

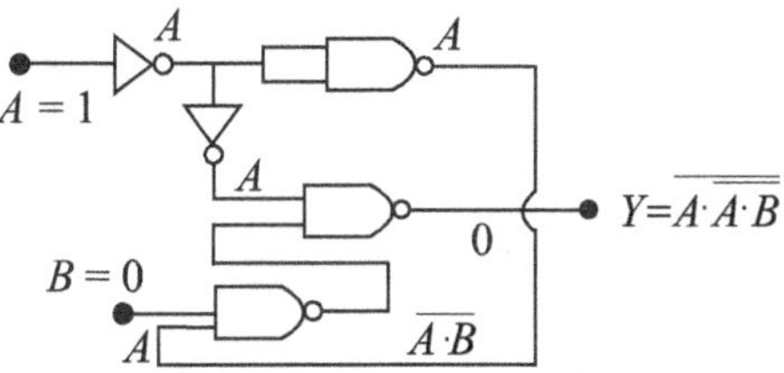

$$Y = \overline{\overline{AB}.A} = \overline{\overline{AB}} + \overline{A} = AB + \overline{A}$$
For $A = 1$, $B = 0$
$$Y = (1) \times 0 + 0$$
$$\Rightarrow Y = 0 + 0 = 0$$

7. (4) For carnot refrigerator

Efficiency $= \dfrac{Q_1 - Q_2}{Q_1}$

Where,
$Q_1 = $ heat lost from sorrounding
$Q_2 = $ heat absorbed from reservoir at low temperature.

Also, $\dfrac{Q_1 - Q_2}{Q_1} = \dfrac{w}{Q_1}$

$$\Rightarrow \dfrac{1}{10} = \dfrac{w}{Q_1}$$

$$\Rightarrow Q_1 = w \times 10 = 100\, J$$
So, $Q_1 - Q_2 = w$
$$\Rightarrow Q_2 = Q_1 - w$$
$$\Rightarrow 100 - 10 = Q_2 = 90\, J$$

8. (1) Given, Path difference, $\Delta x = \dfrac{\lambda}{8}$

Phase differences, $\Delta\phi = \dfrac{2\pi}{\lambda}\Delta x$

$$= \dfrac{2\pi}{\lambda} \times \dfrac{\lambda}{8} = \dfrac{\pi}{4}$$

$$I = I_0 \cos^2\left(\dfrac{\Delta\phi}{2}\right)$$

$$\Rightarrow \dfrac{I}{I_0} = \cos^2\left(\dfrac{\frac{\pi}{4}}{2}\right) = \cos^2\left(\dfrac{\pi}{8}\right)$$

$$\Rightarrow \dfrac{I}{I_0} = 0.853$$

9. (1)

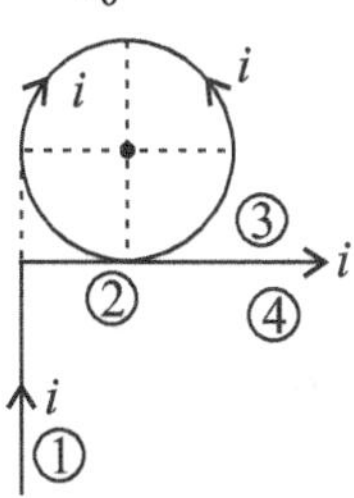

$$B_0 = B_1 + B_2 + B_3 + B_4$$

$$= \dfrac{\mu_0 I}{4\pi R}[\sin 90° - \sin 45°] + \dfrac{\mu_0 I}{2R} + \dfrac{\mu_0 I}{4\pi R}$$

$$[\sin 45° + \sin 90°]$$

$$= -\dfrac{\mu_0 I}{4\pi R}\left(1 - \dfrac{1}{\sqrt{2}}\right) + \dfrac{\mu_0 I}{2R} + \dfrac{\mu_0 I}{4\pi R}\left(1 + \dfrac{1}{\sqrt{2}}\right)$$

$$\overrightarrow{B_0^\odot} = \dfrac{\mu_0 I}{2\pi R}\left(\pi + \dfrac{1}{\sqrt{2}}\right)^\odot$$

10. (4) Let t be the time taken by the particle dropped from height h to collide with particle thrown upward.

Using,
$$v^2 - u^2 = 2gh$$
$$\Rightarrow v^2 - 0^2 = 2gh$$
$$\Rightarrow v = \sqrt{2gh}$$

Downward distance travelled
$$S_1 = \dfrac{1}{2}gt^2 = \dfrac{1}{2}g.\dfrac{h}{2g} = \dfrac{h}{4}$$

Distance of collision point from ground
$$s_2 = h - \dfrac{h}{4} = \dfrac{3h}{4}$$

Speed of (A) just before collision
$$v_1 = gt = \sqrt{\dfrac{gh}{2}}$$

And speed of(B) just before collision
$$v_2 = \sqrt{2gh} - \sqrt{\dfrac{gh}{2}}$$

Using principle of conservation of linear momentum
$$mv_1 + mv_2 = 2mv_f$$

$$\Rightarrow v_f = \dfrac{m\left(\sqrt{2gh} - \sqrt{\dfrac{gh}{2}}\right) - m\sqrt{\dfrac{gh}{2}}}{2m} = 0$$

After collision, time taken (t_1) for combined mass to reach the ground is

$$\Rightarrow \dfrac{3h}{4} = \dfrac{1}{2}gt_1^2$$

$$\Rightarrow t_1 = \sqrt{\dfrac{3h}{2g}}$$

11. (4) Amplitude of electric field (E) and Magnetic field (B) of an electromagnetic wave are related by the relation

—

$$\Rightarrow E = Bc$$
$$\Rightarrow E = 5 \times 10^{-8} \times 3 \times 10^8 = 15\, N/C$$
$$\Rightarrow \vec{E} = 15\hat{i}\, V/m$$

12. (3) Given, Initial velocity, $u = v_0\hat{i} + v_0\hat{j}$

Acceleration, $a = \dfrac{qE_0}{m} = \dfrac{eE_0}{m}$

Using $v = u + at$

$$v = v_0\hat{i} + v_0\hat{j} + \frac{eE_0}{m}t\hat{k}$$

$$\therefore |\vec{v}| = \sqrt{2v_0^2 + \left(\frac{eE_0 t}{m}\right)^2}$$

de-Broglie wavelength, $\lambda = \dfrac{h}{p}$

$$\Rightarrow \lambda = \frac{h}{mv} \quad (\because p = mv)$$

Initial wavelength, $\lambda_0 = \dfrac{h}{mv_0\sqrt{2}}$

Final wavelength,

$$\lambda = \frac{h}{m\sqrt{2v_0^2 + \left(\dfrac{eE_0 t}{m}\right)^2}}$$

$$\frac{\lambda}{\lambda_0} = \frac{1}{\sqrt{1 + \left(\dfrac{eE_0 t}{\sqrt{2}mv_0}\right)^2}}$$

$$\Rightarrow \lambda = \frac{\lambda_0}{\sqrt{1 + \dfrac{e^2 E_0^2 t^2}{2m^2 v_0^2}}}$$

13. (3) Given, Length of simple pendulum, $l = 25.0$ cm
Time of 40 oscillation, $T = 50s$
Time period of pendulum

$$T = 2\pi\sqrt{\frac{\ell}{g}}$$

$$\Rightarrow T^2 = \frac{4\pi^2 \ell}{g} \Rightarrow g = \frac{4\pi^2 \ell}{T^2}$$

$$\Rightarrow \text{Fractional error in g} = \frac{\Delta g}{g} = \frac{\Delta l}{l} + \frac{2\Delta T}{T}$$

$$\Rightarrow \frac{\Delta g}{g} = \left(\frac{0.1}{25.0}\right) + 2\left(\frac{1}{50}\right) = 0.044$$

$$\therefore \text{Percentage error in } g = \frac{\Delta g}{g} \times 100 = 4.4\%$$

14. (1) For series connection of a resistor and inductor, time
variation of current is $I = I_0(1 - e^{-t/T_c})$

Here, $T_C = \dfrac{L}{R}$

$$q = \int\limits_{0}^{T_c} i\, dt$$

$$\Rightarrow \int dq = \int \frac{E}{R}\left(1 - e^{-t/t_c}\right) dt$$

$$\Rightarrow q = \frac{\in}{R}\left[t + t_C e^{-t/t_c}\right]_0^{t_c}$$

$$\Rightarrow q = \frac{\in}{R}\left[t_C + \frac{t_C}{e} - t_C\right]$$

$$\Rightarrow q = \frac{\in}{R}\frac{L}{Re}$$

$$\therefore q = \frac{\in L}{R^2 e}$$

15. (2) Electric field at a point outside the sphere is given by

$$E = \frac{1}{4\pi \in_0}\frac{Q}{r^2}$$

But $\rho = \dfrac{Q}{\dfrac{4}{3}\pi R^3}$

$$\therefore E = \frac{\rho R^3}{3\in_0 r^2}$$

At surface $r = R$

$$\therefore E = \frac{\rho R^3}{3\in_0}$$

Let ρ_1 and ρ_2 are the charge densities of two sphere.

$$E_1 = \frac{\rho R_1}{3\varepsilon_0} \text{ and } E_2 = \frac{\rho_2 R_2}{3\varepsilon_0}$$

$$\because \frac{E_1}{E_2} = \frac{\rho_1 R_1}{\rho_2 R_2} = \frac{R_1}{R_2}$$

This gives $\rho_1 = \rho_2 = \rho$
Potential at a point outside the sphere

$$V = \frac{1}{4\pi\varepsilon_0}\frac{Q}{r}$$

$$= \frac{\rho R^3}{3\varepsilon_0 r}\left(\because \rho = \frac{Q}{\dfrac{4}{3}\pi R^3}\right)$$

At surface, $r = R$

$$V = \frac{\rho R^2}{3\varepsilon_0} \text{ so, } V_1 = \frac{\rho R_1^2}{3\varepsilon_0} \text{ and } V_2 = \frac{\rho R_2^2}{3\varepsilon_0}$$

$$\therefore \frac{V_1}{V_2} = \left(\frac{R_1}{R_2}\right)^2$$

16. (4) Given, Position vector,
$$\vec{r} = \cos\omega t\,\hat{i} + \sin\omega t\,\hat{j}$$

Velocity, $\vec{v} = \dfrac{d\vec{r}}{dt} = \omega(-\sin\omega t\,\hat{i} + \cos\omega t\,\hat{j})$

Acceleration,

$\vec{a} = \dfrac{d\vec{v}}{dt} = -\omega^2(\cos\omega t\,\hat{i} + \sin\omega t\,\hat{j})$

$\vec{a} = -\omega^2\vec{r}$

$\therefore \vec{a}$ is antiparallel to $\vec{r}$

Also $\vec{v}.\vec{r} = 0$

$\therefore \vec{v} \perp \vec{r}$

Thus, the particle is performing uniform circular motion.

17. (1)

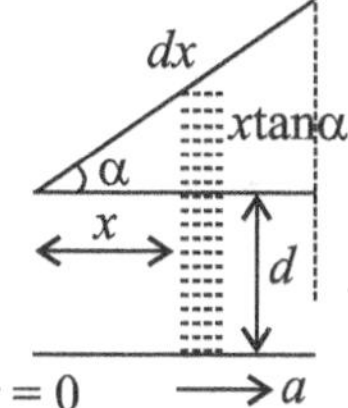

Consider an infinitesimal strip of capacitor of thickness dx at a distance x as shown.

Capacitance of parallel plate capacitor of area A is given by $C = \dfrac{\varepsilon_0 A}{t}$

[Here t = seperation between plates]
So, capacitance of thickness dx will be

$\therefore dC = \dfrac{\varepsilon_0 a\,dx}{d + x\tan\alpha}$

Total capacitance of system can be obtained by integrating with limits x = 0 to x = a

$\therefore C_{eq} = \int dC = a\varepsilon_0 \int\limits_{x=0}^{x=a} \dfrac{dx}{x\tan\alpha + d}$

[By Binomial expansion]

$\Rightarrow C_{eq} = \dfrac{a\varepsilon_0}{d}\int\limits_0^a\left(1 - \dfrac{x\tan\alpha}{d}\right)dx = \dfrac{a\varepsilon_0}{d}\left(x - \dfrac{x^2\tan\alpha}{2d}\right)_0^a$

$\Rightarrow C_{eq} = \dfrac{a^2\varepsilon_0}{d}\left(1 - \dfrac{a\tan\alpha}{2d}\right) = \dfrac{\varepsilon_0 a^2}{d}\left(1 - \dfrac{\alpha a}{2d}\right)$

18. (2)

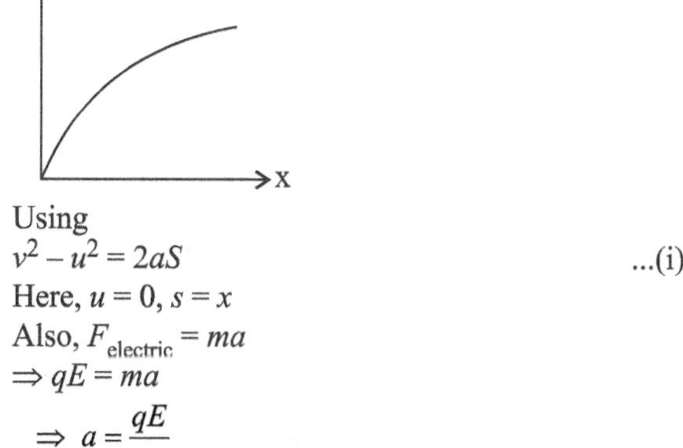

Using
$v^2 - u^2 = 2aS$ ...(i)
Here, $u = 0$, $s = x$
Also, $F_{electric} = ma$
$\Rightarrow qE = ma$
$\Rightarrow a = \dfrac{qE}{m}$

Substituting the values in (i) we get

$v^2 = \dfrac{2qE}{m}.x$

19. (4) Given,

Resistance of galvanometer, $G = 100\,\Omega$
Current, $i_g = 1\,mA$
A galvanometer can be converted into voltmeter by connecting a large resistance R in series with it.
Total resistance of the combination $= G + R$
According to Ohm's law, $V = i_g(G + R)$
$\therefore 10 = 1 \times 10^{-3}(100 + R_0)$
$\Rightarrow 10000 - 100 = 9900\,\Omega = R_0$
$\Rightarrow R_0 = 9.9\,k\Omega$

20. (4)

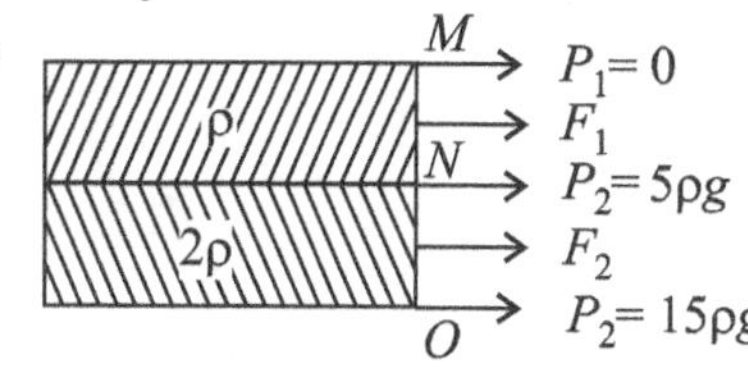

Let P_1, P_2 and P_3 be the pressure at points M, N and O respectively.
Pressure is given by $P = \rho g h$
Now, $P_1 = 0$ ($\because h = 0$)
$P_2 = \rho g(5)$
$P_3 = \rho g(15)$
   $= 15\,\rho g$

Force on upper part, $F_1 = \dfrac{(P_1 + P_2)}{2}A$

Force on lower part, $F_2 = \dfrac{(P_2 + P_3)}{2}A$

$\therefore \dfrac{F_1}{F_2} = \dfrac{5\rho g}{20\rho g} = \dfrac{5}{20} = \dfrac{1}{4}$

21. (08.00)

Let the ball takes time t to reach the ground

Using, $S = ut + \dfrac{1}{2}gt^2$

$\Rightarrow S = 0 \times t + \dfrac{1}{2}gt^2$

$\Rightarrow 200 = gt^2$

$[\because 2S = 100m]$

$\Rightarrow t = \sqrt{\dfrac{200}{g}}$ ...(i)

In last $\dfrac{1}{2}s$, body travels a distance of 19 m, so in $\left(t - \dfrac{1}{2}\right)$ distance travelled $= 81$

Now, $\dfrac{1}{2}g\left(t - \dfrac{1}{2}\right)^2 = 81$

$\therefore g\left(t - \dfrac{1}{2}\right)^2 = 81 \times 2$

$$\Rightarrow \left(t - \frac{1}{2}\right) = \sqrt{\frac{81 \times 2}{g}}$$

$$\therefore \frac{1}{2} = \frac{1}{\sqrt{g}}(\sqrt{200} - \sqrt{81 \times 2}) \qquad \text{using (i)}$$

$$\Rightarrow \sqrt{g} = 2(10\sqrt{2} - 9\sqrt{2})$$

$$\Rightarrow \sqrt{g} = 2\sqrt{2}$$

$$\therefore g = 8 \; m/s^2$$

22. (486.00)

The wavelength of the spectral line of hydrogen spectrum is given by formula

$$\frac{1}{\lambda} = R\left(\frac{1}{n_f^2} - \frac{1}{n_i^2}\right)$$

Where, R = Rydberg constant
For the first member of Balmer series $n_F = 2$, $n_i = 3$

$$\therefore \frac{1}{\lambda} = R\left(\frac{1}{2^2} - \frac{1}{3^2}\right) \qquad \text{...(i)}$$

For last member of Balmer series, $n_f = 2$, $n_i = 4$

$$\text{So, } \frac{1}{\lambda'} = R\left[\frac{1}{4} - \frac{1}{16}\right] \qquad \text{...(ii)}$$

Dividing (i) by (ii), we get

$$\Rightarrow \frac{\lambda'}{\lambda} = \frac{5 \times 16}{9 \times 4 \times 3}$$

$$\Rightarrow \lambda' = \frac{5 \times 4 \times 656.1}{9 \times 3}(nm) = 486\,nm$$

23. (30.00)

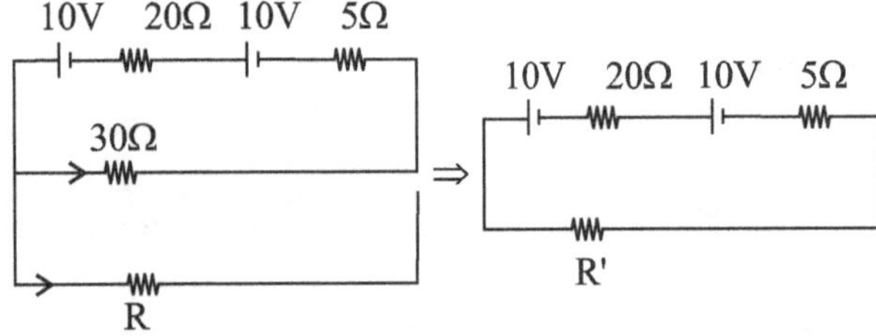

The resistance of 30Ω is in parallel with R. Their effective resistance

$$\frac{1}{R'} = \frac{1}{30} + \frac{1}{R}$$

$$R' = \frac{30R}{30 + R} \qquad \text{...(i)}$$

Also, V = IR

$$\Rightarrow 10 = \frac{20 \times 20}{R' + 25}$$

$$\Rightarrow R' + 25 = 40$$

$$\Rightarrow R' = 15$$

$$R' = 15 = \frac{30R}{30 + R} \qquad \text{Using (i)}$$

$$\Rightarrow 30 + R = 2R$$

$$\Rightarrow R = 30 \; \Omega$$

24. (50.00)

Let Q_1, Q_2, Q_3 be the temperatures of container C_1, C_2 and C_3 respectively.
Using principle of calorimetry in container C_1, we have

$$(\theta_1 - 60) = 2\,ms(60 - \theta)$$
$$\Rightarrow \theta_1 - 60 = 120 - 2\theta$$
$$\Rightarrow \theta_1 = 180 - 2\theta \qquad \text{...(i)}$$

For container C_2
$$ms\,(\theta_2 - 30) = 2ms\,(30 - \theta)$$
$$\Rightarrow \theta_2 = 90 - 2\theta3 \qquad \text{...(ii)}$$

For container C_3
$$2ms\,(\theta_1 - 60) = ms\,(60 - \theta)$$
$$\Rightarrow 2\theta_1 - 120 = 60 - \theta$$
$$\Rightarrow 2\theta_1 + \theta = 180 \qquad \text{...(iii)}$$

Also, $\theta_1 + \theta_2 + \theta_3 = 3\theta$ ...(iv)
Adding (i), (ii) and (iii)

$$3\theta_1 + 3\theta_2 + 3\theta_3 = 450$$
$$\Rightarrow \theta_1 + \theta_2 + \theta_3 = 150$$
$$\Rightarrow 3\theta = 150 \Rightarrow \theta = 50 \; ^\circ C$$

25. (16.00)

Using law of conservation of energy
Total energy at height 10 R = total energy at earth

$$-\frac{GM_E m}{10R} + \frac{1}{2}mV_0^2 = -\frac{GM_E m}{R} + \frac{1}{2}mV^2$$

$$\left[\because \text{Gravitational potential energy} = -\frac{GMm}{r}\right]$$

$$\Rightarrow \frac{GM_E}{R}\left(1 - \frac{1}{10}\right) + \frac{V_0^2}{2} = \frac{V^2}{2}$$

$$\Rightarrow V^2 = V_0^2 + \frac{9}{5}gR$$

$$\Rightarrow V = \sqrt{V_0^2 + \frac{9}{5}gR} \approx 16 \; km/s$$

$$[\because V_0 = 12 \text{ km/s given}]$$

CHEMISTRY

26. (4)

27. (3) During the reduction of Fe_2O_3 to FeO, Fe_2O_3 is first reduced to Fe_3O_4 and then to FeO, thus follows reaction (b).

In order to remove impurity of the ore limestone is added along with ore which is decomposed to CaO.

The resulted CaO reacts with SiO_2 to form $CaSiO_3$ i.e. follows reaction (a) and is removed as a slag.

28. (1)

	^1_1H	$^2_1H(D)$	$^3_1H(T)$
Number of neutron	0	1	2
	(x)	(y)	(z)

Total number of neutrons in three isotopes of hydrogen $= 0 + 1 + 2 = 3$

29. (1) Reactant should not be adsorbed strongly which might result into immobilisation that inhibit further adsorption on the catalyst's surface.

30. (4) Maltose on hydrolysis gives two moles of α-D-glucose.

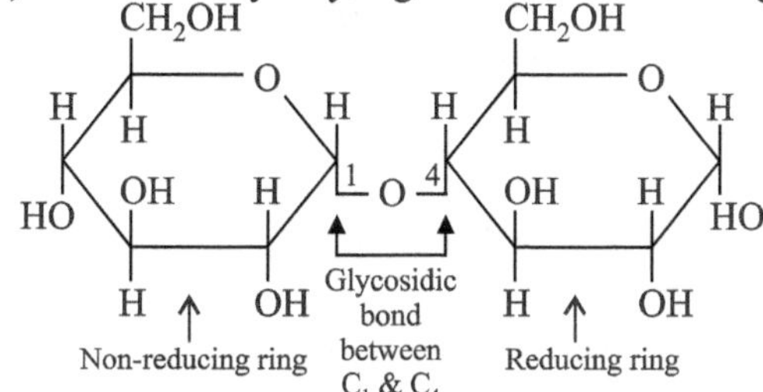

31. (3) Formation of Bakelite follows electrophilic substitution reaction of phenol with formaldehyde followed by dehydration.

32. (3) $r = \dfrac{a_0 n^2}{Z}$

For Li^{2+}, $r = \dfrac{a_0 (2)^2}{3} = \dfrac{4a_0}{3}$

33. (3)
$$3Mg + N_2 \longrightarrow \underset{(B)}{Mg_3N_2} \xrightarrow{H_2O} 3Mg(OH)_2 + 2NH_3$$
(A)

$$4NH_3 + CuSO_4 \longrightarrow \underset{\text{(Dark blue coloured)}}{[Cu(NH_3)_4]SO_4}$$

34. (3) $[Pt(NH_3)_2Cl(NO_2)]$ and $[Pt(NH_3)_4ClBr]^{2+}$ are the Ma_4bc and Ma_2bc type of complexes.

Each shows two geometrical isomers i.e., cis and trans isomers.

35. (3) Arrhenius equation, $k = Ae^{-Ea/RT}$

$$\log k = \log A - \dfrac{E_a}{2.303\,RT}$$

$$\text{slope} = -\dfrac{E_a}{2.303\,R}$$

∴ More negative the slope greater will be the E_a.

So correct order is $E_c > E_a > E_d > E_b$

36. (2)

37. (4)

			No. of unpaired e^-	μ
(A)	$Ni(CO)_4$;	$Ni = 3d^8 4s^2 (SFL)$	0	0
(B)	$[Ni(H_2O)_6]\,;Cl_2$	$Ni^{2+} = 3d^8 (WFL)$	2	$\sqrt{8}$ BM
(C)	$Na_2[Ni(CN)_4]$;	$Ni^{2+} = 3d^8 (SFL)$	0	0
(D)	$PdCl_2(PPh_3)_2$;	$Pd^{2+} = 4d^8$	0	0

Correct order of the calculated spin only magnetic moments of complexes A to D is (A) ≈ (C) ≈ (D) < B

38. (1) Generally, bond energy $\propto \dfrac{1}{\text{Bond length}}$

So bond energy order is C–F > C–Cl > C–Br > C–I

39. (3) Kjeldahl's method can not be used for nitrogen determination of compounds having nitro group or azo group or nitrogen present in rings as the nitrogen of these compounds can not be converted to $(NH_4)_2SO_4$ under the condition of this method.

40. (1) In (A), –OH group is present, so inter-molecular H-bonding is possible while in (B), due to methoxy group there is no possibility of Inter-molecular H-bonding. So A is having higher boiling point than B.

41. (2) Temperature plays a significant role on pH measurements. As the temperature rises, molecular vibrations increase which results in greater ability of water to ionise and form more hydrogen ions.

As a result, the pH will drop. So assertion is incorrect. The dissociation of water molecules into ions is bond breaking and is therefore an endothermic process (energy must be absorbed to break the bonds). So reason is also incorrect.

42. (1) AgBr shows both Schottky as well as Frenkel defects.

43. (2) $P_4 + 3NaOH + 3H_2O \longrightarrow PH_3 + \underset{(X)}{3NaH_2PO_2}$

$\underset{(X)}{NaH_2PO_2} \xrightarrow{\ HCl\ } \underset{(Y)}{H_3PO_2}$

Basicity of $H_3PO_2 = 1$

44. (3)

3-oxo-hexane dicarboxylic acid

45. (3)

Correct increasing order of atomic radii is
F < O < C < Cl < Br

46. (13)

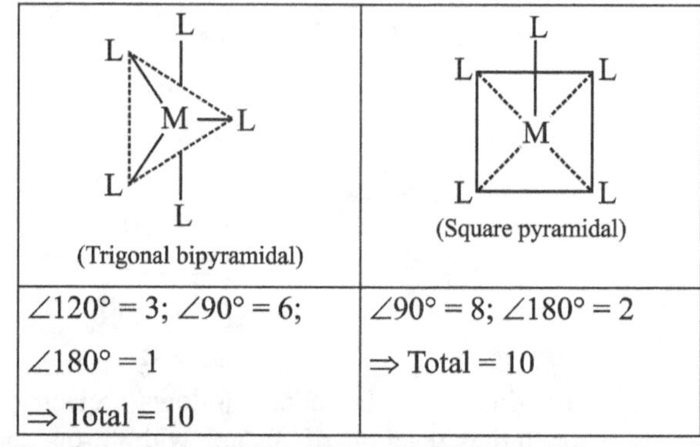

Number of atoms present in molecule (C) in one plane = 13

47. (2.15) At equilibrium state $E_{cell} = 0$; $E^0_{cell} = 0.01$ V

$$Sn + Pb^{2+} \longrightarrow Sn^{2+} + Pb$$

$$E = E^0_{cell} - \frac{0.06}{n} \log \frac{[P]}{[R]}$$

$$0 = 0.01 - \frac{0.06}{2} \log \frac{[Sn^{2+}]}{[Pb^{2+}]}$$

$$0.01 = \frac{0.06}{2} \log \frac{[Sn^{2+}]}{[Pb^{2+}]}$$

$$\frac{1}{3} = \log \frac{[Sn^{2+}]}{[Pb^{2+}]}$$

$$\frac{[Sb^{2+}]}{[Pb^{2+}]} = 10^{1/3} = 2.15$$

48. (6.25) $\Delta U = nC_v\Delta T$

$5000 = 4 \times C_v (500 - 300)$

$C_v = 6.25 \ JK^{-1} \ mol^{-1}$

49. (20.0)

(Trigonal bipyramidal)	(Square pyramidal)
$\angle 120° = 3$; $\angle 90° = 6$;	$\angle 90° = 8$; $\angle 180° = 2$
$\angle 180° = 1$	$\Rightarrow$ Total = 10
$\Rightarrow$ Total = 10	

Total number of 180°, 90° and 120° L–M–L bond angles
$= 10 + 10 = 20$

50. (2130)

$NaClO_3(s) + Fe(s) \longrightarrow NaCl(s) + FeO(s) + O_2(g)$

Moles of $NaClO_3$ = Moles of O_2

Moles of $O_2 = \dfrac{PV}{RT} = \dfrac{1 \times 492}{0.082 \times 300} = 20$ mol

Mass of $NaClO_3 = 20 \times 106.5 = 2130$ g

MATHEMATICS

51. **(1)** Using L' Hospital rule,

$$\lim_{x \to 0} \frac{x\sin(10x)}{1} = 0$$

52. **(4)** Given equation of curve is

$$x^2 + 2xy - 3y^2 = 0$$
$$\Rightarrow 2x + 2y + 2xy' - 6yy' = 0$$
$$\Rightarrow x + y + xy' - 3yy' = 0$$
$$\Rightarrow y'(x - 3y) = -(x + y)$$
$$\Rightarrow \frac{dy}{dx} = \frac{x + y}{3y - x}$$

Slope of normal $= \dfrac{-dx}{dy} = \dfrac{x - 3y}{x - 3y}$

Normal at point $(2, 2) = \dfrac{2 - 6}{2 + 2} = -1$

Equation of normal to curve $= y - 2 = -1\,(x - 2)$
$$\Rightarrow x + y = 4$$
$\therefore$ Perpendicular distance from origin

$$= \left|\frac{0 + 0 - 4}{\sqrt{2}}\right| = 2\sqrt{2}$$

53. **(3)** $\vec{a} \times (\vec{b} \times \vec{c}) = \vec{a} \times (\vec{b} \times \vec{a})$

$$\Rightarrow -(\vec{a}.\vec{b})\vec{c} = (\vec{a}.\vec{a})\vec{b} - (\vec{a}.\vec{b})\vec{a}$$
$$\Rightarrow -4\vec{c} = 6(\hat{i} - \hat{j} + \hat{k}) - 4(\hat{i} - 2\hat{j} - \hat{k})$$
$$\Rightarrow -4\vec{c} = 2\hat{i} - 2\hat{j} + 2\hat{k}$$
$$\Rightarrow \vec{c} = \frac{1}{2}(\hat{i} + \hat{j} + \hat{k})$$
$$\Rightarrow \vec{b}.\vec{c} = -\frac{1}{2}$$

54. **(1)** Point of intersection of $y = x^2$ and $y = -2x + 3$ is obtained by $x^2 + 2x - 3 = 0$

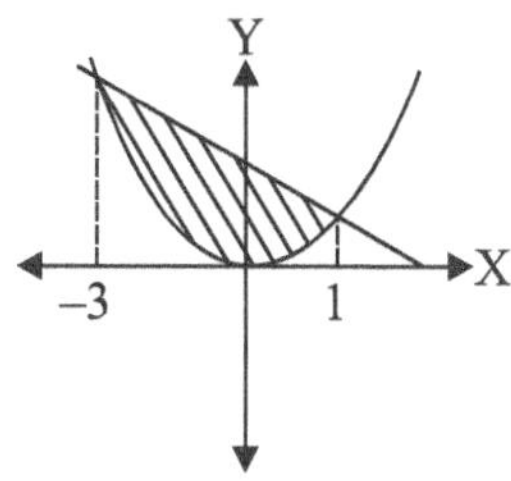

$$\Rightarrow x = -3, 1$$

So, required area $= \displaystyle\int_{-3}^{1} (\text{line} - \text{parabola})\,dz$

$$= \int_{-3}^{1} (3 - 2x - x^2)\,dx$$

$$= \left[3x - x^2 - \frac{x^3}{3}\right]_{-3}^{1}$$

$$= (3)4 - 2\left(\frac{1^2 - 3^2}{2}\right) - \left(\frac{1^3 + 3^3}{3}\right)$$

$$= 12 + 8 - \frac{28}{3} = \frac{32}{3}$$

55. **(3)** Characteristics equation of matrix 'A' is $|A - \lambda I| = 0$

$$\begin{vmatrix} 2 - \lambda & 2 \\ 9 & 4 - \lambda \end{vmatrix} = 0 \quad \Rightarrow \quad \lambda^2 - 6\lambda - 10 = 0$$

$$\therefore \quad A^2 - 6A - 10I = 0$$
$$\Rightarrow A^{-1}(A^2) - 6A^{-1} - 10IA^{-1} = 0$$
$$\Rightarrow 10A^{-1} = A - 6I$$

56. **(1)** Let $x_1, x_2, \ldots, x_{20}$ be 20 observations, then

$$\text{Mean} = \frac{x_1 + x_2 + \ldots + x_{20}}{20} = 10$$

$$\Rightarrow \frac{\displaystyle\sum_{i=1}^{20} x_i}{20} = 10 \qquad\qquad \ldots\text{(i)}$$

$$\text{Variance} = \frac{\Sigma x_i^2}{n} - (\bar{x})^2$$

$$\Rightarrow \frac{\Sigma x_i^2}{20} - 100 = 4 \qquad\qquad \ldots\text{(ii)}$$

$$\Sigma x_i^2 = 104 \times 20 = 2080$$

$$\text{Actual mean} = \frac{200 - 9 + 11}{20} = \frac{202}{20}$$

$$\text{Variance} = \frac{2080 - 81 + 121}{20} - \left(\frac{202}{20}\right)^2$$

$$= \frac{2120}{20} - (10.1)^2 = 106 - 102.01 = 3.99$$

57. **(1)** Since, $x^2 = 4b(y + b)$
$$x^2 = 4by + 4b^2$$
$$2x = 4by'$$
$$\Rightarrow b = \frac{x}{2y'}$$

So, differential equation is

$$x^2 = \frac{2x}{y'}.y + \left(\frac{x}{y'}\right)^2$$

$$x(y')^2 = 2yy' + x$$

58. **(2)** Let the hyperbola is $\dfrac{x^2}{a^2} - \dfrac{y^2}{b^2} = 1$

If a hyperbola passes through vertices at $(\pm 6, 0)$, then

$\therefore \quad a = 6$

As hyperbola passes through the point $P(10, 16)$

$\therefore \quad \dfrac{100}{36} - \dfrac{256}{b^2} = 1 \;\Rightarrow\; b^2 = 144$

$\therefore \quad$ Required hyperbola is $\dfrac{x^2}{36} - \dfrac{y^2}{144} = 1$

Equation of normal is $\dfrac{a^2 x}{x_1} + \dfrac{b^2 y}{y_1} = a^2 + b^2$

$\therefore \quad$ At P(10, 16) normal is

$\dfrac{36x}{10} + \dfrac{144y}{16} = 36 + 144$

$\therefore \quad 2x + 5y = 100.$

59. (4) $(\sim p \wedge q) \to (p \vee q)$

$\Rightarrow \;\; \sim \{(\sim p \wedge q) \wedge (\sim p \wedge \sim q)\}$

$\Rightarrow \;\; \sim \{\sim p \wedge f\}$

60. (4) $T_{10} = \dfrac{1}{20} = a + 9d$ ...(i)

$T_{20} = \dfrac{1}{10} = a + 19d$ ...(ii)

Solving equations (i) and (ii), we get

$a = \dfrac{1}{200}, d = \dfrac{1}{200}$

$\Rightarrow \;\; S_{200} = \dfrac{200}{2}\left[\dfrac{2}{200} + \dfrac{199}{200}\right] = \dfrac{201}{2} = 100\dfrac{1}{2}$

61. (2) Let $\alpha = \omega$, $b = 1 + \omega^3 + \omega^6 + \ldots = 101$

$a = (1 + \omega)(1 + \omega^2 + \omega^4 + \ldots \omega^{198} + \omega^{200})$

$= (1 + \omega)\dfrac{\left(1 - (\omega^2)^{101}\right)}{1 - \omega^2} = \dfrac{(\omega+1)(\omega^{202} - 1)}{(\omega^2 - 1)}$

$\Rightarrow \;\; a = \dfrac{(1+\omega)(1-\omega)}{1 - \omega^2} = 1$

Required equation $= x^2 - (101 + 1)x + (101) \times 1 = 0$

$\Rightarrow \;\; x^2 - 102x + 101 = 0$

62. (Bonus) For a constant function $f(x)$, option (1), (3) and (4) doesn't hold and by LMVT theorem, option (2) is incorrect.

63. (4) $P(\text{exactly one}) = \dfrac{2}{5}$

$\Rightarrow \;\; P(A) + P(B) - 2P(A \cap B) = \dfrac{2}{5}$

$P(A \text{ or } B) = P(A \cup B) = \dfrac{1}{2}$

$\Rightarrow \;\; P(A) + P(B) - P(A \cap B) = \dfrac{1}{2}$

$\therefore \quad P(A \cap B) = \dfrac{1}{2} - \dfrac{2}{5} = \dfrac{5-4}{10} = \dfrac{1}{10} = 0.10$

64. (2) $f(x) = \dfrac{1}{\sqrt{2x^3 - 9x^2 + 12x + 4}}$

$f'(x) = \dfrac{-1}{2}\left(\dfrac{(6x^2 - 18x + 12)}{(2x^3 - 9x^2 - 12x + 4)^{3/2}}\right)$

$= \dfrac{-6(x-1)(x-2)}{2(2x^3 - 9x^2 + 12x + 4)^{3/2}}$

$f(1) = \dfrac{1}{3}$ and $f(2) = \dfrac{1}{\sqrt{8}}$

It is increasing function

$\dfrac{1}{3} < I < \dfrac{1}{\sqrt{8}}$

$\dfrac{1}{9} < I^2 < \dfrac{1}{8}$

65. (2) $f(x)\begin{cases}\dfrac{x}{x^2+1}; & x \in (1,2) \\[2mm] \dfrac{2x}{x^2+1}; & x \in [2,3)\end{cases}$

$f'(x)\begin{cases}\dfrac{1-x^2}{1+x^2}; & x \in (1,2) \\[2mm] \dfrac{1-2x^2}{1+x^2}; & x \in [2,3)\end{cases}$

$\therefore \quad f(x)$ is a decreasing function

$\therefore \quad y \in \left(\dfrac{2}{5}, \dfrac{1}{2}\right) \cup \left(\dfrac{6}{10}, \dfrac{4}{5}\right]$

$\Rightarrow \;\; y \in \left(\dfrac{2}{5}, \dfrac{1}{2}\right) \cup \left(\dfrac{3}{5}, \dfrac{4}{5}\right]$

66. (2) $\vec{n} = \dfrac{-7}{3} - 1, \dfrac{-4}{3} - 2, \dfrac{-1}{3} - 3$

$\vec{n} = \dfrac{10}{3}, \dfrac{10}{3}, \dfrac{10}{3}$

D.r of normal to the plane $(1, 1, 1)$

Midpoint of P and Q is $\left(\dfrac{-2}{3}, \dfrac{1}{3}, \dfrac{4}{3}\right)$

$\therefore \quad$ Equation of required plane Q

$\vec{r}.\vec{n} = \vec{a}.\vec{n}$

$\vec{r}.(\hat{i} + \hat{j} + \hat{k}) = \dfrac{-2}{3} + \dfrac{1}{3} + \dfrac{4}{3}$

$\therefore \quad$ Equation of plane is $x + y + z = 1$

67. (3) $D = \begin{vmatrix} \lambda & 2 & 2 \\ 2\lambda & 3 & 5 \\ 4 & \lambda & 6 \end{vmatrix}$

$D = \lambda^2 + 6\lambda - 16$

$D = (\lambda + 8)(2 - \lambda)$

For no solutions, $D = 0$

$\Rightarrow \lambda = -8, 2$

when $\lambda = 2$

$$D_1 = \begin{vmatrix} 5 & 2 & 2 \\ 8 & 3 & 5 \\ 10 & 2 & 6 \end{vmatrix}$$

$= 5[18 - 10] - 2[48 - 50] + 2(16 - 30]$

$= 40 + 4 - 28 \neq 0$

There exist no solutions for $\lambda = 2$

68. (2) Let $3^x = y$

$\therefore \quad y(y - 1) + 2 = |y - 1| + |y - 2|$

Case 1: when $y > 2$

$y^2 - y + 2 = y - 1 + y - 2$

$y^2 - 3y + 5 = 0$

$\because \quad D < 0$ [$\therefore$ Equation not satisfy.]

Case 2: when $1 \leq y \leq 2$

$y^2 - y^2 + 2 = y - 1 - y + 2$

$y^2 - y + 1 = 0$

$\because \quad D < 0$ [$\therefore$ Equation not satisfy.]

Case 3: when $y \leq 1$

$y^2 - y + 2 = -y + 1 - y + 2$

$y^2 + y - 1 = 0$

$\therefore y = \dfrac{-1 + \sqrt{5}}{2}$

$= \dfrac{-1 - \sqrt{5}}{2}$ [$\therefore$ Equation not Satisfy]

$\therefore$ Only one $-1 + \dfrac{\sqrt{5}}{2}$ satisfy equation

69. (4) Using Binomial expansion

$(x + a)^n + (x - a)^n = 2(T_1 + T_3 + T_5 + T_7 ...)$

$\therefore \left(x + \sqrt{x^2 - 1}\right)^6 + \left(x - \sqrt{x^2 - 1}\right)^6 = 2(T_1 + T_3 + T_5 + T_7)$

$2[{}^6C_0 x^5 + {}^6C_2 x^4 (x^2 - 1) + {}^6C_4 x^2 (x^2 - 1)^2$
$\qquad\qquad\qquad\qquad + {}^6C_6 (x^2 - 1)^3]$

$= 2[x^6 + 15(x^6 - x^4) + 15x^2(x^4 - 2x^2 + 1)$
$\qquad\qquad\qquad\qquad + (-1 + 3x^2 - 3x^4 + x^6)]$

$= 2(32x^6 - 48x^4 + 18x^2 - 1)$

$\alpha = -96$ and $\beta = 36$

$\therefore \quad \alpha - \beta = -132$

70. (3) Slope of tangent of $x^2 + y^2 = 1$ at $\left(\dfrac{1}{\sqrt{2}}, \dfrac{1}{\sqrt{2}}\right)$

$\dfrac{1}{\sqrt{2}} x + \dfrac{1}{\sqrt{2}} y - 1 = 0$

$x + y\sqrt{2} = 0$, which is perpendicular to $x - y + c = 0$

At $\left(\dfrac{1}{\sqrt{2}}, \dfrac{1}{\sqrt{2}}\right)$ which is tangent of $(x - 3)^2 + y^2 = 1$

So, $m = 1 \quad \Rightarrow \quad y = x + c$

Now, distance of $(3, 0)$ from $y = x + c$ is

$\left| \dfrac{c + 3}{\sqrt{2}} \right| = 1$

$\Rightarrow \quad c = -3 \pm \sqrt{2}$

$\Rightarrow \quad (c + 3)^2 = 2$

$\Rightarrow \quad c^2 + 6c + 9 = 2$

$\therefore \quad c^2 + 6c + 7 = 0$

71. (0.5) Let the coordinates of $P = P(t^2, t)$

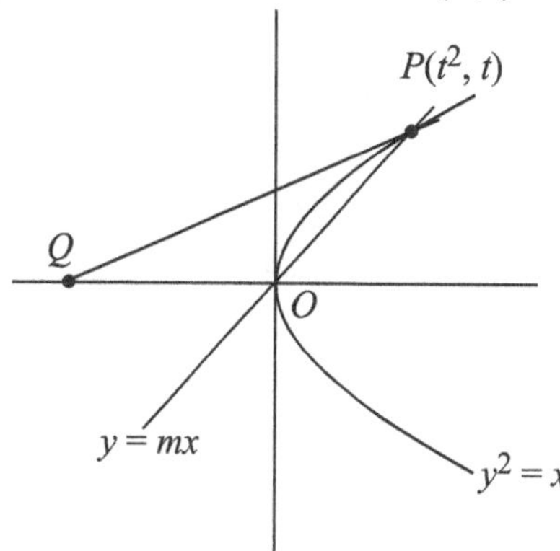

Tangent at $P(t^2, t)$ is $ty = \dfrac{x + t^2}{2}$

$\Rightarrow \quad 2ty = x + t^2$

$Q(-t^2, 0),\ O(0, 0)$

$\therefore \quad$ Area of $\triangle OPQ = \dfrac{1}{2} \begin{vmatrix} 0 & 0 & 1 \\ t^2 & t & 1 \\ -t^2 & 0 & 1 \end{vmatrix} = 4$

$\Rightarrow \quad |t|^3 = 8$

$t = \pm 2 \ (t > 0)$

$\therefore \quad 4y = x + 4$ is a tangent

$\therefore \quad P$ is $(4, 2)$

Now, $y = mx \quad \therefore \quad m = \dfrac{1}{2}$

72. (2454) EXAMINATION

2N, 2A, 2I, E, X, M, T, O

Case I : If all are different, then

$${}^8p_4 = \dfrac{8!}{4!} = 8.7.6.5 = 1680$$

Case II : If two are same and two are different, then

$${}^3C_1 \cdot {}^7C_2 \cdot \dfrac{4!}{2!} = 3.21.12 = 756$$

Case III : If two are same and other two are same, then

$${}^3C_2 \cdot \dfrac{4!}{2!2!} = 3.6 = 18$$

$\therefore \quad$ Total cases $= 1680 + 756 + 18 = 2454$

73. **(504)** $\left[\sum_{n=1}^{7}\dfrac{n(n+1)(2n+1)}{4}\right]\dfrac{1}{4}\left[\sum_{n=1}^{7}(2n^3+3n^2+n)\right]$

$$=\dfrac{1}{4}\left[2\left(\dfrac{7.8}{2}\right)^2+3\left(\dfrac{7.8.15}{6}\right)+\dfrac{7.8}{2}\right]$$

$$\Rightarrow\quad \dfrac{1}{4}[2\times49\times16+28\times15+28]$$

$$=\dfrac{1}{4}[1568+420+28]=504$$

74. **(3)** Let $f(x)=ax^3+bx^2+cx+d$

$$f(-1)=10 \text{ and } f(1)=-6$$

$$-a+b-c+d=10 \qquad\qquad …(i)$$

$$a+b+c+d=-6 \qquad\qquad …(ii)$$

Solving equations (i) and (ii), we get

$$a=\dfrac{1}{4}, d=\dfrac{35}{4}$$

$$b=\dfrac{-3}{4}, c=-\dfrac{9}{4}$$

$$\Rightarrow\quad f(x)=a(x^3-3x^2-9x)+d$$

$$f'(x)=\dfrac{3}{4}\,(x^2-2x-3)=0$$

$\Rightarrow\quad x=3,-1$

Local minima exist at $x=3$

75. **(1)** $\dfrac{\sqrt{2}\sin\alpha}{\sqrt{2}\cos\alpha}=\dfrac{1}{7}$ and $\sqrt{\dfrac{1-\cos^2\beta}{2}}=\dfrac{1}{10}$

$$\Rightarrow\quad \dfrac{\sqrt{2}\sin\beta}{\sqrt{2}}=\dfrac{1}{\sqrt{10}}$$

$$\therefore\quad \tan\alpha=\dfrac{1}{7} \text{ and } \sin\beta=\dfrac{1}{\sqrt{10}}$$

$$\tan\beta=\dfrac{1}{3}$$

$$\therefore\quad \tan2\beta=\dfrac{2\tan\beta}{1-\tan^2\beta}=\dfrac{2.\dfrac{1}{3}}{1-\dfrac{1}{9}}=\dfrac{\dfrac{2}{3}}{\dfrac{8}{9}}=\dfrac{3}{4}$$

$$\tan(\alpha+2\beta)=\dfrac{\tan\alpha+\tan2\beta}{1-\tan\alpha\tan2\beta}$$

$$=\dfrac{\dfrac{1}{7}+\dfrac{3}{4}}{1-\dfrac{1}{7}.\dfrac{3}{4}}=\dfrac{\dfrac{4+21}{28}}{\dfrac{25}{28}}=1$$

PHYSICS

1. (1) Using Einstein's photoelectric equation,

$$E = \omega_0 + KE_{max}$$
$$\Rightarrow \omega_0 = KE_{max} - E$$

$$p = \sqrt{2mKE} \Rightarrow KE = \frac{p^2}{2m}$$

$$r = \frac{p}{eB} \Rightarrow p = reB$$

$$K_{max} = \frac{r^2 e^2 B^2}{2m}$$

$$KE_{max} = \frac{12420}{\lambda} - \omega_0$$

$$\Rightarrow \omega_0 = \frac{12420}{6561} - \frac{r^2 eB^2}{2m}(In\,eV)$$

$$= 1.89(eV) - \frac{\left(10^{-4}\right)\left(1.6\times10^{-19}\right)9\times10^5}{2\times9.07\times10^{-31}}$$

$$= (1.89 - 0.79)\,eV = 1.1\,eV$$

2. (2) Dimension of $[h] = [ML^2T^{-1}]$

$[C] = [LT^{-1}]$

$[G] = [M^{-1}L^3T^{-2}]$

Hence dimension of

$$\left[\sqrt{\frac{hC^5}{G}}\right] = \frac{\left[ML^2T^{-1}\right]\cdot\left[L^5T^{-5}\right]}{\left[M^{-1}L^3T^{-2}\right]}$$

$$= [ML^2T^{-2}] = \text{energy}$$

3. (3) Work done, $W = \int \vec{F}\cdot\vec{ds}$

$$= \left(-x\hat{i} + y\hat{j}\right)\cdot\left(dx\,\hat{i} + dy\hat{j}\right)$$

$$\Rightarrow W = -\int_1^0 x\,dx + \int_0^1 y\,dy$$

$$= \left(0 + \frac{1}{2}\right) + \frac{1}{2} = 1J$$

4. (2) According to question, area of cross-section at A, aA = 40 cm^2 and at B, aB = 20 cm^2

Let velocity of liquid flow at A, = V_A and at B, = V_B

Using equation of continuity $a_A V_A = a_B V_B$

$$40V_A = 20V_B$$
$$\Rightarrow 2V_A = V_B$$

Now, using Bernoulli's equation

$$P_A + \frac{1}{2}\rho V_A^2 = P_B + \frac{1}{2}\rho V_B^2 \Rightarrow P_A - P_B = \frac{1}{2}\rho\left(V_B^2 - V_A^2\right)$$

$$\Rightarrow \Delta P = \frac{1}{2}1000\left(V_B^2 - \frac{V_B^2}{4}\right) \Rightarrow \Delta P = 500\times\frac{3V_B^2}{4}$$

$$\Rightarrow V_B = \sqrt{\frac{(\Delta P)\times4}{1500}} = \sqrt{\frac{(700)\times4}{1500}}\,\text{m/s} = 1.37\times10^2\,\text{cm/s}$$

Volume flow rate $Q = a_B \times v_B$

$$= 20 \times 100 \times V_B = 2732 \text{ cm}^3/\text{s} \approx 2720 \text{ cm}^3/\text{s}$$

5. (1) Let a be the radius of the wire

Magnetic field at point A (inside)

$$B_A = \frac{\mu_0 ir}{2\pi a^2} = \frac{\mu_0 i\dfrac{a}{3}}{2\pi a^2} = \frac{\mu_0 i}{\pi a^2}\frac{a}{6} = \frac{\mu_0 i}{6\pi a}$$

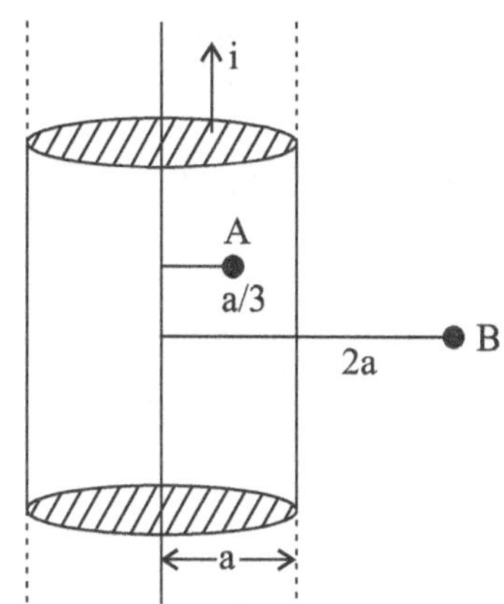

Magnetic field at point B (outside)

$$B_B = \frac{\mu_0 i}{2\pi(2a)}$$

$$\therefore \frac{B_A}{B_B} = \frac{\dfrac{\mu_0 i}{6\pi a}}{\dfrac{\mu_0 i}{2\pi(2a)}} = \frac{4}{6} = \frac{2}{3}$$

6. (4) Given: $\vec{E}_1 = E_0\hat{j}\cos\left(\omega t - kx\right)$

i.e., Travelling in $+ve$ x-direction $\vec{E}\times\vec{B}$ should be in x-direction

$\therefore$ $\vec{B}$ is in $\hat{K}$

$$\therefore \vec{B}_1 = \frac{E_0}{C}\cos\left(\omega t - kx\right)\hat{k} \quad \left(\because B_0 = \frac{E_0}{C}\right)$$

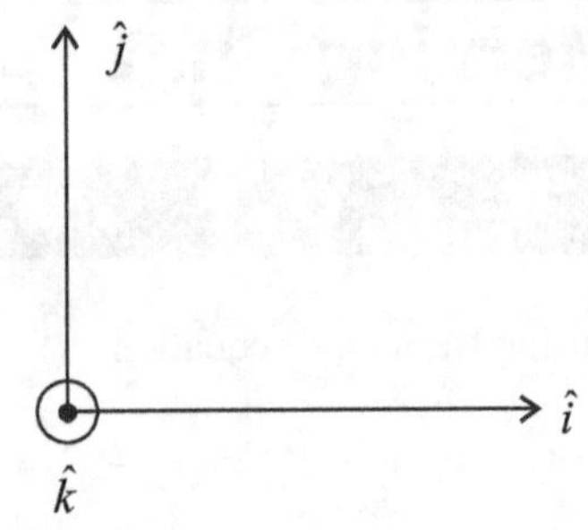

$$\vec{E}_2 = E_0 \hat{k} \cos(\omega t - ky)$$

$$\vec{B}_2 = \frac{E_0}{C} \hat{i} \cos(\omega t - ky)$$

$\therefore$ Travelling in $+ve$ y-axis

$\vec{E} \times \vec{B}$ should be in y-axis

$\therefore$ Net force $\vec{F} = q\vec{E} + q(\vec{v} \times \vec{B})$

$$q(\vec{E}_1 + \vec{E}_2) + q(0.8c\hat{j} \times (\vec{B}_1 + \vec{B}_2))$$

If $t = 0$ and $x = y = 0$

$$\vec{E}_1 = E_0 \hat{j} \qquad \vec{E}_2 = E_0 \hat{k}$$

$$\vec{B}_1 = \frac{E_0}{c} \hat{k} \qquad \vec{B}_2 = \frac{E_0}{c} \hat{i}$$

$$\therefore \vec{F}_{net} = qE_0(\hat{j} + \hat{k}) + q \times 0.8c \times \frac{E_0}{C} \hat{j} \times (\hat{k} + \hat{i})$$

$$= qE_0(\hat{j} + \hat{k}) + 0.8qE_0(\hat{i} - \hat{k})$$

$$= qE_0(0.8\hat{i} + \hat{j} + 0.2\hat{k})$$

7. **(2)** Electric field at A $\left(R' = \dfrac{R}{2} \right)$

$$E_A . ds = \frac{q}{\varepsilon_0}$$

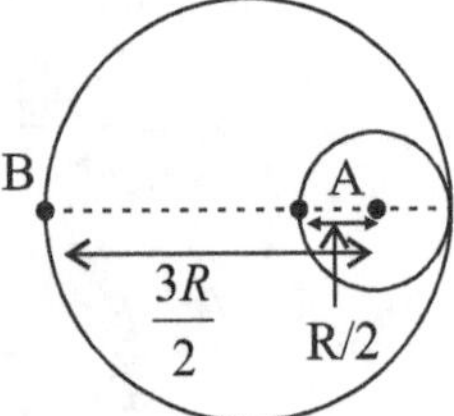

$$\Rightarrow \vec{E}_A = \frac{\rho \times \dfrac{4}{3}\pi \left(\dfrac{R}{2} \right)^3}{\varepsilon_0 \cdot 4\pi \left(\dfrac{R}{2} \right)^2}$$

$$\Rightarrow \vec{E}_A = \frac{\sigma(R/2)}{3\varepsilon_0} = \left(\frac{\sigma R}{6\varepsilon_0} \right)$$

Electric fields at 'B'

$$\vec{E}_B = \frac{k \times \rho \times \dfrac{4}{3}\pi R^3}{R^2} - \frac{k \times \rho \times \dfrac{4}{3}\pi \left(\dfrac{R}{2} \right)^3}{\left(\dfrac{3R}{2} \right)^2}$$

$$\Rightarrow \vec{E}_B = \frac{\sigma R}{3\varepsilon_0} - \left(\frac{1}{4\pi\varepsilon_0} \right) \frac{(\sigma)}{\left(\dfrac{3R}{2} \right)^2} \frac{4\pi}{3} \left(\frac{R}{2} \right)^3$$

$$\Rightarrow \vec{E}_B = \frac{\sigma R}{3\varepsilon_0} - \frac{\sigma R}{54\varepsilon_0}$$

$$\Rightarrow E_B = \frac{17}{54}\left(\frac{\sigma R}{\varepsilon_0} \right)$$

$$\left| \frac{E_A}{E_B} \right| = \frac{1 \times 54}{6 \times 17} = \left(\frac{9}{17} \right) = \frac{9}{17} \times \frac{2}{2} = \frac{18}{34}$$

8. **(1)**

9. **(3)** Since $\vec{r} \cdot \vec{p} = 0$

$\vec{E}$ must be antiparallel to $\vec{p}$

$\therefore \hat{E}$ is parallel to $\left(\hat{i} + 3\hat{j} - 2\hat{k} \right)$

10. **(4)** Specific heat of gas at constant volume

$$C_v = \frac{1}{2} fR; f = \text{degree of freedom}$$

For gas A (diatomic)

$f = 5$ (3 translational + 2 rotational)

$$\therefore C_v^A = \frac{5}{2}R$$

For gas B (diatomic) in addition to (3 translational + 2 rotational) 2 vibrational degree of freedom.

$$\therefore \quad C_v^B = \frac{7}{2}R \text{ Hence } \frac{C_v^A}{C_v^B} = \frac{\dfrac{5}{2}R}{\dfrac{7}{2}R} = \frac{5}{7}$$

11. **(3)** As per question, when KE of particle E, wavelength λ and when KE becomes $E + \Delta E$ wavelength becomes $\lambda/2$

Using, $\lambda = \dfrac{h}{\sqrt{2mKE}}$

$$\frac{\lambda}{2} = \frac{h}{\sqrt{2m(KE + \Delta E)}}$$

$$\Rightarrow \frac{\lambda}{/2} = \sqrt{\frac{KE + \Delta E}{KE}}$$

$$\Rightarrow 4 = \frac{KE + \Delta E}{KE}$$

$$\Rightarrow \quad 4KE - KE = \Delta E$$

$$\therefore \quad \Delta E = 3\,KE = 3\,E$$

12. **(3)** For process $3 \to 1$ volume is constant

$\therefore$ Graph given in option (4) is wrong.

And process $1 \rightarrow 2$ is adiabatic $\therefore$ graph in option (1) is wrong

$\because \quad v = $ constant

$P\uparrow, T\uparrow$

For Process $2 \rightarrow 3$ Pressure constant *i.e.*, $P = $ constant

$\therefore \quad V\downarrow T\downarrow$

Hence graph (3) is the correct $V - T$ graph of given $P - V$ graph

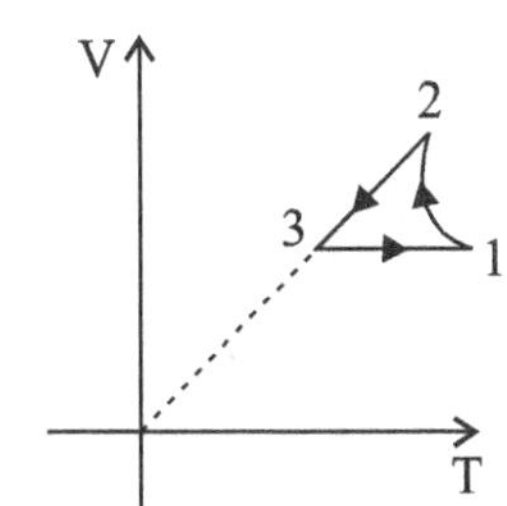

13. (2)

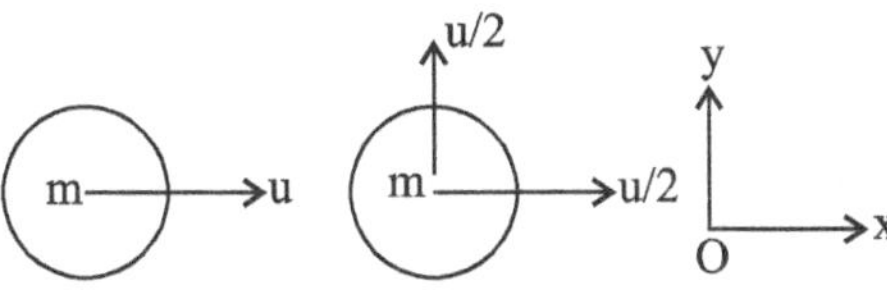

x-direction

$$mu + \frac{mu}{2} = 2mv_x' \Rightarrow V_x' = \frac{3u}{4}$$

y-direction $0 + \dfrac{mu}{2} = 2mv_y' \Rightarrow v_y' = \dfrac{u}{4}$

$$K.E._i = \frac{1}{2}m\,u^2 + \frac{1}{2}m\left[\left(\frac{u}{2}\right)^2 + \left(\frac{u}{2}\right)^2\right]$$

$$= \frac{1}{2}mu^2 + \frac{mu^2}{4} = \frac{3mu^2}{4}$$

$$K.E._f = \frac{1}{2}(2m)\left(v_x'\right)^2 + \frac{1}{2}(2m)\left(v_y'\right)^2$$

$$= \frac{1}{2}2m\left[\left(\frac{3u}{4}\right)^2 + \left(\frac{u}{4}\right)^2\right] = \frac{5}{8}mu^2$$

$\therefore$ Loss in $KE = KE_f - KE_i$

$$= mu^2\left(\frac{6}{8} - \frac{5}{8}\right) = \frac{mu^2}{8}$$

14. (2) From circuit diagram,

$$\frac{1}{R_1} = \frac{1}{1} + \frac{1}{4} \Rightarrow R_1 = \frac{4}{5}$$

$$\frac{1}{R_2} = \frac{1}{2} + \frac{1}{3} \Rightarrow R_2 = \frac{6}{5}$$

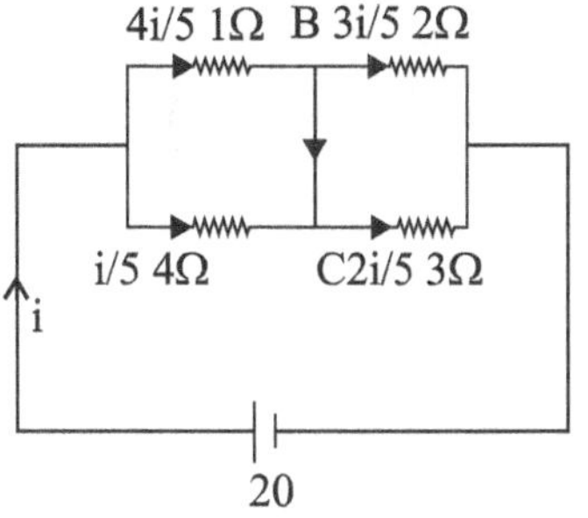

$$R_{\text{eff}} = R_1 + R_2 = \frac{4}{5} + \frac{6}{5} = 2\Omega$$

$$i = \frac{v}{R_{\text{eff}}} = \frac{20}{2} = 10A$$

$$\therefore \quad I_{BC} = \frac{4i}{5} - \frac{3i}{5} = \frac{i}{5} = 2A$$

15. (1)

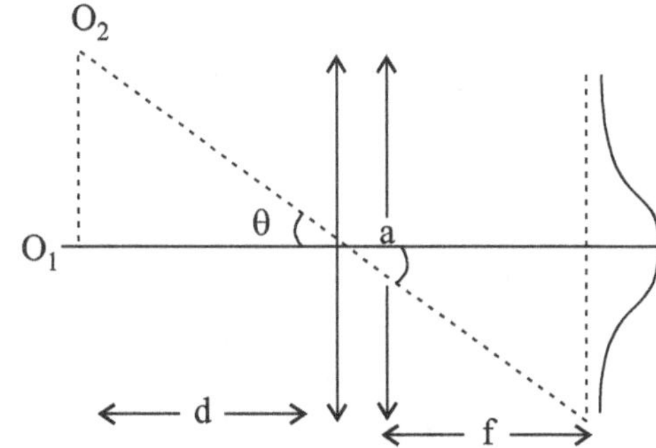

Smallest angular separation between two distant objects here moon and earth,

$$\theta = 1.22\frac{\lambda}{a}$$

a = aperture diameter of telescope

Distance $O_1O_2 = (\theta)d$

Minimum separation between objects on the surface of moon,

$$= \left(1.22\frac{\lambda}{a}\right)d$$

$$= \frac{(1.22)(5500\times10^{-10})\times4\times10^5\times10^3}{5}$$

$$= 5368 \times 10^{-2}\text{ m} = 53.68\text{ m} \approx 60\text{ m}$$

16. (4) When screw on a screw-gauge is given six rotations, it moves by 3mm on the main scale

$$\therefore \quad \text{Pitch} = \frac{3}{6} = 0.5\,\text{mm}$$

$$\therefore \quad \text{Least count L.C.} = \frac{\text{Pitch}}{CSD} = \frac{0.5\,\text{mm}}{50}$$

$$= \frac{1}{100}\text{mm} = 0.01\,mm = 0.001\,cm$$

17. **(3)** (A) By work energy theorem

$$W_{mg} + W_{ele} = \frac{1}{2}m(2v)^2 - \frac{1}{2}m(v)^2$$

$$0 + qE_0 2a = \frac{3}{2}mv^2$$

$$\Rightarrow E_0 = \frac{3}{4}\frac{mv^2}{qa}$$

(B) Rate of work done at P = power of electric force

$$= qE_0 V = \frac{3}{4}\frac{mv^3}{a}$$

(C) At, Q, $\dfrac{dw}{dt} = 0$ for both the fields

(D) The difference of magnitude of angular momentum of the particle at P and Q,

$$\Delta \vec{L} = \left(-m2v2a\hat{k}\right) - \left(-mva\hat{k}\right)$$

$$\left|\Delta \vec{L}\right| = 3mva$$

18. **(1)** Moment of inertia,

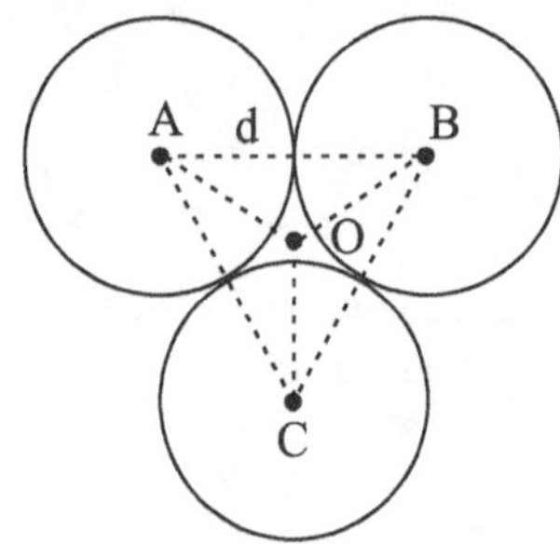

$$I_1 = \frac{2}{5}m\left(\frac{d}{2}\right)^2 + m(AO)^2$$

and $AO = \dfrac{d}{\sqrt{3}}$

Moment of inertia about 'O'

$$I_0 = 3I_1 = 3\left[\frac{2}{5}m\left(\frac{d}{2}\right)^2 + m\left(\frac{d}{\sqrt{3}}\right)^2\right]$$

$$\Rightarrow I_0 = \frac{13}{10}Md^2$$

And $I_A = 2\left[\dfrac{2}{5}M\left(\dfrac{d}{2}\right)^2 + Md^2\right] + \dfrac{2}{5}M\left(\dfrac{d}{2}\right)^2$

$$\Rightarrow I_A = \frac{23}{10}Md^2$$

$$\therefore \frac{I_O}{I_A} = \frac{\frac{13}{10}Md^2}{\frac{23}{10}Md^2} = \frac{13}{23}$$

19. **(4)** Apparent depth,

$$D = \frac{t_1}{\mu_1} + \frac{t_2}{\mu_2} = \frac{h}{\sqrt{2}} + \frac{h}{2\sqrt{2}} = \frac{3h}{2\sqrt{2}} = \frac{3h\sqrt{2}}{4}$$

20. **(4)** From law of conservation of momentum, $\vec{p}_i = \vec{p}_f$

$$m_1 u_1 + m_2 u_2 = MV_f$$

$$\Rightarrow v_f = \frac{\left(mv + \dfrac{mv}{4}\right)}{\dfrac{3m}{2}} = \frac{5v}{6}$$

Clearly, $v_f < v_i$ $\therefore$ Path will be elliptical

21. **(12)** Right hand diode is reversed biased and left hand diode is forward biased.

Hence Voltage at 'A'

$$V_A = 12.7 - 0.7 = 12 \text{ volt}$$

22. **(10)** Given $dI = 0.25 - 0 = 0.25$ A

$dt = 0.025$ ms

Induced voltage

$E_{ind} = 100$ v

Self-inductance, L = ?

Using, $E_{\text{ind}} = \dfrac{\Delta \phi}{\Delta t}$

$$\Rightarrow 100 = \frac{L(0.25 - 0)}{.025 \times 10^{-3}}$$

$$\Rightarrow L = 10^{-3} \text{ H} = 10 \text{ mH}$$

23. **(3)** Distance X varies with time t as $x^2 = at^2 + 2bt + c$

$$\Rightarrow 2x\frac{dx}{dt} = 2at + 2b$$

$$\Rightarrow x\frac{dx}{dt} = at + b \Rightarrow \frac{dx}{dt} = \frac{(at+b)}{x}$$

$$\Rightarrow x\frac{d^2x}{dt^2} + \left(\frac{dx}{dt}\right)^2 = a$$

$$\Rightarrow \frac{d^2x}{dt^2} = \frac{a - \left(\dfrac{dx}{dt}\right)^2}{x} = \frac{a - \left(\dfrac{at+b}{x}\right)^2}{x}$$

$$= \frac{ax^2 - (at+b)^2}{x^3} = \frac{ac - b^2}{x^3}$$

$$\Rightarrow \quad a \propto x^{-3}$$

Hence, n = 3

24. (4) Given : Wire length, $l = 0.3$ m

Mass of the body, m = 10 kg

Breaking stress, $\sigma = 4.8 \times 10^7$ Nm^{-2}

Area of cross-section, a = 10^{-2} cm^2

Maximum angular speed ω = ?

$T = Ml\omega^2$

$$\sigma = \frac{T}{A} = \frac{ml\omega^2}{A}$$

$$\frac{ml\omega^2}{A} \leq 48 \times 10^7$$

$$\Rightarrow \omega^2 \leq \frac{\left(48 \times 10^7\right)A}{ml}$$

$$\Rightarrow \omega^2 \leq \frac{\left(48 \times 10^7\right)\left(10^{-6}\right)}{10 \times 3} = 16 \Rightarrow \omega_{max} = 4 \text{ rad/s}$$

25. (15) Here, length of bar, l = 1 m

angle, $\theta = 30°$

$$\Delta PE = \Delta KE \text{ or } mgh = \frac{1}{2}I\omega^2$$

$$\Rightarrow (mg)\frac{l}{2}\sin 30° = \frac{1}{2}\left(\frac{ml^2}{3}\right)\omega^2$$

$$\Rightarrow mg\frac{l}{2} \times \frac{1}{2} = \frac{1}{2}\left(\frac{ml^2}{3}\right)\omega^2$$

$$\Rightarrow \omega = \sqrt{15} \text{ rad/s}$$

CHEMISTRY

26. (3) $$PbCl_2 \rightleftharpoons Pb^{2+}(aq) + 2Cl^-(aq)$$

Given; $K_{sp} = 1.6 \times 10^{-5}$

$$[Pb^{2+}] = \frac{300 \times 0.134}{400} = 0.1005$$

$$[Cl^-] = \frac{100 \times 0.4}{400} = 0.1$$

$$Q = [Pb^{2+}][Cl^-]^2$$
$$= 0.1005 \times (0.1)^2$$
$$= 1.005 \times 10^{-3}$$

$$Q > K_{sp}$$

27. (1) In isomers of hydrocarbon heat of combustion is inversely proportional to the stability.

Stability order : $A > B > C$

Order of heat of combustion : $A < B < C$

28. (2) $$A + BO_2 \longrightarrow B + AO_2$$

$\Delta G = -ve$

when the temperature is above 1400 °C, A reduces BO_2.

29. (3) $_5B : 1s^2\ 2s^2\ 2p^1$

$_4Be : 1s^2\ 2s^2$

First ionisation enthalpy of B is lower than Be because Be has a stable electronic configuration. It required more energy to remove the first electron from $2s$ (in Be) than $2p$ (in B) because $2s\ e^-$ has more penetration power than $2p$. Therefore options (I), (II) and (III) are correct. Atomic radius of B is less than Be.

30. (1) $$\mu = \sqrt{n(n+2)} \text{ B.M.}$$

$$1.73 = \sqrt{n(n+2)}$$

$n = 1$

$$O_2^+ = \sigma 1s^2\ \sigma^* 1s^2\ \sigma 2s^2\ \sigma^* 2s^2\ \sigma 2p_z^2\ \pi 2p_x^2$$
$$= \pi 2p_y^2\ \pi^* 2p_x^1 = \pi^* 2p_y^\circ$$

$$O_2^- = \sigma 1s^2\ \sigma^* 1s^2\ \sigma 2s^2\ \sigma^* 2s^2\ \sigma 2p_z^2\ \pi 2p_x^2$$
$$= \pi 2p_y^2\ \pi^* 2p_x^2 = \pi^* 2p_y^1$$

31. (4) $2\pi r = n\lambda$

$$r = \frac{n^2 a_0}{Z}$$

$$2\pi \times \frac{4^2}{1} a_0 = 4\lambda$$

$$\lambda = 2\pi \times \frac{4}{1} a_0$$

$$\lambda = 8\pi a_0$$

32. (4) $CCl_4 \rightarrow$ Non-conductor in solid and liquid phase.

Melting point of CCl_4 is –23 °C. It does not conduct electricity in both solid and liquid state.

33. (2)

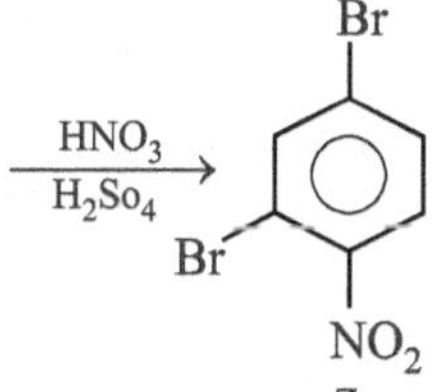

34. **(4)** $\mu = \sqrt{n(n+2)}$ B.M. $= 3.83$ B.M.

$n = 3$ (n = No. of unpaired e^-)

Therefore, oxidation number of Cr should be +3.

Hence complex is $Cr(H_2O)_6Cl_3$.

Complex shows geometrical isomerism therefore formula of complex is $[Cr(H_2O)_4Cl_2]Cl.2H_2O$.

IUPAC Name:

Tetraaquadichlorido chromium(III) Chloridedihydrate

35. **(1)** A – Aspartame

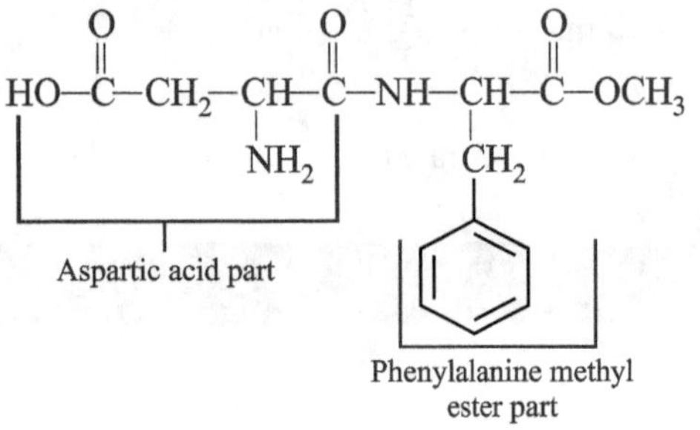

$$HO-\overset{\overset{O}{\|}}{C}-CH_2-\underset{\underset{NH_2}{|}}{CH}-\overset{\overset{O}{\|}}{C}-NH-\underset{\underset{CH_2}{|}}{CH}-\overset{\overset{O}{\|}}{C}-OCH_3$$

Aspartic acid part

Phenylalanine methyl ester part

B – Saccharine

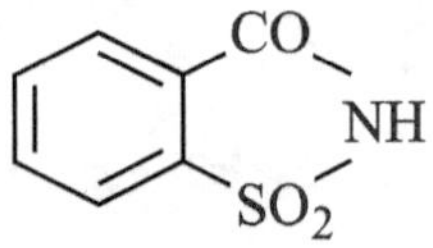

C – Sucralose

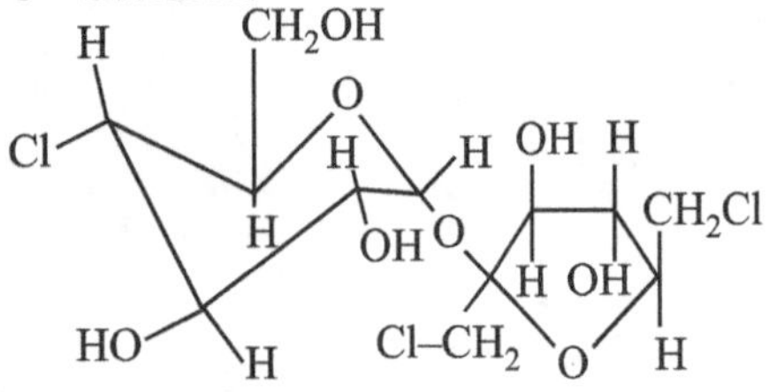

D – Alitame

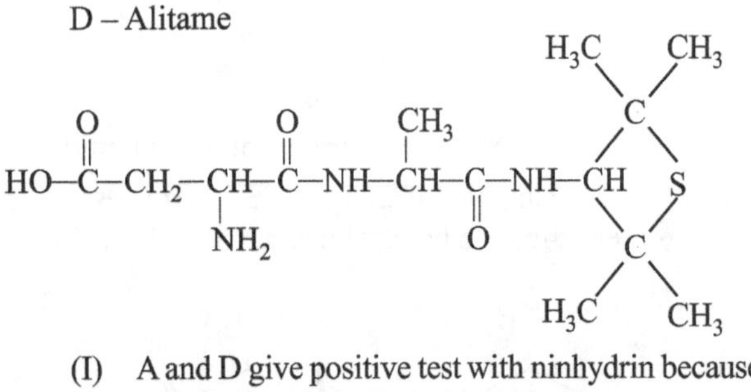

$$HO-\overset{\overset{O}{\|}}{C}-CH_2-\underset{\underset{NH_2}{|}}{CH}-\overset{\overset{O}{\|}}{C}-NH-\underset{\underset{CH_3}{|}}{CH}-\overset{\overset{O}{\|}}{C}-NH-CH$$

(I) A and D give positive test with ninhydrin because both have free carboxylic and amine groups.

(II) C form precipitate with $AgNO_3$ in the lassaigne extract of the sugar because it has chlorine atoms.

(III) B and D give positive test with sodium nitroprusside because both have sulphur atoms.

36. **(3)** Generally, non-metal oxides are acidic in nature and metal oxides are basic in nature, Al_2O_3 is amphoteric.

37. **(3)** $\Delta H_{atomisation} = \Delta H_{vap} + $ Bond energy

Hence $x > y$

38. **(2)** $Eu^{2+} : [Xe]4f^7$; $Ce^{3+} : [Xe]4f^1$

39. **(1)** $A \xrightarrow{700K(k_1)}$ Product

$A \xrightarrow[\text{Catalyst}]{500K(k_2)}$ Product

Given: $k_1 = k_2$

$$Ae^{-\frac{E_{a_1}}{RT_1}} = Ae^{-\frac{E_{a_2}}{RT_2}}$$

$$\frac{E_{a_1}}{T_1} = \frac{E_{a_2}}{T_2}$$

$$E_{a_2} = E_{a_1} - 30$$

$$\Rightarrow E_{a1} = E_{a_2} + 30$$

$$\frac{E_{a_2} + 30}{T_1} = \frac{E_{a_2}}{T_2}$$

$$\frac{E_{a_2} + 30}{700} = \frac{E_{a_2}}{500}$$

$$\Rightarrow 150 = 2E_{a_2}$$

$$E_{a_2} = 75 kJ/mol$$

40. **(3)** Basicity order can be determined by the cummulative effect of the factors on the electron density of concerned atom.

41. **(4)**

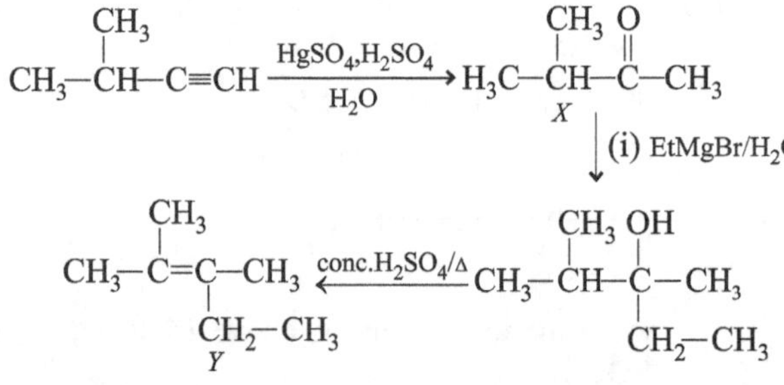

$$CH_3-\underset{\underset{CH_3}{|}}{CH}-C\equiv CH \xrightarrow[H_2O]{HgSO_4,H_2SO_4} H_3C-\underset{\underset{X}{}}{\overset{\overset{CH_3}{|}}{CH}}-\overset{\overset{O}{\|}}{C}-CH_3$$

$\downarrow$ (i) $EtMgBr/H_2O$

$$CH_3-\underset{\underset{\underset{Y}{CH_2-CH_3}}{|}}{\overset{\overset{CH_3}{|}}{C}}=C-CH_3 \xleftarrow{conc.H_2SO_4/\Delta} CH_3-\underset{\underset{CH_2-CH_3}{|}}{\overset{\overset{CH_3\ OH}{|\ \ |}}{CH-C}}-CH_3$$

42. **(3)** Aniline and phenol form complex with lewis acid. Chlorobenzene produces highest yield in Friedel craft reaction among the given options.

43. **(1)** In H_3PO_4 oxidation state of P is +5, which cannot be oxidised further to a higher oxidation state. Hence, it cannot act as reducing agent.

44. **(3)** Number of Geometrical isomers (n) in square planar $[Pd(F)(Cl)(Br)(I)]^{2-} = 3$

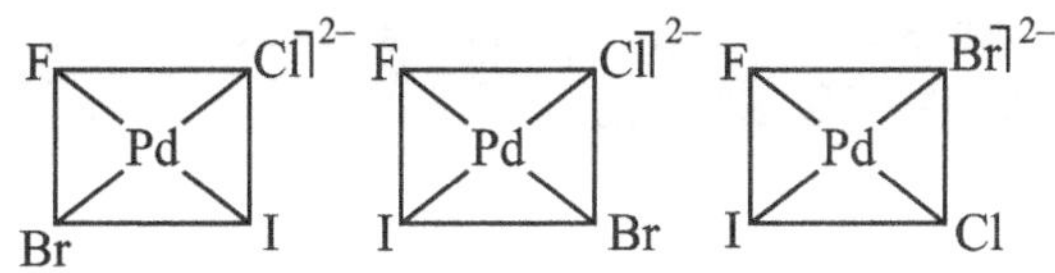

$[Fe(CN)_6]^{3-6} = [Fe(CN)_6]^{3-}$

$Fe^{3+} = 3d^5$

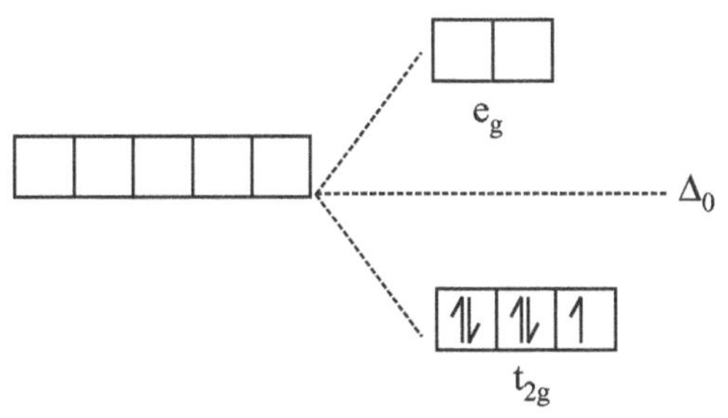

$\mu = \sqrt{n(n+2)} = 1.73$ B.M.

$CFSE = -0.4\,\Delta_0 \times nt_{2g} + 0.6\Delta_0 \times n_{eg}$

$= -0.4\,\Delta_0 \times 5 = -2.0\,\Delta_0$

45. (2)

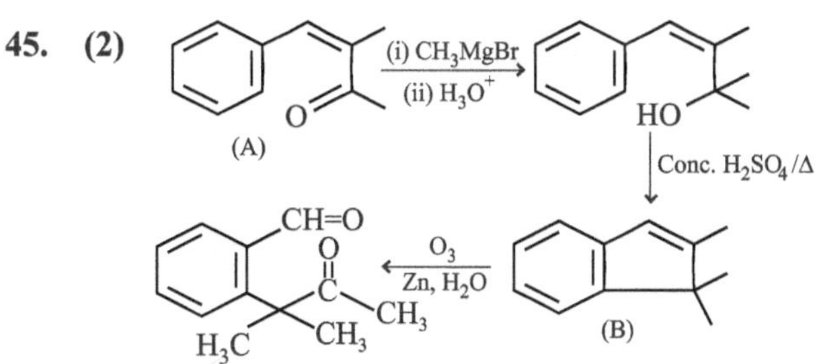

46. (14.00)

Mass percent of $HNO_3 = 63$

Thus, 100 g of nitric acid solution contains 63 g of nitric acid by mass.

No. of moles $= \dfrac{63\,g}{63\,g\,mol^{-1}} = 1$

Volume of 100 g of nitric acid solution

$= \dfrac{Mass}{Density} = \dfrac{100\ g}{1.4\ g/mL} = 71.4$ mL

$Molarity = \dfrac{No.\ of\ moles}{volume\ (mL)} \times 1000$

$= \dfrac{1}{71.4} \times 1000 = 14$ M

47. (100.00)

10^{-3} molar $MgSO_4 \equiv 10^{-3}$ moles of $MgSO_4$ present in 1 L solutions.

10^{-3} M $MgSO_4 \equiv 10^{-3}$ M $CaCO_3$

10^{-3} M $CaCO_3 = 10^{-3} \times 100$g $CaCO_3$ in 1L water

$ppm_{(in\ term\ of\ CaCO_3)} = \dfrac{10^{-3} \times 100}{1000} \times 10^6$

$ppm_{(in\ term\ of\ CaCO_3)} = 100$ ppm

48. (1.75)

$\Delta T_f = i k_f m$

$0.2 = 2 \times 2 \times \dfrac{w}{58.5} \times \dfrac{1000}{600}$

$w = \dfrac{0.2 \times 58.5 \times 600}{1000 \times 4} = \dfrac{1.2 \times 58.5}{40} = 1.75$ g

49. (5.68)

No. of moles of silver deposited.

$= \dfrac{108}{108} = 1$ mol

$Ag^+ + e^- \rightarrow Ag$

1 F charge is required to deposit 1 mole of Ag

$H_2O \rightarrow \dfrac{1}{2}O_2 + 2H^+ + 2e^-$

2 F charge deposit $\rightarrow \dfrac{1}{2}$ moles of oxygen

1 F charge will deposit $\rightarrow \dfrac{1}{4}$ moles of oxygen

$V_{O_2} = \dfrac{nRT}{P}$

$= \dfrac{1}{4} \times \dfrac{0.08314 L\,bar\,K^{-1}mol^{-1} \times 273K}{1\,bar}$

$= \dfrac{1}{4} \times 22.7$

$V_{O_2} = 5.675$ L

50. (37.84)

Molecular formula of histamine is $C_5H_9N_3$

Molecular mass of histamine

$= 5 \times 12 + 9 \times 1 + 3 \times 14 = 111$

Mass percentage of nitrogen in histamine

$= \dfrac{42}{111} \times 100 = 37.84\%$

MATHEMATICS

51. (4) Since, function $f(x)$ is twice differentiable and continuous in $x \in [a, b]$. Then, by LMVT for $x \in [a, c]$

$$\frac{f(c) - f(a)}{c - a} = f'(\alpha), \alpha \in (a, c)$$

Again by LMVT for $x \in [c, b]$

$$\frac{f(b) - f(c)}{b - c} = f'(\beta), \beta \in (c, b)$$

$\because$ $f''(x) < 0 \Rightarrow f'(x)$ is decreasing

$$f'(\alpha) > f'(\beta) \Rightarrow \frac{f(c) - f(a)}{c - a} > \frac{f(b) - f(c)}{b - c}$$

$$\Rightarrow \frac{f(c) - f(a)}{f(b) - f(c)} > \frac{c - a}{b - c} \qquad (\because f(x) \text{ is increasing})$$

52. (4) $\displaystyle\int_0^1 (a + bx + cx^2)\,dx = ax + \frac{bx^2}{2} + \frac{cx^3}{3}\Big|_0^1 = a + \frac{b}{2} + \frac{c}{3}$

Now, $f(1) = a + b + c, f(0) = a$ and $f\left(\dfrac{1}{2}\right) = a + \dfrac{b}{2} + \dfrac{c}{4}$

Now, $\dfrac{1}{6}\left(f(1) + f(0) + 4f\left(\dfrac{1}{2}\right)\right)$

$$= \frac{1}{6}\left(a + b + c + a + 4\left(a + \frac{b}{2} + \frac{c}{4}\right)\right)$$

$$= \frac{1}{6}(6a + 3b + 2c) = a + \frac{b}{2} + \frac{c}{3}$$

Hence, $\displaystyle\int_0^1 f(x) = \frac{1}{6}\left\{f(0) + f(1) + 4f\left(\frac{1}{2}\right)\right\}$

53. (2) Let $z = x + iy$

Then, $\left|\dfrac{z - i}{z + 2i}\right| = 1 \Rightarrow x^2 + (y - 1)^2$

$= x^2 + (y + 2)^2 \Rightarrow -2y + 1 = 4y + 4$

$$\Rightarrow 6y = -3 \Rightarrow y = -\frac{1}{2}$$

$\because$ $|z| = \dfrac{5}{2} \Rightarrow x^2 + y^2 = \dfrac{25}{4}$

$$\Rightarrow x^2 = \frac{24}{4} = 6$$

$\therefore$ $z = x + iy \qquad \Rightarrow z = \pm\sqrt{6} - \dfrac{i}{2}$

$$|z + 3i| = \sqrt{6 + \frac{25}{4}} = \sqrt{\frac{49}{4}}$$

$$\Rightarrow |z + 3i| = \frac{7}{2}$$

54. (2) $\Delta = 0 \Rightarrow \begin{vmatrix} 1 & 4 & -2 \\ 1 & 7 & -5 \\ 1 & 5 & \alpha \end{vmatrix} = 0$

$\Rightarrow (7\alpha + 25) - (4\alpha + 10) + (-20 + 14) = 0$

$\Rightarrow 3\alpha + 9 = 0 \Rightarrow \alpha = -3$

Also, $D_z = 0 \Rightarrow \begin{vmatrix} 1 & 4 & 1 \\ 1 & 7 & \beta \\ 1 & 5 & 5 \end{vmatrix} = 0$

$\Rightarrow 1(35 - 5\beta) - (15) + 1(4\beta - 7) = 0 \Rightarrow \beta = 13$

Hence, $\alpha + \beta = -3 + 13 = 10$

55. (1) Let $e^x = t \in (0, \infty)$

Given equation

$$t^4 + t^3 - 4t^2 + t + 1 = 0$$

$$\Rightarrow t^2 + t - 4 + \frac{1}{t} + \frac{1}{t^2} = 0$$

$$\Rightarrow \left(t^2 + \frac{1}{t^2}\right) + \left(t + \frac{1}{t}\right) - 4 = 0$$

Let $t + \dfrac{1}{t} = y$

$(y^2 - 2) + y - 4 = 0 \Rightarrow y^2 + y - 6 = 0$

$y^2 + y - 6 = 0 \Rightarrow y = -3, 2$

$$\Rightarrow y = 2 \qquad \Rightarrow t + \frac{1}{t} = 2$$

$$\Rightarrow e^x + e^{-x} = 2$$

$x = 0$, is the only solution of the equation

Hence, there only one solution of the given equation.

56. (3) $\displaystyle\int_0^{2\pi} \frac{x \sin^8 x}{\sin^8 x + \cos^8 x}\,dx$

$$= \int_0^\pi \left[\frac{x \sin^8 x}{\sin^8 x + \cos^8 x} + \frac{(2\pi - x)\sin^8 x}{\sin^8 x + \cos^8 x}\right] dx$$

$$\left[\because \int_0^{2a} f(x)\,dx = \int_0^a f(x)\,dx + \int_0^a f(2a - x)\,dx\right]$$

$$= \int_0^\pi \frac{2\pi \sin^8 x}{\sin^8 x + \cos^8 x}\,dx$$

$$= 2\pi \int_0^{\pi/2} \left[\frac{\sin^8 x}{\sin^8 x + \cos^8 x} + \frac{\cos^8 x}{\sin^8 x + \cos^8 x}\right] dx$$

$$= 2\pi \int_0^{\pi/2} 1\,dx = 2\pi \times \frac{\pi}{2} = \pi^2$$

57. (3) $\text{LHL} = \displaystyle\lim_{x \to 0} \frac{\sin(a + 2)x + \sin x}{x}$

$$= \lim_{x \to 0}\left(\frac{\sin(a + 2)x}{(a + 2)x}\right)(a + 2) + \lim_{x \to 0}\frac{\sin x}{x} = a + 3$$

$f(0) = b$

$$\text{RHL} = \lim_{h \to 0}\left(\frac{(1+3h)^{\frac{1}{3}}-1}{h}\right) = 1$$

∵   Function $f(x)$ is continuous

∴ $\lim_{x \to 0^-} f(x) = \lim_{x \to 0^+} f(x) = f(0)$

∴ $a + 3 = 1 \Rightarrow a = -2$

and $b = 1$

Hence, $a + 2b = 0$

58. (2) $P(\text{second } A - \text{card appears before the third } B- \text{card})$

$= P(AA) + P(ABA) + P(BAA) + P(ABBA) + P(BBAA)$
$\hspace{8cm} + P(BABA)$

$$= \frac{1}{4} + \frac{1}{8} + \frac{1}{8} + \frac{1}{16} + \frac{1}{16} + \frac{1}{16} = \frac{11}{16}$$

59. (4) Number of five digit numbers with 2 at 10th place

$\hspace{2cm} = 8 \times 8 \times 7 \times 6 = 2688$

∵   It is given that, number of five digit number with 2 at 10th place $= 336k$

∴ $336\, k = 2688 \Rightarrow k = 8$

60. (1) Eccentricity of ellipse

$$e_1 = \sqrt{1 - \frac{4}{18}} = \sqrt{\frac{7}{9}} = \frac{\sqrt{7}}{3}$$

Eccentricity of hyperbola

$$e_2 = \sqrt{1 + \frac{4}{9}} = \sqrt{\frac{13}{9}} = \frac{\sqrt{13}}{3}$$

Since, the point (e_1, e_2) is on the ellipse
$15x^2 + 3y^2 = k.$

Then, $15e_1^2 + 3e_2^2 = k$

$$\Rightarrow \quad k = 15\left(\frac{7}{9}\right) + 3\left(\frac{13}{9}\right)$$

$$\Rightarrow \quad k = 16$$

61. (4) Let the thickness of ice layer be $= x$ cm

Total volume $V = \dfrac{4}{3}\,\pi(10+x)^3$

$$\frac{dV}{dt} = 4\pi(10+x)^2 \frac{dx}{dt} \hspace{2cm} ...(i)$$

Since, it is given that

$$\frac{dV}{dt} = 50 \text{ cm}^3 / \text{min} \hspace{2cm} ...(ii)$$

From (i) and (ii), $50 = 4\pi(10+x)\dfrac{dx}{dt}$

$$\Rightarrow \quad 50 = 4\pi(10+5)^2 \frac{dx}{dt} \quad [\because \text{ thickness of ice } x = 5]$$

$$\Rightarrow \quad \frac{dx}{dt} = \frac{1}{18\pi} \text{ cm}/\text{min}$$

62. (1) Mean of the observation $(x_i - 5) = \dfrac{\Sigma(x_i - 5)}{10} = 1$

∴ $\lambda = \{\text{Mean } (x_i - 5)\} + 2 = 3$

Variance of the observation

$$\mu = \text{var }(x_i - 5) = \frac{\Sigma(x_i-5)^2}{10} - \frac{\Sigma(x_i-5)}{10} = 3$$

63. (2) Let p and q the statements such that $p = \sqrt{5}$ is an integer $q = 5$ is an irrational number.

Then, negation of the given statement

$\sqrt{5}$ is not an integer and 5 is not an irrational Number

$\sim (p \vee q) = \sim p \wedge \sim q$

64. (4)

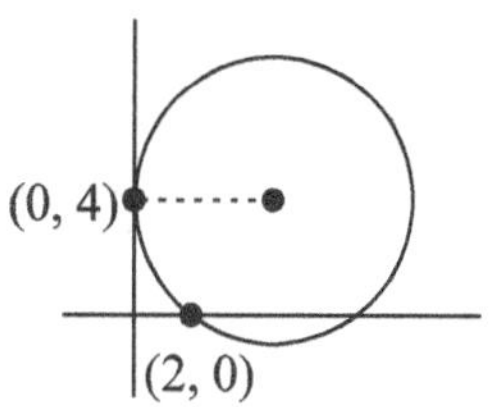

Equation of family of circle

$$(x-0)^2 + (y-4)^2 + \lambda x = 0$$

Passes through the point (2, 0) then

$$4 + 16 + 2\lambda = 0 \Rightarrow \lambda = -10$$

Hence, the equation of circle

$$x^2 + y^2 - 10x - 8y + 16 = 0$$

$$\Rightarrow \quad (x-5)^2 + (y-4)^2 = 25$$

Centre (5, 4).

$$R = \sqrt{\frac{1}{2}\text{coeff. of } x + \frac{1}{2}\text{coeff. of } y - \text{constant}}$$

$$= \sqrt{25 + 16 - 16} = 5$$

Perpendicular distance of $4x + 3y - 8 = 0$ from the centre of circle

$$= \left|\frac{20 + 16 - 8}{\sqrt{16+9}}\right| = \frac{28}{5} \neq 5$$

Hence, $4x + 3y - 8 = 0$ can not be tangent to the circle.

65. (1) $|A| = \begin{vmatrix} 1 & 1 & 2 \\ 1 & 3 & 4 \\ 1 & -1 & 3 \end{vmatrix} = ((9+4) - 1(3-4) + 2(-1-3))$

$$= 13 + 1 - 8 = 6$$

$|adjB| = |adj(adjA)| = |A|^{(n-1)^2} = |A|^4 = (36)^2$

$|C| = |3A| = 3^3 \times 6$

Hence, $\dfrac{|adjB|}{|C|} = \dfrac{36 \times 36}{3^3 \times 6} = 8$

66. (1) $f'(x) = \tan^{-1}(\sec x + \tan x)$

$$= \tan^{-1}\left(\frac{1+\sin x}{\cos x}\right) = \tan^{-1}\left(\frac{1 - \cos\left(\frac{\pi}{2} + x\right)}{\sin\left(\frac{\pi}{2} + x\right)}\right)$$

$$= \tan^{-1}\left(\frac{2\sin^2\left(\frac{\pi}{4}+\frac{x}{2}\right)}{2\sin\left(\frac{\pi}{4}+\frac{x}{2}\right)\cos\left(\frac{\pi}{4}+\frac{x}{2}\right)}\right)$$

$$= \tan^{-1}\left(\tan\left(\frac{\pi}{4}+\frac{x}{2}\right)\right) = \frac{\pi}{4}+\frac{x}{2}$$

Integrate both sides, we get

$$\int(f'(x))\,dx = \int\left(\frac{\pi}{4}+\frac{x}{2}\right)dx$$

$$f(x) = \frac{\pi}{4}x + \frac{x^2}{4} + C$$

$\because \;\; f(0) = 0$

$$C = 0 \;\Rightarrow\; f(x) = \frac{\pi}{4}x + \frac{x^2}{4}$$

So, $\;\; f(1) = \dfrac{\pi+1}{4}$

67. (2) $\cos^3\dfrac{\pi}{8}\left[4\cos^3\dfrac{\pi}{8}-3\cos\dfrac{\pi}{8}\right]$

$$+\sin^3\frac{\pi}{8}\left[3\sin\frac{\pi}{8}-4\sin^3\frac{\pi}{8}\right]$$

$$= 4\cos^6\frac{\pi}{8}-4\sin^6\frac{\pi}{8}-3\cos^4\frac{\pi}{8}+3\sin^4\frac{\pi}{8}$$

$$= 4\left[\left(\cos^2\frac{\pi}{8}-\sin^2\frac{\pi}{8}\right)\right]$$

$$\left[\left(\sin^4\frac{\pi}{8}+\cos^4\frac{\pi}{8}+\sin^2\frac{\pi}{8}\cos^2\frac{\pi}{8}\right)\right]$$

$$-3\left[\left(\cos^2\frac{\pi}{8}-\sin^2\frac{\pi}{8}\right)\left(\cos^2\frac{\pi}{8}+\sin^2\frac{\pi}{8}\right)\right]$$

$$= \cos\frac{\pi}{4}\left[4\left(1-\sin^2\frac{\pi}{8}\cos^2\frac{\pi}{8}\right)-3\right]$$

$$= \frac{1}{\sqrt{2}}\left[1-\frac{1}{2}\right] = \frac{1}{2\sqrt{2}}$$

68. (1) Coordinates of centroides

$$C = \left(\frac{x_1+x_2+x_3}{3}, \frac{y_1+y_2+y_3}{3}\right)$$

$$= \left(\frac{3+1+2}{3}, \frac{-1+3+4}{3}\right) = (2,2)$$

The given equation of lines are

$$\begin{aligned}x+3y-1 &= 0 &\quad\text{...(i)}\\ 3x-y+1 &= 0 &\quad\text{...(ii)}\end{aligned}$$

Then, from (i) and (ii)

point of intersection $P\left(-\dfrac{1}{5}, \dfrac{2}{5}\right)$

equation of line DP

$$8x-11y+6 = 0$$

69. (1) $I = \displaystyle\int \frac{dx}{(x+4)^{8/7}(x-3)^{6/7}}$

$$= \int\left(\frac{x-3}{x+4}\right)^{-\frac{6}{7}}\frac{1}{(x+4)^2}\,dx$$

Let $\dfrac{x-3}{x+4} = t^7$,

Differentiate on both sides, we get

$$\frac{7}{(x+4)^2}\,dx = 7t^6\,dt$$

Hence, $I = \displaystyle\int t^{-6}t^6\,dt = t+C = \left(\frac{x-3}{x+4}\right)^{\frac{1}{7}}+C$

70. (1) $2^{\frac{1}{4}+\frac{2}{16}+\frac{3}{48}+\dots\infty}$

$$= 2^{\frac{1}{4}+\frac{1}{8}+\frac{1}{16}+\dots\infty} = \sqrt{2}$$

71. (8) Let $P(1,-1,3),\, Q(2,-4,11),\, R(-1,2,3)$
and $S(3,-2,10)$

Then, $\overrightarrow{PQ} = \hat{i}-3\hat{j}+8\hat{k}$

$$\overrightarrow{RS} = 4\hat{i}-4\hat{j}+7\hat{k}$$

Projection of $\overrightarrow{PQ}$ on $\overrightarrow{RS}$

$$= \frac{\overrightarrow{PQ}.\overrightarrow{RS}}{|\overrightarrow{RS}|} = \frac{4+12+56}{\sqrt{(4)^2+(4)^2+(7)^2}} = 8$$

72. (1) $\begin{vmatrix} a+1 & a & a \\ a & a+1 & a \\ a & a & a+1 \end{vmatrix} = 0$

$$\Rightarrow\;\; 3a+1 = 0 \;\Rightarrow\; a = -\frac{1}{3}$$

The given vectors

$$\vec{p} = \frac{2}{3}\hat{i}-\frac{1}{3}\hat{j}-\frac{1}{3}\hat{k} = \frac{1}{3}(2\hat{i}-\hat{j}-\hat{k})$$

$$\vec{q} = \frac{1}{3}(-\hat{i}+2\hat{j}-\hat{k})$$

$$\vec{r} = \frac{1}{3}(-\hat{i}-\hat{j}+2\hat{k})$$

Now, $\vec{p}.\vec{q} = \dfrac{1}{9}(-2-2+1) = -\dfrac{1}{3}$

$$\vec{r}\times\vec{q} = \frac{1}{9}\begin{vmatrix} i & j & k \\ -1 & 2 & -1 \\ -1 & -1 & 2 \end{vmatrix}$$

$$= \frac{1}{9}(i(4-1)-j(-2-1)+k(1+2))$$

$$= \frac{1}{9}(3i+3j+3k) = \frac{i+j+k}{3}$$

$$|\vec{r} \times \vec{q}| = \frac{1}{3}\sqrt{3} \quad \Rightarrow \quad |\vec{r} \times \vec{q}|^2 = \frac{1}{3}$$

$$3(\vec{p}.\vec{q})^2 - \lambda |\vec{r} \times \vec{q}|^2 = 0$$

$$\Rightarrow \quad 3.\frac{1}{9} - \lambda.\frac{1}{3} = 0 \quad \Rightarrow \quad \lambda = 1$$

73. **(615)** General term of the expansion $= \dfrac{10!}{\alpha!\beta!\gamma!} x^{\beta+2\gamma}$

For coefficient of x^4; $\beta + 2\gamma = 4$
Here, three cases arise
Case-1 : When $\gamma = 0$, $\beta = 4$, $\alpha = 6$

$$\Rightarrow \quad \frac{10!}{6!\,4!\,0!} = 210$$

Case-2 : When $\gamma = 1$, $\beta = 2$, $\alpha = 7$

$$\Rightarrow \quad \frac{10!}{7!\,2!\,1!} = 360$$

Case-3 : When $\gamma = 2$, $\beta = 0$, $\alpha = 8$

$$\Rightarrow \quad \frac{10!}{8!\,0!\,2!} = 45$$

Hence, total = 615

74. **(8)** $\log_{1/2}|\sin x| = 2 - \log_{1/2}|\cos x|$

$$\Rightarrow \quad \log_{1/2}|\sin x\,\cos x| = 2$$

$$\Rightarrow \quad |\sin x\,\cos x| = \frac{1}{4}$$

$$\Rightarrow \quad \sin 2x = \pm\frac{1}{2}$$

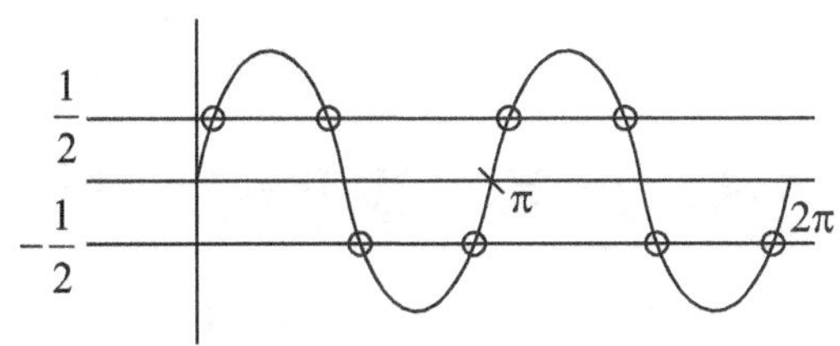

Hence, total number of solutions = 8.

75. **(3)** $(x + 1)dy = ((x + 1)^2 + (y - 3))dx = 0$

$$\Rightarrow \quad \frac{dy}{dx} = (1+x) + \left(\frac{y-3}{1+x}\right)$$

$$\frac{dy}{dx} - \frac{1}{(1+x)}\,y = (1+x) - \frac{3}{(1+x)}$$

$$\text{I.F.} = e^{-\int \frac{1}{(1+x)}dx} = \frac{1}{(1+x)}$$

$$\therefore \quad \frac{d}{dx}\left(\frac{y}{1+x}\right) = 1 - \frac{3}{(1+x)^2}$$

$$\frac{y}{1+x} = x + 3(1+x)^{-1} + C$$

$$y = (1+x)\left[x + \frac{3}{(1+x)} + C\right]$$

$$\because \quad \text{At } x = 2, y = 0$$

$$\therefore \quad 0 = 3(2 + 1 + C) \quad \Rightarrow \quad C = -3$$

Then, $y = (1+x)\left[x + \dfrac{3}{1+x} - 3\right]$

Now, at $x = 3$, $y = (1+3)\left[3 + \dfrac{3}{1+3} - 3\right] = 3$

PHYSICS

1. **(3)** Both the diodes are reverse biased, so, there is no flow of current through 5Ω and 20Ω resistances. Now, two resistors of 10Ω and two resistors of 5Ω are in series.

Hence current I through the network

$$I = \frac{V}{R_{eq}} = \frac{9}{10+5+10+5}$$

$$\Rightarrow \quad I = \frac{9}{30} = 0.3A$$

2. **(1)** Fundamental frequency, $f = 70$ Hz.

The fundamental frequency of wire vibrating under tension T is given by

$$f = \frac{1}{2L}\sqrt{\frac{T}{\mu}}$$

Here, μ = mass per unit length of the wire

$\qquad L$ = length of wire

$$70 = \frac{1}{2L}\sqrt{\frac{540}{6\times10^{-3}}}$$

$$\Rightarrow \quad L \approx 2.14 \text{ m}$$

3. **(4)** Acceleration of electron in electric field, $a = \dfrac{eE}{m}$

Using equation

$$v = u + at$$

$$\Rightarrow \quad v = 0 + \frac{eE}{m}t$$

$$\Rightarrow \quad v = \frac{eEt}{m} \qquad\qquad \text{..... (i)}$$

De-broglie wavelength λ is given by

$$\lambda = \frac{h}{mv} = \frac{h}{m\left(\dfrac{eEt}{m}\right)} \qquad \text{[using (i)]}$$

$$\Rightarrow \quad \lambda = \frac{h}{eEt}$$

Differentiating w.r.t. t

$$\frac{d\lambda}{dt} = \frac{d\left(\dfrac{h}{eEt}\right)}{dt} \quad \Rightarrow \quad \frac{d\lambda}{dt} = \frac{-h}{eEt^2}$$

4. **(1)** Given, Inductance, $L = 40$ mH

Capacitance, $C = 100$ μF

Impedance, $Z = X_C - X_L$

$$\Rightarrow \quad Z = \frac{1}{\omega C} - \omega L \quad \left(\because X_c = \frac{1}{\omega C} \text{ and } X_L = \omega L\right)$$

$$= \frac{1}{314\times100\times10^{-6}} - 314\times40\times10^{-3}$$

$$= 19.28\Omega$$

Current, $\quad i = \dfrac{V_0}{Z}\sin(\omega t + \pi/2)$

$$\Rightarrow \quad i = \frac{10}{19.28}\cos\omega t = 0.52\cos(314\,t)$$

5. **(3)** Torque on circular loop, $\tau = MB\sin\theta$

where, $\quad M$ = magnetic moment

$\qquad\qquad B$ = magnetic field

Now, using $\tau = I\alpha$

$\therefore \quad \tau = MB\sin\theta = I\alpha$

$$\Rightarrow \quad \pi R^2 IB\theta = \frac{mR^2\alpha}{2}$$

$(\because m = IA$ and moment of inertia of circular loop,

$$I = \frac{mR^2}{2})$$

$$\Rightarrow \quad \pi R^2 IB\,\theta = \frac{mR^2}{2}\omega\theta$$

$$\Rightarrow \quad \omega = \sqrt{\frac{2\pi IB}{m}} \quad \Rightarrow \quad \frac{2\pi}{T} = \sqrt{\frac{2\pi IB}{m}}$$

$$\Rightarrow \quad T = \sqrt{\frac{2\pi m}{IB}}$$

6. **(3)** In case I diode is reverse biased, so no current flows

$\therefore \quad Q_A = CV$

In case II, current will flow as diode is forward biased. So, it offers negligible resistance to the flow of current and thus be replaced by short circuit. Now, the charge of capacitor will leak through the resistance and decay exponentially with time.

During discharging of capacitor

Potential difference across the capacitor at any instant

$$V' = Ve^{-\frac{t}{CR}}$$

But $t = CR$

$$V' = Ve^{-1} = \frac{V}{e}$$

$$\therefore \quad \text{Charge } Q_B = CV' = \frac{CV}{e}$$

7. (1) Using principal of conservation of energy

$$(m_1 - m_2)gh = \frac{1}{2}(m_1 + m_2)v^2 + \frac{1}{2}I\omega^2$$

$$\Rightarrow \quad (m_1 - m_2)gh = \frac{1}{2}(m_1 + m_2)(\omega R)^2 + \frac{1}{2}I\omega^2$$

$$(\because v = \omega R)$$

$$\Rightarrow \quad (m_1 - m_2)gh = \frac{\omega^2}{2}\left[(m_1 + m_2)R^2 + I\right]$$

$$\Rightarrow \quad \omega = \sqrt{\frac{2(m_1 - m_2)gh}{(m_1 + m_2)R^2 + I}}$$

8. (3) Given,

Refractive index, $\mu = \dfrac{4}{3}$

$$\frac{4}{3}\sin\theta = 1\sin 90°$$

$$\Rightarrow \sin\theta = \frac{3}{4}$$

$$\cos\theta = \frac{\sqrt{7}}{4}$$

Solid angle, $\Omega = 2\pi(1 - \cos\theta) = 2\pi(1 - \sqrt{7}/4)$

Fraction of energy transmitted

$$= \frac{2\pi(1 - \cos\theta)}{4\pi} = \frac{1 - \sqrt{7}/4}{2} = 0.17$$

Percentage of light emerges out of surface

$$= 0.17 \times 100 = 17\%$$

9. (3) Free body diagram in the frame of disc

$$\therefore \quad m\omega^2(\ell_0 + x) = kx$$

$$\Rightarrow \quad x = \frac{m\ell_0\omega^2}{k - m\omega^2}$$

For $k \gg m\omega^2$

$$\Rightarrow \quad \frac{x}{\ell_0} = \frac{m\omega^2}{k}$$

10. (4) For the drops to be in equilibrium upward force on drop = downward force on drop

$$T.2\pi R = \frac{4}{3}\pi R^3 dg - \frac{2}{3}\pi R^3 \rho g$$

$$\Rightarrow \quad T(2\pi R) = \frac{2}{3}\pi R^3 (2d - \rho)g$$

$$\Rightarrow \quad T = \frac{R^2}{3}(2d - \rho)g \quad \Rightarrow \quad R = \sqrt{\frac{3T}{(2d - \rho)g}}$$

11. (1) Escape velocity of the planet A is $V_A = \sqrt{\dfrac{2GM_A}{R_A}}$

where M_A and R_A be the mass and radius of the planet A.

According to given problem

$$M_B = \frac{M_A}{2}, \quad R_B = \frac{R_A}{2}$$

$$\therefore \; V_B = \sqrt{\frac{2G\dfrac{M_A}{2}}{\dfrac{R_A}{2}}} \quad \therefore \; \frac{V_A}{V_B} = \sqrt{\frac{\dfrac{2GM_A}{R_A}}{\dfrac{2GM_A/2}{R_A/2}}} = \frac{n}{4} = 1$$

$$\Rightarrow \quad n = 4$$

12. (2) Given,

Linear mass density, $\rho(x) = a + b\left(\dfrac{x}{L}\right)^2$

$$X_{CM} = \frac{\int x\,dm}{\int dm}$$

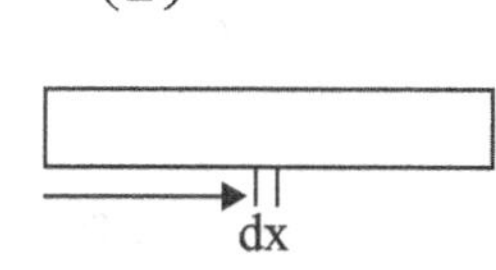

$$\int dm = \int_0^L \rho(x)\,dx$$

$$= \int_0^L \left[a + b\left(\frac{x}{L}\right)^2\right]dx = aL + \frac{bL}{3}$$

$$\int_0^L x\,dm = \int_0^L \left(ax + \frac{bx^3}{L^2}\right)dx = \left(\frac{aL^2}{2} + \frac{bL^2}{4}\right)$$

$$\therefore \quad X_{CM} = \frac{\left(\dfrac{aL^2}{2} + \dfrac{bL^2}{4}\right)}{aL + \dfrac{bL}{3}}$$

$$\Rightarrow \quad X_{CM} = \frac{3L}{4}\left(\frac{2a + b}{3a + b}\right)$$

13. (Bonus)

$$D_1 = A_1 + B_1 + C_1 = 24.36 + 0.0724 + 256.2 = 280.6$$

$$D_2 = A_2 + B_2 + C_2 = 24.44 + 16.082 + 240.2 = 280.7$$

$D_3 = A_3 + B_3 + C_3 = 25.2 + 19.2812 + 236.183 = 280.7$

$D_4 = A_4 + B_4 + C_4 = 25 + 236.191 + 19.5 = 281$

None of the option matches.

14. **(Bonus)**

Mean free path of a gas molecule is given by

$$\lambda = \frac{1}{\sqrt{2}\pi d^2 n}$$

Here, n = number of collisions per unit volume

d = diameter of the molecule

If average speed of molecule is v then

Mean free time, $\tau = \dfrac{\lambda}{v}$

$$\Rightarrow \tau = \frac{1}{\sqrt{2}\pi n d^2 v} = \frac{1}{\sqrt{2}\pi n d^2}\sqrt{\frac{M}{3RT}}$$

$$\left(\because v = \sqrt{\frac{3RT}{M}}\right)$$

$$\therefore \ \tau \propto \frac{\sqrt{M}}{d^2} \quad \therefore \ \frac{\tau_1}{\tau_2} = \frac{\sqrt{M_1}}{d_1^2} \times \frac{d_2^2}{\sqrt{M_2}}$$

$$= \sqrt{\frac{40}{140}} \times \left(\frac{0.1}{0.07}\right)^2 = 1.09$$

15. **(1)** If force F acts along the length L of the wire of cross-section A, then energy stored in unit volume of wire is given by

Energy density $= \dfrac{1}{2}$ stress × strain

$$= \frac{1}{2} \times \frac{F}{A} \times \frac{F}{AY} \quad \left(\because \text{ stress } = \frac{F}{A} \text{ and strain } = \frac{X}{AY}\right)$$

$$= \frac{1}{2}\frac{F^2}{A^2 Y} = \frac{1}{2}\frac{F^2 \times 16}{(\pi d^2)^2 Y} = \frac{1}{2}\frac{F^2 \times 16}{\pi d^4 Y}$$

If u_1 and u_2 are the densities of two wires, then

$$\frac{u_1}{u_2} = \left(\frac{d_2}{d_1}\right)^4 \quad \Rightarrow \frac{d_1}{d_2} = (4)^{1/4} \Rightarrow \frac{d_1}{d_2} = \sqrt{2} : 1$$

16. **(2)** According to Bohr's Theory the wavelength of the radiation emitted from hydrogen atom is given by

$$\frac{1}{\lambda} = RZ^2 \left[\frac{1}{n_1^2} - \frac{1}{n_2^2}\right]$$

$$\because \quad Z = 3$$

$$\therefore \ \frac{1}{\lambda} = 9R\left(1 - \frac{1}{9}\right)$$

$$\Rightarrow \ \lambda = \frac{1}{8R} = \frac{1}{8 \times 10973731.6} \quad (\because R = 10973731.6 \ \text{m}^{-1})$$

$$\Rightarrow \ \lambda = 11.39 \ \text{nm}$$

17. **(1)** Using principal of conservation of linear momentum for horizontal motion, we have

$$2mv_x = mu + mu \cos 60°$$

$$v_x = \frac{3u}{4}$$

For vertical motion

$$h = 0 + \frac{1}{2}gT^2 \quad \Rightarrow \quad T = \sqrt{\frac{2h}{g}}$$

Let R is the horizontal distance travelled by the body.

$$R = v_x T + \frac{1}{2}(0)(T)^2 \quad (\text{For horizontal motion})$$

$$R = v_x T = \frac{3u}{4} \times \sqrt{\frac{2h}{g}}$$

$$\Rightarrow \quad R = \frac{3\sqrt{3}u^2}{8g}$$

18. **(2)** Magnetic field inside the solenoid is given by

$$B = \mu_0 nI \qquad \text{.... (i)}$$

Here, n = number of turns per unit length

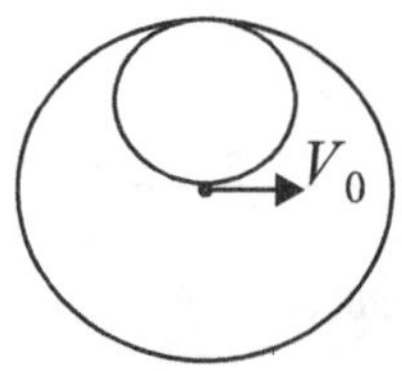

The path of charge particle is circular. The maximum possible radius of electron $= \dfrac{R}{2}$

$$\therefore \quad \frac{mV_{\max}}{qB} = \frac{R}{2}$$

$$\Rightarrow \quad V_{\max} = \frac{qBR}{2m} = \frac{eR\mu_0 nI}{2m} \qquad (\text{using (i)})$$

19. **(3)** Using $S = ut + \dfrac{1}{2}at^2$

$$y = u_y t + \frac{1}{2}a_y t^2 \quad (\text{along } y \text{ Axis})$$

$$\Rightarrow \quad 32 = 0 \times t + \frac{1}{2}(4)t^2$$

$$\Rightarrow \quad \frac{1}{2} \times 4 \times t^2 = 32$$

$$\Rightarrow \quad t = 4\,s$$

$$S_x = u_x t + \frac{1}{2}a_x t^2 \qquad \text{(Along } x \text{ Axis)}$$

$$\Rightarrow \quad x = 3 \times 4 + \frac{1}{2} \times 6 \times 4^2 = 60$$

20. (1) Direction of polarisation $= \hat{E} = \hat{k}$

Direction of propagation $= \widehat{E} \times \widehat{B} = \dfrac{\hat{i} + \hat{j}}{\sqrt{2}}$

But $\vec{E}.\vec{B} = 0$ $\therefore$ $\hat{B} = \dfrac{\hat{i} - \hat{j}}{\sqrt{2}}$

21. (1818) For an adiabatic process,
$TV^{\gamma-1} = $ constant

$$\therefore \quad T_1 V_1^{\gamma-1} = T_2 V_2^{\gamma-1}$$

$$\Rightarrow \quad T_2 = (300) \times \left(\frac{V_1}{\frac{V_1}{16}}\right)^{1.4-1}$$

$$\Rightarrow \quad T_2 = 300 \times (16)^{0.4}$$

Ideal gas equation, $PV = nRT$

$$\therefore \quad V = \frac{nRT}{P}$$

$\Rightarrow \quad V = kT$ (since pressure is constant for isobaric process)

So, during isobaric process

$$V_2 = kT_2 \qquad \qquad \text{...(i)}$$

$$2V_2 = kT_f \qquad \qquad \text{...(ii)}$$

Dividing (i) by (ii)

$$\frac{1}{2} = \frac{T_2}{T_f}$$

$$T_f = 2T_2 = 300 \times 2 \times (16)^{0.4} = 1818\,K$$

22. (–48)

Flux of electric field $\vec{E}$ through any area $\vec{A}$ is defined as

$$\phi = \int \vec{E}.\vec{A} \cos\theta$$

Here, $\theta = $ angle between electric field and area vector of a surface

For surface $ABCD$ Angle, $\theta = 90°$

$$\therefore \quad \phi_1 = \int E.A \cos 90° = 0$$

For surface $BCGF$ $\phi_n = \int \vec{E}.\overrightarrow{dA}$

$$\therefore \quad \phi_{11} = \left[4 \times \hat{i} - (y^2 + 1)\hat{j}\right].4\hat{i} = 16x$$

$$\phi_{11} = 48\,\frac{Nm^2}{C}$$

$$\phi_1 - \phi_{11} = -48$$

23. (40) For the given meter bridge

$$\frac{R}{S} = \frac{\ell_1}{100 - \ell_1} \quad \text{Where, } \ell_1 = \text{balancing length}$$

$$\Rightarrow \quad \frac{R}{S} = \frac{25}{75} = \frac{1}{3} \qquad \qquad \text{...(i)}$$

New resistance,

$$R' = \frac{\rho \frac{\ell}{2}}{\frac{A}{4}} = \rho \frac{\ell \times 2}{A} \qquad \left(\because R = \rho \frac{\ell}{A}\right)$$

$$\Rightarrow \quad R' = 2R$$

$$\frac{R'}{S} = \frac{\ell_2}{100 - \ell_2}$$

$$\Rightarrow \quad \frac{2R}{S} = \frac{\ell_2}{100 - \ell_2}$$

$$\Rightarrow \quad 2 \times \frac{1}{3} = \frac{\ell_2}{100 - \ell_2} \qquad \text{Using (i)}$$

$$\Rightarrow \quad \ell_2 = 40\,cm$$

24. (40) Current in the circuit, $I = \dfrac{12 - 8}{400} = 10^{-2}\,A$

Power dissipited in each diode, $P = VI$

$$\Rightarrow \quad P = 4 \times 10^{-2} = 40\,mW$$

25. (750) Fringe width, $\beta = \dfrac{\lambda D}{d}$ where, $\lambda = $ wavelength, $D = $ distance of screen from slits, $d = $ distance between slits

ATQ

$$15 \times \frac{\lambda_1 D}{d} = 10 \times \frac{\lambda_2 D}{d}$$

$$\Rightarrow \quad 15\lambda_1 = 10\lambda_2$$

$$\Rightarrow \quad \lambda_2 = 1.5\lambda_1, \; 15\lambda_1 = 1.5 \times 500\,nm$$

$$\Rightarrow \quad \lambda_2 = 750\,nm$$

CHEMISTRY

26. **(3)**

(Reaction scheme: P = 3-methylaniline (m-toluidine); with Br_2, H_2O gives 2,4,6-tribromo-3-methylaniline ($C_7H_6NBr_3$); with $NaNO_2$/HCl gives diazonium salt ($N_2^+Cl^-$); with β-Naphthol/$NaOH$ gives azo coupled coloured compounds.)

Coloured compounds

27. **(2)** LiCl is soluble in pyridine.

28. **(2)** $Cr(OH)_3 \rightarrow \underset{s}{Cr^{3+}} + \underset{3s}{3OH^-}$

$$K_{sp} = s.(3s)^3$$

$$\Rightarrow 6 \times 10^{-31} = 27.s^4$$

$$\Rightarrow s = \left(\frac{6}{27} \times 10^{-31}\right)^{1/4}$$

$$[OH^-] = 3s = 3 \times \left(\frac{6}{27} \times 10^{-31}\right)^{1/4}$$

$$= (18 \times 10^{-31})^{1/4} \text{ M}$$

29. **(2)** In $Cl–CH=CH–NO_2$ double bond character in carbon-chlorine bond is maximum due to resonance and so the bond length is shortest.

30. **(4)** $\underset{(A)}{H_3N_3B_3Cl_3} + LiBH_4 \xrightarrow{THF} \underset{(B)}{B_3N_3H_6} + LiCl + BCl_3$

$$\underset{(A)}{H_3N_3B_3Cl_3} + 3MeMgBr \longrightarrow \underset{(C)}{H_3N_3B_3(Me)_3}$$
$$+ 3MgBrCl$$

31. **(4)** A large difference between first and second ionisation enthalpies ($4560 - 496 = 4064$ kJ mol^{-1}) confirms the metal to be an alkali metal and thus is monovalent and form hydroxide of the type M(OH).

$$\underset{1 \text{ mol} \quad 1 \text{ mol}}{MOH + HCl \rightarrow MCl + H_2O}$$

$$\underset{1 \text{ mol} \quad 1/2 \text{ mol}}{2\,MOH + H_2SO_4 \rightarrow M_2SO_4 + H_2O}$$

32. **(4)** Basic strength of amines depends upon availability of lone pair of electrons. Aliphatic amines are more basic than aromatic amines.

33. **(1)**

(Reaction scheme: cyclohexane $\xrightarrow{Br_2, h\nu}$ bromocyclohexane $\xrightarrow[\Delta]{alc.\ KOH}$ cyclohexene $\xrightarrow[Me_2S]{O_3}$ hexanedial $\xrightarrow[\Delta]{OH^-}$ cyclopentene carbaldehyde)

34. **(3)** As, $\mu_s = \sqrt{n(n+2)}$

$$Na_4[Fe(CN)_6] \rightarrow Fe^{2+}$$
$$\Rightarrow S.F.L. \Rightarrow t_{2g}^6 e_g^0 \Rightarrow \mu_s = 0$$
$$[Cr(H_2O)_6]\,Br_2 \rightarrow Cr^{2+}$$
$$\Rightarrow W.F.L. \Rightarrow t_{2g}^3 e_g^1 \Rightarrow \mu_s = \sqrt{24} \text{ B.M.}$$
$$(Et_4N)_2[CoCl_4] \rightarrow Co^{2+}$$
$$\Rightarrow W.F.L. \Rightarrow e^4 t_2^3 \Rightarrow \mu_s = \sqrt{15} \text{ B.M.}$$
$$Na_3[Fe(C_2O_4)_3] \rightarrow Fe^{3+}$$
$$\Rightarrow S.F.L. \Rightarrow t_{2g}^5 e_g^0 \Rightarrow \mu_s = \sqrt{3} \text{ B.M.}$$

35. **(2)** $Zn + 2NaOH \rightarrow Na_2ZnO_2 + H_2$

$$Zn + 2HCl \rightarrow ZnCl_2 + H_2$$

NaOH and HCl reacts with a certain amount of zinc to produce equal number of moles of H_2.

36. **(4)** Equilibrium constant

$$= \frac{[B]}{[A]} \approx 2$$

37. **(2)** Initially, adsorption of gases at the surface of charcoal occurs rapidly which results in a sudden decrease in pressure. As the number of vacant sites at the surface of adsorbent decreases with the passage of time, rate of adsorption decreases. Therefore, pressure tends to be constant.

38. **(4)** $(CH_3)_2CH–CH=CH_2 \xrightarrow{HCl} (CH_3)_2CH–\overset{+}{C}H–CH_3$

$$\xrightarrow{Hydride\ shift} CH_3–\overset{+}{\underset{CH_3}{C}}–CH_2–CH_3 \rightarrow CH_3–\overset{Cl}{\underset{CH_3}{C}}–CH_2–CH_3$$

There is no chiral carbon in the product of this reaction.

39. **(4)** $CH_3–\overset{OH}{\underset{}{CH}}–CH_2–COOH$ and
(3-Hydroxybutanoic acid)

$$CH_3–CH_2–\overset{OH}{\underset{}{CH}}–CH_2–COOH$$
(3-Hydroxypentanoic acid)

Both monomers of PHBV have chiral centre.

40. **(3)** In benzene each carbon atom is sp^2 hybridised. Therefore total 18 sp^2 hybrid orbitals are present in benzene.

41. **(1)** In distilled water, there are only neutral water molecules therefore, it does not conduct electricity.

42. **(2)** Molisch's test is used to check the presence of carbohydrates while Barfoed test is used for detecting the monosaccharides. Biuret test is used to detect the peptide bonds. Therefore, A and B (monosaccharide) are carbohydrates while C is a protein.

43. **(1)** A system at higher temperature has greater entropy (randomness). ΔS is related with q and T as:

$$\Delta S = \int \frac{dq}{T}$$

44. **(2)** Biochemical oxygen demand is the amount of oxygen required by bacteria to break down the organic matter present in a given volume of a sample of water.

45. **(4)**

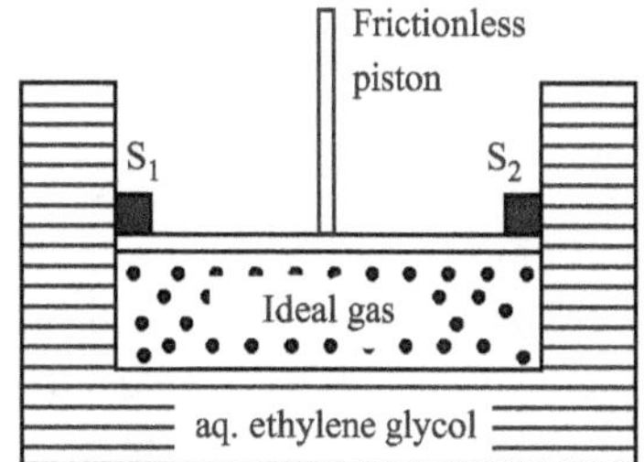

c is-Form

46. **(10.00)**

$$\text{ppm} = \frac{10.3\times10^{-3}}{1.03\times1000}\times10^6 = 10$$

47. **(66.67)**

$$CH_3-\overset{\overset{O}{\|}}{C}-CH_2-CH_3 \xrightarrow{CH_3MgBr} CH_3-\overset{\overset{O^-}{|}}{\underset{\underset{CH_3}{|}}{C}}-CH_2-CH_3$$

$$\xrightarrow{H_3O^+} CH_3-\overset{\overset{OH}{|}}{\underset{\underset{CH_3}{|}}{C}}-CH_2-CH_3 \xrightarrow[573\ K]{Cu} CH_3-\overset{}{\underset{\underset{CH_3}{|}}{C}}=CH-CH_3$$

B   2-methyl-2-butene

Compound A is $CH_3-\overset{\overset{O}{\|}}{C}-CH_2-CH_3(C_4H_8O)$

Mass percentage of carbon

$$=\left(\frac{12\times4}{48+16+8}\times100\right) = 66.67$$

48. **(3.98)**

For a first order reaction, $kt = \ln\dfrac{[A]}{[A_0]}$

At 300 K, $k_1 \times 60 = \ln\dfrac{[A]}{[A_0]}$ ...(1)

At 400 K, $k_2 \times 40 = \ln\dfrac{[A]}{[A_0]}$ ...(2)

From equation (1) and (2),

$$\frac{k_2}{k_1} = \frac{60}{40}$$

$$\ln\frac{k_2}{k_1} = \frac{E_a}{R}\left[\frac{1}{T_1}-\frac{1}{T_2}\right]$$

$$\ln\left(\frac{60}{40}\right) = \frac{E_a}{8.3}\times\frac{100}{400\times300}$$

$$\ln\left(\frac{3}{2}\right) \times 8.3 \times 1200 = E_a$$

$$\Rightarrow \qquad E_a = 0.4 \times 8.3 \times 1200$$

$$\Rightarrow \qquad E_a = 3984 \text{ J/mol.}$$

$$\Rightarrow \qquad E_a = 3.984 \text{ kJ/mol.}$$

49. **(2.18)**

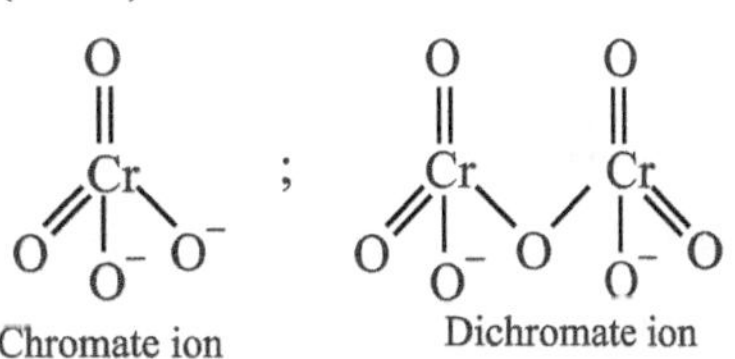

$K_f = 2.0$ K kg mol^{-1}; m = 0.5

$\Delta T_f = K_f m = 0.5 \times 2$

$T_{initial} = 272$ K

$n = 0.1$ mol

$V = 1$ dm^3

$$P_{gas} = \frac{nRT}{V} = \frac{0.1\times0.08\times272}{1} = 2.176 \text{ atm}$$

After releasing piston $P_1V_1 = P_2V_2$

$2.176 \times 1 = 1 \times V_2$

$V_2 = 2.18$ dm^3

50. **(12.00)**

Chromate ion   Dichromate ion

$\Rightarrow$ Total number of Cr and O bonds is 12.

MATHEMATICS

51. (3) The given system of linear equations

$$7x + 6y - 2z = 0 \qquad \text{...(i)}$$
$$3x + 4y + 2z = 0 \qquad \text{...(ii)}$$
$$x - 2y - 6z = 0 \qquad \text{...(iii)}$$

Now, determinant of coefficient matrix

$$\Delta = \begin{vmatrix} 7 & 6 & -2 \\ 3 & 4 & 2 \\ 1 & -2 & -6 \end{vmatrix}$$

$$= 7(-20) - 6(-20) - 2(-10)$$
$$= -140 + 120 + 20 = 0$$

So, there are infinite non-trivial solutions.

From eqn. (i) + 3 × (iii); we get

$$10x - 20z = 0 \implies x = 2z$$

Hence, there are infinitely many solutions (x, y, z) satisfying $x = 2z$.

52. (Bonus) Total number of ways placing 10 different balls in 4 distinct boxes = 4^{10}

Since, two of the 4 distinct boxes contains exactly 2 and 3 balls.

Then, there are three cases to place exactly 2 and 3 balls in 2 of the 4 boxes.

Case-1: When boxes contains balls in order 2, 3, 0, 5
Then, number of ways of placing the balls

$$= \frac{10!}{2! \times 3! \times 0! \times 5!} \times 4!$$

Case-2: When boxes contains ball in order 2, 3, 1, 4.
Then, number of ways of placing the balls

$$= \frac{10!}{2! \times 3! \times 1! \times 4!} \times 4!$$

Case-3: When boxes contains ball in order 2, 3, 2, 3
Then, number of ways of placing the balls

$$= \frac{10!}{(2!)^2 \times (3!)^2 \times 2! \times 3!} \times 4!$$

Therefore, number of ways of placing the balls that contains exactly 2 and 3 balls.

$$= \frac{10!}{2! \times 3! \times 0! \times 5!} \times 4! + \frac{10!}{2! \times 3! \times 1! \times 4!} \times 4!$$

$$+ \frac{10!}{(2!)^2 \times 2! \times (3!)^2 \times 2!} \times 4!$$

$$= 2^5 \times 17 \times 945$$

Hence, the required probability

$$= \frac{2^5 \times 17 \times 945}{4^{10}} = \frac{17 \times 945}{2^{15}}$$

53. (1) It is given that functions f and g are differentiable and fog is identity function.

$$\therefore \quad (fog)(x) = x \implies f(g(x)) = x$$

Differentiating both sides, we get

$$f'(g(x)) \cdot g'(x) = 1$$

Now, put $x = a$, then

$$f'(g(a)) \cdot g'(a) = 1$$
$$f'(b) \cdot 5 = 1$$
$$f'(b) = \frac{1}{5}$$

54. (1)

$$F(x) = \int_1^x t^2 g(t)\,dt$$

Differentiate by using Leibnitz's rule, we get

$$F'(x) = x^2 g(x) = x^2 \int_1^x f(u)\,du \qquad \text{...(i)}$$

At $x = 1$,

$$F'(1) = 1 \int_1^1 f(u)\,du = 0$$

Now, differentiate eqn (i)

$$F''(x) = x^2 f(x) - 2x \int_1^x f(u)\,du$$

At $x = 1$,

$$F''(1) = 1.f(1) - 2 \times 1. \int_1^1 f(u)\,du$$

$$= f(1) - 2 \times 0 = f(1)$$
$$F''(1) = 3$$

Then, for $F'(1) = 0$, $F''(1) = 3 > 0$

Hence, $x = 1$ is a point of local minima.

55. (4) Let G.P. be $a, ar, ar^2 \dots$

$$\sum_{n=1}^{100} a_{2n+1} = a_3 + a_5 + \dots + a_{201} = 200$$

$$\implies \frac{ar^2(r^{200} - 1)}{r^2 - 1} = 200 \qquad \text{...(i)}$$

$$\sum_{n=1}^{100} a_{2n} = a_2 + a_4 + \dots + a_{200} = 100$$

$$\implies \frac{ar(r^{200} - 1)}{r^2 - 1} = 100 \qquad \text{...(ii)}$$

From equations (i) and (ii), $r = 2$ and

$$a_2 + a_3 + \dots + a_{200} + a_{201} = 300$$
$$\implies r(a_1 + \dots + a_{200}) = 300$$

$$\Rightarrow \sum_{n=1}^{200} a_n = \frac{300}{r} = 150$$

56. **(1)** $\displaystyle\lim_{x\to 0} x\left[\frac{4}{x}\right] = A \Rightarrow \lim_{x\to 0} x\left[\frac{4}{x} - \left\{\frac{4}{x}\right\}\right] = A$

$$\Rightarrow \lim_{x\to 0} 4 - x\left\{\frac{4}{x}\right\} = A \Rightarrow 4 - 0 = A$$

As, $f(x) = [x^2]\sin(\pi x)$ will be discontinuous at non-integers

And, when $x = \sqrt{A+1} \Rightarrow x = \sqrt{5}$,

which is not an integer.

Hence, $f(x)$ is discontinuous when x is equal to $\sqrt{A+1}$

57. **(3)** $z = x + iy$

$|x| + |y| = 4$

$|z| = \sqrt{x^2 + y^2}$

Minimum value of

$|z| = 2\sqrt{2}$

Maximum value of

$|z| = 4$

$|z| \in \left[\sqrt{8}, \sqrt{16}\right]$

So, $|z|$ can't be $\sqrt{7}$.

58. **(2)** $y = 1 + \cos^2\theta + \cos^4\theta + \dots$

$$\Rightarrow y = \frac{1}{1 - \cos^2\theta} \Rightarrow \frac{1}{y} = \sin^2\theta$$

$$x = 1 - \tan^2\theta + \tan^4\theta + \dots$$

$$x = \frac{1}{1 - (-\tan^2\theta)} = \frac{1}{\sec^2\theta}$$

$$\Rightarrow x = \cos^2\theta$$

$$y = \frac{1}{\sin^2\theta} \Rightarrow y = \frac{1}{1 - x}$$

$$\therefore \quad y(1 - x) = 1$$

59. **(Bonus)** It is given that

$$x = 2\sin\theta - \sin 2\theta \qquad \dots(i)$$

$$y = 2\cos\theta - \cos 2\theta \qquad \dots(ii)$$

Differentiating (i) w.r.t. θ, we get

$$\frac{dx}{d\theta} = 2\cos\theta - 2\cos 2\theta$$

Differentiating (ii) w.r.t. θ; we get

$$\frac{dy}{d\theta} = -2\sin\theta + 2\sin 2\theta$$

From (ii) ÷ (i), we get

$$\therefore \quad \frac{dy}{dx} = \frac{\sin 2\theta - \sin\theta}{\cos\theta - \cos 2\theta}$$

$$= \frac{2\sin\dfrac{\theta}{2}.\cos\dfrac{3\theta}{2}}{2\sin\dfrac{\theta}{2}.\sin\dfrac{3\theta}{2}} = \cot\frac{3\theta}{2} \qquad \dots(iii)$$

Again, differentiating eqn. (iii), we get

$$\frac{d^2y}{dx^2} = \frac{-3}{2}\operatorname{cosec}^2\frac{3\theta}{2}.\frac{d\theta}{dx}$$

$$\frac{d^2y}{dx^2} = \frac{\dfrac{-3}{2}\operatorname{cosec}^2\dfrac{3\theta}{2}}{2(\cos\theta - \cos 2\theta)}$$

$$\frac{d^2y}{dx^2}\Big|_{(\theta = \pi)} = -\frac{3}{4(-1-1)} = \frac{3}{8}$$

60. **(2)** Coordinates of $P\left(\dfrac{1}{2},0\right), Q\left(\dfrac{\sqrt{3}}{2},0\right), R\left(\dfrac{\sqrt{3}}{2},1-\dfrac{\sqrt{3}}{2}\right)$

and $S\left(\dfrac{1}{2},\dfrac{1}{2}\right)$

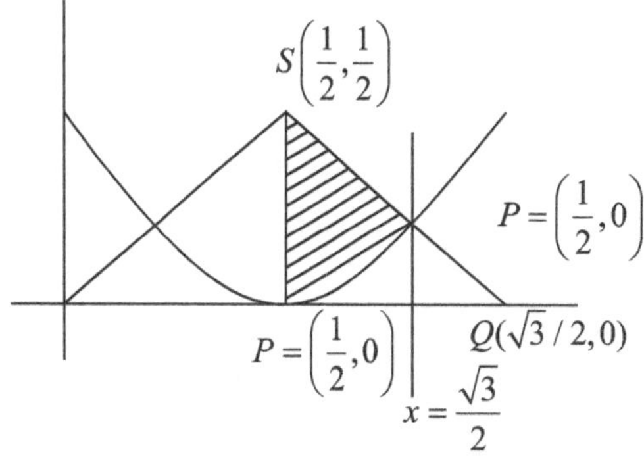

Required area = Area of trapezium $PQRS$

$$- \int_{1/2}^{\sqrt{3}/2}\left(x - \frac{1}{2}\right)^2 dx$$

$$= \frac{1}{2}\left(\frac{\sqrt{3}-1}{2}\right)\left(\frac{1}{2}+1-\frac{\sqrt{3}}{2}\right) - \frac{1}{3}\left(\left(x-\frac{1}{2}\right)^3\right)_{1/2}^{\sqrt{3}/2}$$

$$= \frac{\sqrt{3}}{4} - \frac{1}{3}$$

61. **(1)** Let $\dfrac{x^2}{a^2} + \dfrac{y^2}{b^2} = 1; a > b$

$$2b = \frac{4}{\sqrt{3}} \Rightarrow b = \frac{2}{\sqrt{3}}$$

Equation of tangent $\equiv y = mx \pm \sqrt{a^2 m^2 + b^2}$

Comparing with $\equiv y = \dfrac{-x}{6} + \dfrac{4}{3}$

$m = \dfrac{-1}{6}$ and $a^2 m^2 + b^2 = \dfrac{16}{9}$

$\Rightarrow \quad \dfrac{a^2}{36} + \dfrac{4}{3} = \dfrac{16}{9} \quad \Rightarrow \quad \dfrac{a^2}{36} = \dfrac{16}{9} - \dfrac{4}{3} = \dfrac{4}{9}$

$\Rightarrow \quad a^2 = 16 \quad \Rightarrow \quad a = \pm 4$

Now, eccentricity of ellipse $(e) = \sqrt{1 - \dfrac{b^2}{a^2}}$

$\Rightarrow \quad e = \sqrt{1 - \dfrac{4}{3 \times 16}} = \sqrt{\dfrac{11}{12}} = \dfrac{1}{2}\sqrt{\dfrac{11}{3}}$

62. (1) $ax^2 - 2bx + 5 = 0$,

If α and α are roots of equations, then sum of roots

$$2\alpha = \dfrac{2b}{a} \quad \Rightarrow \quad \alpha = \dfrac{b}{a}$$

and product of roots $= \alpha^2 = \dfrac{5}{a} \quad \Rightarrow \quad \dfrac{b^2}{a^2} = \dfrac{5}{a}$

$\Rightarrow \quad b^2 = 5a \qquad (a \ne 0) \qquad \ldots$(i)

For $x^2 - 2bx - 10 = 0$

$\quad \alpha + \beta = 2b \qquad\qquad \ldots$(ii)

and $\alpha\beta = -10 \qquad\qquad \ldots$(iii)

$\alpha = \dfrac{b}{a}$ is also root of $x^2 - 2bx - 10 = 0$

$\Rightarrow \quad b^2 - 2ab^2 - 10a^2 = 0$

By eqn. (i) $\Rightarrow 5a - 10a^2 - 10a^2 = 0$

$\Rightarrow \quad 20a^2 = 5a$

$\Rightarrow \quad a = \dfrac{1}{4}$ and $b^2 = \dfrac{5}{4}$

$\alpha^2 = 20$ and $\beta^2 = 5$

Now, $\alpha^2 + \beta^2 = 5 + 20 = 25$

63. (2) Let parabola $y^2 = 8x$ at point $\left(\dfrac{1}{2}, -2\right)$ is $(2t^2, 4t)$

$\Rightarrow \quad t = \dfrac{-1}{2}$

Parameter of other end of

focal chord is 2

So, coordinates of

B is $(8, 8)$

$\Rightarrow$ Equation of tangent

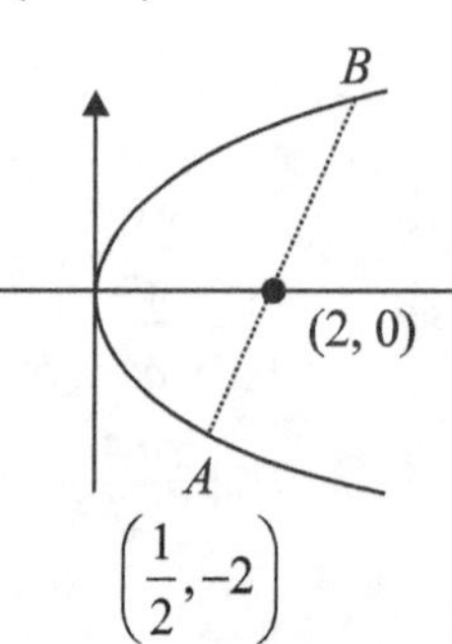

at B is $8y - 4(x + 8) = 0$

$\Rightarrow \quad 2y - x = 8$

$\Rightarrow \quad x - 2y + 8 = 0$

64. (4) The given differential equation,

$$\dfrac{dy}{dx} = \dfrac{xy}{x^2 + y^2}$$

Put $y = vx \quad \Rightarrow \quad \dfrac{dy}{dx} = v + x\dfrac{dv}{dx}$

Then, $v + x\dfrac{dv}{dx} = \dfrac{vx^2}{x^2 + v^2 x^2} = \dfrac{v}{1 + v^2}$

$\Rightarrow \quad \dfrac{1 + v^2}{v^3} dv = -\dfrac{1}{x} dx$

$\Rightarrow \quad \displaystyle\int \left(\dfrac{1}{v^3} + \dfrac{1}{v}\right) dv = \int \dfrac{-1}{x} dx$

$\Rightarrow \quad \dfrac{-1}{2}\left(\dfrac{1}{v^2}\right) + \ln v = -\ln x + c$

$\Rightarrow \quad -\dfrac{x^2}{2y^2} = -\ln y + c \qquad \left[\because v = \dfrac{y}{x}\right]$

When $x = 1, y = 1$, then $-\dfrac{1}{2} = c$

$\Rightarrow \quad x^2 = y^2(1 + 2\ln y)$

At $y = e, \ x^2 = e^2(3)$

$\Rightarrow \quad x = \pm\sqrt{3}e$

So, $\ x = \sqrt{3}e$

65. (4) If $f(x) = \begin{vmatrix} x+a & x+2 & x+1 \\ x+b & x+3 & x+2 \\ x+c & x+4 & x+3 \end{vmatrix}$

$R_1 = R_1 + R_3 - 2R_2$

$\Rightarrow \quad f(x) = \begin{vmatrix} 1 & 0 & 0 \\ x+b & x+3 & x+2 \\ x+c & x+4 & x+3 \end{vmatrix}$

$\Rightarrow \quad f(x) = 1 \quad \Rightarrow \quad f(50) = 1$

66. (2) $A = \{x : x \in (-2, 2)\}$

$B = \{x : x \in (-\infty, -1] \cup [5, \infty)\}$

$A \cap B = \{x : x \in (-2, -1]\}$

$A \cup B = \{x : x \in (-\infty, 2) \cup [5, \infty)\}$

$A - B = \{x : x \in (-1, 2)\}$

$B - A = \{x : x \in (-\infty, -2] \cup [5, \infty)\}$

67. **(2)** General term of the given expansion

$$T_{r+1} = {}^{16}C_r \left(\frac{x}{\sin\theta}\right)^{16-r}\left(\frac{1}{x\cos\theta}\right)^r$$

For $r = 8$ term is free from 'x'

$$T_9 = {}^{16}C_8 \frac{1}{\sin^8\theta\cos^8\theta}$$

$$T_9 = {}^{16}C_8 \frac{2^8}{(\sin 2\theta)^8}$$

When $\theta \in \left[\dfrac{\pi}{8},\dfrac{\pi}{4}\right]$, then least value of the term independent of x,

$$l_1 = {}^{16}C_8\, 2^8 \qquad [\because \text{min. value of } l_1 \text{ at } \theta = \pi/4]$$

When $\theta \in \left[\dfrac{\pi}{16},\dfrac{\pi}{8}\right]$, then least value of the term independent of x,

$$l_2 = {}^{16}C_8 = \frac{2^8}{\left(\dfrac{1}{\sqrt2}\right)^8} = {}^{16}C_8.2^8.2^4$$

$$[\because \text{min. value of } l_2 \text{ at } \theta = \pi/8]$$

Now, $\dfrac{l_2}{l_1} = \dfrac{{}^{16}C_8.2^8.2^4}{{}^{16}C_8.2^8} = 16$

68. **(4)** $\sum P(K) = 1 \Rightarrow 6K^2 + 5K = 1$

$$6K^2 + 5K - 1 = 0$$
$$6K^2 + 6K - K - 1 = 0$$
$$\Rightarrow (6K-1)(K+1) = 0$$
$$\Rightarrow K = \frac{1}{6} \; (K = -1 \text{ rejected})$$

$$P(X>2) = K + 2K + 5K^2$$
$$= \frac{1}{6} + \frac{2}{6} + \frac{5}{36} = \frac{6+12+5}{36} = \frac{23}{36}$$

69. **(3)**

p	q	$\sim q$	$p \wedge \sim q$	$p \rightarrow (p \wedge \sim q)$
T	T	F	F	F
T	F	T	T	T
F	T	F	F	T
F	F	T	F	T

70. **(3)** $I = \displaystyle\int \frac{d\theta}{\cos^2\theta(\tan 2\theta + \sec 2\theta)}$

$$= \int \frac{\sec^2\theta}{\dfrac{1+\tan^2\theta}{1-\tan^2\theta} + \dfrac{2\tan\theta}{1-\tan^2\theta}}\, d\theta$$

$$= \int \frac{\sec^2\theta(1-\tan^2\theta)}{(1+\tan\theta)^2}\, d\theta$$

$$= \int \frac{\sec^2\theta(1-\tan\theta)}{1+\tan\theta}\, d\theta$$

Let $\tan\theta = t \Rightarrow \sec^2\theta\, d\theta = dt$, then

$$I = \int\left(\frac{1-t}{1+t}\right) dt = \int\left(-1 + \frac{2}{1+t}\right) dt$$
$$= -t + 2\log(1+t) + C$$
$$= -\tan\theta + 2\log(1+\tan\theta) + C$$

Hence, by comparison $\lambda = -1$ and $f(x) = 1 + \tan\theta$

71. **(51)** $\displaystyle\sum_{r=0}^{25}(4r+1)\,{}^{25}C_r = 4\sum_{r=0}^{25} r.\,{}^{25}C_r + \sum_{r=0}^{25}{}^{25}C_r$

$$= 4\sum_{r=1}^{25} r\times\frac{25}{r}\,{}^{24}C_{r-1} + 2^{25} = 100\sum_{r=1}^{25}{}^{24}C_{r-1} + 2^{25}$$

$$= 100.2^{24} + 2^{25} = 2^{25}(50+1) = 51.2^{25}$$

Hence, by comparison $k = 51$

72. **(14)** First common term of both the series is 23 and common difference is $7 \times 4 = 28$

$\because$ Last term ≤ 407

$$\Rightarrow 23 + (n-1) \times 28 \leq 407$$
$$\Rightarrow (n-1)\times 28 \leq 384$$
$$\Rightarrow n \leq \frac{384}{28} + 1$$
$$\Rightarrow n \leq 14.71$$

Hence, $n = 14$

73. **(30)** $\vec{b}.\vec{c} = 10 \Rightarrow |\vec{b}||\vec{c}|\cos\left(\frac{\pi}{3}\right) = 10$

$$\Rightarrow 5.|\vec{c}|.\frac{1}{2} = 10 \Rightarrow |\vec{c}| = 4$$

Since, $\vec{a}$ is perpendicular to the vector $\vec{b} \times \vec{c}$, then

$$\vec{a}.(\vec{b}\times\vec{c}) = 0$$

Now, $\left|\vec{a}\times(\vec{b}\times\vec{c})\right| = |\vec{a}|\left|\vec{b}\times\vec{c}\right|\sin\left(\frac{\pi}{2}\right)$

$$= \sqrt3\times|\vec{b}||\vec{c}|\sin\frac{\pi}{3}\times 1 = \sqrt3\times 5\times 4\times\frac{\sqrt3}{2} = 30$$

Hence, $\left|\vec{a}\times(\vec{b}\times\vec{c})\right| = 30$.

74. **(3)** Since, the line $\dfrac{x+1}{2} = \dfrac{y-3}{4} = \dfrac{z+1}{3}$ contains the point $(-1, 3, -1)$ and line $\dfrac{x+3}{2} = \dfrac{y+2}{6} = \dfrac{z-1}{\lambda}$ contains the point $(-3, -2, 1)$.

Then, the distance between the plane

$23x - 10y - 2z + 48 = 0$ and the plane containing the lines = perpendicular distance of plane

$23x - 10y - 2z + 48 = 0$ either from $(-1, 3, -1)$ or $(-3, -2, 1)$.

$$= \left| \frac{23(-1) - 10(3) - 2(-1)}{\sqrt{(23)^2 + (10)^2 + (-2)^2}} \right| = \frac{3}{\sqrt{633}}$$

It is given that distance between the planes

$$= \frac{k}{\sqrt{633}} \quad \Rightarrow \quad \frac{k}{\sqrt{633}} = \frac{3}{\sqrt{633}} \quad \Rightarrow \quad k = 3$$

75. **(36)** The given equation of circle

$$x^2 - 6x + y^2 + 8 = 0$$

$$(x-3)^2 + y^2 = 1 \qquad \text{...(i)}$$

So, centre of circle (i) is $C_1(3, 0)$ and radius $r_1 = 1$.

And the second equation of circle

$$x^2 - 8y + y^2 + 16 - k = 0 \ (k > 0)$$

$$x^2 + (y-4)^2 = \left(\sqrt{k}\right)^2 \qquad \text{...(ii)}$$

So, centre of circle (ii) is $C_2(0, 4)$ and radius $r_2 = \sqrt{k}$

Two circles touches each other when

$$C_1 C_2 = |r_1 \pm r_2| \quad \Rightarrow \quad 5 = \left|1 \pm \sqrt{k}\right|$$

Distance between $C_2(3, 0)$ and $C_1(0, 4)$ is

either $\sqrt{k} + 1$ or $\left|\sqrt{k} - 1\right|$ $(C_1 C_2 = 5)$

$\Rightarrow \quad \sqrt{k} + 1 = 5 \quad$ or $\quad \left|\sqrt{k} - 1\right| = 5$

$\Rightarrow \quad k = 16 \quad$ or $\quad k = 36$

Hence, maximum value of k is 36

The given equation of circles

$$x^2 - 6x + y^2 + 8 = 0$$

$$\Rightarrow \quad (x-3)^2 + y^2 = 1$$

JEE MAIN 2020
(Held on 2-09-2020 Morning Shift)

1. An amplitude modulated wave is represented by the expression $v_m = 5(1 + 0.6\cos 6280t)\sin(211 \times 10^4 t)$ volts The minimum and maximum amplitudes of the amplitude modulated wave are, respectively :

(1) $\dfrac{3}{2}$ V, 5 V

(2) $\dfrac{5}{2}$ V, 8 V

(3) 5 V, 8 V

(4) 3 V, 5 V

2. Magnetic materials used for making permanent magnets (P) and magnets in a transformer (T) have different properties of the following, which property best matches for the type of magnet required?

(1) T : Large retentivity, small coercivity

(2) P : Small retentivity, large coercivity

(3) T : Large retentivity, large coercivity

(4) P : Large retentivity, large coercivity

3.

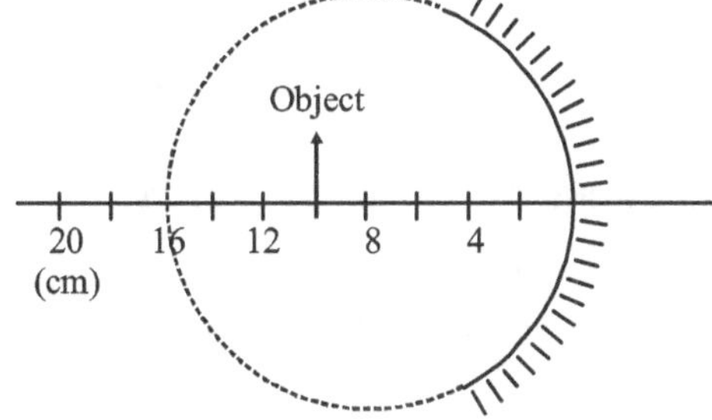

A spherical mirror is obtained as shown in the figure from a hollow glass sphere. If an object is positioned in front of the mirror, what will be the nature and magnification of the image of the object? (Figure drawn as schematic and not to scale)

(1) Inverted, real and magnified

(2) Erect, virtual and magnified

(3) Erect, virtual and unmagnified

(4) Inverted, real and unmagnified

4. The least count of the main scale of a vernier callipers is 1 mm. Its vernier scale is divided into 10 divisions and coincide with 9 divisions of the main scale. When jaws are touching each other, the 7th division of vernier scale coincides with a division of main scale and the zero of vernier scale is lying right side of the zero of main scale. When this vernier is used to measure length of a cylinder the zero of the vernier scale between 3.1 cm and 3.2 cm and 4th VSD coincides with a main scale division. The length of the cylinder is : (VSD is vernier scale division)

(1) 3.2 cm (2) 3.21 cm (3) 3.07 cm (4) 2.99 cm

5. A bead of mass m stays at point $P(a, b)$ on a wire bent in the shape of a parabola $y = 4Cx^2$ and rotating with angular speed ω (see figure). The value of ω is (neglect friction) :

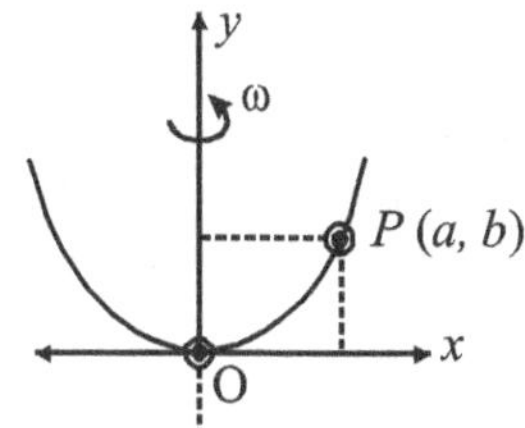

(1) $2\sqrt{2gC}$

(2) $2\sqrt{gC}$

(3) $\sqrt{\dfrac{2gC}{ab}}$

(4) $\sqrt{\dfrac{2g}{C}}$

6. A particle of mass m with an initial velocity $u\,\hat{i}$ collides perfectly elastically with a mass $3\,m$ at rest. It moves with a velocity $v\,\hat{j}$ after collision, then, v is given by :

(1) $v = \sqrt{\dfrac{2}{3}}u$

(2) $v = \dfrac{u}{\sqrt{3}}$

(3) $v = \dfrac{u}{\sqrt{2}}$

(4) $v = \dfrac{1}{\sqrt{6}}u$

7. Consider four conducting materials copper, tungsten, mercury and aluminium with resistivity ρ_C, ρ_T, ρ_M and ρ_A respectively. Then :

(1) $\rho_C > \rho_A > \rho_T$

(2) $\rho_M > \rho_A > \rho_C$

(3) $\rho_A > \rho_T > \rho_C$

(4) $\rho_A > \rho_M > \rho_C$

8. Two identical strings X and Z made of same material have tension T_X and T_Z in them. If their fundamental frequencies are 450 Hz and 300 Hz, respectively, then the ratio T_X/T_Z is:

(1) 2.25 (2) 0.44 (3) 1.25 (4) 1.5

9. A gas mixture consists of 3 moles of oxygen and 5 moles of argon at temperature T. Assuming the gases to be ideal and the oxygen bond to be rigid, the total internal energy (in units of RT) of the mixture is :

(1) 15 (2) 13 (3) 20 (4) 11

10. Train A and train B are running on parallel tracks in the opposite directions with speeds of 36 km/hour and 72 km/hour, respectively. A person is walking in train A in the direction opposite to its motion with a speed of 1.8 km/hour. Speed (in ms^{-1}) of this person as observed from train B will be close to : (take the distance between the tracks as negligible)

(1) 29.5 ms^{-1}

(2) 28.5 ms^{-1}

(3) 31.5 ms^{-1}

(4) 30.5 ms^{-1}

11. A beam of protons with speed 4×10^5 ms^{-1} enters a uniform magnetic field of 0.3 T at an angle of 60° to the magnetic field. The pitch of the resulting helical path of protons is close to : (Mass of the proton = 1.67×10^{-27} kg, charge of the proton = 1.69×10^{-19} C)

(1) 2 cm   (2) 5 cm   (3) 12 cm   (4) 4 cm

12.

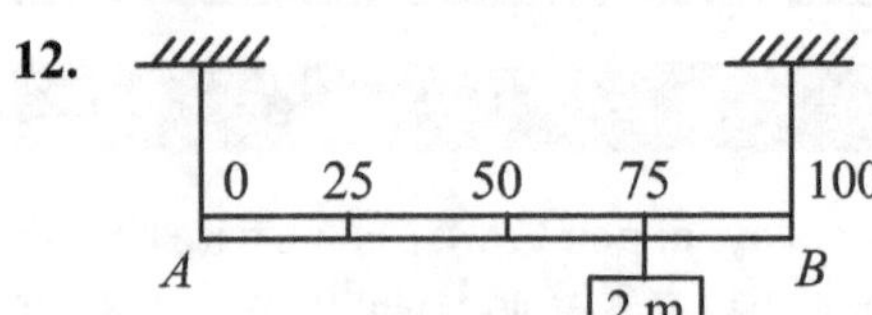

Shown in the figure is rigid and uniform one meter long rod AB held in horizontal position by two strings tied to its ends and attached to the ceiling. The rod is of mass 'm' and has another weight of mass 2 m hung at a distance of 75 cm from A. The tension in the string at A is :

(1) 0.5 mg   (2) 2 mg   (3) 0.75 mg   (4) 1 mg

13. A plane electromagnetic wave, has frequency of 2.0×10^{10} Hz and its energy density is 1.02×10^{-8} J/m^3 in vacuum. The amplitude of the magnetic field of the wave is close to

$(\dfrac{1}{4\pi\varepsilon_0} = 9 \times 10^9 \dfrac{Nm^2}{C^2}$ and speed of light $= 3 \times 10^8$ ms$^{-1})$:

(1) 150 nT   (2) 160 nT   (3) 180 nT   (4) 190 nT

14. A cylindrical vessel containing a liquid is rotated about its axis so that the liquid rises at its sides as shown in the figure. The radius of vessel is 5 cm and the angular speed of rotation is ω rad s^{-1}. The difference in the height, h (in cm) of liquid at the centre of vessel and at the side will be :

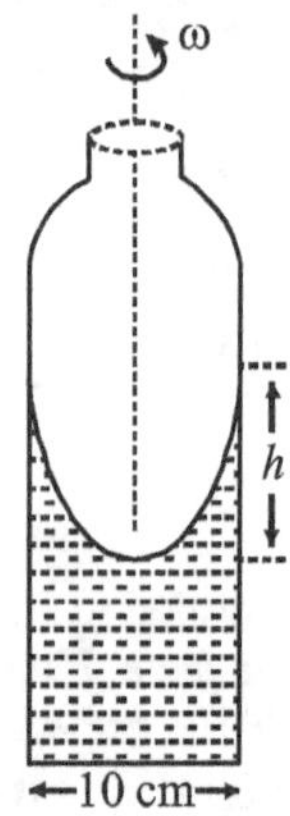

(1) $\dfrac{2\omega^2}{25g}$ (2) $\dfrac{5\omega^2}{2g}$ (3) $\dfrac{25\omega^2}{2g}$ (4) $\dfrac{2\omega^2}{5g}$

15. In a reactor, 2 kg of $_{92}U^{235}$ fuel is fully used up in 30 days. The energy released per fission is 200 MeV. Given that the Avogadro number, N = 6.023×10^{26} per kilo mole and 1 eV = 1.6×10^{-19} J. The power output of the reactor is close to:

(1) 35 MW   (2) 60 MW   (3) 125 MW   (4) 54 MW

16. If speed V, area A and force F are chosen as fundamental units, then the dimension of Young's modulus will be :

(1) FA^{2}V^{-1} (2) FA^{2}V^{-3}
(3) FA^{2}V^{-2} (4) FA^{-1}V^0

17. A uniform cylinder of mass M and radius R is to be pulled over a step of height a ($a < R$) by applying a force F at its centre 'O' perpendicular to the plane through the axes of the cylinder on the edge of the step (see figure). The minimum value of F required is :

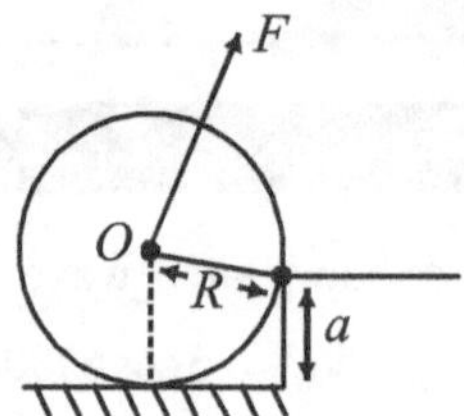

(1) $Mg\sqrt{1-\left(\dfrac{R-a}{R}\right)^2}$ (2) $Mg\sqrt{\left(\dfrac{R}{R-a}\right)^2 - 1}$

(3) $Mg\dfrac{a}{R}$ (4) $Mg\sqrt{1-\dfrac{a^2}{R^2}}$

18. Interference fringes are observed on a screen by illuminating two thin slits 1 mm apart with a light source (λ = 632.8 nm). The distance between the screen and the slits is 100 cm. If a bright fringe is observed on a screen at a distance of 1.27 mm from the central bright fringe, then the path difference between the waves, which are reaching this point from the slits is close to :

(1) 1.27 µm   (2) 2.87 nm   (3) 2 nm   (4) 2.05 µm

19. The mass density of a spherical galaxy varies as $\dfrac{K}{r}$ over a large distance 'r' from its centre. In that region, a small star is in a circular orbit of radius R. Then the period of revolution, T depends on R as :

(1) $T^2 \propto R$ (2) $T^2 \propto R^3$

(3) $T^2 \propto \dfrac{1}{R^3}$ (4) $T \propto R$

20. A charged particle (mass m and charge q) moves along X axis with velocity V_0. When it passes through the origin it enters a region having uniform electric field $\vec{E} = -E\hat{j}$ which extends upto $x = d$. Equation of path of electron in the region $x > d$ is :

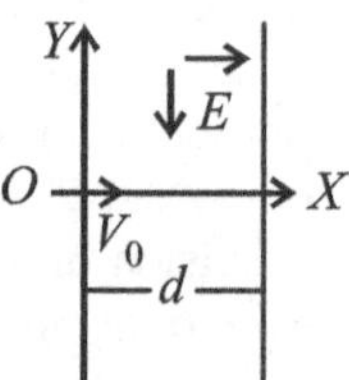

(1) $y = \dfrac{qEd}{mV_0^2}(x-d)$ (2) $y = \dfrac{qEd}{mV_0^2}\left(\dfrac{d}{2} - x\right)$

(3) $y = \dfrac{qEd}{mV_0^2}x$ (4) $y = \dfrac{qEd^2}{mV_0^2}x$

21. A circular coil of radius 10 cm is placed in a uniform magnetic field of 3.0×10^{-5} T with its plane perpendicular to the field initially. It is rotated at constant angular speed about an axis along the diameter of coil and perpendicular to magnetic field so that it undergoes half of rotation in 0.2 s. The maximum value of EMF induced (in μV) in the coil will be close to the integer __________.

22. An engine takes in 5 mole of air at 20°C and 1 atm, and compresses it adiabatically to $1/10^{th}$ of the original volume. Assuming air to be a diatomic ideal gas made up of rigid molecules, the change in its internal energy during this process comes out to be X kJ. The value of X to the nearest integer is __________.

23.

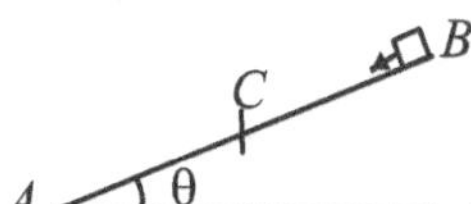

A small block starts slipping down from a point B on an inclined plane AB, which is making an angle θ with the horizontal section BC is smooth and the remaining section CA is rough with a coefficient of friction μ. It is found that the block comes to rest as it reaches the bottom (point A) of the inclined plane. If $BC = 2AC$, the coefficient of friction is given by $\mu = k \tan\theta$. The value of k is __________.

24. A 5 μF capacitor is charged fully by a 220 V supply. It is then disconnected from the supply and is connected in series to another uncharged 2.5 μF capacitor. If the energy change during the charge redistribution is $\dfrac{X}{100}$ J then value of X to the nearest integer is __________.

25. When radiation of wavelength λ is used to illuminate a metallic surface, the stopping potential is V. When the same surface is illuminated with radiation of wavelength 3λ, the stopping potential is $\dfrac{V}{4}$. If the theshold wavelength for the metallic surface is $n\lambda$ then value of n will be __________.

CHEMISTRY

26. The figure that is **not** a direct manifestation of the quantum nature of atoms is :

(1)

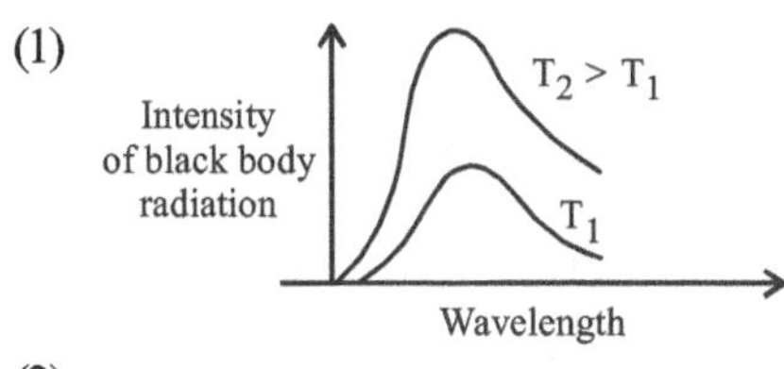

(2)

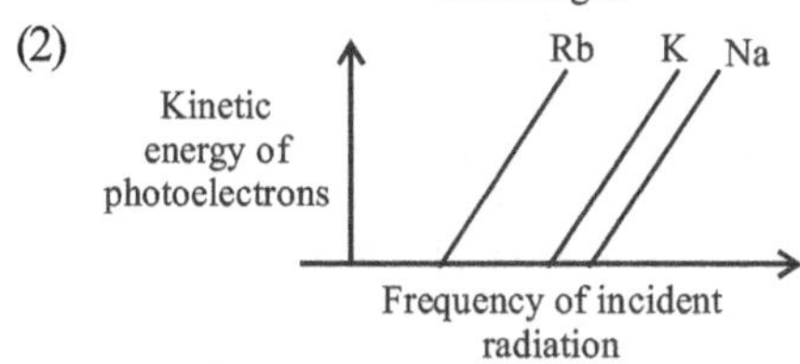

(3)

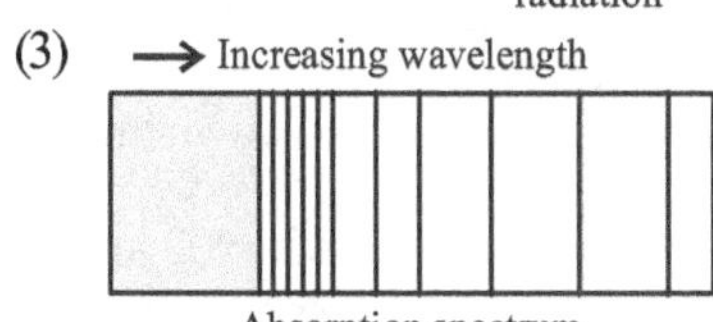

(4)

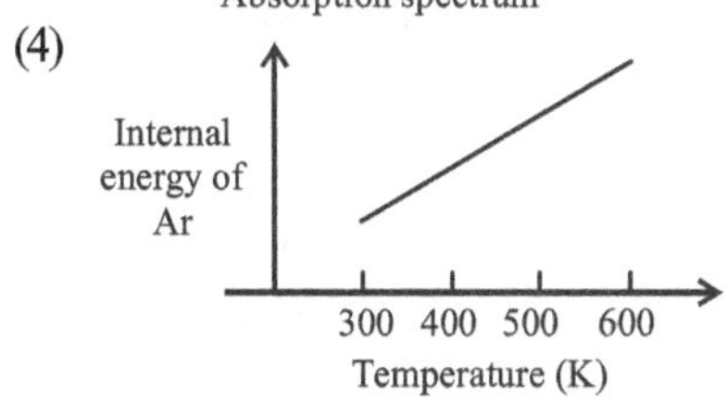

27. Consider that a d^6 metal ion (M^{2+}) forms a complex with aqua ligands, and the spin only magnetic moment of the complex is 4.90 BM. The geometry and the crystal field stabilization energy of the complex is :

(1) octahedral and $-2.4\Delta_0 + 2P$

(2) tetrahedral and $-0.6\,\Delta_t$

(3) octahedral and $-1.6\,\Delta_0$

(4) tetrahedral and $-1.6\Delta_t + 1P$

28. In Carius method of estimation of halogen, 0.172 g of an organic compound showed presence of 0.08 g of bromine. Which of these is the **correct** structure of the compound?

(1) $H_3C - CH_2 - Br$

(2) *4-bromoaniline* (NH_2 para to Br)

(3) *2-bromo-4-bromoaniline* (aniline with Br at 2 and 4 positions)

(4) $H_3C - Br$

29. For octahedral Mn(II) and tetrahedral Ni(II) complexes, consider the following statements :

(I) both the complexes can be high spin.

(II) Ni(II) complex can very rarely below spin.

(III) with strong field ligands, Mn(II) complexes can be low spin.

(IV) aqueous solution of Mn(II) ions is yellow in color.

The correct statements are :

(1) (I) and (II) only   (2) (I), (III) and (IV) only

(3) (I), (II) and (III) only   (4) (II), (III) and (IV) only

30. The major aromatic product C in the following reaction sequence will be :

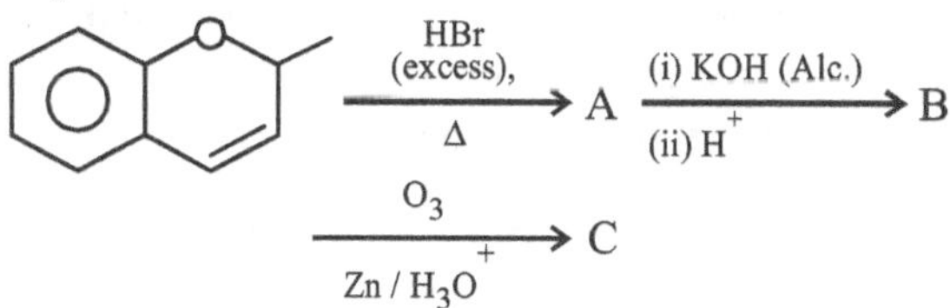

(1) [structure: benzene ring with OH and CHO]

(2) [structure: benzene ring with OH and CO_2H]

(3) [structure: benzene ring with Br and CO_2H]

(4) [structure: benzene ring with Br and CHO]

31. Which of the following compounds will show retention in configuration on nucleophic substitution by OH^- ion ?

(1) $CH_3 - \overset{\overset{\displaystyle Br}{|}}{\underset{\underset{\displaystyle C_6H_{13}}{|}}{C}} - H$

(2) $CH_3 - \underset{\underset{\displaystyle C_6H_5}{|}}{CH} - Br$

(3) $CH_3 - \underset{\underset{\displaystyle CH_3}{|}}{CH} - Br$

(4) $CH_3 - \underset{\underset{\displaystyle C_2H_5}{|}}{CH} - CH_2Br$

32. The major product in the following reaction is :

[structure: methylenecyclopentane with gem-dimethyl, reagent H_3O^+, Heat]

(1) [cyclopentene with isopropyl group]

(2) [cyclohexene with two methyl groups]

(3) [cyclohexene with gem-dimethyl]

(4) [cyclopentane with $C(OH)(CH_3)$ and methyl]

33. The increasing order of the following compounds towards HCN addition is :

[structure (i): H_3CO on benzene ring with CHO (meta)]

[structure (ii): benzene ring with CHO and NO_2 (ortho)]

          (i)   (ii)

[structure (iii): benzene ring with CHO and OCH_3 (ortho)]

[structure (iv): O_2N and CHO on benzene ring (meta)]

          (iii)   (iv)

(1) (i) < (iii) < (iv) < (ii)   **(2)** (iii) < (iv) < (i) < (ii)
(3) (iii) < (i) < (iv) < (ii)   **(4)** (iii) < (iv) < (ii) < (i)

34. In general, the property (magnitudes only) that shows an opposite trend in comparison to other properties across a period is :
(1) Ionization enthalpy   **(2)** Electronegativity
(3) Electron gain enthalpy   **(4)** Atomic radius

35. Consider the following reactions :

(i)   Glucose + ROH $\xrightarrow{\text{dry HCl}}$ Acetal $\xrightarrow[\text{(CH}_3\text{CO)}_2\text{O}]{x \text{ eq. of}}$

     acetyl derivative

(ii)   Glucose $\xrightarrow{\text{Ni/H}_2}$ A $\xrightarrow[\text{(CH}_3\text{CO)}_2\text{O}]{y \text{ eq. of}}$ acetyl derivative

(iii)   Glucose $\xrightarrow[\text{(CH}_3\text{CO)}_2\text{O}]{z \text{ eq. of}}$ acetyl derivative

'x', 'y' and 'z' in these reactions are respectively.
(1) 5, 4 & 5   **(2)** 4, 6 & 5
(3) 4, 5 & 5   **(4)** 5, 6 & 5

36. The metal mainly used in devising photoelectric cells is :
(1) Na   **(2)** Li   **(3)** Rb   **(4)** Cs

37. For the following **Assertion** and **Reason**, the correct option is
Assertion (A) : When Cu (II) and sulphide ions are mixed, they react together extremely quickly to give a solid.
Reason (R) : The equilibrium constant of Cu^{2+} (aq) + S^{2-} (aq) $\rightleftharpoons$ CuS (s) is high because the solubility product is low.
(1) **(A)** is false and **(R)** is true
(2) Both **(A)** and **(R)** are false
(3) Both **(A)** and **(R)** are true but **(R)** is not the explanation for **(A)**
(4) Both **(A)** and **(R)** are true and **(R)** is the explanation for **(A)**

38. On heating compound (A) gives a gas (B) which is a constituent of air. This gas when treated with H_2 in the presence of a catalyst gives another gas (C) which is basic in nature. (A) should **not** be :
(1) NaN_3 **(2)** $Pb(NO_3)_2$
(3) $(NH_4)_2Cr_2O_7$ **(4)** NH_4NO_2

39. An open beaker of water in equilibrium with water vapour is in a sealed container. When a few grams of glucose are added to the beaker of water, the rate at which water molecules :
(1) leaves the vapour increases
(2) leaves the solution increases
(3) leaves the solution decreases
(4) leaves the vapour decreases

40. The statement that is **not** true about ozone is :
(1) in the stratosphere, CFCs release chlorine free radicals (Cl) which reacts with O_3 to give chlorine dioxide radicals.
(2) in the atmosphere, it is depleted by CFCs.
(3) in the stratosphere, it forms a protective shield against UV radiation.
(4) it is a toxic gas and its reaction with NO gives NO_2.

41. Which of the following is used for the preparation of colloids?
(1) Ostwald Process   **(2)** Van Arkel Method
(3) Bredig' s Arc Method   **(4)** Mond Process

42. If AB_4 molecule is a polar molecule, a possible geometry of AB_4 is :
(1) Square pyramidal   **(2)** Tetrahedral
(3) Rectangular planar   **(4)** Square planar

43. The IUPAC name for the following compound is :

[structure: $H_3C-CH(CHO)-CH=CH-CH(CH_3)-COOH$]

(1) 2, 5-dimethyl-5-carboxy-hex-3-enal
(2) 2, 5-dimethyl-6-carboxy-hex-3-enal
(3) 2, 5-dimethyl-6-oxo-hex-3-enoic acid
(4) 6-formyl-2-methyl-hex-3-enoic acid

44. Which one of the following graphs is **not** correct for ideal gas?

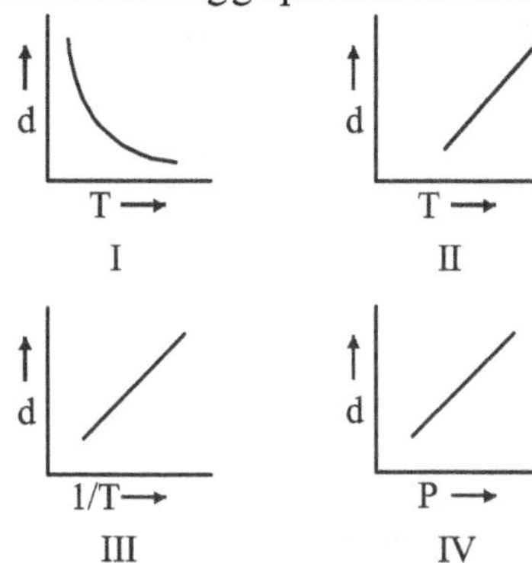

d = Density, P = Pressure, T = Temperature

(1) I (2) II (3) IV (4) III

45. While titrating dilute HCl solution with aqueous NaOH, which of the following will **not** be required?

(1) Burette and porcelain tile
(2) Pipette and distilled water
(3) Clamp and phenolphthalein
(4) Bunsen burner and measuring cylinder

46. The number of chiral carbons present in the molecule given below is __________.

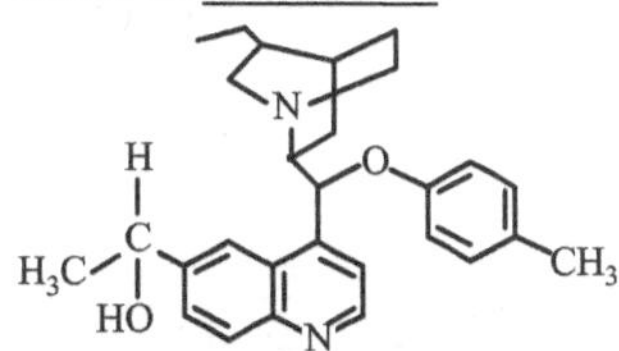

47. The oxidation states of iron atoms in compounds (A), (B) and (C), respectively, are x, y and z. The sum of x, y and z is __________.

$$Na_4[Fe(CN)_5(NOS)] \qquad Na_4[FeO_4] \qquad [Fe_2(CO)_9]$$
$$\text{(A)} \qquad\qquad \text{(B)} \qquad\qquad \text{(C)}$$

48. The Gibbs energy change (in J) for the given reaction at $[Cu^{2+}] = [Sn^{2+}] = 1$ M and 298 K is :

$$Cu(s) + Sn^{2+}\ (aq.) \rightarrow Cu^{2+}\ (aq.) + Sn(s);$$

$(E^0_{Sn^{2+}|Sn} = -0.16$ V, $E^0_{Cu^{2+}|Cu} = 0.34$ V,

Take F = 96500 C mol^{-1})

49. The mass of gas adsorbed, x, per unit mass of adsorbate, m, was measured at various pressures, p. A graph between $\log \dfrac{x}{m}$ and $\log p$ gives a straight line with slope equal to 2 and the intercept equal to 0.4771. The value of $\dfrac{x}{m}$ at a pressure of 4 atm is : (Given log 3 = 0.4771)

50. The internal energy change (in J) when 90 g of water undergoes complete evaporation at 100°C is __________ . (Given : ΔH_{vap} for water at 373 K = 41 kJ/ mol, R = 8.314 JK^{-1} mol^{-1})

MATHEMATICS

51. The domain of the function $f(x) = \sin^{-1}\left(\dfrac{|x|+5}{x^2+1}\right)$ is $(-\infty, -a] \cup [a, \infty]$. Then a is equal to :

(1) $\dfrac{\sqrt{17}}{2}$

(2) $\dfrac{\sqrt{17}-1}{2}$

(3) $\dfrac{1+\sqrt{17}}{2}$

(4) $\dfrac{\sqrt{17}}{2}+1$

52. If $R = \{(x, y): x, y \in \mathbf{Z}, x^2 + 3y^2 \le 8\}$ is a relation on the set of integers $\mathbf{Z}$, then the domain of R^{-1} is :

(1) $\{-2, -1, 1, 2\}$
(2) $\{0, 1\}$
(3) $\{-2, -1, 0, 1, 2\}$
(4) $\{-1, 0, 1\}$

53. Box I contains 30 cards numbered 1 to 30 and Box II contains 20 cards numbered 31 to 50. A box is selected at random and a card is drawn from it. The number on the card is found to be a non-prime number. The probability that the card was drawn from Box I is :

(1) $\dfrac{2}{3}$ (2) $\dfrac{8}{17}$ (3) $\dfrac{4}{17}$ (4) $\dfrac{2}{5}$

54. Area (in sq. units) of the region outside $\dfrac{|x|}{2} + \dfrac{|y|}{3} = 1$ and inside the ellipse $\dfrac{x^2}{4} + \dfrac{y^2}{9} = 1$ is :

(1) $6(\pi - 2)$

(2) $3(\pi - 2)$

(3) $3(4 - \pi)$

(4) $6(4 - \pi)$

55. Let $y = y(x)$ be the solution of the differential equation,

$$\dfrac{2 + \sin x}{y+1} \cdot \dfrac{dy}{dx} = -\cos x, \ y > 0, \ y(0) = 1.$$ If $y(\pi) = a$ and $\dfrac{dy}{dx}$ at $x = \pi$ is b, then the ordered pair (a, b) is equal to :

(1) $\left(2, \dfrac{3}{2}\right)$

(2) $(1, -1)$

(3) $(1, 1)$

(4) $(2, 1)$

56. Let $\alpha > 0$, $\beta > 0$ be such that $\alpha^3 + \beta^2 = 4$. If the maximum value of the term independent of x in the binomial expansion of $(\alpha x^{\frac{1}{9}} + \beta x^{-\frac{1}{6}})^{10}$ is $10k$, then k is equal to :

(1) 336 (2) 352 (3) 84 (4) 176

57. Let A be a 2×2 real matrix with entries from $\{0, 1\}$ and $|A| \ne 0$. Consider the following two statements :

(P) If $A \ne I_2$, then $|A| = -1$
(Q) If $|A| = 1$, then tr$(A) = 2$,

where I_2 denotes 2×2 identity matrix and tr(A) denotes the sum of the diagonal entries of A. Then :

(1) (P) is false and (Q) is true
(2) Both (P) and (Q) are false
(3) (P) is true and (Q) is false
(4) Both (P) and (Q) are true

58. The sum of the first three terms of a G.P. is S and their product is 27. Then all such S lie in :
(1) $(-\infty, -9] \cup [3, \infty)$ (2) $[-3, \infty)$
(3) $(-\infty, -3] \cup [9, \infty)$ (4) $(-\infty, 9]$

59. If $|x| < 1, |y| < 1$ and $x \neq y$, then the sum to infinity of the following series
$$(x+y)+(x^2+xy+y^2)+(x^3+x^2y+xy^2+y^3)+.... \text{ is :}$$
(1) $\dfrac{x+y-xy}{(1+x)(1+y)}$ (2) $\dfrac{x+y+xy}{(1+x)(1+y)}$
(3) $\dfrac{x+y-xy}{(1-x)(1-y)}$ (4) $\dfrac{x+y+xy}{(1-x)(1-y)}$

60. Let α and β be the roots of the equation, $5x^2+6x-2=0$. If $S_n = \alpha^n + \beta^n$, $n = 1, 2, 3, ...,$ then :
(1) $6S_6 + 5S_5 = 2S_4$ (2) $6S_6 + 5S_5 + 2S_4 = 0$
(3) $5S_6 + 6S_5 = 2S_4$ (4) $5S_6 + 6S_5 + 2S_4 = 0$

61. Let S be the set of all $\lambda \in \mathbf{R}$ for which the system of linear equations
$$2x-y+2z=2 \qquad x-2y+\lambda z=-4$$
$$x+\lambda y+z=4$$
has no solution. Then the set S
(1) contains more than two elements.
(2) is an empty set.
(3) is a singleton.
(4) contains exactly two elements.

62. A line parallel to the straight line $2x-y=0$ is tangent to the hyperbola $\dfrac{x^2}{4}-\dfrac{y^2}{2}=1$ at the point (x_1, y_1). Then $x_1^2 + 5y_1^2$ is equal to :
(1) 6 (2) 8 (3) 10 (4) 5

63. If the tangent to the curve $y = x + \sin y$ at a point (a, b) is parallel to the line joining $\left(0, \dfrac{3}{2}\right)$ and $\left(\dfrac{1}{2}, 2\right)$, then :
(1) $b = a$ (2) $|b-a| = 1$
(3) $|a+b| = 1$ (4) $b = \dfrac{\pi}{2} + a$

64. Let $X = \{x \in \mathbf{N} : 1 \leq x \leq 17\}$ and $Y = \{ax+b : x \in X$ and $a, b \in \mathbf{R}, a > 0\}$. If mean and variance of elements of Y are 17 and 216 respectively then $a+b$ is equal to :
(1) 7 (2) –7
(3) –27 (4) 9

65. The value of $\left(\dfrac{1+\sin\dfrac{2\pi}{9}+i\cos\dfrac{2\pi}{9}}{1+\sin\dfrac{2\pi}{9}-i\cos\dfrac{2\pi}{9}}\right)^3$ is :

(1) $\dfrac{1}{2}(1-i\sqrt{3})$ (2) $\dfrac{1}{2}(\sqrt{3}-i)$
(3) $-\dfrac{1}{2}(\sqrt{3}-i)$ (4) $-\dfrac{1}{2}(1-i\sqrt{3})$

66. The contrapositive of the statement "If I reach the station in time, then I will catch the train" is :
(1) If I do not reach the station in time, then I will catch the train.
(2) If I do not reach the station in time, then I will not catch the train.
(3) If I will catch the train, then I reach the station in time.
(4) If I will not catch the train, then I do not reach the station in time.

67. If $p(x)$ be a polynomial of degree three that has a local maximum value 8 at $x=1$ and a local minimum value 4 at $x=2$; then $p(0)$ is equal to :
(1) 6 (2) -12 (3) -24 (4) 12

68. If a function $f(x)$ defined by
$$f(x) = \begin{cases} ae^x + be^{-x}, & -1 \leq x < 1 \\ cx^2, & 1 \leq x \leq 3 \\ ax^2 + 2cx, & 3 < x \leq 4 \end{cases}$$
be continuous for some $a, b, c \in \mathbf{R}$ and $f'(0)+f'(2)=e$, then the value of a is :
(1) $\dfrac{1}{e^2-3e+13}$ (2) $\dfrac{e}{e^2-3e-13}$
(3) $\dfrac{e}{e^2+3e+13}$ (4) $\dfrac{e}{e^2-3e+13}$

69. The plane passing through the points $(1, 2, 1), (2, 1, 2)$ and parallel to the line, $2x = 3y, z = 1$ also through the point :
(1) $(0, 6, -2)$ (2) $(-2, 0, 1)$
(3) $(0, -6, 2)$ (4) $(2, 0, -1)$

70. Let $P(h, k)$ be a point on the curve $y = x^2 + 7x + 2$, nearest to the line, $y = 3x - 3$. Then the equation of the normal to the curve at P is :
(1) $x + 3y + 26 = 0$ (2) $x + 3y - 62 = 0$
(3) $x - 3y - 11 = 0$ (4) $x - 3y + 22 = 0$

71. If $\displaystyle\lim_{x \to 1}\dfrac{x+x^2+x^3+...+x^n-n}{x-1} = 820, (n \in \mathbf{N})$ then the value of n is equal to __________.

72. The integral $\displaystyle\int_0^2 \left|\,|x-1|-x\right| dx$ is equal to __________.

73. The number of integral values of k for which the line, $3x+4y=k$ intersects the circle, $x^2+y^2-2x-4y+4=0$ at two distinct points is __________.

74. If the letters of the word 'MOTHER' be permuted and all the words so formed (with or without meaning) be listed as in a dictionary, then the position of the word 'MOTHER' is __________.

75. Let $\vec{a}, \vec{b}$ and $\vec{c}$ be three unit vectors such that $|\vec{a}-\vec{b}|^2 + |\vec{a}-\vec{c}|^2 = 8$. Then $|\vec{a}+2\vec{b}|^2 + |\vec{a}+2\vec{c}|^2$ is equal to __________.

JEE MAIN 2020

(Held on 2-09-2020 Evening Shift)

PHYSICS

1. A capillary tube made of glass of radius 0.15 mm is dipped vertically in a beaker filled with methylene iodide (surface tension $= 0.05\,\text{Nm}^{-1}$, density $= 667\,\text{kg m}^{-3}$) which rises to height h in the tube. It is observed that the two tangents drawn from liquid-glass interfaces (from opp. sides of the capillary) make an angle of $60°$ with one another. Then h is close to ($g = 10\,\text{ms}^{-2}$).

   (1) 0.049 m   (2) 0.087 m   (3) 0.137 m   (4) 0.172 m

2. An inductance coil has a reactance of $100\,\Omega$. When an AC signal of frequency 1000 Hz is applied to the coil, the applied voltage leads the current by $45°$. The self-inductance of the coil is :

   (1) $1.1 \times 10^{-2}\,\text{H}$ (2) $1.1 \times 10^{-1}\,\text{H}$

   (3) $5.5 \times 10^{-5}\,\text{H}$ (4) $6.7 \times 10^{-7}\,\text{H}$

3. The height 'h' at which the weight of a body will be the same as that at the same depth 'h' from the surface of the earth is (Radius of the earth is R and effect of the rotation of the earth is neglected) :

   (1) $\dfrac{\sqrt{5}}{2}R - R$ (2) $\dfrac{R}{2}$

   (3) $\dfrac{\sqrt{5}R - R}{2}$ (4) $\dfrac{\sqrt{3}R - R}{2}$

4. The figure shows a region of length 'l' with a uniform magnetic field of 0.3 T in it and a proton entering the region with velocity $4 \times 10^5\,\text{ms}^{-1}$ making an angle $60°$ with the field. If the proton completes 10 revolution by the time it cross the region shown, 'l' is close to (mass of proton $= 1.67 \times 10^{-27}$ kg, charge of the proton $= 1.6 \times 10^{-19}$ C)

   (1) 0.11 m

   (2) 0.88 m

   (3) 0.44 m

   (4) 0.22 m

5. If momentum (P), area (A) and time (T) are taken to be the fundamental quantities then the dimensional formula for energy is :

   (1) $[\text{P}^2\text{AT}^{-2}]$ (2) $[\text{PA}^{-1}\text{T}^{-2}]$

   (3) $[\text{PA}^{1/2}\text{T}^{-1}]$ (4) $[\text{P}^{1/2}\text{AT}^{-1}]$

6. When the temperature of a metal wire is increased from $0°\text{C}$ to $10°\text{C}$, its length increased by 0.02%. The percentage change in its mass density will be closest to :

   (1) 0.06   (2) 2.3   (3) 0.008   (4) 0.8

7. A 10 µF capacitor is fully charged to a potential difference of 50 V. After removing the source voltage it is connected to an uncharged capacitor in parallel. Now the potential difference across them becomes 20 V. The capacitance of the second capacitor is :

   (1) 15 µF   (2) 30 µF   (3) 20 µF   (4) 10 µF

8. In a hydrogen atom the electron makes a transition from $(n + 1)^{\text{th}}$ level to the nth level. If $n \gg 1$, the frequency of radiation emitted is proportional to :

   (1) $\dfrac{1}{n}$ (2) $\dfrac{1}{n^3}$ (3) $\dfrac{1}{n^2}$ (4) $\dfrac{1}{n^4}$

9. A heat engine is involved with exchange of heat of 1915 J, -40 J, $+125$ J and $-Q$ J, during one cycle achieving an efficiency of 50.0%. The value of Q is :

   (1) 640 J   (2) 40 J   (3) 980 J   (4) 400 J

10. A wire carrying current I is bent in the shape $ABCDEFA$ as shown, where rectangle $ABCDA$ and $ADEFA$ are perpendicular to each other. If the sides of the rectangles are of lengths a and b, then the magnitude and direction of magnetic moment of the loop $ABCDEFA$ is :

    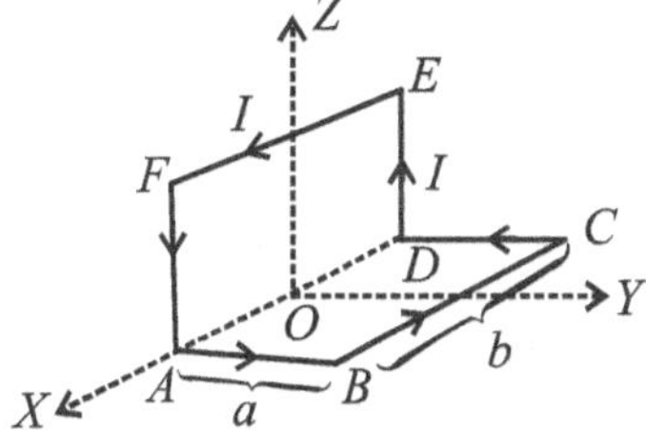

    (1) abI, along $\left(\dfrac{\hat{j}}{\sqrt{2}} + \dfrac{\hat{k}}{\sqrt{2}}\right)$

    (2) $\sqrt{2}abI$, along $\left(\dfrac{\hat{j}}{\sqrt{2}} + \dfrac{\hat{k}}{\sqrt{2}}\right)$

    (3) $\sqrt{2}abI$, along $\left(\dfrac{\hat{j}}{\sqrt{5}} + \dfrac{2\hat{k}}{\sqrt{5}}\right)$

    (4) abI, along $\left(\dfrac{\hat{j}}{\sqrt{5}} + \dfrac{2\hat{k}}{\sqrt{5}}\right)$

11. A particle is moving 5 times as fast as an electron. The ratio of the de-Broglie wavelength of the particle to that of the electron is 1.878×10^{-4}. The mass of the particle is close to :

    (1) 4.8×10^{-27} kg   (2) 9.1×10^{-31} kg

    (3) 1.2×10^{-28} kg   (4) 9.7×10^{-28} kg

12. In a plane electromagnetic wave, the directions of electric field and magnetic field are represented by $\hat{k}$ and $2\hat{i} - 2\hat{j}$, respectively. What is the unit vector along direction of propagation of the wave.

(1) $\dfrac{1}{\sqrt{2}}(\hat{i} + \hat{j})$

(2) $\dfrac{1}{\sqrt{2}}(\hat{j} + \hat{k})$

(3) $\dfrac{1}{\sqrt{5}}(\hat{i} + 2\hat{j})$

(4) $\dfrac{1}{\sqrt{5}}(2\hat{i} + \hat{j})$

13. In the following digitial circuit, what will be the output at 'Z', when the input (A, B) are $(1, 0), (0, 0), (1, 1), (0, 1)$:

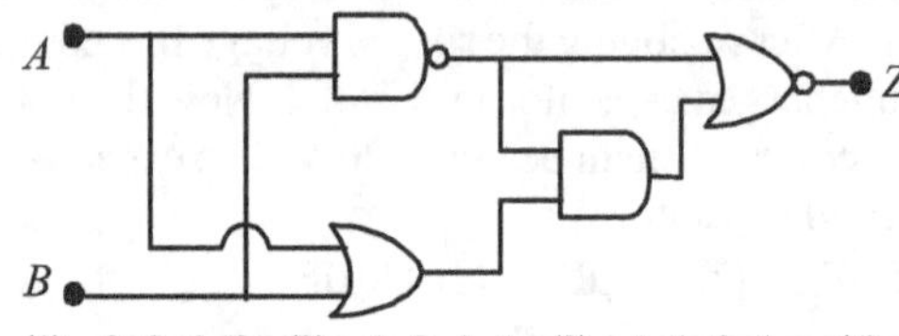

(1) $0, 0, 1, 0$ (2) $1, 0, 1, 1$ (3) $1, 1, 0, 1$ (4) $0, 1, 0, 0$

14. A small point mass carrying some positive charge on it, is released from the edge of a table. There is a uniform electric field in this region in the horizontal direction. Which of the following options then correctly describe the trajectory of the mass ? (Curves are drawn schematically and are not to scale).

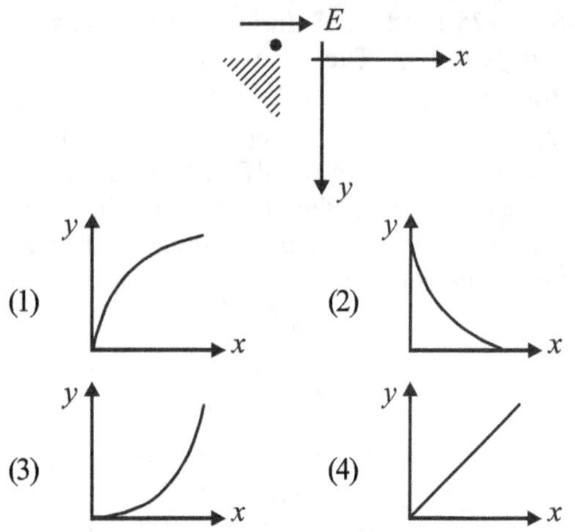

15. A potentiometer wire PQ of 1 m length is connected to a standard cell E_1. Another cell E_2 of emf 1.02 V is connected with a resistance 'r' and switch S (as shown in figure). With switch S open, the null position is obtained at a distance of 49 cm from Q. The potential gradient in the potentiometer wire is :

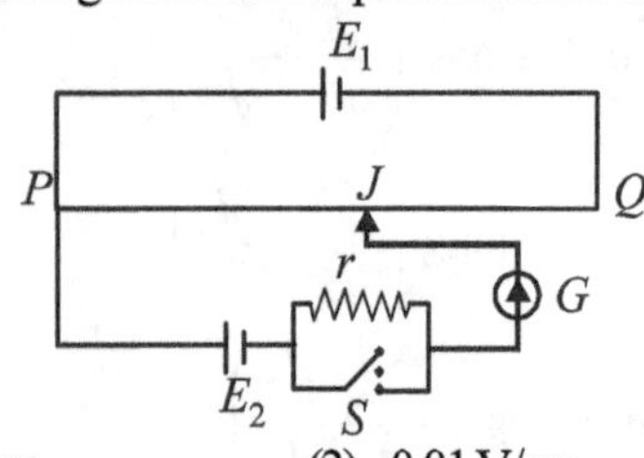

(1) 0.02 V/cm

(2) 0.01 V/cm

(3) 0.03 V/cm

(4) 0.04 V/cm

16. In a Young's double slit experiment, 16 fringes are observed in a certain segment of the screen when light of wavelength 700 nm is used. If the wavelength of light is changed to 400 nm, the number of fringes observed in the same segment of the screen would be :

(1) 24 (2) 30 (3) 18 (4) 28

17. A charge Q is distributed over two concentric conducting thin spherical shells radii r and R $(R > r)$. If the surface charge densities on the two shells are equal, the electric potential at the common centre is :

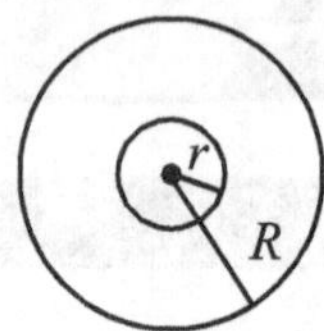

(1) $\dfrac{1}{4\pi\varepsilon_0}\dfrac{(R+r)}{2(R^2 + r^2)}Q$

(2) $\dfrac{1}{4\pi\varepsilon_0}\dfrac{(2R+r)}{(R^2 + r^2)}Q$

(3) $\dfrac{1}{4\pi\varepsilon_0}\dfrac{(R+2r)Q}{2(R^2 + r^2)}$

(4) $\dfrac{1}{4\pi\varepsilon_0}\dfrac{(R+r)}{(R^2 + r^2)}Q$

18. The displacement time graph of a particle executing S.H.M. is given in figure : (sketch is schematic and not to scale)

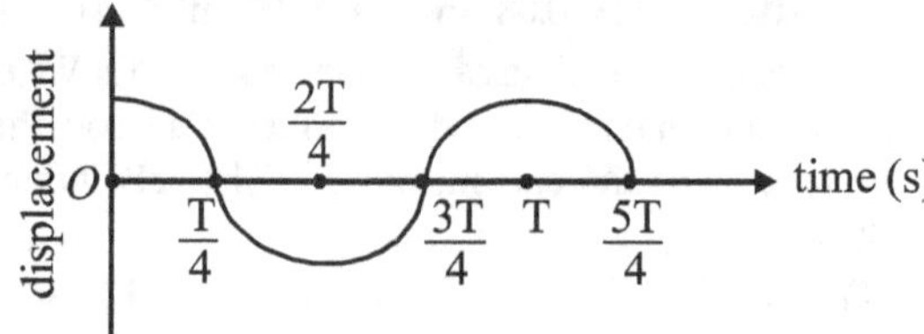

Which of the following statements is/are true for this motion?

(a) The force is zero at $t = \dfrac{3T}{4}$

(b) The acceleration is maximum at $t = T$

(c) The speed is maximum at $t = \dfrac{T}{4}$

(d) The P.E. is equal to K.E. of the oscillation at $t = \dfrac{T}{2}$

(1) (a), (b) and (d)

(2) (b), (c) and (d)

(3) (a), (b) and (c)

(4) (a) and (d)

19. Two uniform circular discs are rotating independently in the same direction around their common axis passing through their centres. The moment of inertia and angular velocity of the first disc are 0.1 kg-m^2 and 10 rad s^{-1} respectively while those for the second one are 0.2 kg-m^2 and 5 rad s^{-1} respectively. At some instant they get stuck together and start rotating as a single system about their common axis with some angular speed. The kinetic energy of the combined system is :

(1) $\dfrac{10}{3}$ J (2) $\dfrac{20}{3}$ J (3) $\dfrac{5}{3}$ J (4) $\dfrac{2}{3}$ J

20. An ideal gas in a closed container is slowly heated. As its temperature increases, which of the following statements are true?

(a) The mean free path of the molecules decreases

(b) The mean collision time between the molecules decreases

(c) The mean free path remains unchanged

(d) The mean collision time remains unchanged

(1) (b) and (c)

(2) (a) and (b)

(3) (c) and (d)

(4) (a) and (d)

21. An ideal cell of emf 10 V is connected in circuit shown in figure. Each resistance is 2 Ω. The potential difference (in V) across the capacitor when it is fully charged is __________.

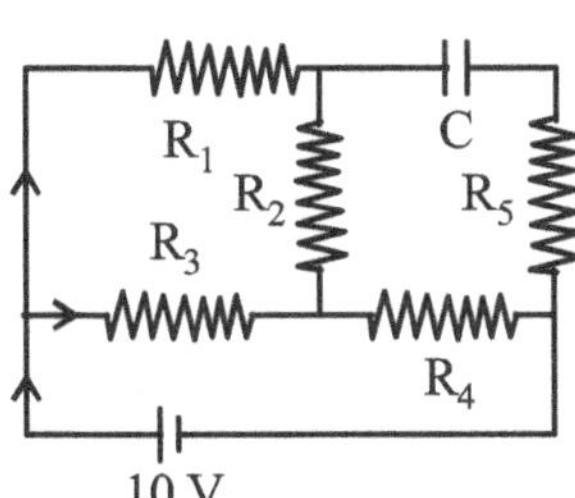

22. A square shaped hole of side $l = \dfrac{a}{2}$ is carved out at a distance $d = \dfrac{a}{2}$ from the centre 'O' of a uniform circular disk of radius a. If the distance of the centre of mass of the remaining portion from O is $-\dfrac{a}{X}$, value of X (to the nearest integer) is __________.

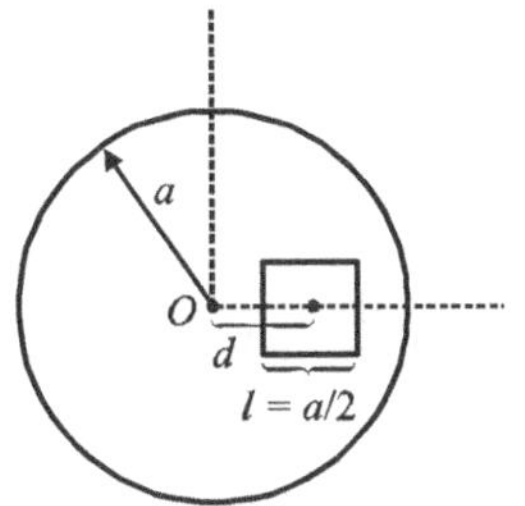

23. A light ray enters a solid glass sphere of refractive index $\mu = \sqrt{3}$ at an angle of incidence 60°. The ray is both reflected and refracted at the farther surface of the sphere. The angle (in degrees) between the reflected and refracted rays at this surface is __________.

24. A particle of mass m is moving along the x-axis with initial velocity $u\hat{i}$. It collides elastically with a particle of mass 10 m at rest and then moves with half its initial kinetic energy (see figure). If $\sin\theta_1 = \sqrt{n}\,\sin\theta_2$, then value of n is __________.

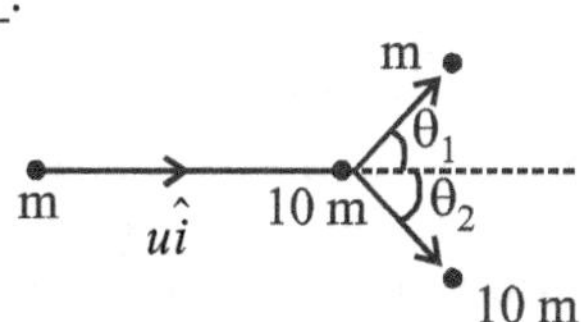

25. A wire of density 9×10^{-3} kg cm^{-3} is stretched between two clamps 1 m apart. The resulting strain in the wire is 4.9×10^{-4}. The lowest frequency of the transverse vibrations in the wire is (Young's modulus of wire $Y = 9 \times 10^{10}$ Nm^{-2}), (to the nearest integer), __________.

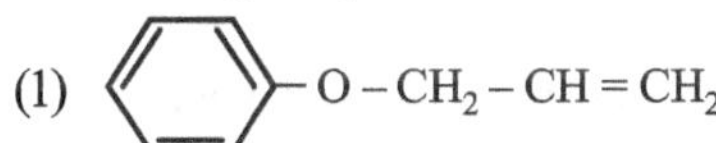

CHEMISTRY

26. If you spill a chemical toilet cleaning liquid on your hand, your first aid would be :
(1) vinegar   (2) aqueous NaOH
(3) aqueous $NaHCO_3$ (4) aqueous NH_3

27. An organic compound 'A' ($C_9H_{10}O$) when treated with conc. HI undergoes cleavage to yield compounds 'B' and 'C'. 'B' gives yellow precipitate with $AgNO_3$ whereas 'C' tautomerizes to 'D'. 'D' gives positive iodoform test. 'A' could be :

(1) ![benzene ring] $- O - CH_2 - CH = CH_2$

(2) ![benzene ring] $- O - CH = CH - CH_3$

(3) ![benzene ring] $- CH_2 - O - CH = CH_2$

(4) $H_3C -$![benzene ring] $- O - CH = CH_2$

28. The size of a raw mango shrinks to a much smaller size when kept in a concentrated salt solution. Which one of the following processes can explain this ?
(1) Osmosis   (2) Dialysis
(3) Diffusion   (4) Reverse osmosis

29. Amongst the following statements regarding adsorption, those that are valid are :
(a) ΔH becomes less negative as adsorption proceeds.
(b) On a given adsorbent, ammonia is adsorbed more than nitrogen gas.
(c) On adsorption, the residual force acting along the surface of the adsorbent increases.
(d) With increase in temperature, the equilibrium concentration of adsorbate increases.
(1) (d) and (a)   (2) (b) and (c)
(3) (a) and (b)   (4) (c) and (d)

30. The major product obtained from E2-elimination of 3-bromo-2-fluoropentane is :

(1) $CH_3CH_2 - \overset{\overset{\displaystyle Br}{|}}{CH} - CH = CH_2$

(2) $CH_3CH_2CH = \overset{\overset{\displaystyle }{}}{C} - F$ with CH_3

(3) $CH_3 - CH = CH - \overset{\overset{\displaystyle F}{|}}{CH} - CH_3$

(4) $CH_3 - CH_2 - \overset{\overset{\displaystyle Br}{|}}{C} = CH - CH_3$

31. Simplified absorption spectra of three complexes ((i), (ii) and (iii)) of M^{n+} ion are provided below; their λ_{max} values are marked as A, B and C respectively. The correct match between the complexes and their λ_{max} values is :

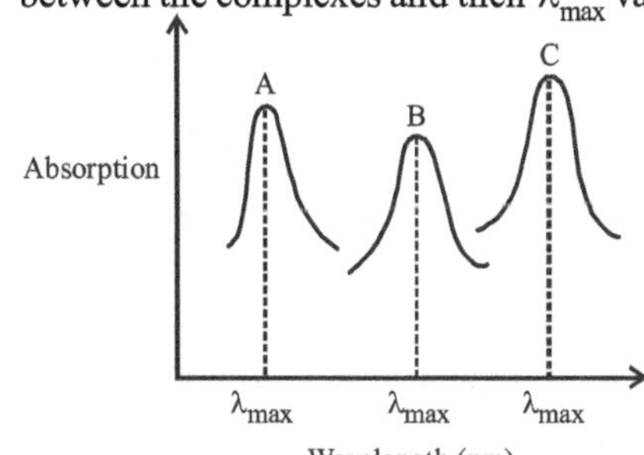

(i) $[M(NCS)_6]^{(-6+n)}$

(ii) $[MF_6]^{(-6+n)}$

(iii) $[M(NH_3)_6]^{n+}$

(1) A-(iii), B-(i), C-(ii)

(2) A-(ii), B-(i), C-(iii)

(3) A-(ii), B-(iii), C-(i)

(4) A-(i), B-(ii), C-(iii)

32. The correct observation in the following reactions is :

$$\text{Sucrose} \xrightarrow[\substack{\text{Cleavage} \\ \text{(Hydrolysis)}}]{\text{Glycosidic bond}} A + B \xrightarrow{\substack{\text{Seliwanoff's} \\ \text{reagent}}} ?$$

(1) Formation of blue colour

(2) Gives no colour

(3) Formation of red colour

(4) Formation of violet colour

33. Two elements A and B have similar chemical properties. They don't form solid hydrogencarbonates, but react with nitrogen to form nitrides. A and B, respectively, are :

(1) Na and Rb

(2) Na and Ca

(3) Cs and Ba

(4) Li and Mg

34. The results given in the below table were obtained during kinetic studies of the following reaction :

$$2A + B \rightarrow C + D$$

Experiment	$[A]/$ $mol\,L^{-1}$	$[B]/$ $mol\,L^{-1}$	Initial rate/ $mol\,L^{-1}\,min^{-1}$
I	0.1	0.1	6.00×10^{-3}
II	0.1	0.2	2.40×10^{-2}
III	0.2	0.1	1.20×10^{-2}
IV	X	0.2	7.20×10^{-2}
V	0.3	Y	2.88×10^{-1}

X and Y in the given table are respectively :

(1) 0.4, 0.4

(2) 0.4, 0.3

(3) 0.3, 0.4

(4) 0.3, 0.3

35. The major product of the following reaction is :

(1)

(2)

(3)

(4)

36. Arrange the following labelled hydrogens in decreasing order of acidity :

(1) $(ii) > (i) > (iii) > (iv)$

(2) $(iii) > (ii) > (iv) > (i)$

(3) $(ii) > (iii) > (iv) > (i)$

(4) $(iii) > (ii) > (i) > (iv)$

37. Consider the reaction sequence given below :

$$\text{rate} = k[t\text{-BuBr}] \quad \text{----------- (1)}$$

$$\text{rate} = k[t\text{-BuBr}][OH^{\ominus}] \quad \text{----- (2)}$$

Which of the following statements is true ?

(1) Changing the base from $OH^{\ominus}$ to $^{\ominus}OR$ will have no effect on reaction (2).

(2) Changing the concentration of base will have no effect on reaction (1).

(3) Doubling the concentration of base will double the rate of both the reactions.

(4) Changing the concentration of base will have no effect on reaction (2).

38. Three elements X, Y and Z are in the 3rd period of the periodic table. The oxides of X, Y and Z, respectively, are basic, amphoteric and acidic. The correct order of the atomic numbers of X, Y and Z is :

(1) $Z < Y < X$

(2) $X < Y < Z$

(3) $X < Z < Y$

(4) $Y < X < Z$

39. The one that is not expected to show isomerism is :

(1) $[Ni(NH_3)_4(H_2O)_2]^{2+}$

(2) $[Ni(en)_3]^{2+}$

(3) $[Ni(NH_3)_2Cl_2]$

(4) $[Pt(NH_3)_2Cl_2]$

40. Two compounds A and B with same molecular formula (C_3H_6O) undergo Grignard's reaction with methylmagnesium bromide to give products C and D. Products C and D show following chemical tests.

Test	C	D
Ceric ammonium nitrate Test	Positive	Positive
Lucas Test	Turbidity obtained after five minutes	Turbidity obtained immediately
Iodoform Test	Positive	Negative

C and D respectively are :

(1) $C = H_3C - CH_2 - \overset{\overset{\textstyle OH}{\textstyle |}}{CH} - CH_3;$

$$D = H_3C - \underset{\underset{CH_3}{|}}{\overset{\overset{CH_3}{|}}{C}} - OH$$

(2) $C = H_3C - CH_2 - CH_2 - CH_2 - OH;$

$$D = H_3C - CH_2 - \underset{\underset{OH}{|}}{CH} - CH_3$$

(3) $C = H_3C - CH_2 - CH_2 - CH_2 - OH;$

$$D = H_3C - \underset{\underset{CH_3}{|}}{\overset{\overset{CH_3}{|}}{C}} - OH$$

(4) $C = H_3C - \underset{\underset{CH_3}{|}}{\overset{\overset{CH_3}{|}}{C}} - OH;$

$$D = H_3C - CH_2 - \underset{\underset{OH}{|}}{CH} - CH_3$$

41. Cast iron is used for the manufacture of :
(1) wrought iron and pig iron
(2) pig iron, scrap iron and steel
(3) wrought iron, pig iron and steel
(4) wrought iron and steel

42. The shape/ structure of $[XeF_5]^-$ and XeO_3F_2, respectively, are :
(1) pentagonal planar and trigonal bipyramidal
(2) octahedral and square pyramidal
(3) trigonal bipyramidal and pentagonal planar
(4) trigonal bipyramidal and trigonal bipyramidal

43. Match the type of interaction in column A with the distance dependence of their interaction energy in column B :

A	B
(I) ion-ion	(A) $\dfrac{1}{r}$
(II) dipole-dipole	(B) $\dfrac{1}{r^2}$
(III) London dispersion	(C) $\dfrac{1}{r^3}$
	(D) $\dfrac{1}{r^6}$

(1) (I)-(B), (II)-(D), (III)-(C) (2) (I)-(A), (II)-(B), (III)-(D)
(3) (I)-(A), (II)-(B), (III)-(C) (4) (I)-(A), (II)-(C), (III)-(D)

44. The molecular geometry of SF_6 is octahedral. What is the geometry of SF_4 (including lone pair(s) of electrons, if any)?
(1) Tetrahedral   (2) Trigonal bipyramidal
(3) Pyramidal   (4) Square planar

45. The number of subshells associated with $n = 4$ and $m = -2$ quantum numbers is :
(1) 8   (2) 2   (3) 16   (4) 4

46. The work function of sodium metal is 4.41×10^{-19} J. If photons of wavelength 300 nm are incident on the metal, the kinetic energy of the ejected electrons will be $(h = 6.63 \times 10^{-34}$ J s; $c = 3 \times 10^8$ m/s) _______ $\times 10^{-21}$ J.

47. The oxidation states of transition metal atoms in $K_2Cr_2O_7$, $KMnO_4$ and K_2FeO_4, respectively, are x, y and z. The sum of x, y and z is _______ .

48. For the disproportionation reaction
$$2Cu^+(aq) \rightleftharpoons Cu(s) + Cu^{2+}(aq) \text{ at } 298 \text{ K, ln K}$$
(where K is the equilibrium constant) is _______ $\times 10^{-1}$.
Given
$(E^0_{Cu^{2+}/Cu^+} = 0.16$ V ; $E^0_{Cu^+/Cu} = 0.52$ V ; $\dfrac{RT}{F} = 0.025)$

49. The ratio of the mass percentages of 'C & H' and 'C & O' of a saturated acyclic organic compound 'X' are $4 : 1$ and $3 : 4$ respectively. Then, the moles of oxygen gas required for complete combustion of two moles of organic compound 'X' is _______ .

50. The heat of combustion of ethanol into carbon dioxids and water is $- 327$ kcal at constant pressure. The heat evolved (in cal) at constant volume and $27°C$ (if all gases behave ideally) is $(R = 2$ cal mol^{-1} K^{-1}) _______ .

MATHEMATICS

51. Let $A = \{X = (x, \ y, \ z)^T : PX = 0 \text{ and } x^2 + y^2 + z^2 = 1\}$,
where $P = \begin{bmatrix} 1 & 2 & 1 \\ -2 & 3 & -4 \\ 1 & 9 & -1 \end{bmatrix}$, then the set A :

(1) is a singleton
(2) is an empty set
(3) contains more than two elements
(4) contains exactly two elements

52. Let $f : \mathbf{R} \to \mathbf{R}$ be a function which satisfies $f(x+y) = f(x) + f(y), \ \forall \ x, y \in \mathbf{R}$. If $f(1) = 2$ and $g(n) = \displaystyle\sum_{k=1}^{(n-1)} f(k), \ n \in \mathbf{N}$, then the value of n, for which $g(n) = 20$, is :

(1) 5   (2) 20   (3) 4   (4) 9

53. Which of the following is a tautology?
(1) $(\sim p) \wedge (p \vee q) \to q$ (2) $(q \to p) \vee \sim (p \to q)$
(3) $(\sim q) \vee (p \wedge q) \to q$ (4) $(p \to q) \wedge (q \to p)$

54. If the equation $\cos^4 \theta + \sin^4 \theta + \lambda = 0$ has real solutions for θ, then λ lies in the interval :

(1) $\left(-\dfrac{5}{4}, -1 \right)$ (2) $\left[-1, -\dfrac{1}{2} \right]$

(3) $\left(-\dfrac{1}{2}, -\dfrac{1}{4} \right)$ (4) $\left[-\dfrac{3}{2}, \dfrac{5}{4} \right]$

55. Let $f(x)$ be a quadratic polynomial such that $f(-1) + f(2) = 0$. If one of the roots of $f(x) = 0$ is 3, then its other root lies in:
(1) $(-1, 0)$ (2) $(1, 3)$ (3) $(-3, -1)$ (4) $(0, 1)$

56. If a curve $y = f(x)$, passing through the point $(1, 2)$, is the solution of the differential equation,

$$2x^2 dy = (2xy + y^2)\,dx, \text{ then } f\left(\frac{1}{2}\right) \text{ is equal to :}$$

(1) $\dfrac{1}{1 + \log_e 2}$ (2) $\dfrac{1}{1 - \log_e 2}$

(3) $1 + \log_e 2$ (4) $\dfrac{-1}{1 + \log_e 2}$

57. $\displaystyle \lim_{x \to 0} \left(\tan\left(\frac{\pi}{4} + x\right) \right)^{1/x}$ is equal to :

(1) e (2) 2 (3) 1 (4) e^2

58. The set of all possible values of θ in the interval $(0, \pi)$ for which the points $(1, 2)$ and $(\sin\theta, \cos\theta)$ lie on the same side of the line $x + y = 1$ is :

(1) $\left(0, \dfrac{\pi}{2}\right)$ (2) $\left(\dfrac{\pi}{4}, \dfrac{3\pi}{4}\right)$ (3) $\left(0, \dfrac{3\pi}{4}\right)$ (4) $\left(0, \dfrac{\pi}{4}\right)$

59. Let $f : (-1, \infty) \to \mathbf{R}$ be defined by $f(0) = 1$ and

$$f(x) = \frac{1}{x} \log_e(1 + x), \; x \neq 0. \text{ Then the function } f :$$

(1) decreases in $(-1, 0)$ and increases in $(0, \infty)$.
(2) increases in $(-1, \infty)$.
(3) increases in $(-1, 0)$ and decreases in $(0, \infty)$.
(4) decreases in $(-1, \infty)$.

60. Let $a, b, c \in \mathbf{R}$ be all non-zero and satisfy

$a^3 + b^3 + c^3 = 2$. If the matrix $A = \begin{pmatrix} a & b & c \\ b & c & a \\ c & a & b \end{pmatrix}$ satisfies

$A^T A = I$, then a value of abc can be :

(1) $-\dfrac{1}{3}$ (2) $\dfrac{1}{3}$ (3) 3 (4) $\dfrac{2}{3}$

61. The imaginary part of $(3 + 2\sqrt{-54})^{1/2} - (3 - 2\sqrt{-54})^{1/2}$ can be :

(1) $-\sqrt{6}$ (2) $-2\sqrt{6}$ (3) 6 (4) $\sqrt{6}$

62. The equation of the normal to the curve

$y = (1 + x)^{2y} + \cos^2(\sin^{-1} x)$ at $x = 0$ is :
(1) $y + 4x = 2$ (2) $y = 4x + 2$
(3) $x + 4y = 8$ (4) $2y + x = 4$

63. A plane passing through the point $(3, 1, 1)$ contains two lines whose direction ratios are $1, -2, 2$ and $2, 3, -1$ respectively. If this plane also passes through the point $(\alpha, -3, 5)$, then α is equal to :
(1) 5 (2) -10 (3) 10 (4) -5

64. Let E^C denote the complement of an event E. Let E_1, E_2 and E_3 be any pairwise independent events with $P(E_1) > 0$ and $P(E_1 \cap E_2 \cap E_3) = 0$. Then $P(E_2^C \cap E_3^C / E_1)$ is equal to :

(1) $P(E_2^C) + P(E_3)$ (2) $P(E_3^C) - P(E_2^C)$
(3) $P(E_3) - P(E_2^C)$ (4) $P(E_3^C) - P(E_2)$

65. The area (in sq. units) of an equilateral triangle inscribed in the parabola $y^2 = 8x$, with one of its vertices on the vertex of this parabola, is :

(1) $64\sqrt{3}$ (2) $256\sqrt{3}$ (3) $192\sqrt{3}$ (4) $128\sqrt{3}$

66. If the sum of first 11 terms of an A.P., $a_1, a_2, a_3, ...$ is 0 $(a_1 \neq 0)$, then the sum of the A.P., $a_1, a_3, a_5, ..., a_{23}$ is ka_1, where k is equal to :

(1) $-\dfrac{121}{10}$ (2) $\dfrac{121}{10}$ (3) $\dfrac{72}{5}$ (4) $-\dfrac{72}{5}$

67. Let S be the sum of the first 9 terms of the series :
$\{x + ka\} + \{x^2 + (k+2)a\} + \{x^3 + (k+4)a\}$
$+ \{x^4 + (k+6)a\} + ...$ where $a \neq 0$ and $x \neq 1$. If

$$S = \frac{x^{10} - x + 45a(x - 1)}{x - 1}, \text{ then } k \text{ is equal to :}$$

(1) -5 (2) 1 (3) -3 (4) 3

68. Let $n > 2$ be an integer. Suppose that there are n Metro stations in a city located along a circular path. Each pair of stations is connected by a straight track only. Further, each pair of nearest stations is connected by blue line, whereas all remaining pairs of stations are connected by red line. If the number of red lines is 99 times the number of blue lines, then the value of n is :
(1) 201 (2) 200 (3) 101 (4) 199

69. Consider a region $R = \{(x, y) \in \mathbf{R}^2 : x^2 \leq y \leq 2x\}$. If a line $y = \alpha$ divides the area of region R into two equal parts, then which of the following is **true**?
(1) $\alpha^3 - 6\alpha^2 + 16 = 0$ (2) $3\alpha^2 - 8\alpha^{3/2} + 8 = 0$
(3) $3\alpha^2 - 8\alpha + 8 = 0$ (4) $\alpha^3 - 6\alpha^{3/2} - 16 = 0$

70. For some $\theta \in \left(0, \dfrac{\pi}{2}\right)$, if the eccentricity of the hyperbola, $x^2 - y^2 \sec^2\theta = 10$ is $\sqrt{5}$ times the eccentricity of the ellipse, $x^2 \sec^2\theta + y^2 = 5$, then the length of the latus rectum of the ellipse, is :

(1) $2\sqrt{6}$ (2) $\sqrt{30}$ (3) $\dfrac{2\sqrt{5}}{3}$ (4) $\dfrac{4\sqrt{5}}{3}$

71. If $\displaystyle y = \sum_{k=1}^{6} k \cos^{-1}\left\{\frac{3}{5} \cos kx - \frac{4}{5} \sin kx\right\}$, then $\dfrac{dy}{dx}$ at $x = 0$ is

______.

72. For a positive integer n, $\left(1 + \dfrac{1}{x}\right)^n$ is expanded in increasing powers of x. If three consecutive coefficients in this expansion are in the ratio, $2 : 5 : 12$, then n is equal to

______.

73. Let $[t]$ denote the greatest integer less than or equal to t. Then the value of $\displaystyle \int_1^2 |2x - [3x]|\, dx$ is ______.

74. Let the position vectors of points 'A' and 'B' be $\hat{i} + \hat{j} + \hat{k}$ and $2\hat{i} + \hat{j} + 3\hat{k}$, respectively. A point 'P' divides the line segment AB internally in the ratio $\lambda : 1 \, (\lambda > 0)$. If O is the region and $\overrightarrow{OB} \cdot \overrightarrow{OP} - 3|\overrightarrow{OA} \times \overrightarrow{OP}|^2 = 6$, then λ is equal to

______.

75. If the variance of the terms in an increasing A.P., $b_1, b_2, b_3, ..., b_{11}$ is 90, then the common difference of this A.P. is ______.

JEE MAIN 2020

(Held on 3-09-2020 Morning Shift)

PHYSICS

1. In a radioactive material, fraction of active material remaining after time t is 9/16. The fraction that was remaining after $t/2$ is :

(1) $\dfrac{4}{5}$ (2) $\dfrac{3}{5}$ (3) $\dfrac{3}{4}$ (4) $\dfrac{7}{8}$

2. An elliptical loop having resistance R, of semi major axis a, and semi minor axis b is placed in a magnetic field as shown in the figure. If the loop is rotated about the x-axis with angular frequency ω, the average power loss in the loop due to Joule heating is :

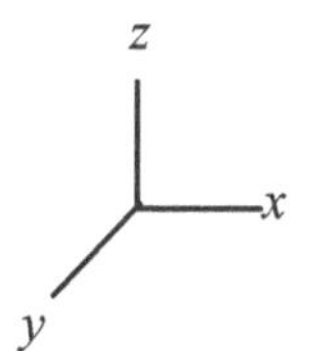 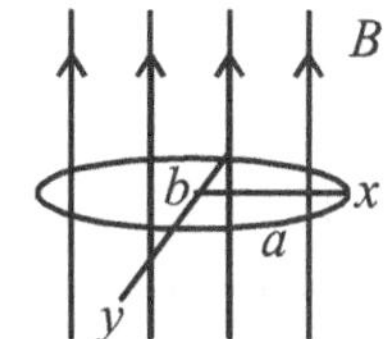

(1) $\dfrac{\pi^2 a^2 b^2 B^2 \omega^2}{2R}$ (2) zero

(3) $\dfrac{\pi a b B \omega}{R}$ (4) $\dfrac{\pi^2 a^2 b^2 B^2 \omega^2}{R}$

3. 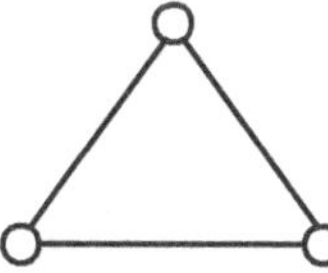

Consider a gas of triatomic molecules. The molecules are assumed to be triangular and made of massless rigid rods whose vertices are occupied by atoms. The internal energy of a mole of the gas at temperature T is :

(1) $\dfrac{5}{2}RT$ (2) $\dfrac{3}{2}RT$ (3) $\dfrac{9}{2}RT$ (4) $3RT$

4. Two isolated conducting spheres S_1 and S_2 of radius $\dfrac{2}{3}R$ and $\dfrac{1}{3}R$ have 12 μC and –3 μC charges, respectively, and are at a large distance from each other. They are now connected by a conducting wire. A long time after this is done the charges on S_1 and S_2 are respectively :

(1) 4.5 μC on both   (2) +4.5 μC and –4.5 μC

(3) 3 μC and 6 μC   (4) 6 μC and 3 μC

5. Moment of inertia of a cylinder of mass M, length L and radius R about an axis passing through its centre and perpendicular to the axis of the cylinder is $I = M\left(\dfrac{R^2}{4} + \dfrac{L^2}{12}\right)$. If such a cylinder is to be made for a given mass of a material, the ratio L/R for it to have minimum possible I is :

(1) $\dfrac{2}{3}$ (2) $\dfrac{3}{2}$ (3) $\sqrt{\dfrac{3}{2}}$ (4) $\sqrt{\dfrac{2}{3}}$

6. Model a torch battery of length l to be made up of a thin cylindrical bar of radius 'a' and a concentric thin cylindrical shell of radius 'b' filled in between with an electrolyte of resistivity ρ (see figure). If the battery is connected to a resistance of value R, the maximum Joule heating in R will take place for :

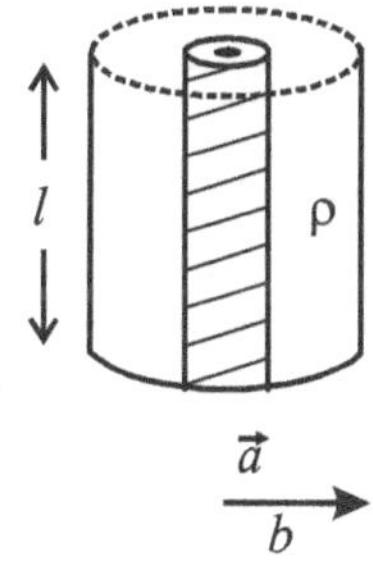

(1) $R = \dfrac{\rho}{2\pi l}\left(\dfrac{b}{a}\right)$ (2) $R = \dfrac{\rho}{2\pi l}\,\ln\left(\dfrac{b}{a}\right)$

(3) $R = \dfrac{\rho}{\pi l}\,\ln\left(\dfrac{b}{a}\right)$ (4) $R = \dfrac{2\rho}{\pi l}\,\ln\left(\dfrac{b}{a}\right)$

7. Magnitude of magnetic field (in SI units) at the centre of a hexagonal shape coil of side 10 cm, 50 turns and carrying current I (Ampere) in units of $\dfrac{\mu_0 I}{\pi}$ is :

(1) $250\sqrt{3}$ (2) $50\sqrt{3}$ (3) $500\sqrt{3}$ (4) $5\sqrt{3}$

8. A balloon filled with helium (32°C and 1.7 atm.) bursts. Immediately afterwards the expansion of helium can be considered as :

(1) irreversible isothermal   (2) irreversible adiabatic

(3) reversible adiabatic   (4) reversible isothermal

9. A 750 Hz, 20 V (rms) source is connected to a resistance of 100 Ω, an inductance of 0.1803 H and a capacitance of 10 μF all in series. The time in which the resistance (heat capacity 2 J/°C) will get heated by 10°C. (assume no loss of heat to the surroundings) is close to :

(1) 418 s (2) 245 s (3) 365 s (4) 348 s

10. The magnetic field of a plane electromagnetic wave is

$$\vec{B} = 3 \times 10^{-8} \sin[200\pi(y+ct)]\hat{i}\, T$$

where $c = 3 \times 10^8$ ms^{-1} is the speed of light.

The corresponding electric field is :

(1) $\vec{E} = 9\sin[200\pi(y+ct)]\hat{k}$ V/m

(2) $\vec{E} = -10^{-6}\sin[200\pi(y+ct)]\hat{k}$ V/m

(3) $\vec{E} = 3\times 10^{-8}\sin[200\pi(y+ct)]\hat{k}$ V/m

(4) $\vec{E} = -9\sin[200\pi(y+ct)]\hat{k}$ V/m

11. A charged particle carrying charge 1 μC is moving with velocity $(2\hat{i}+3\hat{j}+4\hat{k})$ ms^{-1}. If an external magnetic field of $(5\hat{i}+3\hat{j}-6\hat{k})\times 10^{-3}$ T exists in the region where the particle is moving then the force on the particle is $\vec{F}\times 10^{-9}$ N. The vector $\vec{F}$ is :

(1) $-0.30\hat{i}+0.32\hat{j}-0.09\hat{k}$

(2) $-30\hat{i}+32\hat{j}-9\hat{k}$

(3) $-300\hat{i}+320\hat{j}-90\hat{k}$

(4) $-3.0\hat{i}+3.2\hat{j}-0.9\hat{k}$

12. In the circuit shown in the figure, the total charge is 750 μC and the voltage across capacitor C_2 is 20 V. Then the charge on capacitor C_2 is :

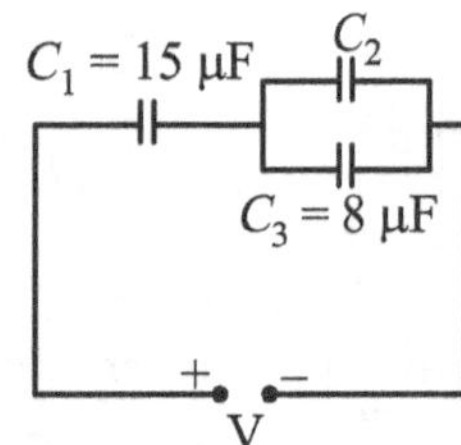

(1) 450 μC (2) 590 μC (3) 160 μC (4) 650 μC

13. In a Young's double slit experiment, light of 500 nm is used to produce an interference pattern. When the distance between the slits is 0.05 mm, the angular width (in degree) of the fringes formed on the distance screen is close to :

(1) 0.17°   (2) 0.57°
(3) 1.7°   (4) 0.07°

14. A block of mass $m = 1$ kg slides with velocity $v = 6$ m/s on a frictionless horizontal surface and collides with a uniform vertical rod and sticks to it as shown. The rod is pivoted about O and swings as a result of the collision making angle θ before momentarily coming to rest. If the rod has mass $M = 2$ kg, and length $l = 1$ m, the value of θ is approximately: (take $g = 10$ m/s^2)

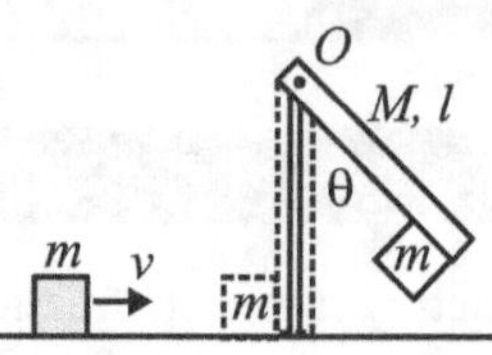

(1) 63°   (2) 55°   (3) 69°   (4) 49°

15. Using screw gauge of pitch 0.1 cm and 50 divisions on its circular scale, the thickness of an object is measured. It should correctly be recorded as :

(1) 2.121 cm   (2) 2.124 cm
(3) 2.125 cm   (4) 2.123 cm

16. A uniform thin rope of length 12 m and mass 6 kg hangs vertically from a rigid support and a block of mass 2 kg is attached to its free end. A transverse short wave-train of wavelength 6 cm is produced at the lower end of the rope. What is the wavelength of the wavetrain (in cm) when it reaches the top of the rope ?

(1) 3   (2) 6   (3) 12   (4) 9

17. When the wavelength of radiation falling on a metal is changed from 500 nm to 200 nm, the maximum kinetic energy of the photoelectrons becomes three times larger. The work function of the metal is close to :

(1) 0.81 eV   (2) 1.02 eV
(3) 0.52 eV   (4) 0.61 eV

18. When a diode is forward biased, it has a voltage drop of 0.5 V. The safe limit of current through the diode is 10 mA. If a battery of emf 1.5 V is used in the circuit, the value of minimum resistance to be connected in series with the diode so that the current does not exceed the safe limit is :

(1) 300 Ω   (2) 50 Ω
(3) 100 Ω   (4) 200 Ω

19. Pressure inside two soap bubbles are 1.01 and 1.02 atmosphere, respectively. The ratio of their volumes is :

(1) 4 : 1   (2) 0.8 : 1   (3) 8 : 1   (4) 2 : 1

20. A satellite is moving in a low nearly circular orbit around the earth. Its radius is roughly equal to that of the earth's radius R_e. By firing rockets attached to it, its speed is instantaneously increased in the direction of its motion so that it become $\sqrt{\dfrac{3}{2}}$ times larger. Due to this the farthest distance from the centre of the earth that the satellite reaches is R. Value of R is :

(1) $4R_e$ (2) $2.5R_e$
(3) $3R_e$ (4) $2R_e$

21. An observer can see through a small hole on the side of a jar (radius 15 cm) at a point at height of 15 cm from the bottom (see figure). The hole is at a height of 45 cm. When the jar is filled with a liquid up to a height of 30 cm the same observer can see the edge at the bottom of the jar. If the refractive index of the liquid is $N/100$, where N is an integer, the value of N is __________.

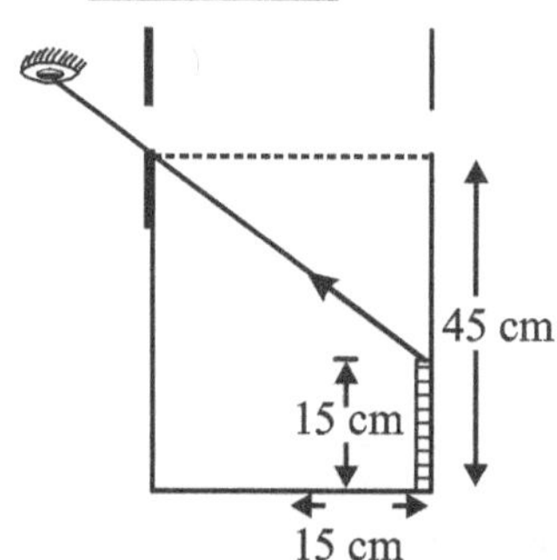

22. A cricket ball of mass 0.15 kg is thrown vertically up by a bowling machine so that it rises to a maximum height of 20 m after leaving the machine. If the part pushing the ball applies a constant force F on the ball and moves horizontally a distance of 0.2 m while launching the ball, the value of F (in N) is ($g = 10$ ms^{-2}) __________.

23. A person of 80 kg mass is standing on the rim of a circular platform of mass 200 kg rotating about its axis at 5 revolutions per minute (rpm). The person now starts moving towards the centre of the platform. What will be the rotational speed (in rpm) of the platform when the person reaches its centre __________.

24. When a long glass capillary tube of radius 0.015 cm is dipped in a liquid, the liquid rises to a height of 15 cm within it. If the contact angle between the liquid and glass to close to 0°, the surface tension of the liquid, in milliNewton m^{-1}, is [$\rho_{(liquid)} = 900$ kgm^{-3}, $g = 10$ ms^{-2}] (Give answer in closest integer) __________.

25. A bakelite beaker has volume capacity of 500 cc at 30°C. When it is partially filled with V_m volume (at 30°C) of mercury, it is found that the unfilled volume of the beaker remains constant as temperature is varied. If $\gamma_{(beaker)} = 6 \times 10^{-6}\,°C^{-1}$ and $\gamma_{(mercury)} = 1.5 \times 10^{-4}\,°C^{-1}$, where γ is the coefficient of volume expansion, then V_m (in cc) is close to __________.

CHEMISTRY

26. Henry's constant (in kbar) for four gases α, β, γ and δ in water at 298 K is given below :

	α	β	γ	δ
K_H	50	2	2×10^{-5}	0.5

(density of water = 10^3 kg m^{-3} at 298 K)

This table implies that :

(1) α has the highest solubility in water at a given pressure

(2) solubility of γ at 308 K is lower than at 298 K

(3) The pressure of a 55.5 molal solution of γ is 1 bar

(4) The pressure of a 55.5 molal solution of δ is 250 bar

27. Which of the following compounds produces an optically inactive compound on hydrogenation?

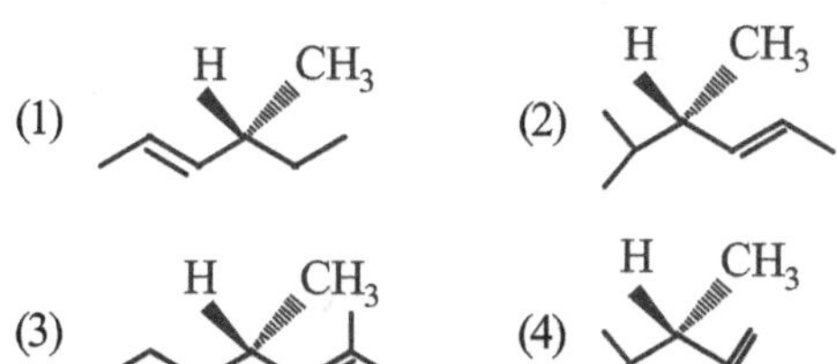

28. An organic compound [A], molecular formula $C_{10}H_{20}O_2$ was hydrolyzed with dilute sulphuric acid to give a carboxylic acid [B] and an alcohol [C]. Oxidation of [C] with $CrO_3 - H_2SO_4$ produced [B]. Which of the following structures are not possible for [A]?

(1) $CH_3 - CH_2 - CH - OCOCH_2CH - CH_2CH_3$ with CH_3 substituents

$$CH_3 - CH_2 - \underset{CH_3}{\overset{CH_3}{CH}} - OCOCH_2\underset{}{CH} - CH_2CH_3$$

(2) $$CH_3 - CH_2 - \underset{CH_3}{CH} - COOCH_2 - \overset{CH_3}{CH} - CH_2CH_3$$

(3) $CH_3CH_2CH_2COOCH_2CH_2CH_2CH_3$

(4) $(CH_3)_3 - C - COOCH_2C(CH_3)_3$

29. The mechanism of S_N1 reaction is given as :

$$R - X \longrightarrow \underset{\text{Ion pair}}{\overset{\oplus}{R}\,\overset{\ominus}{X}} \longrightarrow \underset{\substack{\text{Solvent} \\ \text{Separated ion} \\ \text{pair}}}{\overset{\oplus}{R}\|\overset{\ominus}{X}} \overset{Y^{\ominus}}{\longrightarrow} R - Y + X^{\ominus}$$

A student writes general characteristics based on the given mechanism as :

(a) The reaction is favoured by weak nucleophiles.

(b) $\overset{\oplus}{R}$ would be easily formed if the substituents are bulky.

(c) The reaction is accompanied by racemization.

(d) The reaction is favoured by non-polar solvents.

Which observations are correct?

(1) (a) and (b) (2) (a) and (c)
(3) (a), (b) and (c) (4) (b) and (d)

30. Which one of the following compounds possesses the most acidic hydrogen?

(1) 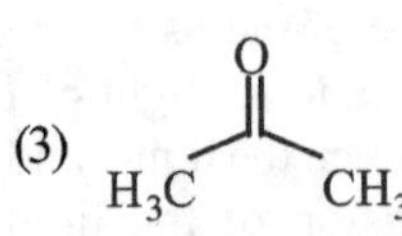

(2) $H_3C - C \equiv C - H$

(3) $\underset{H_3C \quad\quad CH_3}{\overset{O}{\parallel}\;C}$

(4) $MeO \overset{O}{\underset{O}{\parallel}} C \underset{H}{\overset{OMe}{\underset{OMe}{\parallel}}}$

31. Thermal power plants can lead to :
(1) Acid rain
(2) Blue baby syndrome
(3) Ozone layer depletion
(4) Eutrophication

32. An acidic buffer is obtained on mixing :
(1) 100 mL of 0.1 M CH_3COOH and 100 mL of 0.1 M NaOH
(2) 100 mL of 0.1 M HCl and 200 mL of 0.1 M NaCl
(3) 100 mL of 0.1 M CH_3COOH and 200 mL of 0.1 M NaOH
(4) 100 mL of 0.1 M HCl and 200 mL of 0.1 M CH_3COONa

33. If the boiling point of H_2O is 373 K, the boiling point of H_2S will be :
(1) less than 300 K
(2) equal to 373 K
(3) more than 373 K
(4) greater than 300 K but less than 373 K

34. Tyndall effect is observed when :
(1) The diameter of dispersed particles is much larger than the wavelength of light used.
(2) The diameter of dispersed particles is much smaller than the wavelength of light used.
(3) The refractive index of dispersed phase is greater than that of the dispersion medium.
(4) The diameter of dispersed particles is similar to the wavelength of light used.

35. Glycerol is separated in soap industries by :
(1) Fractional distillation
(2) Differential extraction
(3) Steam distillation
(4) Distillation under reduced pressure

36. The electronic spectrum of $[Ti(H_2O)_6]^{3+}$ shows a single broad peak with a maximum at 20,300 cm^{-1}. The crystal field stabilization energy (CFSE) of the complex ion, in kJ mol^{-1}, is : (1 kJ mol^{-1} = 83.7 cm^{-1})
(1) 145.5 (2) 242.5
(3) 83.7 (4) 97

37. The Kjeldahl method of Nitrogen estimation fails for which of the following reaction products?

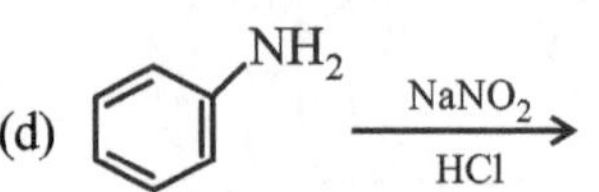

38. The atomic number of the element unnilennium is :
(1) 109 (2) 102
(3) 108 (4) 119

39. It is true that :
(1) A second order reaction is always a multistep reaction
(2) A zero order reaction is a multistep reaction
(3) A first order reaction is always a single step reaction
(4) A zero order reaction is a single step reaction

40. Let C_{NaCl} and C_{BaSO_4} be the conductances (in S) measured for saturated aqueous solutions of NaCl and $BaSO_4$, respectively, at a temperature T.
Which of the following is **false**?
(1) Ionic mobilities of ions from both salts increase with T
(2) $C_{BaSO_4}(T_2) > C_{BaSO_4}(T_1)$ for $T_2 > T_1$
(3) $C_{NaCl}(T_2) > C_{NaCl}(T_1)$ for $T_2 > T_1$
(4) $C_{NaCl} \gg C_{BaSO_4}$ at a given T

41. The complex that can show optical activity is :
(1) $trans\text{-}[Cr(Cl_2)(ox)_2]^{3-}$
(2) $trans\text{-}[Fe(NH_3)_2(CN)_4]^-$
(3) $cis\text{-}[Fe(NH_3)_2(CN)_4]^-$
(4) $cis\text{-}[CrCl_2(ox)_2]^{3-}$ (ox = oxalate)

42. Aqua regia is used for dissolving noble metals (Au, Pt, etc.). The gas evolved in this process is :
(1) NO (2) N_2O_5
(3) N_2 (4) N_2O_3

43. In a molecule of pyrophosphoric acid, the number of P – OH, P = O and P – O – P bonds/ moiety(ies) respectively are :
(1) 2, 4 and 1 (2) 3, 3 and 3
(3) 4, 2 and 0 (4) 4, 2 and 1

44. The antifertility drug "Novestrol" can react with :
  (1) $ZnCl_2/HCl$; $FeCl_3$; Alcoholic HCN
  (2) Br_2/ water; $ZnCl_2/HCl$; $FeCl_3$
  (3) Alcoholic HCN; NaOCl; $ZnCl_2/HCl$
  (4) Br_2/ water; $ZnCl_2/HCl$; NaOCl

45. Of the species, NO, NO^+, NO^{2+} and NO^-, the one with minimum bond strength is :
  (1) NO^+ (2) NO   (3) NO^{2+} (4) NO^-

46. The mole fraction of glucose $(C_6H_{12}O_6)$ in an aqueous binary solution is 0.1. The mass percentage of water in it, to the nearest integer, is __________.

47. The photoelectric current from Na (work function, $w_0 = 2.3$ eV) is stopped by the output voltage of the cell $Pt(s)|H_2(g, 1\ bar)|HCl(aq., pH = 1)|AgCl(s)|Ag(s)$.
The pH of aq. HCl required to stop the photoelectric current from $K(w_0 = 2.25$ eV), all other conditions remaining the same, is __________ $\times 10^{-2}$ (to the nearest integer).

Given,
$$2.303\frac{RT}{F} = 0.06\ V;\ E^0_{AgCl|Ag|Cl^-} = 0.22\ V$$

48. An element with molar mass 2.7×10^{-2} kg mol^{-1} forms a cubic unit cell with edge length 405 pm. If its density is 2.7×10^3 kg m^{-3}, the radius of the element is approximately __________ $\times 10^{-12}$ m (to the nearest integer).

49. The total number of monohalogenated organic products in the following (including stereoisomers) reaction is __________.

$$A \xrightarrow[\text{(ii) } X_2/\Delta]{\text{(i) } H_2/Ni/\Delta}$$

(Simplest optically active alkene)

50. The volume strength of 8.9 M H_2O_2 solution calculated at 273 K and 1 atm is __________. (R = 0.0821 L atm K^{-1} mol^{-1}) (rounded off to the nearest integer)

MATHEMATICS

51. If $y^2 + \log_e(\cos^2 x) = y$, $x \in \left(-\dfrac{\pi}{2}, \dfrac{\pi}{2}\right)$, then :
  (1) $y''(0) = 0$
  (2) $|y'(0)| + |y''(0)| = 1$
  (3) $|y''(0)| = 2$
  (4) $|y'(0)| + |y''(0)| = 3$

52. $2\pi - \left(\sin^{-1}\dfrac{4}{5} + \sin^{-1}\dfrac{5}{13} + \sin^{-1}\dfrac{16}{65}\right)$ is equal to :
  (1) $\dfrac{\pi}{2}$ (2) $\dfrac{5\pi}{4}$ (3) $\dfrac{3\pi}{2}$ (4) $\dfrac{7\pi}{4}$

53. If the first term of an A.P. is 3 and the sum of its first 25 terms is equal to the sum of its next 15 terms, then the common difference of this A.P. is :
  (1) $\dfrac{1}{6}$
  (2) $\dfrac{1}{5}$
  (3) $\dfrac{1}{4}$
  (4) $\dfrac{1}{7}$

54. A hyperbola having the transverse axis of length $\sqrt{2}$ has the same foci as that of the ellipse $3x^2 + 4y^2 = 12$, then this hyperbola does **not** pass through which of the following points?
  (1) $\left(\dfrac{1}{\sqrt{2}}, 0\right)$
  (2) $\left(-\sqrt{\dfrac{3}{2}}, 1\right)$
  (3) $\left(1, -\dfrac{1}{\sqrt{2}}\right)$
  (4) $\left(\sqrt{\dfrac{3}{2}}, \dfrac{1}{\sqrt{2}}\right)$

55. The proposition $p \to \sim (p \wedge \sim q)$ is equivalent to :
  (1) q
  (2) $(\sim p) \vee q$
  (3) $(\sim p) \wedge q$
  (4) $(\sim p) \vee (\sim q)$

56. Let P be a point on the parabola, $y^2 = 12x$ and N be the foot of the perpendicular drawn from P on the axis of the parabola. A line is now drawn through the mid-point M of PN, parallel to its axis which meets the parabola at Q. If the y-intercept of the line NQ is $\dfrac{4}{3}$, then :
  (1) $PN = 4$
  (2) $MQ = \dfrac{1}{3}$
  (3) $MQ = \dfrac{1}{4}$
  (4) $PN = 3$

57. Consider the two sets :
$A = \{m \in \mathbf{R}$: both the roots of $x^2 - (m+1)x + m + 4 = 0$ are real$\}$ and $B = [-3, 5)$.
Which of the following is **not** true?
  (1) $A - B = (-\infty, -3) \cup (5, \infty)$
  (2) $A \cap B = \{-3\}$
  (3) $B - A = (-3, 5)$
  (4) $A \cup B = \mathbf{R}$

58. If α and β are the roots of the equation $x^2 + px + 2 = 0$ and $\dfrac{1}{\alpha}$ and $\dfrac{1}{\beta}$ are the roots of the equation $2x^2 + 2qx + 1 = 0$, then $\left(\alpha - \dfrac{1}{\alpha}\right)\left(\beta - \dfrac{1}{\beta}\right)\left(\alpha + \dfrac{1}{\beta}\right)\left(\beta + \dfrac{1}{\alpha}\right)$ is equal to :
  (1) $\dfrac{9}{4}(9 + q^2)$
  (2) $\dfrac{9}{4}(9 - q^2)$
  (3) $\dfrac{9}{4}(9 + p^2)$
  (4) $\dfrac{9}{4}(9 - p^2)$

59. If $\Delta = \begin{vmatrix} x-2 & 2x-3 & 3x-4 \\ 2x-3 & 3x-4 & 4x-5 \\ 3x-5 & 5x-8 & 10x-17 \end{vmatrix} = Ax^3 + Bx^2 + Cx + D,$

then $B + C$ is equal to :

(1) -1 (2) 1
(3) -3 (4) 9

60. The area (in sq. units) of the region

$$\{(x, y) : 0 \le y \le x^2 + 1,\ 0 \le y \le x+1,\ \tfrac{1}{2} \le x \le 2\} \text{ is :}$$

(1) $\dfrac{23}{16}$ (2) $\dfrac{79}{24}$ (3) $\dfrac{79}{16}$ (4) $\dfrac{23}{6}$

61. The foot of the perpendicular drawn from the point $(4, 2, 3)$ to the line joining the points $(1, -2, 3)$ and $(1, 1, 0)$ lies on the plane :

(1) $2x + y - z = 1$ (2) $x - y - 2z = 1$
(3) $x - 2y + z = 1$ (4) $x + 2y - z = 1$

62. The solution curve of the differential equation,

$$(1 + e^{-x})(1 + y^2)\frac{dy}{dx} = y^2, \text{ which passes through the point}$$

$(0, 1)$, is :

(1) $y^2 + 1 = y\left(\log_e\left(\dfrac{1 + e^{-x}}{2} \right) + 2 \right)$

(2) $y^2 + 1 = y\left(\log_e\left(\dfrac{1 + e^{x}}{2} \right) + 2 \right)$

(3) $y^2 = 1 + y\log_e\left(\dfrac{1 + e^{x}}{2} \right)$

(4) $y^2 = 1 + y\log_e\left(\dfrac{1 + e^{-x}}{2} \right)$

63. A die is thrown two times and the sum of the scores appearing on the die is observed to be a multiple of 4. Then the conditional probability that the score 4 has appeared atleast once is :

(1) $\dfrac{1}{4}$ (2) $\dfrac{1}{3}$

(3) $\dfrac{1}{8}$ (4) $\dfrac{1}{9}$

64. $\displaystyle\int_{-\pi}^{\pi} |\pi - |x|| \, dx$ is equal to :

(1) $\sqrt{2}\pi^2$ (2) $2\pi^2$

(3) π^2 (4) $\dfrac{\pi^2}{2}$

65. For the frequency distribution :

Variate (x) : x_1 x_2 $x_3 \ldots x_{15}$
Frequency (f) : f_1 f_2 $f_3 \ldots f_{15}$

where $0 < x_1 < x_2 < x_3 < \ldots < x_{15} = 10$ and $\displaystyle\sum_{i=1}^{15} f_i > 0$, the standard deviation **cannot** be :

(1) 4 (2) 1 (3) 6 (4) 2

66. The lines $\vec{r} = (\hat{i} - \hat{j}) + l(2\hat{i} + \hat{k})$ and
$\vec{r} = (2\hat{i} - \hat{j}) + m(\hat{i} + \hat{j} - \hat{k})$

(1) do not intersect for any values of l and m
(2) intersect for all values of l and m
(3) intersect when $l = 2$ and $m = \dfrac{1}{2}$
(4) intersect when $l = 1$ and $m = 2$

67. Let $[t]$ denote the greatest integer $\le t$. If for some $\lambda \in \mathbf{R} - \{0, 1\}$, $\displaystyle\lim_{x \to 0} \left| \frac{1 - x + |x|}{\lambda - x + [x]} \right| = L$, then L is equal to :

(1) 1 (2) 2 (3) $\dfrac{1}{2}$ (4) 0

68. The value of $(2 \cdot {}^1P_0 - 3 \cdot {}^2P_1 + 4 \cdot {}^3P_2 - \ldots$ up to 51th term$)$ $+ (1! - 2! + 3! - \ldots$ up to 51th term$)$ is equal to :

(1) $1 - 51(51)!$ (2) $1 + (51)!$
(3) $1 + (52)!$ (4) 1

69. The function, $f(x) = (3x - 7)x^{2/3},\ x \in \mathbf{R},$ is increasing for all x lying in :

(1) $(-\infty, 0) \cup \left(\dfrac{14}{15}, \infty \right)$ (2) $(-\infty, 0) \cup \left(\dfrac{3}{7}, \infty \right)$

(3) $\left(-\infty, \dfrac{14}{15} \right)$ (4) $\left(-\infty, -\dfrac{14}{15} \right) \cup (0, \infty)$

70. If the number of integral terms in the expansion of $(3^{1/2} + 5^{1/8})^n$ is exactly 33, then the least value of n is :

(1) 264 (2) 128 (3) 256 (4) 248

71. The value of $(0.16)\log_{2.5}\left(\dfrac{1}{3} + \dfrac{1}{3^2} + \dfrac{1}{3^3} + \ldots \text{ to } \infty \right)$ is equal to __________ .

72. Let $A = \begin{bmatrix} x & 1 \\ 1 & 0 \end{bmatrix},\ x \in \mathbf{R}$ and $A^4 = [a_{ij}]$. If $a_{11} = 109$, then a_{22} is equal to __________ .

73. The diameter of the circle, whose centre lies on the line $x + y = 2$ in the first quadrant and which touches both the lines $x = 3$ and $y = 2$, is __________ .

74. If $\left(\dfrac{1+i}{1-i} \right)^{m/2} = \left(\dfrac{1+i}{i-1} \right)^{n/3} = 1,\ (m, n \in \mathbf{N})$, then the greatest common divisor of the least values of m and n is __________ .

75. If $\displaystyle\lim_{x \to 0} \left\{ \frac{1}{x^8}\left(1 - \cos\frac{x^2}{2} - \cos\frac{x^2}{4} + \cos\frac{x^2}{2}\cos\frac{x^2}{4} \right) \right\} = 2^{-k}$, then the value of k is __________ .

PHYSICS

1. Concentric metallic hollow spheres of radii R and $4R$ hold charges Q_1 and Q_2 respectively. Given that surface charge densities of the concentric spheres are equal, the potential difference $V(R) - V(4R)$ is :

(1) $\dfrac{3Q_1}{16\pi\varepsilon_0 R}$ (2) $\dfrac{3Q_2}{4\pi\varepsilon_0 R}$ (3) $\dfrac{Q_2}{4\pi\varepsilon_0 R}$ (4) $\dfrac{3Q_1}{4\pi\varepsilon_0 R}$

2. The electric field of a plane electromagnetic wave propagating along the x direction in vacuum is $\vec{E} = E_0 \hat{j} \cos(\omega t - kx)$. The magnetic field $\vec{B}$, at the moment $t = 0$ is :

(1) $\vec{B} = \dfrac{E_0}{\sqrt{\mu_0 \varepsilon_0}} \cos(kx)\hat{k}$

(2) $\vec{B} = E_0 \sqrt{\mu_0 \varepsilon_0} \cos(kx)\hat{j}$

(3) $\vec{B} = E_0 \sqrt{\mu_0 \varepsilon_0} \cos(kx)\hat{k}$

(4) $\vec{B} = \dfrac{E_0}{\sqrt{\mu_0 \varepsilon_0}} \cos(kx)\hat{j}$

3. A block of mass m attached to a massless spring is performing oscillatory motion of amplitude 'A' on a frictionless horizontal plane. If half of the mass of the block breaks off when it is passing through its equilibrium point, the amplitude of oscillation for the remaining system become fA. The value of f is :

(1) $\dfrac{1}{\sqrt{2}}$ (2) 1 (3) $\dfrac{1}{2}$ (4) $\sqrt{2}$

4. A particle is moving unidirectionally on a horizontal plane under the action of a constant power supplying energy source. The displacement (s) - time (t) graph that describes the motion of the particle is (graphs are drawn schematically and are not to scale) :

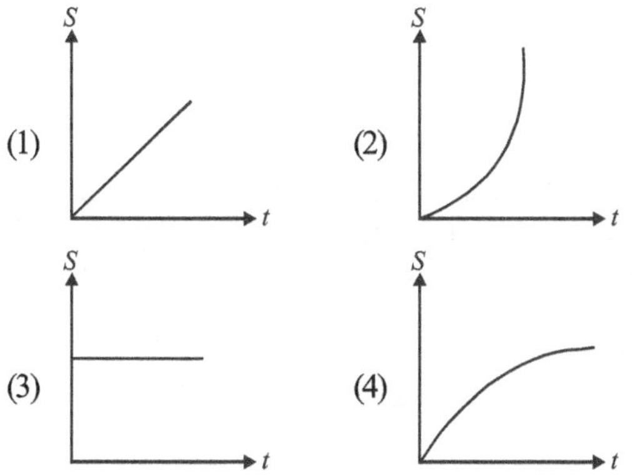

5. A uniform magnetic field B exists in a direction perpendicular to the plane of a square loop made of a metal wire. The wire has a diameter of 4 mm and a total length of 30 cm. The magnetic field changes with time at a steady rate $dB/dt = 0.032$ Ts^{-1}. The induced current in the loop is close to (Resistivity of the metal wire is $1.23 \times 10^{-8}\,\Omega$m)

(1) 0.43 A   (2) 0.61 A   (3) 0.34 A   (4) 0.53 A

6. The mass density of a planet of radius R varies with the distance r from its centre as $\rho(r) = \rho_0 \left(1 - \dfrac{r^2}{R^2}\right)$. Then the gravitational field is maximum at :

(1) $r = \sqrt{\dfrac{3}{4}}R$ (2) $r = R$

(3) $r = \dfrac{1}{\sqrt{3}}R$ (4) $r = \sqrt{\dfrac{5}{9}}R$

7. A metallic sphere cools from 50°C to 40°C in 300 s. If atmospheric temperature around is 20°C, then the sphere's temperature after the next 5 minutes will be close to :

(1) 31°C   (2) 33°C   (3) 28°C   (4) 35°C

8. The radius R of a nucleus of mass number A can be estimated by the formula $R = (1.3 \times 10^{-15})A^{1/3}$ m. It follows that the mass density of a nucleus is of the order of : ($M_{\text{prot.}} \cong M_{\text{neut.}} \approx 1.67 \times 10^{-27}$ kg)

(1) 10^3 kg m^{-3} (2) 10^{10} kg m^{-3}
(3) 10^{24} kg m^{-3} (4) 10^{17} kg m^{-3}

9. If a semiconductor photodiode can detect a photon with a maximum wavelength of 400 nm, then its band gap energy is :
Planck's constant, $h = 6.63 \times 10^{-34}$ J.s.
Speed of light, $c = 3 \times 10^8$ m/s

(1) 1.1 eV   (2) 2.0 eV   (3) 1.5 eV   (4) 3.1 eV

10. Two light waves having the same wavelength λ in vacuum are in phase initially. Then the first wave travels a path L_1 through a medium of refractive index n_1 while the second wave travels a path of length L_2 through a medium of refractive index n_2. After this the phase difference between the two waves is :

(1) $\dfrac{2\pi}{\lambda}\left(\dfrac{L_2}{n_1} - \dfrac{L_1}{n_2}\right)$ (2) $\dfrac{2\pi}{\lambda}\left(\dfrac{L_1}{n_1} - \dfrac{L_2}{n_2}\right)$

(3) $\dfrac{2\pi}{\lambda}(n_1 L_1 - n_2 L_2)$ (4) $\dfrac{2\pi}{\lambda}(n_2 L_1 - n_1 L_2)$

11. Two resistors 400Ω and 800Ω are connected in series across a 6 V battery. The potential difference measured by a voltmeter of 10 kΩ across 400Ω resistor is close to :

(1) 2 V   (2) 1.8 V   (3) 2.05 V   (4) 1.95 V

12. To raise the temperature of a certain mass of gas by 50°C at a constant pressure, 160 calories of heat is required. When the same mass of gas is cooled by 100°C at constant volume, 240 calories of heat is released. How many degrees of freedom does each molecule of this gas have (assume gas to be ideal)?
(1) 5   (2) 6   (3) 3   (4) 7

13. Which of the following will NOT be observed when a multimeter (operating in resistance measuring mode) probes connected across a component, are just reversed ?
  (1) Multimeter shows an equal deflection in both cases i.e. before and after reversing the probes if the chosen component is resistor.
  (2) Multimeter shows NO deflection in both cases i.e. before and after reversing the probes if the chosen component is capacitor.
  (3) Multimeter shows a deflection, accompanied by a splash of light out of connected and NO deflection on reversing the probes if the chosen component is LED.
  (4) Multimeter shows NO deflection in both cases i.e. before and after reversing the probes if the chosen component is metal wire.

14. A calorimter of water equivalent 20 g contains 180 g of water at 25°C. 'm' grams of steam at 100°C is mixed in it till the temperature of the mixture is 31°C. The value of 'm' is close to (Latent heat of water = 540 cal g^{-1}, specific heat of water = 1 cal g^{-1} °C^{-1})
(1) 2   (2) 4   (3) 3.2   (4) 2.6

15. A block of mass 1.9 kg is at rest at the edge of a table, of height 1 m. A bullet of mass 0.1 kg collides with the block and sticks to it. If the velocity of the bullet is 20 m/s in the horizontal direction just before the collision then the kinetic energy just before the combined system strikes the floor, is [Take g = 10 m/s^2. Assume there is no rotational motion and losss of energy after the collision is negligiable.
(1) 20 J   (2) 21 J   (3) 19 J   (4) 23 J

16. Amount of solar energy received on the earth's surface per unit area per unit time is defined a solar constant. Dimension of solar constant is :
(1) ML^2T^{-2} (2) ML^0T^{-3}
(3) $M^2L^0T^{-1}$ (4) MLT^{-2}

17. A perfectly diamagnetic sphere has a small spherical cavity at its centre, which is filled with a paramagnetic substance. The whole system is placed in a uniform magnetic field $\vec{B}$. Then the field inside the paramagnetic substance is :

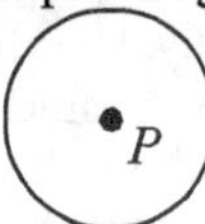

(1) $\vec{B}$
(2) zero
(3) much large than $|\vec{B}|$ and parallel to $\vec{B}$
(4) much large than $|\vec{B}|$ but opposite to $\vec{B}$

18. Hydrogen ion and singly ionized helium atom are accelerated, from rest, through the same potential difference. The ratio of final speeds of hydrogen and helium ions is close to :
(1) 1 : 2   (2) 10 : 7   (3) 2 : 1   (4) 5 : 7

19. Two sources of light emit X-rays of wavelength 1 nm and visible light of wavelength 500 nm, respectively. Both the sources emit light of the same power 200 W. The ratio of the number density of photons of X-rays to the number density of photons of the visible light of the given wavelengths is :
(1) $\dfrac{1}{500}$ (2) 250   (3) $\dfrac{1}{250}$ (4) 500

20.

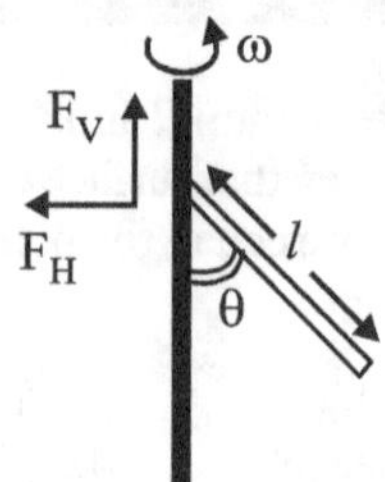

A uniform rod of length 'l' is pivoted at one of its ends on a vertical shaft of negligible radius. When the shaft rotates at angular speed ω the rod makes an angle θ with it (see figure). To find θ equate the rate of change of angular momentum (direction going into the paper) $\dfrac{ml^2}{12}\omega^2\sin\theta\cos\theta$ about the centre of mass (CM) to the torque provided by the horizontal and vertical forces F_H and F_V about the CM. The value of θ is then such that :
(1) $\cos\theta = \dfrac{2g}{3l\omega^2}$ (2) $\cos\theta = \dfrac{g}{2l\omega^2}$
(3) $\cos\theta = \dfrac{g}{l\omega^2}$ (4) $\cos\theta = \dfrac{3g}{2l\omega^2}$

21. If minimum possible work is done by a refrigerator in converting 100 grams of water at 0°C to ice, how much heat (in calories) is released to the surroundings at temperature 27°C (Latent heat of ice = 80 Cal/gram) to the nearest integer?

22. When an object is kept at a distance of 30 cm from a concave mirror, the image is formed at a distance of 10 cm from the mirror. If the object is moved with a speed of 9 cms^{-1}, the speed (in cms^{-1}) with which image moves at that instant is __________.

23. A block starts moving up an inclined plane of inclination 30° with an initial velocity of v_0. It comes back to its initial position with velocity $\dfrac{v_0}{2}$. The value of the coefficient of kinetic friction between the block and the inclined plane is close to $\dfrac{I}{1000}$. The nearest integer to I is __________.

24. An massless equilateral triangle EFG of side 'a' (As shown in figure) has three particles of mass m situated at its vertices. The moment of inertia of the system about the line EX perpendicular to EG in the plane of EFG is $\dfrac{N}{20}ma^2$ where N is an integer. The value of N is __________.

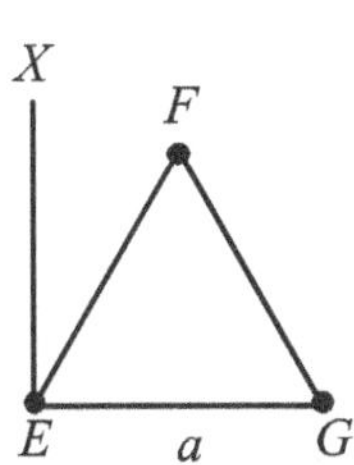

25. A galvanometer coil has 500 turns and each turn has an average area of $3 \times 10^{-4}\,m^2$. If a torque of 1.5 Nm is required to keep this coil parallel to a magnetic field when a current of 0.5 A is flowing through it, the strength of the field (in T) is __________.

CHEMISTRY

26. Among the statements (I - IV), the **correct** ones are :
(I) Be has smaller atomic radius compared to Mg.
(II) Be has higher ionization enthalpy than Al.
(III) Charge/radius ratio of Be is greater than that of Al.
(IV) Both Be and Al form mainly covalent compounds.
(1) (I), (II) and (IV)
(2) (I), (III) and (IV)
(3) (II), (III) and (IV)
(4) (I), (II) and (III)

27. An ionic micelle is formed on the addition of :
(1) liquid diethyl ether to aqueous NaCl solution
(2) excess water to liquid

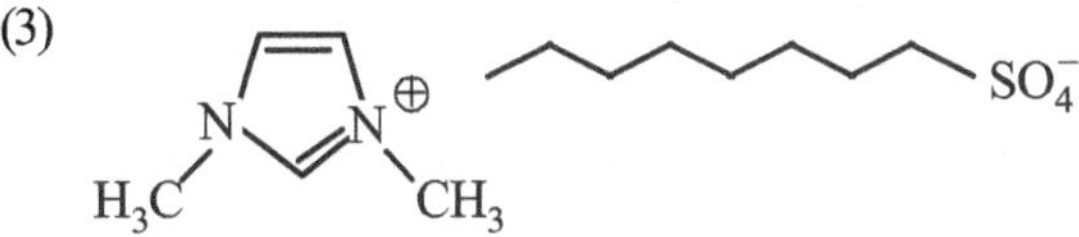
excess water to liquid

(3)

(4) sodium stearate to pure toluene

28. The increasing order of the reactivity of the following compounds in nucleophilic addition reaction is :
Propanal, Benzaldehyde, Propanone, Butanone
(1) Benzaldehyde < Butanone < Propanone < Propanal
(2) Butanone < Propanone < Benzaldehyde < Propanal
(3) Propanal < Propanone < Butanone < Benzaldehyde
(4) Benzaldehyde < Propanal < Propanone < Butanone

29. 100 mL of 0.1 M HCl is taken in a beaker and to it 100 mL of 0.1 M NaOH is added in steps of 2 mL and the pH is continuously measured. Which of the following graphs **correctly** depicts the change in pH?

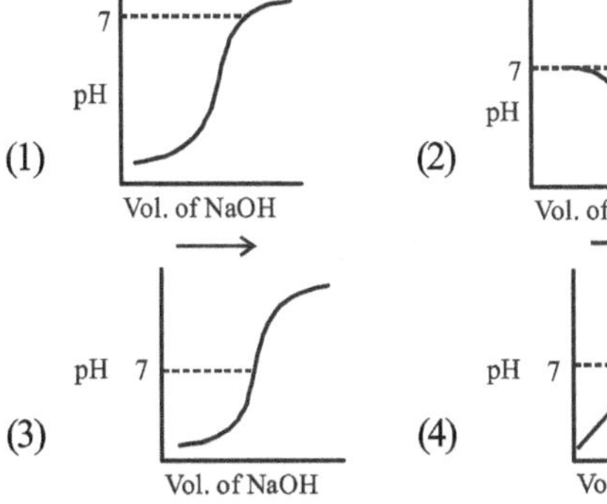

30. A mixture of one mole each of H_2, He and O_2 each are enclosed in a cylinder of volume V at temperature T. If the partial pressure of H_2 is 2 atm, the total pressure of the gases in the cylinder is :
(1) 6 atm
(2) 38 atm
(3) 14 atm
(4) 22 atm

31. Consider the hypothetical situation where the azimuthal quantum number, l, takes values $0, 1, 2, \ldots\ n+1$, where n is the principal quantum number. Then, the element with atomic number :
(1) 9 is the first alkali metal
(2) 13 has a half-filled valence subshell
(3) 8 is the first noble gas
(4) 6 has a $2p$-valence subshell

32. Consider the following reaction :

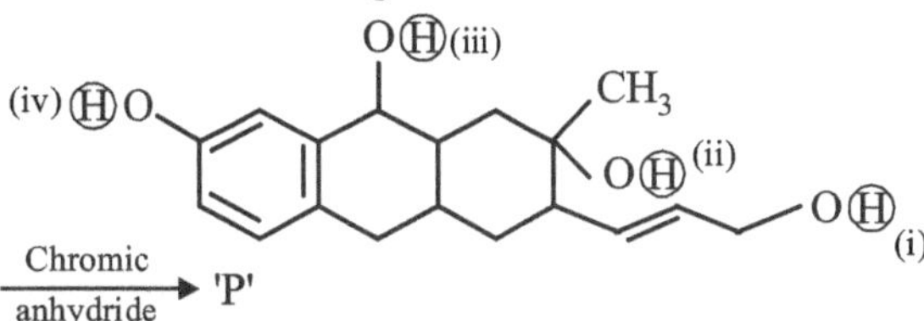

The product 'P' gives positive ceric ammonium nitrate test. This is because of the presence of which of these –OH group(s)?
(1) (ii) only
(2) (iii) and (iv)
(3) (iv) only
(4) (ii) and (iv)

33. Consider the following molecules and statements related to them :

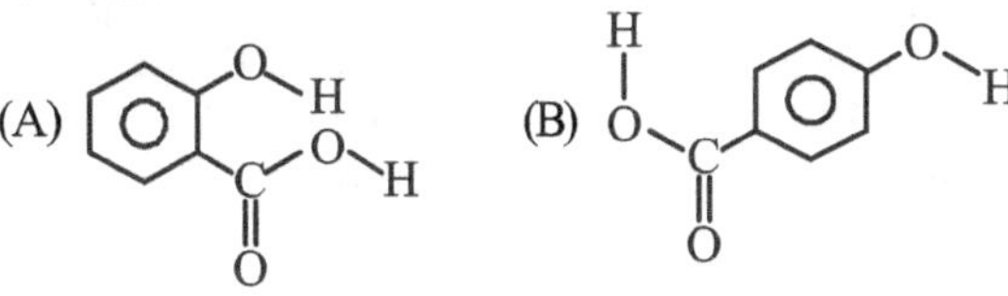

(a) (B) is more likely to be crystalline than (A)
(b) (B) has higher boiling point than (A)
(c) (B) dissolves more readily than (A) in water
Identify the **correct** option from below :
(1) (a) and (b) are true
(2) (a) and (c) are true
(3) only (a) is true
(4) (b) and (c) are true

34. The **incorrect** statement is :
(1) Manganate and permanganate ions are tetrahedral
(2) In manganate and permanganate ions, the π-bonding takes place by overlap of p-orbitals of oxygen and d-orbitals of manganese
(3) Manganate and permanganate ions are paramagnetic
(4) Manganate ion is green in colour and permanganate ion is purple in colour

35. The **incorrect** statement(s) among (1) - (4) regarding acid rain is (are) :
(a) It can corrode water pipes.
(b) It can damage structures made up of stone.
(c) It cannot cause respiratory ailments in animals
(d) It is not harmful for trees
(1) (a), (c) and (d)
(2) (c) only
(3) (a), (b) and (d)
(4) (c) and (d)

36. The compound A in the following reactions is :

$A \xrightarrow[\text{(ii) Conc. } H_2SO_4/\Delta]{\text{(i) } CH_3MgBr/H_2O}$

$B \xrightarrow[\text{(ii) } Zn/H_2O]{\text{(i) } O_3} C + D$

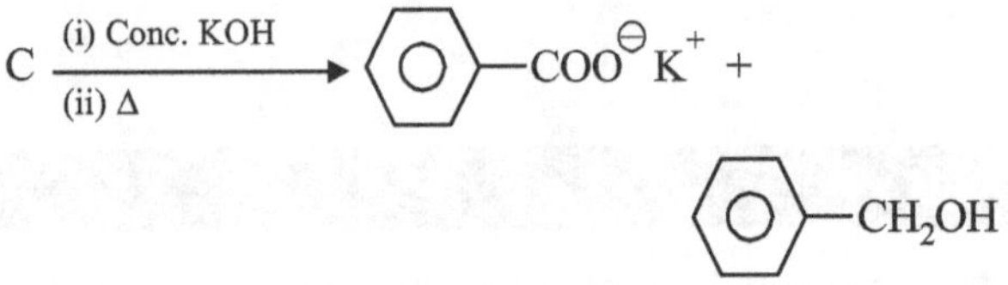

$D \xrightarrow[\Delta]{Ba(OH)_2} H_3C-\overset{CH_3}{\overset{|}{C}}=CH-\overset{O}{\overset{\|}{C}}-CH_3$

(1) $C_6H_5-\overset{O}{\overset{\|}{C}}-CH_3$

(2) $C_6H_5-\overset{O}{\overset{\|}{C}}-CH(CH_3)_2$

(3) $C_6H_5-CH_2-\overset{O}{\overset{\|}{C}}-CH_3$

(4) $C_6H_5-\overset{O}{\overset{\|}{C}}-CH_2CH_3$

37. The strengths of 5.6 volume hydrogen peroxide (of density 1 g/ mL) in terms of mass percentage and molarity (M), respectively, are :
(Take molar mass of hydrogen peroxide as 34 g/ mol)
(1) 1.7 and 0.5 (2) 0.85 and 0.25
(3) 1.7 and 0.25 (4) 0.85 and 0.5

38. The decreasing order of reactivity of the following compounds towards nucleophilic substitution (S_N2) is :

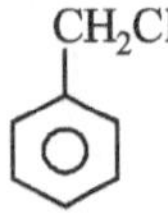
(I)

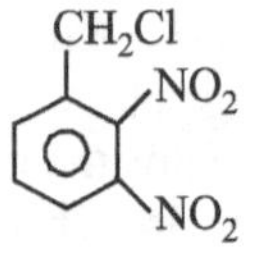
(II)

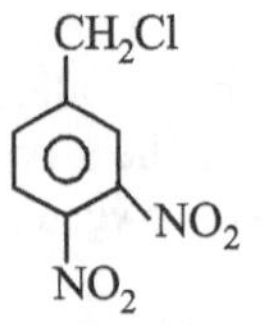
(III)

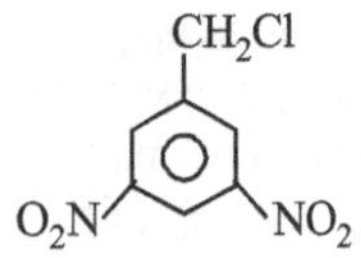
(IV)

(1) (II) > (III) > (I) > (IV)
(2) (II) > (III) > (IV) > (I)
(3) (III) > (II) > (IV) > (I)
(4) (IV) > (II) > (III) > (I)

39. For the reaction $2A + 3B + \frac{3}{2}C \rightarrow 3P$, which statement is **correct**?

(1) $\frac{dn_A}{dt} = \frac{3}{2}\frac{dn_B}{dt} = \frac{3}{4}\frac{dn_C}{dt}$

(2) $\frac{dn_A}{dt} = \frac{dn_B}{dt} = \frac{dn_C}{dt}$

(3) $\frac{dn_A}{dt} = \frac{2}{3}\frac{dn_B}{dt} = \frac{4}{3}\frac{dn_C}{dt}$

(4) $\frac{dn_A}{dt} = \frac{2}{3}\frac{dn_B}{dt} = \frac{3}{4}\frac{dn_C}{dt}$

40. The five successive ionization enthalpies of an element are 800, 2427, 3658, 25024 and 32824 kJ mol^{-1}. The number of valence electrons in the element is :
(1) 5 (2) 4 (3) 3 (4) 2

41. Complex A has a composition of $H_{12}O_6Cl_3Cr$. If the complex on treatment with conc. H_2SO_4 loses 13.5% of its original mass, the correct molecular formula of A is :
[Given : atomic mass of Cr = 52 amu and Cl = 35 amu]
(1) $[Cr(H_2O)_6]Cl_3$
(2) $[Cr(H_2O)_3Cl_3]\cdot 3H_2O$
(3) $[Cr(H_2O)_5Cl]Cl_2\cdot H_2O$
(4) $[Cr(H_2O)_4Cl_2]Cl\cdot 2H_2O$

42. The *d*-electron configuration of $[Ru(en)_3]Cl_2$ and $[Fe(H_2O)_6]Cl_2$, respectively are :
(1) $t_{2g}^6 e_g^0$ and $t_{2g}^6 e_g^0$ (2) $t_{2g}^4 e_g^2$ and $t_{2g}^6 e_g^0$
(3) $t_{2g}^6 e_g^0$ and $t_{2g}^4 e_g^2$ (4) $t_{2g}^4 e_g^2$ and $t_{2g}^4 e_g^2$

43. Three isomers A, B and C (mol. formula $C_8H_{11}N$) give the following results :

A and C $\xrightarrow{\text{Diazotization}}$ P + Q $\xrightarrow[\text{(ii) Oxidation } (KMnO_4 + H^+)]{\text{(i) Hydrolysis}}$ R (product of A) + S (product of C)

R has lower boiling point than S

$B \xrightarrow{C_6H_5SO_2Cl}$ alkali-insoluble product

A, B and C, respectively are :

(1) 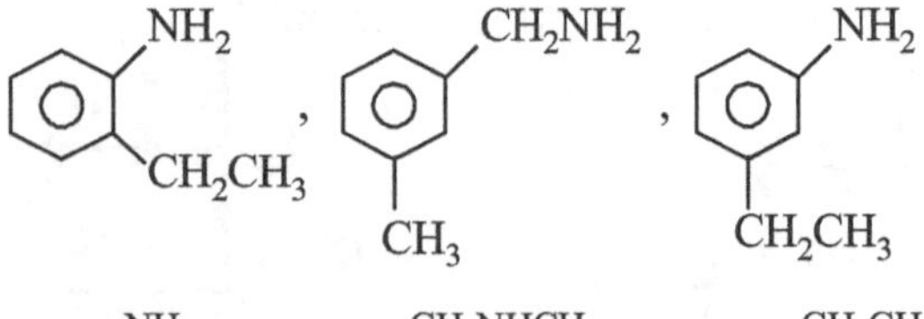

(2) 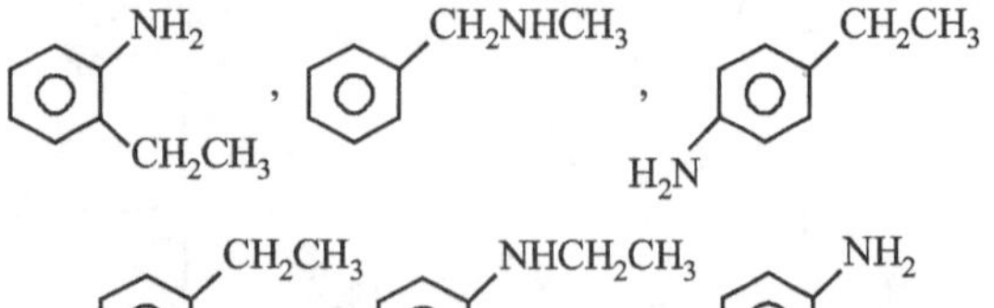

(3) 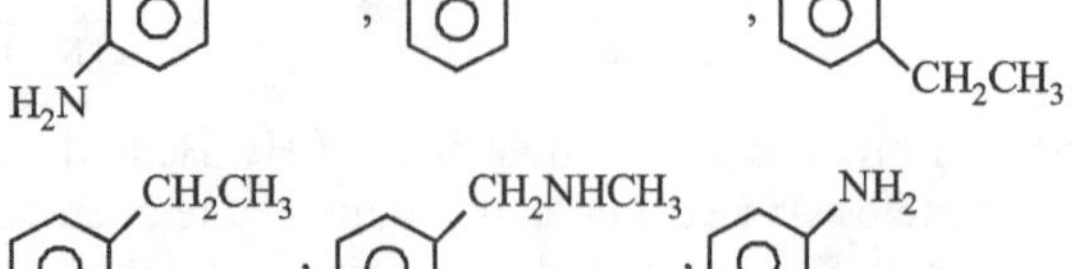

(4) 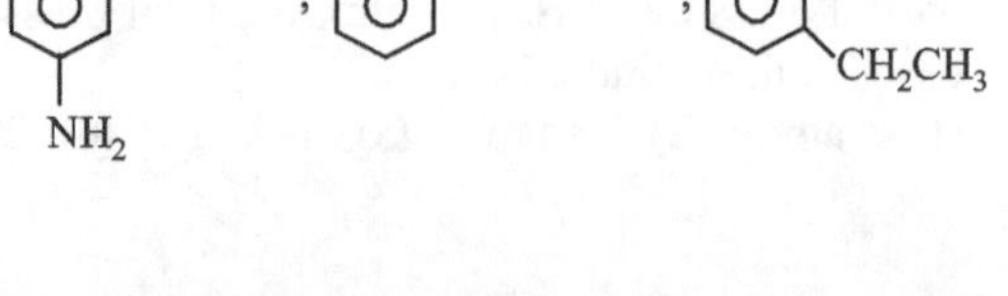

44. Match the following drugs with their therapeutic actions :
(i)   Ranitidine   (A) Antidepressant
(ii) Nardil (Phenelzine)   (B) Antibiotic
(iii) Chloramphenicol   (C) Antihistamine
(iv) Dimetane   (D) Antacid
      (Brompheniramine)
                              (E) Analgesic
(1) (i)-(A); (ii)-(C); (iii)-(B); (iv)-(E)
(2) (i)-(D); (ii)-(A); (iii)-(B); (iv)-(C)
(3) (i)-(E); (ii)-(A); (iii)-(C); (iv)-(D)
(4) (i)-(D); (ii)-(C); (iii)-(A); (iv)-(E)

45. The major product in the following reaction is :

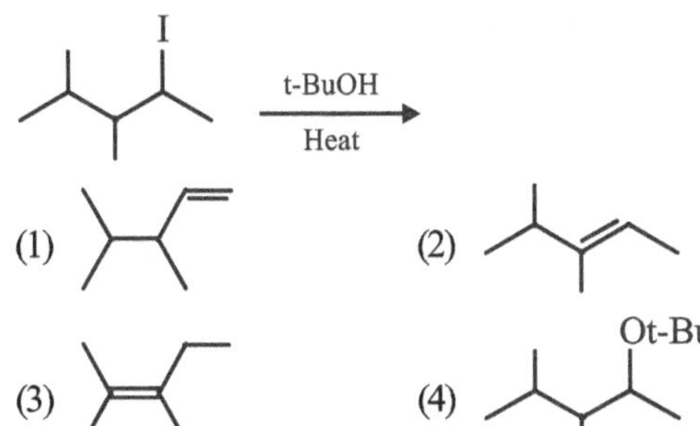

46. If 250 cm^3 of an aqueous solution containing 0.73 g of a protein A is isotonic with one litre of another aqueous solution containing 1.65 g of a protein B, at 298 K, the ratio of the molecular masses of A and B is __________ $\times 10^{-2}$ (to the nearest integer).

47. An acidic solution of dichromate is electrolyzed for 8 minutes using 2A current. As per the following equation

$$Cr_2O_7^{2-} + 14H^+ + 6e^- \rightarrow 2Cr^{3+} + 7H_2O$$

The amount of Cr^{3+} obtained was 0.104 g. The efficiency of the process (in %) is (Take : F = 96000 C, At. mass of chromium = 52) __________.

48. The number of $\rangle C = O$ groups present in a tripeptide Asp - Glu - Lys is __________.

49. 6.023×10^{22} molecules are present in 10 g of a substance 'x'. The molarity of a solution containing 5 g of substance 'x' in 2 L solution is __________ $\times 10^{-3}$.

50. The volume (in mL) of 0.1 N NaOH required to neutralise 10 mL of 0.1 N phosphinic acid is __________.

MATHEMATICS

51. Let A be a 3×3 matrix such that $\text{adj} A = \begin{bmatrix} 2 & -1 & 1 \\ -1 & 0 & 2 \\ 1 & -2 & -1 \end{bmatrix}$ and

$B = \text{adj(adj } A)$. If $|A| = \lambda$ and $|(B^{-1})^T| = \mu$, then the ordered pair, $(|\lambda|, \mu)$ is equal to :

(1) $\left(3, \dfrac{1}{81}\right)$ (2) $\left(9, \dfrac{1}{9}\right)$ (3) $(3, 81)$ (4) $\left(9, \dfrac{1}{81}\right)$

52. The set of all real values of λ for which the quadratic equations, $(\lambda^2 + 1)x^2 - 4\lambda x + 2 = 0$ always have exactly one root in the interval $(0, 1)$ is :
(1) $(0, 2)$ (2) $(2, 4]$ (3) $(1, 3]$ (4) $(-3, -1)$

53. If $\int \sin^{-1}\left(\sqrt{\dfrac{x}{1+x}}\right) dx = A(x)\tan^{-1}(\sqrt{x}) + B(x) + C$, where

C is a constant of integration, then the ordered pair $(A(x), B(x))$ can be :

(1) $(x+1, -\sqrt{x})$ (2) $(x+1, \sqrt{x})$

(3) $(x-1, -\sqrt{x})$ (4) $(x-1, \sqrt{x})$

54. If the term independent of x in the expansion of $\left(\dfrac{3}{2}x^2 - \dfrac{1}{3x}\right)^9$ is k, then $18k$ is equal to :
(1) 5   (2) 9   (3) 7   (4) 11

55. Let $x_i (1 \le i \le 10)$ be ten observations of a random variable X.

If $\displaystyle\sum_{i=1}^{10}(x_i - p) = 3$ and $\displaystyle\sum_{i=1}^{10}(x_i - p)^2 = 9$ where

$0 \ne p \in \mathbf{R}$, then the standard deviation of these observations is :

(1) $\sqrt{\dfrac{3}{5}}$ (2) $\dfrac{4}{5}$ (3) $\dfrac{9}{10}$ (4) $\dfrac{7}{10}$

56. If $x^3 dy + xy\, dx = x^2 dy + 2y\, dx$; $y(2) = e$ and $x > 1$, then $y(4)$ is equal to :

(1) $\dfrac{3}{2} + \sqrt{e}$ (2) $\dfrac{3}{2}\sqrt{e}$ (3) $\dfrac{1}{2} + \sqrt{e}$ (4) $\dfrac{\sqrt{e}}{2}$

57. If z_1, z_2 are complex numbers such that $\text{Re}(z_1) = |z_1 - 1|$, $\text{Re}(z_2) = |z_2 - 1|$ and $\arg(z_1 - z_2) = \dfrac{\pi}{6}$, then $\text{Im}(z_1 + z_2)$ is equal to :

(1) $\dfrac{2}{\sqrt{3}}$ (2) $2\sqrt{3}$ (3) $\dfrac{\sqrt{3}}{2}$ (4) $\dfrac{1}{\sqrt{3}}$

58. $\displaystyle\lim_{x \to a} \dfrac{(a+2x)^{\frac{1}{3}} - (3x)^{\frac{1}{3}}}{(3a+x)^{\frac{1}{3}} - (4x)^{\frac{1}{3}}}$ $(a \ne 0)$ is equal to :

(1) $\left(\dfrac{2}{3}\right)^{\frac{4}{3}}$ (2) $\left(\dfrac{2}{3}\right)\left(\dfrac{2}{9}\right)^{\frac{1}{3}}$

(3) $\left(\dfrac{2}{9}\right)^{\frac{4}{3}}$ (4) $\left(\dfrac{2}{9}\right)\left(\dfrac{2}{3}\right)^{\frac{1}{3}}$

59. Let p, q, r be three statements such that the truth value of $(p \wedge q) \to (\sim q \vee r)$ is F. Then the truth values of p, q, r are respectively :
(1) T, F, T   (2) T, T, T
(3) F, T, F   (4) T, T, F

60. In the sum of the series

$$20 + 19\frac{3}{5} + 19\frac{1}{5} + 18\frac{4}{5} + \cdots \text{ upto } n^{\text{th}} \text{ term is } 488 \text{ and then}$$

n^{th} term is negative, then :

(1) $n = 60$ (2) n^{th} term is -4

(3) $n = 41$ (4) n^{th} term is $-4\frac{2}{5}$

61. Let e_1 and e_2 be the eccentricities of the ellipse, $\dfrac{x^2}{25} + \dfrac{y^2}{b^2} = 1 \ (b < 5)$ and the hyperbola, $\dfrac{x^2}{16} - \dfrac{y^2}{b^2} = 1$ respectively satisfying $e_1 e_2 = 1$. If α and β are the distances between the foci of the ellipse and the foci of the hyperbola respectively, then the ordered pair (α, β) is equal to :

(1) $(8, 12)$ (2) $\left(\dfrac{20}{3}, 12\right)$

(3) $\left(\dfrac{24}{5}, 10\right)$ (4) $(8, 10)$

62. If the value of the integral $\displaystyle\int_0^{1/2} \dfrac{x^2}{(1-x^2)^{3/2}}\, dx$ is $\dfrac{k}{6}$, then k is equal to :

(1) $2\sqrt{3} - \pi$ (2) $2\sqrt{3} + \pi$

(3) $3\sqrt{2} + \pi$ (4) $3\sqrt{2} - \pi$

63. Suppose $f(x)$ is a polynomial of degree four, having critical points at $-1, 0, 1$. If $T = \{x \in \mathbf{R} \mid f(x) = f(0)\}$, then the sum of squares of all the elements of T is :

(1) 4   (2) 6   (3) 2   (4) 8

64. If the surface area of a cube is increasing at a rate of 3.6 cm²/sec, retaining its shape; then the rate of change of its volume (in cm³/sec.), when the length of a side of the cube is 10 cm, is :

(1) 18   (2) 10   (3) 20   (4) 9

65. Let $a, b, c \in \mathbf{R}$ be such that $a^2 + b^2 + c^2 = 1$. If

$$a\cos\theta - b\cos\left(\theta + \frac{2\pi}{3}\right) = c\cos\left(\theta + \frac{4\pi}{3}\right), \text{ where } \theta = \frac{\pi}{9},$$

then the angle between the vectors $a\hat{i} + b\hat{j} + c\hat{k}$ and $b\hat{i} + c\hat{j} + a\hat{k}$ is :

(1) $\dfrac{\pi}{2}$ (2) $\dfrac{2\pi}{3}$ (3) $\dfrac{\pi}{9}$ (4) 0

66. The probability that a randomly chosen 5-digit number is made from exactly two digits is :

(1) $\dfrac{135}{10^4}$ (2) $\dfrac{121}{10^4}$ (3) $\dfrac{150}{10^4}$ (4) $\dfrac{134}{10^4}$

67. If a $\triangle ABC$ has vertices $A(-1, 7)$, $B(-7, 1)$ and $C(5, -5)$, then its orthocentre has coordinates :

(1) $\left(-\dfrac{3}{5}, \dfrac{3}{5}\right)$ (2) $(-3, 3)$

(3) $\left(\dfrac{3}{5}, -\dfrac{3}{5}\right)$ (4) $(3, -3)$

68. Let R_1 and R_2 be two relations defined as follows :

$R_1 = \{(a, b) \in \mathbf{R}^2 : a^2 + b^2 \in Q\}$ and

$R_2 = \{(a, b) \in \mathbf{R}^2 : a^2 + b^2 \notin Q\}$, where Q is the set of all rational numbers. Then :

(1) Neither R_1 nor R_2 is transitive.

(2) R_2 is transitive but R_1 is not transitive.

(3) R_1 is transitive but R_2 is not transitive.

(4) R_1 and R_2 are both transitive.

69. The plane which bisects the line joining the points $(4, -2, 3)$ and $(2, 4, -1)$ at right angles also passes through the point:

(1) $(4, 0, 1)$ (2) $(0, -1, 1)$

(3) $(4, 0, -1)$ (4) $(0, 1, -1)$

70. Let the latus ractum of the parabola $y^2 = 4x$ be the common chord to the circles C_1 and C_2 each of them having radius $2\sqrt{5}$. Then, the distance between the centres of the circles C_1 and C_2 is :

(1) $8\sqrt{5}$ (2) 8

(3) 12   (4) $4\sqrt{5}$

71. The total number of 3-digit numbers, whose sum of digits is 10, is __________.

72. Let a plane P contain two lines

$$\vec{r} = \hat{i} + \lambda(\hat{i} + \hat{j}), \ \lambda \in \mathbf{R} \text{ and } \vec{r} = -\hat{j} + \mu(\hat{j} - \hat{k}), \ \mu \in \mathbf{R}.$$

If $Q(\alpha, \beta, \gamma)$ is the foot of the perpendicular drawn from the point $M(1, 0, 1)$ to P, then $3(\alpha + \beta + \gamma)$ equals __________.

73. If the tangent to the curve, $y = e^x$ at a point (c, e^c) and the normal to the parabola, $y^2 = 4x$ at the point $(1, 2)$ intersect at the same point on the x-axis, then the value of c is __________.

74. If m arithmetic means (A.Ms) and three geometric means (G.Ms) are inserted between 3 and 243 such that 4th A.M. is equal to 2nd G.M., then m is equal to __________.

75. Let S be the set of all integer solutions, (x, y, z), of the system of equations

$$x - 2y + 5z = 0$$

$$-2x + 4y + z = 0$$

$$-7x + 14y + 9z = 0$$

such that $15 \le x^2 + y^2 + z^2 \le 150$. Then, the number of elements in the set S is equal to __________.

JEE MAIN 2020

(Held on 4-09-2020 Morning Shift)

PHYSICS

1. Two charged thin infinite plane sheets of uniform surface charge density σ_+ and σ_-, where $|\sigma_+| > |\sigma_-|$, intersect at right angle. Which of the following best represents the electric field lines for this system ?

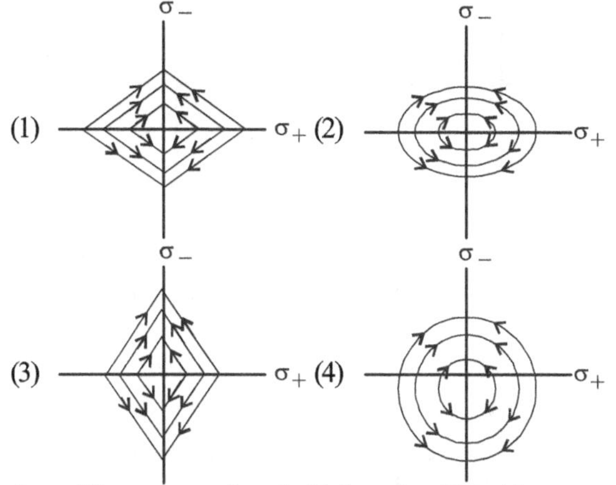

2. A small bar magnet placed with its axis at 30° with an external field of 0.06 T experiences a torque of 0.018 Nm. The minimum work required to rotate it from its stable to unstable equilibrium position is :
   (1) 6.4×10^{-2} J
   (2) 9.2×10^{-3} J
   (3) 7.2×10^{-2} J
   (4) 11.7×10^{-3} J

3. The specific heat of water $= 4200$ J kg^{-1} K^{-1} and the latent heat of ice $= 3.4 \times 10^5$ J kg^{-1}. 100 grams of ice at 0°C is placed in 200 g of water at 25°C. The amount of ice that will melt as the temperature of water reaches 0°C is close to (in grams) :
   (1) 61.7   (2) 63.8   (3) 69.3   (4) 64.6

4. Take the breakdown voltage of the zener diode used in the given circuit as 6V. For the input voltage shown in figure below, the time variation of the output voltage is :
   (Graphs drawn are schematic and not to scale)

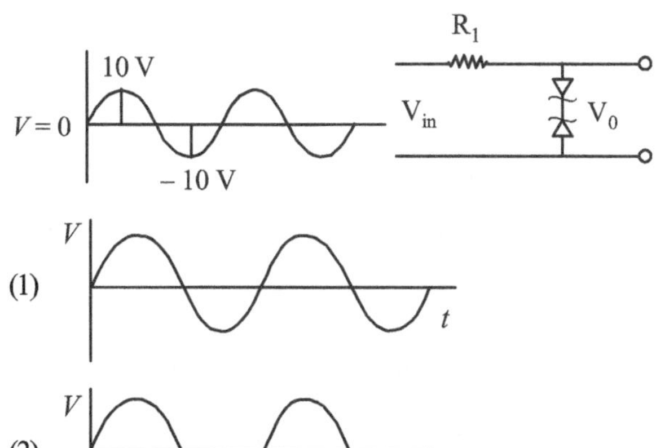

5. Match the C_p/C_v ratio for ideal gases with different type of molecules :

Column-I Molecule Type	Column-II C_p/C_v
(A) Monatomic	(I) 7/5
(B) Diatomic rigid molecules	(II) 9/7
(C) Diatomic non-rigid molecules	(III) 4/3
(D) Triatomic rigid molecules	(IV) 5/3

   (1) (A)-(IV), (B)-(II), (C)-(I), (D)-(III)
   (2) (A)-(III), (B)-(IV), (C)-(II), (D)-(I)
   (3) (A)-(IV), (B)-(I), (C)-(II), (D)-(III)
   (4) (A)-(II), (B)-(III), (C)-(I), (D)-(IV)

6. A beam of plane polarised light of large cross-sectional area and uniform intensity of 3.3 Wm^{-2} falls normally on a polariser (cross sectional area 3×10^{-4} m^2) which rotates about its axis with an angular speed of 31.4 rad/s. The energy of light passing through the polariser per revolution, is close to :
   (1) 1.0×10^{-5} J
   (2) 1.0×10^{-4} J
   (3) 1.5×10^{-4} J
   (4) 5.0×10^{-4} J

7. A wire A, bent in the shape of an arc of a circle, carrying a current of 2 A and having radius 2 cm and another wire B, also bent in the shape of arc of a circle, carrying a current of 3 A and having radius of 4 cm, are placed as shown in the figure. The ratio of the magnetic fields due to the wires A and B at the common centre O is :

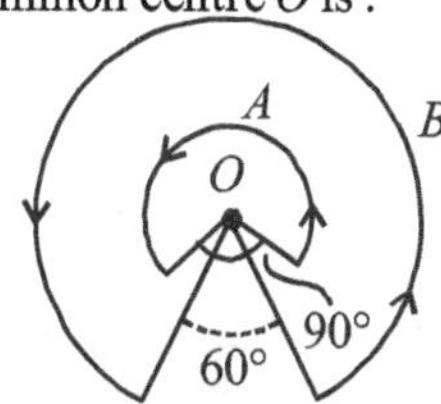

   (1) 4 : 6   (2) 6 : 4   (3) 2 : 5   (4) 6 : 5

8. A small bar magnet is moved through a coil at constant speed from one end to the other. Which of the following series of observations will be seen on the galvanometer G attached across the coil ?

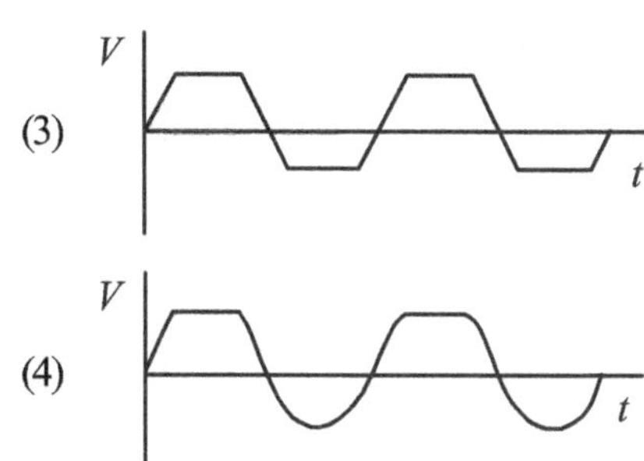

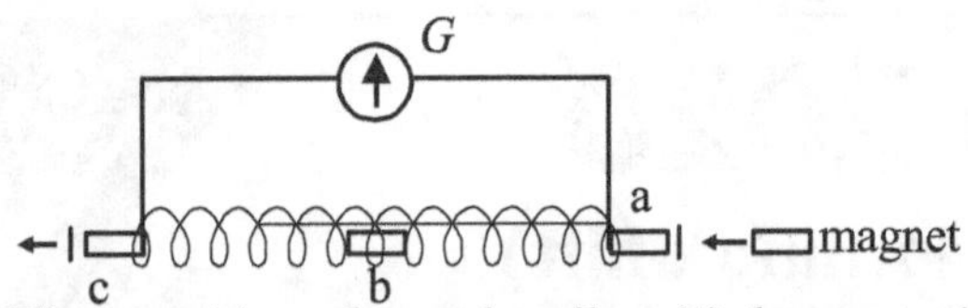

Three positions shown describe : (1) the magnet's entry (2) magnet is completely inside and (3) magnet's exit.

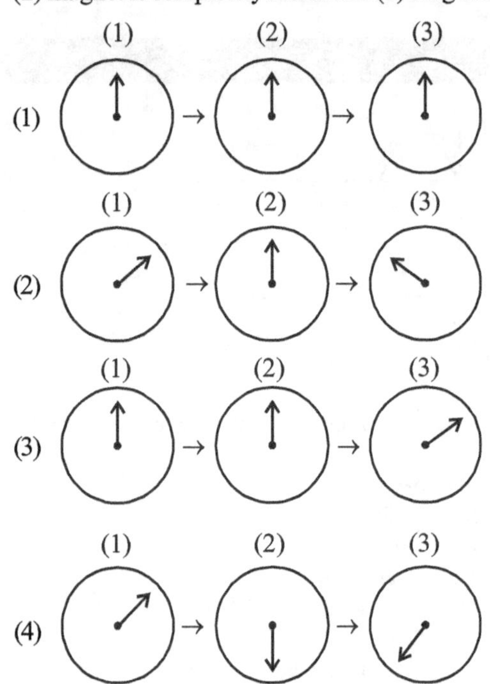

9. A two point charges $4q$ and $-q$ are fixed on the x-axis at $x = -\dfrac{d}{2}$ and $x = \dfrac{d}{2}$, respectively. If a third point charge 'q' is taken from the origin to $x = d$ along the semicircle as shown in the figure, the energy of the charge will :

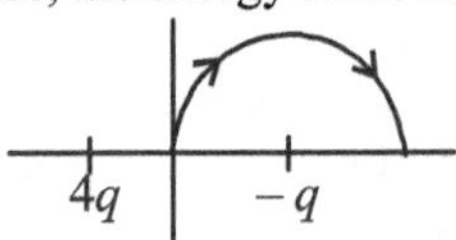

(1) increase by $\dfrac{3q^2}{4\pi\varepsilon_0 d}$ (2) increase by $\dfrac{2q^2}{3\pi\varepsilon_0 d}$

(3) decrease by $\dfrac{q^2}{4\pi\varepsilon_0 d}$ (4) decrease by $\dfrac{4q^2}{3\pi\varepsilon_0 d}$

10. A battery of 3.0 V is connected to a resistor dissipating 0.5 W of power. If the termial voltage of the battery is 2.5 V, the power dissipated within the internal resistance is:
(1) 0.50 W   (2) 0.072 W   (3) 0.10 W   (4) 0.125 W

11. For a transverse wave travelling along a straight line, the distance between two peaks (crests) is 5 m, while the distance between one crest and one trough is 1.5 m. The possible wavelengths (in m) of the waves are :

(1) $1, 3, 5, ...$ (2) $\dfrac{1}{1}, \dfrac{1}{3}, \dfrac{1}{5}, ...$

(3) $1, 2, 3, ...$ (4) $\dfrac{1}{2}, \dfrac{1}{4}, \dfrac{1}{6}, ...$

12. A Tennis ball is released from a height h and after freely falling on a wooden floor it rebounds and reaches height $\dfrac{h}{2}$. The velocity versus height of the ball during its motion may be represented graphically by :
(graph are drawn schematically and on not to scale)

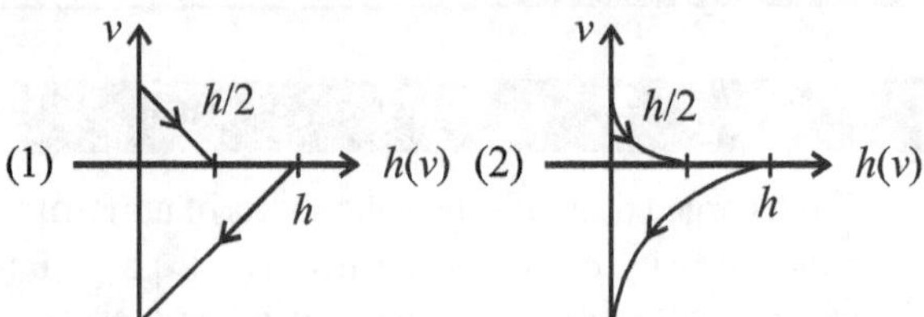

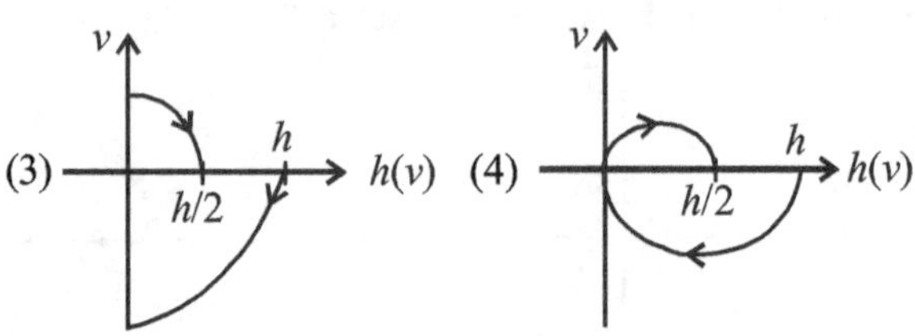

13. Particle A of mass $m_A = \dfrac{m}{2}$ moving along the x-axis with velocity v_0 collides elastically with another particle B at rest having mass $m_B = \dfrac{m}{3}$. If both particles move along the x-axis after the collision, the change $\Delta\lambda$ in de-Broglie wavelength of particle A, in terms of its de-Broglie wavelength (λ_0) before collision is :

(1) $\Delta\lambda = \dfrac{3}{2}\lambda_0$ (2) $\Delta\lambda = \dfrac{5}{2}\lambda_0$

(3) $\Delta\lambda = 2\lambda_0$ (4) $\Delta\lambda = 4\lambda_0$

14. Starting from the origin at time $t = 0$, with initial velocity $5\hat{j}$ ms^{-1}, a particle moves in the x–y plane with a constant acceleration of $(10\hat{i} + 4\hat{j})$ ms^{-2}. At time t, its coordiantes are $(20$ m$, y_0$ m$)$. The values of t and y_0 are, respectively :
(1) 2 s and 18 m   (2) 4 s and 52 m
(3) 2 s and 24 m   (4) 5 s and 25 m

15. On the x-axis and at a distance x from the origin, the gravitational field due to a mass distribution is given by $\dfrac{Ax}{(x^2 + a^2)^{3/2}}$ in the x-direction. The magnitude of gravitational potential on the x-axis at a distance x, taking its value to be zero at infinity, is :

(1) $\dfrac{A}{(x^2 + a^2)^{1/2}}$ (2) $\dfrac{A}{(x^2 + a^2)^{3/2}}$

(3) $A(x^2 + a^2)^{1/2}$ (4) $A(x^2 + a^2)^{3/2}$

16. Dimensional formula for thermal conductivity is (here K denotes the temperature :
(1) MLT^{-2}K   (2) MLT^{-2}K^{-2}
(3) MLT^{-3}K   (4) MLT^{-3}K^{-1}

17. Blocks of masses $m, 2m, 4m$ and $8m$ are arranged in a line on a frictionless floor. Another block of mass m, moving with speed v along the same line (see figure) collides with mass m in perfectly inelastic manner. All the subsequent collisions are also perfectly inelastic. By the time the last block of mass $8m$ starts moving the total energy loss is $p\%$ of the original energy. Value of 'p' is close to :

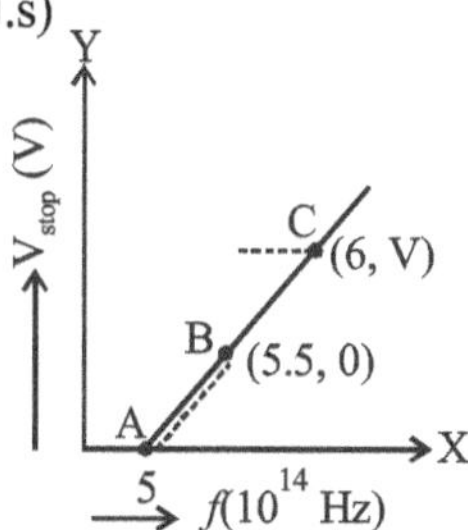

(1) 77   (2) 94   (3) 37   (4) 87

18. Chosse the **correct** option relating wavelengths of different parts of electromagnetic wave spectrum :
(1) $\lambda_{visible} < \lambda_{micro\ waves} < \lambda_{radio\ waves} < \lambda_{x-rays}$
(2) $\lambda_{radio\ waves} > \lambda_{micro\ waves} > \lambda_{visible} > \lambda_{x-rays}$
(3) $\lambda_{x-rays} < \lambda_{micro\ waves} < \lambda_{radio\ waves} < \lambda_{visible}$
(4) $\lambda_{visible} > \lambda_{x-rays} > \lambda_{radio\ waves} > \lambda_{micro\ waves}$

19. Given figure shows few data points in a photo electric effect experiment for a certain metal. The minimum energy for ejection of electron from its surface is : (Plancks constant $h = 6.62 \times 10^{-34}$ J.s)

(1) 2.27 eV   (2) 2.59 eV   (3) 1.93 eV   (4) 2.10 eV

20. An air bubble of radius 1 cm in water has an upward acceleration 9.8 cm s^{-2}. The density of water is 1 gm cm^{-3} and water offers negligible drag force on the bubble. The mass of the bubble is (g = 980 cm/s^2)
(1) 4.51 gm   (2) 3.15 gm   (3) 4.15 gm   (4) 1.52 gm

21. A closed vessel contains 0.1 mole of a monatomic ideal gas at 200 K. If 0.05 mole of the same gas at 400 K is added to it, the final equilibrium temperature (in K) of the gas in the vessel will be close to __________.

22. In the line spectra of hydrogen atom, difference between the largest and the shortest wavelengths of the Lyman series is 304 Å. The corresponding difference for the Paschan series in Å is : __________.

23. In a compound microscope, the magnified virtual image is formed at a distance of 25 cm from the eye-piece. The focal length of its objective lens is 1 cm. If the magnification is 100 and the tube length of the microscope is 20 cm, then the focal length of the eye-piece lens (in cm) is __________.

24. ABC is a plane lamina of the shape of an equilateral triangle. D, E are mid points of AB, AC and G is the centroid of the lamina. Moment of inertia of the lamina about an axis passing through G and perpendicular to the plane ABC is I_0. If part ADE is removed, the moment of inertia of the remaining part about the same axis is $\dfrac{NI_0}{16}$ where N is an integer. Value of N is __________.

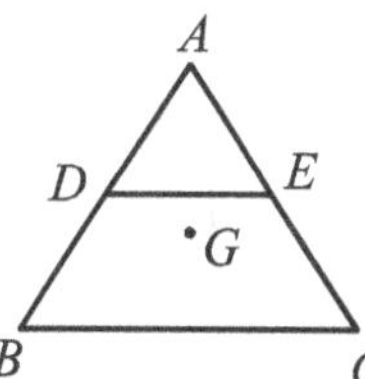

25. A circular disc of mass M and radius R is rotating about its axis with angular speed ω_1. If another stationary disc having radius $\dfrac{R}{2}$ and same mass M is dropped co-axially on to the rotating disc. Gradually both discs attain constant angular speed ω_2. The energy lost in the process is $p\%$ of the initial energy. Value of p is __________.

CHEMISTRY

26. The elements with atomic numbers 101 and 104 belong to, respectively :
(1) Group 11 and Group 4   (2) Actinoids and Group 6
(3) Actinoids and Group 4   (4) Group 6 and Actinoids

27. Which of the following will react with $CHCl_3$ + alc. KOH?
(1) Adenine and proline   (2) Thymine and proline
(3) Adenine and lysine   (4) Adenine and thymine

28. The number of isomers possible for $[Pt(en)(NO_2)_2]$ is :
(1) 2   (2) 4   (3) 1   (4) 3

29. The region in the electromagnetic spectrum where the Balmer series lines appear is :
(1) Visible   (2) Microwave
(3) Infrared   (4) Ultraviolet

30. For one mole of an ideal gas, which of these statements must be **true**?
(a) U and H each depends only on temperature
(b) Compressibility factor z is not equal to 1
(c) $C_{P,m} - C_{V,m} = R$
(d) $dU = C_V dT$ for any process

(1) (a) and (c)   (2) (b), (c) and (d)
(3) (c) and (d)   (4) (a), (c) and (d)

31. What are the functional groups present in the structure of maltose?
(1) One ketal and hemiketal
(2) Two acetals
(3) One acetal and one hemiacetal
(4) One acetal and one ketal

32. The IUPAC name of the following compound is :

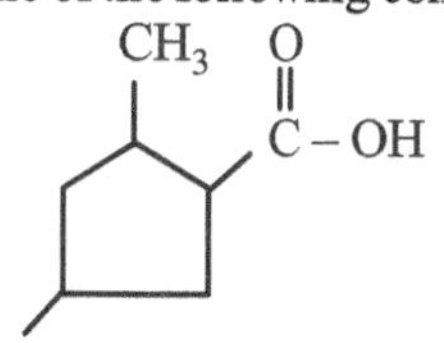

(1) 5-Bromo-3-methylcyclopentanoic acid
(2) 4-Bromo-2-methylcyclopentane carboxylic acid
(3) 3-Bromo-5-methylcyclopentanoic acid
(4) 3-Bromo-5-methylcyclopentane carboxylic acid

33. On combustion of Li, Na and K in excess of air, the major oxides formed, respectively, are :
(1) Li_2O_2, Na_2O_2 and K_2O_2 (2) Li_2O, Na_2O_2 and KO_2
(3) Li_2O, Na_2O and K_2O_2 (4) Li_2O, Na_2O_2 and K_2O

34. On heating, lead (II) nitrate gives a brown gas (A). The gas (A) on cooling changes to a colourless solid/liquid (B). (B) on heating with NO changes to a blue solid (C). The oxidation number of nitrogen in solid (C) is :
(1) +5   (2) +2   (3) +3   (4) +4

35. For the equilibrium $A \rightleftharpoons B$, the variation of the rate of the forward (a) and reverse (b) reaction with time is given by :

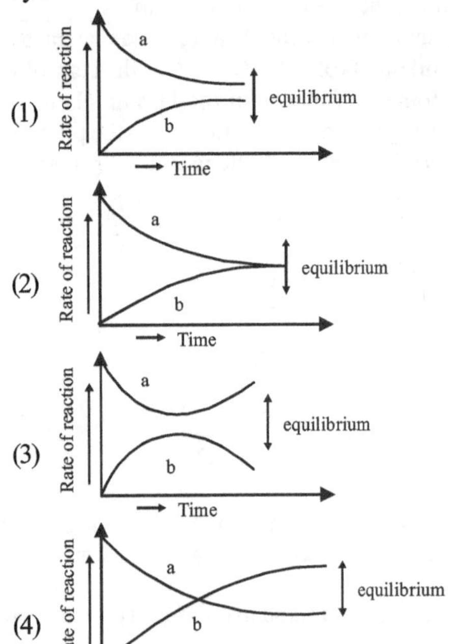

36. Among statements (1) - (4), the **correct** ones are :
(a) Lime stone is decomposed to CaO during the extraction of iron from its oxides.
(b) In the extraction of silver, silver is extracted as an anionic complex.
(c) Nickel is purified by Mond's process.
(d) Zr and Ti are purified by Van Arkel method.
(1) (a), (b), (c) and (d)   (2) (a), (c) and (d) only
(3) (b), (c) and (d) only   (4) (c) and (d) only

37. An organic compound (A) (molecular formula $C_6H_{12}O_2$) was hydrolysed with dil. H_2SO_4 to give a carboxylic acid (B) and an alcohol (C). 'C' gives white turbidity immediately when treated with anhydrous $ZnCl_2$ and conc. HCl. The organic compound (A) is :

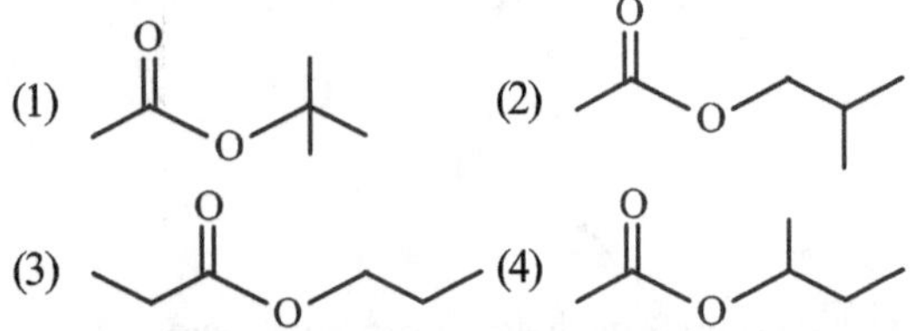

38. When neopentyl alcohol is heated with an acid, it slowly converted into an 85 : 15 mixture of alkenes A and B, respectively. What are these alkenes?

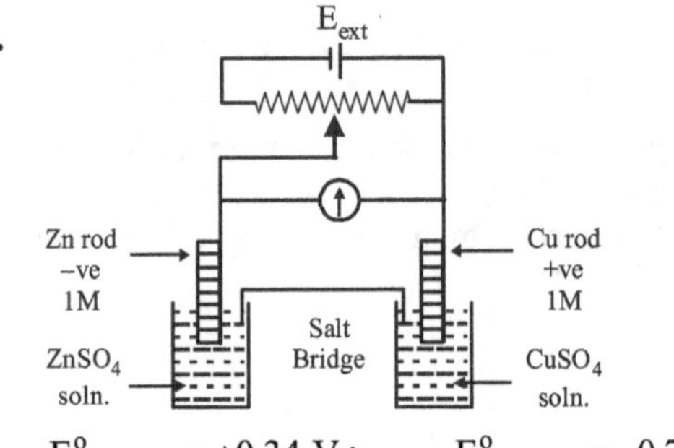

39.

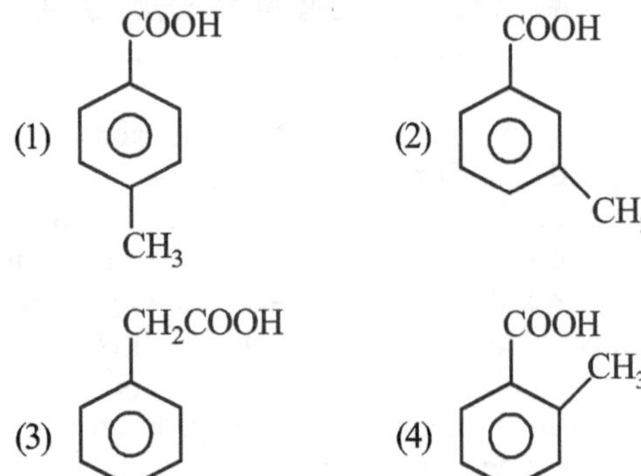

$E^o_{Cu^{2+}|Cu} = +0.34$ V ; $E^o_{Zn^{2+}|Zn} = -0.76$ V

Identify the **incorrect** statement from the options below for the above cell :
(1) If $E_{ext} > 1.1$ V, e^- flows from Cu to Zn
(2) If $E_{ext} > 1.1$ V, Zn dissolves at Zn electrode and Cu deposits at Cu electrode
(3) If $E_{ext} < 1.1$ V, Zn dissolves at anode and Cu deposits at cathode
(4) If $E_{ext} = 1.1$ V, no flow of e^- or current occurs

40. [P] on treatment with Br_2/$FeBr_3$ in CCl_4 produced a single isomer $C_8H_7O_2Br$ while heating [P] with sodalime gave toluene. The compound [P] is :

(1) COOH with CH_3 (para)   (2) COOH with CH_3 (meta)

(3) CH_2COOH (4) COOH with CH_3 (ortho)

41. Match the following :
(i) Foam   (A) smoke
(ii) Gel   (B) cell fluid
(iii) Aerosol   (C) jellies
(iv) Emulsion   (D) rubber
                       (E) froth
                       (F) milk

(1) (i)-(B), (ii)-(C), (iii)-(E), (iv)-(D)
(2) (i)-(D), (ii)-(B), (iii)-(A), (iv)-(E)
(3) (i)-(E), (ii)-(C), (iii)-(A), (iv)-(F)
(4) (i)-(D), (ii)-(B), (iii)-(E), (iv)-(F)

42. The pair in which both the species have the same magnetic moment (spin only) is :
(1) $[Cr(H_2O)_6]^{2+}$ and $[Fe(H_2O)_6]^{2+}$
(2) $[Co(OH)_4]^{2-}$ and $[Fe(NH_3)_6]^{2+}$
(3) $[Mn(H_2O)_6]^{2+}$ and $[Cr(H_2O)]^{2+}$
(4) $[Cr(H_2O)_6]^{2+}$ and $[CoCl_4]^{2-}$

43. The intermolecular potential energy for the molecules A, B, C and D given below suggests that :

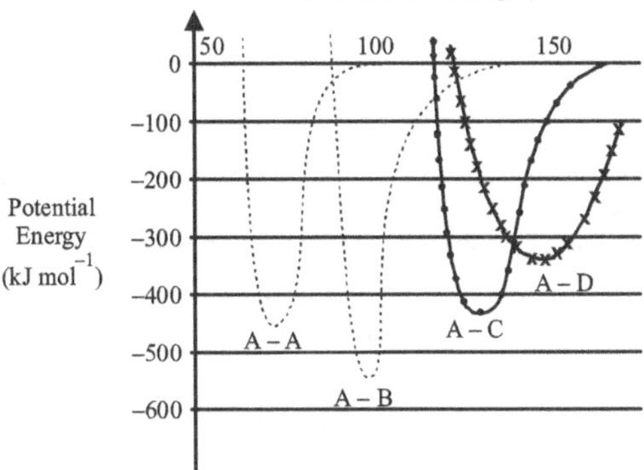

(1) A-D has the shortest bond length
(2) A-A has the largest bond enthalpy
(3) D is more electronegative than other atoms
(4) A-B has the stiffest bond

44. The decreasing order of reactivity of the following organic molecules towards $AgNO_3$ solution is :

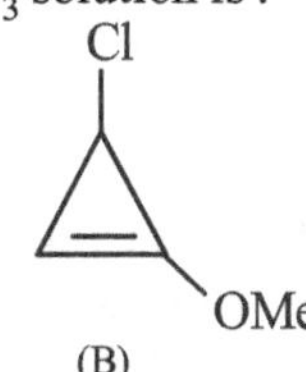

CH₃CHCH₃ with Cl **(C)**   CH₃CHCH₂NO₂ with Cl **(D)**

(1) (C) > (D) > (A) > (B)   (2) (A) > (B) > (D) > (C)
(3) (A) > (B) > (C) > (D)   (4) (B) > (A) > (C) > (D)

45. The ionic radii of O^{2-}, F^-, Na^+ and Mg^{2+} are in the order:
(1) $F^- > O^{2-} > Na^+ > Mg^{2+}$ (2) $O^{2-} > F^- > Na^+ > Mg^{2+}$
(3) $Mg^{2+} > Na^+ > F^- > O^{2-}$ (4) $O^{2-} > F^- > Mg^{2+} > Na^+$

46. A 20.0 mL solution containing 0.2 g impure H_2O_2 reacts completely with 0.316 g of $KMnO_4$ in acid solution. The purity of H_2O_2 (in %) is _______ (mol. wt. of H_2O_2 = 34; mol. wt. of $KMnO_4$ = 158)

47. The number of chiral centres present in [B] is _______ .

48. The mass of ammonia in grams produced when 2.8 kg of dinitrogen quantitatively reacts with 1 kg of dihydrogen is _______ .

49. If 75% of a first order reaction was completed in 90 minutes, 60% of the same reaction would be completed in approximately (in minutes) _______ .
(Take : log 2 = 0.30; log 2.5 = 0.40)

50. At 300 K, the vapour pressure of a solution containing 1 mole of n-hexane and 3 moles of n-heptane is 550 mm of Hg. At the same temperature, if one more mole of n-heptane is added to this solution, the vapour pressure of the solution increases by 10 mm of Hg. What is the vapour pressure in mm Hg of n-heptane in its pure state _______ ?

MATHEMATICS

51. If $1 + (1 - 2^2 \cdot 1) + (1 - 4^2 \cdot 3) + (1 - 6^2 \cdot 5) + \ldots + (1 - 20^2 \cdot 19)$ $= \alpha - 220\beta$, then an ordered pair (α, β) is equal to :
(1) (10, 97)   (2) (11, 103) (3) (10, 103)   (4) (11, 97)

52. Let $y = y(x)$ be the solution of the differential equation, $xy' - y = x^2(x \cos x + \sin x)$, $x > 0$. If $y(\pi) = \pi$, then $y''\left(\dfrac{\pi}{2}\right) + y\left(\dfrac{\pi}{2}\right)$ is equal to :
(1) $2 + \dfrac{\pi}{2}$
(2) $1 + \dfrac{\pi}{2} + \dfrac{\pi^2}{4}$
(3) $2 + \dfrac{\pi}{2} + \dfrac{\pi^2}{4}$
(4) $1 + \dfrac{\pi}{2}$

53. The value of $\displaystyle\sum_{r=0}^{20} {}^{50-r}C_6$ is equal to :
(1) ${}^{51}C_7 - {}^{30}C_7$
(2) ${}^{50}C_7 - {}^{30}C_7$
(3) ${}^{50}C_6 - {}^{30}C_6$
(4) ${}^{51}C_7 + {}^{30}C_7$

54. Two vertical poles $AB = 15$ m and $CD = 10$ m are standing apart on a horizontal ground with points A and C on the ground. If P is the point of intersection of BC and AD, then the height of P (in m) above the line AC is :
(1) 20/3   (2) 5   (3) 10/3   (4) 6

55. A triangle ABC lying in the first quadrant has two vertices as $A(1, 2)$ and $B(3, 1)$. If $\angle BAC = 90°$, and ar $(\triangle ABC) = 5\sqrt{5}$ sq. units, then the abscissa of the vertex C is:
(1) $1 + \sqrt{5}$ (2) $1 + 2\sqrt{5}$ (3) $2 + \sqrt{5}$ (4) $2\sqrt{5} - 1$

56. The mean and variance of 8 observations are 10 and 13.5, respectively. If 6 of these observations are 5, 7, 10, 12, 14, 15, then the absolute difference of the remaining two observations is :
(1) 9   (2) 5   (3) 3   (4) 7

57. Let $[t]$ denote the greatest integer $\le t$. Then the equation in x, $[x]^2 + 2[x + 2] - 7 = 0$ has :
(1) exactly two solutions
(2) exactly four integral solutions
(3) no integral solution
(4) infinitely many solutions

58. The integral $\displaystyle\int\left(\dfrac{x}{x\sin x+\cos x}\right)^2 dx$ is equal to (where C is a constant of integration) :

(1) $\tan x-\dfrac{x\sec x}{x\sin x+\cos x}+C$

(2) $\sec x+\dfrac{x\tan x}{x\sin x+\cos x}+C$

(3) $\sec x-\dfrac{x\tan x}{x\sin x+\cos x}+C$

(4) $\tan x+\dfrac{x\sec x}{x\sin x+\cos x}+C$

59. If $A=\begin{bmatrix}\cos\theta & i\sin\theta \\ i\sin\theta & \cos\theta\end{bmatrix},\left(\theta=\dfrac{\pi}{24}\right)$ and $A^5=\begin{bmatrix}a & b \\ c & d\end{bmatrix}$, where $i=\sqrt{-1}$, then which one of the following is **not** true?

(1) $0\le a^2+b^2\le 1$ (2) $a^2-d^2=0$

(3) $a^2-c^2=1$ (4) $a^2-b^2=\dfrac{1}{2}$

60. Let x_0 be the point of local maxima of $f(x)=\vec{a}\cdot(\vec{b}\times\vec{c})$, where $\vec{a}=x\hat{i}-2\hat{j}+3\hat{k}$, $\vec{b}=-2\hat{i}+x\hat{j}-\hat{k}$ and $\vec{c}=7\hat{i}-2\hat{j}+x\hat{k}$. Then the value of $\vec{a}\cdot\vec{b}+\vec{b}\cdot\vec{c}+\vec{c}\cdot\vec{a}$ at $x=x_0$ is :

(1) -4 (2) -30 (3) 14 (4) -22

61. If $(a+\sqrt{2}b\cos x)(a-\sqrt{2}b\cos y)=a^2-b^2$, where $a>b>0$, then $\dfrac{dx}{dy}$ at $\left(\dfrac{\pi}{4},\dfrac{\pi}{4}\right)$ is :

(1) $\dfrac{a-2b}{a+2b}$ (2) $\dfrac{a-b}{a+b}$ (3) $\dfrac{a+b}{a-b}$ (4) $\dfrac{2a+b}{2a-b}$

62. Given the following two statements :

$(S_1):(q\vee p)\to(p\leftrightarrow\sim q)$ is a tautology.

$(S_2):\sim q\wedge(\sim p\leftrightarrow q)$ is a fallacy. Then :

(1) both (S_1) and (S_2) are correct
(2) only (S_1) is correct
(3) only (S_2) is correct
(4) both (S_1) and (S_2) are not correct

63. Let $f(x)=|x-2|$ and $g(x)=f(f(x))$, $x\in[0,4]$.

Then $\displaystyle\int_0^3(g(x)-f(x))\,dx$ is equal to :

(1) 1 (2) 0 (3) $\dfrac{1}{2}$ (4) $\dfrac{3}{2}$

64. Let $u=\dfrac{2z+i}{z-ki}$, $z=x+iy$ and $k>0$. If the curve represented by $\text{Re}(u)+\text{Im}(u)=1$ intersects the y-axis at the points P and Q where $PQ=5$, then the value of k is :

(1) $3/2$ (2) $1/2$ (3) 4 (4) 2

65. A survey shows that 63% of the people in a city read newspaper A whereas 76% read newspaper B. If $x\%$ of the people read both the newspapers, then a possible value of x can be :

(1) 29 (2) 37 (3) 65 (4) 55

66. Let f be a twice differentiable function on $(1,6)$. If $f(2)=8$, $f'(2)=5,f'(x)\ge 1$ and $f''(x)\ge 4$, for all $x\in(1,6)$, then :

(1) $f(5)+f'(5)\le 26$ (2) $f(5)+f'(5)\ge 28$

(3) $f'(5)+f''(5)\le 20$ (4) $f(5)\le 10$

67. Let $f(x)=\displaystyle\int\dfrac{\sqrt{x}}{(1+x)^2}\,dx\,(x\ge 0)$. Then $f(3)-f(1)$ is equal to :

(1) $-\dfrac{\pi}{12}+\dfrac{1}{2}+\dfrac{\sqrt{3}}{4}$ (2) $\dfrac{\pi}{6}+\dfrac{1}{2}-\dfrac{\sqrt{3}}{4}$

(3) $-\dfrac{\pi}{6}+\dfrac{1}{2}+\dfrac{\sqrt{3}}{4}$ (4) $\dfrac{\pi}{12}+\dfrac{1}{2}-\dfrac{\sqrt{3}}{4}$

68. Let $\dfrac{x^2}{a^2}+\dfrac{y^2}{b^2}=1\,(a>b)$ be a given ellipse, length of whose latus rectum is 10. If its eccentricity is the maximum value of the function, $\phi(t)=\dfrac{5}{12}+t-t^2$, then a^2+b^2 is equal to :

(1) 145 (2) 116 (3) 126 (4) 135

69. Let $P(3,3)$ be a point on the hyperbola, $\dfrac{x^2}{a^2}-\dfrac{y^2}{b^2}=1$. If the normal to it at P intersects the x-axis at $(9,0)$ and e is its eccentricity, then the ordered pair (a^2,e^2) is equal to :

(1) $\left(\dfrac{9}{2},3\right)$ (2) $\left(\dfrac{3}{2},2\right)$ (3) $\left(\dfrac{9}{2},2\right)$ (4) $(9,3)$

70. Let α and β be the roots of $x^2-3x+p=0$ and γ and δ be the roots of $x^2-6x+q=0$. If $\alpha,\beta,\gamma,\delta$ form a geometric progression. Then ratio $(2q+p):(2q-p)$ is :

(1) $3:1$ (2) $9:7$ (3) $5:3$ (4) $33:31$

71. Suppose a differentiable function $f(x)$ satisfies the identity $f(x+y)=f(x)+f(y)+xy^2+x^2y$, for all real x and y. If $\displaystyle\lim_{x\to 0}\dfrac{f(x)}{x}=1$, then $f'(3)$ is equal to __________.

72. If the system of equations $x-2y+3z=9$, $2x+y+z=b$, $x-7y+az=24$, has infinitely many solutions, then $a-b$ is equal to __________.

73. The probability of a man hitting a target is $\dfrac{1}{10}$. The least number of shots required, so that the probability of his hitting the target at least once is greater than $\dfrac{1}{4}$, is __________.

74. If the equation of a plane P, passing through the intersection of the planes, $x+4y-z+7=0$ and $3x+y+5z=8$ is $ax+by+6z=15$ for some $a,b\in\mathbf{R}$, then the distance of the point $(3,2,-1)$ from the plane P is __________.

75. Let $(2x^2+3x+4)^{10}=\displaystyle\sum_{r=0}^{20}a_rx^r$. Then $\dfrac{a_7}{a_{13}}$ is equal to __________.

JEE MAIN 2020

(Held on 4-09-2020 Evening Shift)

PHYSICS

1. A particle of charge q and mass m is subjected to an electric field $E = E_0(1 - ax^2)$ in the x-direction, where a and E_0 are constants. Initially the particle was at rest at $x = 0$. Other than the initial position the kinetic energy of the particle becomes zero when the distance of the particle from the origin is :

(1) a

(2) $\sqrt{\dfrac{2}{a}}$

(3) $\sqrt{\dfrac{3}{a}}$

(4) $\sqrt{\dfrac{1}{a}}$

2. A series L-R circuit is connected to a battery of emf V. If the circuit is switched on at $t = 0$, then the time at which the energy stored in the inductor reaches $\left(\dfrac{1}{n}\right)$ times of its maximum value, is :

(1) $\dfrac{L}{R}\ln\left(\dfrac{\sqrt{n}}{\sqrt{n}-1}\right)$

(2) $\dfrac{L}{R}\ln\left(\dfrac{\sqrt{n}+1}{\sqrt{n}-1}\right)$

(3) $\dfrac{L}{R}\ln\left(\dfrac{\sqrt{n}}{\sqrt{n}+1}\right)$

(4) $\dfrac{L}{R}\ln\left(\dfrac{\sqrt{n}-1}{\sqrt{n}}\right)$

3. Consider two uniform discs of the same thickness and different radii $R_1 = R$ and $R_2 = \alpha R$ made of the same material. If the ratio of their moments of inertia I_1 and I_2, respectively, about their axes is $I_1 : I_2 = 1 : 16$ then the value of α is :

(1) $2\sqrt{2}$

(2) $\sqrt{2}$

(3) 2

(4) 4

4. The electric field of a plane electromagnetic wave is given by $\vec{E} = E_0(\hat{x} + \hat{y})\sin(kz - \omega t)$

Its magnetic field will be given by :

(1) $\dfrac{E_0}{c}(-\hat{x} + \hat{y})\sin(kz - \omega t)$

(2) $\dfrac{E_0}{c}(\hat{x} + \hat{y})\sin(kz - \omega t)$

(3) $\dfrac{E_0}{c}(\hat{x} - \hat{y})\sin(kz - \omega t)$

(4) $\dfrac{E_0}{c}(\hat{x} - \hat{y})\cos(kz - \omega t)$

5. The driver of a bus approaching a big wall notices that the frequency of his bus's horn changes from 420 Hz to 490 Hz when he hears it after it gets reflected from the wall. Find the speed of the bus if speed of the sound is 330 ms^{-1}.

(1) 91 kmh^{-1}

(2) 81 kmh^{-1}

(3) 61 kmh^{-1}

(4) 71 kmh^{-1}

6. Find the Binding energy per neucleon for $^{120}_{50}$Sn. Mass of proton $m_p = 1.00783$ U, mass of neutron $m_n = 1.00867$ U and mass of tin nucleus $m_{\text{Sn}} = 119.902199$ U.
(take 1U = 931 MeV)

(1) 7.5 MeV

(2) 9.0 MeV

(3) 8.0 MeV

(4) 8.5 MeV

7. Identify the operation performed by the circuit given below:

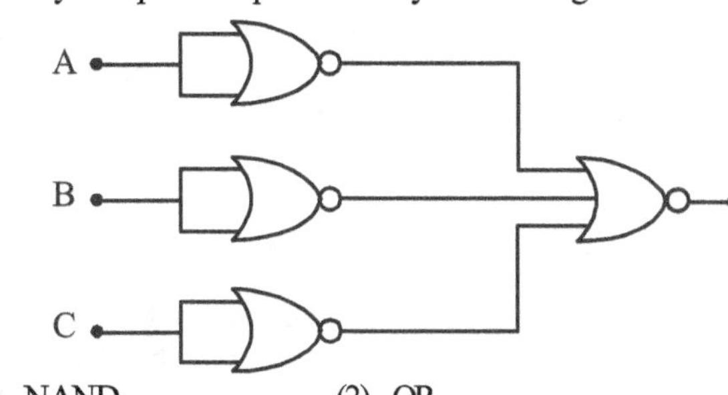

(1) NAND

(2) OR

(3) AND

(4) NOT

8. A capacitor C is fully charged with voltage V_0. After disconnecting the voltage source, it is connected in parallel with another uncharged capacitor of capacitance $\dfrac{C}{2}$. The energy loss in the process after the charge is distributed between the two capacitors is :

(1) $\dfrac{1}{2}CV_0^2$

(2) $\dfrac{1}{3}CV_0^2$

(3) $\dfrac{1}{4}CV_0^2$

(4) $\dfrac{1}{6}CV_0^2$

9. In a photoelectric effect experiment, the graph of stopping potential V versus reciprocal of wavelength obtained is shown in the figure. As the intensity of incident radiation is increased :

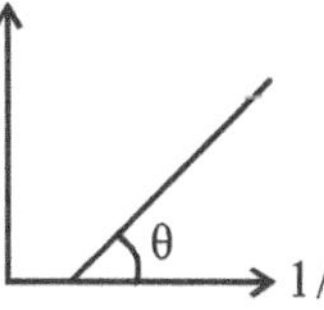

(1) Straight line shifts to right

(2) Slope of the straight line get more steep

(3) Straight line shifts to left

(4) Graph does not change

10. A circular coil has moment of inertia $0.8\ kg\ m^2$ around any diameter and is carrying current to produce a magnetic moment of $20\ Am^2$. The coil is kept initially in a vertical position and it can rotate freely around a horizontal diameter. When a uniform magnetic field of $4\ T$ is applied along the vertical, it starts rotating around its horizontal diameter. The angular speed the coil acquires after rotating by $60°$ will be :

(1) $10\ rad\ s^{-1}$ (2) $10\pi\ rad\ s^{-1}$

(3) $20\pi\ rad\ s^{-1}$ (4) $20\ rad\ s^{-1}$

11. A small ball of mass m is thrown upward with velocity u from the ground. The ball experiences a resistive force mkv^2 where v is its speed. The maximum height attained by the ball is :

(1) $\dfrac{1}{2k}\tan^{-1}\dfrac{ku^2}{g}$ (2) $\dfrac{1}{k}\ln\left(1+\dfrac{ku^2}{2g}\right)$

(3) $\dfrac{1}{k}\tan^{-1}\dfrac{ku^2}{2g}$ (4) $\dfrac{1}{2k}\ln\left(1+\dfrac{ku^2}{g}\right)$

12. Two identical cylindrical vessels are kept on the ground and each contain the same liquid of density d. The area of the base of both vessels is S but the height of liquid in one vessel is x_1 and in the other, x_2. When both cylinders are connected through a pipe of negligible volume very close to the bottom, the liquid flows from one vessel to the other until it comes to equilibrium at a new height. The change in energy of the system in the process is :

(1) $gdS(x_2^2+x_1^2)$ (2) $gdS(x_2+x_1)^2$

(3) $\dfrac{3}{4}gdS(x_2-x_1)^2$ (4) $\dfrac{1}{4}gdS(x_2-x_1)^2$

13. A body is moving in a low circular orbit about a planet of mass M and radius R. The radius of the orbit can be taken to be R itself. Then the ratio of the speed of this body in the orbit to the escape velocity from the planet is :

(1) $\dfrac{1}{\sqrt{2}}$ (2) 2 (3) 1 (4) $\sqrt{2}$

14. A cube of metal is subjected to a hydrostatic pressure of $4\ GPa$. The percentage change in the length of the side of the cube is close to :

(Given bulk modulus of metal, $B=8\times10^{10}\ Pa$)

(1) 5 (2) 0.6 (3) 20 (4) 1.67

15. A quantity x is given by (IFv^2/WL^4) in terms of moment of inertia I, force F, velocity v, work W and Length L. The dimensional formula for x is same as that of :

(1) planck's constant   (2) force constant

(3) energy density   (4) coefficient of viscosity

16.

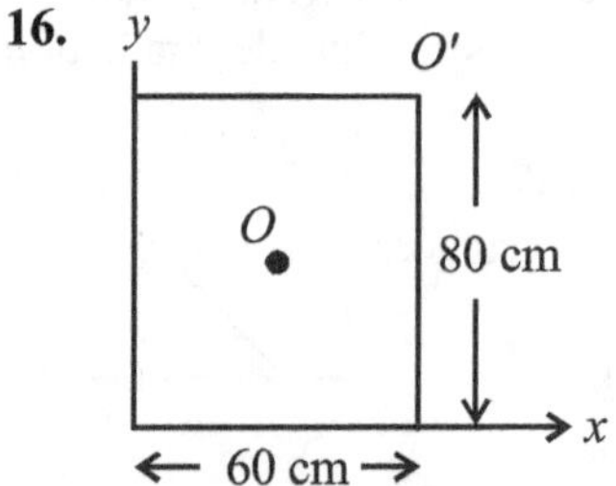

For a uniform rectangular sheet shown in the figure, the ratio of moments of inertia about the axes perpendicular to the sheet and passing through O (the centre of mass) and O' (corner point) is :

(1) 2/3   (2) 1/4   (3) 1/8   (4) 1/2

17. Match the thermodynamic processes taking place in a system with the correct conditions. In the table : ΔQ is the heat supplied, ΔW is the work done and ΔU is change in internal energy of the system.

Process	Condition
(I) Adiabatic	(A) $\Delta W=0$
(II) Isothermal	(B) $\Delta Q=0$
(III) Isochoric	(C) $\Delta U\neq0,\ \Delta W\neq0,\ \Delta Q\neq0$
(IV) Isobaric	(D) $\Delta U=0$

(1) (I)-(A), (II)-(B), (III)-(D), (IV)-(D)

(2) (I)-(B), (II)-(A), (III)-(D), (IV)-(C)

(3) (I)-(A), (II)-(A), (III)-(B), (IV)-(C)

(4) (I)-(B), (II)-(D), (III)-(A), (IV)-(C)

18. The value of current i_1 flowing from A to C in the circuit diagram is :

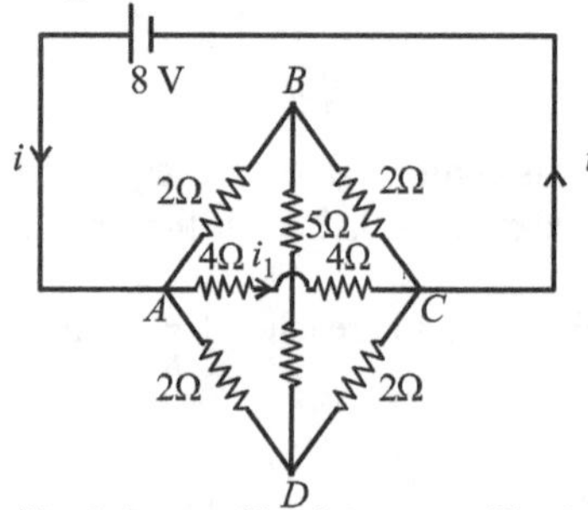

(1) 2 A   (2) 4 A   (3) 1 A   (4) 5 A

19. A person pushes a box on a rough horizontal platform surface. He applies a force of $200\ N$ over a distance of $15\ m$. Thereafter, he gets progressively tired and his applied force reduces linearly with distance to $100\ N$. The total distance through which the box has been moved is $30\ m$. What is the work done by the person during the total movement of the box ?

(1) 3280 J   (2) 2780 J

(3) 5690 J   (4) 5250 J

20. A paramagnetic sample shows a net magnetisation of $6\ A/m$ when it is placed in an external magnetic field of $0.4\ T$ at a temperature of $4\ K$. When the sample is placed in an external magnetic field of $0.3\ T$ at a temperature of $24\ K$, then the magnetisation will be :

(1) 1 A/m   (2) 4 A/m   (3) 2.25 A/m   (4) 0.75 A/m

21. The speed verses time graph for a particle is shown in the figure. The distance travelled (in m) by the particle during the time interval $t=0$ to $t=5$ s will be __________.

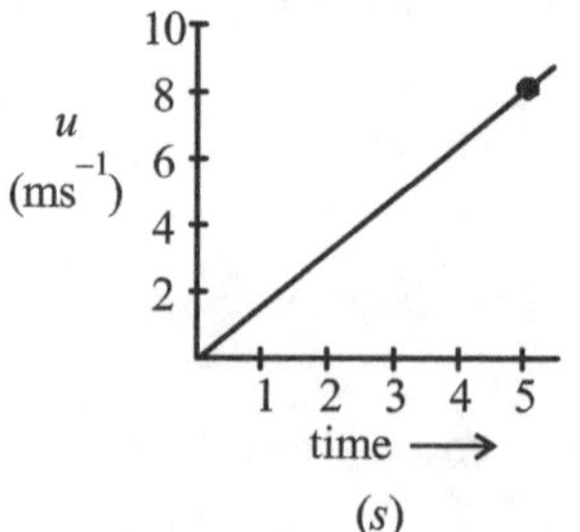

22.

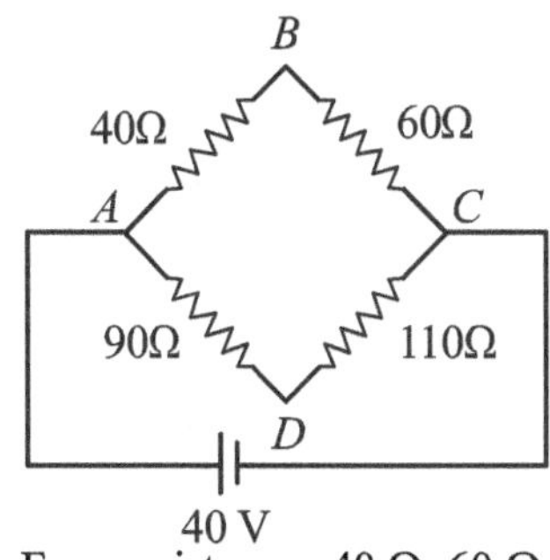

Four resistances 40 Ω, 60 Ω, 90 Ω and 110 Ω make the arms of a quadrilateral $ABCD$. Across AC is a battery of emf 40 V and internal resistance negligible. The potential difference across BD in V is ___________.

23. The distance between an object and a screen is 100 cm. A lens can produce real image of the object on the screen for two different positions between the screen and the object. The distance between these two positions is 40 cm. If the power of the lens is close to $\left(\dfrac{N}{100}\right)D$ where N is an integer, the value of N is ___________.

24. The change in the magnitude of the volume of an ideal gas when a small additional pressure ΔP is applied at a constant temperature, is the same as the change when the temperature is reduced by a small quantity ΔT at constant pressure. The initial temperature and pressure of the gas were 300 K and 2 atm. respectively. If $|\Delta T| = C\,|\Delta P|$, then value of C in (K/atm.) is ___________.

25. Orange light of wavelength 6000×10^{-10} m illuminates a single slit of width 0.6×10^{-4} m. The maximum possible number of diffraction minima produced on both sides of the central maximum is ___________.

CHEMISTRY

1. The reaction in which the hybridisation of the underlined atom is affected is :

(1) $\underline{\text{H}_3\text{P}}\text{O}_2 \xrightarrow{\text{Disproportionation}}$

(2) $\text{H}_2\underline{\text{S}}\text{O}_4 + \text{NaCl} \xrightarrow{420\ \text{K}}$

(3) $\underline{\text{N}}\text{H}_3 \xrightarrow{\text{H}^+}$

(4) $\underline{\text{Xe}}\text{F}_4 + \text{SbF}_5 \longrightarrow$

2. 250 mL of a waste solution obtained from the workshop of a goldsmith contains 0.1 M AgNO_3 and 0.1 M AuCl. The solution was electrolyzed at 2 V by passing a current of 1 A for 15 minutes. The metal/metals electrodeposited will be :

$$\left(E^0_{\text{Ag}^+/\text{Ag}} = 0.80\ \text{V},\ E^0_{\text{Au}^+/\text{Au}} = 1.69\ \text{V}\right)$$

(1) only gold
(2) silver and gold in proportion to their atomic weights
(3) only silver
(4) silver and gold in equal mass proportion

3. An alkaline earth metal 'M' readily forms water soluble sulphate and water insoluble hydroxide. Its oxide MO is very stable to heat and does not have rock-salt structure. M is :

(1) Sr   (2) Ca   (3) Mg   (4) Be

4. The incorrect statement(s) among (1) - (3) is (are) :

(a) W(VI) is more stable than Cr(VI).
(b) in the presence of HCl, permanganate titrations provide satisfactory results.
(c) some lanthanoid oxides can be used as phosophorus.

(1) (b) and (c) only   (2) (a) and (b) only
(3) (b) only   (4) (a) only

5. The shortest wavelength of H atom in the Lyman series is λ_1. The longest wavelength in the Balmer series is He^+ is :

(1) $\dfrac{36\lambda_1}{5}$ (2) $\dfrac{5\lambda_1}{9}$

(3) $\dfrac{9\lambda_1}{5}$ (4) $\dfrac{27\lambda_1}{5}$

6. Which of the following compounds will form the precipitate with aq. AgNO_3 solution most readily?

(1)

(2)

(3)

(4)

7. If the equilibrium constant for $A \rightleftharpoons B + C$ is $K_{eq}^{(1)}$ and that of $B + C \rightleftharpoons P$ is $K_{eq}^{(2)}$, the equilibrium constant for $A \rightleftharpoons P$ is :

(1) $K_{eq}^{(1)} / K_{eq}^{(2)}$ (2) $K_{eq}^{(2)} - K_{eq}^{(1)}$

(3) $K_{eq}^{(1)} + K_{eq}^{(2)}$ (4) $K_{eq}^{(1)}\ K_{eq}^{(2)}$

8. The major product [R] in the following sequence of reactions is :

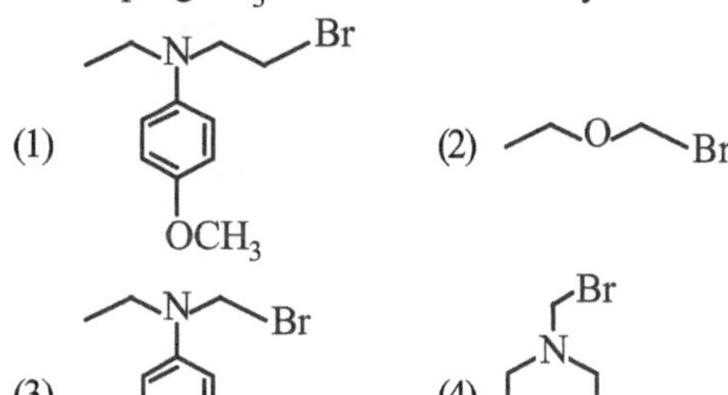

(1)
$$H_2C = \underset{\underset{CH(CH_3)_2}{|}}{C} - CH_2 - CH_3$$

(2)
$$\underset{\underset{(CH_3)_2CH}{|}}{\overset{H_3C}{\diagdown}} C = CH - CH_3$$

(3)
$$\underset{\underset{H_3CCH_2}{\diagup}}{\overset{H_3C}{\diagdown}} C = C(CH_3)_2$$

(4)
$$\underset{\underset{(CH_3)_2CH}{|}}{\overset{H_3C}{\diagdown}} CH - CH = CH_2$$

9. The Crystal Field Stabilization Energy (CFSE) of $[CoF_3(H_2O)_3]$ $(\Delta_0 < P)$ is :

(1) $-0.8\Delta_0 + 2P$ (2) $-0.4\Delta_0$

(3) $-0.8\Delta_0$ (4) $-0.4\Delta_0 + P$

10. The processes of calcination and roasting in metallurgical industries, respectively, can lead to :

(1) Global warming and photochemical smog

(2) Global warming and acid rain

(3) Photochemical smog and ozone layer depletion

(4) Photochemical smog and global warming

11. Five moles of an ideal gas at 1 bar and 298 K is expanded into vacuum to double the volume. The work done is :

(1) $C_V(T_2 - T_1)$ (2) $-RT(V_2 - V_1)$

(3) $-RT \ln V_1/V_1$ (4) zero

12. The one that can exhibit highest paramagnetic behaviour among the following is :

gly = glycinato; bpy = 2, 2'-bipyridine

(1) $[Pd(gly)_2]$

(2) $[Fe(en)(bpy)(NH_3)_2]^{2+}$

(3) $[Co(OX)_2(OH)_2]^-$ $(\Delta_0 > P)$

(4) $[Ti(NH_3)_6]^{3+}$

13. In the following reaction sequence, [C] is :

$$\underset{\underset{CH_3}{|}}{\overset{\overset{NH_2}{|}}{\bigcirc}} \xrightarrow[\text{(ii) } Cu_2Cl_2 + HCl]{\text{(i) } NaNO_2 + HCl, \ 0\text{-}5\ °C} [A] \xrightarrow{Cl_2, \ h\nu} [B]$$

$$\xrightarrow{Na + dry \ ether} [C] \text{ (Major product)}$$

(1) $Cl - \bigcirc - CH_2 - CH_2 - \bigcirc - Cl$

(2) $Cl - \bigcirc - CH_2 - \bigcirc - CH_2 - Cl$

(3) $\underset{\underset{Cl}{|}}{CH_2} - \bigcirc - \bigcirc - \underset{\underset{Cl}{|}}{CH_2}$

(4) $CH_3 - \bigcirc - \bigcirc - CH_3$

14. The process that is NOT endothermic in nature is :

(1) $Ar(g) + e^- \rightarrow Ar^-(g)$ (2) $H(g) + e^- \rightarrow H^-(g)$

(3) $O^-(g) + e^- \rightarrow O^{2-}(g)$ (4) $Na(g) \rightarrow Na^+(g) + e^-$

15. The mechanism of action of "Terfenadine" (Seldane) is :

(1) Activates the histamine receptor

(2) Inhibits the secretion of histamine

(3) Helps in the secretion of histamine

(4) Inhibits the action of histamine receptor

16. The major product [B] in the following reactions is :

$$CH_3 - CH_2 - \underset{\underset{CH_3}{|}}{CH} - CH_2 - OCH_2 - CH_3$$

$$\xrightarrow[\text{Heat}]{HI} [A] \text{alcohol} \xrightarrow[\Delta]{H_2SO_4} [B]$$

(1) $CH_2 = CH_2$

(2) $CH_3 - CH = \underset{\underset{CH_3}{|}}{C} - CH_3$

(3) $CH_3 - CH_2 - \underset{\underset{CH_3}{|}}{C} = CH_2$

(4) $CH_3 - CH_2 - CH = CH - CH_3$

17. A sample of red ink (a colloidal suspension) is prepared by mixing eosin dye, egg white, HCHO and water. The component which ensures stabilitiy of the ink sample is :

(1) Egg white   (2) Water

(3) HCHO   (4) Eosin dye

18. Among the following compounds, which one has the shortest C – Cl bond?

(1) $\underset{\underset{CH_3}{|}}{\overset{\overset{H_3C}{\diagdown}}{H_3C}} C - Cl$ (2) $HC \equiv \underset{\underset{CH_2}{||}}{C} - Cl$

(3) $H_3C - Cl$ (4) $\underset{\underset{CH_2}{||}}{CH} - Cl$

19. The molecule in which hybrid MOs involve only one d-orbital of the central atom is :

(1) $[Ni(CN)_4]^{2-}$ (2) BrF_5

(3) XeF_4 (4) $[CrF_6]^{3-}$

20. The major product [C] of the following reaction sequence will be :

$$CH_2 = CH - CHO \xrightarrow[\text{(ii) } SOCl_2]{\text{(i) } NaBH_4} [A] \xrightarrow[\substack{Anhy. \\ AlCl_3}]{\bigcirc} [B] \xrightarrow{DBr} [C]$$

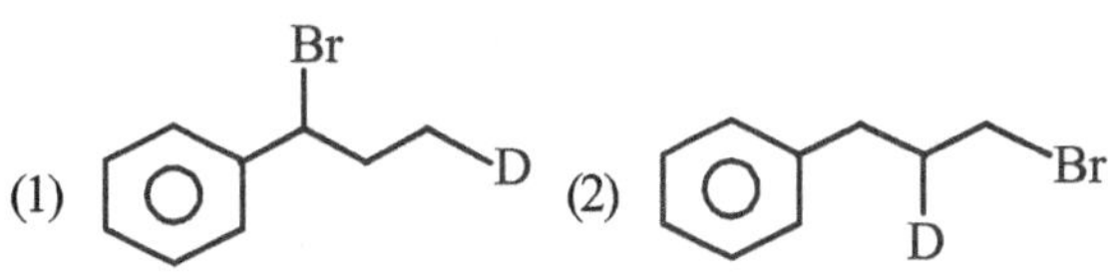

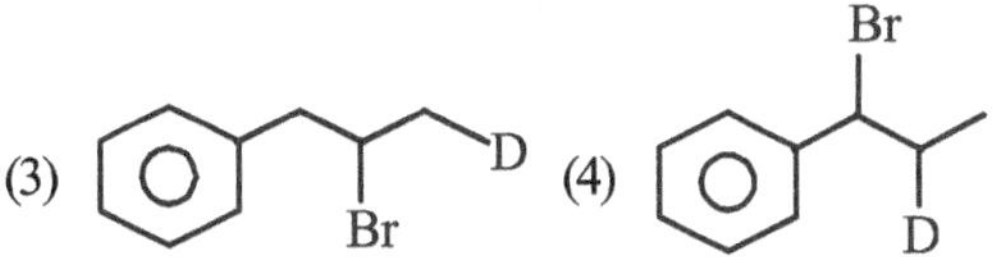

21. The osmotic pressure of a solution of $NaCl$ is 0.10 atm and that of a glucose solution is 0.20 atm. The osmotic pressure of a solution formed by mixing 1 L of the sodium chloride solution with 2 L of the glucose solution is $x \times 10^{-3}$ atm. x is __________. (nearest integer)

22. The number of chiral centres present in threonine is __________.

23. A 100 mL solution was made by adding 1.43 g of $Na_2CO_3 \cdot xH_2O$. The normality of the solution is 0.1 N. The value of x is __________.
(The atomic mass of Na is 23 g/ mol)

24. The number of molecules with energy greater than the threshold energy for a reaction increases five fold by a rise of temperature from 27°C to 42°C. Its energy of activation in J/ mol is __________. (Take $\ln 5 = 1.6094$; $R = 8.314 \, \mathrm{J\,mol^{-1}K^{-1}}$)

25. Consider the following equations :

$$2Fe^{2+} + H_2O_2 \rightarrow x\,A + y\,B$$

(in basic medium)

$$2MnO_4^- + 6H^+ + 5H_2O_2 \rightarrow x'C + y'D + z'E$$

(in acidic medium)

The sum of the stoichiometric coefficients x, y, x', y' and z' for products A, B, C, D and E, respectively, is __________.

MATHEMATICS

1. The circle passing through the intersection of the circles,
$x^2 + y^2 - 6x = 0$ and $x^2 + y^2 - 4y = 0$, having its centre on the line, $2x - 3y + 12 = 0$, also passes through the point:
(1) $(-1, 3)$ (2) $(-3, 6)$
(3) $(-3, 1)$ (4) $(1, -3)$

2. Let $x = 4$ be a directrix to an ellipse whose centre is at the origin and its eccentricity is $\dfrac{1}{2}$. If $P(1, \beta), \beta > 0$ is a point on this ellipse, then the equation of the normal to it at P is :
(1) $4x - 3y = 2$ (2) $8x - 2y = 5$
(3) $7x - 4y = 1$ (4) $4x - 2y = 1$

3. The minimum value of $2^{\sin x} + 2^{\cos x}$ is :
(1) $2^{-1+\frac{1}{\sqrt{2}}}$ (2) $2^{-1+\sqrt{2}}$ (3) $2^{1-\sqrt{2}}$ (4) $2^{1-\frac{1}{\sqrt{2}}}$

4. The angle of elevation of a cloud C from a point P, 200 m above a still lake is 30°. If the angle of depression of the image of C in the lake from the point P is 60°, then PC (in m) is equal to :
(1) 100   (2) $200\sqrt{3}$
(3) 400   (4) $400\sqrt{3}$

5. If the system of equations
$x + y + z = 2$ $\quad 2x + 4y - z = 6$ $\quad 3x + 2y + \lambda z = \mu$
has infinitely many solutions, then :
(1) $\lambda + 2\mu = 14$ (2) $2\lambda - \mu = 5$
(3) $\lambda - 2\mu = -5$ (4) $2\lambda + \mu = 14$

6. The area (in sq. units) of the largest rectangle $ABCD$ whose vertices A and B lie on the x-axis and vertices C and D lie on the parabola, $y = x^2 - 1$ below the x-axis, is :

(1) $\dfrac{2}{3\sqrt{3}}$ (2) $\dfrac{1}{3\sqrt{3}}$ (3) $\dfrac{4}{3}$ (4) $\dfrac{4}{3\sqrt{3}}$

7. The function $f(x) = \begin{cases} \dfrac{\pi}{4} + \tan^{-1} x, & |x| \le 1 \\ \dfrac{1}{2}(|x| - 1), & |x| > 1 \end{cases}$ is :
(1) continuous on $\mathbf{R} - \{1\}$ and differentiable on $\mathbf{R} - \{-1, 1\}$.
(2) both continuous and differentiable on $\mathbf{R} - \{1\}$.
(3) continuous on $\mathbf{R} - \{-1\}$ and differentiable on $\mathbf{R} - \{-1, 1\}$.
(4) both continuous and differentiable on $\mathbf{R} - \{-1\}$.

8. If for some positive integer n, the coefficients of three consecutive terms in the binomial expansion of $(1+x)^{n+5}$ are in the ratio $5 : 10 : 14$, then the largest coefficient in this expansion is :
(1) 462   (2) 330   (3) 792   (4) 252

9. Suppose the vectors x_1, x_2 and x_3 are the solutions of the system of linear equations, $Ax = b$ when the vector b on the right side is equal to b_1, b_2 and b_3 respectively. If

$$x_1 = \begin{bmatrix} 1 \\ 1 \\ 1 \end{bmatrix}, x_2 = \begin{bmatrix} 0 \\ 2 \\ 1 \end{bmatrix}, x_3 = \begin{bmatrix} 0 \\ 0 \\ 1 \end{bmatrix}, b_1 = \begin{bmatrix} 1 \\ 0 \\ 0 \end{bmatrix}, b_2 = \begin{bmatrix} 0 \\ 2 \\ 0 \end{bmatrix} \quad \text{and}$$

$$b_3 = \begin{bmatrix} 0 \\ 0 \\ 2 \end{bmatrix}, \text{ then the determinant of } A \text{ is equal to :}$$

(1) 4   (2) 2   (3) $\dfrac{1}{2}$ (4) $\dfrac{3}{2}$

10. Contrapositive of the statement :

'If a function f is differentiable at a, then it is also continuous at a', is :

(1) If a function f is continuous at a, then it is not differentiable at a.

(2) If a function f is not continuous at a, then it is not differentiable at a.

(3) If a function f is not continuous at a, then it is differentiable at a

(4) If a function f is continuous at a, then it is differentiable at a.

11. The solution of the differential equation

$$\frac{dy}{dx} - \frac{y+3x}{\log_e(y+3x)} + 3 = 0 \text{ is :}$$

(where C is a constant of integration.)

(1) $\quad x - \dfrac{1}{2}(\log_e(y+3x))^2 = C$

(2) $\quad x - \log_e(y+3x) = C$

(3) $\quad y + 3x - \dfrac{1}{2}(\log_e x)^2 = C$

(4) $\quad x - 2\log_e(y+3x) = C$

12. In a game two players A and B take turns in throwing a pair of fair dice starting with player A and total of scores on the two dice, in each throw is noted. A wins the game if he throws a total of 6 before B throws a total of 7 and B wins the game if he throws a total of 7 before A throws a total of six. The game stops as soon as either of the players wins. The probability of A winning the game is :

(1) $\dfrac{5}{31}$ (2) $\dfrac{31}{61}$ (3) $\dfrac{5}{6}$ (4) $\dfrac{30}{61}$

13. The distance of the point $(1, -2, 3)$ from the plane

$x - y + z = 5$ measured parallel to the line $\dfrac{x}{2} = \dfrac{y}{3} = \dfrac{z}{-6}$

is :

(1) $\dfrac{7}{5}$ (2) 1 (3) $\dfrac{1}{7}$ (4) 7

14. Let $\lambda \neq 0$ be in $\mathbf{R}$. If α and β are roots of the equation,

$x^2 - x + 2\lambda = 0$ and α and γ are the roots of the equation,

$3x^2 - 10x + 27\lambda = 0$, then $\dfrac{\beta\gamma}{\lambda}$ is equal to :

(1) 27 (2) 18 (3) 9 (4) 36

15. The integral

$$\int_{\pi/6}^{\pi/3} \tan^3 x \cdot \sin^2 3x (2\sec^2 x \cdot \sin^2 3x + 3\tan x \cdot \sin 6x)\, dx$$

is equal to :

(1) $\dfrac{7}{18}$ (2) $-\dfrac{1}{9}$ (3) $-\dfrac{1}{18}$ (4) $\dfrac{9}{2}$

16. Let $a_1, a_2, \ldots, a_n$ be a given A.P. whose common difference is an integer and $S_n = a_1 + a_2 + \ldots + a_n$. If $a_1 = 1$, $a_n = 300$ and $15 \leq n \leq 50$, then the ordered pair (S_{n-4}, a_{n-4}) is equal to :

(1) $(2490, 249)$ (2) $(2480, 249)$

(3) $(2480, 248)$ (4) $(2490, 248)$

17. If a and b are real numbers such that $(2+\alpha)^4 = a + b\alpha$, where $\alpha = \dfrac{-1+i\sqrt{3}}{2}$, then $a + b$ is equal to :

(1) 9 (2) 24 (3) 33 (4) 57

18. If the perpendicular bisector of the line segment joining the points $P(1, 4)$ and $Q(k, 3)$ has y-intercept equal to -4, then a value of k is :

(1) -2 (2) -4 (3) $\sqrt{14}$ (4) $\sqrt{15}$

19. Let $f : (0, \infty) \to (0, \infty)$ be a differentiable function such that $f(1) = e$ and $\displaystyle\lim_{t \to x} \frac{t^2 f^2(x) - x^2 f^2(t)}{t - x} = 0$.

If $f(x) = 1$, then x is equal to :

(1) $\dfrac{1}{e}$ (2) $2e$ (3) $\dfrac{1}{2e}$ (4) e

20. Let $\displaystyle\bigcup_{i=1}^{50} X_i = \bigcup_{i=1}^{n} Y_i = T$, where each X_i contains 10 elements and each Y_i contains 5 elements. If each element of the set T is an element of exactly 20 of sets X_i's and exactly 6 of sets Y_i's, then n is equal to

(1) 15 (2) 50 (3) 45 (4) 30

21. A test consists of 6 multiple choice questions, each having 4 alternative answers of which only one is correct. The number of ways, in which a candidate answers all six questions such that exactly four of the answers are correct, is __________.

22. If $\vec{a} = 2\hat{i} + \hat{j} + 2\hat{k}$, then the value of

$|\hat{i} \times (\vec{a} \times \hat{i})|^2 + |\hat{j} \times (\vec{a} \times \hat{j})|^2 + |\hat{k} \times (\vec{a} \times \hat{k})|^2$ is equal to __________.

23. Let $\{x\}$ and $[x]$ denote the fractional part of x and the greatest integer $\leq x$ respectively of a real number x. If $\displaystyle\int_0^n \{x\}\, dx$, $\displaystyle\int_0^n [x]\, dx$ and $10(n^2 - n)$, $(n \in \mathbf{N}, n > 1)$ are three consecutive terms of a G.P., then n is equal to __________.

24. If a variance of the following frequency distribution :

Class	10-20	20-30	30-40
Frequency	2	x	2

is 50, then x is equal to __________.

25. Let PQ be a diameter of the circle $x^2 + y^2 = 9$. If α and β are the lengths of the perpendiculars from P and Q on the straight line, $x + y = 2$ respectively, then the maximum value of $\alpha\beta$ is __________.

JEE MAIN 2020

(Held on 5-09-2020 Morning Shift)

PHYSICS

1. Assume that the displacement (s) of air is proportional to the pressure difference (Δp) created by a sound wave. Displacement (s) further depends on the speed of sound (v), density of air (ρ) and the frequency (f). If $\Delta p \sim 10$ Pa, $v \sim 300$ m/s, $p \sim q$ kg/m³ and $f \sim 1000$ Hz, then s will be of the order of (take the multiplicative constant to be 1)

(1) $\dfrac{3}{100}$ mm

(2) 10 mm

(3) $\dfrac{1}{10}$ mm

(4) 1 mm

2. Acitvities of three radioactive substances A, B and C are represented by the curves A, B and C, in the figure. Then their half-lives $T_{\frac{1}{2}}(A) : T_{\frac{1}{2}}(B) : T_{\frac{1}{2}}(C)$ are in the ratio :

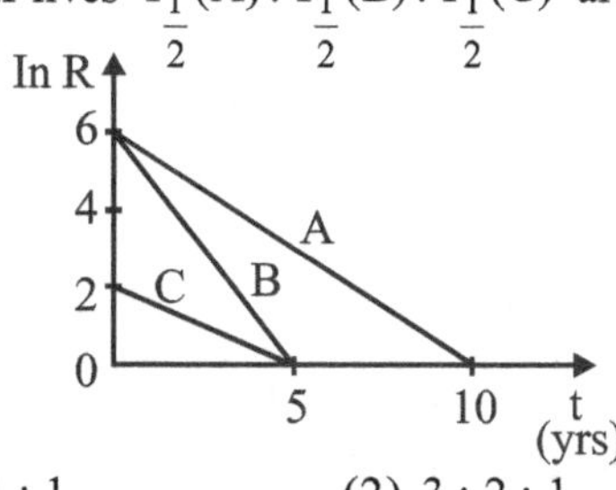

(1) 2 : 1 : 1

(2) 3 : 2 : 1

(3) 2 : 1 : 3

(4) 4 : 3 : 1

3. A balloon is moving up in air vertically above a point A on the ground. When it is at a height h_1, a girl standing at a distance d (point B) from A (see figure) sees it at an angle 45° with respect to the vertical. When the balloon climbs up a further height h_2, it is seen at an angle 60° with respect to the vertical if the girl moves further by a distance 2.464 d (point C). Then the height h_2 is (given tan 30° = 0.5774):

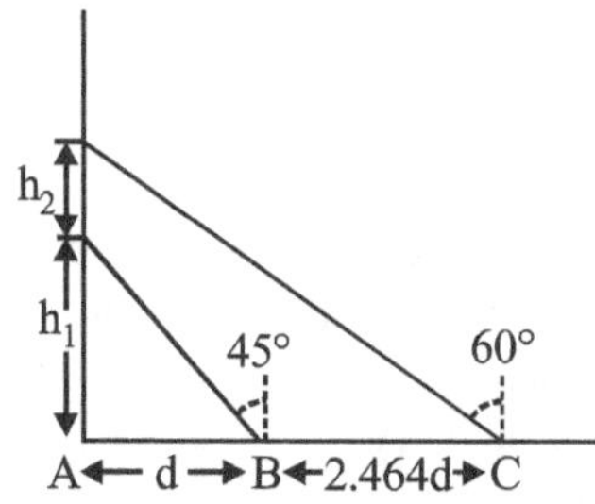

(1) 1.464 d

(2) 0.732 d

(3) 0.464 d

(4) d

4. An electron is constrained to move along the y-axis with a speed of 0.1 c (c is the speed of light) in the presence of electromagnetic wave, whose electric field is $\vec{E} = 30\,\hat{j}$ $\sin(1.5 \times 10^7 t - 5 \times 10^{-2} x)$ V/m. The maximum magnetic force experienced by the electron will be : (given $c = 3 \times 10^8$ ms^{-1} & electron charge $= 1.6 \times 10^{-19}$ C)

(1) 3.2×10^{-18} N

(2) 2.4×10^{-18} N

(3) 4.8×10^{-19} N

(4) 1.6×10^{-19} N

5. A helicopter rises from rest on the ground vertically upwards with a constant acceleration g. A food packet is dropped from the helicopter when it is at a height h. The time taken by the packet to reach the ground is close to [g is the accelertion due to gravity] :

(1) $t = \dfrac{2}{3}\sqrt{\left(\dfrac{h}{g}\right)}$

(2) $t = 1.8\sqrt{\dfrac{h}{g}}$

(3) $t = 3.4\sqrt{\left(\dfrac{h}{g}\right)}$

(4) $t = \sqrt{\dfrac{2h}{3g}}$

6. A galvanometer of resistance G is converted into a voltmeter of ragne $0 - 1$V by connecting a resistance R_1 in series with it. The additional resistance R_1 in series with it. The additional resistance that should be connected in series with R_1 to increase the range of the voltmeter to $0 - 2$V will be :

(1) G

(2) R_1

(3) $R_1 - G$

(4) $R_1 + G$

7. Two capacitors of capacitances C and 2C are charged to potential differences V and 2V, respectively. These are then connected in parallel in such a manner that the positive terminal of one is connected to the negative terminal of the other. The final energy of this configuration is :

(1) $\dfrac{25}{6}CV^2$

(2) $\dfrac{3}{2}CV^2$

(3) zero

(4) $\dfrac{9}{2}CV^2$

8. With increasing biasing voltage of a photodiode, the photocurrent magnitude :

(1) remains constant

(2) increases initially and after attaining certain value, it decreases

(3) Increases linearly

(4) increases initially and saturates finally

9. The value of acceleration due to gravity is g_1 at a height $h = \dfrac{R}{2}$ (R = radius of the earth) from the surface of the earth. It is again equal to g_1 and a depth d below the surface of the earth. The ratio $\left(\dfrac{d}{R}\right)$ equals :

(1) $\dfrac{4}{9}$ (2) $\dfrac{5}{9}$

(3) $\dfrac{1}{3}$ (4) $\dfrac{7}{9}$

10. A solid sphere of radius R carries a charge $Q + q$ distributed uniformaly over its volume. A very small point like piece of it of mass m gets detached from the bottom of the sphere and falls down vertically under gravity. This piece carries charge q. If it acquires a speed v when it has fallen through a vertical height y (see figure), then : (assume the remaining portion to be spherical).

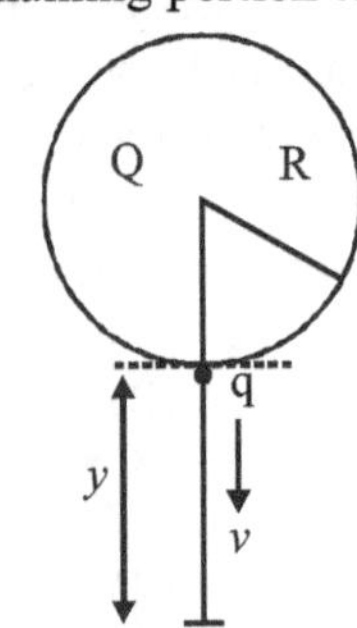

(1) $v^2 = y\left[\dfrac{qQ}{4\pi\varepsilon_0 R^2 ym} + g\right]$

(2) $v^2 = y\left[\dfrac{qQ}{4\pi\varepsilon_0 R(R+y)m} + g\right]$

(3) $v^2 = 2y\left[\dfrac{Qq\,R}{4\pi\varepsilon_0 (R+y)^3 m} + g\right]$

(4) $v^2 = 2y\left[\dfrac{qQ}{4\pi\varepsilon_0 R(R+y)m} + g\right]$

11. A wheel is rotating freely with an angular speed ω on a shaft. The moment of inertia of the wheel is I and the moment of inertia of the shaft is negligible. Another wheel of moment of inertia 3I initially at rest is suddenly coupled to the same shaft. The resultant fractional loss in the kinetic energy of the system is :

(1) $\dfrac{5}{6}$ (2) $\dfrac{1}{4}$

(3) 0 (4) $\dfrac{3}{4}$

12. For a concave lens of focal length f, the relation between object and image distances u and v, respectively, from its pole can best be represented by ($u = v$ is the reference line):

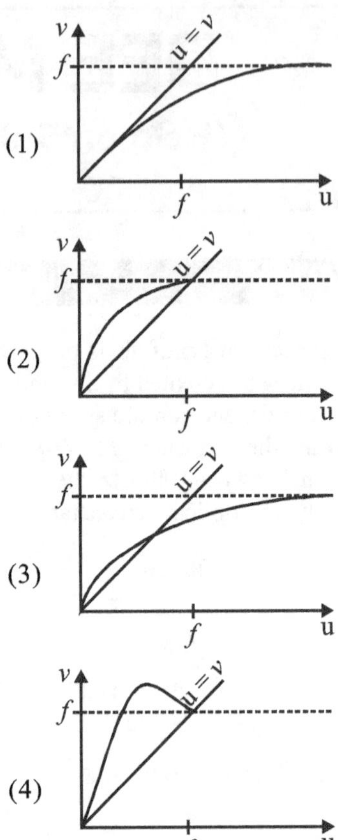

(1)

(2)

(3)

(4)

13. Three different processes that can occur in an ideal monoatomic gas are shown in the P vs V diagram. The paths are lebelled as $A \rightarrow B$, $A \rightarrow C$ and $A \rightarrow D$. The change in internal energies during these process are taken as E_{AB}, E_{AC} and E_{AD} and the workdone as W_{AB}, W_{AC} and W_{AD}. The correct relation between these parameters are :

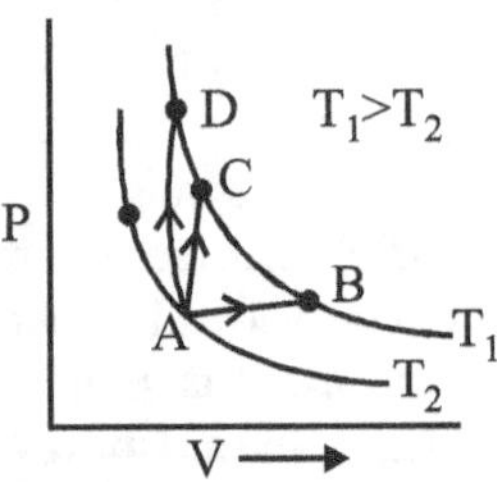

(1) $E_{AB} = E_{AC} < E_{AD}$, $W_{AB} > 0$, $W_{AC} = 0$, $W_{AD} < 0$
(2) $E_{AB} = E_{AC} = E_{AD}$, $W_{AB} > 0$, $W_{AC} = 0$, $W_{AD} > 0$
(3) $E_{AB} < E_{AC} < E_{AD}$, $W_{AB} > 0$, $W_{AC} > W_{AD}$
(4) $E_{AB} > E_{AC} > E_{AD}$, $W_{AB} < W_{AC} < W_{AD}$

14. Number of molecules in a volume of 4 cm^3 of a perfect monoatomic gas at some temperature T and at a pressure of 2 cm of mercury is close to? (Given, mean kinetic energy of a molecule (at T) is 4×10^{-14} erg, $g = 980$ cm/s^2, density of mercury = 13.6 g/cm^3)
(1) 4.0×10^{18} (2) 4.0×10^{16}
(3) 5.8×10^{16} (4) 5.8×10^{18}

15. A square loop of side $2a$, and carrying current I, is kept in XZ plane with its centre at origin. A long wire carrying the same current I is placed parallel to the z-axis and passing through the point $(0, b, 0)$, $(b \gg a)$. The magnitude of the torque on the loop about z-axis is given by :

(1) $\dfrac{\mu_0 I^2 a^2}{2\pi b}$

(2) $\dfrac{\mu_0 I^2 a^3}{2\pi b^2}$

(3) $\dfrac{2\mu_0 I^2 a^2}{\pi b}$

(4) $\dfrac{2\mu_0 I^2 a^3}{\pi b^2}$

16. A physical quantity z depends on four observables a, b, c and d, as $z = \dfrac{a^2 b^{\frac{2}{3}}}{\sqrt{c}\, d^3}$. The percentages of error in the measurement of a, b, c and d are 2%, 1.5%, 4% and 2.5% respectively. The percentage of error in z is :

(1) 12.25%
(2) 16.5%
(3) 13.5%
(4) 14.5%

17. A hollow spherical shell at outer radius R floats just submerged under the water surface. The inner radius of the shell is r. If the specific gravity of the shell material is $\dfrac{27}{8}$ w.r.t water, the value of r is :

(1) $\dfrac{8}{9} R$

(2) $\dfrac{4}{9} R$

(3) $\dfrac{2}{3} R$

(4) $\dfrac{1}{3} R$

18. In a resonance tube experiment when the tube is filled with water up to a height of 17.0 cm from bottom, it resonates with a given tuning fork. When the water level is raised the next resonance with the same tuning fork occurs at a height of 24.5 cm. If the velocity of sound in air is 330 m/s, the tuning fork frequency is :

(1) 2200 Hz
(2) 550 Hz
(3) 1100 Hz
(4) 3300 Hz

19. An electrical power line, having a total resistance of $2\ \Omega$, delivers 1 kW at 220 V. The efficiency of the transmission line is approximately :

(1) 72%
(2) 91%
(3) 85%
(4) 96%

20. A bullet of mass 5 g, travelling with a speed of 210 m/s, strikes a fixed wooden target. One half of its kinetics energy is converted into heat in the bullet while the other half is converted into heat in the wood. The rise of temperature of the bullet if the specific heat of its material is 0.030 cal/(g – °C) (1 cal = 4.2 × 10^7 ergs) close to :

(1) 87.5°C
(2) 83.3°C
(3) 119.2°C
(4) 38.4°C

21. A force $\vec{F} = (\hat{i} + 2\hat{j} + 3\hat{k})\,$N acts at a point $(4\hat{i} + 3\hat{j} - \hat{k})\,$m. Then the magnitude of torque about the point $(\hat{i} + 2\hat{j} + \hat{k})\,$m will be $\sqrt{x}\,$ N-m. The value of x is ______.

22. A beam of electrons of energy E scatters from a target having atomic spacing of 1Å. The first maximum intensity occurs at $\theta = 60°$. Then E (in eV) is ______.
(Plank constant $h = 6.64 \times 10^{-34}$ Js, 1 eV = 1.6×10^{-19} J, electron mass $m = 9.1 \times 10^{-31}$ kg)

23. A particle of mass 200 MeV/c^2 collides with a hydrogen atom at rest. Soon after the collision the particle comes to rest, and the atom recoils and goes to its first excited state. The initial kinetic energy of the particle (in eV) is $\dfrac{N}{4}$. The value of N is :
(Given the mass of the hydrogen atom to be 1 GeV/c^2)

24. A compound microscope consists of an objective lens of focal length 1 cm and an eye piece of focal length 5 cm with a separation of 10 cm.
The distance between an object and the objective lens, at which the strain on the eye is minimum is $\dfrac{n}{40}$ cm.
The value of n is ______.

25. Two concentric circular coils, C_1 and C_2, are placed in the XY plane. C_1 has 500 turns, and a radius of 1 cm. C_2 has 200 turns and radius current 20 cm. C_2 carries a time dependent current $I(t) = (5t^2 - 2t + 3)$ A Where t is in s.
The emf induced in C_1 (in mV), at the instant $t = 1$ s is $\dfrac{4}{x}$.
The value of x is ______.

<h2 style="text-align:center">CHEMISTRY</h2>

26. Which of the following derivatives of alcohols is unstable in an aqueous base?

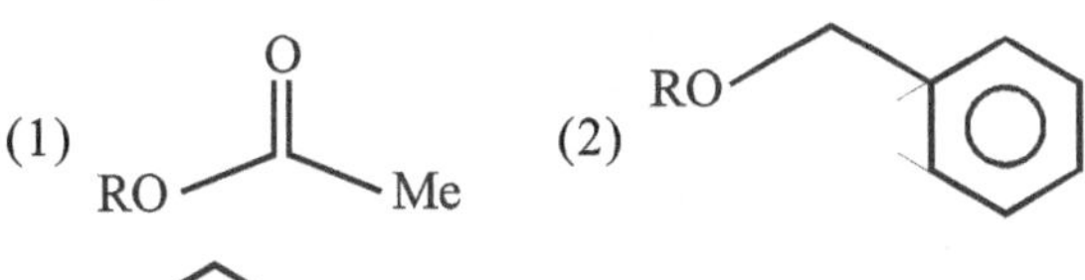

(4) RO – CMe$_3$

27. The values of the crystal field stabilization energies for a high spin d^6 metal ion in octahedral and tetrahedral fields, respectively, are :

(1) $-0.4\ \Delta_o$ and $-0.6\ \Delta_t$
(2) $-2.4\ \Delta_o$ and $-0.6\ \Delta_t$
(3) $-1.6\ \Delta_o$ and $-0.4\ \Delta_t$
(4) $-0.4\ \Delta_o$ and $-0.27\ \Delta_t$

28. Consider the following reaction :

$$N_2O_4(g) \rightleftharpoons 2NO_2(g); \Delta H^0 = +58\ \text{kJ}$$

For each of the following cases ((i), (ii)), the direction in which the equilibrium shifts is :
(i) Temperature is decreases
(ii) Pressure is increased by adding N_2 at constant T.
(1) (i) towards product, (ii) towards product
(2) (i) towards reactant, (ii) towards product
(3) (i) towards reactant, (ii) no change
(4) (i) towards product, (ii) no change

29. The increasing order of the acidity of the α-hydrogen of the following compounds is :

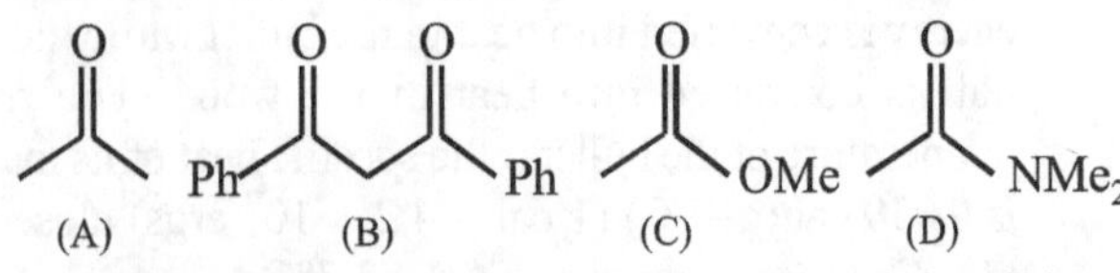

(1) (D) < (C) < (A) < (B)   (2) (B) < (C) < (A) < (D)
(3) (A) < (C) < (D) < (B)   (4) (C) < (A) < (B) < (D)

30. A diatomic molecule X_2 has a body-centred cubic (*bcc*) structure with a cell edge of 300 pm. The density of the molecule is 6.17 g cm^{-3}. The number of molecules present in 200 g of X_2 is :
(Avogadroconstant $(N_A) = 6 \times 10^{23}$ mol^{-1})

(1) 40 N_A (2) 8 N_A
(3) 4 N_A (4) 2 N_A

31. The potential energy curve for the H_2 molecule as a function of internuclear distance is :

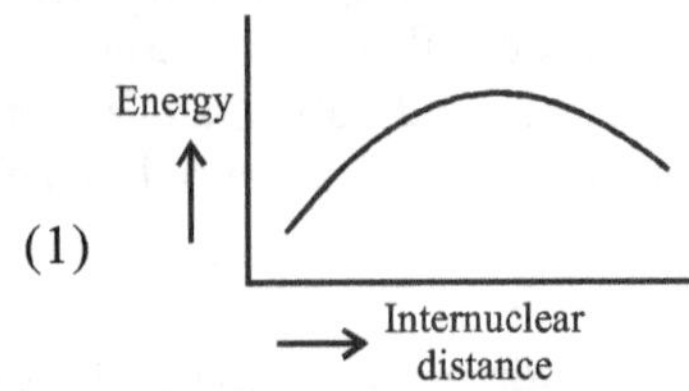

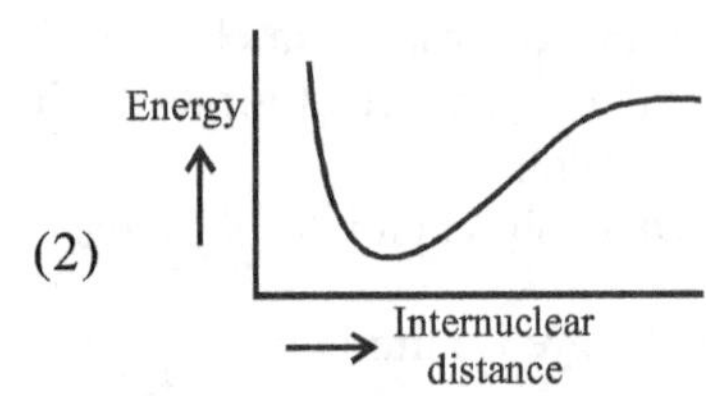

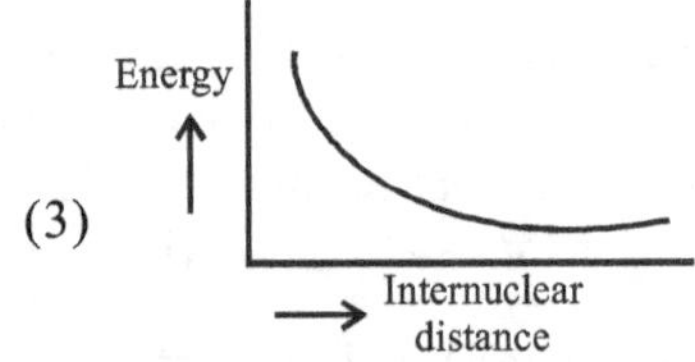

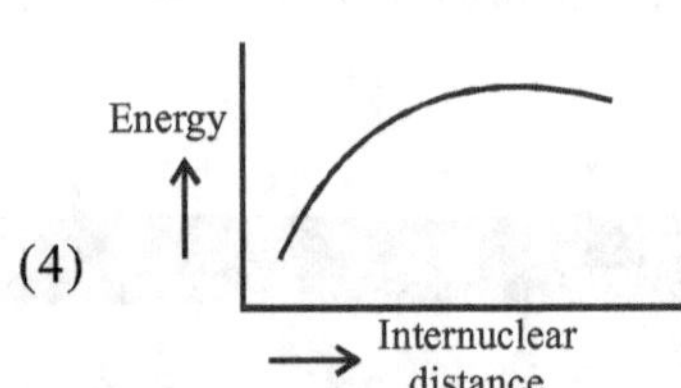

32. Identify the correct molecular picture showing what happens at the critical micellar concentration (CMC) of an aqueous solution of a surfactant (◯ polar head, ∿ non-polar tail, • water).

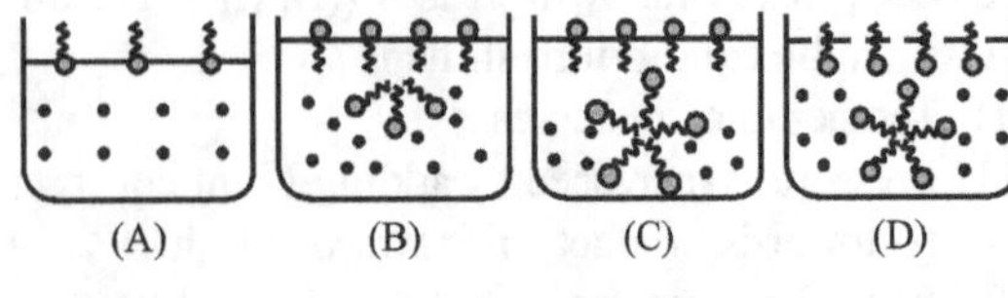

(1) (D)   (2) (B)
(3) (A)   (4) (C)

33. The difference between the radii of 3rd and 4th orbits of Li^{2+} is ΔR_1. The difference between the radii of 3rd and 4th orbits of He^+ is ΔR_2. Ratio $\Delta R_1 : \Delta R_2$ is :
(1) 8 : 3   (2) 3 : 8
(3) 2 : 3   (4) 3 : 2

34. In the sixth period, the orbitals that are filled are :
(1) $6s, 4f, 5d, 6p$ (2) $6s, 5d, 5f, 6p$
(3) $6s, 5f, 6d, 6p$ (4) $6s, 6p, 6d, 6f$

35. The most appropriate reagent for conversion of C_2H_5CN into $CH_3CH_2CH_2NH_2$ is :
(1) $NaBH_4$ (2) CaH_2
(3) $LiAlH_4$ (4) $Na(CN)BH_3$

36. If a person is suffering from the deficiency of nor-adrenaline, what kind of drug can be suggested?
(1) Anti-inflammatory   (2) Antidepressant
(3) Antihistamine   (4) Analgesic

37. Which of the following is not an essential amino acid?
(1) Tyrosine   (2) Leucine
(3) Valine   (4) Lysine

38. The correct electronic configuration and spin-only magnetic moment (BM) of $Gd^{3+}(Z = 64)$, respectively, are:
(1) $[Xe]\,4f^7$ and 8.9   (2) $[Xe]\,4f^7$ and 7.9
(3) $[Xe]\,5f^7$ and 8.9   (4) $[Xe]\,5f^7$ and 7.9

39. The increasing order of basicity of the following compounds is:

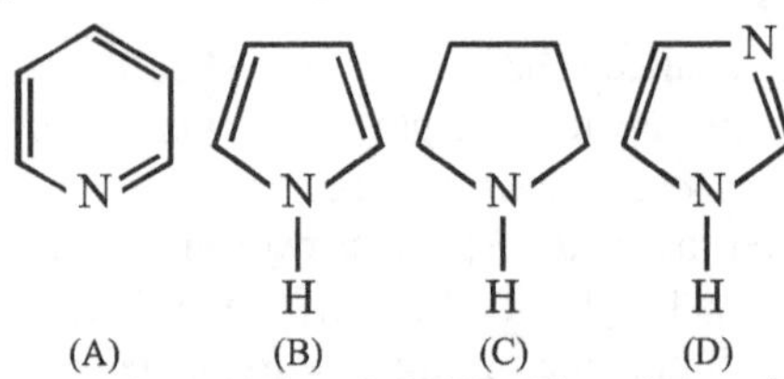

(1) (A) < (B) < (C) < (D)   (2) (B) < (A) < (D) < (C)
(3) (D) < (A) < (B) < (C)   (4) (B) < (A) < (C) < (D)

40. A flask contains a mixture of compounds A and B. Both compounds decompose by first-order kinetics. The half-lives for A and B are 300 s and 180 s, respectively. If the concentrations of A and B are equal initially, the time required for the concentration of A to be four times that of B (in s) is: (Use ln 2 = 0.693)
(1) 180   (2) 900
(3) 300   (4) 120

41. The structure of PCl_5 in the solid state is:
(1) tetrahedral $[PCl_4]^+$ and octahedral $[PCl_6]^-$
(2) square planar $[PCl_4]^+$ and octahedral $[PCl_6]^-$
(3) square pyramidal
(4) trigonal bipyramidal

42. An Ellingham diagram provides information about:
(1) the conditions of pH and potential under which a species is thermodynamically stable.
(2) the temperature dependence of the standard Gibbs energies of formation of some metal oxides.
(3) the pressure dependence of the standard electrode potentials of reduction reactions involved in the extraction of metals.
(4) the kinetics of the reduction process.

43. In the following reaction sequence the major products A and B are :

[reaction scheme: p-xylene + glutaric anhydride (cyclic) $\xrightarrow[\text{AlCl}_3]{\text{anhydrous}}$ A $\xrightarrow[\text{2. H}_3\text{PO}_4]{\text{1. Zn–Hg/HCl}}$ B]

(1) A = [aryl ketone with CO_2H] ; B = [octahydronaphthalene]

(2) A = [aryl ketone with CO_2H] ; B = [bicyclic ketone]

(3) A = [aryl ketone with CO_2H] ; B = [methyl dihydronaphthalenone]

(4) A = [aryl ketone with CO_2H] ; B = [methyl dihydronaphthalenone]

44. The equation that represents the water-gas shift reaction is:

(1) $CH_4(g) + H_2O(g) \xrightarrow[\text{Ni}]{1270K} CO(g) + 3H_2(g)$

(2) $2C(s) + O_2(g) + 4N_2(g) \xrightarrow{1273K} 2CO(g) + 4N_2(g)$

(3) $C(s) + H_2O(g) \xrightarrow{1270K} CO(g) + H_2(g)$

(4) $CO(g) + H_2O(g) \xrightarrow[\text{Catalyst}]{673K} CO_2(g) + H_2(g)$

45. The condition that indicates a polluted environment is:
(1) eutrophication
(2) 0.03% of CO_2 in the atmosphere
(3) BOD value of 5 ppm
(4) pH of rain water to be 5.6

46. The minimum number of moles of O_2 required for complete combustion of 1 mole of propane and 2 moles of butane is ______.

47. The totole number of coordination sites in ethylenediaminetetraacetate ($EDTA^{4-}$) is ______.

48. The number of chiral carbons (s) present in peptide, Ile-Age-Pro, is ______.

49. A soft drink was bottled with a partial prssure of CO_2 of 3 bar over the liquid at room temperature. The partial pressure of CO_2 over the solution approaches a value of 30 bar when 44g of CO_2 is dissolved in 1 kg of water at room temperature. The approximate pH of the soft drink is ______ $\times 10^{-1}$.
(First dissociation constant of $H_2CO_3 = 4.0 \times 10^{-7}$; log 2 = 0.3; density of the soft drink = 1g mL^{-1})

50. An oxidation-reduction reaction in which 3 electrons are transferred has a ΔG^0 of 17.37 kJ mol^{-1} at 25°C. The value of E^0_{cell} (in V) is ______ $\times 10^{-2}$.
(1 F = 96,500 C mol^{-1})

MATHEMATICS

51. If $y = y(x)$ is the solution of the differential equation $\dfrac{5+e^x}{2+y}\cdot\dfrac{dy}{dx}+e^x = 0$ satisfying $y(0) = 1$, then a value of $y(\log_e 13)$ is :
(1) 1
(2) – 1
(3) 0
(4) 2

52. The product of the roots of the equation $9x^2 - 18|x| + 5 = 0$, is :
(1) $\dfrac{5}{9}$
(2) $\dfrac{25}{81}$
(3) $\dfrac{5}{27}$
(4) $\dfrac{25}{9}$

53. The negation of the Boolean expression $x \leftrightarrow \sim y$ is equivalent to:
(1) $(x \wedge y) \vee (\sim x \wedge \sim y)$
(2) $(x \wedge y) \wedge (\sim x \vee \sim y)$
(3) $(x \wedge \sim y) \vee (\sim x \wedge y)$
(4) $(\sim x \wedge y) \vee (\sim x \wedge \sim y)$

54. The mean and variance of 7 observations are 8 and 16, respectively. If five observations are 2, 4, 10, 12, 14, then the absolute difference of the remaining two observations is :
(1) 1
(2) 4
(3) 2
(4) 3

55. If $2^{10} + 2^9\cdot 3^1 + 2^8\cdot 3^2 + \ldots + 2\times 3^9 + 3^{10} = S - 2^{11}$ then S is equal to:
(1) $3^{11} - 2^{12}$
(2) 3^{11}
(3) $\dfrac{3^{11}}{2} + 2^{10}$
(4) $2\cdot 3^{11}$

56. If $3^{2\sin 2\alpha - 1}$, 14 and $3^{4-2\sin 2\alpha}$ are the first three terms of an A.P. for some α, then the sixth term of this A.P is:
(1) 66
(2) 81
(3) 65
(4) 78

57. If the volume of a parallelopiped, whose coterminus edges are given by the vectors $\vec{a} = \hat{i} + \hat{j} + n\hat{k}$, $\vec{b} = 2\hat{i} + 4\hat{j} - n\hat{k}$ and $\vec{c} = \hat{i} + n\hat{j} + 3\hat{k}\,(n \geq 0)$, is 158 cu.units, then:
(1) $\vec{a}\cdot\vec{c} = 17$
(2) $\vec{b}\cdot\vec{c} = 10$
(3) $n = 7$
(4) $n = 9$

58. If S is the sum of the first 10 terms of the series

$$\tan^{-1}\left(\frac{1}{3}\right) + \tan^{-1}\left(\frac{1}{7}\right) + \tan^{-1}\left(\frac{1}{13}\right) + \tan^{-1}\left(\frac{1}{21}\right) + \dots,$$

then tan (S) is equal to:

(1) $\dfrac{5}{6}$ (2) $\dfrac{5}{11}$

(3) $-\dfrac{6}{5}$ (4) $\dfrac{10}{11}$

59. If the four complex numbers z, $\overline{z}$, $\overline{z} - 2\,\text{Re}(\overline{z})$ and $z - 2\text{Re}(z)$ represent the vertices of a square of side 4 units in the Argand plane, then $|z|$ is equal to :

(1) $4\sqrt{2}$ (2) 4

(3) $2\sqrt{2}$ (4) 2

60. A survey shows that 73% of the persons working in an office like coffee, whereas 65% like tea. If x denotes the percentage of them, who like both coffee and tea, then x cannot be :

(1) 63   (2) 36

(3) 54   (4) 38

61. If the co-ordinates of two points A and B are $(\sqrt{7}, 0)$ and $(-\sqrt{7}, 0)$ respectively and P is any point on the conic, $9x^2 + 16y^2 = 144$, then PA + PB is equal to :

(1) 16   (2) 8

(3) 6   (4) 9

62. If the point P on the curve, $4x^2 + 5y^2 = 20$ is farthest from the point $Q(0, -4)$, then PQ^2 is equals to :

(1) 36   (2) 48

(3) 21   (4) 29

63. Let $\lambda \in R$. The system of linear equations

$$2x_1 - 4x_2 + \lambda x_3 = 1$$
$$x_1 - 6x_2 + x_3 = 2$$
$$\lambda x_1 - 10x_2 + 4x_3 = 3$$

(1) exactly one negative value of λ
(2) exactly one positive value of λ
(3) every value of λ
(4) exactly two value of λ

64. If the minimum and the maximum values of the function

$$f : \left[\frac{\pi}{4}, \frac{\pi}{2}\right] \to R \text{ , defined by}$$

$$f(\theta) = \begin{vmatrix} -\sin^2\theta & -1-\sin^2\theta & 1 \\ -\cos^2\theta & -1-\cos^2\theta & 1 \\ 12 & 10 & -2 \end{vmatrix} \quad \text{are } m \text{ and } M$$

respectively, then the ordered pair (m, M) is equal to :

(1) $(0, 2\sqrt{2})$ (2) $(-4, 0)$

(3) $(-4, 4)$ (4) $(0, 4)$

65. If (a, b, c) is the image of the point $(1, 2, -3)$ in the line,

$$\frac{x+1}{2} = \frac{y-3}{-2} = \frac{z}{-1}, \text{ then } a + b + c \text{ is equals to:}$$

(1) 2   (2) -1

(3) 3   (4) 1

66. If the function $f(x)\begin{cases} k_1(x-\pi)^2 - 1, & x \le \pi \\ k_2\cos x, & x > \pi \end{cases}$ is twice differentiable, then the ordered pair (k_1, k_2) is equal to:

(1) $\left(\dfrac{1}{2}, 1\right)$ (2) $(1, 0)$

(3) $\left(\dfrac{1}{2}, -1\right)$ (4) $(1, 1)$

67. If the common tangent to the parabolas, $y^2 = 4x$ and $x^2 = 4y$ also touches the circle, $x^2 + y^2 = c^2$, then c is equal to:

(1) $\dfrac{1}{2\sqrt{2}}$ (2) $\dfrac{1}{\sqrt{2}}$

(3) $\dfrac{1}{4}$ (4) $\dfrac{1}{2}$

68. If α is the positive root of the equation, $p(x) = x^2 - x - 2 = 0$, then $\displaystyle\lim_{x \to \alpha^+} \frac{\sqrt{1 - \cos(p(x))}}{x + \alpha - 4}$ is equal to:

(1) $\dfrac{3}{2}$ (2) $\dfrac{3}{\sqrt{2}}$

(3) $\dfrac{1}{\sqrt{2}}$ (4) $\dfrac{1}{2}$

69. If $\int (e^{2x} + 2e^x - e^{-x} - 1)e^{(e^x + e^{-x})} \, dx = g(x)e^{(e^x + e^{-x})} + c$, where c is a constant of integeration, then $g(0)$ is equal to:

(1) e (2) e^2

(3) 1   (4) 2

70. The value of $\displaystyle\int_{-\pi/2}^{\pi/2} \frac{1}{1 + e^{\sin x}} dx$ is:

(1) $\dfrac{\pi}{4}$ (2) π

(3) $\dfrac{\pi}{2}$ (4) $\dfrac{3\pi}{2}$

71. Let $f(x) = x.\left[\dfrac{x}{2}\right]$, for $-10 < x < 10$, where $[t]$ denotes the greatest integer function. Then the number of points of discontinuity of f is equal to ______.

72. If the line, $2x - y + 3 = 0$ is at a distance $\dfrac{1}{\sqrt{5}}$ and $\dfrac{2}{\sqrt{5}}$ from the lines $4x - 2y + \alpha = 0$ and $6x - 3y + \beta = 0$, respectively, then the sum of all possible value of α and β is ______.

73. The number of words, with or without meaning, that can be formed by taking 4 letters at a time from the letters of the word 'SYLLABUS' such that two letters are distinct and two letters are alike, is ______.

74. The natural number m, for which the coefficient of x in the binomial expansion of $\left(x^m + \dfrac{1}{x^2}\right)^{22}$ is 1540, is ______.

75. Four fair dice are thrown independently 27 times. Then the expected number of times, at least two dice show up a three or a five, is ______.

JEE MAIN 2020

(Held on 05-09-2020 Evening Shift)

PHYSICS

1. A spaceship in space sweeps stationary interplanetary dust. As a result, its mass increases at a rate $\dfrac{dM(t)}{dt} = bv^2(t)$, where $v(t)$ is its instantaneous velocity. The instantaneous acceleration of the satellite is :

(1) $-bv^3(t)$ (2) $-\dfrac{bv^3}{M(t)}$ (3) $-\dfrac{2bv^3}{M(t)}$ (4) $-\dfrac{bv^3}{2M(t)}$

2. Ten charges are placed on the circumference of a circle of radius R with constant angular separation between successive charges. Alternate charges 1, 3, 5, 7, 9 have charge $(+q)$ each, while 2, 4, 6, 8, 10 have charge $(-q)$ each. The potential V and the electric field E at the centre of the circle are respectively :
(Take $V = 0$ at infinity)

(1) $V = \dfrac{10q}{4\pi\varepsilon_0 R}; E = 0$

(2) $V = 0; E = \dfrac{10q}{4\pi\varepsilon_0 R^2}$

(3) $V = 0; E = 0$

(4) $V = \dfrac{10q}{4\pi\varepsilon_0 R}; E = \dfrac{10q}{4\pi\varepsilon_0 R^2}$

3. An infinitely long straight wire carrying current I, one side opened rectangular loop and a conductor C with a sliding connector are located in the same plane, as shown in the figure. The connector has length l and resistance R. It slides to the right with a velocity v. The resistance of the conductor and the self inductance of the loop are negligible. The induced current in the loop, as a function of separation r, between the connector and the straight wire is :

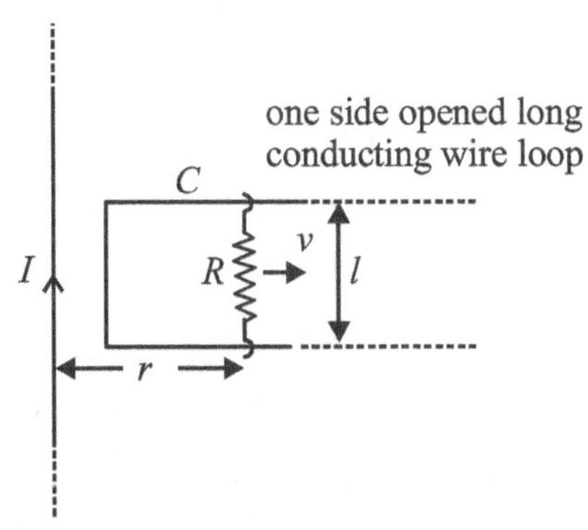

(1) $\dfrac{\mu_0}{4\pi}\dfrac{Ivl}{Rr}$ (2) $\dfrac{\mu_0}{\pi}\dfrac{Ivl}{Rr}$ (3) $\dfrac{2\mu_0}{\pi}\dfrac{Ivl}{Rr}$ (4) $\dfrac{\mu_0}{2\pi}\dfrac{Ivl}{Rr}$

4. In the circuit shown, charge on the 5 µF capacitor is :

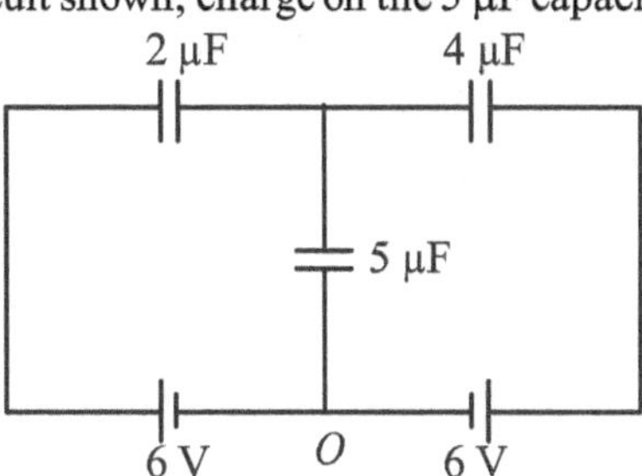

(1) $18.00\,\mu C$ (2) $10.90\,\mu C$ (3) $16.36\,\mu C$ (4) $5.45\,\mu C$

5. A galvanometer is used in laboratory for detecting the null point in electrical experiments. If, on passing a current of 6 mA it produces a deflection of $2°$, its figure of merit is close to :

(1) $333°$ A/div.   (2) 6×10^{-3} A/div.
(3) $666°$ A/div.   (4) 3×10^{-3} A/div.

6. The correct match between the entries in column I and column II are :

I Radiation	II Wavelength
(A) Microwave	(i) 100 m
(B) Gamma rays	(ii) 10^{-15} m
(C) A.M. radio waves	(iii) 10^{-10} m
(D) X-rays	(iv) 10^{-3} m

(1) (A)-(ii), (B)-(i), (C)-(iv), (D)-(iii)
(2) (A)-(i), (B)-(iii), (C)-(iv), (D)-(ii)
(3) (A)-(iii), (B)-(ii), (C)-(i), (D)-(iv)
(4) (A)-(iv), (B)-(ii), (C)-(i), (D)-(iii)

7. Two coherent sources of sound, S_1 and S_2, produce sound waves of the same wavelength, $\lambda = 1$ m, in phase. S_1 and S_2 are placed 1.5 m apart (see fig.). A listener, located at L, directly in front of S_2 finds that the intensity is at a minimum when he is 2 m away from S_2. The listener moves away from S_1, keeping his distance from S_2 fixed. The adjacent maximum of intensity is observed when the listener is at a distance d from S_1. Then, d is :

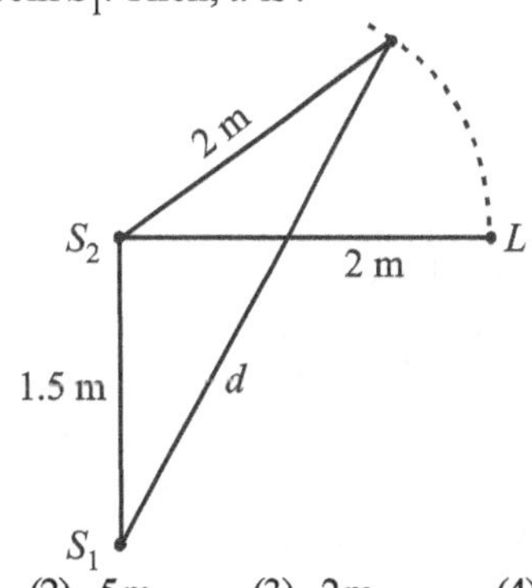

(1) 12 m   (2) 5 m   (3) 2 m   (4) 3 m

8. Two different wires having lengths L_1 and L_2, and respective temperature coefficient of linear expansion α_1 and α_2, are joined end-to-end. Then the effective temperature coefficient of linear expansion is :

(1) $\dfrac{\alpha_1 L_1 + \alpha_2 L_2}{L_1 + L_2}$

(2) $2\sqrt{\alpha_1 \alpha_2}$

(3) $\dfrac{\alpha_1 + \alpha_2}{2}$

(4) $4 \dfrac{\alpha_1 \alpha_2}{\alpha_1 + \alpha_2} \dfrac{L_2 L_1}{(L_2 + L_1)^2}$

9. The velocity (v) and time (t) graph of a body in a straight line motion is shown in the figure. The point S is at 4.333 seconds. The total distance covered by the body in 6 s is:

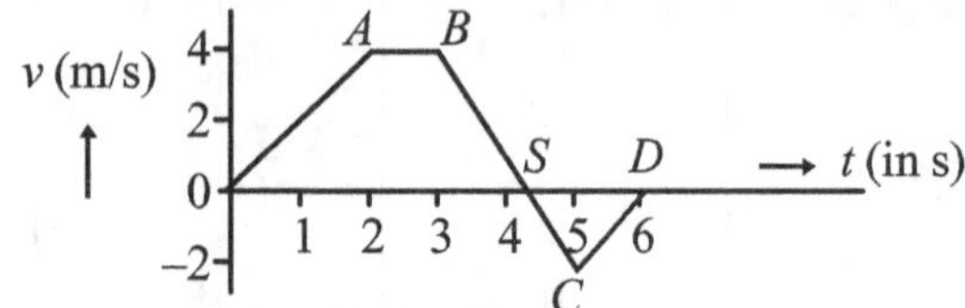

(1) $\dfrac{37}{3}$ m   (2) 12 m   (3) 11 m   (4) $\dfrac{49}{4}$ m

10. In an experiment to verify Stokes law, a small spherical ball of radius r and density ρ falls under gravity through a distance h in air before entering a tank of water. If the terminal velocity of the ball inside water is same as its velocity just before entering the water surface, then the value of h is proportional to :
(ignore viscosity of air)

(1) r^4 (2) r (3) r^3 (4) r^2

11. A parallel plate capacitor has plate of length 'l', width 'w' and separation of plates is 'd'. It is connected to a battery of emf V. A dielectric slab of the same thickness 'd' and of dielectric constant $k = 4$ is being inserved between the plates of the capacitor. At what length of the slab inside plates, will the energy stored in the capacitor be two times the initial energy stored?

(1) $2l/3$ (2) $l/3$ (3) $l/4$ (4) $l/2$

12. A driver in a car, approaching a vertical wall notices that the frequency of his car horn, has changed from 440 Hz to 480 Hz, when it gets reflected from the wall. If the speed of sound in air is 345 m/s, then the speed of the car is :

(1) 54 km/hr   (2) 36 km/hr   (3) 18 km/hr   (4) 24 km/hr

13. A ring is hung on a nail. It can oscillate, without slipping or sliding (i) in its plane with a time period T_1 and, (ii) back and forth in a direction perpendicular to its plane, with a period T_2. The ratio $\dfrac{T_1}{T_2}$ will be :

(1) $\dfrac{2}{\sqrt{3}}$ (2) $\dfrac{2}{3}$ (3) $\dfrac{3}{\sqrt{2}}$ (4) $\dfrac{\sqrt{2}}{3}$

14. Two Zener diodes (A and B) having breakdown voltages of 6 V and 4 V respectively, are connected as shown in the circuit below. The output voltage V_0 variation with input voltage linearly increasing with time, is given by :
($V_{input} = 0$ V at $t = 0$)
(figures are qualitative)

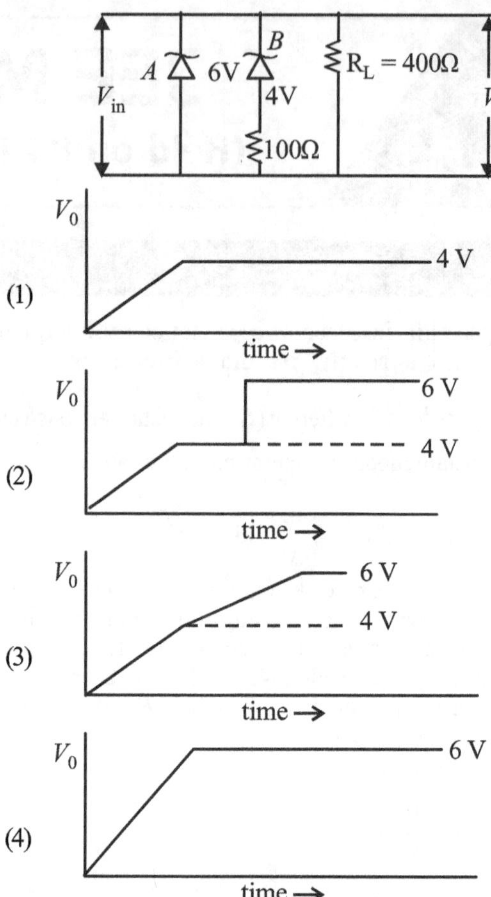

15. A radioactive nucleus decays by two different processes. The half life for the first process is 10 s and that for the second is 100 s. The effective half life of the nucleus is close to :

(1) 9 sec.   (2) 6 sec.   (3) 55 sec.   (4) 12 sec.

16. The quantities $x = \dfrac{1}{\sqrt{\mu_0 \varepsilon_0}}$, $y = \dfrac{E}{B}$ and $z = \dfrac{1}{CR}$ are defined where C-capacitance, R-Resistance, l-length, E-Electric field, B-magnetic field and ε_0, μ_0, - free space permittivity and permeability respectively. Then :

(1) x, y and z have the same dimension.
(2) Only x and z have the same dimension.
(3) Only x and y have the same dimension.
(4) Only y and z have the same dimension.

17. In an adiabatic process, the density of a diatomic gas becomes 32 times its initial value. The final pressure of the gas is found to be n times the initial pressure. The value of n is :

(1) 32   (2) 326   (3) 128   (4) $\dfrac{1}{32}$

18. The acceleration due to gravity on the earth's surface at the poles is g and angular velocity of the earth about the axis passing through the pole is ω. An object is weighed at the equator and at a height h above the poles by using a spring balance. If the weights are found to be same, then h is : ($h \ll R$, where R is the radius of the earth)

(1) $\dfrac{R^2 \omega^2}{2g}$ (2) $\dfrac{R^2 \omega^2}{g}$ (3) $\dfrac{R^2 \omega^2}{4g}$ (4) $\dfrac{R^2 \omega^2}{8g}$

19. In the circuit, given in the figure currents in different branches and value of one resistor are shown. Then potential at point B with respect to the point A is :

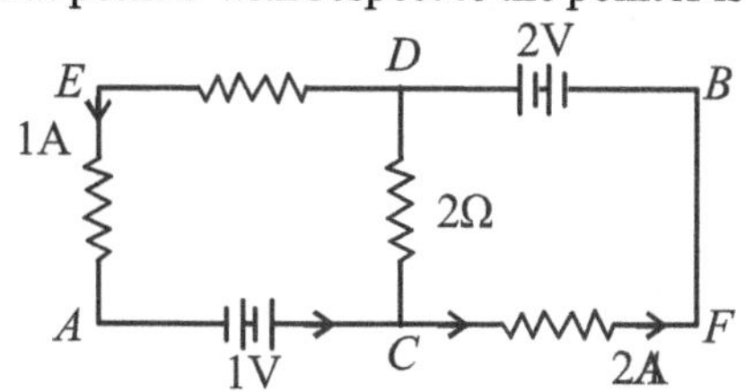

(1) $+2\,V$ (2) $-2\,V$ (3) $-1\,V$ (4) $+1\,V$

20. An iron rod of volume $10^{-3}\,m^3$ and relative permeability 1000 is placed as core in a solenoid with 10 turns/cm. If a current of 0.5 A is passed through the solenoid, then the magnetic moment of the rod will be :

(1) $50 \times 10^2\,Am^2$ (2) $5 \times 10^2\,Am^2$

(3) $500 \times 10^2\,Am^2$ (4) $0.5 \times 10^2\,Am^2$

21. A body of mass 2 kg is driven by an engine delivering a constant power of 1 J/s. The body starts from rest and moves in a straight line. After 9 seconds, the body has moved a distance (in m) _________ .

22. Nitrogen gas is at 300°C temperature. The temperature (in K) at which the rms speed of a H_2 molecule would be equal to the rms speed of a nitrogen molecule, is _________ . (Molar mass of N_2 gas 28 g);

23. A prism of angle A = 1° has a refractive index $\mu = 1.5$. A good estimate for the minimum angle of deviation (in degrees) is close to $N/10$. Value of N is _________ .

24. The surface of a metal is illuminated alternately with photons of energies $E_1 = 4$ eV and $E_2 = 2.5$ eV respectively. The ratio of maximum speeds of the photoelectrons emitted in the two cases is 2. The work function of the metal in (eV) is _________ .

25. A thin rod of mass 0.9 kg and length 1 m is suspended, at rest, from one end so that it can freely oscillate in the vertical plane. A particle of move 0.1 kg moving in a straight line with velocity 80 m/s hits the rod at its bottom most point and sticks to it (see figure). The angular speed (in rad/s) of the rod immediately after the collision will be _________ .

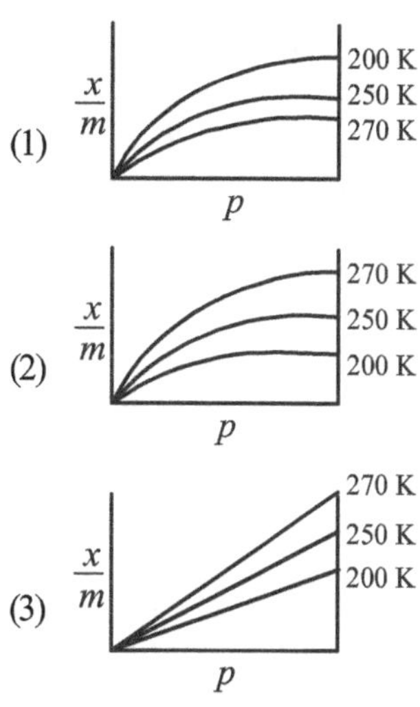

CHEMISTRY

26. The final major product of the following reaction is :

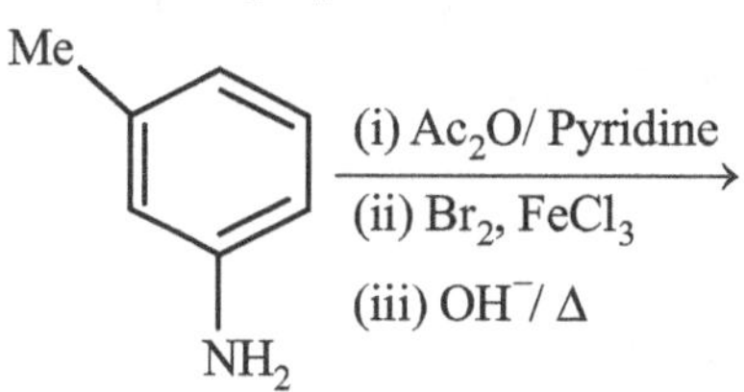

(i) Ac_2O/ Pyridine

(ii) Br_2, $FeCl_3$

(iii) OH^- / Δ

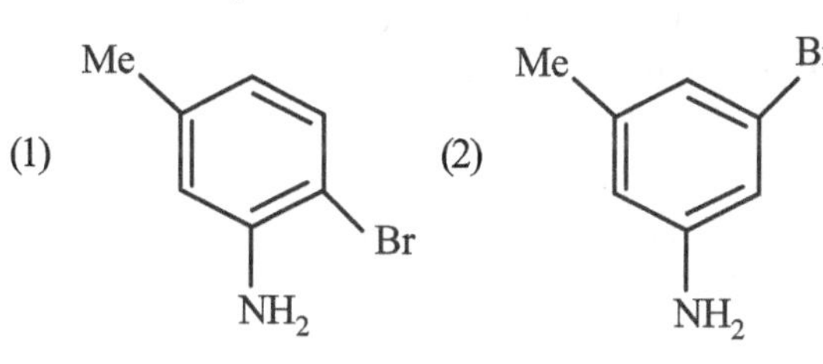

(1)   (2)

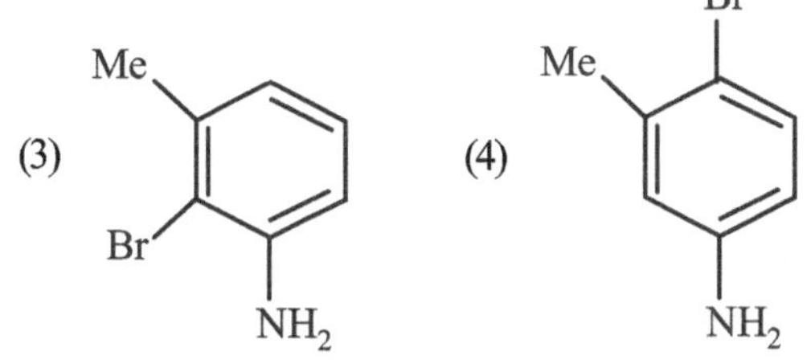

(3)   (4)

27. Among the following compounds, geometrical isomerism is exhibited by :

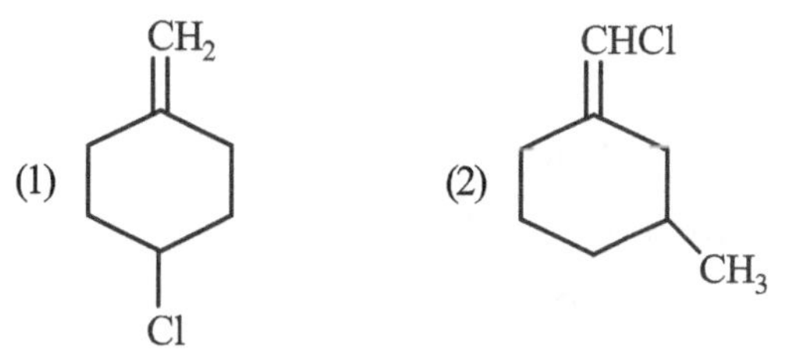

(1)   (2)

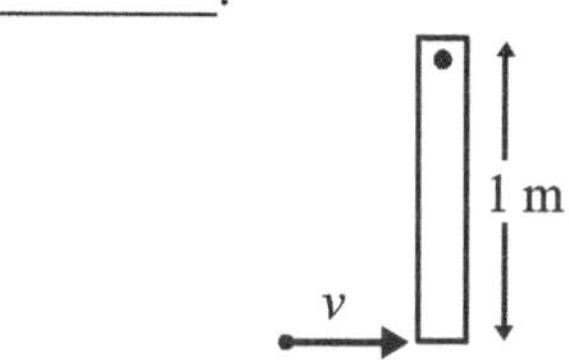

(3)   (4)

28. Adsorption of a gas follows Freundlich adsorption isotherm. If x is the mass of the gas adsorbed on mass m of the adsorbent, the correct plot of $\dfrac{x}{m}$ versus p is :

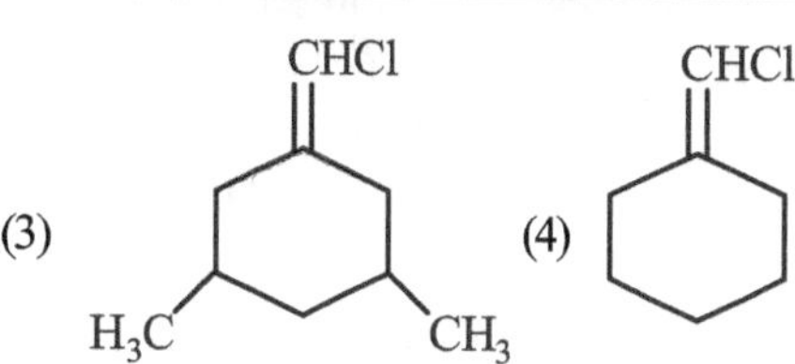

(1)

(2)

(3)

(4)

29. An element crystallises in a face-centred cubic (*fcc*) unit cell with cell edge a. The distance between the centres of two nearest octahedral voids in the crystal lattice is :

(1) $\dfrac{a}{\sqrt{2}}$ (2) a (3) $\sqrt{2}a$ (4) $\dfrac{a}{2}$

30. Consider the complex ions, *trans*-$[Co(en)_2Cl_2]^+$ (A) and *cis*-$[Co(en)_2Cl_2]^+$ (B). The correct statement regarding them is :

(1) both (A) and (B) cannot be optically active.
(2) (A) can be optically active, but (B) cannot be optically active.
(3) both (A) and (B) can be optically active.
(4) (A) cannot be optically active, but (B) can be optically active.

31. The increasing order of boiling points of the following compounds is :

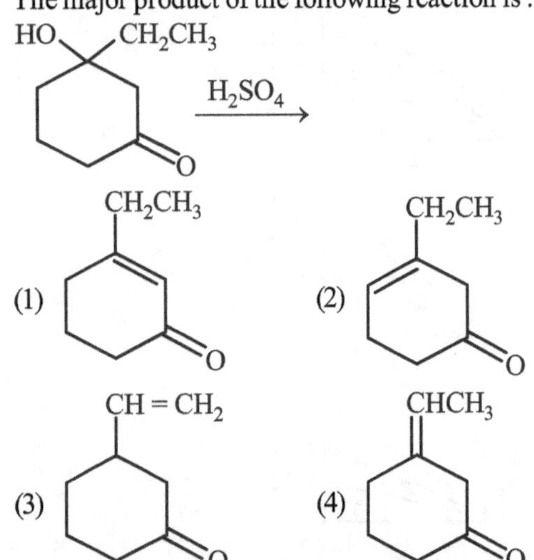

(1) I < III < IV < II   (2) I < IV < III < II
(3) IV < I < II < III   (4) III < I < II < IV

32. The correct order of the ionic radii of O^{2-}, N^{3-}, F^-, Mg^{2+}, Na^+ and Al^{3+} is :

(1) $N^{3-} < O^{2-} < F^- < Na^+ < Mg^{2+} < Al^{3+}$

(2) $Al^{3+} < Na^+ < Mg^{2+} < O^{2-} < F^- < N^{3-}$

(3) $Al^{3+} < Mg^{2+} < Na^+ < F^- < O^{2-} < N^{3-}$

(4) $N^{3-} < F^- < O^{2-} < Mg^{2+} < Na^+ < Al^{3+}$

33. Which one of the following polymers is not obtained by condensation polymerisation?
(1) Nylon 6,6   (2) Buna - N
(3) Bakelite   (4) Nylon 6

34. The major product of the following reaction is :

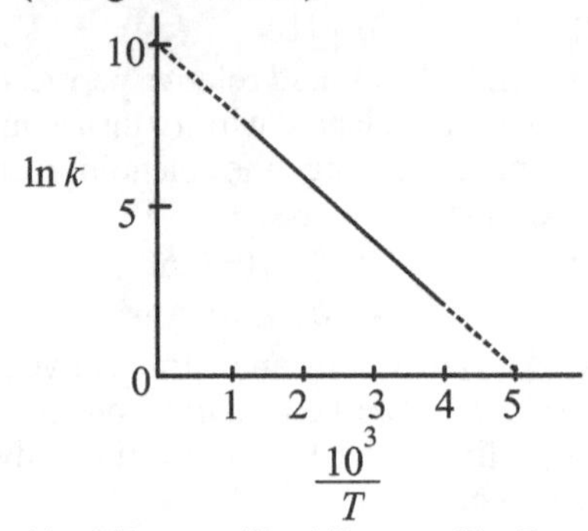

35. Hydrogen peroxide, in the pure state, is :
(1) non-planar and almost colorless
(2) linear and blue in color
(3) linear and almost colorless
(4) planar and blue in color

36. The rate constant (k) of a reaction is measured at different temperatures (T), and the data are plotted in the given figure. The activation energy of the reaction in kJ mol^{-1} is : (R is gas constant)

(1) $2/R$ (2) $1/R$ (3) R (4) $2R$

37. Lattice enthalpy and enthalpy of solution of NaCl are 788 kJ mol^{-1} and 4 kJ mol^{-1}, respectively. The hydration enthalpy of NaCl is :
(1) -780 kJ mol^{-1} (2) 780 kJ mol^{-1}
(3) -784 kJ mol^{-1} (4) 784 kJ mol^{-1}

38. The one that is NOT suitable for the removal of permanent hardness of water is :
(1) Clark's method
(2) Ion-exchange method
(3) Calgon's method
(4) Treatment with sodium carbonate

39. The compound that has the largest H – M – H bond angle (M = N, S, C), is :
(1) H_2O (2) NH_3 (3) H_2S (4) CH_4

40. Boron and silicon of very high purity can be obtained through :
(1) liquation   (2) zone refining
(3) vapour phase refining (4) electrolytic refining

41. The correct statement about probability density (except at infinite distance from nucleus) is :
(1) It can be zero for $1s$ orbital
(2) It can be negative for $2p$ orbital
(3) It can be zero for $3p$ orbital
(4) It can never be zero for $2s$ orbital

42. The major product formed in the following reaction is :

$$CH_3CH = CHCH(CH_3)_2 \xrightarrow{\text{HBr}}$$

(1) $CH_3CH(Br)CH_2CH(CH_3)_2$

(2) $CH_3CH_2CH(Br)CH(CH_3)_2$

(3) $Br(CH_2)_3CH(CH_3)_2$

(4) $CH_3CH_2CH_2C(Br)(CH_3)_2$

43. The variation of molar conductivity with concentration of an electrolyte (X) in aqueous solution is shown in the given figure.

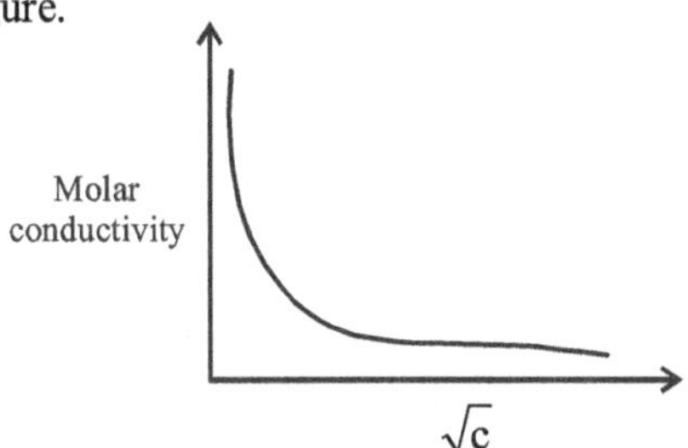

The electrolyte X is :
(1) HCl
(2) NaCl
(3) KNO_3
(4) CH_3COOH

44. The following molecule acts as an :

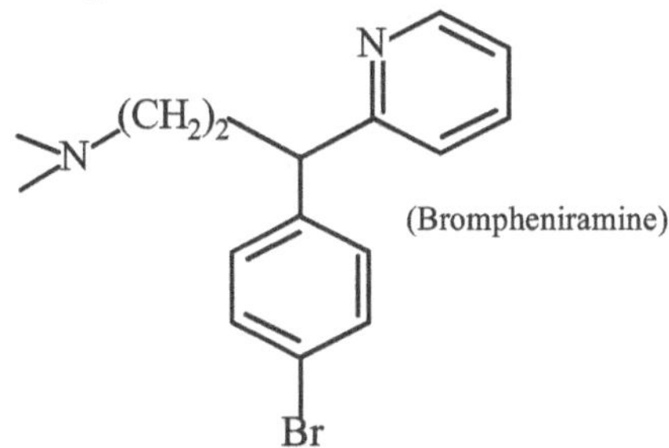

(1) Antiseptic
(2) Anti-depressant
(3) Anti-bacterial
(4) Anti-histamine

45. Reaction of ammonia with excess Cl_2 gives :
(1) NH_4Cl and N_2
(2) NH_4Cl and HCl
(3) NCl_3 and NH_4Cl
(4) NCl_3 and HCl

46. The volume, in mL, of 0.02 M $K_2Cr_2O_7$ solution required to react with 0.288 g of ferrous oxalate in acidic medium is __________ . (Molar mass of Fe = 56 g mol^{-1})

47. For a dimerization reaction, $2A(g) \rightarrow A_2(g)$, at 298 K, $\Delta U^{\ominus} = -20$ kJ mol^{-1}, $\Delta S^{\ominus} = -30$ J K^{-1} mol^{-1}, then the $\Delta G^{\ominus}$ will be __________ J.

48. Considering that $\Delta_0 > P$, the magnetic moment (in BM) of $[Ru(H_2O)_6]^{2+}$ would be __________ .

49. For a reaction $X + Y \rightleftharpoons 2Z$, 1.0 mol of X, 1.5 mol of Y and 0.5 mol of Z were taken in a 1 L vessel and allowed to react. At equilibrium, the concentration of Z was 1.0 mol L^{-1}. The equilibrium constant of the reaction is $\dfrac{x}{15}$. The value of x is __________ .

50. The number of chiral carbons present in sucrose is __________ .

MATHEMATICS

51. If the system of linear equations

$x + y + 3z = 0$

$x + 3y + k^2z = 0$

$3x + y + 3z = 0$

has a non-zero solution (x, y, z) for some $k \in \mathbf{R}$, then $x + \left(\dfrac{y}{z}\right)$ is equal to :

(1) -3
(2) 9
(3) 3
(4) -9

52. If α and β are the roots of the equation, $7x^2 - 3x - 2 = 0$, the the value of $\dfrac{\alpha}{1-\alpha^2} + \dfrac{\beta}{1-\beta^2}$ is equal to :

(1) $\dfrac{27}{32}$
(2) $\dfrac{1}{24}$
(3) $\dfrac{3}{8}$
(4) $\dfrac{27}{16}$

53. If $x = 1$ is a critical point of the function $f(x) = (3x^2 + ax - 2 - a)e^x$, then :

(1) $x = 1$ and $x = -\dfrac{2}{3}$ are local minima of f.

(2) $x = 1$ and $x = -\dfrac{2}{3}$ are local maxima of f.

(3) $x = 1$ is a local maxima and $x = -\dfrac{2}{3}$ is a local minima of f.

(4) $x = 1$ is a local minima and $x = -\dfrac{2}{3}$ is a local maxima of f.

54. The area (in sq. units) of the region $A = \{(x, y) : (x-1)[x] \le y \le 2\sqrt{x}, 0 \le x \le 2\}$, where $[t]$ denotes the greatest integer function, is :

(1) $\dfrac{8}{3}\sqrt{2} - \dfrac{1}{2}$
(2) $\dfrac{4}{3}\sqrt{2} + 1$
(3) $\dfrac{8}{3}\sqrt{2} - 1$
(4) $\dfrac{4}{3}\sqrt{2} - \dfrac{1}{2}$

55. If the sum of the second, third and fourth terms of a positive term G.P. is 3 and the sum of its sixth, seventh and eighth terms is 243, then the sum of the first 50 terms of this G.P. is:

(1) $\dfrac{1}{26}(3^{49} - 1)$
(2) $\dfrac{1}{26}(3^{50} - 1)$
(3) $\dfrac{2}{13}(3^{50} - 1)$
(4) $\dfrac{1}{13}(3^{50} - 1)$

56. The value of $\left(\dfrac{-1+i\sqrt{3}}{1-i}\right)^{30}$ is :

(1) -2^{15}
(2) $2^{15}i$
(3) $-2^{15}i$
(4) 6^5

57. If $L = \sin^2\left(\dfrac{\pi}{16}\right) - \sin^2\left(\dfrac{\pi}{8}\right)$ and $M = \cos^2\left(\dfrac{\pi}{16}\right) - \sin^2\left(\dfrac{\pi}{8}\right)$, then :

(1) $L = -\dfrac{1}{2\sqrt{2}} + \dfrac{1}{2}\cos\dfrac{\pi}{8}$
(2) $L = \dfrac{1}{4\sqrt{2}} - \dfrac{1}{4}\cos\dfrac{\pi}{8}$
(3) $M = \dfrac{1}{4\sqrt{2}} + \dfrac{1}{4}\cos\dfrac{\pi}{8}$
(4) $M = \dfrac{1}{2\sqrt{2}} + \dfrac{1}{2}\cos\dfrac{\pi}{8}$

58. If $a+x=b+y=c+z+1$, where a, b, c, x, y, z are non-zero distinct real numbers, then $\begin{vmatrix} x & a+y & x+a \\ y & b+y & y+b \\ z & c+y & z+c \end{vmatrix}$ is equal to :

(1) $y\,(b-a)$ (2) $y\,(a-b)$
(3) 0 (4) $y\,(a-c)$

59. If the line $y = mx + c$ is a common tangent to the hyperbola $\dfrac{x^2}{100} - \dfrac{y^2}{64} = 1$ and the circle $x^2 + y^2 = 36$, then which one of the following is true?

(1) $c^2 = 369$ (2) $5m = 4$
(3) $4c^2 = 369$ (4) $8m + 5 = 0$

60. Which of the following points lies on the tangent to the curve $x^4 e^y + 2\sqrt{y+1} = 3$ at the point $(1, 0)$?

(1) $(2, 2)$ (2) $(2, 6)$
(3) $(-2, 6)$ (4) $(-2, 4)$

61. The statement $(p \to (q \to p)) \to (p \to (p \vee q))$ is :

(1) equivalent to $(p \wedge q) \vee (\sim q)$
(2) a contradiction
(3) equivalent to $(p \vee q) \wedge (\sim p)$
(4) a tautology

62. $\displaystyle \lim_{x \to 0} \frac{x(e^{(\sqrt{1+x^2+x^4}-1)/x} - 1)}{\sqrt{1+x^2+x^4} - 1}$

(1) is equal to $\sqrt{e}$ (2) is equal to 1
(3) is equal to 0 (4) does not exist

63. If the sum of the first 20 terms of the series $\log_{(7^{1/2})} x + \log_{(7^{1/3})} x + \log_{(7^{1/4})} x + \cdots$ is 460, then x is equal to :

(1) 7^2 (2) $7^{1/2}$ (3) e^2 (4) $7^{46/21}$

64. The derivative of $\tan^{-1}\left(\dfrac{\sqrt{1+x^2}-1}{x}\right)$ with respect to $\tan^{-1}\left(\dfrac{2x\sqrt{1-x^2}}{1-2x^2}\right)$ at $x = \dfrac{1}{2}$ is :

(1) $\dfrac{2\sqrt{3}}{5}$ (2) $\dfrac{\sqrt{3}}{12}$ (3) $\dfrac{2\sqrt{3}}{3}$ (4) $\dfrac{\sqrt{3}}{10}$

65. If $\displaystyle \int \frac{\cos\theta}{5 + 7\sin\theta - 2\cos^2\theta} d\theta = A\log_e |B(\theta)| + C$, where C is a constant of integration, then $\dfrac{B(\theta)}{A}$ can be :

(1) $\dfrac{2\sin\theta + 1}{\sin\theta + 3}$ (2) $\dfrac{2\sin\theta + 1}{5(\sin\theta + 3)}$

(3) $\dfrac{5(\sin\theta + 3)}{2\sin\theta + 1}$ (4) $\dfrac{5(2\sin\theta + 1)}{\sin\theta + 3}$

66. Let $y = y(x)$ be the solution of the differential equation
$$\cos x \frac{dy}{dx} + 2y\sin x = \sin 2x, \quad x \in \left(0, \frac{\pi}{2}\right).$$
If $y(\pi/3) = 0$, then $y(\pi/4)$ is equal to :

(1) $2 - \sqrt{2}$ (2) $2 + \sqrt{2}$ (3) $\sqrt{2} - 2$ (4) $\dfrac{1}{\sqrt{2}} - 1$

67. If the length of the chord of the circle, $x^2 + y^2 = r^2 \, (r > 0)$ along the line, $y - 2x = 3$ is r, then r^2 is equal to :

(1) $\dfrac{9}{5}$ (2) 12 (3) $\dfrac{24}{5}$ (4) $\dfrac{12}{5}$

68. If the mean and the standard deviation of the data 3, 5, 7, a, b are 5 and 2 respectively, then a and b are the roots of the equation :

(1) $x^2 - 10x + 18 = 0$ (2) $2x^2 - 20x + 19 = 0$
(3) $x^2 - 10x + 19 = 0$ (4) $x^2 - 20x + 18 = 0$

69. If for some $\alpha \in \mathbf{R}$, the lines $L_1 : \dfrac{x+1}{2} = \dfrac{y-2}{-1} = \dfrac{z-1}{1}$ and $L_2 : \dfrac{x+2}{\alpha} = \dfrac{y+1}{5-\alpha} = \dfrac{z+1}{1}$ are coplanar, then the line L_2 passes through the point :

(1) $(10, 2, 2)$ (2) $(2, -10, -2)$
(3) $(10, -2, -2)$ (4) $(-2, 10, 2)$

70. There are 3 sections in a question paper and each section contains 5 questions. A candidate has to answer a total of 5 questions, choosing at least one question from each section. Then the number of ways, in which the candidate can choose the questions, is :

(1) 3000   (2) 1500   (3) 2255   (4) 2250

71. The coefficient of x^4 in the expansion of $(1 + x + x^2 + x^3)^6$ in powers of x, is ____________.

72. In a bombing attack, there is 50% chance that a bomb will hit the target. At least two independent hits are required to destroy the target completely. Then the minimum number of bombs, that must be dropped to ensure that there is at least 99% chance of completely destroying the target, is ____________.

73. If the lines $x + y = a$ and $x - y = b$ touch the curve $y = x^2 - 3x + 2$ at the points where the curve intersects the x-axis, then $\dfrac{a}{b}$ is equal to ________.

74. Let the vectors $\vec{a}, \vec{b}, \vec{c}$ be such that $|\vec{a}| = 2$, $|\vec{b}| = 4$ and $|\vec{c}| = 4$. If the projection of $\vec{b}$ on $\vec{a}$ is equal to the projection of $\vec{c}$ on $\vec{a}$ and $\vec{b}$ is perpendicular to $\vec{c}$, then the value of $|\vec{a} + \vec{b} - \vec{c}|$ is ________.

75. Let $A = \{a, b, c\}$ and $B = \{1, 2, 3, 4\}$. Then the number of elements in the set $C = \{f : A \to B \mid 2 \in f(A) \text{ and } f \text{ is not one-one}\}$ is ____________.

JEE MAIN 2020

(Held on 6-09-2020 Morning Shift)

PHYSICS

1. A screw gauge has 50 divisions on its circular scale. The circular scale is 4 units ahead of the pitch scale marking, prior to use. Upon one complete rotation of the circular scale, a displacement of 0.5 mm is noticed on the pitch scale. The nature of zero error involved, and the least count of the screw gauge, are respectively :
(1) Negative, 2 μm (2) Positive, 10 μm
(3) Positive, 0.1 mm (4) Positive, 0.1 μm

2. A sound source S is moving along a straight track with speed v, and is emitting sound of frequency v_0 (see figure). An observer is standing at a finite distance, at the point O, from the track. The time variation of frequency heard by the observer is best represented by:
(t_0 represents the instant when the distance between the source and observer is minimum)

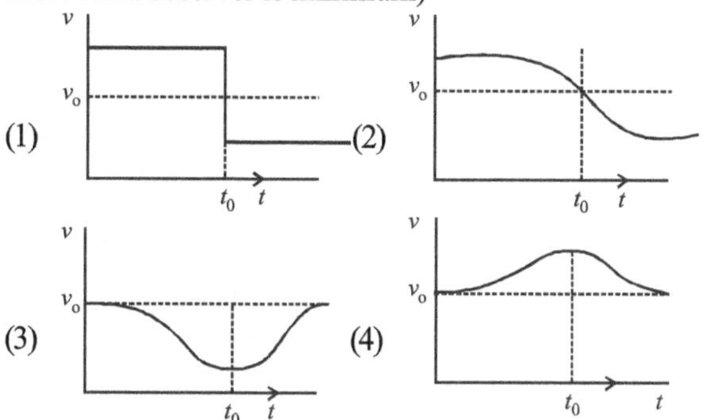

3. In the figure below, P and Q are two equally intense coherent sources emitting radiation of wavelength 20 m. The separation between P and Q is 5 m and the phase of P is ahead of that of Q by 90°. A, B and C are three distinct points of observation, each equidistant from the midpoint of PQ. The intensities of radiation at A, B, C will be in the ratio :

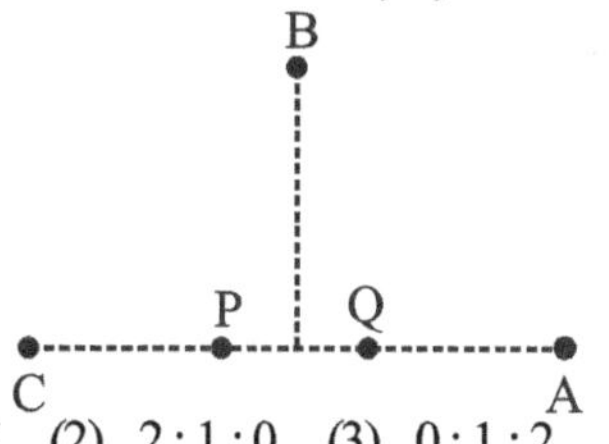

(1) $0:1:4$ (2) $2:1:0$ (3) $0:1:2$ (4) $4:1:0$

4. If the potential energy between two molecules is given by $U = -\dfrac{A}{r^6} + \dfrac{B}{r^{12}}$, then at equilibrium, separation between molecules, and the potential energy are:

(1) $\left(\dfrac{B}{2A}\right)^{\frac{1}{6}}, -\dfrac{A^2}{2B}$ (2) $\left(\dfrac{B}{A}\right)^{\frac{1}{6}}, 0$

(3) $\left(\dfrac{2B}{A}\right)^{\frac{1}{6}}, -\dfrac{A^2}{4B}$ (4) $\left(\dfrac{2B}{A}\right)^{\frac{1}{6}}, -\dfrac{A^2}{2B}$

5. An AC circuit has $R = 100\ \Omega$, $C = 2\ \mu F$ and $L = 80\ mH$, connected in series. The quality factor of the circuit is :
(1) 2 (2) 0.5 (3) 20 (4) 400

6. Charges Q_1 and Q_2 are at points A and B of a right angle triangle OAB (see figure). The resultant electric field at point O is perpendicular to the hypotenuse, then Q_1/Q_2 is proportional to :

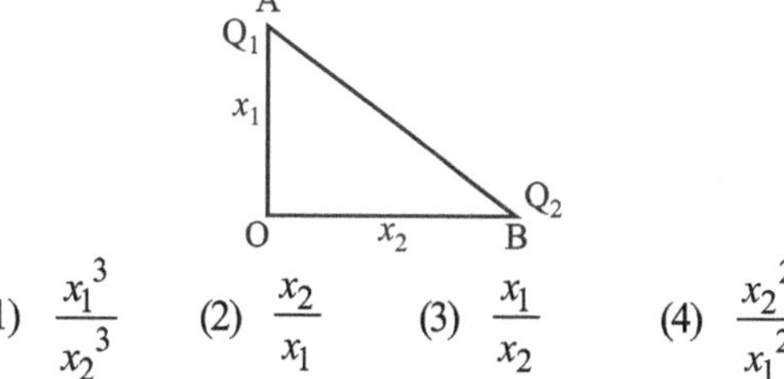

(1) $\dfrac{x_1^{\,3}}{x_2^{\,3}}$ (2) $\dfrac{x_2}{x_1}$ (3) $\dfrac{x_1}{x_2}$ (4) $\dfrac{x_2^{\,2}}{x_1^{\,2}}$

7. Shown in the figure is a hollow icecream cone (it is open at the top). If its mass is M, radius of its top, R and height, H, then its moment of inertia about its axis is :

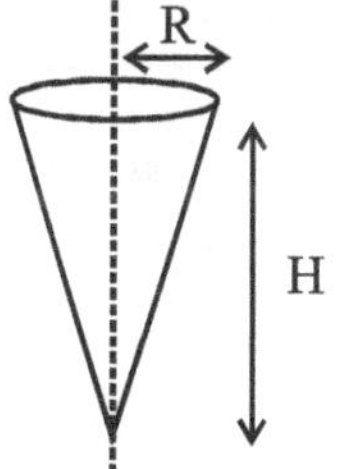

(1) $\dfrac{MR^2}{2}$ (2) $\dfrac{M(R^2 + H^2)}{4}$

(3) $\dfrac{MH^2}{3}$ (4) $\dfrac{MR^2}{3}$

8. Four point masses, each of mass m, are fixed at the corners of a square of side l. The square is rotating with angular frequency ω, about an axis passing through one of the corners of the square and parallel to its diagonal, as shown in the figure. The angular momentum of the square about this axis is :

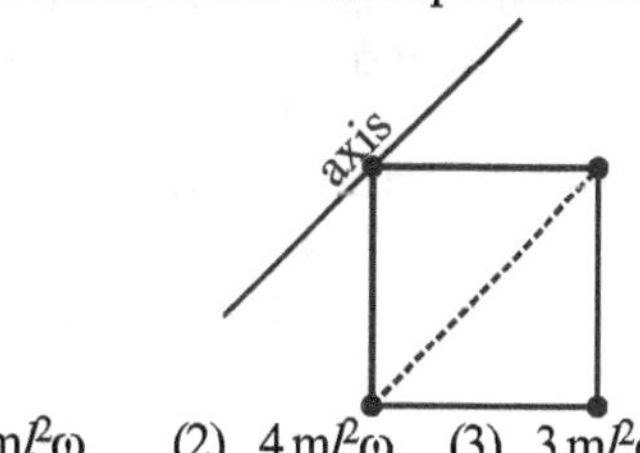

(1) $ml^2\omega$ (2) $4ml^2\omega$ (3) $3ml^2\omega$ (4) $2ml^2\omega$

9. For the given input voltage waveform $V_{in}(t)$, the output voltage waveform $V_o(t)$, across the capacitor is correctly depicted by :

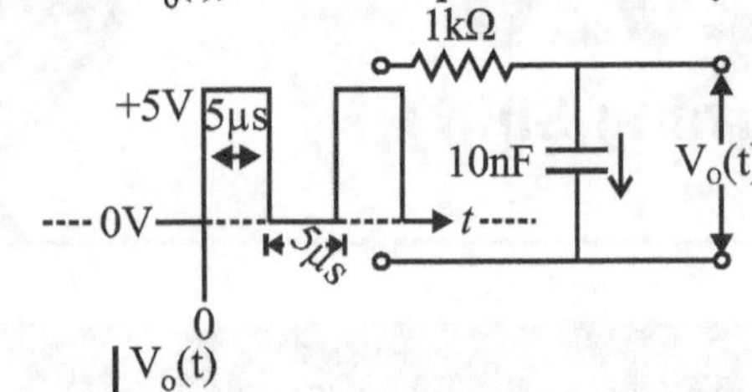

(1) 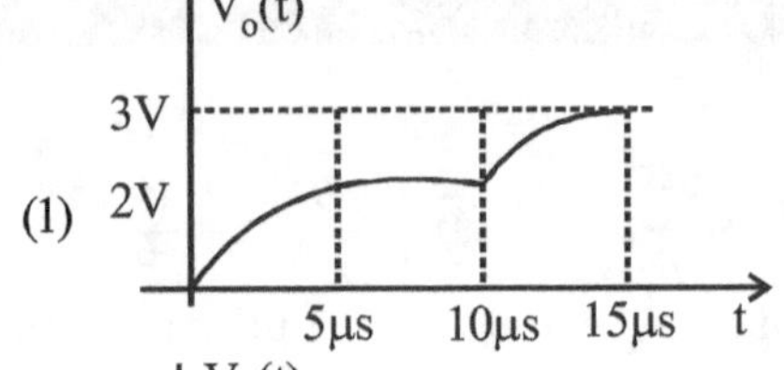

(2) 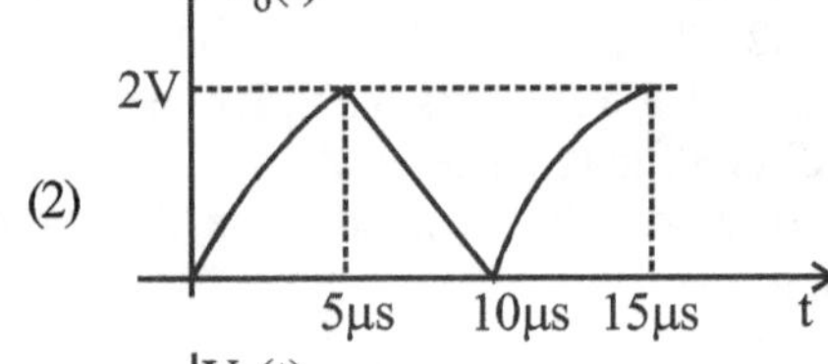

(3) 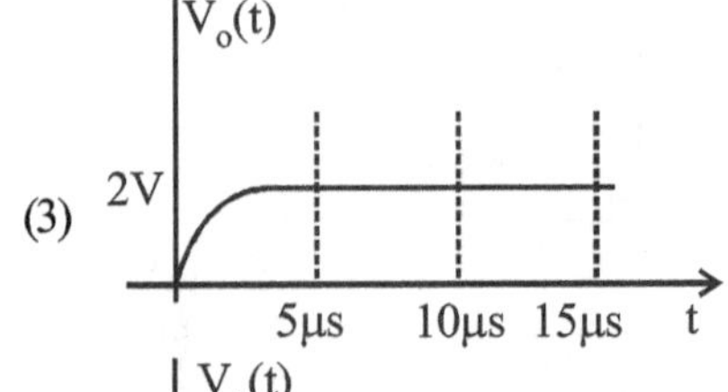

(4) 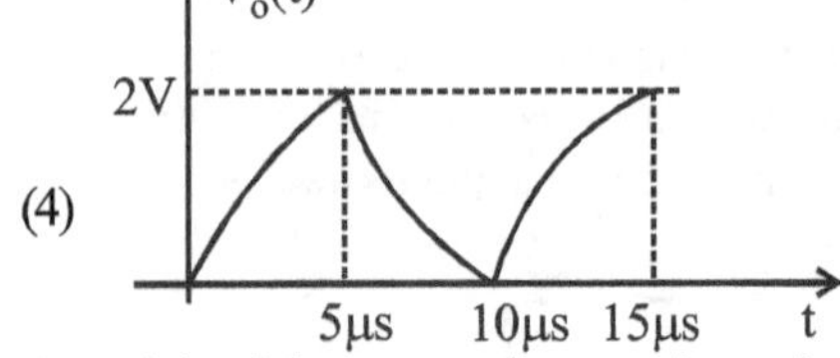

10. A particle of charge q and mass m is moving with a velocity $-v\,\hat{i}\,(v \neq 0)$ towards a large screen placed in the Y-Z plane at a distance d. If there is a magnetic field $\vec{B} = B_0\hat{k}$, the minimum value of v for which the particle will not hit the screen is:

(1) $\dfrac{qdB_0}{3m}$ (2) $\dfrac{2qdB_0}{m}$ (3) $\dfrac{qdB_0}{m}$ (4) $\dfrac{qdB_0}{2m}$

11. An insect is at the bottom of a hemispherical ditch of radius 1 m. It crawls up the ditch but starts slipping after it is at height h from the bottom. If the coefficient of friction between the ground and the insect is 0.75, then h is : ($g = 10$ ms^{-2})

(1) 0.20 m   (2) 0.45 m   (3) 0.60 m   (4) 0.80 m

12. A satellite is in an elliptical orbit around a planet P. It is observed that the velocity of the satellite when it is farthest from the planet is 6 times less than that when it is closest to the planet. The ratio of distances between the satellite and the planet at closest and farthest points is :

(1) 1 : 6   (2) 1 : 3   (3) 1 : 2   (4) 3 : 4

13. An electron, a doubly ionized helium ion (He^{++}) and a proton are having the same kinetic energy. The relation between their respective de-Broglie wavelengths λ_e, $\lambda_{He^{++}}$ and λ_p is :

(1) $\lambda_e > \lambda_{He^{++}} > \lambda_p$ (2) $\lambda_e < \lambda_{He^{++}} = \lambda_p$

(3) $\lambda_e > \lambda_p > \lambda_{He^{++}}$ (4) $\lambda_e < \lambda_p < \lambda_{He^{++}}$

14. A clock has a continuously moving second's hand of 0.1 m length. The average acceleration of the tip of the hand (in units of ms^{-2}) is of the order of:

(1) 10^{-3} (2) 10^{-4} (3) 10^{-2} (4) 10^{-1}

15. You are given that mass of $^7_3$Li $= 7.0160$ u,

Mass of $^4_2$He $= 4.0026$ u

and Mass of $^1_1$H $= 1.0079$ u.

When 20 g of $^7_3$Li is converted into $^4_2$He by proton capture, the energy liberated, (in kWh), is :
[Mass of nucleon $= 1$ GeV/c^2]

(1) 4.5×10^5 (2) 8×10^6 (3) 6.82×10^5 (4) 1.33×10^6

16. A point like object is placed at a distance of 1 m in front of a convex lens of focal length 0.5 m. A plane mirror is placed at a distance of 2 m behind the lens. The position and nature of the final image formed by the system is :

(1) 2.6 m from the mirror, real

(2) 1 m from the mirror, virtual

(3) 1 m from the mirror, real

(4) 2.6 m from the mirror, virtual

17. Identify the correct output signal Y in the given combination of gates (as shown) for the given inputs A and B.

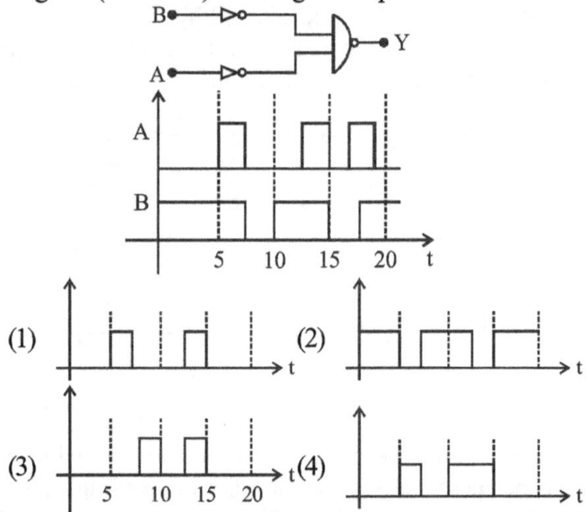

(1)   (2)

(3)   (4)

18. Molecules of an ideal gas are known to have three translational degrees of freedom and two rotational degrees of freedom. The gas is maintained at a temperature of T. The total internal energy, U of a mole of this gas, and the value of $\gamma\left(=\dfrac{C_p}{C_v}\right)$ are given, respectively, by:

(1) $U = \dfrac{5}{2}RT$ and $\gamma = \dfrac{6}{5}$ (2) $U = 5RT$ and $\gamma = \dfrac{7}{5}$

(3) $U = \dfrac{5}{2}RT$ and $\gamma = \dfrac{7}{5}$ (4) $U = 5RT$ and $\gamma = \dfrac{6}{5}$

19. An object of mass m is suspended at the end of a massless wire of length L and area of cross-section, A. Young modulus of the material of the wire is Y. If the mass is pulled down slightly its frequency of oscillation along the vertical direction is:

(1) $f = \dfrac{1}{2\pi}\sqrt{\dfrac{mL}{YA}}$ (2) $f = \dfrac{1}{2\pi}\sqrt{\dfrac{YA}{mL}}$

(3) $f = \dfrac{1}{2\pi}\sqrt{\dfrac{mA}{YL}}$ (4) $f = \dfrac{1}{2\pi}\sqrt{\dfrac{YL}{mA}}$

20. An electron is moving along $+x$ direction with a velocity of $6 \times 10^6 \, ms^{-1}$. It enters a region of uniform electric field of $300 \, V/cm$ pointing along $+y$ direction. The magnitude and direction of the magnetic field set up in this region such that the electron keeps moving along the x direction will be :
(1) $3 \times 10^{-4} \, T$, along $+z$ direction
(2) $5 \times 10^{-3} \, T$, along $-z$ direction
(3) $5 \times 10^{-3} \, T$, along $+z$ direction
(4) $3 \times 10^{-4} \, T$, along $-z$ direction

21. The density of a solid metal sphere is determined by measuring its mass and its diameter. The maximum error in the density of the sphere is $\left(\dfrac{x}{100}\right)$ %. If the relative errors in measuring the mass and the diameter are 6.0% and 1.5% respectively, the value of x is ______.

22. Two bodies of the same mass are moving with the same speed, but in different directions in a plane. They have a completely inelastic collision and move together thereafter with a final speed which is half of their initial speed. The angle between the initial velocities of the two bodies (in degree) is ______.

23. Suppose that intensity of a laser is $\left(\dfrac{315}{\pi}\right) \, W/m^2$. The rms electric field, in units of V/m associated with this source is close to the nearest integer is ______.
($\epsilon_0 = 8.86 \times 10^{-12} \, C^2 Nm^{-2}$; $c = 3 \times 10^8 \, ms^{-1}$)

24. Initially a gas of diatomic molecules is contained in a cylinder of volume V_1 at a pressure P_1 and temperature 250 K. Assuming that 25% of the molecules get dissociated causing a change in number of moles. The pressure of the resulting gas at temperature 2000 K, when contained in a volume $2V_1$ is given by P_2. The ratio P_2/P_1 is ______.

25. A part of a complete circuit is shown in the figure. At some instant, the value of current I is 1 A and it is decreasing at a rate of $10^2 A \, s^{-1}$. The value of the potential difference $V_P - V_Q$, (in volts) at that instant, is ______.

L=50 mH I   R = 2 Ω
P ——oooooo——|⊢——WWWW—— Q
30 V

CHEMISTRY

26. The correct statement with respect to dinitrogen is:
(1) N_2 is paramagnetic in nature.
(2) it can combine with dioxygen at 25 °C.
(3) liquid dinitrogen is not used in cryosurgery.
(4) it can be used as an inert diluent for reactive chemicals.

27. Consider the following reactions:

'A' $\xrightarrow{\text{ozonolysis}}$ 'B' + 'C'
(C_7H_{14})

'B' $\xrightarrow[\Delta]{(I_2 + NaOH)}$ yellow ppt

$\xrightarrow[\Delta]{Ag_2O}$ silver mirror

'C' $\xrightarrow[\Delta]{(I_2 + NaOH)}$ no yellow ppt

$\xrightarrow{LiAlH_4}$ 'D' $\xrightarrow[\text{& Conc. HCl}]{\text{Anhydrous ZnCl}_2}$ gives white turbidity within 5 minutes

'A' is :

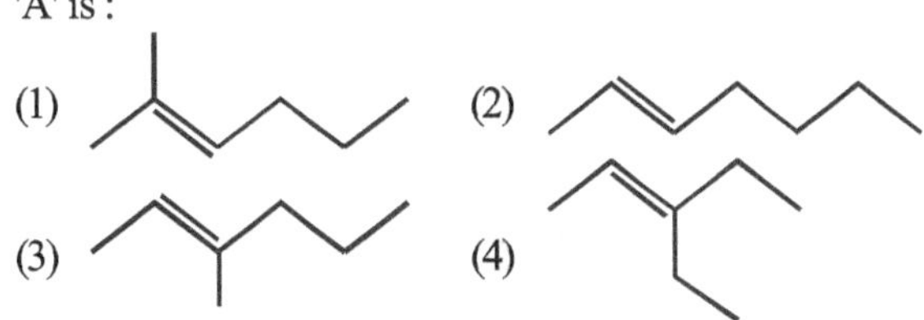

(1)   (2)   (3)   (4)

28. The major product obtained from the following reaction is:

O_2N—⬡—$C \equiv C$—⬡—OCH_3 $\xrightarrow[H_2O]{Hg^{2+}/H^+}$

(1)

29. A solution of two components containing n_1 moles of the 1st component and n_2 moles of the 2nd component is prepared. M_1 and M_2 are the molecular weights of component 1 and 2 respectively. If d is the density of the solution in $g \, mL^{-1}$, C_2 is the molarity and x_2 is the mole fraction of the 2nd component, then C_2 can be expressed as:

(1) $C_2 = \dfrac{1000 \, x_2}{M_1 + x_2(M_2 - M_1)}$

(2) $C_2 = \dfrac{d \, x_2}{M_2 + x_2(M_2 - M_1)}$

(3) $C_2 = \dfrac{1000 \, d \, x_2}{M_1 + x_2(M_2 - M_1)}$

(4) $C_2 = \dfrac{d \, x_1}{M_2 + x_2(M_2 - M_1)}$

30. The INCORRECT statement is :
(1) bronze is an alloy of copper and tin.
(2) cast iron is used to manufacture wrought iron.
(3) german silver is an alloy of zinc, copper and nickel.
(4) brass is an alloy of copper and nickel.

31. Consider the **Assertion** and **Reason** given below.

Assertion (A) : Ethene polymerized in the presence of Ziegler Natta Catalyst at high temperature and pressure is used to make buckets and dustbins.

Reason (R) : High density polymers are closely packed and are chemically inert.

Choose the correct answer from the following :

(1) **(A)** is correct but **(R)** is wrong.

(2) Both **(A)** and **(R)** are correct and **(R)** is not the correct explanation of **(A)**.

(3) Both **(A)** and **(R)** are correct but **(R)** is the correct explanation of **(A)**.

(4) **(A)** and **(R)** both are wrong.

32. Arrange the following solutions in the decreasing order of pOH :

(A) 0.01 M HCl   (B) 0.01 M NaOH

(C) 0.01 M CH_3COONa (D) 0.01 M NaCl

(1) (A) > (C) > (D) > (B)   (2) (A) > (D) > (C) > (B)

(3) (B) > (C) > (D) > (A)   (4) (B) > (D) > (C) > (A)

33. Among the sulphates of alkaline earth metals, the solubilities of $BeSO_4$ and $MgSO_4$ in water, respectively, are :

(1) poor and poor   (2) high and poor

(3) high and high   (4) poor and high

34. The major products of the following reaction are:

$$CH_3-\underset{\underset{OSO_2CH_3}{|}}{\overset{\overset{CH_3}{|}}{CH}}-CH-CH_3 \xrightarrow[\text{(ii)}O_3/H_2O_2]{\text{(i)}KO^tBu/\Delta}$$

(1) (acetone) + CH_3CHO

(2) (acetone) + CH_3COOH

(3) (isobutyraldehyde) + HCHO

(4) (isobutyric acid) + HCOOH

35. The major product of the following reaction is :

(4-methyl, 1-nitrobenzene) $\xrightarrow{2HBr}$

(1) (product 1)

(2) (product 2)

(3) (product 3)

(4) (product 4)

36. The presence of soluble fluoride ion upto 1 ppm concentration in drinking water, is :

(1) harmful for teeth   (2) harmful to skin

(3) harmful to bones   (4) safe for teeth

37. The increasing order of pK_b values of the following compounds is :

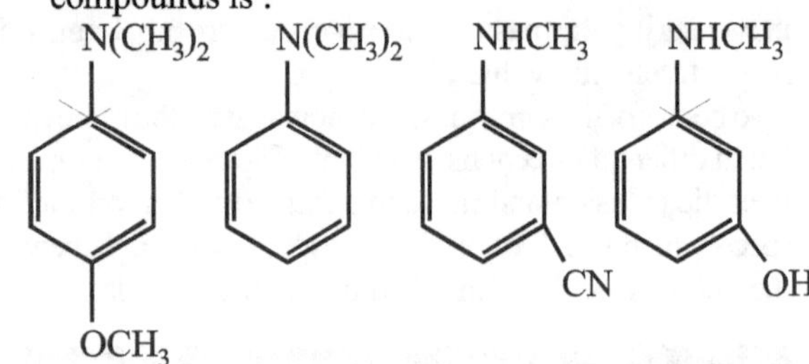

(1) II < IV < III < I   (2) I < II < IV < III

(3) II < I < III < IV   (4) I < II < III < IV

38. Which of the following compounds shows geometrical isomerism?

(1) 2-methylpent-2-ene   (2) 4-methylpent-2-ene

(3) 4-methylpent-1-ene   (4) 2-methylpent-1-ene

39. The set that contains atomic numbers of only transition elements, is :

(1) 37, 42, 50, 64   (2) 21, 25, 42, 72

(3) 9, 17, 34, 38   (4) 21, 32, 53, 64

40. The variation of equilibrium constant with temperature is given below:

Temperature   **Equilibrium Constant**

$T_1 = 25\,°C$ $K_1 = 10$

$T_2 = 100\,°C$ $K_2 = 100$

The values of $\Delta H°$, $\Delta G°$ at T_1 and $\Delta G°$ at T_2 (in kj mol^{-1}) respectively, are close to

[use R = 8.314 J K^{-1} mol^{-1}]

(1) 28.4, −7.14 and −5.71   (2) 0.64, −7.14 and −5.71

(3) 28.4, −5.71 and −14.29   (4) 0.64, −5.71 and −14.29

41. Kraft temperature is the temperature:

(1) below which the aqueous solution of detergents starts freezing.

(2) below which the formation of micelles takes place.

(3) above which the aqueous solution of detergents starts boiling.

(4) above which the formation of micelles takes place.

42. For the reaction

$$Fe_2N(s) + \frac{3}{2}H_2(g) \rightleftharpoons 2Fe(s) + NH_3(g)$$

(1) $K_c = K_p(RT)$ (2) $K_c = K_p(RT)^{\frac{-1}{2}}$

(3) $K_c = K_p(RT)^{\frac{1}{2}}$ (4) $K_c = K_p(RT)^{\frac{3}{2}}$

43. The species that has a spin-only magnetic moment of 5.9 BM, is : (T_d = tetrahedral)
(1) $[Ni(CN)_4]^{2-}$ (square planar)
(2) $[NiCl_4]^{2-}$ (T_d)
(3) $Ni(CO)_4$ (T_d)
(4) $[MnBr_4]^{2-}$ (T_d)

44. The lanthanoid that does NOT show + 4 oxidation state is:
(1) Dy   (2) Ce   (3) Eu   (4) Tb

45. Consider the following reactions
$A \rightarrow P1$; $B \rightarrow P2$; $C \rightarrow P3$; $D \rightarrow P4$,
The order of the above reactions are (i), (ii), (iii), and (iv), respectively. The following graph is obtained when log [rate] vs. log[conc.] are plotted :

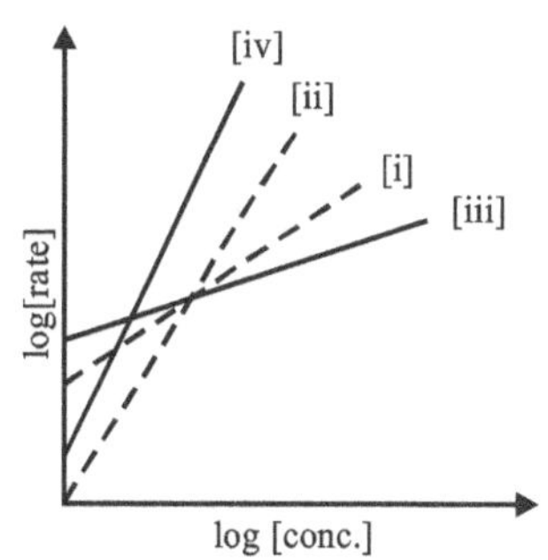

Among the following, the correct sequence for the order of the reactions is:
(1) (iv) > (i) > (ii) > (iii)   (2) (i) > (ii) > (iii) > (iv)
(3) (iii) > (i) > (ii) > (iv)   (4) (iv) > (ii) > (i) > (iii)

46. In an estimation of bromine by Carius method, 1.6 g of an organic compound gave 1.88 g of AgBr. The mass percentage of bromine in the compound is ______.
(Atomic mass, Ag = 108, Br = 80 g mol^{-1})

47. Potassium chlorate is prepared by the electrolysis of KCl in basic solution $6\,OH^- + Cl^- \rightarrow ClO_3^- + 3\,H_2O + 6\,e^-$
If only 60% of the current is utilized in the reaction, the time (rounded to the nearest hour) required to produce 10 g of $KClO_3$ using a current of 2 A is ______.
(Given : F = 96,500 C mol^{-1}; molar mass of $KClO_3$ = 122 g mol^{-1})

48. The number of Cl = O bonds in perchloric acid is, "______."

49. The elevation of boiling point of 0.10 m aqueous $CrCl_3.xNH_3$ solution is two times that of 0.05 m aqueous $CaCl_2$ solution. The value of x is ______.
[Assume 100% ionisation of the complex and $CaCl_2$, coordination number of Cr as 6, and that all NH_3 molecules are present inside the coordination sphere]

50. A spherical balloon of radius 3 cm containing helium gas has a pressure of 48×10^{-3} bar. At the same temperature, the pressure, of a spherical balloon of radius 12 cm containing the same amount of gas will be ______ $\times 10^{-6}$ bar.

MATHEMATICS

51. If α and β be two roots of the equation $x^2 - 64x + 256 = 0$.
Then the value of $\left(\dfrac{\alpha^3}{\beta^5}\right)^{\frac{1}{8}} + \left(\dfrac{\beta^3}{\alpha^5}\right)^{\frac{1}{8}}$ is:
(1) 2   (2) 3   (3) 1   (4) 4

52. The area (in sq. units) of the region
$A = \{(x, y) : |x| + |y| \le 1, 2y^2 \ge |x|\}$ is :
(1) $\dfrac{1}{3}$ (2) $\dfrac{7}{6}$ (3) $\dfrac{1}{6}$ (4) $\dfrac{5}{6}$

53. The general solution of the differential equation
$\sqrt{1 + x^2 + y^2 + x^2 y^2} + xy\dfrac{dy}{dx} = 0$ is :
(where C is a constant of integration)

(1) $\sqrt{1+y^2} + \sqrt{1+x^2} = \dfrac{1}{2}\log_e\left(\dfrac{\sqrt{1+x^2}+1}{\sqrt{1+x^2}-1}\right) + C$

(2) $\sqrt{1+y^2} - \sqrt{1+x^2} = \dfrac{1}{2}\log_e\left(\dfrac{\sqrt{1+x^2}+1}{\sqrt{1+x^2}-1}\right) + C$

(3) $\sqrt{1+y^2} + \sqrt{1+x^2} = \dfrac{1}{2}\log_e\left(\dfrac{\sqrt{1+x^2}-1}{\sqrt{1+x^2}+1}\right) + C$

(4) $\sqrt{1+y^2} - \sqrt{1+x^2} = \dfrac{1}{2}\log_e\left(\dfrac{\sqrt{1+x^2}-1}{\sqrt{1+x^2}+1}\right) + C$

54. Let L_1 be a tangent to the parabola $y^2 = 4(x + 1)$ and L_2 be a tangent to the parabola $y^2 = 8(x + 2)$ such that L_1 and L_2 intersect at right angles. Then L_1 and L_2 meet on the straight line :
(1) $x + 3 = 0$ (2) $2x + 1 = 0$
(3) $x + 2 = 0$ (4) $x + 2y = 0$

55. If $f(x + y) = f(x)f(y)$ and $\displaystyle\sum_{x=1}^{\infty} f(x) = 2$, $x, y \in N$, where N is the set of all natural numbers, then the value of $\dfrac{f(4)}{f(2)}$ is :
(1) $\dfrac{2}{3}$ (2) $\dfrac{1}{9}$ (3) $\dfrac{1}{3}$ (4) $\dfrac{4}{9}$

56. If $I_1 = \displaystyle\int_0^1 (1 - x^{50})^{100} dx$ and $I_2 = \displaystyle\int_0^1 (1 - x^{50})^{101} dx$ such that $I_2 = \alpha I_1$ then α equals to :
(1) $\dfrac{5049}{5050}$ (2) $\dfrac{5050}{5049}$
(3) $\dfrac{5050}{5051}$ (4) $\dfrac{5051}{5050}$

57. Out of 11 consecutive natural numbers if three numbers are selected at random (without repetition), then the probability that they are in A.P. with positive common difference, is:
(1) $\dfrac{15}{101}$ (2) $\dfrac{5}{101}$ (3) $\dfrac{5}{33}$ (4) $\dfrac{10}{99}$

58. A ray of light coming from the point $(2, 2\sqrt{3})$ is incident at an angle $30°$ on the line $x = 1$ at the point A. The ray gets reflected on the line $x = 1$ and meets x-axis at the point B. Then, the line AB passes through the point:

(1) $\left(3, -\dfrac{1}{\sqrt{3}}\right)$ 　　　　(2) $\left(4, -\dfrac{\sqrt{3}}{2}\right)$

(3) $(3, -\sqrt{3})$ 　　　　(4) $(4, -\sqrt{3})$

59. Which of the following points lies on the locus of the foot of perpendicular drawn upon any tangent to the ellipse,

$$\frac{x^2}{4} + \frac{y^2}{2} = 1 \text{ from any of its foci?}$$

(1) $(-2, \sqrt{3})$ (2) $(-1, \sqrt{2})$ (3) $(-1, \sqrt{3})$ (4) $(1, 2)$

60. The region represented by $\{z = x + iy \in C : |z| - \text{Re}(z) \le 1\}$ is also given by the inequality:

(1) $y^2 \ge 2(x+1)$ 　　　　(2) $y^2 \le 2\left(x + \dfrac{1}{2}\right)$

(3) $y^2 \le x + \dfrac{1}{2}$ 　　　　(4) $y^2 \ge x + 1$

61. The position of a moving car at time t is given by $f(t) = at^2 + bt + c, t > 0$, where a, b and c are real numbers greater than 1. Then the average speed of the car over the time interval $[t_1, t_2]$ is attained at the point :

(1) $(t_2 - t_1)/2$ 　　　　(2) $a(t_2 - t_1) + b$
(3) $(t_1 + t_2)/2$ 　　　　(4) $2a(t_1 + t_2) + b$

62. $\displaystyle\lim_{x \to 1}\left(\frac{\displaystyle\int_0^{(x-1)^2} t\cos(t^2)\,dt}{(x-1)\sin(x-1)}\right)$

(1) is equal to $\dfrac{1}{2}$ 　　　　(2) is equal to 1

(3) is equal to $-\dfrac{1}{2}$ 　　　　(4) does not exist

63. If $\displaystyle\sum_{i=1}^{n}(x_i - a) = n$ and $\displaystyle\sum_{i=1}^{n}(x_i - a)^2 = na$, $(n, a > 1)$, then the standard deviation of n observations $x_1, x_2, ..., x_n$ is :

(1) $a - 1$ 　　(2) $n\sqrt{a-1}$ 　(3) $\sqrt{n(a-1)}$ 　(4) $\sqrt{a-1}$

64. If $\{p\}$ denotes the fractional part of the number p, then

$\left\{\dfrac{3^{200}}{8}\right\}$, is equal to :

(1) $\dfrac{5}{8}$ 　　　(2) $\dfrac{7}{8}$ 　　　(3) $\dfrac{3}{8}$ 　　　(4) $\dfrac{1}{8}$

65. The shortest distance between the lines $\dfrac{x-1}{0} = \dfrac{y+1}{-1} = \dfrac{z}{1}$ and $x + y + z + 1 = 0$, $2x - y + z + 3 = 0$ is :

(1) 1 　　　(2) $\dfrac{1}{\sqrt{3}}$ 　　　(3) $\dfrac{1}{\sqrt{2}}$ 　　　(4) $\dfrac{1}{2}$

66. The negation of the Boolean expression $p \vee (\sim p \wedge q)$ is equivalent to :

(1) $p \wedge \sim q$ 　　　　(2) $\sim p \wedge \sim q$
(3) $\sim p \vee \sim q$ 　　　　(4) $\sim p \vee q$

67. Two families with three members each and one family with four members are to be seated in a row. In how many ways can they be seated so that the same family members are not separated?

(1) $2!\,3!\,4!$ 　(2) $(3!)^3 \cdot (4!)$ (3) $(3!)^2 \cdot (4!)$ 　(4) $3!\,(4!)^3$

68. Let m and M be respectively the minimum and maximum values of

$$\begin{vmatrix} \cos^2 x & 1 + \sin^2 x & \sin 2x \\ 1 + \cos^2 x & \sin^2 x & \sin 2x \\ \cos^2 x & \sin^2 x & 1 + \sin 2x \end{vmatrix}$$

Then the ordered pair (m, M) is equal to :

(1) $(-3, 3)$ 　(2) $(-3, -1)$ (3) $(-4, -1)$ 　(4) $(1, 3)$

69. Let a, b, c, d and p be any non zero distinct real numbers such that $(a^2 + b^2 + c^2)p^2 - 2(ab + bc + cd)p + (b^2 + c^2 + d^2) = 0$. Then :

(1) a, c, p are in A.P. 　　(2) a, c, p are in G.P.
(3) a, b, c, d are in G.P. 　(4) a, b, c, d are in A.P.

70. The values of λ and μ for which the system of linear equations

$x + y + z = 2$
$x + 2y + 3z = 5$
$x + 3y + \lambda z = \mu$

has infinitely many solutions are, respectively :

(1) 6 and 8 　(2) 5 and 7 　(3) 5 and 8 　(4) 4 and 9

71. Set A has m elements and set B has n elements. If the total number of subsets of A is 112 more than the total number of subsets of B, then the value of $m \cdot n$ is ______.

72. Let $f : \mathbb{R} \to \mathbb{R}$ be defined as

$$f(x) = \begin{cases} x^5 \sin\left(\dfrac{1}{x}\right) + 5x^2, & x < 0 \\ 0, & x = 0 \\ x^5 \cos\left(\dfrac{1}{x}\right) + \lambda x^2, & x > 0 \end{cases}$$

The value of λ for which $f''(0)$ exists, is ______.

73. If $\vec{a}$ and $\vec{b}$ are unit vectors, then the greatest value of $\sqrt{3}\,|\vec{a} + \vec{b}| + |\vec{a} - \vec{b}|$ is ______.

74. Let AD and BC be two vertical poles at A and B respectively on a horizontal ground. If AD = 8 m, BC = 11 m and AB = 10 m; then the distance (in meters) of a point M on AB from the point A such that $MD^2 + MC^2$ is minimum is ______.

75. The angle of elevation of the top of a hill from a point on the horizontal plane passing through the foot of the hill is found to be 45°. After walking a distance of 80 meters towards the top, up a slope inclined at an angle of 30° to the horizontal plane, the angle of elevation of the top of the hill becomes 75°. Then the height of the hill (in meters) is ______.

JEE MAIN 2020

(Held on 6-09-2020 Evening Shift)

PHYSICS

1.

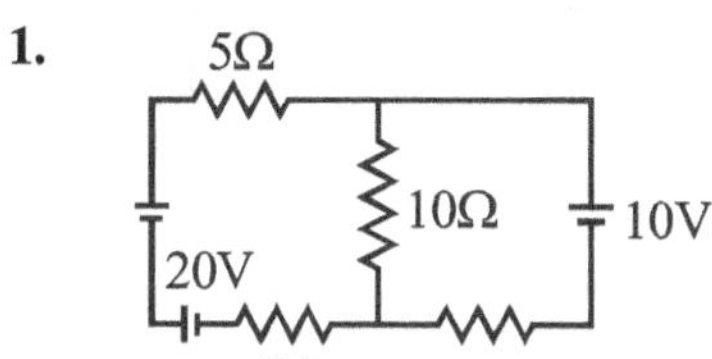

In the figure shown, the current in the 10 V battery is close to :
(1) 0.71 A from positive to negative terminal
(2) 0.42 A from positive to negative terminal
(3) 0.21 A from positive to negative terminal
(4) 0.36 A from negative to positive terminal

2. A charged particle going around in a circle can be considered to be a current loop. A particle of mass m carrying charge q is moving in a plane wit speed v under the influence of magnetic field $\vec{B}$. The magnetic moment of this moving particle :

(1) $\dfrac{mv^2 \vec{B}}{2 B^2}$

(2) $-\dfrac{mv^2 \vec{B}}{2 \pi B^2}$

(3) $-\dfrac{mv^2 \vec{B}}{B^2}$

(4) $-\dfrac{mv^2 \vec{B}}{2 B^2}$

3. Three rods of identical cross-section and lengths are made of three different materials of thermal conductivity K_1, K_2 and K_3, respectively. They are joined together at their ends to make a long rod (see figure). One end of the long rod is maintained at 100°C and the other at 0°C (see figure). If the joints of the rod are at 70°C and 20°C in steady state and there is no loss of energy from the surface of the rod, the correct relationship between K_1, K_2 and K_3 is :

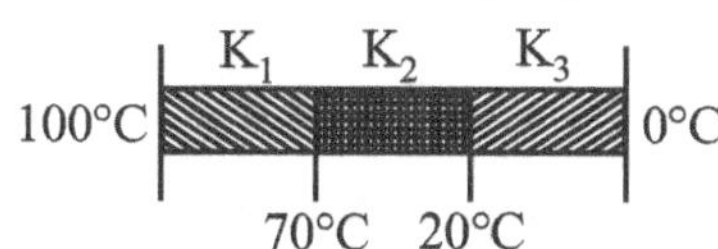

(1) $K_1 : K_3 = 2 : 3, K_1 < K_3 = 2 : 5$
(2) $K_1 < K_2 < K_3$
(3) $K_1 : K_2 = 5 : 2, K_1 : K_3 = 3 : 5$
(4) $K_1 > K_2 > K_3$

4. Two identical electric point dipoles have dipole moments $\vec{P_1} = P\hat{i}$ and $\vec{P_2} = -P\hat{i}$ and are held on the x axis at distance 'a' from each other. When released, they move along x-axis with the direction of their dipole moments remaining unchanged. If the mass of each dipole is 'm', their speed when they are infinitely far apart is :

(1) $\dfrac{P}{a}\sqrt{\dfrac{1}{\pi\varepsilon_0 ma}}$

(2) $\dfrac{P}{a}\sqrt{\dfrac{1}{2\pi\varepsilon_0 ma}}$

(3) $\dfrac{P}{a}\sqrt{\dfrac{2}{\pi\varepsilon_0 ma}}$

(4) $\dfrac{P}{a}\sqrt{\dfrac{2}{2\pi\varepsilon_0 ma}}$

5. For a plane electromagnetic wave, the magnetic field at a point x and time t is

$$\vec{B}(x, t) = [1.2 \times 10^{-7} \sin(0.5 \times 10^3 x + 1.5 \times 10^{11} t)\hat{k}]\text{T}$$

The instantaneous electric field $\vec{E}$ corresponding to $\vec{B}$ is: (speed of light $c = 3 \times 10^8$ ms^{-1})

(1) $\vec{E}(x, t) = [-36\sin(0.5 \times 10^3 x + 1.5 \times 10^{11} t)\hat{j}]\dfrac{V}{m}$

(2) $\vec{E}(x, t) = [36\sin(1 \times 10^3 x + 0.5 \times 10^{11} t)\hat{j}]\dfrac{V}{m}$

(3) $\vec{E}(x, t) = [36\sin(0.5 \times 10^3 x + 1.5 \times 10^{11} t)\hat{k}]\dfrac{V}{m}$

(4) $\vec{E}(x, t) = [36\sin(1 \times 10^3 x + 1.5 \times 10^{11} t)\hat{i}]\dfrac{V}{m}$

6. Two planets have masses M and $16 M$ and their radii are a and $2a$, respectively. The separation between the centres of the planets is $10a$. A body of mass m is fired from the surface of the larger planet towards the smaller planet along the line joining their centres. For the body to be able to reach the surface of smaller planet, the minimum firing speed needed is :

(1) $2\sqrt{\dfrac{GM}{a}}$ (2) $4\sqrt{\dfrac{GM}{a}}$ (3) $\sqrt{\dfrac{GM^2}{ma}}$ (4) $\dfrac{3}{2}\sqrt{\dfrac{5GM}{a}}$

7. A particle moving in the xy plane experiences a velocity dependent force $\vec{F} = k(v_y\hat{i} + v_x\hat{j})$, where v_x and v_y are x and y components of its velocity $\vec{v}$. if $\vec{a}$ is the acceleration of the particle, then which of the following statements is true for the particle?

(1) quantity $\vec{v} \times \vec{a}$ is constant in time

(2) $\vec{F}$ arises due to a magnetic field

(3) kinetic energy of particle is constant in time

(4) quantity $\vec{v} \cdot \vec{a}$ is constant in time

8. Particle A of mass m_1 moving with velocity $(\sqrt{3}\hat{i}+\hat{j})$ ms^{-1} collides with another particle B of mass m_2 which is at rest initially. Let $\vec{V_1}$ and $\vec{V_2}$ be the velocities of particles A and B after collision respectively. If $m_1 = 2m_2$ and after collision $\vec{V_1}=(\hat{i}+\sqrt{3}\hat{j})$ ms^{-1}, the angle between $\vec{V_1}$ and $\vec{V_2}$ is :

(1) 15°   (2) 60°   (3) −45°   (4) 105°

9. When a car si at rest, its driver sees raindrops falling on it vertically. When driving the car with speed v, he sees that raindrops are coming at an angle 60° from the horizontal. On furter increasing the speed of the car to $(1+\beta)v$, this angle changes to 45°. The value of β is close to:

(1) 0.50   (2) 0.41   (3) 0.37   (4) 0.73

10. Given the masses of various atomic particles $m_p = 1.0072$ u, $m_n = 1.0087$ u, $m_e = 0.000548$ u, $m_{\bar{v}} = 0$, $m_d = 2.0141$ u, where p $\equiv$ proton, n $\equiv$ neutron, e $\equiv$ electron, $\bar{v} \equiv$ antineutrino and d $\equiv$ deuteron. Which of the following process is allowed by momentum and energy conservation?

(1) n + n → deuterium atom (electron bound to the nucleus)
(2) p → n + e$^+$ + $\bar{v}$
(3) n + p → d + γ
(4) e$^+$ + e$^-$ → γ

11. A circuit to verify Ohm's law uses ammeter and voltmeter in series or parallel connected correctly to the resistor. In the circuit :

(1) ammeter is always used in parallel and voltmeter is series
(2) Both ammeter and voltmeter must be connected in parallel
(3) ammeter is always connected in series and voltmeter in parallel
(4) Both, ammeter and voltmeter must be connected in series

12. Consider the force F on a charge 'q' due to a uniformly charged spherical shell of radius R carrying charge Q distributed uniformly over it. Which one of the following statements is true for F, if 'q' is placed at distance r from the centre of the shell?

(1) $F = \dfrac{1}{4\pi\varepsilon_0}\dfrac{Qq}{R^2}$ for $r < R$

(2) $\dfrac{1}{4\pi\varepsilon_0}\dfrac{Qq}{R^2} > F > 0$ for $r < R$

(3) $F = \dfrac{1}{4\pi\varepsilon_0}\dfrac{Qq}{R^2}$ for $r > R$

(4) $F = \dfrac{1}{4\pi\varepsilon_0}\dfrac{Qq}{R^2}$ for all r

13. A student measuring the diameter of a pencil of circular cross-section with the help of a vernier scale records the following four readings 5.50 mm, 5.55 mm, 5.45 mm, 5.65 mm, The average of these four reading is 5.5375 mm and the standard deviation of the data is 0.07395 mm. The average diameter of the pencil should therefore be recorded as :

(1) (5.5375 ± 0.0739) mm   (2) (5.5375 ± 0.0740) mm
(3) (5.538 ± 0.074) mm   (4) (5.54 ± 0.07) mm

14. A double convex lens has power P and same radii of curvature R of both the surfaces. The radius of curvature of a surface of a plano-convex lens made of the same material with power $1.5\,P$ is :

(1) $2R$ (2) $\dfrac{R}{2}$ (3) $\dfrac{3R}{2}$ (4) $\dfrac{R}{3}$

15. A square loop of side $2a$ and carrying current I is kept is xz plane with its centre at origin. A long wire carrying the same current I is placed parallel to z-axis and passing through point $(0, b, 0)$, $(b \gg a)$. The magnitude of torque on the loop about z-axis will be :

(1) $\dfrac{2\mu_0 I^2 a^2}{\pi b}$ (2) $\dfrac{2\mu_0 I^2 a^2 b}{\pi(a^2+b^2)}$

(3) $\dfrac{\mu_0 I^2 a^2 b}{2\pi(a^2+b^2)}$ (4) $\dfrac{\mu_0 I^2 a^2}{2\pi b}$

16. A fluid is flowing through a horizontal pipe of varying cross-section, with speed v ms^{-1} at a point where the pressure is P Pascal. At another point where pressure is $\dfrac{P}{2}$ Pascal its speed is V ms^{-1}. If the density of the fluid is ρ kg m^{-3} and the flow is streamline, then V is equal to :

(1) $\sqrt{\dfrac{P}{\rho}+v}$ (2) $\sqrt{\dfrac{2P}{\rho}+v^2}$

(3) $\sqrt{\dfrac{P}{2\rho}+v^2}$ (4) $\sqrt{\dfrac{P}{\rho}+v^2}$

17. When a particle of mass m is attached to a vertical spring of spring constant k and released, its motion is described by $y(t) = y_0\sin^2\omega t$, where 'y' is measured from the lower end of unstretched spring. Then ω is :

(1) $\dfrac{1}{2}\sqrt{\dfrac{g}{y_0}}$ (2) $\sqrt{\dfrac{g}{y_0}}$ (3) $\sqrt{\dfrac{g}{2y_0}}$ (4) $\sqrt{\dfrac{2g}{y_0}}$

18. In a dilute gas at pressure P and temperature T, the mean time between successive collisions of a molecule varies with T is :

(1) T (2) $\dfrac{1}{\sqrt{T}}$ (3) $\dfrac{1}{T}$ (4) $\sqrt{T}$

19. Assuming the nitrogen molecule is moving with r.m.s.velocity at 400 K, the de-Broglie wavelength of nitrongen molecule is close to :

(Given : nitrogen molecule weight : 4.64×10^{-26} kg, Boltzman constant : 1.38×10^{-23} J/K, Planck constant : 6.63×10^{-34} J.s)

(1) 0.24 Å   (2) 0.20 Å
(3) 0.34 Å   (4) 0.44 Å

20. The linear mass density of a thin rod AB of length L varies from A to B as $\lambda(x) = \lambda_0\left(1+\dfrac{x}{L}\right)$, where x is the distance from A. If M is the mass of the rod then its moment of inertia about an axis passing through A and perpendicular to the rod is :

(1) $\frac{5}{12}ML^2$ (2) $\frac{7}{18}ML^2$

(3) $\frac{2}{5}ML^2$ (4) $\frac{3}{7}ML^2$

21. The output characteristics of a transistor is shown in the figure. When V_{CE} is 10 V and $I_C = 4.0$ mA, then value of β_{ac} is ______.

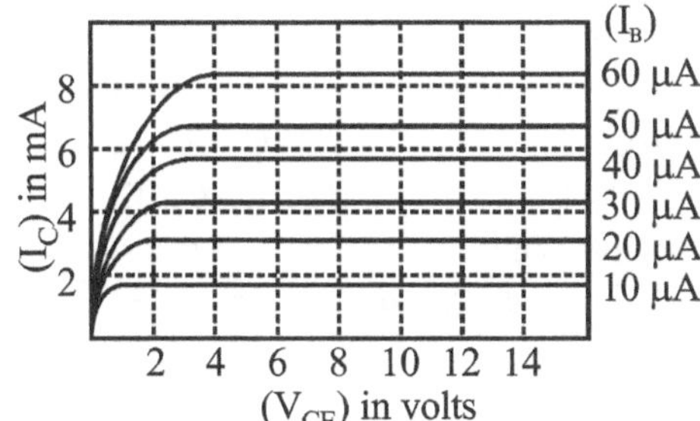

22. The centre of mass of a solid hemisphere of radius 8 cm is x cm from the centre of the flat surface. Then value of x is ______.

23. An engine operates by taking a monatomic ideal gas through the cycle shown in the figure. The percentage efficiency of the engine is close is ______.

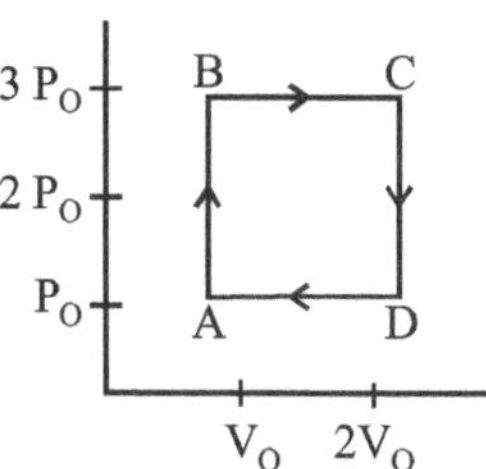

24. A young's double-slit experiment is performed using monocromatic light of wavelength λ. The inntensity of light at a point on the screen, where the path difference is λ, is K units. The intensity of light at a point where the path difference is $\frac{\lambda}{6}$ is given by $\frac{nK}{12}$, where n is an integer. The value of n is ______.

25. In a series LR circuit, power of 400 W is dissipated from a source of 250 V, 50 Hz. The power factor of the circuit is 0.8. In order to bring the power factor to unity, a capacitor of value C is added in series to the L and R. Taking the value C as $\left(\frac{n}{3\pi}\right)\mu F$, then value of n is ______.

CHEMISTRY

26. For a reaction, $4M(s) + nO_2(g) \rightarrow 2M_2O_n(s)$, the free energy change is plotted as a function of temperature. The temperature below which the oxide is stable could be inferred from the plot as the point at which :
  (1) the slope change from negative to positive
  (2) the free energy change shows a change from negative to positive value
  (3) the slop changes from positive to negative
  (4) the slop changes from positive to zero

27. The average molar mass of chlorine is 35.5 g mol⁻¹. The ratio of ^{35}Cl to ^{37}Cl in naturally occrring chlorine is close to :
  (1) 4 : 1 (2) 3 : 1 (3) 2 : 1 (4) 1 : 1

28. Which one of the following statements is not true?
  (1) Lactose contains α-glycosidic linkage between C_1 of galactose and C_4 of glucose.
  (2) Lactose is a reducing sugar and it gives Fehling's test.
  (3) Lactose ($C_{11}H_{22}O_{11}$) is a disaccharide and it contains 8 hydroxyl groups.
  (4) On acid hydrolysis, lactose gives one molecule of D(+)-glucose and one molecule of D(+)-galactose

29. The value of Kc is 64 at 800 K for the reaction
  $N_2(g) + 3H_2(g) \rightleftharpoons 2NH_3(g)$. The value of K_c for the following reaction is :
  $$NH_3(g) \rightleftharpoons \frac{1}{2}N_2(g) + \frac{3}{2}H_2(g)$$
  (1) 1/64 (2) 8 (3) 1/4 (4) 1/8

30. Dihydrogen of high purity (> 99.95%) is obtained through:
  (1) the reaction of Zn with dilute HCl.
  (2) the electrolysis of acidified water using Pt electrodes.
  (3) the electrolysis of bringe solution.
  (4) the electrolysis of warm $Ba(OH)_2$ solution using Ni electrodes.

31. The reaction of NO with N_2O_4 at 250 K gives :
  (1) N_2O (2) NO_2 (3) N_2O_3 (4) N_2O_5

32. The correct match between Item - I (starting material) and Item - II (reagent) for the preparation of benzaldehyde is :

Item - I	Item - II
(I) Benzene	(P) HCl and $SnCl_2$, H_3O^+
(II) Benzonitrile	(Q) H_2, Pd-$BaSO_4$, S and quinoline
(III) Benzoyl Chloride	(R) CO, HCl and $AlCl_3$

  (1) (I) - (Q), (II) - (R) and (III) - (P)
  (2) (I) - (P), (II) - (Q) and (III) - (R)
  (3) (I) - (R), (II) - (P) and (III) - (Q)
  (4) (I) - (R), (II) - (Q) and (III) - (P)

33. A crystal is made up of metal ions 'M₁' and 'M₂' and oxide ions. Oxide ions. form a *ccp* lattice structure. The cation 'M₁' occpies 50% of octahedral voids and the cation 'M₂' occupies 12.5% of tetrahedral voids of oxide lattice. The oxidation numbers of 'M₁' and 'M₂' are, respectively :
  (1) +2, +4 (2) +1, +3 (3) +3, +1 (4) +4, +2

34. The element that can be refined by distillation is :
  (1) nickel (2) zinc (3) tin (4) gallium

35. For a d^4 metal ion in an octahedral field, the correct electronic configuration is :

(1) $t_{2g}^3 e_g^1$ when $\Delta_0 < P$ (2) $t_{2g}^3 e_g^1$ when $\Delta_0 > P$

(3) $t_{2g}^4 e_g^0$ when $\Delta_0 < P$ (4) $e_g^2 t_{2g}^2$ when $\Delta_0 < P$

36. Match the following :

Column-I	Column-II
Test / Method	**Reagent**
(i) Lucas Test	(A) $C_6H_5SO_2Cl$ / aq. KOH
(ii) Dumans method	(B) HNO_3 / $AgNO_3$
(iii) Kjeldahl's method	(C) CuO / CO_2
(iv) Hinsberg Test	(D) Conc. HCl and $ZnCl_2$
	(E) H_2SO_4

(1) (I)-(D), (II)-(C), (III)-(B), (IV)-(A)

(2) (I)-(B), (II)-(D), (III)-(E), (IV)-(A)

(3) (I)-(D), (II)-(C), (III)-(E), (IV)-(A)

(4) (I)-(B), (II)-(A), (III)-(C), (IV)-(D)

37. Match the following compounds (Column-I) with their uses (Column-II) :

Column-I	Column-II
(I) $Ca(OH)_2$	(A) casts of statutes
(II) NaCl	(B) white wash
(III) $CaSO_4 \cdot \frac{1}{2} H_2O$	(C) antacid
(IV) $CaCO_3$	(D) washing soda preparation

(1) (I)-(D), (II)-(A), (III)-(C), (IV)-(B)

(2) (I)-(B), (II)-(D), (III)-(A), (IV)-(C)

(3) (I)-(B), (II)-(C), (III)-(D), (IV)-(A)

(4) (I)-(C), (II)-(D), (III)-(B), (IV)-(A)

38. The IUPAC name of the following compound is:

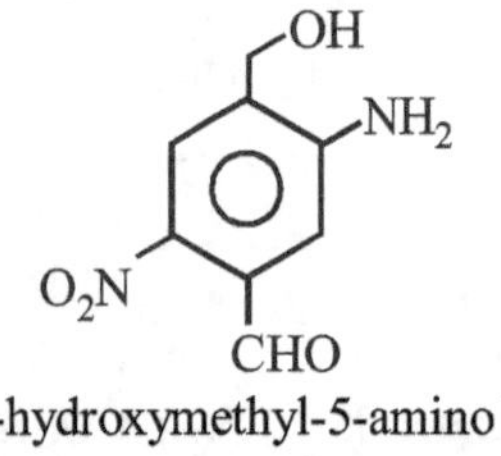

(1) 2-nitro-4-hydroxymethyl-5-amino benzaldehyde

(2) 3-amino-4-hydroxymethyl-5-nitrobenzaldehyde

(3) 5-amino-4-hydroxymethyl-2-nitrobenzaldehyde

(4) 4-amino-2-formyl-5-hydroxymethyl nitrobenzene

39. Which of the following compounds can be prepared in good yield by Gabriel phthalimide synthesis?

(1) 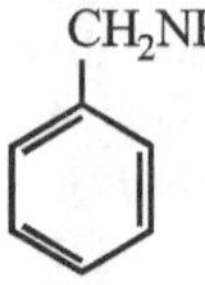 [structure: benzene ring with CH_2NH_2]

(2) $CH_3 - CH_2 - NHCH_3$

(3) 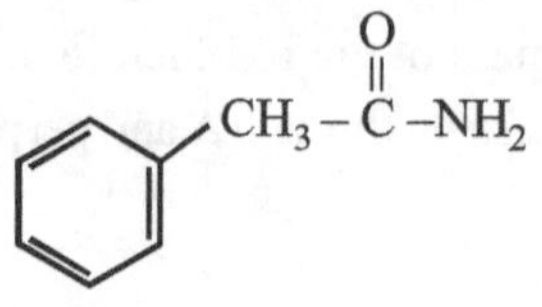 [structure: benzene ring with $CH_3 - \overset{\overset{O}{\|}}{C} - NH_2$]

(4) 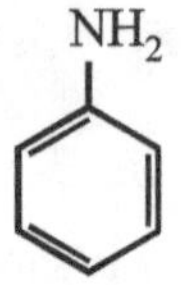 [structure: benzene ring with NH_2]

40. A set of solutions is prepared using 180g of water as a solvent and 10g of different non-volatile solutes A, B and C. The relative lowering of vapour pressure in the presence of these solutes are in the order [Given, molar mass of $A = 100\,g\,mol^{-1}$; $B = 200\,g\,mol^{-1}$; $C = 10{,}000\,g\,mol^{-1}$]

(1) $B > C > A$ (2) $C > B > A$

(3) $A > B > C$ (4) $A > C > B$

41. For the given cell;

$Cu(s)|Cu^{2+}(C_1 M)\|Cu^{2+}(C_2 M)|Cu(s)$

change in Gibbs energy (ΔG) is negative, if :

(1) $C_1 = C_2$ (2) $C_2 = \dfrac{C_1}{\sqrt{2}}$

(3) $C_1 = 2C_2$ (4) $C_2 = \sqrt{2}\,C_1$

42. Reaction of an inorganic sulphite X with dilute H_2SO_4 generates compound Y. Reaction of Y with NaOH gives X. Further, the reaction of X with Y and water affords compound Z. Y and Z, respectively, are:

(1) SO_2 and Na_2SO_3 (2) SO_3 and $NaHSO_3$

(3) SO_2 and $NaHSO_3$ (4) S and Na_2SO_3

43. The increasing order of the boiling point of the major products A, B and C of the following reactions will be:

(a) 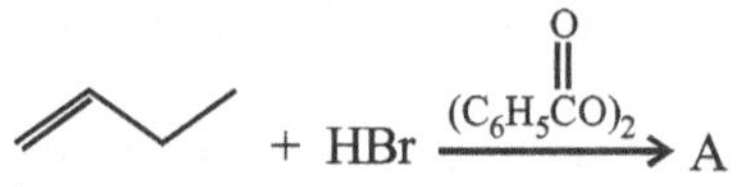 [alkene] $+ HBr \xrightarrow{(C_6H_5CO)_2} A$

(b) 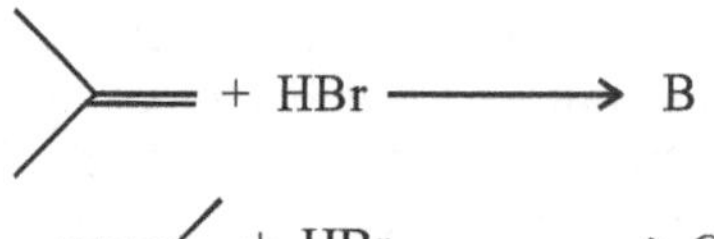 [alkene] $+ HBr \longrightarrow B$

(c) [alkene] $+ HBr \longrightarrow C$

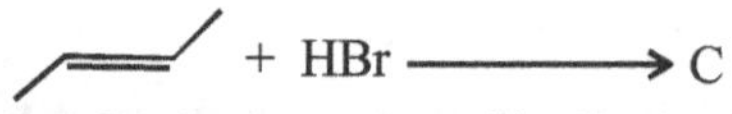

(1) $B < C < A$ (2) $C < A < B$

(3) $A < B < C$ (4) $A < C < B$

44. Mischmetal is an alloy consisting mainly of:

(1) lanthanoid metals

(2) actinoid and transition metals

(3) lanthanoid and actinoid metals

(4) actinoid metals

45. The correct match between Item-I and Item - II is:

Item - I	Item - II
(a) Natural rubber	(I) 1, 3-butadiene + styrene
(b) Neoprene	(II) 1, 3-butadiene + acrylonitrile
(c) Buna-N	(III) Chloroprene
(d) Buna-S	(IV) Isoprene

(1) (A) - (III), (B) - (IV), (C) - (I), (D) - (II)
(2) (A) - (III), (B) - (IV), (C) - (II), (D) - (I)
(3) (A) - (IV), (B) - (III), (C) - (II), (D) - (I)
(4) (A) - (IV), (B) - (III), (C) - (I), (D) - (II)

46. If the solubility product of AB_2 is $3.20 \times 10^{-11} M^3$, then the solubility of AB_2 in pure water is ______ $\times 10^{-4}$ mol L^{-1}. [Assuming that neither kind of ion reacts with water]

47. For Freundlich adsorption isotherm, a plot of log (x/m) (y-axis) and log p (x - axis) gives a straight line. The intercept and slope for the line is 0.4771 and 2, respectively. The mass of gas, adsorbed per gram of adsorbent if the initial pressure is 0.04 atm, is ______ $\times 10^{-4}$g. (log 3 = 0.4771)

48. A solution of phenol in chloroform when treated with aqueous NaOH gives compound P as a major product. The mass percentage of carbon in P is ______ . (to the nearest integer) (Atomic mass: C = 12; H = 1; O = 16)

49. The atomic number of Unnilunium is ______ .

50. The rate of a reaction decreased by 3.555 times when the temperature was changed from 40°C to 30°C. The activation energy (in kJ mol^{-1}) of the reaction is ______. Take; R = 8.314 J mol^{-1} K^{-1} In 3.555 = 1.268

MATHEMATICS

51. The integral $\int_1^2 e^x \cdot x^x (2 + \log_e x)\, dx$ equals:

(1) $e(4e+1)$
(2) $4e^2 - 1$
(3) $e(4e-1)$
(4) $e(2e-1)$

52. The area (in sq. units) of the region enclosed by the curves $y = x^2 - 1$ and $y = 1 - x^2$ is equal to:

(1) $\dfrac{4}{3}$
(2) $\dfrac{8}{3}$
(3) $\dfrac{7}{2}$
(4) $\dfrac{16}{3}$

53. The angle of elevation of the summit of a mountain from a point on the ground is 45°. After climbing up on km towards the summit at an inclination of 30° from the ground, the angle of elevation of the summit is found to be 60°. Then the height (in km) of the summit from the ground is:

(1) $\dfrac{\sqrt{3}-1}{\sqrt{3}+1}$
(2) $\dfrac{\sqrt{3}+1}{\sqrt{3}-1}$
(3) $\dfrac{1}{\sqrt{3}-1}$
(4) $\dfrac{1}{\sqrt{3}+1}$

54. The set of all real values of λ for which the function

$$f(x) = (1 - \cos^2 x) \cdot (\lambda + \sin x), \quad x \in \left(-\frac{\pi}{2}, \frac{\pi}{2}\right), \text{ has exactly}$$

one maxima and exactly minima, is:

(1) $\left(-\dfrac{1}{2}, \dfrac{1}{2}\right) - \{0\}$
(2) $\left(-\dfrac{3}{2}, \dfrac{3}{2}\right)$
(3) $\left(-\dfrac{1}{2}, \dfrac{1}{2}\right)$
(4) $\left(-\dfrac{3}{2}, \dfrac{3}{2}\right) - \{0\}$

55. If α and β are the roots of the equation $2x(2x + 1) = 1$, then β is equal to:

(1) $2\alpha(\alpha + 1)$
(2) $-2\alpha(\alpha + 1)$
(3) $2\alpha(\alpha - 1)$
(4) $2\alpha^2$

56. For all twice differentiable functios $f : R \to R$, with $f(0) = f(1) = f'(0) = 0$

(1) $f''(x) \neq 0$ at every point $x \in (0,1)$
(2) $f''(x) = 0$, for some $x \in (0,1)$
(3) $f''(0) = 0$
(4) $f''(x) = 0$, at every point $x \in (0,1)$

57. If $y = \left(\dfrac{2}{\pi} x - 1\right) \operatorname{cosec} x$ is the solution of the differential equation, $\dfrac{dy}{dx} + p(x)y = \dfrac{2}{\pi} \operatorname{cosec} x, 0 < x < \dfrac{\pi}{2}$, then the function $p(x)$ is equal to:

(1) $\cot x$
(2) $\operatorname{cosec} x$
(3) $\sec x$
(4) $\tan x$

58. Let L denote the line in the xy-plane with x and y intercepts as 3 and 1 respectively. Then the image of the point $(-1, -4)$ in this line is:

(1) $\left(\dfrac{11}{5}, \dfrac{28}{5}\right)$
(2) $\left(\dfrac{29}{5}, \dfrac{8}{5}\right)$
(3) $\left(\dfrac{8}{5}, \dfrac{29}{5}\right)$
(4) $\left(\dfrac{29}{5}, \dfrac{11}{5}\right)$

59. If the tangent to the curve, $y = f(x) = x\log_e x$, $(x > 0)$ at a point $(c, f(c))$ is parallel to the line segement joining the points $(1, 0)$ and (e, e), then c is equal to:

(1) $\dfrac{e-1}{e}$
(2) $e^{\left(\frac{1}{e-1}\right)}$
(3) $e^{\left(\frac{1}{1-e}\right)}$
(4) $\dfrac{e}{e-1}$

60. Let $f : R \to R$ be a function defined by $f(x) = \max\{x, x^2\}$. Let S denote the set of all points in R, where f is not differentiable. Then:

(1) $\{0, 1\}$
(2) $\{0\}$
(3) ϕ (an empty set)
(4) $\{1\}$

61. Let $\theta = \dfrac{\pi}{5}$ and $A = \begin{bmatrix} \cos\theta & \sin\theta \\ -\sin\theta & \cos\theta \end{bmatrix}$. If $B = A + A^4$, then det (B):

(1) is one
(2) lies in (2, 3)
(3) is zero
(4) lies in (1, 2)

62. A plane P meets the coordinate axes at A, B and C respectively. The centroid of $\triangle ABC$ is given to be $(1,1,2)$. Then the equation of the line through this centroid and perpendicular to the plane P is:

(1) $\dfrac{x-1}{2} = \dfrac{y-1}{1} = \dfrac{z-2}{1}$
(2) $\dfrac{x-1}{1} = \dfrac{y-1}{1} = \dfrac{z-2}{2}$
(3) $\dfrac{x-1}{2} = \dfrac{y-1}{2} = \dfrac{z-2}{1}$
(4) $\dfrac{x-1}{1} = \dfrac{y-1}{2} = \dfrac{z-2}{2}$

63. The common difference of the A.P. $b_1, b_2, ..., b_m$ is 2 more than the common difference of A.P. $a_1, a_2, ..., a_n$. If $a_{40} = -159$, $a_{100} = -399$ and $b_{100} = a_{70}$, then b_1 is equal to:

(1) 81 (2) -127 (3) -81 (4) 127

64. If the normal at an end of a latus rectum of an ellipse passes through an extermity of the minor axis, then the eccentricity e of the ellipse satisfies:

(1) $e^4 + 2e^2 - 1 = 0$ (2) $e^2 + e - 1 = 0$
(3) $e^4 + e^2 - 1 = 0$ (4) $e^2 + 2e - 1 = 0$

65. For a suitably chosen real constant a, let a function, $f : R - \{-a\} \to R$ be defined by $f(x) = \dfrac{a-x}{a+x}$. Further suppose that for any real number $x \neq -a$ and $f(x) \neq -a$, $(fof)(x) = x$. Then $f\left(-\dfrac{1}{2}\right)$ is equal to:

(1) $\dfrac{1}{3}$ (2) $-\dfrac{1}{3}$ (3) -3 (4) 3

66. If the constant term in the binomial expansion of $\left(\sqrt{x} - \dfrac{k}{x^2}\right)^{10}$ is 405, then $|k|$ equals:

(1) 9 (2) 1 (3) 3 (4) 2

67. The centre of the circle passing through the point $(0, 1)$ and touching the parabola $y = x^2$ at the point $(2,4)$ is:

(1) $\left(\dfrac{-53}{10}, \dfrac{16}{5}\right)$ (2) $\left(\dfrac{6}{5}, \dfrac{53}{10}\right)$

(3) $\left(\dfrac{3}{10}, \dfrac{16}{5}\right)$ (4) $\left(\dfrac{-16}{5}, \dfrac{53}{10}\right)$

68. Let $z = x + iy$ be a non-zero complex number such that $z^2 = i|z|^2$, where $i = \sqrt{-1}$, then z lies on the:

(1) line, $y = -x$ (2) imaginary axis
(3) line, $y = x$ (4) real axis

69. Consider the statement: "For an integer n, if $n^3 - 1$ is even, then n is odd." The contrapositive statement of this statement is:

(1) For an integer n, if n is even, then $n^3 - 1$ is odd.
(2) For an intetger n, if $n^3 - 1$ is not even, then n is not odd.
(3) For an integer n, if n is even, then $n^3 - 1$ is even.
(4) For an integer n, if n is odd, then $n^3 - 1$ is even.

70. The probabilities of three events A, B and C are given by $P(A) = 0.6$, $P(B) = 0.4$ and $P(C) = 0.5$. If $P(A \cup B) = 0.8$, $P(A \cap C) = 0.3$, $P(A \cap B \cap C) = 0.2$, $P(B \cap C) = \beta$ and $P(A \cup B \cup C) = \alpha$, where $0.85 \leq \alpha \leq 0.95$, then β lies in the interval:

(1) $[0.35, 0.36]$ (2) $[0.25, 0.35]$
(3) $[0.20, 0.25]$ (4) $[0.36, 0.40]$

71. Suppose that a function $f : R \to R$ satisfies $f(x+y) = f(x)f(y)$ for all $x, y \in R$ and $f(1) = 3$. If $\sum_{i=1}^{n} f(i) = 363$, then n is equal to ______.

72. The sum of distinct values of λ for whcih the system of equations
$(\lambda - 1)x + (3\lambda + 1)y + 2\lambda z = 0$
$(\lambda - 1)x + (4\lambda - 2)y + (\lambda + 3)z = 0$
$2x + (3\lambda + 1)y + 3(\lambda - 1)z = 0,$
has non-zero solutions, is ______.

73. If $\vec{x}$ and $\vec{y}$ be two non-zero vectors such that $|\vec{x} + \vec{y}| = |\vec{x}|$ and $2\vec{x} + \lambda \vec{y}$ is perpendicular to $\vec{y}$, then the value of λ is ______.

74. Consider the data on x taking the values 0, 2, 4, 8, ..., 2^n with frequencies $^nC_0, {}^nC_1, {}^nC_2, ..., {}^nC_n$ respectively. If the mean of this data is $\dfrac{728}{2^n}$, then n is equal to ______.

75. The number of words (with or without meaning) that can be formed from all the letters of the word "LETTER" in which vowels never come together is ______.

JEE Main 2020 (2-09-2020) Morning Shift

PHYSICS

1. **(2)** From the given expression,

$V_m = 5\,(1 + 0.6\cos 6280t)\sin(211 \times 10^4 t)$

Modulation index, $\mu = 0.6$

$\because A_m = \mu A_c$

$$\frac{A_{max} + A_{min}}{2} = A_c = 5 \qquad \text{...(i)}$$

$$\frac{A_{max} - A_{min}}{2} = A_m = 3 \qquad \text{...(ii)}$$

From equation (i) + (ii),

Maximum amplitude, $A_{max} = 8$.

From equation (i) − (ii),

Minimum amplitude $A_{min} = 2$.

2. **(4)** Permanent magnets (P) are made of materials with large retentivity and large coercivity. Transformer cores (T) are made of materials with low retentivity and low coercivity.

3. **(4)** Object is placed beyond radius of curvature (R) of concave mirror hence image formed is real, inverted and diminished or unmagnified.

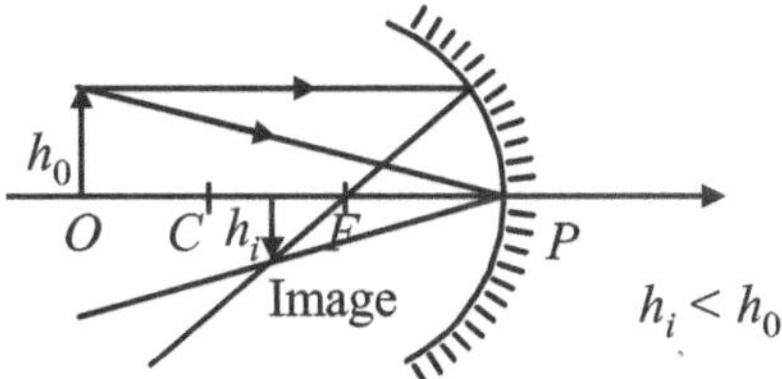

4. **(3)** L.C. of vernier callipers = 1 MSD − 1 VSD

$$= \left(1 - \frac{9}{10}\right) \times 1 = 0.1 \text{ mm} = 0.01 \text{ cm}$$

Here 7th division of vernier scale coincides with a division of main scale and the zero of vernier scale is lying right side of the zero of main scale.

Zero error = $7 \times 0.1 = 0.7$ mm = 0.07 cm.

Length of the cylinder = measured value − zero error

$= (3.1 + 4 \times 0.01) - 0.07 = 3.07$ cm.

5. **(1)** $y = 4Cx^2 \Rightarrow \dfrac{dy}{dx} = \tan\theta = 8Cx$

At P, $\tan\theta = 8Ca$

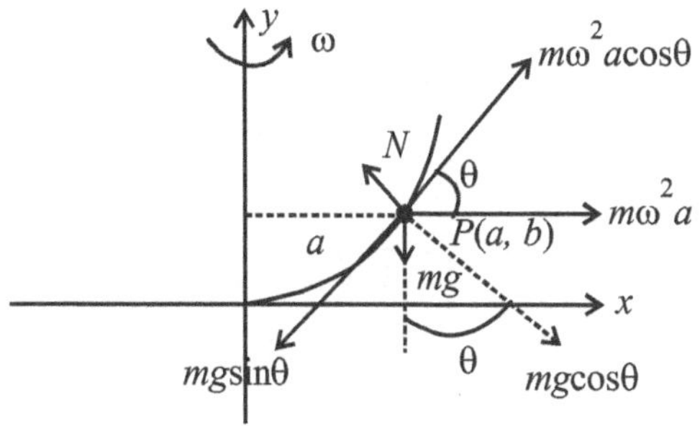

For steady circular motion

$m\omega^2 a\cos\theta = mg\sin\theta$

$$\Rightarrow \omega = \sqrt{\frac{g\tan\theta}{a}}$$

$$\therefore \omega = \sqrt{\frac{g \times 8aC}{a}} = 2\sqrt{2gC}$$

6. **(3)** From conservation of linear momentum

$mu\hat{i} + 0 = mv\hat{j} + 3m\vec{v'}$

$$\vec{v'} = \frac{u}{3}\hat{i} - \frac{v}{3}\hat{j}$$

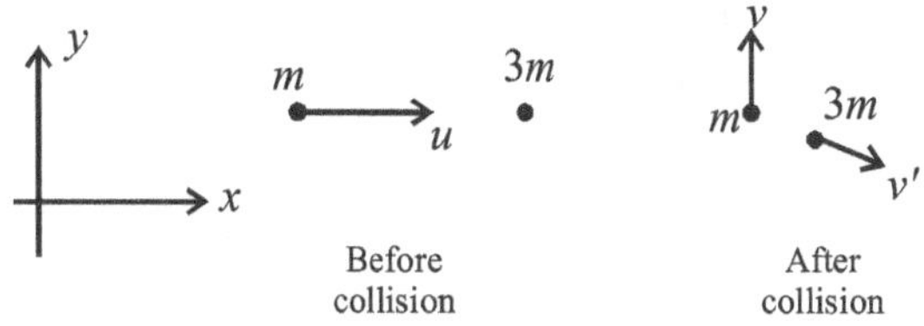

From kinetic energy conservation,

$$\frac{1}{2}mu^2 = \frac{1}{2}mv^2 + \frac{1}{2}(3m)\left(\left(\frac{u}{3}\right)^2 + \left(\frac{v}{3}\right)^2\right)$$

or, $mu^2 = mv^2 + \dfrac{mu^2}{3} + \dfrac{mv^2}{3}$

$$\therefore v = \frac{u}{\sqrt{2}}$$

7. **(2)** $\rho_M = 98 \times 10^{-8}$

$\rho_A = 2.65 \times 10^{-8}$

$\rho_C = 1.724 \times 10^{-8}$

$\rho_T = 5.65 \times 10^{-8}$

$\therefore \rho_M > \rho_T > \rho_A > \rho_C$

8. **(1)** Using $f = \dfrac{1}{2\ell}\sqrt{\dfrac{T}{\mu}}$,

where, $T =$ tension and $\mu = \dfrac{\text{mass}}{\text{length}}$

$f_x = \dfrac{1}{2\ell}\sqrt{\dfrac{T_x}{\mu}}$ and $f_z = \dfrac{1}{2\ell}\sqrt{\dfrac{T_z}{\mu}}$

$\dfrac{f_x}{f_z} = \dfrac{450}{300} = \sqrt{\dfrac{T_x}{T_z}}$

$\therefore \dfrac{T_x}{T_z} = \dfrac{9}{4} = 2.25.$

9. **(1)** Total energy of the gas mixture,

$E_{\text{mix}} = \dfrac{f_1 n_1 R T_1}{2} + \dfrac{f_2 n_2 R T_2}{2}$

$= 3 \times \dfrac{5}{2} RT + \dfrac{5}{2} \times 3RT = 15RT$

10. **(1)** According to question, train A and B are running on parallel tracks in the opposite direction.

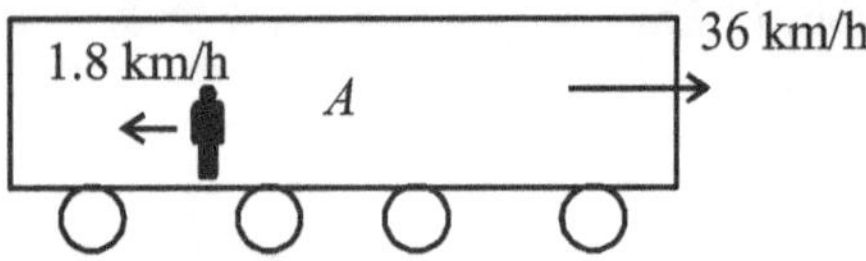

$V_A = 36$ km/h $= 10$ m/s

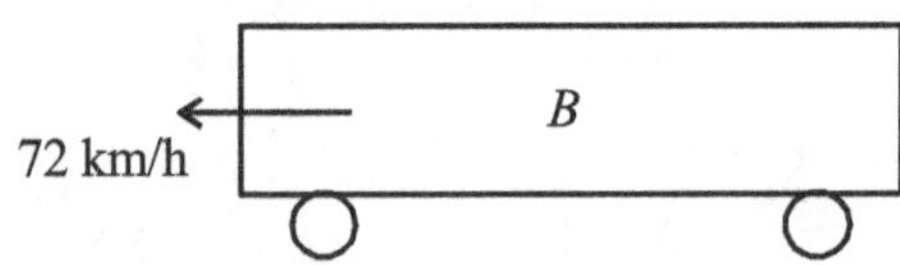

$V_B = -72$ km/h $= -20$ m/s

$V_{MA} = -1.8$ km/h $= -0.5$ m/s

$V_{\text{man}, B} = V_{\text{man}, A} + V_{A, B}$

$\qquad = V_{\text{man}, A} + V_A - V_B = -0.5 + 10 - (-20)$

$\qquad = -0.5 + 30 = 29.5$ m/s.

11. **(4)** Pitch $= (v \cos \theta) T$ and $T = \dfrac{2\pi m}{qB}$

$\therefore$ Pitch $= (V \cos \theta) \dfrac{2\pi m}{qB}$

$= (4 \times 10^5 \cos 60°) \dfrac{2\pi}{0.3} \left(\dfrac{1.67 \times 10^{-27}}{1.69 \times 10^{-19}} \right) = 4$ cm

12. **(4)** Net torque, τ_{net} about B is zero at equilibrium

$\therefore T_A \times 100 - mg \times 50 - 2mg \times 25 = 0$

$\Rightarrow T_A \times 100 = 100mg$

$\Rightarrow T_A = 1mg$ (Tension in the string at A)

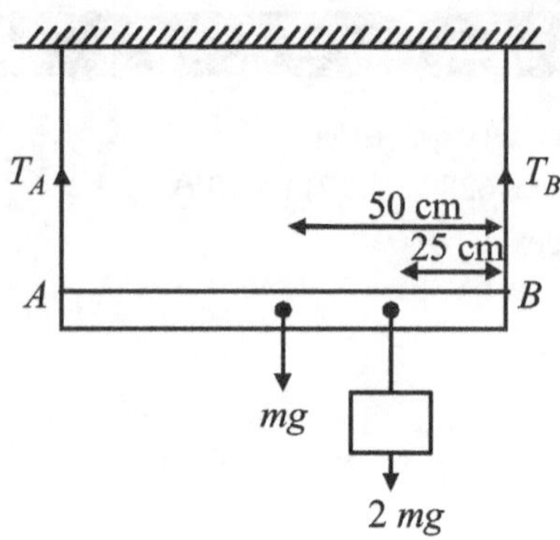

13. **(2)** Energy density $= \dfrac{1}{2} \dfrac{B^2}{\mu_0}$

$\Rightarrow B = \sqrt{2 \times \mu_0 \times \text{Energy density}}$

$\mu_0 = \dfrac{1}{C^2 \varepsilon_0} = 4\pi \times 10^{-7}$

$\therefore B = \sqrt{2 \times 4\pi \times 10^{-7} \times 1.02 \times 10^{-8}} = 160 \times 10^{-9}$

$\qquad = 160$ nT

14. **(3)** Here, $\rho \, dr \omega^2 r = \rho g \, dh$

$\Rightarrow \omega^2 \displaystyle\int_0^R r \, dr = g \displaystyle\int_0^h dh$

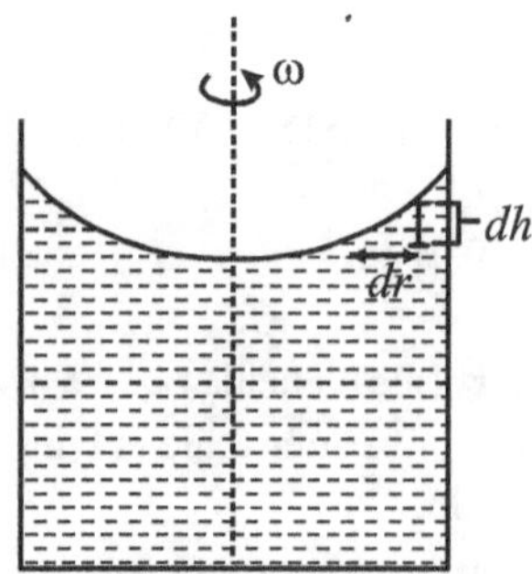

$\Rightarrow \dfrac{\omega^2 R^2}{2} = gh$ (Given $R = 5$ cm)

$\therefore h = \dfrac{\omega^2 R^2}{2g} = \dfrac{25\omega^2}{2g}$

15. (2) Power output of the reactor,

$$P = \frac{\text{energy}}{\text{time}}$$

$$= \frac{2}{235} \times \frac{6.023 \times 10^{26} \times 200 \times 1.6 \times 10^{-19}}{30 \times 24 \times 60 \times 60} \simeq 60\,\text{MW}$$

16. (4) Young's modulus, $Y = \dfrac{\text{stress}}{\text{strain}}$

$$\Rightarrow Y = \frac{F}{A} \bigg/ \frac{\Delta\ell}{\ell_0} = FA^{-1}V^0$$

17. (1)

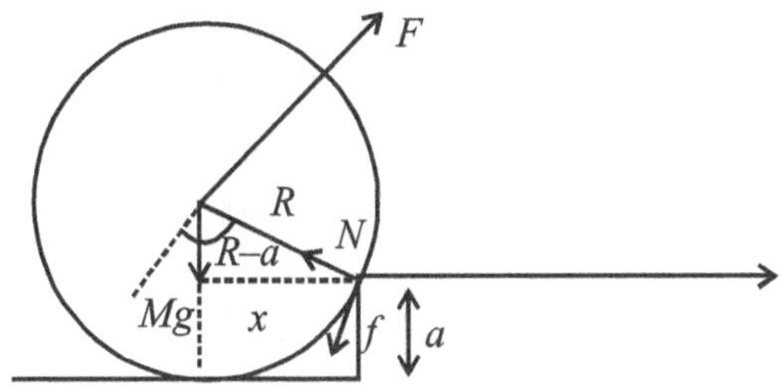

For step up, $F \times R \geq Mg \times x$

$x = \sqrt{R^2 - (R-a)^2}$ from figure

$$F_{\min} = \frac{Mg}{R} \times \sqrt{R^2 - (R-a)^2} = Mg\sqrt{1 - \left(\frac{R-a}{R}\right)^2}$$

18. (1) Path difference, $\Delta P = d\sin\theta = d\theta$
d = distance between slits = 1 mm = 10^{-3} mm
D = distance between the slits and screen = 100 cm = 1 m
y = distance between central bright fringe and observed fringe = 1.27 mm

$$\therefore \Delta P = \frac{dy}{D} = \frac{10^{-3} \times 1.270\,\text{mm}}{1\,\text{m}} = 1.27\,\mu\text{m}$$

19. (1) According to question, mass density of a spherical galaxy varies as $\dfrac{k}{r}$.

Mass, $M = \int \rho\, dV$

$$\Rightarrow M = \int_0^{r=R_0} \frac{k}{r} 4\pi r^2\, dr$$

$$\Rightarrow M = 4\pi k \int_0^{R_0} r\, dr$$

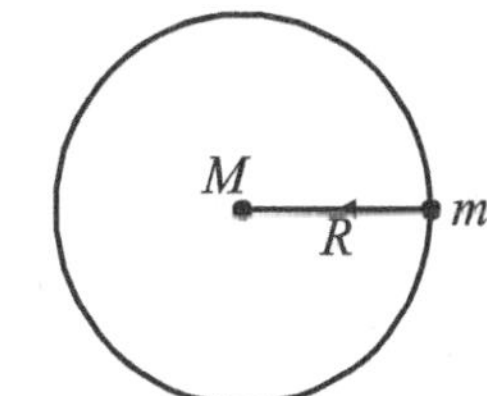

$$\text{or, } M = \frac{4\pi k R_0^2}{2} = 2\pi k R^2$$

$$F_G = \frac{GMm}{R_0^2} = m\omega_0^2 R \ (= F_C)$$

$$\Rightarrow \frac{G\dfrac{4\pi k R^2}{2}}{R^2} = \omega_0^2 R \Rightarrow \omega_0 = \sqrt{\frac{2\pi KG}{R}} \quad \left(\because \omega = \frac{2\pi}{T}\right)$$

$$\therefore T = \frac{2\pi}{\omega_0} = \frac{2\pi\sqrt{R}}{\sqrt{2\pi KG}} = \sqrt{\frac{2\pi R}{KG}} \Rightarrow T^2 = \frac{2\pi R}{KG}$$

$\because 2\pi$, K and G are constants

$\therefore T^2 \propto R.$

20. (2) $F_x = 0$, $a_x = 0$, $(v)_x = $ constant

Time taken to reach at $'P' = \dfrac{d}{v_0} = t_0$ (let) ...(i)

$(\text{Along} - y)$, $y_0 = 0 + \dfrac{1}{2} \cdot \dfrac{qE}{m} \cdot t_0^2$ ...(ii)

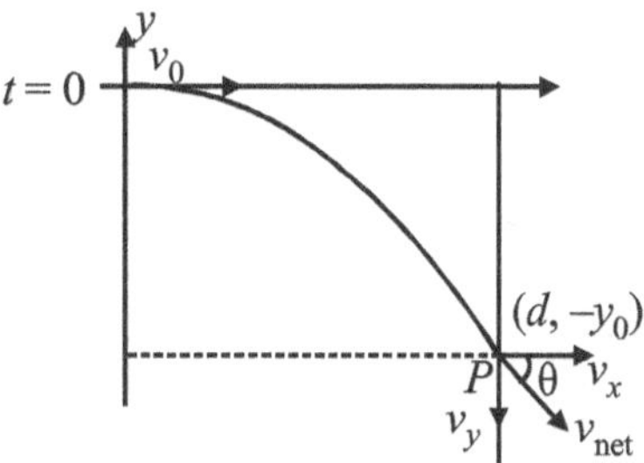

$$\tan\theta = \frac{v_y}{v_x} = \frac{qEt_0}{m \cdot v_0}, \left(t = \frac{d}{v_0}\right)$$

$$\tan\theta = \frac{qEd}{m \cdot v_0^2}, \ \text{Slope} = \frac{-qEd}{mv_0^2}$$

No electric field $\Rightarrow F_{\text{net}} = 0$, $\vec{v} = $ const.

$$y = mx + c, \left\{\begin{array}{l} m = \dfrac{qEd}{mv_0^2} \\ (d, -y_0) \end{array}\right.$$

$$-y_0 = \frac{-qEd}{mv_0^2}, d + c \Rightarrow c = -y_0 + \frac{qEd^2}{mv_0^2}$$

$$y = \frac{-qEd}{mv_0^2} x - y_0 + \frac{qEd^2}{mv_0^2}$$

$$y_0 = \frac{1}{2} \cdot \frac{qE}{m}\left(\frac{d}{v_0}\right)^2 = \frac{1}{2}\frac{qEd^2}{mv_0^2}$$

$$y = \frac{-qEdx}{mv_0^2} - \frac{1}{2}\frac{qEd^2}{mv_0^2} + \frac{qEd^2}{mv_0^2}$$

$$y = \frac{-qEd}{mv_0^2} + \frac{1}{2}\frac{qEd^2}{mv_0^2} \Rightarrow y = \frac{qEd}{mv_0^2}\left(\frac{d}{2} - x\right)$$

21. (15)

Here, $B = 3.0 \times 10^{-5}\,\text{T}$, $R = 10\,\text{cm} = 0.1\,\text{m}$

$$\omega = \frac{2\pi}{2T} = \frac{\pi}{0.2}$$

Flux as a function of time $\phi = \vec{B}\cdot\vec{A} = AB\cos(\omega t)$

Emf induced, $e = \dfrac{-d\phi}{dt} = AB\omega\sin(\omega t)$

Max. value of Emf $= AB\omega = \pi R^2 B\omega$

$$= 3.14 \times 0.1 \times 0.1 \times 3 \times 10^{-5} \times \frac{\pi}{0.2}$$

$$= 15 \times 10^{-6}\,\text{V} = 15\,\mu\text{V}$$

22. (46)

For adiabatic process, $TV^{\gamma-1} = \text{constant}$

or, $T_1 V_1^{\gamma-1} = T_2 V_2^{\gamma-1}$

$T_1 = 20°\text{C} + 273 = 293\,\text{K}$, $V_2 = \dfrac{V_1}{10}$ and $\gamma = \dfrac{7}{5}$

$$T_1(V_1)^{\gamma-1} = T_2\left(\frac{V_1}{10}\right)^{\gamma-1}$$

$$\Rightarrow 293 = T_2\left(\frac{1}{10}\right)^{2/5} \Rightarrow T_2 = 293(10)^{2/5} \simeq 736\,\text{K}$$

$\Delta T = 736 - 293 = 443\,\text{K}$

During the process, change in internal energy

$$\Delta U = NC_V\Delta T = 5 \times \frac{5}{2} \times 8.3 \times 443 \simeq 46 \times 10^3\,\text{J} = X\,\text{kJ}$$

$\therefore X = 46\cdot$

23. (3)

If $AC = l$ then according to question, $BC = 2l$ and $AB = 3l$.

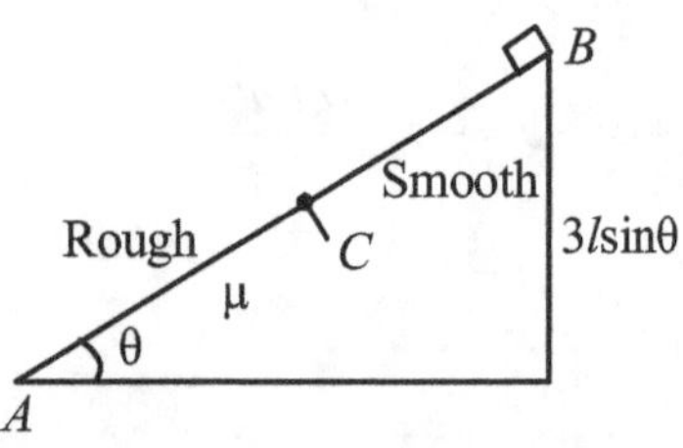

Here, work done by all the forces is zero.

$W_{\text{friction}} + W_{mg} = 0$

$mg(3l)\sin\theta - \mu mg\cos\theta(l) = 0$

$\Rightarrow \mu mg\cos\theta l = 3mgl\sin\theta$

$\Rightarrow \mu = 3\tan\theta = k\tan\theta$

$\therefore k = 3$

24. (4)

Given, $C_1 = 5\,\mu\text{F}$ and $V_1 = 220\,\text{Volt}$

When capacitor C_1 fully charged it is disconnected from the supply and connected to uncharged capacitor C_2.

$C_2 = 2.5\,\mu\text{F}$, $V_2 = 0$

Energy change during the charge redistribution,

$$\Delta U = U_i - U_f = \frac{1}{2}\frac{C_1 C_2}{C_1 + C_2}(V_1 - V_2)^2$$

$$= \frac{1}{2} \times \frac{5 \times 2.5}{(5+2.5)}(220-0)^2\,\mu\text{J}$$

$$= \frac{5}{2\times 3} \times 22 \times 22 \times 100 \times 10^{-6}\,\text{J}$$

$$= \frac{5 \times 11 \times 22}{3} \times 10^{-4}\,\text{J} = \frac{55 \times 22}{3} \times 10^{-4}\,\text{J}$$

$$= \frac{1210}{3} \times 10^{-4}\,\text{J} = \frac{1210}{3} \times 10^{-3}\,\text{J} \simeq 4 \times 10^{-2}\,\text{J}$$

According to questions, $\dfrac{x}{100} = 4 \times 10^{-2}$

$\therefore x = 4$

25. (9)

When radiation of wavelength A, λ_A is used to illuminate, stopping potential $V_A = V$

$$\frac{hc}{\lambda} = \phi + eV \qquad\qquad \text{...(i)}$$

When radiation of wavelength B, λ_B is used to illuminate, stopping potential, $V_B = \dfrac{V}{4}$

$$\frac{hc}{3\lambda} = \phi + \frac{eV}{4} \qquad\qquad \text{...(ii)}$$

From eq. (i) – (ii),

$$\frac{hc}{\lambda}\left(1 - \frac{1}{3}\right) = \frac{3}{4}eV$$

$$\Rightarrow \frac{hc}{\lambda}\frac{2}{3} = \frac{3}{4}eV \Rightarrow eV = \frac{8}{9}\frac{hc}{\lambda}$$

$$\frac{hc}{\lambda} = \phi + \frac{8}{9}\frac{hc}{\lambda}$$

$$\therefore \phi = \frac{hc}{9\lambda} = \frac{hc}{n\lambda}\text{, so, } n = 9.$$

CHEMISTRY

26. **(4)** (a), (b) and (c) are according to quantum theory but (d) is statement of kinetic theory of gases.

27. **(2)** Spin only magnetic moment $= 4\cdot9 = \sqrt{n(n+2)}$

$\therefore$ number of unpaired electrons $= 4$

Two possible arrangements are

Octahedral

$+0.6\,\Delta_0$
$-0.4\,\Delta_0$

Tetrahedral

$+0.4\,\Delta_t$
$-0.6\,\Delta_t$

eg.

$CFSE = t_{2g}$
$= 4 \times (-0.4)\Delta_0 + 2\,(0.6)\Delta_0$
$= -0.4\Delta_0$

$CFSE = 3 \times (-0.6)\Delta_t + 3 \times (0.4)\Delta_t$
$= -0.6\Delta_t$

So, option (b) is correct.

28. **(2)** Mole of bromine $= \dfrac{0.08}{80} = 10^{-3}$ mole

Molar mass of compound is given by the following equation,

$$\frac{0.172}{M} = 10^{-3}$$

$$\Rightarrow M = \frac{0.172}{10^{-2}} = 172\ \text{g}$$

$\because$ Molar mass of C_6H_6NBr
$= (6 \times 12) + (1 \times 6) + (1 \times 14) + (1 \times 80) = 172$ g.

Thus option (b) is the correct structure of compound.

29. **(3)** With weak field ligands Mn(II) will be of high spin and with strong field ligands it will be of low spin. Ni(II) tetrahedral complexes will be generally of high spin due to sp^3 hybridisation. Mn(II) is of light pink colour in aqueous solution.

30. **(1)**

31. **(4)** $CH_3 - CH - CH_2Br \xrightarrow{S_N1} CH_3 - CH - \overset{+}{C}H_2$

$\xrightarrow{1,\,2H^- \text{shift}} CH_3 - \overset{+}{C} - CH_3 \longrightarrow CH_3 - \underset{OH}{C} - CH_3$

32. **(2)**

Rearrangement $\xrightarrow{\hspace{1cm}}$ $\xrightarrow{-H^+}$

33. **(3)** $-I$ effect of NO_2 increases reactivity towards nucleophilic addition reaction with HCN. $-OCH_3$ group is electron donating due to resonance effect which decreases the reactivity towards nucleophillic addition.

34. **(4)** On moving left to right along a period in the periodic table atomic radius decreases while electronegativity, electron gain enthalpy and ionisation enthalpy increases, along a period.

35. **(2)** (i)

$$\begin{array}{l} CHO \\ (CHOH)_4 \\ CH_2OH \end{array} \xrightarrow[\text{dry HCl}]{ROH} \cdots \xrightarrow{4\text{ eq. of } Ac_2O} \cdots$$

(ii) $\begin{array}{l} CHO \\ (CHOH)_4 \\ CH_2OH \end{array} \xrightarrow{H_2/Ni} \begin{array}{l} CH_2OH \\ (CHOH)_4 \\ CH_2OH \end{array} \xrightarrow{6\text{ eq. of } Ac_2O} \begin{array}{l} CH_2OAc \\ (CH-OAc)_4 \\ CH_2OAc \end{array}$

(iii) $\begin{array}{l} CHO \\ (CHOH)_4 \\ CH_2OH \end{array} \xrightarrow{5\text{ eq. of } Ac_2O} \begin{array}{l} CH_2O \\ (CH-OAc)_4 \\ CH_2OAc \end{array}$

Thus $x = 4$, $y = 6$ and $z = 5$

36. **(4)** Cesium has lowest ionisation enthalpy and hence it shows photoelectric effect to the maximum extent. So, it is used in photo electric cell.

37. **(3)** Cu^{2+} ions get precipitated every quickely due to low K_{sp} value even at very low concentration of S^{2-} ion.

$$CuS(s) \rightleftharpoons Cu^{2+} + S^{2-}$$

$K_{sp} = [Cu^{2+}][S^{2-}]$

$Cu^{2+} + S^{2-} \rightleftharpoons CuS(s)$

$K_{eq} = \dfrac{1}{[Cu^{2+}][S^{2-}]} = \dfrac{1}{K_{sp}}$

Due to high value of K_{eq}, CuS precipitated easily.

38. **(2)** $Pb(NO_3)_2$ does not produce nitrogen gas on heating.

(a) $NaN_3 \xrightarrow{300°C} 3N_2 + 2Na$

(b) $Pb(NO_3)_2 \xrightarrow{\Delta} PbO + 2NO_2$

(c) $(NH_4)_2Cr_2O_7 \xrightarrow{\Delta} N_2 + Cr_2O_3 + H_2O$

(d) $NH_4NO_2 \xrightarrow{\Delta} N_2 + 2H_2O$

39. **(1)** The vapour pressure of solution will be less than the vapour pressure of pure solvent, so some vapour molecules will get condensed to maintain new equilibrium.

40. **(2)** In presence of sunlight CFC's molecule divides and release chlorine free radical, which react with ozone give chlorine monoxide radical (ClO$^\bullet$) and oxygen.

$CF_2Cl_2(g) \xrightarrow{UV} \overset{\bullet}{Cl}(g) + \overset{\bullet}{C}F_2Cl(g)$

$Cl^\bullet(g) + O_3(g) \longrightarrow ClO^\bullet(g) + O_2(g)$

$ClO^\bullet(g) + O(g) \longrightarrow Cl^\bullet(g) + O_2(g)$

41. **(3)** Bredig's Arc method is used for preparation of colloidal sol's of less reactive metal like Au, Ag, Pt.

42. **(1)** For AB_4 compound possible geometry are

No. of Bond pair	No. of lone pair	Hybridisation
4	0	sp^3
4	1	sp^3d
4	2	sp^3d^2

Structure with sp^3d^2 hybridisation is polar due to lone pair moment while in other possibilities molecules is non-polar. Square pyramidal can be polar due to lone pair moment as the bond pair moments will get cancelled out.

43. **(3)**

(2, 5-dimethyl 1-6-oxo-hex-3-enoic acid)

44. **(2)** For ideal gas

$PV = nRT$

$PV = \dfrac{m}{M}RT \qquad \left(\because n = \dfrac{m}{M}\right)$

$PM = \dfrac{m}{V}RT ; \quad PM = dRT ; \quad d = \left[\dfrac{PM}{R}\right]\dfrac{1}{T}$

$\Rightarrow d \propto \dfrac{1}{T} ; \quad d \propto P$

So, graph between d Vs T is not straight line.

45. **(4)** In this acid base titration bunsen burner and measuring cylinder are of no use while other laboratory equipments will be required i.e., phenol phthalein, burette and pipette.

46. **(5)**

(* = Chiral carbon)

47. **(6)**
The oxidation states of iron in these compounds will be -
In A, $x + 5(-1) + (-1) = -4 \Rightarrow x = +2$
In B, $y + 4(-2) = -4 \Rightarrow y = +4$
In C, $z = 0$
The sum of oxidation states will be $= 4 + 2 + 0 = 6$.

48. **(96500)**

$E^0_{cell} = E^0_{Sn^{2+}/Sn} - E^0_{Cu^{2+}/Cu}$
$\qquad = -0.16 - 0.34 = -0.50 \text{ V}$

$\Delta G^0 = -nE^0_{cell}$
$\qquad = -2 \times 96500 \times (-0.5) = 96500 \text{ J}$

49. **(6)**

$\left(\dfrac{x}{m}\right) = k(p)^{\frac{1}{n}}$

$\log\left(\dfrac{x}{m}\right) = \log k + \dfrac{1}{n}\log p$

Slope $= \dfrac{1}{n} = 2$, so $n = \dfrac{1}{2}$.

Intercept $\Rightarrow \log k = 0.477$. So $k = $ Antilog $(0.477) = 3$

So, $\left(\dfrac{x}{m}\right) = k(p)^{\frac{1}{n}} = 3(4)^{\frac{1}{2}} = 6$.

50. **(189494)**

$\Delta H = \Delta U + \Delta n_g RT$

$n = \dfrac{90}{18} = 5 \text{ mol}$

$H_2O(l) \rightleftharpoons H_2O(g) \qquad\qquad \Delta n = 1$
$41000 = \Delta U + 1 \times 8.314 \times 373$
$\Rightarrow \Delta U = 37898.875 \text{ J}$
For 5 moles, $\Delta U = 37898.87 \times 5 = 189494 \text{ J}$

MATHEMATICS

51. **(3)** $\because f(x) = \sin^{-1}\left(\dfrac{|x|+5}{x^2+1}\right)$

$\therefore -1 \le \dfrac{|x|+5}{x^2+1} \le 1$

$\Rightarrow |x|+5 \le x^2+1$ $\qquad\qquad$ $[\because x^2+1 \neq 0]$

$\Rightarrow x^2-|x|-4 \ge 0$

$\Rightarrow \left(|x|-\dfrac{1-\sqrt{17}}{2}\right)\left(|x|-\dfrac{1+\sqrt{17}}{2}\right) \ge 0$

$\Rightarrow x \in \left(-\infty,\,-\dfrac{1+\sqrt{17}}{2}\right] \cup \left[\dfrac{1+\sqrt{17}}{2},\,\infty\right)$

$\therefore a = \dfrac{1+\sqrt{17}}{2}$

52. **(4)** Since, $R = \{(x,y): x,y \in \mathbf{Z},\ x^2+3y^2 \le 8\}$

$\therefore R = \{(1,1),(2,1),(1,-1),(0,1),(1,0)\}$

$\Rightarrow D_{R^{-1}} = \{-1,0,1\}$

53. **(2)** Let B_1 and B_2 be the boxes and N be the number of non-prime number.

$\because P(B_1) = P(B_2) = \dfrac{1}{2}$

and P (non-prime number)

$= P(B_1) \times P\left(\dfrac{N}{B_1}\right) + P(B_2) \times P\left(\dfrac{N}{B_2}\right)$

$= \dfrac{1}{2} \times \dfrac{20}{30} + \dfrac{1}{2} \times \dfrac{15}{20}$

So,

$P\left(\dfrac{B_1}{N}\right) = \dfrac{P(B_1) \times P\left(\dfrac{N}{B_1}\right)}{P(B_1) \times P\left(\dfrac{N}{B_1}\right) + P(B_2) \times P\left(\dfrac{N}{B_2}\right)}$

$= \dfrac{\dfrac{1}{2} \times \dfrac{20}{30}}{\dfrac{1}{2} \times \dfrac{20}{30} + \dfrac{1}{2} \times \dfrac{15}{20}} = \dfrac{\dfrac{1}{3}}{\dfrac{1}{3} + \dfrac{15}{40}} = \dfrac{8}{17}.$

54. **(1)**

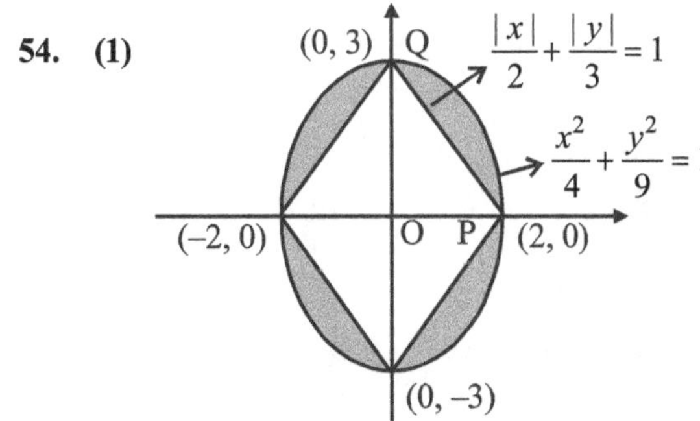

$\because$ Area of ellipse $= \pi ab = \pi \times 2 \times 3 = 6\pi$

$\therefore$ Required area $=$ Area of ellipse

$\qquad\qquad\qquad\qquad -4$ (Area of triangle OPQ)

$= 6\pi - 4\left(\dfrac{1}{2} \times 2 \times 3\right)$

$= 6\pi - 12 = 6(\pi-2)$ sq. units

55. **(3)** The given differential equation is

$\dfrac{2+\sin x}{y+1}\dfrac{dy}{dx} = -\cos x,\ y > 0$

$\Rightarrow \dfrac{dy}{y+1} = -\dfrac{\cos x}{2+\sin x}dx$

Integrate both sides,

$\int \dfrac{dy}{y+1} = \int \dfrac{(-\cos x)dx}{2+\sin x}$

$\ln|y+1| = -\ln|2+\sin x| + \ln C$

$\Rightarrow \ln|y+1| + \ln|2+\sin x| = \ln C$

$\Rightarrow \ln|(y+1)(2+\sin x)| = \ln C$

$\because y(0) = 1 \Rightarrow \ln 4 = \ln C \Rightarrow C = 4$

$\therefore (y+1)(2+\sin x) = 4$

$\Rightarrow y = \dfrac{4}{2+\sin x} - 1$

$\therefore y = \dfrac{2-\sin x}{2+\sin x} \Rightarrow y(\pi) = \dfrac{2-\sin \pi}{2+\sin \pi} = 1$

$\Rightarrow a = 1$

Now, $\dfrac{dy}{dx} = \dfrac{(2+\sin x)(-\cos x)-(2-\sin x)\cdot \cos x}{(2+\sin x)^2}$

$\left.\dfrac{dy}{dx}\right|_{x=\pi} = 1 \Rightarrow b = 1.$

Ordered pair $(a,b) = (1,1)$.

56. **(1)** General term of

$(\alpha x^{\frac{1}{9}} + \beta x^{\frac{-1}{6}})^{10} = {}^{10}C_r(\alpha x^{\frac{1}{9}})^{10-r}(\beta x^{\frac{-1}{6}})^r$

$= {}^{10}C_r \alpha^{10-r}\beta^r (x)^{\frac{10-r}{9}-\frac{r}{6}}$

Term independent of x if $\dfrac{10-r}{9} - \dfrac{r}{6} = 0 \Rightarrow r = 4.$

$\therefore$ Term independent of $x = {}^{10}C_4 \alpha^6 \beta^4$

Since $\alpha^3 + \beta^2 = 4$

Then, by AM-GM inequality

$\dfrac{\alpha^3+\beta^2}{2} \ge (\alpha^3 b^2)^{\frac{1}{2}}$

$\Rightarrow (2)^2 \geq \alpha^3 \beta^2 \Rightarrow \alpha^6 \beta^4 \leq 16$

$\because$ The maximum value of the term independent of $x = 10k$

$\therefore 10k = {}^{10}C_4 \cdot 16 \Rightarrow k = 336.$

57. (4) Let $A = \begin{bmatrix} a & b \\ c & d \end{bmatrix}$, where $a, b, c, d \in \{0, 1\}$

$\Rightarrow |A| = ad - bc \neq 0$

$\Rightarrow$ either $ad = 1$, $bc = 0$ or $ad = 0$ and $bc = 1$

(P) If $A \neq I_2 \Rightarrow ad \neq 1$

$\Rightarrow ad = 0$ and $bc = 1 \Rightarrow |A| = -1$

$\therefore$ P is true.

(Q) If $|A| = 1 \Rightarrow ad = 1$

$\Rightarrow ad = 1$ and $bc = 0$

$\Rightarrow \text{tr}(A) = 2$

$\therefore$ Q is true.

58. (3) Let terms of G.P. be $\dfrac{a}{r}$, a, ar

$\therefore a\left(\dfrac{1}{r} + 1 + r\right) = S$ ...(i)

and $a^3 = 27$

$\Rightarrow a = 3$ ...(ii)

Put $a = 3$ in eqn. (1), we get

$S = 3 + 3\left(r + \dfrac{1}{r}\right)$

If $f(x) = x + \dfrac{1}{x}$, then $f(x) \in (-\infty, -2] \cup [2, \infty)$

$\Rightarrow 3f(x) \in (-\infty, -6] \cup [6, \infty)$

$\Rightarrow 3 + 3f(x) \in (-\infty, -3] \cup [9, \infty)$

Then, it concludes that

$S \in (-\infty, -3] \cup [9, \infty)$

59. (3) $S = (x+y) + (x^2 + y^2 + xy) + (x^3 + x^2y + xy^2 + y^3) + ...\infty$

$= \dfrac{1}{x-y}\left[(x^2 - y^2) + (x^3 - y^3) + (x^4 - y^4 + ...\infty)\right]$

$= \dfrac{1}{x-y}\left[\dfrac{x^2}{1-x} - \dfrac{y^2}{1-y}\right] = \dfrac{(x-y)(x+y-xy)}{(x-y)(1-x)(1-y)}$

$$\left[\because S_\infty = \dfrac{a}{1-r}\right]$$

$= \dfrac{x+y-xy}{(1-x)(1-y)}$

60. (3) Since, α and β are the roots of the equaton

$5x^2 + 6x - 2 = 0$

Then, $5\alpha^2 + 6\alpha - 2 = 0$, $5\beta^2 + 6\beta - 2 = 0$

$5\alpha^2 + 6\alpha = 2$

$5S_6 + 6S_5 = 5(\alpha^6 + \beta^6) + 6(\alpha^5 + \beta^5)$

$\qquad = (5\alpha^4 + 6\alpha^5) + (5\beta^6 + 6\beta^5)$

$\qquad = \alpha^4(5\alpha^2 + 6\alpha) + \beta^4(5\beta^2 + 6\beta)$

$\qquad = 2(\alpha^4 + \beta^4) = 2S_4$

61. (4) $\Delta = \begin{vmatrix} 2 & -1 & 2 \\ 1 & -2 & \lambda \\ 1 & \lambda & 1 \end{vmatrix} = -(\lambda - 1)(2\lambda + 1)$

$\Delta_1 = \begin{vmatrix} 2 & -1 & 2 \\ -4 & -2 & \lambda \\ 4 & \lambda & 1 \end{vmatrix} = -2(\lambda^2 + 6\lambda - 4)$

For no solution $\Delta = 0$ and at least one of Δ_1, Δ_2 and Δ_3 is non-zero.

$\therefore \Delta = 0 \Rightarrow \lambda = 1, -\dfrac{1}{2}$ and $\Delta_1 \neq 0$

Hence, $S = \left\{1, -\dfrac{1}{2}\right\}$

62. (1) The tangent to the hyperbola at the point (x_1, y_1) is,

$xx_1 - 2yy_1 - 4 = 0$

The given equation of tangent is

$2x - y = 0$

$\Rightarrow \dfrac{x_1}{2y_1} = 2$

$\Rightarrow x_1 = 4y_1$ ...(i)

Since, point (x_1, y_1) lie on hyperbola.

$\therefore \dfrac{x_1^2}{4} - \dfrac{y_1^2}{2} - 1 = 0$ ...(ii)

On solving eqs. (i) and (ii)

$y_1^2 = \dfrac{2}{7}, \; x_1^2 = \dfrac{32}{7}$

$\therefore x_1^2 + 5y_1^2 = \dfrac{32}{7} + 5 \times \dfrac{2}{7} = 6$

63. (2) The given curve $y = x + \sin y$

$\because$ The point (a, b) lie on the curve

$\therefore b = a + \sin b$

$\Rightarrow \dfrac{dy}{dx} = 1 + \cos y \dfrac{dy}{dx} \Rightarrow (1 - \cos y)\dfrac{dy}{dx} = 1$

$\Rightarrow \dfrac{dy}{dx} = \dfrac{1}{1-\cos y}$

$\therefore \left(\dfrac{dy}{dx}\right)_{(a,b)} = \dfrac{1}{1-\cos b}$

Slope of the line joining the points $\left(0, \dfrac{3}{2}\right)$ and $\left(\dfrac{1}{2}, 2\right)$

$= \dfrac{2-\dfrac{3}{2}}{\dfrac{1}{2}-0} = 1$

Now, according to the question,

$\left(\dfrac{dy}{dx}\right)_{(a,b)} = 1 \Rightarrow \dfrac{1}{1-\cos b} = 1$

$\Rightarrow 1-\cos b = 1 \Rightarrow b = \dfrac{\pi}{2}$

Now, $b = a + \sin b$

$\Rightarrow a = b - \sin b = \dfrac{\pi}{2} - 1$

$|b-a| = \left|\dfrac{\pi}{2} - \dfrac{\pi}{2} + 1\right| = 1$

64. (2) $\because \bar{x} = \dfrac{1+2+3+....+17}{17} = \dfrac{17 \times 18}{17 \times 2} = 9$

$\bar{y} = a\bar{x} + b = \dfrac{a(1+2+3+.....+17)}{17} + b = 17$

$\Rightarrow \dfrac{a \cdot (17 \cdot 18)}{17 \cdot 2} + b = 17 \Rightarrow 9a + b = 17$ ...(i)

$\text{Var}(x) = \sigma A^2 = \dfrac{\Sigma x^2}{n} - (\bar{x})^2$

$= \dfrac{1^2 + 2^2 + ... + 17^2}{17} - (9)^2$

$= \dfrac{17 \cdot 18 \cdot 35}{6 \cdot 17} - (9)^2 = 105 - 81 = 24$

$\text{Var}(y) = a^2 \text{Var}(x) = a^2 \cdot 24 = 216$

$a^2 = \dfrac{216}{24} = 9 \Rightarrow a = 3$

$\therefore$ From (i), $b = 17 - 9a = 17 - 27 = -10$

$\therefore a + b = 3 + (-10) = -7$

65. (3) $\left(\dfrac{1 + \cos\dfrac{5\pi}{18} + i\sin\dfrac{5\pi}{18}}{1 + \cos\dfrac{5\pi}{18} - i\sin\dfrac{5\pi}{18}}\right)^3$

$= \left(\dfrac{2\cos^2\dfrac{5\pi}{36} + i2\sin\dfrac{5\pi}{36}\cdot\cos\dfrac{5\pi}{36}}{2\cos^2\dfrac{5\pi}{36} - i2\sin\dfrac{5\pi}{36}\cdot\cos\dfrac{5\pi}{36}}\right)^3$

$= \left(\dfrac{\cos\dfrac{5\pi}{36} + i\sin\dfrac{5\pi}{36}}{\cos\dfrac{5\pi}{36} - i\sin\dfrac{5\pi}{36}}\right)^3 = \left(\cos\dfrac{5\pi}{36} + i\sin\dfrac{5\pi}{36}\right)^6$

$= \cos\left(6 \times \dfrac{5\pi}{36}\right) + i\sin\left(6 \times \dfrac{5\pi}{36}\right) = \cos\dfrac{5\pi}{6} + i\sin\dfrac{5\pi}{6}$

$= -\dfrac{\sqrt{3}}{2} + i\dfrac{1}{2} = -\dfrac{1}{2}(\sqrt{3} - i)$

66. (4) Contrapositive of $p \to q$ is $\sim q \to \sim p$

i.e. contrapositive of 'if p then q' is 'if not q then not p'.

67. (2) Let $p'(x) = \lambda(x-1)(x-2)$ where $\lambda > 0$

$p(x) = \lambda\left[\dfrac{x^3}{3} - \dfrac{3x^2}{2} + 2x\right] + C$

Since $p(1) = 8 \Rightarrow \lambda\left(\dfrac{1}{3} - \dfrac{3}{2} + 2\right) + C = 8$

$\Rightarrow \dfrac{5\lambda}{6} + C = 8$ ...(i)

Also, $p(2) = 4 \Rightarrow \lambda\left(\dfrac{8}{3} - 6 + 4\right) + C = 4$

$\Rightarrow \dfrac{2}{3}\lambda + C = 4$ ...(ii)

From (i) and (ii), we get

$C = -12$ and $\lambda = 24$

$\Rightarrow p(0) = 0 + C = -12$

68. (4) Since, function $f(x)$ is continuous at $x = 1, 3$

$\therefore f(1) = f(1^+)$

$\Rightarrow ae + be^{-1} = c$ ...(i)

$f(3) = f(3^+)$

$\Rightarrow 9c = 9a + 6c \Rightarrow c = 3a$ ...(ii)

From (i) and (ii),

$b = ae(3 - e)$ ...(iii)

$$f'(x) = \begin{bmatrix} ae^x - be^{-x} & -1 < x < 1 \\ 2cx & 1 < x < 3 \\ 2ax + 2c & 3 < x < 4 \end{bmatrix}$$

$f'(0) = a - b,\ f'(2) = 4c$

Given, $f'(0) + f'(2) = e$

$a - b + 4c = e$ ...(iv)

From eqs. (i), (ii), (iii) and (iv),

$a - 3ae + ae^2 + 12a = e$

$\Rightarrow 13a - 3ae + ae^2 = e$

$\Rightarrow a = \dfrac{e}{e^2 - 3e + 13}$

69. (2) Let plane passes through $(2, 1, 2)$ be

$a(x - 2) + b(y - 1) + (z - 2) = 0$

It also passes through $(1, 2, 1)$

$\therefore -a + b - c = 0 \Rightarrow a - b + c = 0$

The given line is

$\dfrac{x}{3} = \dfrac{y}{2} = \dfrac{z-1}{0}$ is parallel to plane

$\therefore 3a + 2b + c(0) = 0$

$\Rightarrow \dfrac{a}{0-2} = \dfrac{b}{3-0} = \dfrac{c}{2+3}$

$\Rightarrow \dfrac{a}{2} = \dfrac{b}{-3} = \dfrac{c}{2+3}$

$\Rightarrow \dfrac{a}{2} = \dfrac{b}{-3} = \dfrac{c}{-5}$

$\therefore$ plane is $2x - 4 - 3y + 3 - 5z + 10 = 0$

$\Rightarrow 2x - 3y - 5z + 9 = 0$

The plane satisfies the point $(-2, 0, 1)$.

70. (1)

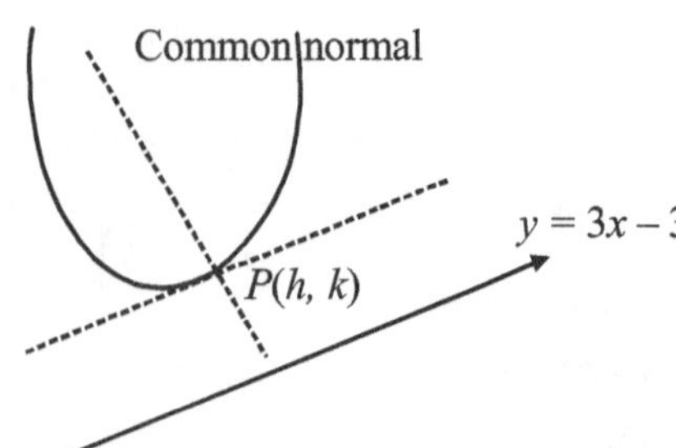

The given curve is, $y = x^2 + 7x + 2$

$\Rightarrow \dfrac{dy}{dx} = 2x + 7$

$\left(\dfrac{dy}{dx}\right)_{(h, k)} = 2h + 7$

The tangent at $P(h, k)$ will be parallel to given line

$2h + 7 = 3 \Rightarrow h = -2$

Point $P(h, k)$ lies on curve

$k = (-2)^2 - 7 \times 2 + 2 = -8$

Slope of normal at point $P(-2, -8) = -\dfrac{1}{3}$

$\therefore$ The equation of normal to the cuve at P is

$x + 3y + 26 = 0$

71. (40)

$$\lim_{x \to 1} \frac{x + x^2 + x^3 + ... + x^n - n}{x - 1} = 820 \left(\frac{0}{0}\ \text{case}\right)$$

$$\lim_{x \to 1} \frac{1 + 2x + 3x^2 + ... + nx^{n-1}}{1} = 820$$

(Using L' Hospital rule)

$\Rightarrow 1 + 2 + 3 + ... + n = 820$

$\Rightarrow \dfrac{n(n+1)}{2} = 820$

$\Rightarrow n^2 + n - 1640 = 0$

$\Rightarrow n = 40,\ n \in N$

72. (1.50)

$$\int_0^2 \big\| x - 1 | - x \big| dx = \int_0^1 |1 - x - x| dx + \int_1^2 \big\| x - 1 - x \big| dx$$

$$= \int_0^1 (1 - 2x)dx + \int_{1/2}^1 (2x - 1)dx + \int_1^2 dx$$

$$= [x - x^2]_0^{\frac{1}{2}} + [x^2 - x]_{\frac{1}{2}}^1 + [x]_1^2$$

$$= \frac{1}{2} - \frac{1}{4} + (1 - 1) - \left(\frac{1}{4} - \frac{1}{2}\right) + 2 - 1 = \frac{1}{4} + \frac{1}{4} + 1 = \frac{3}{2}$$

73. (9)

The given circle is $x^2 + y^2 - 2x - 4y + 4 = 0$

$\therefore$ Centre of circle $(1, 2)$, $r = 1$.

If line cuts circle then $p < r$, where $p = \left|\dfrac{ax_1 + by_1 + c}{\sqrt{a^2 + b^2}}\right|$

$\Rightarrow \left|\dfrac{3 + 8 - k}{5}\right| < 1 \Rightarrow k \in (6, 16)$

$k = 7, 8, 9, 10, 11, 12, 13, 14, 15$

74. (309)

$$\begin{array}{cccccc} M & O & T & H & E & R \\ 3 & 4 & 6 & 2 & 1 & 5 \end{array}$$

$\Rightarrow 2 \times 5! + 2 \times 4! + 3 \times 3! + 2! + 1$

$= 240 + 48 + 18 + 2 + 1 = 309$

75. (2)

$|\vec{a}| = |\vec{b}| = |\vec{c}| = 1$

$|\vec{a} - \vec{b}|^2 + |\vec{a} - \vec{c}|^2 = 8$

$\Rightarrow \vec{a} \cdot \vec{b} + \vec{a} \cdot \vec{c} = -2$

Now, $|\vec{a} + 2\vec{b}|^2 + |\vec{a} + 2\vec{c}|^2$

$= 2|\vec{a}|^2 + 4|\vec{b}|^2 + 4|\vec{c}|^2 + 4(\vec{a} \cdot \vec{b} + \vec{a} \cdot \vec{c}) = 2$

PHYSICS

1. **(2)** Given,

Angle of contact $\theta = 30°$

Surface tension, $T = 0.05 \, \text{Nm}^{-1}$

Radius of capillary tube, $r = 0.15 \, \text{mm} = 0.15 \times 10^{-3} \text{m}$

Density of methylene iodide, $\rho = 667 \, \text{kg m}^{-3}$

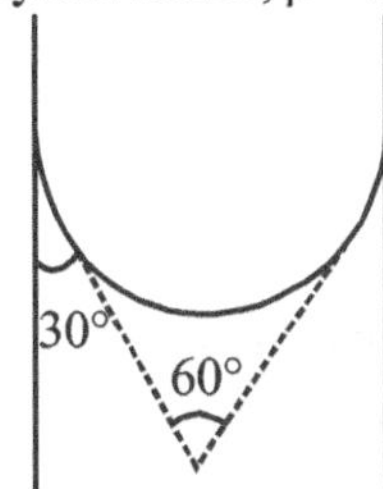

Capillary rise, $h = \dfrac{2T\cos\theta}{\rho g r}$

$$= \dfrac{2 \times 0.05 \times \dfrac{\sqrt{3}}{2}}{667 \times 10 \times 0.15 \times 10^{-3}} = 0.087 \text{ m}$$

2. **(1)** Given,

Reactance of inductance coil, $Z = 100\,\Omega$

Frequency of AC signal, $v = 1000 \, \text{Hz}$

Phase angle, $\phi = 45°$

$$\tan\phi = \dfrac{X_L}{R} = \tan 45° = 1$$

$$\Rightarrow X_L = R$$

Reactance, $Z = 100 = \sqrt{X_L^2 + R^2}$

$$\Rightarrow 100 = \sqrt{R^2 + R^2}$$

$$\Rightarrow \sqrt{2}R = 100 \Rightarrow R = 50\sqrt{2}$$

$$\therefore X_L = 50\sqrt{2}$$

$$\Rightarrow L\omega = 50\sqrt{2} \qquad\qquad (\because X_L = \omega L)$$

$$\Rightarrow L = \dfrac{50\sqrt{2}}{2\pi \times 1000} \qquad\qquad (\because \omega = 2\pi v)$$

$$= \dfrac{25\sqrt{2}}{\pi} \text{ mH} = 1.1 \times 10^{-2} \, \text{H}$$

3. **(3)** The acceleration due to gravity at a height h is given by

$$g = \dfrac{GM}{(R+h)^2}$$

Here, $G = $ gravitation constant

$M = $ mass of earth

The acceleration due to gravity at depth h is

$$g' = \dfrac{GM}{R^2}\left(1 - \dfrac{h}{R}\right)$$

Given, $g = g'$

$$\therefore \dfrac{GM}{(R+h)^2} = \dfrac{GM}{R^2}\left(1 - \dfrac{h}{R}\right)$$

$$\therefore R^3 = (R+h)^2(R-h) = (R^2 + h^2 + 2hR)(R-h)$$

$$\Rightarrow R^3 = R^3 + h^2 R + 2hR^2 - R^2 h - h^3 - 2h^2 R$$

$$\Rightarrow h^3 + h^2(2R - R) - R^2 h = 0$$

$$\Rightarrow h^3 + h^2 R - R^2 h = 0$$

$$\Rightarrow h^2 + hR - R^2 = 0$$

$$\Rightarrow h = \dfrac{-R \pm \sqrt{R^2 + 4(1)R^2}}{2} = \dfrac{-R + \sqrt{5}R}{2} = \dfrac{(\sqrt{5}-1)}{2}R$$

4. **(3)** Time period of one revolution of proton, $T = \dfrac{2\pi m}{qB}$

Here, $m = $ mass of proton

$q = $ charge of proton

$B = $ magnetic field.

Linear distance travelled in one revolution,

$p = T(v\cos\theta)$ (Here, $v = $ velocity of proton)

$\therefore$ Length of region, $l = 10 \times (v\cos\theta)T$

$$\Rightarrow l = 10 \times v\cos 60° \times \dfrac{2\pi m}{qB}$$

$$\Rightarrow l = \dfrac{20\pi m v}{qB} = \dfrac{20 \times 3.14 \times 1.67 \times 10^{-27} \times 4 \times 10^5}{1.6 \times 10^{-19} \times 0.3}$$

$$\Rightarrow l = 0.44 \text{ m}$$

5. **(3)** Energy, $E \propto A^a T^b P^c$

or, $\qquad E = kA^a T^b P^c \qquad\qquad$ ...(i)

where k is a dimensionless constant and a, b and c are the exponents.

Dimension of momentum, $P = M^1 L^1 T^{-1}$

Dimension of area, $A = L^2$

Dimension of time, $T = T^1$

Putting these value in equation (i), we get

$$M^1 L^2 T^{-2} = M^c L^{2a+c} T^{b-c}$$

by comparison

$c = 1$

$2a + c = 2$

$b - c = -2$

$c = 1, a = 1/2, b = -1$

$$\therefore E = A^{1/2} T^{-1} P^1$$

6. **(1)** Change in length of the metal wire (Δl) when its temperature is changed by ΔT is given by

$\Delta l = l\alpha\Delta T$

Here, $\alpha = $ Coefficient of linear expansion

Here, $\Delta l = 0.02\%$, $\Delta T = 10°\text{C}$

$\therefore \alpha = \dfrac{\Delta l}{l\Delta T} = \dfrac{0.02}{100 \times 10} \Rightarrow \alpha = 2 \times 10^{-5}$

Volume coefficient of expansion, $\gamma = 3\alpha = 6 \times 10^{-5}$

$\because \rho = \dfrac{M}{V}$

$\dfrac{\Delta V}{V} \times 100 = \gamma \Delta T = (6 \times 10^{-5} \times 10 \times 100) = 6 \times 10^{-2}$

Volume increase by 0.06% therefore density decrease by 0.06%.

7. **(1)** Given,

Capacitance of capacitor, $C_1 = 10\ \mu F$

Potential difference before removing the source voltage, $V_1 = 50\ V$

If C_2 be the capacitance of uncharged capacitor, then common potential is

$V = \dfrac{C_1 V_1 + C_2 V_2}{C_1 + C_2}$

$\Rightarrow 20 = \dfrac{10 \times 50 + 0}{20 + C} \Rightarrow C = 15\ \mu F$

8. **(2)** Total energy of electron in n^{th} orbit of hydrogen atom

$E_n = -\dfrac{Rhc}{n^2}$

Total energy of electron in $(n+1)^{\text{th}}$ level of hydrogen atom

$E_{n+1} = -\dfrac{Rhc}{(n+1)^2}$

When electron makes a transition from $(n+1)^{\text{th}}$ level to n^{th} level

Change in energy,

$\Delta E = E_{n+1} - E_n$

$h\nu = Rhc \cdot \left[\dfrac{1}{n^2} - \dfrac{1}{(n+1)^2} \right]$ $\qquad (\because E = h\nu)$

$\nu = R \cdot c \left[\dfrac{(n+1)^2 - n^2}{n^2 (n+1)^2} \right]$

$\nu = R \cdot c \left[\dfrac{1 + 2n}{n^2 (n+1)^2} \right]$

For $n \gg 1$

$\Rightarrow \nu = R \cdot c \left[\dfrac{2n}{n^2 \times n^2} \right] = \dfrac{2RC}{n^3} \Rightarrow \nu \propto \dfrac{1}{n^3}$

9. **(3)** Efficiency, $\eta = \dfrac{\text{Work done}}{\text{Heat absorbed}} = \dfrac{W}{\Sigma Q}$

$= \dfrac{Q_1 + Q_2 + Q_3 + Q_4}{Q_1 + Q_3} = 0.5$

Here, $Q_1 = 1915\ J$, $Q_2 = -40\ J$ and $Q_3 = 125\ J$

$\therefore \dfrac{1915 - 40 + 125 + Q_4}{1915 + 125} = 0.5$

$\Rightarrow 1915 - 40 + 125 + Q_4 = 1020$

$\Rightarrow Q_4 = 1020 - 2000$

$\Rightarrow Q_4 = -Q = -980\ J \Rightarrow Q = 980\ J$

10. **(1)** Magnetic moment of loop $ABCD$,

$M_1 = $ area of loop $\times$ current

$\vec{M}_1 = (abI)(\hat{j})$ $\qquad$ (Here, $ab =$ area of rectangle)

Magnetic moment of loop $DEFA$,

$\vec{M}_2 = (abI)(\hat{i})$

Net magnetic moment,

$\vec{M} = \vec{M}_1 + \vec{M}_2 \Rightarrow \vec{M} = abI(\hat{i} + \hat{j})$

$\Rightarrow |\vec{M}| = \sqrt{2}\,abI \left(\dfrac{\hat{j}}{\sqrt{2}} + \dfrac{\hat{k}}{\sqrt{2}} \right)$

11. **(4)** de Broglie wavelength

$\lambda = \dfrac{h}{mv} \Rightarrow m = \dfrac{h}{\lambda v}$

Clearly, $m \propto \dfrac{1}{\lambda v}$

If λ and v be the wavelength and velocity of electron and λ' and v' be the wavelength and velocity of the particle then

$\Rightarrow \dfrac{m'}{m} = \dfrac{v\lambda}{v'\lambda'} = \dfrac{1}{5} \times \dfrac{1}{1.878} \times 10^{-4}$

$\Rightarrow m = 9.7 \times 10^{-28}\ \text{kg}$

12. **(1)** Electromagnetic wave will propagate perpendicular to the direction of Electric and Magnetic fields

$\hat{C} = \hat{E} \times \hat{B}$

Here unit vector $\hat{C}$ is perpendicular to both $\hat{E}$ and $\hat{B}$

Given, $\vec{E} = \hat{k}$, $\vec{B} = 2\hat{i} - 2\hat{j}$

$\therefore \hat{C} = \hat{E} \times \hat{B} = \dfrac{1}{\sqrt{2}} \begin{vmatrix} \hat{i} & \hat{j} & \hat{k} \\ 0 & 0 & 1 \\ 1 & -1 & 0 \end{vmatrix} = \dfrac{\hat{i} + \hat{j}}{\sqrt{2}}$

$\Rightarrow \hat{C} = \dfrac{\hat{i} + \hat{j}}{\sqrt{2}}$

13. **(3)**

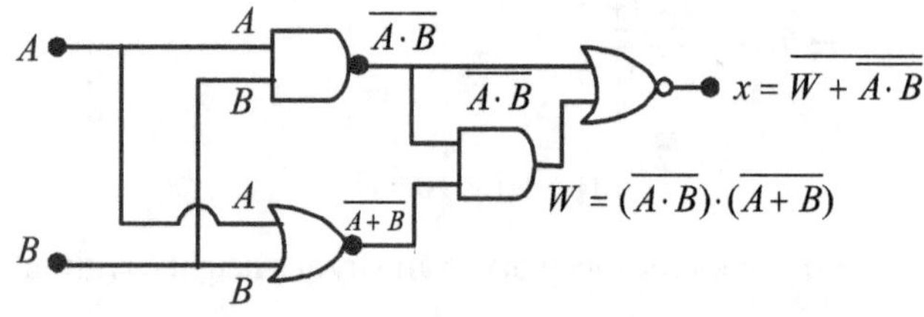

A	B	$\overline{A \cdot B}$	$\overline{A + B}$	$W = (\overline{A \cdot B}) \cdot (\overline{A + B})$	$Q = W + \overline{A \cdot B}$	$\overline{Q} = x$
1	0	1	0	0	1	0
0	1	1	0	0	1	0
1	1	0	0	0	0	1
0	0	1	1	1	0	0

14. **(4)** Net force acting on the particle,

$$\vec{F} = qE\hat{i} + mg\hat{j}$$

Net acceleration of particle is constant, initial velocity is zero therefore path is straight line.

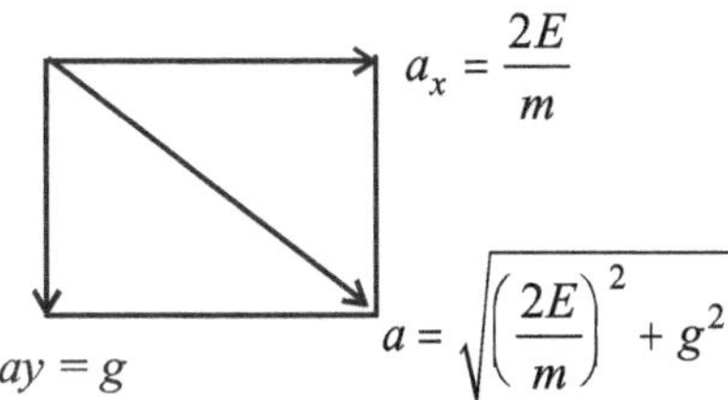

15. **(1)** Potential gradient, $x = \dfrac{\text{Potential drop}}{\text{length}}$

Here, Potential drop $= 1.02$
Balancing length from $P = 100 - 49$

$$\therefore x = \dfrac{1.02}{100 - 49} = 0.02 \text{ volt/cm}$$

16. **(4)** Let n_1 fringes are visible with light of wavelength λ_1 and n_2 with light of wavelength λ_2. Then

$$\beta = \dfrac{n_1 D\lambda_1}{d} = \dfrac{n_2 D\lambda_2}{d} \qquad \left(\because \beta = \dfrac{n\lambda D}{d} \right)$$

$$\Rightarrow \dfrac{n_2}{n_1} = \dfrac{\lambda_1}{\lambda_2} \;\Rightarrow\; n_2 = \dfrac{700}{400} \times 16 = 28$$

17. **(4)** Let σ be the surface charge density of the shells.

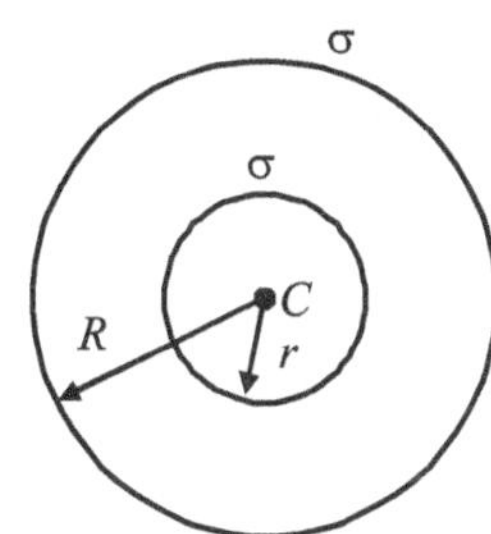

Charge on the inner shell, $Q_1 = \sigma 4\pi r^2$

Charge on the outer shell, $Q_2 = \sigma 4\pi R^2$

$\therefore$ Total charge, $Q = \sigma 4\pi (r^2 + R^2)$

$$\Rightarrow \sigma = \dfrac{Q}{4\pi(r^2 + R^2)}$$

Potential at the common centre,

$$V_C = \dfrac{KQ_1}{r} + \dfrac{KQ_2}{R} \qquad \left(\text{where } K = \dfrac{1}{4\pi\varepsilon_0} \right)$$

$$= \dfrac{K\sigma 4\pi r^2}{r} + \dfrac{K\sigma 4\pi R^2}{R} = K\sigma 4\pi(r + R)$$

$$= \dfrac{KQ4\pi(r+R)}{4\pi(r^2 + R^2)} = \dfrac{1}{4\pi\varepsilon_0} \dfrac{(r+R)Q}{(r^2 + R^2)}$$

18. **(3)** From graph equation of SHM

$$X = A\cos\omega t$$

(a) At $\dfrac{3T}{4}$ particle is at mean position.

$\therefore$ Acceleration $= 0$, Force $= 0$

(b) At T particle again at extreme position so acceleration is maximum.

(c) At $t = \dfrac{T}{4}$, particle is at mean position so velocity is maximum.

Acceleration $= 0$

(d) When KE $=$ PE

$$\Rightarrow \dfrac{1}{2}k(A^2 - x^2) = \dfrac{1}{2}kx^2$$

Here, $A =$ amplitude of SHM
$\qquad x =$ displacement from mean position

$$\Rightarrow A^2 = 2x^2 \Rightarrow x = \dfrac{+A}{\sqrt{2}}$$

$$\Rightarrow \dfrac{A}{\sqrt{2}} = A\cos\omega t \quad \Rightarrow t = \dfrac{T}{2}$$

$\therefore x = -A$ which is not possible

$\therefore A, B$ and C are correct.

19. **(2)** Initial angular momentum $= I_1\omega_1 + I_2\omega_2$

Let ω be angular speed of the combined system.

Final angular momentum $= I_1\omega + I_2\omega$

According to conservation of angular momentum

$$(I_1 + I_2)\omega = I_1\omega_1 + I_2\omega_2$$

$$\Rightarrow \omega = \dfrac{I_1\omega_1 + I_2\omega_2}{I_1 + I_2} = \dfrac{0.1 \times 10 + 0.2 \times 5}{0.1 + 0.2} = \dfrac{20}{3}$$

Final rotational kinetic energy

$$K_f = \dfrac{1}{2}I_1\omega^2 + \dfrac{1}{2}I_2\omega^2 = \dfrac{1}{2}(0.1 + 0.2) \times \left(\dfrac{20}{3} \right)^2$$

$$\Rightarrow K_f = \dfrac{20}{3} \text{ J}$$

20. **(1)** As we know mean free path

$$\lambda = \dfrac{1}{\sqrt{2}\left(\dfrac{N}{V} \right)\pi d^2}$$

Here, $\quad N =$ no. of molecule
$\qquad\quad V =$ volume of container
$\qquad\quad d =$ diameter of molecule

But $PV = nRT = nNKT$

$$\Rightarrow \dfrac{N}{V} = \dfrac{P}{KT} = n$$

$$\lambda = \dfrac{1}{\sqrt{2}} \dfrac{KT}{\pi d^2 P}$$

For constant volume and hence constant number density n of gas molecules $\dfrac{P}{T}$ is constant.

So mean free path remains same.

As temperature increases no. of collision increases so relaxation time decreases.

21. (08.00)

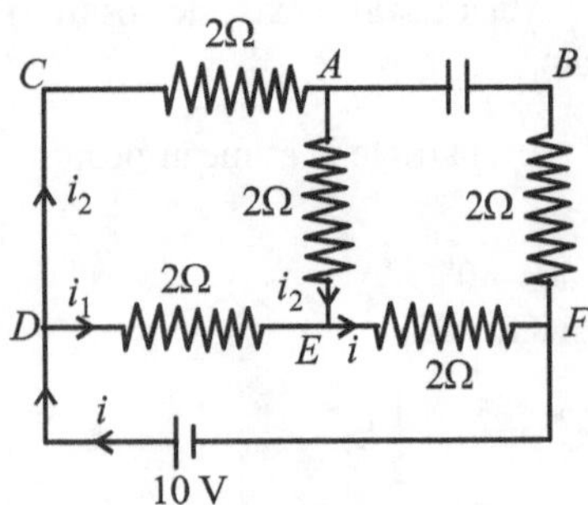

As capacitor is fully charged no current will flow through it.

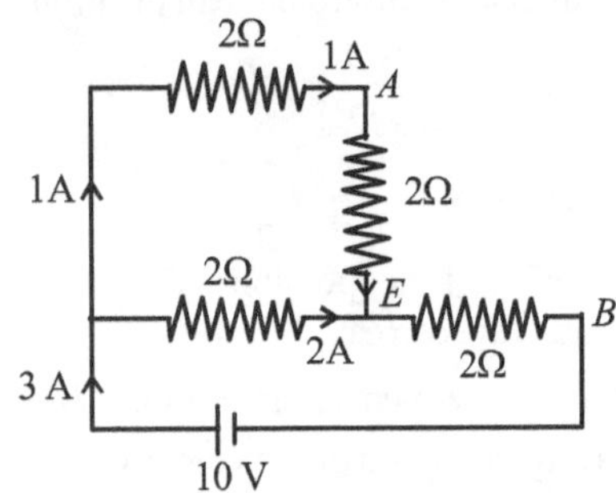

We have the current distribution as shown in the figure.

Equivalent resistance, $R_{eq} = \left(\dfrac{4 \times 2}{4 + 2}\right) + 2$

Net current, $i = \dfrac{10}{\dfrac{4}{3} + 2} = \dfrac{10 \times 3}{10} = 3$ Amp

$i_1 = 2\,A$ and $i_2 = 1\,A$

$V_{AEB} = 1 \times 2 + 3 \times 2 = 8\,V$

22. (23.00)

Let σ be the mass density of circular disc.

Original mass of the disc, $m_0 = \pi a^2 \sigma$

Removed mass, $m = \dfrac{a^2}{4}\sigma$

Remaining, mass, $m' = \left(\pi a^2 - \dfrac{a^2}{4}\right)\sigma$

$= a^2\left(\dfrac{4\pi - 1}{4}\right)\sigma$

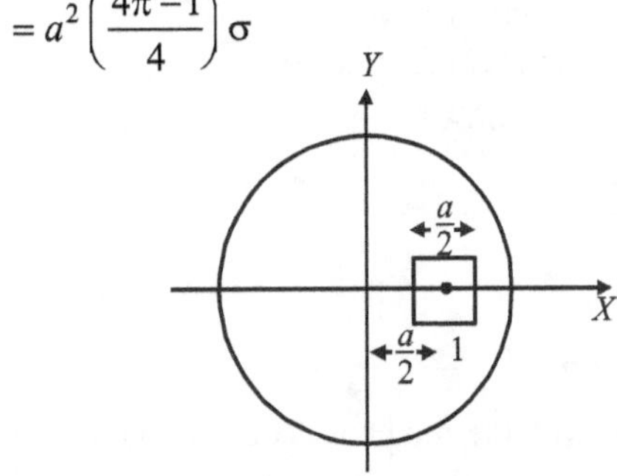

New position of centre of mass

$X_{CM} = \dfrac{m_0 x_0 - m x}{m_0 - m} = \dfrac{\pi a^2 \times 0 - \dfrac{a^2}{4} \times \dfrac{a}{2}}{\pi a^2 - \dfrac{a^2}{4}}$

$= \dfrac{-a^3/8}{\left(\pi - \dfrac{1}{4}\right)a^2} = \dfrac{-a}{2(4\pi - 1)} = \dfrac{-a}{8\pi - 2} = -\dfrac{a}{23}$

$\therefore x = 23$

23. (90.00)

In the figure, QR is the reflected ray and QS is refracted ray. CQ is normal.

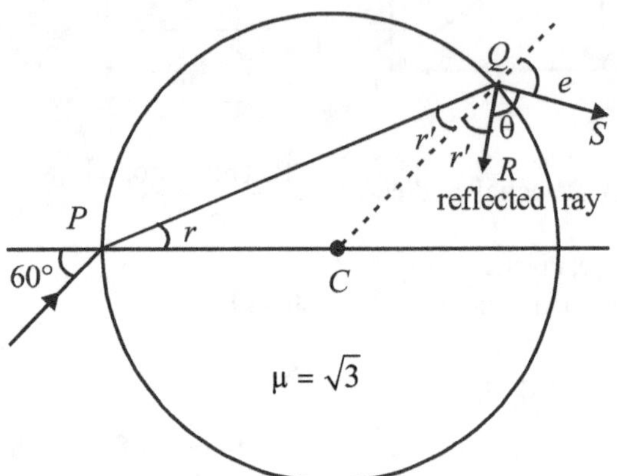

Apply Snell's law at P

$1\sin 60° = \sqrt{3}\sin r$

$\Rightarrow \sin r = \dfrac{1}{2} \Rightarrow r = 30°$

From geometry, $CP = CQ$

$\therefore r' = 30°$

Again apply snell's law at Q,

$\sqrt{3}\sin r' = 1\sin e$

$\Rightarrow \dfrac{\sqrt{3}}{2} = \sin e \Rightarrow e = 60°$

From geometry

$r' + \theta + e = 180°$ (As angles lies on a straight line)

$\Rightarrow 30° + \theta + 60° = 180° \Rightarrow \theta = 90°$.

24. (10.00)

From momentum conservation in perpendicular direction of initial motion.

$mu_1 \sin\theta_1 = 10mv_1 \sin\theta_2$ ...(i)

It is given that energy of m reduced by half. If u_1 be velocity of m after collision, then

$\left(\dfrac{1}{2}mu^2\right)\dfrac{1}{2} = \dfrac{1}{2}mu_1^2$

$\Rightarrow u_1 = \dfrac{u}{\sqrt{2}}$

If v_1 be the velocity of mass 10 m after collision, then

$\dfrac{1}{2} \times 10m \times v_1^2 = \dfrac{1}{2m}\dfrac{u^2}{2} \Rightarrow v_1 = \dfrac{u}{\sqrt{20}}$

From equation (i), we have

$\sin\theta_1 = \sqrt{10}\sin\theta_2$

$\Rightarrow n = 10$

25. (35.00)

Given, Denisty of wire, $\sigma = 9 \times 10^{-3}$ kg cm^{-3}

Young's modulus of wire, $Y = 9 \times 10^{10}$ Nm^{-2}

Strain $= 4.9 \times 10^{-4}$

$$Y = \frac{\text{Stress}}{\text{Strain}} = \frac{T/A}{\text{Strain}}$$

$$\therefore \frac{T}{A} = Y \times \text{Strain} = 9 \times 10^9 \times 4.9 \times 10^{-4}$$

Also, mass of wire, $m = Al\sigma$

Mass per unit length, $\mu = \dfrac{m}{l} = A\sigma$

Fundamental frequency in the string

$$f = \frac{1}{2l}\sqrt{\frac{T}{\mu}} = \frac{1}{2l}\sqrt{\frac{T}{\sigma A}} = \frac{1}{2 \times 1}\sqrt{\frac{9 \times 10^9 \times 4.9 \times 10^{-4}}{9 \times 10^3}}$$

$$= \frac{1}{2}\sqrt{49 \times 10^{9-4-3}} = \frac{1}{2} \times 70 = 35 \text{ Hz}$$

CHEMISTRY

26. (3) In toilet cleaning liquid, the main constituent is HCl, which can cause skin burn, so it should be treated with $NaHCO_3$, which can easily neutralise the acid.

27. (3)

(phenyl)–CH_2–O–CH=CH_2 $\xrightarrow{\text{HI}}$

(A) $C_9H_{10}O$

(phenyl)–CH_2–I + CH_2= CH–OH

(B)

CH_2–I + CH_2= CH–OH $\xleftrightarrow{\text{Tauto-merisation}}$ CH_3–CH=O

(C)   (D) $\downarrow$

                           +ve Iodoform test

$\downarrow AgNO_3$

$AgI\downarrow$ + (phenyl)–CH_2–ONO_2

Yellow ppt.

28. (1) It is an example of osmosis. Osmosis is the movement of solvent across a semipermeable membrane towards a higher concentration of solute (concentrated solution).

29. (3) (i) When gas is adsorbed on metal surface, ΔH becomes less negative with progress of adsorption.

(ii) The gas having greater value of critical temperature (T_C) is adsorbed more compared to lower T_C containing gases. As $T_C(NH_3) > T_C(N_2)$, so NH_3 is adsorbed more than N_2 gas.

30. (2) (reaction scheme) $\xrightarrow[E_2]{\text{Alc. KOH}}$ — the proton more acidic (due to –I effect of F) is eliminated to form the alkene.

31. (1) Stronger the ligand greater is splitting of d orbitals and smaller will be wavelength of light absorbed.

According to spectrochemical series, the splitting power of ligands is $NH_3 > NC\bar{S} > F^-$.

Thus, order of wavelength of light absorbed is

$$\lambda_{NH_3} < \lambda_{NC\bar{S}} < \lambda_{F^-}.$$

32. (3) Seliwanoff reagent $\rightarrow$ [Resorcinol + Conc. HCl]

It is used to distinguish aldoses and ketoses. Ketoses show red colour whereas aldoses show light pink colour with Seliwanoff Reagent.

33. (4) Li and Mg do not form solid bicarbonate, but react with N_2 to give nitrides.

$$6Li + N_2 \xrightarrow{\Delta} 2Li_3N$$

$$3Mg + N_2 \xrightarrow{\Delta} Mg_3N_2$$

34. (3) Rate (R) $= k[A]^a[B]^b$

Exp I $\Rightarrow 6.0 \times 10^{-3} = k[0.1]^a[0.1]^b$

Exp II $\Rightarrow 24.0 \times 10^{-3} = k[0.1]^a[0.2]^b$

Exp III $\Rightarrow 12.0 \times 10^{-3} = k[0.2]^a[0.1]^b$

Exp IV $\Rightarrow 72 \times 10^{-3} = k[X]^a[0.2]^b$

Exp V $\Rightarrow 288 \times 10^{-3} = k[0.3]^a[Y]^b$

From Exp I & II,

$$\Rightarrow \frac{6.0 \times 10^{-3}}{24 \times 10^{-3}} = \frac{k[0.1]^a[0.1]^b}{k[0.1]^a[0.2]^b}$$

$$\Rightarrow \frac{1}{4} = \left(\frac{0.1}{0.2}\right)^b \Rightarrow \left(\frac{1}{2}\right)^2 = \left(\frac{1}{2}\right)^b$$

$$\therefore b = 2$$

Similarly, from exp I & III we get

$$\frac{1}{2} = \left(\frac{1}{2}\right)^a \Rightarrow a = 1$$

From Exp. II & IV,

$$\Rightarrow \frac{24 \times 10^{-3}}{72 \times 10^{-3}} = \frac{k[0.1]^a[0.2]^b}{k[X]^a[0.2]^b}$$

$$\Rightarrow \frac{1}{3} = \left(\frac{0.1}{X}\right)^a \Rightarrow \frac{1}{3} = \left(\frac{0.1}{X}\right)^1$$

$$\therefore X = 0.3$$

From Exp. I & V,

$$\Rightarrow \frac{6.0 \times 10^{-3}}{288 \times 10^{-3}} = \left(\frac{0.1}{0.3}\right)^a\left(\frac{0.1}{Y}\right)^b$$

$$\Rightarrow \frac{1}{48} = \left(\frac{1}{3}\right)^1\left(\frac{0.1}{Y}\right)^2 \Rightarrow \frac{3}{48} = \left(\frac{0.1}{Y}\right)^2 \Rightarrow \frac{1}{16} = \left(\frac{0.1}{Y}\right)^2$$

$$\Rightarrow \left(\frac{1}{4}\right)^2 = \left(\frac{0.1}{Y}\right)^2 \Rightarrow \frac{1}{4} = \frac{0.1}{Y}$$

$$\therefore Y = 0.4$$

35. **(3)**

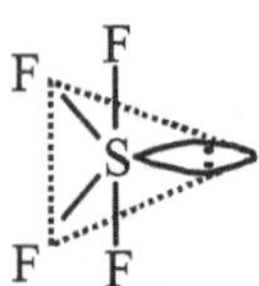

It is an example of electrophilic substitution reaction. Position of electrophile is directed by the strong ring activating group (–OH), present in the ring.

36. **(3)** Acidic strength $\propto$ Stability of conjugate base

General order of acidic strength is

$$R\text{–COOH} > Ph\text{–OH} > R\text{–C} \equiv CH$$

In between (iii) and (iv), (iii) is more acidic due to –M effect of –NO$_2$.

Thus, decreasing order of acidity is (ii) > (iii) > (iv) > (i).

37. **(2)** First reaction is S_N1 in which rate does not depend on conc. of nucleophile but depends on reactant conc. Second reaction is E2 reaction in which rate depends on conc. of base as well as reactant conc.

Therefore, changing the concentration of base will have no effect on rate of reaction (1).

38. **(2)** On moving left to right in a period, the acidic character of oxides increases.

3rd period element oxides.

$$\underbrace{Na_2O \quad MgO}_{Basic} \quad \underbrace{Al_2O_3}_{Amphoteric} \quad \underbrace{SiO_2 \quad P_2O_5 \quad Cl_2O_7}_{Acidic}$$

Acidic character $\propto$ Atomic No.

So, X have minimum atomic number while Z have maximum atomic number.

Thus, the correct order of the atomic number is

$$X < Y < Z$$

39. **(3)**

(a) $[Ni(NH_3)_4(H_2O)_2]^{2+}$ shows geometrical isomerism.

(b) $[Ni(en)_3]^{2+}$ shows optical isomerism.

(c) $[Ni^{2+}(NH_3)_2Cl_2] \Rightarrow Ni^{2+} \Rightarrow 3d^8 4s^0$

$$\Rightarrow sp^3 \text{ hybridisation}$$
$$\Rightarrow \text{tetrahedral}$$

So, $[Ni(NH_3)_2Cl_2]$ does not show isomerism.

(d) $[Pt(NH_3)_2Cl_2]$ shows geometrical isomerism.

40. **(1)**

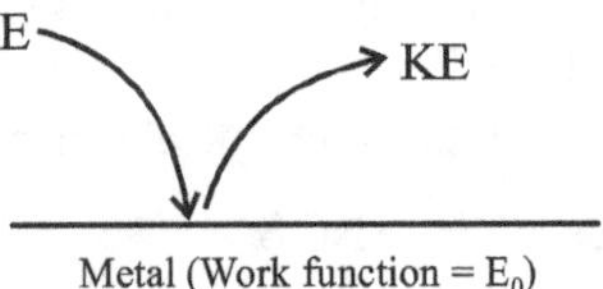

Test	D	C	Conformation
Iodoform Test	–ve	+ve	Presence of OH, R–CH–CH$_3$ group
Lucas Test	Immediate	after 5-10 Min.	Presence of 2° & 3°, –OH group
Ceric Ammonium nitrate Test	+ve	+ve	Presence of –OH group

41. **(4)** Cast iron is made from pig iron which is used for production of wroght iron and steel.

42. **(1)**

(i) XeF_5^- St. No. $=$ Bond pair $+$ Lone Pair $= (5+2) = 7$

So, hybridisation is $= sp^3d^3$

and structure is pentagonal planar.

(ii) XeO_3F_2 St. No. $= 5$

So, hybridisation is $= sp^3d$

and structure is trigonal bipyramidal.

43. **(4)** (I) Ion-ion interaction energy $\propto \left(\dfrac{1}{r}\right)$.

(II) Dipole-dipole interaction energy $\propto \left(\dfrac{1}{r^3}\right)$.

(III) London dispersion $\propto \left(\dfrac{1}{r^6}\right)$.

44. **(2)** SF_4

$$\begin{aligned} \text{Bond pair} &= 4 \\ \underline{\text{Lone pair} = 1} & \\ \text{Steric number} &= 5, \end{aligned}$$

So, hybridisation is sp^3d.

Geometry is trigonal bipyramidal but shape is "See Saw".

45. **(2)** For $n = 4$ possible values of $l = 0, 1, 2, 3$; only $l = 2$ and $l = 3$ can have $m = -2$. So possible subshells are 2.

46. **(222)**

$$E = E_0 + (KE)_{max}$$

$$\frac{hc}{\lambda} = 4.41 \times 10^{-19} + KE$$

$$\frac{6.63 \times 10^{-34} \times 3 \times 10^8}{300 \times 10^{-9}} = 4.41 \times 10^{-19} + KE$$

So, $(KE)_{max} = 6.63 \times 10^{-19} - 4.41 \times 10^{-19}$
$= 2.22 \times 10^{-19} \, J = 222 \times 10^{-21} \, J$

47. **(19)**

Compound	Oxidation state of transition element
(i) $K_2Cr_2O_7$	$x = +6$
(ii) $KMnO_4$	$y = +7$
(iii) K_2FeO_4	$z = +6$

So, $(x + y + z) = 6 + 7 + 6 = 19$.

48. **(144)**

$2Cu^+ (aq) \rightleftharpoons Cu(s) + Cu^{2+} (aq)$

$E^o_{cell} = E^o_{Cu^+/Cu} - E^o_{Cu^{2+}/Cu^+} = 0.52 - 0.16 = 0.36 \, V$

$E^o_{cell} = \dfrac{RT}{nF} \ln K_{eq} \Rightarrow 0.36 = \dfrac{0.025}{1} \ln K$

$\Rightarrow \ln K = 14.4 = 144 \times 10^{-1}$

49. **(5)**

Mass ratio of C : H is $4 : 1 \Rightarrow 12 : 3$ and

C : O is $3 : 4 \Rightarrow 12 : 16$

So,

	mass	mole	mole ratio
C	12	1	1
H	3	3	3
O	16	1	1

Empirical formula $\Rightarrow CH_3O$

As compound is saturated acyclic, so molecular formula is $C_2H_6O_2$.

$$C_2H_6O_2 + \frac{5}{2}O_2(g) \longrightarrow 2CO_2 \ (g) + 3H_2O \ (g)$$

$\underset{2 \text{ mole}}{} \qquad \underset{5 \text{ mole}}{}$

$\therefore$ Number of moles of O_2 required to oxidise 2 moles of (X) = 5.

50. **(− 326400)**

$C_2H_5OH \ (l) + O_2(g) \longrightarrow 2O_2(g) + 3H_2O(l)$;

$\Delta H_C = -327 \, Kcal$

$\Delta H = \Delta U + \Delta n_g RT$

$\Rightarrow -327 \times 10^3 = \Delta U + (-1) \times 2 \times 300$

$\Rightarrow \Delta U = -327 \times 10^3 + 600$

$\therefore \Delta U = -326400 \, cal$

MATHEMATICS

51. **(4)** $\because |P| = 1(-3 + 36) - 2(2 + 4) + 1(-18 - 3) = 0$

Given that $PX = 0$

$\therefore$ System of equations

$x + 2y + z = 0$; $2x - 3y + 4z = 0$

and $x + 9y - z = 0$ has infinitely many solution.

Let $z = k \in \mathbf{R}$ and solve above equations, we get

$x = -\dfrac{11k}{7}, \ y = \dfrac{2k}{7}, \ z = k$

But given that $x^2 + y^2 + z^2 = 1$

$\therefore k = \pm \dfrac{7}{\sqrt{174}}$

$\therefore$ Two solutions only.

52. **(1)** Given : $f(x + y) = f(x) + f(y), \ \forall x, y \in R, \ f(1) = 2$

$\Rightarrow f(2) = f(1) + f(1) = 2 + 2 = 4$

$f(3) = f(1) + f(2) = 2 + 4 = 6$

$f(n - 1) = 2(n - 1)$

Now, $g(n) = \displaystyle\sum_{k=1}^{n-1} f(k)$

$= f(1) + f(2) + f(3) + \dots f(n - 1)$

$= 2 + 4 + 6 + \dots + 2(n - 1) = 2[1 + 2 + 3 + \dots + (n - 1)]$

$= 2 \times \dfrac{(n - 1)(n)}{2} = n^2 - n$

$\because g(n) = 20$ (given)

So, $n^2 - n = 20$

$\Rightarrow n^2 - n - 20 = 0 \Rightarrow (n - 5)(n + 4) = 0$

$\Rightarrow n = 5$ or $n = -4$ (not possible)

53. **(1)** Truth table

p	q	$\sim p$	$p \vee q$	$(\sim p) \wedge (p \vee q)$	$(\sim p) \wedge (p \vee q) \to q$
T	T	F	T	F	T
T	F	F	T	F	T
F	T	T	T	T	T
F	F	T	F	F	T

$\therefore$ (a) $\sim p \wedge (p \vee q) \to q$ be a tautology

Other options are not tautology.

54. **(2)** $\sin^4 \theta + \cos^4 \theta = -\lambda$

$\Rightarrow (\sin^2 \theta + \cos^2 \theta)^2 - 2\sin^2 \theta \cdot \cos^2 \theta = -\lambda$

$\Rightarrow 1 - 2\sin^2 \theta \cos^2 \theta = -\lambda$

$\Rightarrow \lambda = \dfrac{(\sin 2\theta)^2}{2} - 1$

$\Rightarrow$ as $\sin^2 2\theta \in [0, 1] \Rightarrow \lambda \in \left[-1, \dfrac{-1}{2}\right]$

55. **(1)** Let $f(x) = ax^2 + bx + c$

Given : $f(-1) + f(2) = 0$

$a - b + c + 4a + 2b + c = 0$

$\Rightarrow 5a + b + 2c = 0$ ...(i)

and $f(3) = 0 \Rightarrow 9a + 3b + c = 0$ ...(ii)

From equations (i) and (ii),

$$\frac{a}{1-6} = \frac{b}{18-5} = \frac{c}{15-9} \Rightarrow \frac{a}{-5} = \frac{b}{13} = \frac{c}{6}$$

Product of roots, $\alpha\beta = \dfrac{c}{a} = \dfrac{-6}{5}$ and $\alpha = 3$

$$\Rightarrow \beta = \frac{-2}{5} \in (-1, 0)$$

56. **(1)** $\dfrac{dy}{dx} = \dfrac{2xy + y^2}{2x^2}$

It is homogeneous differential equation.

$\therefore$ Put $y = vx$

$$\Rightarrow v + x\frac{dv}{dx} = v + \frac{v^2}{2} \Rightarrow \int 2\frac{dv}{v^2} = \int \frac{dx}{x}$$

$$\Rightarrow \frac{-2}{v} = \log_e x + c \Rightarrow \frac{-2x}{y} = \log_e x + c$$

Put $x = 1, y = 2$, we get $c = -1$

$$\Rightarrow \frac{-2x}{y} = \log_e x - 1$$

Hence, put $x = \dfrac{1}{2} \Rightarrow y = \dfrac{1}{1 + \log_e 2}$

57. **(4)** $\displaystyle\lim_{x \to 0}\left(\frac{1 + \tan x}{1 - \tan x}\right)^{1/x}$

$$\Rightarrow e^{\displaystyle\lim_{x \to 0}\frac{1}{x}\left[\tan\left(\frac{\pi}{4}+x\right)-1\right]} \Rightarrow e^{\displaystyle\lim_{x \to 0}\frac{1}{x}\left(\frac{1+\tan x}{1-\tan x}-1\right)}$$

$$\Rightarrow e^{\displaystyle\lim_{x \to 0}\left(\frac{2\tan x}{1-\tan x}\right)\frac{1}{x}} = e^{\displaystyle\lim_{x \to 0}\left(\frac{\tan x}{x}\right)\left(\frac{2}{1-\tan x}\right)} = e^2$$

58. **(1)** Let $f(x, y) = x + y - 1$

Given $(1, 2)$ and $(\sin\theta, \cos\theta)$ are lies on same side.

$\therefore f(1, 2) \cdot f(\sin\theta, \cos\theta) > 0$

$\Rightarrow 2[\sin\theta + \cos\theta - 1] > 0$

$\Rightarrow \sin\theta + \cos\theta > 1 \Rightarrow \sin\left(\theta + \dfrac{\pi}{4}\right) > \dfrac{1}{\sqrt{2}}$

$\Rightarrow \theta + \dfrac{\pi}{4} \in \left(\dfrac{\pi}{4}, \dfrac{3\pi}{4}\right) \Rightarrow \theta \in \left(0, \dfrac{\pi}{2}\right)$

59. **(4)** $f'(x) = \dfrac{\dfrac{x}{1+x} - \ln(1+x)}{x^2}$

$$= \frac{x - (1+x)\ln(1+x)}{(1+x)x^2} < 0, \ \forall x \in (-1, \infty) - \{0\}$$

[For $x \in (-1, 0), f'(x) < 0$ and for $x \in (0, \infty), f'(x) < 0$]

So, f(x) is increases in $(-1, \infty)$.

60. **(2)** Given : $A^T A = I$

$$\Rightarrow \begin{bmatrix} a & b & c \\ b & c & a \\ c & a & b \end{bmatrix}\begin{bmatrix} a & b & c \\ b & c & a \\ c & a & b \end{bmatrix} = \begin{bmatrix} 1 & 0 & 0 \\ 0 & 1 & 0 \\ 0 & 0 & 1 \end{bmatrix}$$

$$\Rightarrow \begin{bmatrix} \Sigma a^2 & \Sigma ab & \Sigma ab \\ \Sigma ab & \Sigma a^2 & \Sigma ab \\ \Sigma ab & \Sigma ab & \Sigma a^2 \end{bmatrix} = \begin{bmatrix} 1 & 0 & 0 \\ 0 & 1 & 0 \\ 0 & 0 & 1 \end{bmatrix}$$

So, $\Sigma a^2 = 1$ and $\Sigma ab = 0$

Now, $a^3 + b^3 + c^3 - 3abc$

$= (a+b+c)(a^2 + b^2 + c^2 - ab - bc - ca)$

$= (a+b+c)(1 - 0)$

$= \sqrt{(a+b+c)^2} = \sqrt{\Sigma a^2 + 2\Sigma ab} = \pm 1$

$\Rightarrow 2 - 3abc = 1 \Rightarrow abc = \dfrac{1}{3}$

or $2 - 3abc = -1 \Rightarrow abc = 1$.

61. **(2)** $3 + 2\sqrt{-54} = 3 + 6\sqrt{6}i$

Let $\sqrt{3 + 6\sqrt{6}i} = a + ib$

$\Rightarrow a^2 - b^2 = 3$ and $ab = 3\sqrt{6}$

$\Rightarrow a^2 + b^2 = \sqrt{(a^2 - b^2)^2 + 4a^2b^2} = 15$

So, $a = \pm 3$ and $b = \pm\sqrt{6}$

$\sqrt{3 + 6\sqrt{6}\,i} = \pm(3 + \sqrt{6}\,i)$

Similarly, $\sqrt{3 - 6\sqrt{6}\,i} = \pm(3 - \sqrt{6}\,i)$

$\text{Im}\,(\sqrt{3 + 6\sqrt{6}i} - \sqrt{3 - 6\sqrt{6}i}) = \pm 2\sqrt{6}$

62. **(3)** $\because y = (1+x)^{2y} + \cos^2(\sin^{-1} x)$

$y = e^{2y\ln(1+x)} + \cos^2(\cos^{-1}\sqrt{1 - x^2})$

$\quad = e^{2y\ln(1+x)} + (1 - x^2)$

$$\frac{dy}{dx} = (1+x)^{2y}\left[2\ln(1+x)\frac{dy}{dx} + \frac{2y}{1+x}\right] - 2x$$

When $x = 0$, then $y = 2$

$\therefore \dfrac{dy}{dx} = 4$

Slope of normal at $x = 0$ is $-\dfrac{1}{4}$

$\therefore$ Equation of normal : $y - 2 = -\dfrac{1}{4}(x - 0)$

$\Rightarrow x + 4y = 8$

63. **(1)** $\because$ Plane contains two lines

$$\therefore \vec{n} = \begin{vmatrix} \hat{i} & \hat{j} & \hat{k} \\ 1 & -2 & 2 \\ 2 & 3 & -1 \end{vmatrix}$$

$$= \hat{i}(2-6) - \hat{j}(-1-4) + \hat{k}(3+4) \quad = -4\hat{i} + 5\hat{j} + 7\hat{k}$$

So, equation of plane is

$$-4(x-3) + 5(y-1) + 7(z-1) = 0$$
$$\Rightarrow -4x + 12 + 5y - 5 + 7z - 7 = 0$$
$$\Rightarrow -4x + 5y + 7z = 0$$

This also passes through $(\alpha, -3, 5)$

So, $-4\alpha - 15 + 35 = 0$

$$\Rightarrow -4\alpha = -20 \Rightarrow \alpha = 5.$$

64. (4) $\displaystyle P\left(\frac{E_2^C \cap E_3^C}{E_1}\right) = \frac{P\left[E_1 \cap \left(E_2^C \cap E_3^C\right)\right]}{P(E_1)}$

$$= \frac{P(E_1) - P[E_1 \cap (E_2 \cup E_3)]}{P(E_1)}$$

$$[\because P(A \cap B^C) = P(A) - P(A \cap B)]$$

$$= \frac{P(E_1) - P[(E_1 \cap E_2) \cup (E_1 \cap E_3)]}{P(E_1)}$$

$$= \frac{P(E_1) - [P(E_1 \cap E_2) + P(E_1 \cap E_3) - P(E_1 \cap E_2 \cap E_3)]}{P(E_1)}$$

$$= \frac{P(E_1) - P(E_1 \cap E_2) - P(E_1 \cap E_3) + 0}{P(E_1)}$$

$$= 1 - P(E_2) - P(E_3) \qquad [\because P(A \cap B) = P(A) \cdot P(B)]$$

$$= P(E_2^C) - P(E_3) \text{ or } P(E_3^C) - P(E_2)$$

65. (3) Let $A = (2t^2, 4t)$ and $B = (2t^2, -4t)$

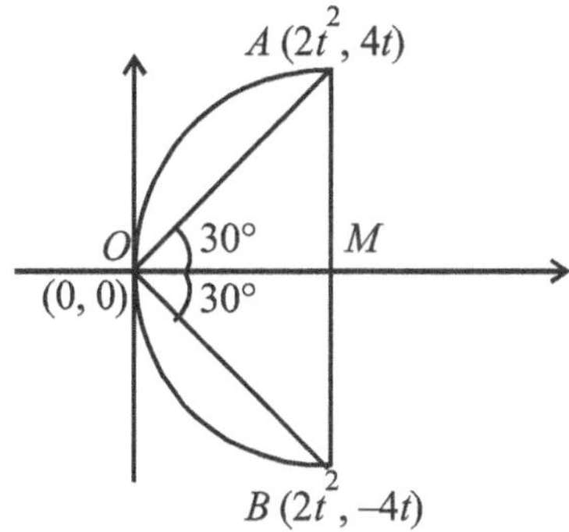

For equilateral triangle $(\angle AOM = 30°)$

$$\tan 30° = \frac{4t}{2t^2} \Rightarrow \frac{1}{\sqrt{3}} = \frac{4t}{2t^2} \Rightarrow t = 2\sqrt{3}$$

$$\text{Area} = \frac{1}{2} \cdot 8(2\sqrt{3}) \cdot 2 \cdot 24 = 192\sqrt{3}.$$

66. (4) Let common difference be d.

$$\because S_{11} = 0 \quad \therefore \frac{11}{2}\{2a_1 + 10 \cdot d\} = 0$$

$$\Rightarrow a_1 + 5d = 0 \Rightarrow d = -\frac{a_1}{5} \qquad \text{...(i)}$$

Now, $S = a_1 + a_3 + a_5 + \dots + a_{23}$

$$= a_1 + (a_1 + 2d) + (a_1 + 4d) + \dots + (a_1 + 22d)$$

$$= 12a_1 + 2d\frac{11 \times 12}{2} = 12\left[a_1 + 11 \cdot \left(-\frac{a_1}{5}\right)\right] \quad \text{(From (i))}$$

$$= 12 \times \left(-\frac{6}{5}\right)a_1 = -\frac{72}{5}a_1$$

67. (3) $S = (x + x^2 + x^3 + \dots 9 \text{ terms})$

$$+ a[k + (k+2) + + (k+4) + \dots 9 \text{ terms}]$$

$$\Rightarrow S = \frac{x(x^9 - 1)}{x-1} + \frac{9}{2}[2ak + 8 \times (2a)]$$

$$\Rightarrow S = \frac{x^{10} - x}{x-1} + \frac{9a(k+8)}{1} = \frac{x^{10} - x + 45a(x-1)}{x-1} \quad \text{(Given)}$$

$$\Rightarrow \frac{x^{10} - x + 9a(k+8)(x-1)}{x-1} = \frac{x^{10} - x + 45a(x-1)}{x-1}$$

$$\Rightarrow 9a(k+8) = 45a \Rightarrow k + 8 = 5 \Rightarrow k = -3.$$

68. (1) Number of two consecutive stations (Blue lines) $= n$

Number of two non-consecutive stations (Red lines)

$$= {}^nC_2 - n$$

Now, according to the question, ${}^nC_2 - n = 99n$

$$\Rightarrow \frac{n(n-1)}{2} - 100n = 0 \Rightarrow n(n-1-200) = 0$$

$$\Rightarrow n - 1 - 200 = 0 \Rightarrow n = 201$$

69. (2) Let $y = x^2$ and $y = 2x$

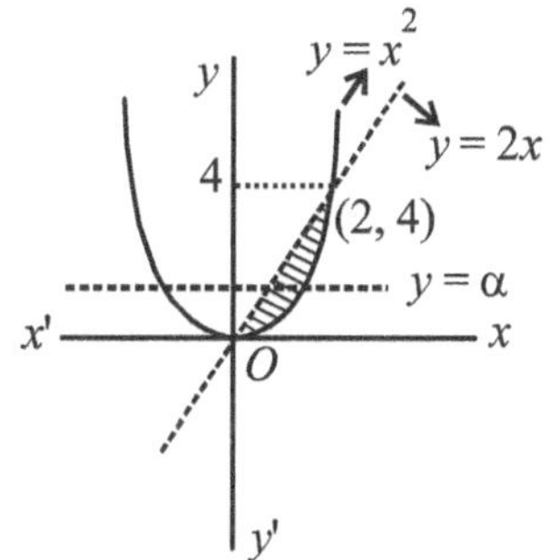

According to question

$$\therefore \int_0^\alpha \left(\sqrt{y} - \frac{y}{2}\right)dy = \int_\alpha^4 \left(\sqrt{y} - \frac{y}{2}\right)dy$$

$$\Rightarrow \left[\frac{y^{3/2}}{\frac{3}{2}}\right]_0^\alpha - \left[\frac{y^2}{4}\right]_0^\alpha = \left[\frac{y^{3/2}}{\frac{3}{2}}\right]_\alpha^4 - \left[\frac{y^2}{4}\right]_\alpha^4$$

$$\Rightarrow \frac{2}{3}\alpha^{3/2} - \frac{\alpha^2}{4} = \frac{2}{3}(8 - \alpha^{3/2}) - \frac{1}{4}(16 - \alpha^2)$$

$$\Rightarrow \frac{4}{3}\alpha^{3/2} - \frac{\alpha^2}{2} = \frac{4}{3} \Rightarrow 8\alpha^{3/2} - 3\alpha^2 = 8$$

$$\therefore 3\alpha^2 - 8\alpha^{3/2} + 8 = 0$$

70. **(4)** Hyperbola : $\dfrac{x^2}{10} - \dfrac{y^2}{10\cos^2\theta} = 1 \Rightarrow e_1 = \sqrt{1 + \cos^2\theta}$

and Ellipse : $\dfrac{x^2}{5\cos^2\theta} + \dfrac{y^2}{5} = 1$

$\Rightarrow e_2 = \sqrt{1 - \cos^2\theta} = \sin\theta$

According to the question, $e_1 = \sqrt{5}\, e_2$

$\Rightarrow 1 + \cos^2\theta = 5\sin^2\theta \Rightarrow \cos^2\theta = \dfrac{2}{3}$

Now length of latus rectum of ellipse

$= \dfrac{2a^2}{b} = \dfrac{10\cos^2\theta}{\sqrt{5}} = \dfrac{20}{3\sqrt{5}} = \dfrac{4\sqrt{5}}{3}$

71. **(91)** $y = \displaystyle\sum_{k=1}^{6} k\cos^{-1}\left\{ \dfrac{3}{5}\cos kx - \dfrac{4}{5}\sin kx \right\}$

Let $\cos a = \dfrac{3}{5}$ and $\sin a = \dfrac{4}{5}$

$\therefore y = \displaystyle\sum_{k=1}^{6} k\cos^{-1}\{\cos a\cos kx - \sin a\sin kx\}$

$= \displaystyle\sum_{k=1}^{6} k\cos^{-1}(\cos(kx + a)) = \sum_{k=1}^{6} k(kx + a) = \sum_{k=1}^{6}(k^2 x + ak)$

$\therefore \dfrac{dy}{dx} = \displaystyle\sum_{k=1}^{6} k^2 = \dfrac{6(7)(13)}{6} = 91.$

72. **(118)**

According to the question,

$^nC_{r-1} : {^nC_r} : {^nC_{r+1}} = 2 : 5 : 12$

$\Rightarrow \dfrac{^nC_r}{^nC_{r-1}} = \dfrac{5}{2} \Rightarrow \dfrac{n-r+1}{r} = \dfrac{5}{2}$

$\Rightarrow 2n - 7r + 2 = 0 \qquad\qquad \text{...(i)}$

$\dfrac{^nC_{r+1}}{^nC_r} = \dfrac{12}{5} \Rightarrow \dfrac{n-r}{r+1} = \dfrac{12}{5}$

$\Rightarrow 5n - 17r - 12 = 0 \qquad\qquad \text{...(ii)}$

Solving eqns. (i) and (ii),

$n = 118, r = 34$

73. **(1)** $\displaystyle\int_1^2 |2x - [3x]|\, dx = \int_1^2 |3x - [3x] - x|\, dx$

$= \displaystyle\int_1^2 |\{3x\} - x|\, dx = \int_1^2 (x - \{3x\})\, dx$

$= \displaystyle\int_1^2 x\, dx - \int_1^2 \{3x\}\, dx = \left[\dfrac{x^2}{2}\right]_1^2 - 3\int_0^{1/3} 3x\, dx$

$= \dfrac{(4-1)}{2} - 9\left[\dfrac{x^2}{2}\right]_0^{1/3} = \dfrac{3}{2} - \dfrac{1}{2} = 1$

74. **(0.8)**

Let position vector of A and B be $\vec{a}$ and $\vec{b}$ respectively.

$\therefore$ Position vector of P is $\overrightarrow{OP} = \dfrac{\lambda\vec{b} + \vec{a}}{\lambda + 1}$

$$
\begin{array}{c}
\overset{\lambda\,:\,1}{\longleftrightarrow}\\
\underset{A}{\circ}\qquad\qquad\underset{P}{|}\qquad\qquad\underset{B}{\circ}\\
(1,1,1)\qquad\qquad\qquad\qquad (2,1,3)
\end{array}
$$

Given $\overrightarrow{OB}\cdot\overrightarrow{OP} - 3\,|\overrightarrow{OA}\times\overrightarrow{OP}|^2 = 6$

$\Rightarrow \vec{b}\cdot\left(\dfrac{\lambda\vec{b}+\vec{a}}{\lambda+1}\right) - 3\left|\vec{a}\times\dfrac{\lambda\vec{b}+\vec{a}}{\lambda+1}\right|^2 = 6$

$\Rightarrow \dfrac{\vec{a}\cdot\vec{b} + \lambda\,|\vec{b}|^2}{\lambda+1} - \dfrac{3\lambda^2}{(\lambda+1)^2}\,|\vec{a}\times\vec{b}|^2 = 6$

$(\because \vec{a}\times\vec{b} = 2\hat{i} - \hat{j} - \hat{k}$ and $\vec{a}\cdot\vec{b} = 6)$

$\Rightarrow \dfrac{6 + 14\lambda}{\lambda+1} - \dfrac{18\lambda^2}{(\lambda+1)^2} = 6 \Rightarrow 6 + \dfrac{8\lambda}{\lambda+1} - \dfrac{18\lambda^2}{(\lambda+1)^2} = 6$

Let $\dfrac{\lambda}{\lambda+1} = t$

$\Rightarrow 18t^2 - 8t = 0 \Rightarrow 2t(9t - 4) = 0$

$\Rightarrow t = 0, \dfrac{4}{9}$

$\therefore \dfrac{\lambda}{\lambda+1} = \dfrac{4}{9} \Rightarrow \lambda = \dfrac{4}{5} = 0.8.$

75. **(3)**

$\text{Variance} = \dfrac{\displaystyle\sum_{i=1}^{11} b_i^2}{11} - \left(\dfrac{\displaystyle\sum_{i=1}^{11} b_i}{11}\right)^2$

Let common difference of A.P. be d

$= \dfrac{\displaystyle\sum_{r=0}^{10}(b_1 + rd)^2}{11} - \left(\dfrac{\displaystyle\sum_{r=0}^{10}(b_1 + rd)}{11}\right)^2$

$= \dfrac{11b_1^2 + 2b_1 d\left(\dfrac{10\times11}{2}\right) + d^2\left(\dfrac{10\times11\times21}{6}\right)}{11}$

PHYSICS

1. **(3)** As we know, for first order decay, $N(t) = N_0 e^{-\lambda t}$

According to question,

$$\frac{N(t)}{N_0} = \frac{9}{16} = e^{-\lambda t}$$

After time, $t/2$;

$$N(t/2) = N_0 e^{-\lambda(t/2)}$$

$$\frac{N(t/2)}{N_0} = \sqrt{e^{-\lambda t}} = \sqrt{\frac{9}{16}}$$

$$\therefore N(t/2) = \frac{3}{4} N_0$$

2. **(1)** As we know, emf $\varepsilon = NAB\omega \cos \omega t$, Here $N = 1$

Average power,

$$<P> = <\frac{\varepsilon^2}{R}> = <\frac{A^2 B^2 \omega^2 \cos^2 \omega t}{R}> = \frac{A^2 B^2 \omega^2}{R}\left(\frac{1}{2}\right)$$

Therefore average power loss in the loop due to Joule heating

$$<P> = \frac{\pi^2 a^2 b^2 B^2}{2R}(\omega^2)$$

3. **(3)** Here degree of freedom, $f = 3 + 3 = 6$ for triatomic non-linear molecule.

Internal energy of a mole of the gas at temperature T,

$$U = \frac{f}{2} nRT = \frac{6}{2} RT = 3RT$$

4. **(1)** Total charge $Q_1 + Q_2 = Q'_1 + Q'_2$

$$= 12\mu C - 3\mu C = 9\mu C$$

Two isolated conducting sphres S_1 and S_2 are now connected by a conducting wire.

$$\therefore V_1 = V_2 = \frac{KQ'_1}{\frac{2}{3}R} = \frac{KQ'_2}{\frac{R}{3}} = 12 - 3 = 9 \text{ }\mu C$$

$$Q'_1 = 2Q'_2 \Rightarrow 2Q'_2 + Q'_2 = 9\mu C$$

$$\therefore Q'_1 = 6\mu C \text{ and } Q'_2 = 3\mu C$$

5. **(3)** Let there be a cylinder of mass m length L and radius R. Now, take elementary disc of radius R and thickness dx at a distance of x from axis OO' then moment of inertia about OO' of this element.

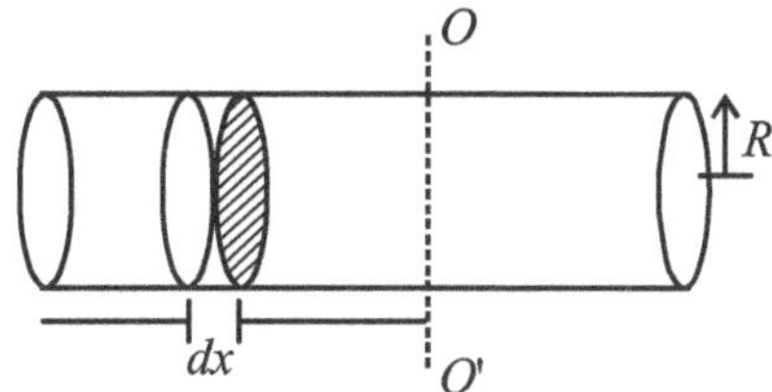

$$dI = \frac{dm R^2}{4} + dm x^2$$

$$\Rightarrow I = \int dI = \int \frac{dm R^2}{4} + \int_{n=L/2}^{n=-L/2} \frac{M}{L} dx \times x^2$$

Given: $I = \frac{MR^2}{4} + \frac{ML^2}{12}$

$$\Rightarrow I = \frac{M}{4} \times \frac{V}{\pi L} + \frac{ML^2}{12} \Rightarrow I = \frac{MV}{4\pi L} + \frac{ML^2}{12}$$

$$\frac{dI}{dL} = -\frac{mV}{4\pi L^2} + \frac{M \times 2L}{12} = 0$$

$$\Rightarrow V = \frac{2}{3}\pi L^3 \Rightarrow \pi R^2 L = \frac{2}{3}\pi L^3$$

$$\therefore \frac{L}{R} = \sqrt{\frac{3}{2}}$$

6. **(2)** Maximum power in external resistance is generated when it is equal to internal resistance of battery i.e., P_R maximum when $r = R$

The maximum Joule heating in R will take place for, the resistance of small element

$$\Delta R = \frac{\rho dr}{2\pi r l} \Rightarrow R = \frac{\rho}{2\pi l}\int_a^b \frac{dr}{r}$$

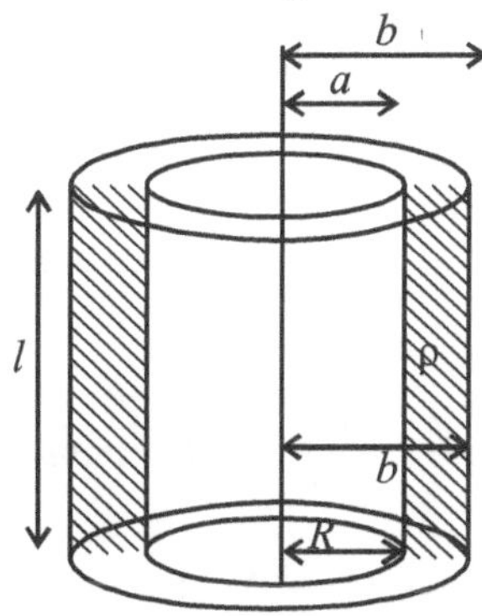

$$\text{or, } R = \frac{\rho}{2\pi l}\ln\frac{b}{a}$$

7. **(3)**

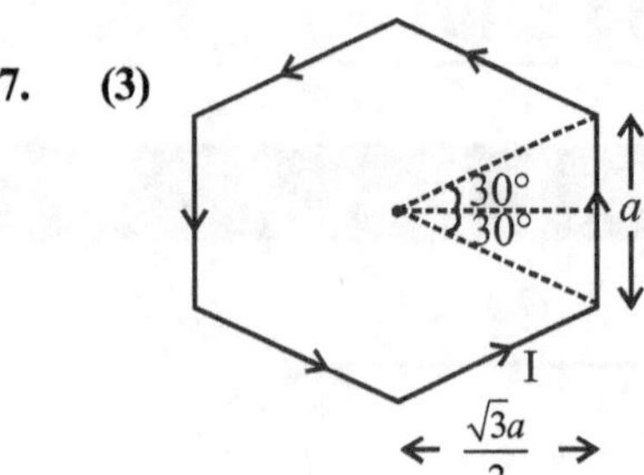

Magnetic field due to one side of hexagon

$$B = \frac{\mu_0 I}{4\pi \frac{\sqrt{3}a}{2}}(\sin 30° + \sin 30°)$$

$$\Rightarrow B = \frac{\mu_0 I}{2\sqrt{3}a}\left(\frac{1}{2}+\frac{1}{2}\right) = \frac{\mu_0 I}{2\sqrt{3}a\pi}$$

Now, magnetic field due to one hexagon coil

$$B = 6 \times \frac{\mu_0 I}{2\sqrt{3}a\pi}$$

Again magnetic field at the centre of hexagonal shape coil of 50 turns,

$$B = 50 \times 6 \times \frac{\mu_0 I}{2\sqrt{3}a\pi} \qquad \left[\because a = \frac{10}{100} = 0.1\ \text{m}\right]$$

or, $B = \dfrac{150\mu_0 I}{\sqrt{3}\times 0.1 \times \pi} = 500\sqrt{3}\,\dfrac{\mu_0 I}{\pi}$

8. **(2)** Bursting of helium balloon is irreversible and in this process $\Delta Q = 0$, so adiabatic.

9. **(4)** Here, $R = 100, X_L = L\omega = 0.1803 \times 750 \times 2\pi = 850\,\Omega,$

$$X_C = \frac{1}{C\omega} = \frac{1}{10^{-5}\times 2\pi \times 750} = 21.23\,\Omega$$

Impedance $Z = \sqrt{R^2 + (X_L - X_C)^2}$

$$= \sqrt{100^2 + (850 - 21.23)^2} = 834.77 \simeq 835$$

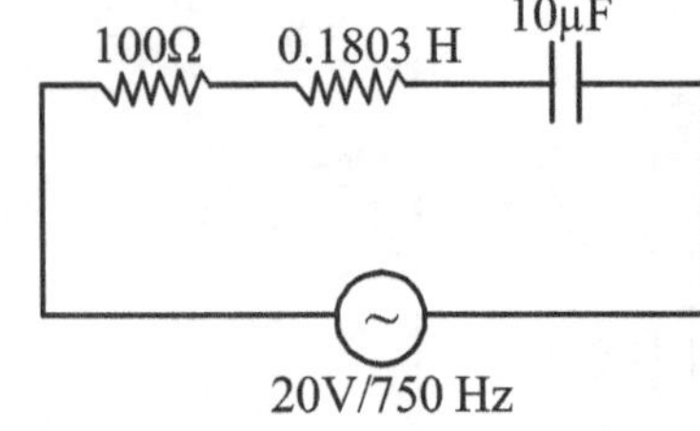

$$H = i_{\text{rms}}^2 Rt = \left(\frac{V_{\text{rms}}}{|Z|}\right)^2 RT = (ms)\Delta t$$

$$\Rightarrow \frac{20}{835}\times\frac{20}{835}\times 100t = (2)\times 10$$

$$\because V_{\text{rms}} = 20\ \text{V and } \Delta t = 10°C$$

$\therefore$ Time, $t = 348.61$ s.

10. **(4)** Given: $\vec{B} = 3 \times 10^{-8}\sin[200\pi(y+ct)]\hat{i}\,T$

$\therefore B_0 = 3 \times 10^{-8}$

$E_0 = CB_0 \Rightarrow E_0 = 3\times 10^8 \times 3 \times 10^{-8} = 9$ V/m

Directiono f wave propagation

$(\vec{E}\times\vec{B}) \parallel \vec{C}$

$\hat{B} = \hat{i}$ and $\hat{C} = -\hat{j}$ $\qquad\qquad \therefore \hat{E} = -\hat{k}$

$\therefore \vec{E} = E_0 \sin[200\pi(y+ct)](-\hat{k})$ V/m

or, $\vec{E} = -9\sin[200\pi(y+ct)]\hat{k}$ V/m

11. **(1)** [Given: $q = 1\mu C = 1\times 10^{-6} C$;

$\vec{V} = (2\hat{i}+3\hat{j}+4\hat{k})$ m/s and

$\vec{B} = (5\hat{i}+3\hat{j}-6\hat{k})\times 10^{-3}$ T]

$$\vec{F} = q(\vec{V}\times\vec{B}) = 10^{-6}\times 10^{-3}\begin{vmatrix} \hat{i} & \hat{j} & \hat{k} \\ 2 & 3 & 4 \\ 5 & 3 & -6 \end{vmatrix}$$

$$= (-30\hat{i}+32\hat{j}-9\hat{k})\times 10^{-9}\ \text{N}$$

$$\therefore \vec{F} = (-30\hat{i}+32\hat{j}-9\hat{k})$$

12. **(2)** According to question,

$$Q = 750\mu C = q_2 + q_3$$

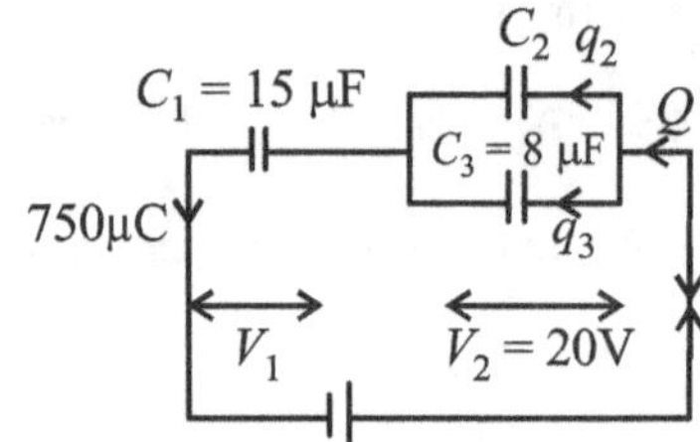

Capacitors C_2 and C_3 are in parallel hence,
Voltage across C_2 = voltage across C_3 = 20 V
Change on capacitor C_3,

$$q_3 = C_3 \times V_3 = 8 \times 20 = 160\mu C$$

$$\therefore q_2 = 750\mu C - 160\mu C = 590\mu C$$

13. **(2)** Given : Wavelength of light, $\lambda = 500$ nm
Distance between the slits, $d = 0.05$ mm
Angular width of the fringe formed,

$$\theta = \frac{\lambda}{d} = \frac{500 \times 10^{-9}}{0.05\times 10^{-3}} = 0.01\ \text{rad} = 0.57°.$$

14. **(1)** Using conservation of angular momentum

$$mvl = \left(ml^2 + \frac{2ml^2}{3}\right)\omega \Rightarrow mvl = \frac{5}{3}ml^2\omega \Rightarrow \omega = \frac{3v}{5l}$$

or, $\omega = \dfrac{3\times 6}{5\times 1} = \dfrac{18}{5}$ rad/s

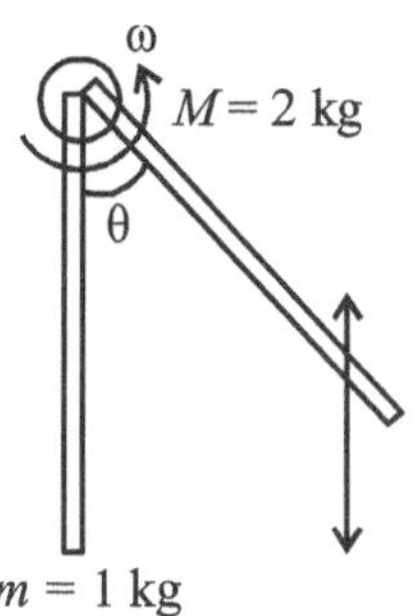

Now using energy conservation, after collision

$$\frac{1}{2}I\omega^2 = 2mg\frac{l}{2}(1-\cos\theta) + mgl(1-\cos\theta)$$

$$\Rightarrow \frac{1}{2}\left(\frac{5}{3}ml^2\right)\frac{9v^2}{25l^2} = 2mgl(1-\cos\theta)$$

$$\Rightarrow \frac{3}{5\times 2}mv^2 = 2mgl(1-\cos\theta)$$

$$\frac{3}{10}\times\frac{36}{2\times 10} = 1-\cos\theta \Rightarrow 1-\frac{27}{50} = \cos\theta$$

or, $\cos\theta = \dfrac{23}{50}$ $\qquad\qquad \therefore \theta \simeq 63°.$

15. **(1)** Thickness = M.S. Reading + Circular Scale Reading (L.C.)

Here LC $= \dfrac{\text{Pitch}}{\text{Circular scale division}} = \dfrac{0.1}{50} = 0.002$ cm per division

So, correct measurement is measurement of integral multiple of L.C.

16. **(3)** Using, $V = f\lambda$

$$\frac{V_1}{\lambda_1} = \frac{V_2}{\lambda_2} \Rightarrow \lambda_2 = \frac{V_2}{V_1}\lambda_1$$

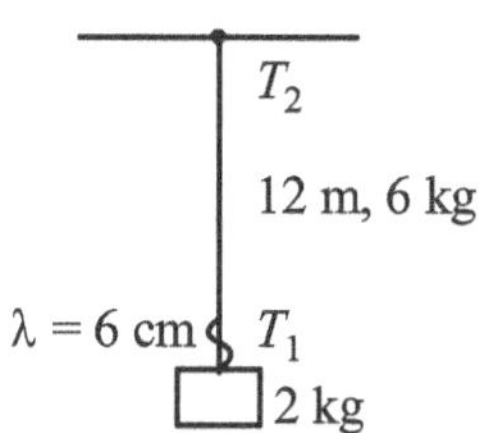

Again using,

$$n = \frac{V}{\lambda} = \sqrt{\frac{T}{M}}\lambda_2 = \sqrt{\frac{T_2}{T_1}}\lambda_1 \qquad T_2 = 8g \text{ (Top)}$$

$$= \sqrt{\frac{8g}{2g}}\lambda_1 = 2\lambda_1 = 12 \text{ cm} \quad T_1 = 2g \text{ (Bottom)}$$

17. **(2)** Using equation, $= \dfrac{hc}{\lambda} - \phi$

$$KE_{\max} = \frac{hc}{\lambda} - \phi = \frac{hc}{500} - \phi \qquad\qquad ...(1)$$

Again, $3KE_{\max} = \dfrac{hc}{200} - \phi$ $\qquad\qquad ...(2)$

Dividing equation (2) by (1),

$$\frac{3KE_{\max}}{KE_{\max}} = \frac{3}{1} = \frac{\dfrac{hc}{200} - \phi}{\dfrac{hc}{500} - \phi}$$

Putting the value of $hc = 1237.5$ and solving we get, work function, $\phi = 0.61$ eV.

18. **(3)** According to question, when diode is forward biased,
$V_{\text{diode}} = 0.5$ V
Safe limit of current, $I = 10$ mA $= 10^{-2}$ A
$R_{\min} = ?$

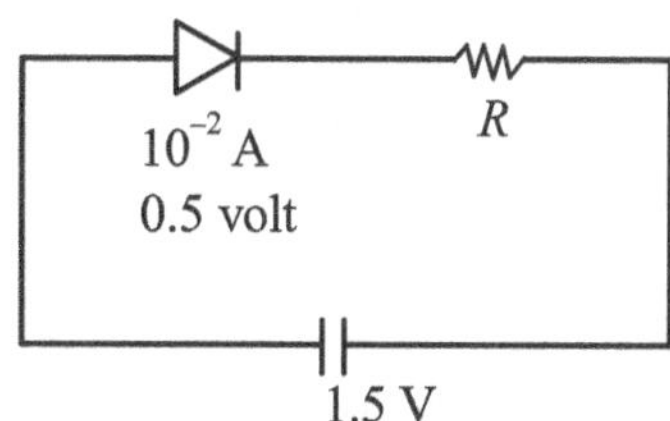

Voltage through resistance
$V_R = 1.5 - 0.5 = 1$ volt
$iR = 1 \ (=V_R)$

$$\therefore R_{\min} = \frac{1}{i} = \frac{1}{10^{-2}} = 100 \ \Omega$$

19. **(3)** According to question, pressure inside, 1st soap bubble,

$$\Delta P_1 = P_1 - P_0 = 0.01 = \frac{4T}{R_1} \qquad\qquad ...(i)$$

And $\Delta P_2 = P_2 - P_0 = 0.02 = \dfrac{4T}{R_2}$ $\qquad ...(ii)$

Dividing, equation (ii) by (i),

$$\frac{1}{2} = \frac{R_2}{R_1} \Rightarrow R_1 = 2R_2$$

Volume $V = \dfrac{4}{3}\pi R^3$

$$\therefore \frac{V_1}{V_2} = \frac{R_1^3}{R_2^3} = \frac{8R_2^3}{R_2^3} = \frac{8}{1}$$

20. (2)

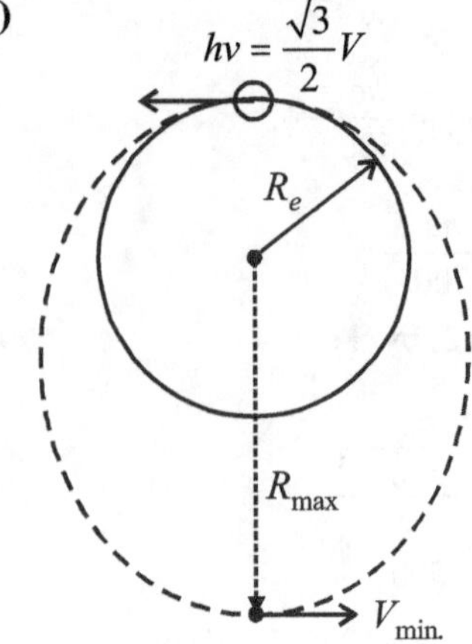

Orbital velocity, $V_0 = \sqrt{\dfrac{GM}{R_e}}$

From energy conversation,

$$-\dfrac{GMm}{R_e} + \dfrac{1}{2}m\left(\sqrt{\dfrac{3}{2}}V\right)^2 = \dfrac{GMm}{R_{max}} + \dfrac{1}{2}mV_{min}^2 \qquad ...(1)$$

From angular momentum conversation

$$\sqrt{\dfrac{3}{2}}VR_e = V_{min}R_{max} \qquad ...(2)$$

Solving equation (1) and (2) we get,

$$R_{max} = 3R_e$$

21. (158)

From figure, $\sin i = \dfrac{15}{\sqrt{15^2 + 30^2}}$ and $\sin r = \sin 45°$

From Snell's law, $\mu \times \sin i = 1 \times \sin r$

$$\Rightarrow \mu \times \dfrac{15}{\sqrt{15^2 + 30^2}} = 1 \times \sin 45° = \dfrac{1}{\sqrt{2}}$$

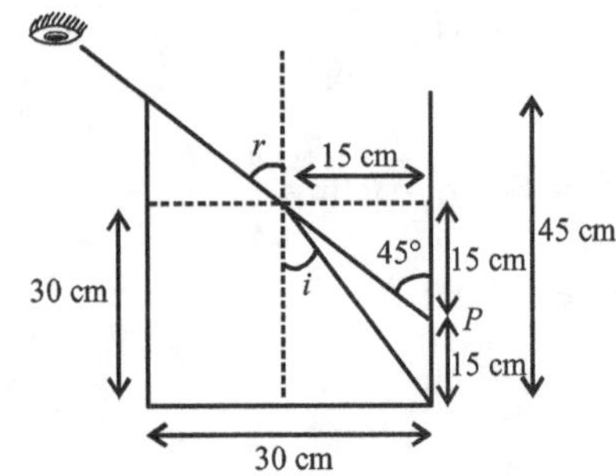

$$\therefore \mu = \dfrac{\dfrac{1}{\sqrt{2}}}{\dfrac{15}{\sqrt{1125}}} = 158 \times 10^{-2} = \dfrac{N}{100}$$

Hence, value of $N \simeq 158$.

22. (150.00)

From work energy theorem, $W = F \cdot s = \Delta KE = \dfrac{1}{2}mv^2$

Here $V^2 = 2gh$

$$\therefore F \cdot s = F \times \dfrac{2}{10} = \dfrac{1}{2} \times \dfrac{15}{100} \times 2 \times 10 \times 20$$

$$\therefore F = 150 \text{ N}.$$

23. (9.00)

Here $M_0 = 200$ kg, $m = 80$ kg

Using conservation of angular momentum, $L_i = L_f$

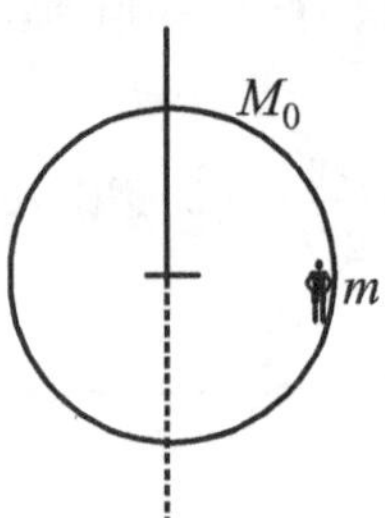

$$I_1\omega_1 = I_2\omega_2$$

$$I_1 = (I_M + I_m) = \left(\dfrac{M_0 R^2}{2} + mR^2\right)$$

$$I_2 = \dfrac{1}{2}M_0 R^2 \text{ and } \omega_1 = 5 \text{ rpm}$$

$$\therefore \omega_2 = \left(\dfrac{M_0 R^2}{2} + mR^2\right) \times \dfrac{5}{\dfrac{M_0 R^2}{2}}$$

$$= \dfrac{5R^2}{R^2} \times \dfrac{(80+100)}{100} = 9 \text{ rpm}.$$

24. (101)

Given : Radius of capillary tube,
$r = 0.015$ cm $= 15 \times 10^{-5}$ mm
$h = 15$ cm $= 15 \times 10^{-2}$ mm

Using, $h = \dfrac{2T\cos\theta}{\rho gr}$ $\qquad [\cos\theta = \cos 0° = 1]$

Surface tension,

$$T = \dfrac{rh\rho g}{2} = \dfrac{15 \times 10^{-5} \times 15 \times 10^{-2} \times 900 \times 10}{2} = 101 \text{ milli}$$

newton m^{-1}

25. (20.00)

Volume capacity of beaker, $V_0 = 500$ cc

$$V_b = V_0 + V_0\gamma_{\text{beaker}}\Delta T$$

When beaker is partially filled with V_m volume of mercury,

$$V_b^1 = V_m + V_m \gamma_m \Delta T$$

Unfilled volume $(V_0 - V_m) = (V_b - V_m^1)$

$$\Rightarrow V_0 \gamma_{beaker} = V_m \gamma_M$$

$$\therefore V_m = \frac{V_0 \gamma_{beaker}}{\gamma_M}$$

or, $V_m = \dfrac{500 \times 6 \times 10^{-6}}{1.5 \times 10^{-4}} = 20$ cc.

CHEMISTRY

26. **(4)** (a) From Henry's law $p = K_H(x)$
Higher the value of K_H smaller will be the solubility of the gas, so γ is more soluble.

(b) Though solubility of gases will decrease with increase in temperature but this conclusion can not be drawn from the given table.

(c) For γ

$(p)_\gamma = (K_H)_\gamma \cdot (x)_\gamma$

$$= 2 \times 10^{-5} \left[\frac{55.5}{55.5 + \dfrac{1000}{18}} \right] = 10^{-5}\ k\,bar = 10^{-2}\,bar$$

(d) For $\delta \Rightarrow$

$p_\delta = (K_H)_\delta \cdot (x)_\delta$

$$= 0.5 \left[\frac{55.5}{55.5 + \dfrac{1000}{18}} \right]$$

$$= 0.5 \times 0.5 = 0.25\ k\,bar = 250\ bar.$$

27. **(4)**

$$\xrightarrow{\text{H}_2/\text{Ni}}$$

Optically inactive
(No chiral centre)

28. **(1)** $CH_3 - CH_2 - \underset{\underset{CH_3}{|}}{CH} - OCOCH_2 - \underset{\underset{(A)}{|}}{CH} - CH_2CH_3 \xrightarrow{H_2SO_4\ (dil.)}$

$CH_3-CH_2-\underset{\underset{\underset{(C)}{CH_3}}{|}}{CH}-OH + HOOC-CH_2-\underset{\underset{(B)}{|}}{\underset{CH_3}{|}}{CH}-CH_2-CH_3$

$$\Big\downarrow \text{CrO}_3/\text{H}^+$$

$CH_3- CH_2 - \underset{\underset{CH_3}{|}}{C} = O$

29. **(3)** Above reaction is S_N1 reaction as it proceeds via formation of carbocation. Polar protic solvent is more suitable for S_N1 and so racemisation takes place.

30. **(4)** Acidic strength $\propto -I, -M$ effect. Due to strong $- I$, and $-M$ effect of $3 - COOCH_3$ group, it has most acidic Hydrogen.

31. **(1)** Burning of fossil fuels (which contain sulphur and nitrogenous matter) such as coal and oil in power stations and furnaces produce sulphur dioxide and nitrogen oxides which causes acid rain.

32. **(4)**

$$HCl + CH_3COONa \longrightarrow CH_3COOH + NaCl$$

Millimoles at start	10	20	0	0
Millimoles after reaction	0	10	10	10

Buffer solution contains CH_3COONa (10 millimole) and CH_3COOH (10 millimole) which is a acidic buffer.

33. **(1)** At room temperature, water is liquid and has boiling point 373 K due to hydrogen bonding. Whereas H_2S is a gas and it has no hydrogen bonding. Hence boiling point of H_2S is less than 300 K (boiling point of H_2S is $-60°C$).

34. **(4)** Tyndall effect is observed only when the following two conditions are satisfied.

(i) The diameter of the dispersed particles is not much smaller than the wavelength of the light used.

(ii) The refractive indices of the dispersed phase and the dispersion medium differ greatly in magnitude.

35. **(4)** Glycerol can be separated from spent-lye in soap industry by using reduce pressure distillation technique.

36. **(4)** $[Ti(H_2O)_6]^{3+} \Rightarrow Ti^{3+} = 3d^1\ 4s^0$

$\therefore$ Electronic configuration is $t_{2g}^1 e_g^0$

$CFSE = [-0.4 n_{t_{2g}} + 0.6 n_{e_g}]\ \Delta_0 + n(p)$

$$= [(-0.4) \times 1 + 0]\ 20300$$

$$= -8120\ cm^{-1}$$

$$= \frac{-8120}{83.7}\ kJ/mol = -97\ kJ/mol$$

37. **(1)**

$$\xrightarrow{\text{Sn/HCl}}$$

(Product will give positive Kjeldhal test due to presence of $-NH_2$ group)

(b)

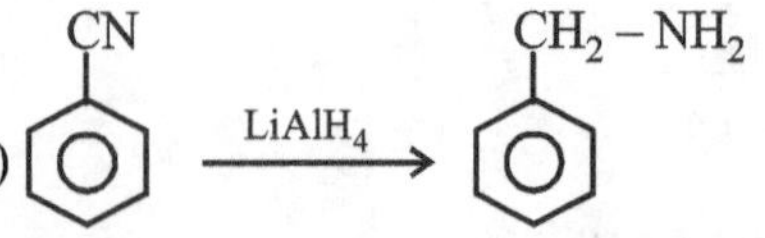

$$\text{CN} \xrightarrow{\text{LiAlH}_4} \text{CH}_2\text{–NH}_2$$

(N-present in product so it will show Kjeldhal Test)

(c)

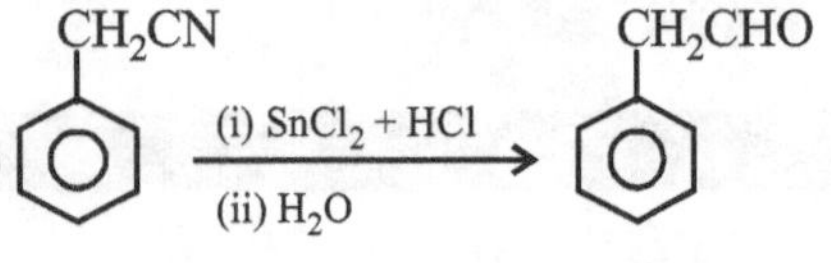

$$\text{CH}_2\text{CN} \xrightarrow[\text{(ii) H}_2\text{O}]{\text{(i) SnCl}_2 + \text{HCl}} \text{CH}_2\text{CHO}$$

(N-absent)

(d)

$$\text{NH}_2 \xrightarrow[\text{HCl}]{\text{NaNO}_2} \overset{+}{\text{N}}_2\text{Cl}^-$$

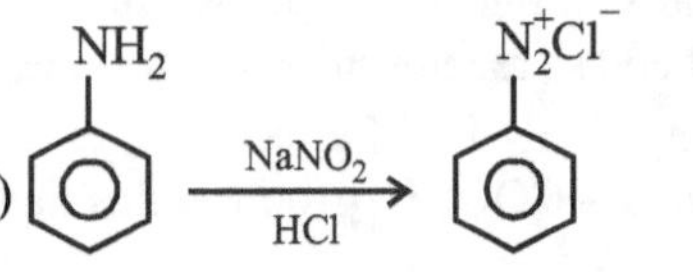

($-\overset{+}{\text{N}}_2$ Never show Kjeldhal test)

38. **(1)** un $= 1$
nil $= 0$
enn $= 9$
So, atomic number $= 109$

39. **(2)** Zero order reaction is always multi step reaction.

40. **(N)** Ionic mobility increases with increase in temperature, which increases the conductance of the solution, while conductance of NaCl solution is independant of temperature above 400°C. Because the temperature is not given, so none of the option is correct.

41. **(4)** Only *cis*-[CrCl$_2$(ox)$_2$]$^{3-}$ shows optical isomerism while its *trans* form do not show optical isomerism due to presence of plane of symmetry.

42. **(1)** Aqua regia is HNO$_3$: HCl
                 1   :   3

$$\text{Au} + 4\text{H}^+ + \text{NO}_3^- + 4\text{Cl}^- \longrightarrow \text{AuCl}_4^- + \text{NO} + 2\text{H}_2\text{O}$$
$$3\text{Pt} + 16\text{H}^+ + 4\text{NO}_3^- + 18\text{Cl}^- \longrightarrow$$
$$3\text{PtCl}_6^{2-} + 4\text{NO} + 8\text{H}_2\text{O}$$

43. **(4)**

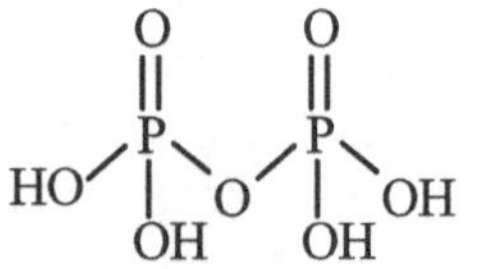

Pyrophosphoric acid

No. of P $=$ O bond $= 2$.
P – OH bond $= 4$
P – O – P bond $= 1$.

44. **(4)**

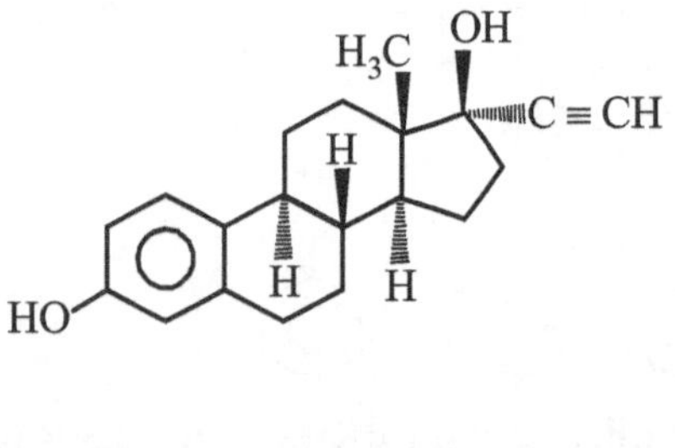

Novestrol has phenolic, alcoholic and terminal alkyne groups, so it can react with Br$_2$ water, ZnCl$_2$/HCl as well as FeCl$_3$.

45. **(4)** Molecular orbital configuration for NO is

$$\sigma 1s^2 \; \sigma^* 1s^2 \; \sigma 2s^2 \; \sigma^* 2s^2 \; \pi 2p_x^2 \; \pi 2p_y^2 \; \sigma 2p_z^2 \; \pi^* 2p_z^1$$

Species	Bond order
NO$^+$	3
NO^{2+}	2.5
NO$^-$	2
NO	2.5

Bond strength is directly proportional to the bond order, so NO$^-$ has minimum bond strength.

46. **(47)**
Let total mole of solution $= 1$
So, mole of glucose $= 0.1$
Mole of H$_2$O $= 0.9$

$$\% \text{ (w/w) of H}_2\text{O} = \left[\frac{0.9 \times 18}{0.9 \times 18 + 0.1 \times 180}\right] \times 100$$
$$= 47.368 = 47.37.$$

47. **(142)**
Sodium metal :

$E = E_0 + (\text{KE})_{max}$; $E_{cell}^0 = 0.22$ V

Cell reaction

Cathode : $\text{AgCl(s)} + e^- \longrightarrow \text{Ag(s)} + \text{Cl}^-\text{(aq)}$

Anode : $\dfrac{1}{2}\text{H}_2\text{(g)} \longrightarrow \text{H}^+\text{(aq)} + e^-$

Overall : $\text{AgCl(s)} + \dfrac{1}{2}\text{H}_2\text{(g)} \longrightarrow \text{Ag(s)} + \text{H}^+\text{(aq)} + \text{Cl}^-\text{(aq)}$

$$E_{cell} = E_{cell}^0 - \frac{0.06}{1}\log[\text{H}^+][\text{Cl}^-]$$

$$E_{cell} = 0.22 - \frac{0.06}{1}\log[10^{-1}][10^{-1}]$$

$$= 0.22 + 0.12 = 0.34 \text{ V}$$

$(\text{KE})_{max} = E_{cell} = 0.34$ eV
So, E $= 2.3 + 0.34 = 2.64$ eV $=$ Energy of photon incident
For potassium metal :
$E = E_0 + (\text{KE})_{max}$
$2.64 = 2.25 + (\text{KE})_{max}$
$(\text{KE})_{max} = 0.39 = E_{cell}$
Cell reaction

Cathode : $\text{AgCl(s)} + e^- \longrightarrow \text{Ag(s)} + \text{Cl}^-\text{(aq)}$

Anode : $\dfrac{1}{2}H_2(g) \longrightarrow H^+(aq) + e^-$

Overall : $AgCl(s) + \dfrac{1}{2}H_2(g) \longrightarrow Ag(s) + H^+(aq) + Cl^-(aq)$

$E_{cell} = E^0_{cell} - \dfrac{0.06}{1}\log[H^+][Cl^-]$

$0.39 = 0.22 - 0.06\log[H^+]^2$

$0.39 = 0.22 - 0.12\log[H^+]$

$0.17 = 0.12 \times pH$

$pH = 17/12 = 1.4166 \simeq 1.42 = 142 \times 10^{-2}$

48. (143)

$$d = \dfrac{Z \times M}{N_A \times \text{Volume}}$$

$$2.7 = \dfrac{Z \times 27}{6.02 \times 10^{23} \times [4.05 \times 10^{-8}]^3}$$

$Z = 4 \Rightarrow fcc$ unit cell

For fcc unit cell $4r = \sqrt{2}a$

$$r = \dfrac{1.414 \times 405}{4} = 143.1675 \text{ pm} = 143.17 \text{ pm}$$

49. 8

$$CH_3-\overset{\overset{\displaystyle H}{|}}{\underset{\underset{\displaystyle CH_2-CH_3}{|}}{C}}-CH=CH_2 \xrightarrow{H_2/Ni} CH_3-\overset{\overset{\displaystyle H}{|}}{\underset{\underset{\underset{\displaystyle CH_3}{|}}{\underset{\displaystyle CH_2}{|}}}{C}}-CH_2-CH_3$$

$\Big\downarrow Cl_2/HCl$

(4) + (1)

2 Pair of enantiomers

$(d + \ell)$ + (1)

(2)   (1)

50. (100)

$$\text{Molarity of } H_2O_2 \text{ solution} = \left\{\dfrac{\text{Volume strength}}{11.2}\right\}$$

Volume strength $= 8.9 \times 11.2 = 99.68\text{ V} \simeq 100\text{ V}$

MATHEMATICS

51. (3) $\quad y^2 + 2\log_e(\cos x) = y \qquad$ ...(i)

$\Rightarrow 2yy' - 2\tan x = y' \qquad$ ...(ii)

From (i), $y(0) = 0$ or 1

$\therefore y'(0) = 0$

Again differentiating (ii) we get,

$2(y')^2 + 2yy'' - 2\sec^2 x = y''$

Put $x = 0, y(0) = 0, 1$ and $y'(0) = 0$,

we get, $|y''(0)| = 2$.

52. (3) $\quad 2\pi - \left(\sin^{-1}\dfrac{4}{5} + \sin^{-1}\dfrac{5}{13} + \sin^{-1}\dfrac{16}{65}\right)$

$= 2\pi - \left(\tan^{-1}\dfrac{4}{3} + \tan^{-1}\dfrac{5}{12} + \tan^{-1}\dfrac{16}{63}\right)$

$$\left[\because \sin^{-1}\dfrac{4}{5} = \tan^{-1}\dfrac{4}{3}\right]$$

$= 2\pi - \left\{\tan^{-1}\left(\dfrac{\dfrac{4}{3} + \dfrac{5}{12}}{1 - \dfrac{4}{3}\cdot\dfrac{5}{12}}\right) + \tan^{-1}\dfrac{16}{63}\right\}$

$= 2\pi - \left(\tan^{-1}\dfrac{63}{16} + \tan^{-1}\dfrac{16}{63}\right)$

$= 2\pi - \left(\tan^{-1}\dfrac{63}{16} + \cot^{-1}\dfrac{63}{16}\right)$

$= 2\pi - \dfrac{\pi}{2} = \dfrac{3\pi}{2}$.

53. (1) Given $a = 3$ and $S_{25} = S_{40} - S_{25}$

$\Rightarrow 2S_{25} = S_{40}$

$\Rightarrow 2 \times \dfrac{25}{2}[6 + 24d] = \dfrac{40}{2}[6 + 39d]$

$\Rightarrow 25[6 + 24d] = 20[6 + 39d]$

$\Rightarrow 5(2 + 8d) = 4(2 + 13d)$

$\Rightarrow 10 + 40d = 8 + 52d$

$\Rightarrow d = \dfrac{1}{6}$

54. (4) The given ellipse :

$$\dfrac{x^2}{4} + \dfrac{y^2}{3} = 1$$

$\because c = \sqrt{a^2 - b^2} = \sqrt{4 - 3} = 1$

$\therefore$ Foci $= (\pm 1, 0)$

Now for hyperbola :

Given : $2a = \sqrt{2} \Rightarrow a = \dfrac{1}{\sqrt{2}}$

$\because c^2 = a^2 + b^2 \Rightarrow 1 = \dfrac{1}{2} + b^2 \Rightarrow b = \dfrac{1}{\sqrt{2}}$

So, equation of hyperbola is

$$\dfrac{x^2}{\dfrac{1}{2}} - \dfrac{y^2}{\dfrac{1}{2}} = 1 \qquad \Rightarrow 2x^2 - 2y^2 = 1$$

So, option (d) does not satisfy it.

55. (b)

p	q	$\sim q$	$p \wedge \sim q$	$\sim p$	$p \to \sim(p \wedge \sim q)$	$\sim p \vee q$
T	T	F	F	F	T	T
T	F	T	T	F	F	F
F	T	F	F	T	T	T
F	F	T	F	T	T	T

$\therefore p \to \sim(p \wedge \sim q)$ is equivalent to $\sim p \vee q$

56. (3)

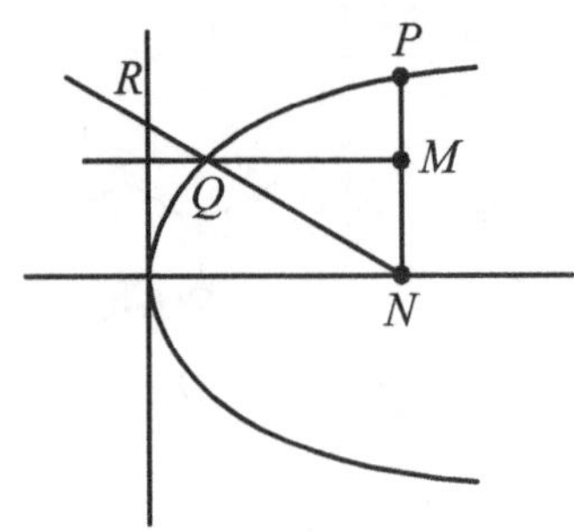

$\because y^2 = 12x$

$\therefore a = 3$

Let $P(at^2, 2at)$

$\Rightarrow N(at^2, 0) \Rightarrow M(at^2, at)$

$\because$ Equation of QM is $y = at$

So, $y^2 = 4ax \Rightarrow x = \dfrac{at^2}{4}$

$\Rightarrow Q\left(\dfrac{at^2}{4}, at\right)$

$\Rightarrow$ Equation of QN is $y = \dfrac{-4}{3t}(x - at^2)$

$\because QN$ passes through $\left(0, \dfrac{4}{3}\right)$, then

$\dfrac{4}{3} = -\dfrac{4}{3t}(-at^2) \Rightarrow at = 1 \Rightarrow t = \dfrac{1}{3}$

Now, $MQ = \dfrac{3}{4}at^2 = \dfrac{1}{4}$ and $PN = 2at = 2$

57. (1) $A = \{m \in \mathbf{R} : x^2 - (m+1)x + m + 4 = 0 \text{ has real roots}\}$

$D \geq 0$

$\Rightarrow (m+1)^2 - 4(m+4) \geq 0$

$\Rightarrow m^2 - 2m - 15 \geq 0$

$A = \{(-\infty, -3] \cup [5, \infty)\}$

$B = [-3, 5) \Rightarrow A - B = (-\infty, -3) \cup [5, \infty)$

58. (4) $\alpha \cdot \beta = 2$ and $\alpha + \beta = -p$ also $\dfrac{1}{\alpha} + \dfrac{1}{\beta} = -q$

$\Rightarrow p = 2q$

Now $\left(\alpha - \dfrac{1}{\alpha}\right)\left(\beta - \dfrac{1}{\beta}\right)\left(\alpha + \dfrac{1}{\beta}\right)\left(\beta + \dfrac{1}{\alpha}\right)$

$= \left[\alpha\beta + \dfrac{1}{\alpha\beta} - \dfrac{\alpha}{\beta} - \dfrac{\beta}{\alpha}\right]\left[\alpha\beta + \dfrac{1}{\alpha\beta} + 2\right]$

$= \dfrac{9}{2}\left[\dfrac{5}{2} - \dfrac{\alpha^2 + \beta^2}{2}\right] = \dfrac{9}{4}[5 - (p^2 - 4)]$

$= \dfrac{9}{4}(9 - p^2)$ $\qquad [\because \alpha^2 + \beta^2 = (\alpha+\beta)^2 - 2\alpha\beta]$

59. (3) $\Delta = \begin{vmatrix} x-2 & 2x-3 & 3x-4 \\ 2x-3 & 3x-4 & 4x-5 \\ 3x-5 & 5x-8 & 10x-17 \end{vmatrix}$

$\Rightarrow \Delta = \begin{vmatrix} x-2 & x-1 & x-1 \\ 2x-3 & x-1 & x-1 \\ 3x-5 & 2x-3 & 5x-9 \end{vmatrix}$ $\begin{bmatrix} C_3 \to C_3 - C_2 \\ C_2 \to C_2 - C_1 \end{bmatrix}$

$\Rightarrow \Delta = \begin{vmatrix} x-2 & x-1 & x-1 \\ x-1 & 0 & 0 \\ 3x-5 & 2x-3 & 5x-9 \end{vmatrix}$ $\begin{bmatrix} R_2 \to R_2 - R_1 \end{bmatrix}$

$\Rightarrow \Delta = -(x-1)[(x-1)(5x-9) - (x-1)(2x-3)]$

$\Rightarrow \Delta = -(x-1)[(5x^2 - 14x + 9) - (2x^2 - 5x + 3)]$

$= -3x^3 + 12x^2 - 15x + 6$

So, $B + C = -3$

60. (2)

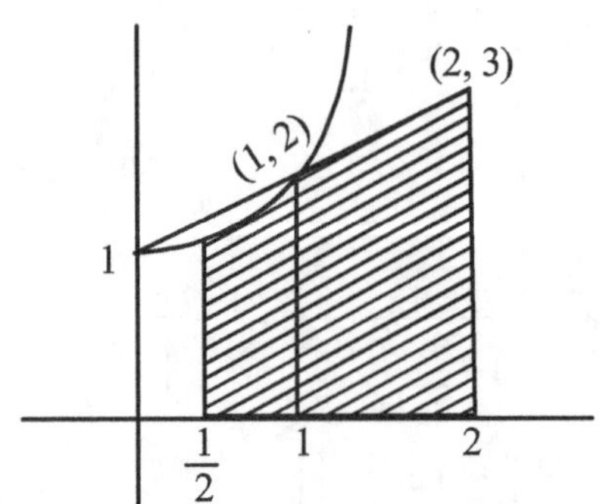

Required area $= \displaystyle\int_{\frac{1}{2}}^{1}(x^2 + 1)\,dx + \int_{1}^{2}(x+1)\,dx$

$$= \left[\frac{x^3}{3} + x\right]_{\frac{1}{2}}^{1} + \left[\frac{x^2}{2} + x\right]_{1}^{2}$$

$$= \left[\frac{4}{3} - \frac{13}{24}\right] + \frac{5}{2} = \frac{79}{24}.$$

61. **(1)** Equation of line through points $(1, -2, 3)$ and $(1, 1, 0)$ is

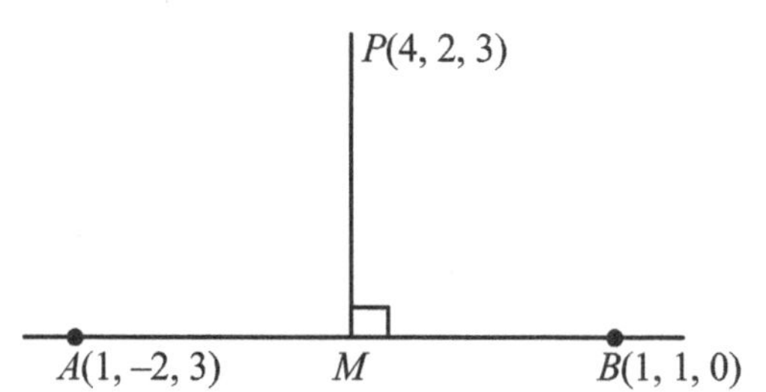

$$\frac{x-1}{0} = \frac{y-1}{-3} = \frac{z-0}{3-0} \qquad (=\lambda \text{ say})$$

$\therefore M(1, -\lambda+1, \lambda)$

Direction ratios of $PM = [-3, -\lambda-1, \lambda-3]$

$\because PM \perp AB$

$\therefore (-3)\cdot 0 + (-1-\lambda)(-1) + (\lambda-3)\cdot 1 = 0$

$\therefore \lambda = 1$

$\therefore$ Foot of perpendicular $= (1, 0, 1)$

This point satisfy the plane $2x + y - z = 1$.

62. **(3)** $\displaystyle \int\left(\frac{y^2+1}{y^2}\right) dy = \int \frac{e^x dx}{e^x+1}$

$$\Rightarrow y - \frac{1}{y} = \log_e |e^x+1| + c$$

$\because$ Passes through $(0, 1)$.

$\therefore c = -\log_e 2$

$$\Rightarrow y^2 - 1 = y \log_e\left(\frac{e^x+1}{2}\right)$$

$$\Rightarrow y^2 = 1 + y \log_e\left(\frac{e^x+1}{2}\right)$$

63. **(4)** E_1 [the event for getting score a multiple of 4]
$= (1, 3), (3, 1), (2, 2), (2, 6), (6, 2), (3, 5), (5, 3), (4, 4) \& (6, 6)$
E_2 [4 has appeared atleast once]
$= (1, 4), (2, 4), (3, 4), (4, 4), (5, 4), (6, 4), (4, 1), (4, 2), (4, 3),$
$(4, 5) \& (4, 6)$

$E_1 \cap E_2 = (4, 4)$

$$P\left(\frac{E_2}{E_1}\right) = \frac{1}{9}$$

64. **(3)** $I = \displaystyle\int_{-\pi}^{\pi} |\pi - |x|| \, dx \qquad [\because |\pi - |x|| \text{ is even}]$

$$= 2\int_0^{\pi} |\pi - |x|| \, dx$$

$$= 2\int_0^{\pi} (\pi - x)\, dx$$

$$= 2\left[\pi x - \frac{x^2}{2}\right]_0^{\pi} = 2\left(\pi^2 - \frac{\pi^2}{2}\right) = \pi^2.$$

65. **(3)** If variate varries from a to b then variance

$$\text{var}(x) \le \left(\frac{b-a}{2}\right)^2$$

$$\Rightarrow \text{var}(x) < \left(\frac{10-0}{2}\right)^2$$

$$\Rightarrow \text{var}(x) < 25$$

$\Rightarrow$ standard deviation < 5

It is clear that standard deviation cann't be 6.

66. **(1)** $L_1 \equiv \vec{r} = (\hat{i} - \hat{j}) + \ell(2\hat{i} + \hat{k})$

$L_2 \equiv \vec{r} = (2\hat{i} - \hat{j}) + m(\hat{i} + \hat{j} - \hat{k})$

Equating coeff. of $\hat{i}, \hat{j}$ and $\hat{k}$ of L_1 and L_2

$2\ell + 1 = m + 2 \qquad \qquad ...(i)$

$-1 = -1 + m \Rightarrow m = 0 \qquad ...(ii)$

$\ell = -m \qquad \qquad ...(iii)$

$\Rightarrow m = \ell = 0$ which is not satisfy eqn. (i) hence lines do not intersect for any value of ℓ and m.

67. **(2)** Given $\displaystyle\lim_{x\to 0}\left|\frac{1-x+|x|}{\lambda - x + [x]}\right| = L$

Here, L.H.L. $= \displaystyle\lim_{h\to 0}\left|\frac{1+h+h}{\lambda + h - 1}\right| = \left|\frac{1}{\lambda-1}\right|$

R.H.L. $= \displaystyle\lim_{h\to 0}\left|\frac{1-h+h}{\lambda + h + 0}\right| = \left|\frac{1}{\lambda}\right|$

Given that limit exists. Hence L.H.L. $=$ R.H.L.

$$\Rightarrow |\lambda - 1| = |\lambda|$$

$$\Rightarrow \lambda = \frac{1}{2} \text{ and } L = \left|\frac{1}{\lambda}\right| = 2$$

68. **(3)** We know, $(r+1)\cdot {}^{r}P_{r-1} = (r+1)\cdot\frac{r!}{1!} = (r+1)!$

So, $(2\cdot {}^{1}P_0 - 3\cdot {}^{2}P_1 + ...51 \text{ terms}) +$
$\qquad\qquad\qquad (1! - 2! + 3! - ... \text{ upto } 51 \text{ terms})$

$= [2! - 3! + 4! - ... + 52!] + [1! - 2! + 3! - ... + 51!]$

$= 52! + 1! = 52! + 1$

69. **(1)** $f(x) = (3x - 7)\cdot x^{2/3}$

$f'(x) = 3x^{2/3} + (3x - 7)\cdot\frac{2}{3}x^{-1/3}$

$$= \frac{15x - 14}{3x^{1/3}}$$

$$\frac{+}{0} \; \overset{\times}{\underset{}{}} \; \frac{-}{\frac{14}{15}} \; \overset{\times}{\underset{}{}} \; +$$

For increasing function

$f'(x) > 0$ then $x \in (-\infty, 0) \cup \left(\dfrac{14}{15}, \infty\right)$

70. **(3)** Here, $\left(3^{\frac{1}{2}} + 5^{\frac{1}{8}}\right)^{n}$

$T_{r+1} = {}^{n}C_{r}(3)^{\frac{n-r}{2}}(5)^{\frac{r}{8}}$

$\because \dfrac{n-r}{2}$ and $\dfrac{r}{8}$ are integer

So, r must be 0, 8, 16, 24 ......

Now $n = t_{33} = a + (n-1)d = 0 + 32 \times 8 = 256$

$\Rightarrow n = 256$

71. **(4)**

$(0.16)^{\log_{2.5}\left(\frac{1}{3}+\frac{1}{3^2}+\frac{1}{3^3}+.....\infty\right)}$

$= 0.16^{\log_{2.5}\left(\frac{\frac{1}{3}}{1-\frac{1}{3}}\right)}$ $\left[\because S_{\infty} = \dfrac{a}{1-r}\right]$

$= 0.16^{\log_{2.5}\left(\frac{1}{2}\right)}$

$= (2.5)^{-2\log_{2.5}\left(\frac{1}{2}\right)} = \left(\dfrac{1}{2}\right)^{-2} = 4.$

72. **(10)**

$A^2 = \begin{bmatrix} x & 1 \\ 1 & 0 \end{bmatrix}\begin{bmatrix} x & 1 \\ 1 & 0 \end{bmatrix} = \begin{bmatrix} x^2+1 & x \\ x & 1 \end{bmatrix}$

$A^4 = \begin{bmatrix} x^2+1 & x \\ x & 1 \end{bmatrix}\begin{bmatrix} x^2+1 & x \\ x & 1 \end{bmatrix}$

$= \begin{bmatrix} (x^2+1)^2+x^2 & x(x^2+1)+x \\ x(x^2+1)+x & x^2+1 \end{bmatrix}$

Given that $(x^2+1)^2 + x^2 = 109$

$x^4 + 3x^2 - 108 = 0$

$\Rightarrow (x^2+12)(x^2-9) = 0$

$\therefore x^2 = 9$

$a_{22} = x^2 + 1 = 9 + 1 = 10.$

73. **(3)**

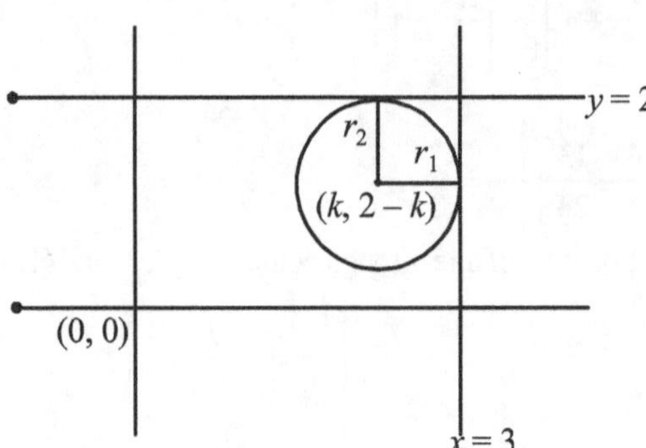

$\Rightarrow$ Radius $(r_1) = 3 - k$

$\because$ Centre lies on $x + y = 2$

Let $x = k$

$\therefore y = 2 - k$

$\Rightarrow$ Centre $= (k, 2-k)$

Also, radius $(r_2) = 2 - (2-k)$

$\therefore 3 - k = 2 - (2-k)$

$\Rightarrow k = \dfrac{3}{2}$

$r = 3 - \dfrac{3}{2} = \dfrac{3}{2}$

Hence, diameter $= 3$.

74. **(4)**

Given that $\left(\dfrac{1+i}{1-i}\right)^{m/2} = \left(\dfrac{1+i}{i-1}\right)^{n/3} = 1$

$\Rightarrow \left(\dfrac{(1+i)^2}{2}\right)^{m/2} = \left(\dfrac{(1+i)^2}{-2}\right)^{n/3} = 1$

$\Rightarrow i^{m/2} = (-i)^{n/3} = 1$

m (least) $= 8$, n (least) $= 12$

$GCD(8, 12) = 4$.

75. **(8)**

$\displaystyle\lim_{x\to 0} \dfrac{\left(1-\cos\dfrac{x^2}{2}\right)\left(1-\cos\dfrac{x^2}{4}\right)}{x^4 \cdot x^4} = 2^{-k}$

$\Rightarrow \displaystyle\lim_{x\to 0} \dfrac{2\sin^2\dfrac{x^2}{4}}{\dfrac{x^4}{16}\times 16} \times \dfrac{2\sin^2\dfrac{x^2}{8}}{\dfrac{x^4}{64}\times 64} = 2^{-k}$

$\Rightarrow \dfrac{4}{16 \times 64} = 2^{-8} = 2^{-k}$ $\left[\because \displaystyle\lim_{\theta\to 0}\dfrac{\sin\theta}{\theta} = 1\right]$

$\therefore k = 8$

PHYSICS

1. **(1)** We have given two metallic hollow spheres of radii R and $4R$ having charges Q_1 and Q_2 respectively.

Potential on the surface of inner sphere (at A)

$$V_A = \frac{kQ_1}{R} + \frac{kQ_2}{4R}$$

Potential on the surface of outer sphere (at B)

$$V_B = \frac{kQ_1}{4R} + \frac{kQ_2}{4R} \qquad \left(\text{Here, } k = \frac{1}{4\pi\varepsilon_0}\right)$$

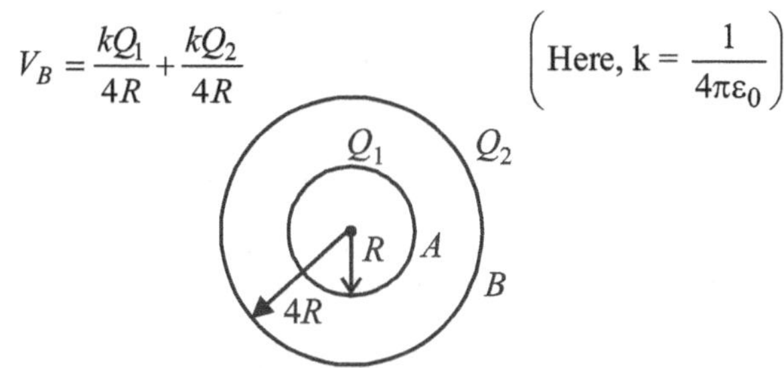

Potential difference,

$$\Delta V = V_A - V_B = \frac{3}{4} \cdot \frac{kQ_1}{R} = \frac{3}{16\pi \in_0} \cdot \frac{Q_1}{R}$$

2. **(3)** Relation between electric field and magnetic field for an electromagnetic wave in vacuum is $B_0 = \dfrac{E_0}{c}$.

In free space, its speed $c = \dfrac{1}{\sqrt{\mu_0 \varepsilon_0}}$

Here, μ_0 = absolute permeability, ε_0 = absolute permittivity

$$\therefore B_0 = \frac{E_0}{c} = \frac{E_0}{1/\sqrt{\mu_0\varepsilon_0}} = E_0\sqrt{\mu_0\varepsilon_0}$$

As the electromagnetic wave is propagating along x direction and electric field is along y direction.

$\therefore \hat{E} \times \hat{B} \parallel \hat{C}$ (Here, $\hat{C}$ = direction of propagation of wave)

$\therefore \vec{B}$ should be in $\hat{k}$ direction.

$\therefore \mathrm{B} = \mathrm{E_o}\sqrt{\mu_o\varepsilon_o}\ \cos(\mathrm{Wt} - \mathrm{Kx})\ \hat{k}$

At $t = 0$

$\mathrm{B} = \mathrm{E_o}\sqrt{\mu_o\varepsilon_o}\ \cos(\mathrm{Kx})\ \hat{k}$

3. **(1)** Potential energy of spring $= \dfrac{1}{2}kx^2$

Here, x = distance of block from mean position,
  k = spring constant

At mean position, potential energy $= \dfrac{1}{2}kA^2$

At equilibrium position, half of the mass of block breaks off, so its potential energy becomes half.

Remaining energy $= \dfrac{1}{2}\left(\dfrac{1}{2}kA^2\right) = \dfrac{1}{2}kA'^2$

Here, A' = New distance of block from mean position

$$\Rightarrow A' = \frac{A}{\sqrt{2}}$$

4. **(2)** We know that

Power, $P = Fv$

But $F = mav = m\dfrac{dv}{dt}v$

$$\therefore P = mv\frac{dv}{dt} \Rightarrow P\,dt = mv\,dv$$

Integrating both sides $\displaystyle\int_0^t P\ dt = m\int_0^v v\ dv$

$$\text{P. } t = \frac{1}{2}mv^2 \Rightarrow v = \left(\sqrt{\frac{2P}{m}}\right)t^{1/2}$$

Distance, $\displaystyle s = \int_0^t v\,dt = \sqrt{\frac{2P}{m}}\int_0^t t^{1/2}\,dt = \sqrt{\frac{2P}{m}} \cdot \frac{t^{3/2}}{3/2}$

$$\Rightarrow s = \sqrt{\frac{8P}{9m}} \cdot t^{3/2} \Rightarrow s \propto t^{3/2}$$

So, graph (b) is correct.

5. **(2)** Given,

Length of wire, $l = 30$ cm

Radius of wire, $r = 2$ mm $= 2 \times 10^{-3}$ m

Resistivity of metal wire, $\rho = 1.23 \times 10^{-8}\ \Omega\mathrm{m}$

Emf generated, $|e| = \dfrac{d\phi}{dt} = \dfrac{dB}{dt}(A) \qquad (\because \phi = \mathrm{B.A.})$

Current, $i = \dfrac{e}{R}$

But, resistance of wire, $R = \rho\dfrac{l}{A}$

$$\therefore i = \left|\frac{dB}{dt}\right|\frac{(A)^2}{\rho l} = \frac{0.032 \times \{\pi \times 2 \times 10^{-3}\}^2}{1.23 \times 10^{-8} \times 0.3} = 0.61\ \mathrm{A}.$$

6. **(4)**

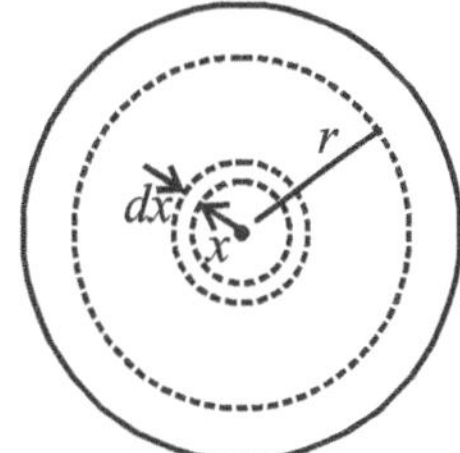

Mass of small element of planet of radius x and thickness dx.

$$dm = \rho \times 4\pi x^2 dx = \rho_0\left(1 - \frac{x^2}{R^2}\right) \times 4\pi x^2 dx$$

Mass of the planet

$$M = 4\pi\rho_0 \int_0^r \left(x^2 - \frac{x^4}{R^2}\right)dx$$

$$\Rightarrow M = 4\pi\rho_0 \left|\frac{r^3}{3} - \frac{r^5}{5R^2}\right|$$

Gravitational field,

$$E = \frac{GM}{r^2} = \frac{G}{r^2} \times 4\pi\rho_0 \left(\frac{r^3}{3} - \frac{r^5}{5R^2} \right)$$

$$\Rightarrow E = 4\pi G\rho_0 \left(\frac{r}{3} - \frac{r^3}{5R^2} \right)$$

E is maximum when $\dfrac{dE}{dr} = 0$

$$\Rightarrow \frac{dE}{dr} = 4\pi G\rho_0 \left(\frac{1}{3} - \frac{3r^2}{5R^2} \right) = 0$$

$$\Rightarrow r = \frac{\sqrt{5}}{3}R$$

7. **(2)** From Newton's Law of cooling,

$$\frac{T_1 - T_2}{t} = K\left[\frac{T_1 + T_2}{2} - T_0 \right]$$

Here, $T_1 = 50°C$, $T_2 = 40°C$
an d $T_0 = 20°C$, $t = 600S = 5$ minutes

$$\Rightarrow \frac{50 - 40}{5\,\text{Min}} = K\left(\frac{50 + 40}{2} - 20 \right) \qquad ...(i)$$

Let T be the temperature of sphere after next 5 minutes. Then

$$\frac{40 - T}{5} = K\left(\frac{40 + T}{2} - 20 \right) \qquad ...(ii)$$

Dividing eqn. (ii) by (i), we get

$$\frac{40 - T}{10} = \frac{40 + T - 40}{50 + 40 - 40} = \frac{T}{50}$$

$$\Rightarrow 40 - T = \frac{T}{5} \Rightarrow 200 - 5T = T$$

$$\therefore T = \frac{200}{6} = 33.3°C$$

8. **(4)** Density of nucleus, $\rho = \dfrac{\text{Mass}}{\text{Volume}} = \dfrac{mA}{\frac{4}{3}\pi R^3}$

$$\Rightarrow \rho = \frac{mA}{\frac{4}{3}\pi(R_0 A^{1/3})^3} \qquad (\because R = R_0 A^{1/3})$$

Here m = mass of a nucleon

$$\therefore \rho = \frac{3 \times 1.67 \times 10^{-27}}{4 \times 3.14 \times (1.3 \times 10^{-15})^3} \quad (\text{Given}, R_0 = 1.3 \times 10^{-15})$$

$$\Rightarrow \rho = 2.38 \times 10^{17} \text{ kg/m}^3$$

9. **(4)** Given,
Wavelength of photon, $\lambda = 400$ nm
A photodiode can detect a wavelength corresponding to the energy of band gap. If the signal is having wavelength greater than this value, photodiode cannot detect it.

$$\therefore \text{ Band gap } E_g = \frac{hc}{\lambda} = \frac{1237.5}{400} = 3.09 \text{ eV}$$

10. **(3)** The distance traversed by light in a medium of refractive index μ in time t is given by
$$d = vt \qquad ...(i)$$

where v is velocity of light in the medium. The distance traversed by light in a vacuum in this time,

$$\Delta = ct = c \times \frac{d}{v} \qquad \text{[from equation (i)]}$$

$$= d\frac{c}{v} = \mu d \qquad ...(ii) \qquad (\because \mu = \frac{c}{v})$$

This distance is the equvalent distance in vacuum and is called optical path.
Optical path for first ray which travels a path L_1 through a medium of refractive index $n_1 = n_1 L_1$
Optical path for second ray which travels a path L_2 through a medium of refractive index $n_2 = n_2 L_2$
Path difference $= n_1 L_1 - n_2 L_2$
Now, phase difference

$$= \frac{2\pi}{\lambda} \times \text{path difference} = \frac{2\pi}{\lambda} \times (n_1 L_1 - n_2 L_2)$$

11. **(4)** The voltmeter of resistance $10k\Omega$ is parallel to the resistance of 400Ω. So, their equivalent resistance is

$$\frac{1}{R'} = \frac{1}{10\ k\Omega} + \frac{1}{400\Omega} = \frac{1}{10000} + \frac{1}{400}$$

$$\Rightarrow \frac{1}{R'} = \frac{1 + 25}{10000} = \frac{26}{10000}$$

$$\Rightarrow R' = \frac{10000}{26}\Omega$$

Using Ohm's law, current in the circuit

$$I = \frac{\text{Voltage}}{\text{Net Resistance}} = \frac{6}{\frac{10000}{26} + 800}$$

Potential difference measured by voltmeter

$$V = IR' = \frac{6}{\frac{10000}{26} + 800} \times \frac{10000}{26}$$

$$\Rightarrow V = \frac{150}{77} = 1.95 \text{ volt}$$

12. **(2)** Let C_p and C_v be the specific heat capacity of the gas at constant pressure and volume.
At constant pressure, heat required
$$\Delta Q_1 = nC_p\Delta T$$
$$\Rightarrow 160 = nC_p \cdot 50 \qquad ...(i)$$
At constant volume, heat required
$$\Delta Q_2 = nC_v\Delta T$$
$$\Rightarrow 240 = nC_v \cdot 100 \qquad ...(ii)$$
Dividing (i) by (ii), we get

$$\frac{160}{240} = \frac{C_p}{C_v} \cdot \frac{50}{100} \Rightarrow \frac{C_p}{C_v} = \frac{4}{3}$$

$$\gamma = \frac{C_p}{C_v} = \frac{4}{3} = 1 + \frac{2}{f} \qquad (\text{Here}, f = \text{degree of freedom})$$

$$\Rightarrow f = 6.$$

13. **(2)** Multimeter shows deflection in both cases i.e. before and after reversing the probes if the chosen component is capacitor.

14. **(1)** Heat given by water $= m_w C_w (T_{\text{mix}} - T_w)$
$$= 200 \times 1 \times (31 - 25)$$
Heat taken by steam $= m\, L_{\text{stem}} + m\, C_w (T_s - T_{\text{mix}})$
$= m \times 540 + m\,(1) \times (100 - 31)$
$= m \times 540 + m\,(1) \times (69)$
From the principal of calorimeter,
Heat lost = Heat gained
$\therefore (200)(31 - 25) = m \times 540 + m(1)(69)$
$\Rightarrow 1200 = m(609) \Rightarrow m \approx 2.$

15. **(2)** Given,
Mass of block, $m_1 = 1.9 \text{ kg}$
Mass of bullet, $m_2 = 0.1 \text{ kg}$
Velocity of bullet, $v_2 = 20 \text{ m/s}$
Let v be the velocity of the combined system. It is an inelastic collision.
Using conservation of linear momentum
$m_1 \times 0 + m_2 \times v_2 = (m_1 + m_2)v$
$\Rightarrow 0.1 \times 20 = (0.1 + 1.9) \times v$
$\Rightarrow v = 1 \text{ m/s}$
Using work energy theorem
Work done = Change in Kinetic energy
Let K be the Kinetic energy of combined system.
$(m_1 + m_2)gh$
$= K - \dfrac{1}{2}(m_1 + m_2)V^2$
$\Rightarrow 2 \times g \times 1 = K - \dfrac{1}{2} \times 2 \times 1^2 \Rightarrow K = 21 \text{ J}$

16. **(2)** Solar constant $= \dfrac{\text{Energy}}{\text{Time Area}}$
Dimension of Energy, $E = ML^2T^{-2}$
Dimension of Time = T
Dimension of Area = L^2
$\therefore$ Dimension of Solar constant
$= \dfrac{M^1 L^2 T^{-2}}{TL^2} = M^1 L^0 T^{-3}.$

17. **(2)** When magnetic field is applied to a diamagnetic substance, it produces magnetic field in opposite direction so net magnetic field inside the cavity of sphere will be zero. So, field inside the paramagnetic substance kept inside the cavity is zero.

18. **(3)** According to work energy theorem, gain in kinetic energy is equal to work done in displacement of charge.
$\therefore \dfrac{1}{2}mv^2 = q\Delta V$
Here, ΔV = potential difference between two positions of charge q.
For same q and ΔV.
$v \propto \dfrac{1}{\sqrt{m}}$
Mass of hydrogen ion $m_H = 1$
Mass of helium ion $m_{He} = 4$
$\therefore \dfrac{v_H}{v_{He}} = \sqrt{\dfrac{4}{1}} = 2 : 1.$

19. **(1)** Given,
Wavelength of X-rays, $\lambda_1 = 1 \text{ nm} = 1 \times 10^{-9} \text{m}$
Wavelength of visible light, $\lambda_2 = 500 \times 10^{-9} \text{m}$
The number of photons emitted per second from a source of monochromatic radiation of wavelength λ and power P is given as
$$n = \frac{P}{E} = \frac{P}{h\nu} = \frac{P\lambda}{hc} \qquad (\because E = h\nu \text{ and } \nu = \frac{c}{\lambda})$$
$\Rightarrow$ Clearly $n \propto \lambda$
$\Rightarrow \dfrac{n_1}{n_2} = \dfrac{\lambda_1}{\lambda_2} = \dfrac{1}{500}$

20. **(4)** Vertical force $= mg$
Horizontal force = Centripetal force $= m\omega^2 \dfrac{l}{2}\sin\theta$
Torque due to vertical force $= mg\dfrac{l}{2}\sin\theta$
Torque due to horizontal force $= m\omega^2 \dfrac{l}{2}\sin\theta\dfrac{l}{2}\cos\theta$

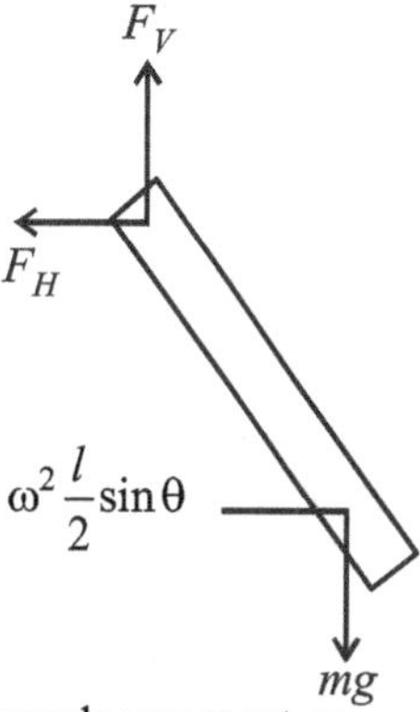

Net Torque = Angular momentum
$$mg\dfrac{l}{2}\sin\theta - m\omega^2 \dfrac{l}{2}\sin\theta\dfrac{l}{2}\cos\theta = \dfrac{ml^2}{12}\omega^2 \sin\theta\cos\theta$$
$\Rightarrow \cos\theta = \dfrac{3}{2}\dfrac{g}{\omega^2 l}$

21. **(8791)**
Given,
Heat absorbed, $Q_2 = mL = 80 \times 100 = 8000 \text{ Cal}$
Temperature of ice, $T_2 = 273 \text{ K}$
Temperature of surrounding,
$T_1 = 273 + 27 = 300 \text{ K}$
$$\text{Efficiency} = \frac{w}{Q_2} = \frac{Q_1 - Q_2}{Q_2} = \frac{T_1 - T_2}{T_2} = \frac{300 - 273}{273}$$
$\Rightarrow \dfrac{Q_1 - 8000}{8000} = \dfrac{27}{273} \Rightarrow Q_1 = 8791 \text{ Cal}$

22. **(1)**
Distance of object, $u = -30 \text{ cm}$
Distance of image, $v = 10 \text{ cm}$
Magnification, $m = \dfrac{-v}{u} = \dfrac{(-10)}{-30} = \dfrac{1}{3}$
Speed of image $= m^2 \times$ speed of object $= \dfrac{1}{9} \times 9 = 1 \text{ cm s}^{-1}$

23. (346)

Acceleration of block while moving up an inclined plane,

$a_1 = g \sin\theta + \mu g \cos\theta$

$\Rightarrow a_1 = g \sin 30° + \mu g \cos 30°$

$= \dfrac{g}{2} + \dfrac{\mu g \sqrt{3}}{2}$ ...(i) $(\because \theta = 30°)$

Using $v^2 - u^2 = 2a(s)$

$\Rightarrow v_0^2 - 0^2 = 2a_1(s)$ $(\because u = 0)$

$\Rightarrow v_0^2 - 2a_1(s) = 0$

$\Rightarrow s = \dfrac{v_0^2}{a_1}$ ...(ii)

Acceleration while moving down an inclined plane

$a_2 = g \sin\theta - \mu g \cos\theta$

$\Rightarrow a_2 = g \sin 30° - \mu g \cos 30°$

$\Rightarrow a_2 = \dfrac{g}{2} - \dfrac{\mu \sqrt{3}}{2} g$ ...(iii)

Using again $v^2 - u^2 = 2as$ for downward motion

$\Rightarrow \left(\dfrac{v_0}{2}\right)^2 = 2a_2(s) \Rightarrow s = \dfrac{v_0^2}{4a_2}$ ...(iv)

Equating equation (ii) and (iv)

$\dfrac{v_0^2}{a_1} = \dfrac{v_0^2}{4a_2} \Rightarrow a_1 = 4a_2$

$\Rightarrow \dfrac{g}{2} + \dfrac{\mu g \sqrt{3}}{2} = 4\left(\dfrac{g}{2} - \dfrac{\mu \sqrt{3}}{2}\right)$

$\Rightarrow 5 + 5\sqrt{3}\mu = 4(5 - 5\sqrt{3}\mu)$ (Substituting, $g = 10$ m/s²)

$\Rightarrow 5 + 5\sqrt{3}\mu = 20 - 20\sqrt{3}\mu \Rightarrow 25\sqrt{3}\mu = 15$

$\Rightarrow \mu = \dfrac{\sqrt{3}}{5} = 0.346 = \dfrac{346}{1000}$

So, $\dfrac{I}{1000} = \dfrac{346}{1000}$

24. (25)

Moment of inertia of the system about axis XE.

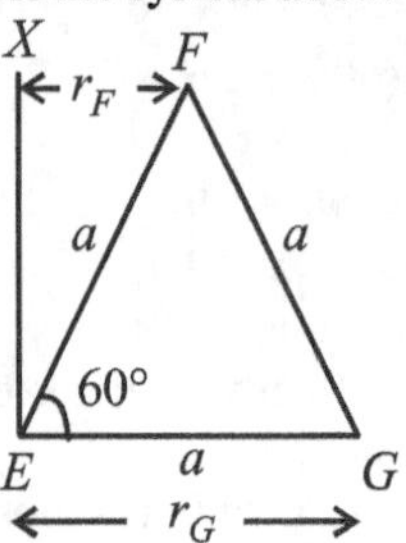

$I = I_E + I_F + I_G$

$\Rightarrow I = m(r_E)^2 + m(r_F)^2 + m(r_G)^2$

$\Rightarrow I = m \times 0^2 + m\left(\dfrac{a}{2}\right)^2 + ma^2 = \dfrac{5}{4}ma^2 = \dfrac{25}{20}ma^2$

$\therefore N = 25.$

25. (20)

Given,

Area of galvanometer coil, $A = 3 \times 10^{-4}\,\text{m}^2$

Number of turns in the coil, $N = 500$

Current in the coil, $I = 0.5$ A

Torque $\tau = |\vec{M} \times \vec{B}| = NiAB \sin(90°) = NiAB$

$\Rightarrow B = \dfrac{\tau}{NiA} = \dfrac{1.5}{500 \times 0.5 \times 3 \times 10^{-4}} = 20\,T$

CHEMISTRY

26. (1) Charge/ radius ratio of Be and Al is same because of diagonal relationship. Remaining statements are correct.

27. (3) Excess water of liquid

N⁺ chain structure with SO₄⁻

Due to presence of hydrophobic chain it forms micelle.

28. (2) Rate of Nucleophillic addition reaction is directly proportional to the –I and –M effect of the substituents present in the substrate. Ketones are less susceptible to the nucleophillic addition, due to the presence of alkyl (R) group which has +I effect. Thus reactivity order

(i)   (ii)   (iii)   (iv)

(i) > (iv) > (ii) > (iii)

29. (3) At equivalence point pH is 7 and pH increases with addition of NaOH so correct graph is (c).

30. (1) $P_{\text{gas}} = \dfrac{n_{\text{gas}} RT}{V}$

As n, T and V constant so $P_{H_2} = P_{O_2} = P_{He} = 2$ atm

So, $P_{\text{Total}} = P_{H_2} + P_{O_2} + P_{He} = 6$ atm

31. (2) Under the given situation for

$n = 1, l = 0, 1, 2$

$n = 2, l = 0, 1, 2, 3$

$n = 3, l = 0, 1, 2, 3, 4$

According to $(n + l)$ rule of order of filling of subshells will be :

$1s\,1p\,1d\,2s\,2p\,3s\,2d\,3f$

Atomic number 6	$1s^2\,1p^4$
Atomic number 9	$1s^2\,1p^6\,1d^1$
Atomic number 8	$1s^2\,1p^6$
Atomic number 13	$1s^2\,1p^6\,1d^5$

Therefore option (b) is correct. Atomic number of first noble gas will be 18 ($1s^2\,1p^6\,1d^{10}$).

32. (a)

Product 'P'

Generally CAN test is done for alcohols which give pink or red colour. But for phenols and phenolic compounds it gives brown or black colour. So, this test helps to diffirentiate phenols from alcohols.

33. (a, b, d) Molecule (A) shows intramolecular H-bonding while molecule (B) shows intermolecular H-bonding. Due to presence of intermolecular H-bonding it has more b. pt. than molecule (A). Molecule (B) also shows intermolecule H-bonding with water which makes it more soluble than A. (B) is crystalline solid while (A) is liquid at room tempertature because of weaker intramolecular hydrogen bonding.

34. (3)

Manganate	Permanganate
MnO_4^{2-}	MnO_4^-

Paramagnetic, green in colour, Tetrahedral & contains $p\pi$-$d\pi$ bond	Diamagnetic, purple in colour, Tetrahedral & contains $p\pi$-$d\pi$ bond

Manganate ion is paramagnetic while permanganate ion is diamagnetic.

35. (4) Acid rain is harmful for trees and animal life. It can also cause respiratory ailments in animals.

36. (3)

37. (1) For H_2O_2

$$Molarity = \frac{Volume\ strength}{11.2} = \frac{5.6}{11.2} = 0.5\ M$$

$$Molarity = \frac{\%(w/w) \times 10 \times d}{GMM}$$

$$\Rightarrow 0.5 = \frac{\%(w/w) \times 10 \times 1}{34}$$

$$\Rightarrow \%(w/w) = \frac{0.5 \times 34}{10} = 1.7.$$

38. (2) S_N2 reactions depend upon $-I$ and $-M$ effect on substrate. On increasing $-I$ and $-M$ effect, rate of S_N2 reaction will increase.

39. (3) For a given reaction,

$$rate = -\frac{1}{2}\frac{dn_A}{dt} = -\frac{1}{3}\frac{dn_B}{dt} = -\frac{2}{3}\frac{dn_C}{dt}$$

$$rate = \frac{dn_A}{dt} = \frac{2}{3}\frac{dn_B}{dt} = \frac{4}{3}\frac{dn_C}{dt}$$

40. (3) As difference in 3rd and 4th ionisation energies is high so atom contains 3 valence electrons.

41. (4) Conc. H_2SO_4 acts as dehydrating agent.
Molar mass of given complex = 266.5 g/mol.
On treating with conc. H_2SO_4 the mass lost by the

$$complex = \frac{13.5}{100}(266.5) \approx 36g = 2\ moles\ of\ H_2O$$

Formula of the complex = $[Cr(H_2O)_4Cl_2]Cl \cdot 2H_2O$

42. (3) $[Ru(en)_3]Cl_2 \Rightarrow Ru^{2+} = 4d^6 = t_{2g}^6, e_g^0$

$$[Fe(H_2O)_6]^{2+} \Rightarrow Fe^{2+} = 3d^6 = t_{2g}^4, e_g^2$$

So, correct answer is (c).

43. **(2)**

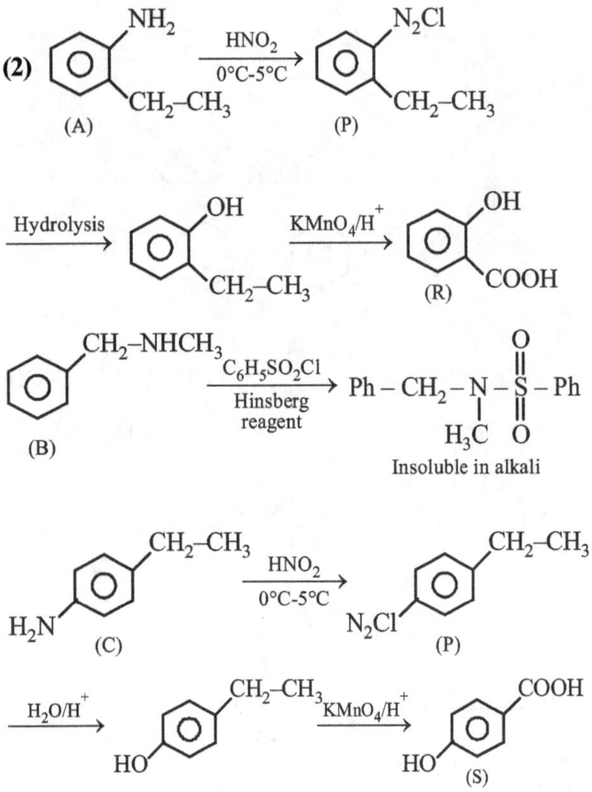

A → (reaction of NH_2-substituted ethylbenzene (A) with HNO_2 at 0°C–5°C gives diazonium salt N_2Cl (P))

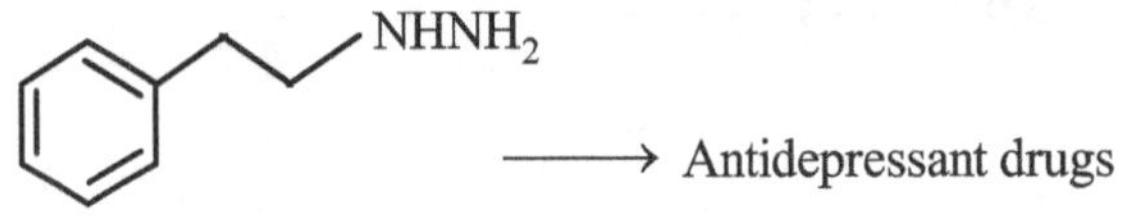

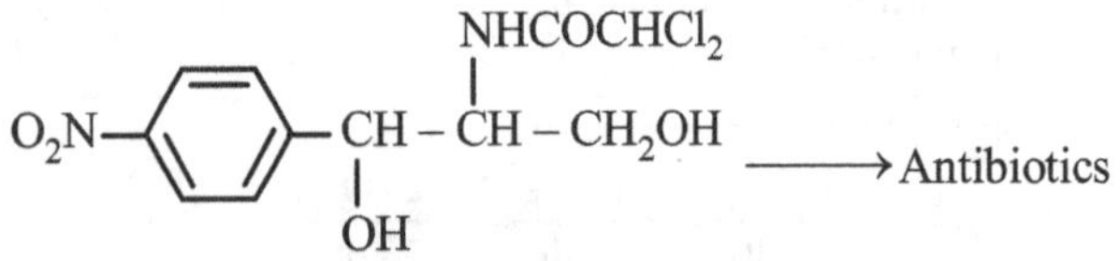

→ **Hydrolysis** → phenol with CH_2–CH_3 (R-precursor) → **$KMnO_4/H^+$** → salicylic acid type product with OH and COOH (R)

(B): benzyl CH_2–$NHCH_3$ → **$C_6H_5SO_2Cl$ / Hinsberg reagent** → $Ph - CH_2 - N - S - Ph$ (with H_3C and two O on S), Insoluble in alkali

(C): H_2N-substituted ethylbenzene → **HNO_2, 0°C–5°C** → N_2Cl-substituted ethylbenzene (P)

→ **H_2O/H^+** → HO-substituted ethylbenzene → **$KMnO_4/H^+$** → HO-substituted benzoic acid (S)

44. **(2)**

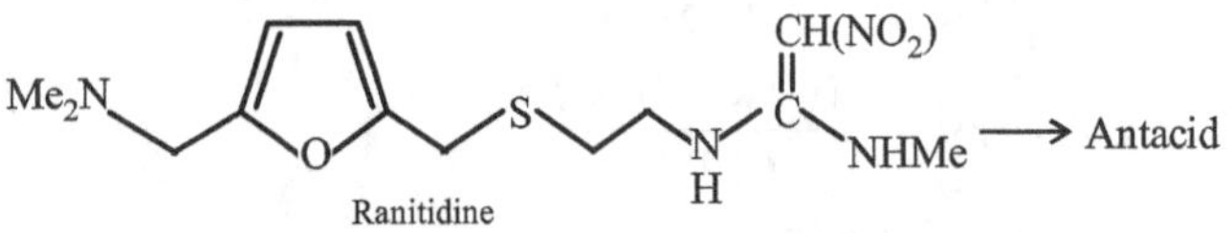

Ranitidine → **Antacid**

Phenelzine (Nardil) → **Antidepressant drugs**

Chloramphenicol → **Antibiotics**

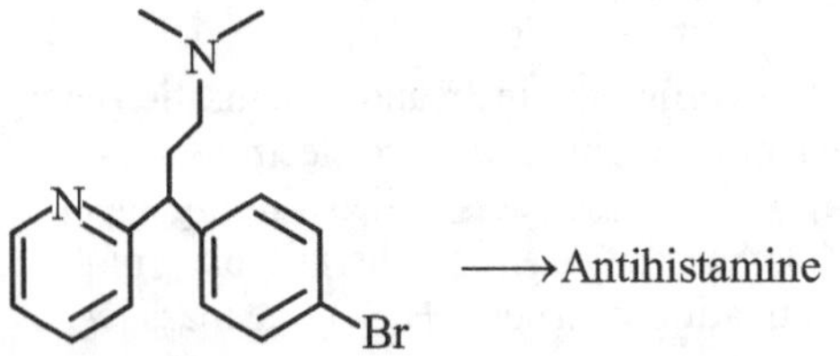

Brompheniramine (Dimetapp. Dimetane) → **Antihistamine**

45. **(3)**

(2-iodo-substituted branched alkane) → **E1 reaction, t-BuOH** → carbocation → **1,2-H$^-$ Shift** → rearranged carbocation → **$-H^+$** → alkene

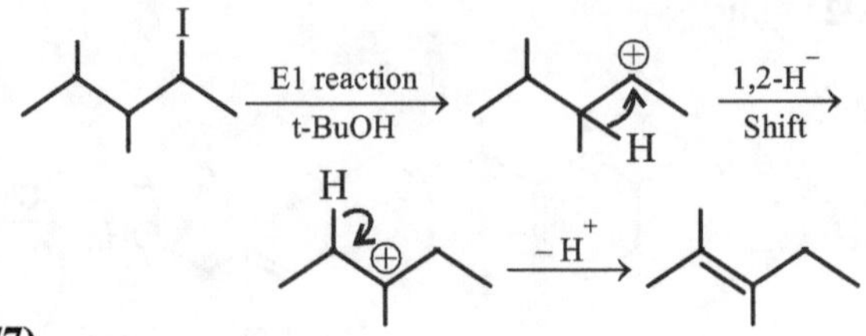

46. **(177)**

$$\pi_A = iC_A RT, \quad \pi_B = iC_B RT$$

For isotonic solution, $\pi_A = \pi_B$

$$i_1 C_1 = i_2 C_2 \qquad \text{(For protein } i = 1)$$

$$\Rightarrow C_1 = C_2$$

$$\Rightarrow \frac{0.73 \times 1000}{M_A \times 250} = \frac{1.65}{M_B \times 1}$$

$$\therefore \frac{M_A}{M_B} = \frac{0.73 \times 4}{1.65} = 1.77 = 177 \times 10^{-2}$$

47. **(60)**

Charge $(Q) = It = 2 \times 8 \times 60 = 960\, C$

$$\Rightarrow \frac{960}{96000} = 0.01\, F$$

$$Cr_2O_7^{2-} + 14H^+ + 6e^- \longrightarrow 2Cr^{3+} + 7H_2O$$

0.01 F → $\frac{1}{3} \times 0.01$ mole

Theoritical mass of $Cr^{3+} = \frac{1}{3} \times \frac{960}{96000} \times 52 = 0.173\, g$

So, efficiency $= \dfrac{W_{actual}}{W_{Theoritical}} \times 100 = \dfrac{0.104}{0.173} \times 100 = 60\%$

48. **5**

Asp – Glu – Lys tripeptide is :

$$H_2N - CH - C - NH - CH - C - NH - CH_2 - COOH$$

(with $\overset{O}{\underset{\parallel}{C}}$ groups; substituents: CH_2–COOH, CH_2–CH_2–COOH, $(CH_2)_4$–NH_2)

No. of CO group = 5

49. **(25)**

Number of mole of $x = \dfrac{6.022 \times 10^{22}}{6.022 \times 10^{23}} = \dfrac{10}{\text{Molar mass of } x}$

So molar mass of $x = 100\, g$

Molarity $= \dfrac{5}{100 \times 2} = 0.025\, M$.

50. **(10)**

Phosphinic acid is hypophosphorous acid (H_3PO_2).

$$NaOH + H_3PO_2 \longrightarrow NaH_2PO_2 + H_2O$$

For neutrization,

$$(N_1 V_1)_{acid} = (N_2 V_2)_{base}$$

$$0.1 \times 10 = 0.1 \times (V_{mL})_{NaOH}$$

$$V_{NaOH} = 10\, mL$$

MATHEMATICS

51. **(1)** $|\operatorname{adj} A| = |A|^2 = 9$ $[\because |\operatorname{adj} A| = |A|^{n-1}]$

$\Rightarrow |A| = \pm 3 = \lambda \Rightarrow |\lambda| = 3$

$\Rightarrow |B| = |\operatorname{adj} A|^2 = 81$

$\mu = |(B^{-1})^T| = |B^{-1}| = |B|^{-1} = \dfrac{1}{|B|} = \dfrac{1}{81}$

52. **(3)** The given quadratic equation is

$(\lambda^2 + 1)x^2 - 4\lambda x + 2 = 0$

$\because$ One root is in the interval $(0, 1)$

$\therefore f(0) f(1) \le 0$

$\Rightarrow 2(\lambda^2 + 1 - 4\lambda + 2) \le 0$

$\Rightarrow 2(\lambda^2 - 4\lambda + 3) \le 0$

$(\lambda - 1)(\lambda - 3) \le 0 \Rightarrow \lambda \in [1, 3]$

But at $\lambda = 1$, both roots are 1 so $\lambda \ne 1$

$\therefore \lambda \in (1, 3]$

53. **(1)** $I = \displaystyle\int \sin^{-1}\left(\dfrac{\sqrt{x}}{\sqrt{1+x}}\right) dx = \int \underset{\text{I}}{\tan^{-1}\sqrt{x}} \cdot \underset{\text{II}}{1}\ dx$

$= x \tan^{-1}\sqrt{x} - \displaystyle\int \dfrac{1}{1+x} \cdot \dfrac{1}{2\sqrt{x}} \cdot x\ dx + C$

$= x \tan^{-1}\sqrt{x} - \dfrac{1}{2}\displaystyle\int \dfrac{t \cdot 2t\, dt}{1+t^2} + C$ (Put $x = t^2 \Rightarrow dx = 2t\, dt$)

$= x \tan^{-1}\sqrt{x} - \displaystyle\int \dfrac{t^2}{1+t^2} dt + C$

$= x \tan^{-1}\sqrt{x} - t + \tan^{-1} t + C$

$= x \tan^{-1}\sqrt{x} - \sqrt{x} + \tan^{-1}\sqrt{x} + C$

$= (x+1)\tan^{-1}\sqrt{x} - \sqrt{x} + C$

$\Rightarrow A(x) = x + 1 \Rightarrow B(x) = -\sqrt{x}$

54. **(3)** General term $= T_{r+1} = {}^9C_r \left(\dfrac{3x^2}{2}\right)^{9-r}\left(-\dfrac{1}{3x}\right)^r$

$= {}^9C_r \left(\dfrac{3}{2}\right)^{9-r}\left(-\dfrac{1}{3}\right)^r x^{18-3r}$

The term is independent of x, then

$18 - 3r = 0 \Rightarrow r = 6$

$\therefore T_7 = {}^9C_6 \left(\dfrac{3}{2}\right)^3 \left(-\dfrac{1}{3}\right)^6 = {}^9C_3 \left(\dfrac{1}{6}\right)^3$

$= \dfrac{9 \times 8 \times 7}{3 \times 2 \times 1}\left(\dfrac{1}{6}\right)^3 = \left(\dfrac{7}{18}\right).$

$\therefore 18k = 18 \times \dfrac{7}{18} = 7.$

55. **(3)** S.D. $= \sqrt{\dfrac{\displaystyle\sum_{i=1}^{10}(x_i - p)^2}{10} - \left(\dfrac{\displaystyle\sum_{i=1}^{10}(x_i - p)}{10}\right)^2}$

$= \sqrt{\dfrac{9}{10} - \left(\dfrac{3}{10}\right)^2} = \dfrac{9}{10}.$

56. **(2)** $x^3 dy + xy\, dyx = 2y\, dx + x^2 dy$

$\Rightarrow (x^3 - x^2) dy = (2 - x) y\, dx$

$\Rightarrow \dfrac{dy}{y} = \dfrac{2-x}{x^2(x-1)} dx$

$\Rightarrow \displaystyle\int \dfrac{dy}{y} = \int \dfrac{2-x}{x^2(x-1)} dx$ ...(i)

Let $\dfrac{2-x}{x^2(x-1)} = \dfrac{A}{x} + \dfrac{B}{x^2} + \dfrac{C}{x-1}$

$\Rightarrow 2 - x = A(x-1) + B(x-1) + Cx^2$

Compare the coefficients of x, x^2 and constant term.
$C = 1$, $B = -2$ and $A = -1$

$\therefore \displaystyle\int \dfrac{dy}{y} = \int \left\{\dfrac{-1}{x} - \dfrac{2}{x^2} + \dfrac{1}{x-1}\right\} dx$

$\Rightarrow \ln y = -\ln x + \dfrac{2}{x} + \ln|x-1| + C$

$\therefore y(2) = e$

$\Rightarrow 1 = -\ln 2 + 1 + 0 + C$ $[\because \log e = 1]$

$\Rightarrow C = \ln 2$

$\Rightarrow \ln y = -\ln x + \dfrac{2}{x} + \ln|x-1| + \ln 2$

At $x = 4$,

$\Rightarrow \ln y(4) = -\ln 4 + \dfrac{1}{2} + \ln 3 + \ln 2$

$\Rightarrow \ln y(4) = \ln\left(\dfrac{3}{2}\right) + \dfrac{1}{2} = \ln\left(\dfrac{3}{2} e^{1/2}\right)$

$[\because \log m + \log n = \log(mn)]$

$\Rightarrow y(4) = \dfrac{3}{2} e^{1/2}$

57. **(2)** Let $z_1 = x_1 + iy_1$ and $z_2 = x_2 + iy_2$

$\because |z_1 - 1| = \text{Re}(z_1)$

$\Rightarrow (x_1 - 1)^2 + y_1^2 = x_1^2$

$\Rightarrow y_1^2 - 2x_1 + 1 = 0$ ...(i)

$|z_2 - 1| = \text{Re}(z_2) \Rightarrow (x_2 - 1)^2 + y_2^2 = x_2^2$

$\Rightarrow y_2^2 - 2x_2 + 1 = 0$ ...(ii)

From eqn. (i) − (ii),

$y_1^2 - y_2^2 - 2(x_1 - x_2) = 0$

$\Rightarrow y_1 + y_2 = 2\left(\dfrac{x_1 - x_2}{y_1 - y_2}\right)$ ...(iii)

$\because \arg(z_1 - z_2) = \dfrac{\pi}{6}$

$\Rightarrow \tan^{-1}\left(\dfrac{y_1 - y_2}{x_1 - x_2}\right) = \dfrac{\pi}{6}$

$\Rightarrow \dfrac{y_1 - y_2}{x_1 - x_2} = \dfrac{1}{\sqrt{3}}$

$\Rightarrow \dfrac{2}{y_1 + y_2} = \dfrac{1}{\sqrt{3}}$ $\left[\text{From, } \dfrac{y_1 - y_2}{x_1 - x_2} = \dfrac{2}{y_1 + y_2}\right]$

$\therefore y_1 + y_2 = 2\sqrt{3} \Rightarrow \text{Im}(z_1 + z_2) = 2\sqrt{3}$

58. **(2)** $\lim\limits_{x \to a} \dfrac{(a + 2x)^{\frac{1}{3}} - (3x)^{\frac{1}{3}}}{(3a + x)^{\frac{1}{3}} - (4x)^{\frac{1}{3}}}$ $\left[\dfrac{0}{0} \text{ case}\right]$

Apply L'Hospital rule

$\lim\limits_{x \to a} \dfrac{\dfrac{1}{3}(a + 2x)^{-2/3} \cdot 2 - \dfrac{1}{3} \cdot (3x)^{-2/3} \cdot 3}{\dfrac{1}{3}(3a + x)^{-2/3} \cdot 1 - \dfrac{1}{3}(4x)^{-2/3} \cdot 4}$

$= \dfrac{\dfrac{1}{3}(3a)^{-2/3} \cdot (2 - 3)}{\dfrac{1}{3}(4a)^{-2/3} \cdot (1 - 4)} = \dfrac{3^{-2/3}}{4^{-2/3}} \cdot \dfrac{1}{3}$

$= \dfrac{2^{4/3}}{9^{1/3}} \cdot \dfrac{1}{3} = \dfrac{2}{3} \cdot \left(\dfrac{2}{9}\right)^{1/3}$

59. **(4)** $(p \wedge q) \to (\sim q \vee r)$

$= \sim(p \wedge q) \vee (\sim q \vee r)$

$= (\sim p \vee \sim q) \vee (\sim q \vee r)$

$= (\sim p \vee \sim q \vee r)$

$\because (\sim p \vee \sim q \vee r)$ is false, then $\sim p$, $\sim q$ and r all these must be false.

$\Rightarrow p$ is true, q is true and r is false.

60. **(2)** $S_n = 20 + 19\dfrac{3}{5} + 19\dfrac{1}{5} + 18\dfrac{4}{5} + ...$

$\because S_n = 488$

$488 = \dfrac{n}{2}\left[2\left(\dfrac{100}{5}\right) + (n - 1)\left(-\dfrac{2}{5}\right)\right]$

$488 = \dfrac{n}{2}(101 - n) \Rightarrow n^2 - 101n + 2440 = 0$

$\Rightarrow n = 61 \text{ or } 40$

For $n = 40 \Rightarrow T_n > 0$

For $n = 61 \Rightarrow T_n < 0$

$n^{\text{th}} \text{ term} = T_{61} = \dfrac{100}{5} + (61 - 1)\left(-\dfrac{2}{5}\right) = -4$

61. **(4)** Equation of ellipse is $\dfrac{x^2}{25} + \dfrac{y^2}{b^2} = 1$

Then, $e_1 = \sqrt{1 - \dfrac{b^2}{25}}$

The equation of hyperbola, $\dfrac{x^2}{16} + \dfrac{y^2}{b^2} = 1$

Then, $e_2 = \sqrt{1 + \dfrac{b^2}{16}}$

$e_1 e_2 = 1$

$\Rightarrow (e_1 e_2)^2 = 1 \Rightarrow \left(1 - \dfrac{b^2}{25}\right)\left(1 + \dfrac{b^2}{16}\right) = 1$

$\Rightarrow 1 + \dfrac{b^2}{16} - \dfrac{b^2}{25} - \dfrac{b^4}{25 \times 16} = 1$

$\Rightarrow \dfrac{9}{16 \cdot 25}b^2 - \dfrac{b^4}{25 \cdot 16} = 0 \Rightarrow b^2 = 9$

$\therefore e_1 = \sqrt{1 - \dfrac{9}{25}} = \dfrac{4}{5}$

And, $e_2 = \sqrt{1 + \dfrac{9}{16}} = \dfrac{5}{4}$

Distance between focii of ellipse

$= \alpha = 2ae_1 = 2(5)(e_1) = 8$

Distance between focii of hyperbola

$= \beta = 2ae_2 = 2(4)(e_2) = 10$

$\therefore (\alpha, \beta) = (8, 10)$

62. **(1)** $\dfrac{k}{6} = \displaystyle\int_0^{\frac{1}{2}} \dfrac{x^2}{(1 - x^2)^{3/2}}\, dx$

Let $x = \sin\theta$; $dx = \cos\theta\, d\theta$,

then $\displaystyle\int_0^{\frac{1}{2}} \frac{x^2}{(1-x^2)^{3/2}}\,dx = \int_0^{\frac{\pi}{6}} \frac{\sin^2\theta\cos\theta}{\cos^3\theta}\,d\theta$

$\therefore \dfrac{k}{6} = \displaystyle\int_0^{\frac{\pi}{6}} \frac{\sin^2\theta}{\cos^3\theta}\cdot\cos\theta\,d\theta$

$\Rightarrow \dfrac{k}{6} = \displaystyle\int_0^{\frac{\pi}{6}} \tan^2\theta\,d\theta = \int_0^{\frac{\pi}{6}} (\sec^2\theta - 1)\,d\theta$

$\Rightarrow \dfrac{k}{6} = (\tan\theta - \theta)_0^{\pi/6} = \left(\dfrac{1}{\sqrt{3}} - \dfrac{\pi}{6}\right) = \dfrac{2\sqrt{3} - x}{6}$

$\Rightarrow k = 2\sqrt{3} - \pi$

63. **(1)** $\because$ The critical points are $-1, 0, 1$

$\therefore f'(x) = k\cdot x(x+1)(x-1) = k(x^3 - x)$

$\Rightarrow f(x) = k\left(\dfrac{x^4}{4} - \dfrac{x^2}{2}\right) + C$

$\Rightarrow f(0) = C$

$\because f(x) = f(0)$

$\Rightarrow k\dfrac{(x^4 - 2x^2)}{4} + C = C$

$\Rightarrow x^2(x^2 - 2) = 0$

$\Rightarrow x = 0, \sqrt{2}, -\sqrt{2}$

$\Rightarrow T = \{0, \sqrt{2}, -\sqrt{2}\}$

64. **(4)** Let the side of cube be a.

$S = 6a^2 \Rightarrow \dfrac{dS}{dt} = 12a\cdot\dfrac{da}{dt} \Rightarrow 3.6 = 12a\cdot\dfrac{da}{dt}$

$\Rightarrow 12(10)\dfrac{da}{dt} = 3.6 \Rightarrow \dfrac{da}{dt} = 0.03$

$V = a^3 \Rightarrow \dfrac{dV}{dt} = 3a^2\cdot\dfrac{da}{dt} = 3(10)^2\cdot\left(\dfrac{3}{100}\right) = 9$

65. **(1)** $a\cos\theta = b\cos\left(\theta + \dfrac{2\pi}{3}\right) = c\cos\left(\theta + \dfrac{4\pi}{3}\right) = k$

$a = \dfrac{k}{\cos\theta},\ b = \dfrac{k}{\cos\left(\theta + \dfrac{2\pi}{3}\right)},\ c = \dfrac{k}{\cos\left(\theta + \dfrac{4\pi}{3}\right)}$

$ab + bc + ca = k^2\dfrac{\left[\cos\left(\theta + \dfrac{4\pi}{3}\right) + \cos\theta + \cos\left(\theta + \dfrac{2\pi}{3}\right)\right]}{\cos\left(\theta + \dfrac{4\pi}{3}\right)\cdot\cos\theta\cdot\cos\left(\theta + \dfrac{2\pi}{3}\right)}$

$= k^2\dfrac{\left[\cos\theta + 2\cos(\theta + \pi)\cdot\cos\left(\dfrac{\pi}{3}\right)\right]}{\cos\theta\cdot\cos\left(\theta + \dfrac{2\pi}{3}\right)\cdot\cos\left(\theta + \dfrac{4\pi}{3}\right)}$

$= k^2\dfrac{\left[\cos\theta - 2\cos\theta\cdot\dfrac{1}{2}\right]}{\cos\theta\cdot\cos\left(\theta + \dfrac{2\pi}{3}\right)\cdot\cos\left(\theta + \dfrac{4\pi}{3}\right)} = 0$

$\cos\phi = \dfrac{(a\hat{i} + b\hat{j} + c\hat{k})\cdot(b\hat{i} + c\hat{j} + a\hat{k})}{\sqrt{a^2 + b^2 + c^2}\cdot\sqrt{b^2 + c^2 + a^2}}$

$= ab + bc + ca = 0$

$\phi = \dfrac{\pi}{2}$

66. **(1)** Total outcomes $= 9(10^4)$

Favourable outcomes

$= {}^9C_2(2^5 - 2) + {}^9C_1(2^4 - 1) = 36(30) + 9(15)$

Probability $= \dfrac{36\times30 + 9\times15}{9\times10^4} = \dfrac{4\times30 + 15}{10^4} = \dfrac{135}{10^4}$

67. **(2)**

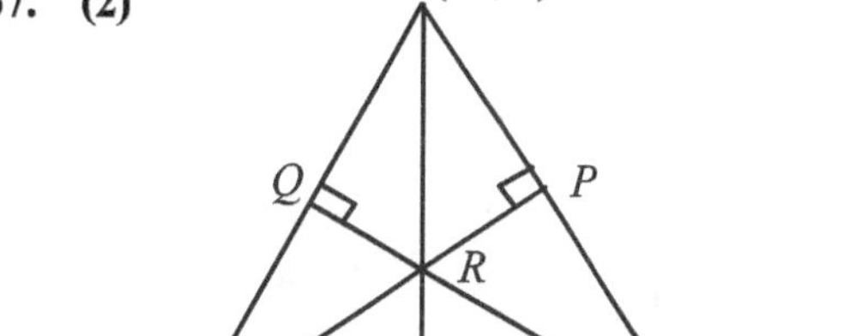

$m_{BC} = \dfrac{6}{-12} = -\dfrac{1}{2}$

$\therefore$ Equation of AS is $y - 7 = 2(x + 1)$

$y = 2x + 9$ ...(i)

$m_{AC} = \dfrac{12}{-6} = -2$

$\therefore$ Equation of BP is $y - 1 = \dfrac{1}{2}(x + 7)$

$y = \dfrac{x}{2} + \dfrac{9}{2}$ ...(ii)

From equs. (i) and (ii),

$2x + 9 = \dfrac{x + 9}{2}$

$\Rightarrow 4x + 18 = x + 9$

$\Rightarrow 3x = 9 \Rightarrow x = -3$

$\therefore y = 3$

68. **(1)** For R_1 let $a = 1+\sqrt{2},\ b = 1-\sqrt{2},\ c = 8^{1/4}$

$aR_1 b \Rightarrow a^2 + b^2 = (1+\sqrt{2})^2 + (1-\sqrt{2})^2 = 6 \in Q$

$bR_1 c \Rightarrow b^2 + c^2 = (1-\sqrt{2})^2 + (8^{1/4})^2 = 3 \in Q$

$aR_1 c \Rightarrow a^2 + c^2 = (1+\sqrt{2})^2 + (8^{1/4})^2 = 3 + 4\sqrt{2} \notin Q$

$\therefore R_1$ is not transitive.

For R_2 let $a = 1+\sqrt{2},\ b = \sqrt{2},\ c = 1-\sqrt{2}$

$aR_2 b \Rightarrow a^2 + b^2 = (1+\sqrt{2})^2 + (\sqrt{2})^2 = 5 + 2\sqrt{2} \notin Q$

$bR_2 c \Rightarrow b^2 + c^2 = (\sqrt{2})^2 + (1-\sqrt{2})^2 = 5 - 2\sqrt{2} \notin Q$

$aR_2 c \Rightarrow a^2 + c^2 = (1+\sqrt{2})^2 + (1-\sqrt{2})^2 = 6 \in Q$

$\therefore R_2$ is not transitive.

69. **(3)** Direction ratios of normal to the plane are $<1, -3, 2>$.
Plane passes through $(3, 1, 1)$.
Equation of plane is,
$1(x-3) - 3(y-1) + 2(z-1) = 0$
$\Rightarrow x - 3y + 2z - 2 = 0$

70. **(2)**

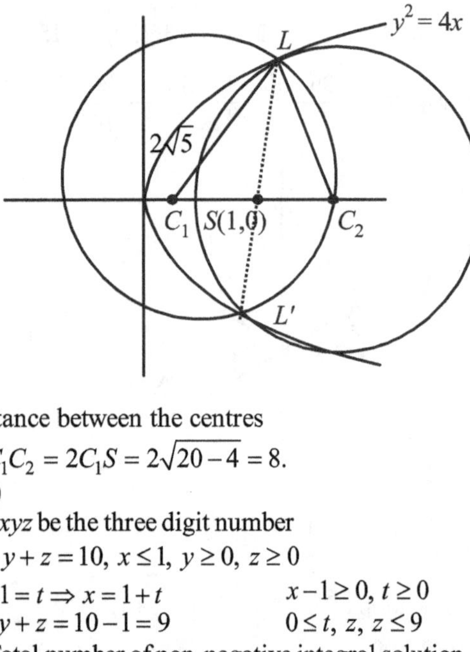

Distance between the centres
$= C_1 C_2 = 2C_1 S = 2\sqrt{20-4} = 8.$

71. **(54)**
Let xyz be the three digit number
$x + y + z = 10,\ x \le 1,\ y \ge 0,\ z \ge 0$

$x - 1 = t \Rightarrow x = 1 + t$ $x - 1 \ge 0,\ t \ge 0$
$t + y + z = 10 - 1 = 9$ $0 \le t,\ z,\ z \le 9$
$\therefore$ Total number of non-negative integral solution

$= {}^{9+3-1}C_{3-1} = {}^{11}C_2 = \dfrac{11 \cdot 10}{2} = 55$

But for $t = 9,\ x = 10$, so required number of integers
$= 55 - 1 = 54.$

72. **(5)**

$$\text{Normal of plane} = \begin{vmatrix} \hat{i} & \hat{j} & \hat{k} \\ 1 & 1 & 0 \\ 0 & 1 & -1 \end{vmatrix}$$

$\vec{n} = -\hat{i} + \hat{j} + \hat{k}$

Direction ratios of normal to the plane $= <-1, 1, 1>$
Equation of plane
$-1(x-1) + 1(y-0) + 1(z-0) = 0$
$\Rightarrow x - y - z - 1 = 0$

If (x, y, z) is foot of perpendicular of $M(1, 0, 1)$ on the plane
then

$$\Rightarrow \frac{x-1}{1} = \frac{y-0}{-1} = \frac{z-1}{-1} = \frac{-(1-0-1-1)}{3}$$

$$\therefore x = \frac{4}{3},\ y = -\frac{1}{3},\ z = \frac{2}{3}$$

$$\alpha + \beta + \gamma = \frac{4}{3} - \frac{1}{3} + \frac{2}{3} = \frac{5}{3}$$

$$\therefore 3(\alpha + \beta + \gamma) = 3 \times \frac{5}{3} = 5.$$

73. **(4)**
For $(1, 2)$ of $y^2 = 4x \Rightarrow t = 1,\ a = 1$
Equation of normal to the parabola
$\Rightarrow tx + y = 2at + at^3$
$\Rightarrow x + y = 3$ intersect x-axis at $(3, 0)$

$$y = e^x \Rightarrow \frac{dy}{dx} = e^x$$

Equation of tangent to the curve
$\Rightarrow y - e^c = e^c(x - c)$
$\because$ Tangent to the curve and normal to the parabola
intersect at same point.
$\therefore 0 - e^c = e^c(3 - c) \Rightarrow c = 4.$

74. **(39)**
Let m arithmetic mean be $A_1, A_2 \ldots A_m$ and G_1, G_2, G_3 be
geometric mean.
The A.P. formed by arithmetic mean is,
$3, A_1, A_2, A_3, \ldots\ldots A_m, 243$

$$\therefore d = \frac{243-3}{m+1} = \frac{240}{m+1}$$

The G.P. formed by geometric mean
$3, G_1, G_2, G_3, 243$

$$r = \left(\frac{243}{3}\right)^{\frac{1}{3+1}} = (81)^{1/4} = 3$$

$\because A_4 = G_2$

$$\Rightarrow 3 + 4\left(\frac{240}{m+1}\right) = 3(3)^2$$

$$\Rightarrow 3 + \frac{960}{m+1} = 27 \Rightarrow m+1 = 40 \Rightarrow m = 39.$$

75. **(8)**
The given system of equations
$x - 2y + 5z = 0$ ...(i)
$-2x + 4y + z = 0$ ...(ii)
$-7x + 14y + 9z = 0$ ...(iii)
From equation, $2 \times$ (i) + (ii) $\Rightarrow z = 0$
Put $z = 0$ in equation (i), we get $x = 2y$
$\because 15 \le x^2 + y^2 + z^2 \le 150$
$\Rightarrow 15 \le 4y^2 + y^2 \le 150$ $[\because x = 2y,\ z = 0]$
$\Rightarrow 3 \le y^2 \le 30$
$\Rightarrow y = \pm 2, \pm 3, \pm 4, \pm 5$
$\Rightarrow 8$ solutions.

PHYSICS

1. **(3)** The electric field produced due to uniformly charged infinite plane is uniform. So option (2) and (4) are wrong. And +ve charge density σ_+ is bigger in magnitude so its field along Y direction will be bigger than field of $-$ve charge density σ_- in X direction. Hence option (3) is correct.

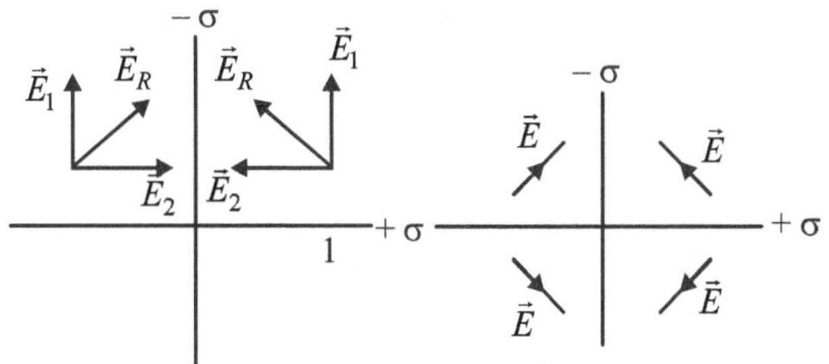

2. **(3)** Here, $\theta = 30°$, $\tau = 0.018$ N-m, $B = 0.06$ T
Torque on a bar magnet :
$$\tau = MB\sin\theta$$
$$0.018 = M \times 0.06 \times \sin 30°$$
$$\Rightarrow 0.018 = M \times 0.06 \times \frac{1}{2} \Rightarrow M = 0.6 \text{ A-m}^2$$
Position of stable equilibrium ($\theta = 0°$)
Position of unstable equilibrium ($\theta = 180°$)
Minimum work required to rotate bar magnet from stable to unstable equilibrium
$$\Delta U = U_f - U_i = -MB\cos 180° - (-MB\cos 0°)$$
$$W = 2MB = 2 \times 0.6 \times 0.06$$
$$\therefore \; W = 7.2 \times 10^{-2} \text{ J}$$

3. **(1)** Here ice melts due to water.
Let the amount of ice melts $= m_{ice}$
$$m_w s_w \Delta\theta = m_{ice} L_{ice}$$
$$\therefore \; m_{ice} = \frac{m_w s_w \Delta\theta}{L_{ice}}$$
$$= \frac{0.2 \times 4200 \times 25}{3.4 \times 10^5} = 0.0617 \text{ kg} = 61.7 \text{ g}$$

4. **(3)** Here two zener diodes are in reverse polarity so if one is in forward bias the other will be in reverse bias and above 6V the reverse bias will too be in conduction mode. Hence when V > 6V the output will be constant. And when V < 6V it will follow the inut voltage.

5. **(3)** As we know,
$$\gamma = \frac{C_p}{C_v} = 1 + \frac{2}{f}, \text{ where } f = \text{degree of freedom}$$
(A) Monatomic, $f = 3$
$$\therefore \gamma = 1 + \frac{2}{3} = \frac{5}{3}$$
(B) Diatomic rigid molecules, $f = 5$
$$\therefore \gamma = 1 + \frac{2}{5} = \frac{7}{5}$$
(C) Diatomic non-rigid molecules, $f = 7$
$$\therefore \gamma = 1 + \frac{2}{7} = \frac{9}{7}$$
(D) Triatomic rigid molecules, $f = 6$
$$\therefore \gamma = 1 + \frac{2}{6} = \frac{4}{3}$$

6. **(4)** Given :
Intensity, $I_0 = 3.3$ Wm^{-2}
Area, $A = 3 \times 10^{-4}$ m^2
Angular speed, $\omega = 31.4$ rad/s
Average energy $= I_0 A < \cos^2\theta >$
$$\because \; <\cos^2\theta> = \frac{1}{2} \text{ per revolution}$$
$$\therefore \text{ Average energy } = \frac{(3.3)(3\times 10^{-4})}{2} \simeq 5 \times 10^{-4} \text{ J}$$

7. **(4)** Given : $I_A = 2$ A, $R_A = 2$ cm, $\theta_A = 2\pi - \dfrac{\pi}{2} = \dfrac{3\pi}{2}$
$I_B = 3$ A, $R_B = 4$ cm, $\theta_B = 2\pi - \dfrac{\pi}{3} = \dfrac{5\pi}{3}$
Using, magnetic field, $B = \dfrac{\mu_0 I\theta}{4\pi R}$
$$\frac{B_A}{B_B} = \frac{I_A}{I_B} \times \frac{\theta_A R_B}{\theta_B R_A} = \frac{2 \times \dfrac{3\pi}{2} \times 4}{3 \times \dfrac{5\pi}{3} \times 2} = \frac{6}{5}$$

8. **(2)** **Case (a) :** When bar magnet is entering with constant speed, flux (ϕ) will change and an e.m.f. is induced, so galvanometer will deflect in positive direction.
Case (b) : When magnet is completely inside, flux (ϕ) will not change, so galvanometer will show null deflection.
Case (c) : When bar magnet is making on exit, again flux (ϕ) will change and an e.m.f. is induced in opposite direction so galvanometer will deflect in negative direction i.e. reverse direction.

9. **(4)** Change in potential energy, $\Delta u = q(V_f - V_i)$
Potential of $-q$ is same as initial and final point of the path.

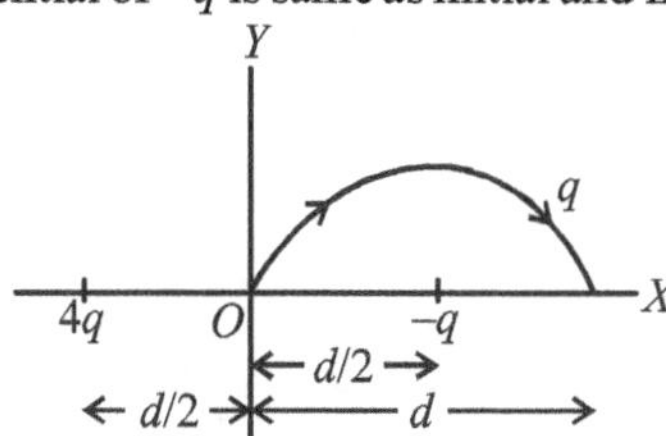

$$\Delta u = q\left(\frac{k4q}{3d/2} - \frac{k4q}{d/2}\right) = -\frac{4q^2}{3\pi\varepsilon_0 d}$$
$-$ve sign shows the energy of the charge is decreasing.

10. **(3)** When resistor is connected power dissipated,
$P_R = 0.5\,\text{W}$
Emf of battery, $E = 3\,\text{V}$
Terminal voltage, $V = 2.5\,\text{V}$

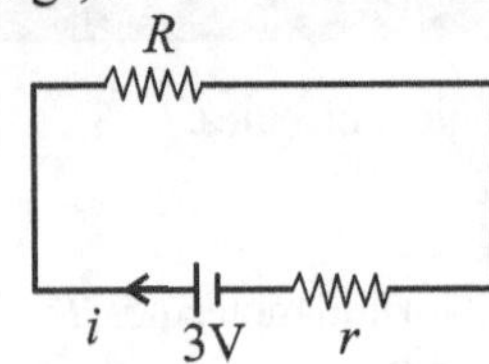

$P_R = i^2 R = 0.5\,\text{W}$
Also, $V = E - ir \Rightarrow 2.5 = 3 - ir \Rightarrow ir = 0.5$
Power dissipated across $'r'$: $P_r = i^2 r$
Now $iR = 2.5$ and $ir = 0.5$

$$\therefore \frac{R}{r} = 5$$

Now $\dfrac{P_R}{P_r} = \dfrac{i^2 R}{i^2 r} \Rightarrow \dfrac{P_R}{P_r} = \dfrac{R}{r} \Rightarrow \dfrac{P_R}{P_r} = 5$

$$\Rightarrow P_r = \frac{P_R}{5} = \frac{0.50}{5}$$

$$\therefore P_r = 0.10\,\text{W}$$

11. **(2)** Given : Distance between one crest and one trough
$= 1.5\,\text{m}$

$$= (2n_1 + 1)\frac{\lambda}{2}$$

Distance between two crests $= 5\,\text{m} = n_2 \lambda$

$$\frac{1.5}{5} = \frac{(2n_1 + 1)}{2n_2} \Rightarrow 3n_2 = 10n_1 + 5$$

Here n_1 and n_2 are integer.
If $\quad n_1 = 1, n_2 = 5 \qquad\qquad \therefore \lambda = 1$
$\qquad n_1 = 4, n_2 = 15 \qquad\quad\ \therefore \lambda = 1/3$
$\qquad n_1 = 7, n_2 = 25 \qquad\quad\ \therefore \lambda = 1/5$

Hence possible wavelengths $\dfrac{1}{1}, \dfrac{1}{3}, \dfrac{1}{5}$ metre.

12. **(3)** For uniformly accelerated/ deaccelerated motion :
$$v^2 = u^2 \pm 2gh$$
As equation is quadratic, so, v-h graph will be a parabola

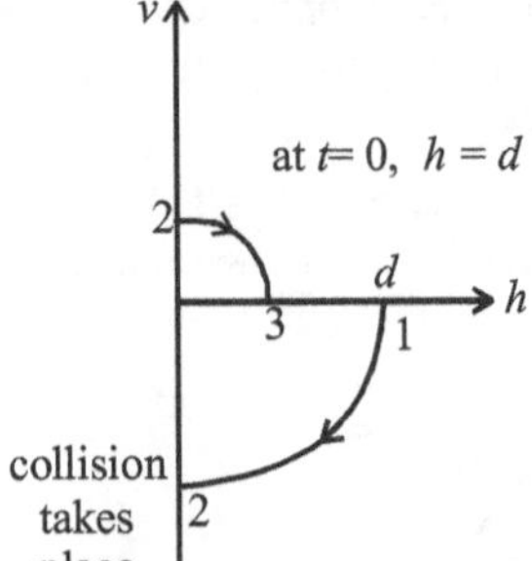

Initially velocity is downwards (−ve) and then after collision it reverses its direction with lesser magnitude, i.e. velocity is upwards (+ve).
Note that time $t = 0$ corresponds to the point on the graph where $h = d$.
Next time collision takes place at 3.

13. **(4)**

$$\begin{array}{cccc} (m/2) & (m/3) & (m/2) & V_B \\ \xrightarrow{\quad} & V_0 \bullet & \xrightarrow{\quad} & \bullet\xrightarrow{\quad} \\ A & B\ (\text{rest}) & (A)\ \ V_A & (B)\ (m/3) \end{array}$$

Before collision $\qquad\qquad\qquad$ After collision

Applying momentum conservation

$$\frac{m}{2} \times V_0 + \frac{m}{3} \times (0) = \frac{m}{2} V_A + \frac{m}{3} V_B$$

$$= \frac{V_0}{2} = \frac{V_A}{2} + \frac{V_B}{3} \qquad\qquad \text{...(i)}$$

Since, collision is elastic

$$e = 1 = \frac{V_B - V_A}{V_0} \Rightarrow V_0 = V_B - V_A \qquad \text{...(ii)}$$

On solving equations (i) and (ii) : $V_A = \dfrac{V_0}{5}$

Now, de-Broglie wavelength of A before collision :

$$\lambda_0 = \frac{h}{m_A V_0} = \frac{h}{\left(\dfrac{m}{2}\right) V_0} \Rightarrow \lambda_0 = \frac{2h}{m V_0}$$

Final de-Broglie wavelength :

$$\lambda_f = \frac{h}{m_A V_0} = \frac{h}{\dfrac{m}{2} \times \dfrac{V_0}{5}} \Rightarrow \lambda_f = \frac{10h}{m V_0}$$

$$\therefore \Delta\lambda = \lambda_f - \lambda_0 = \frac{10h}{m V_0} - \frac{2h}{m V_0}$$

$$\Rightarrow \Delta\lambda = \frac{8h}{m v_0} \Rightarrow \Delta\lambda = 4 \times \frac{2h}{m v_0}$$

$$\therefore \Delta\lambda = 4\lambda_0$$

14. **(1)** Given : $\vec{u} = 5\hat{j}$ m/s

Acceleration, $\vec{a} = 10\hat{i} + 4\hat{j}$ and
final coordinate $(20, y_0)$ in time t.

$$S_x = u_x t + \frac{1}{2} a_x t^2 \qquad\qquad [\because u_x = 0]$$

$$\Rightarrow 20 = 0 + \frac{1}{2} \times 10 \times t^2 \Rightarrow t = 2\ \text{s}$$

$$S_y = u_y \times t + \frac{1}{2} a_y t^2$$

$$y_0 = 5 \times 2 + \frac{1}{2} \times 4 \times 2^2 = 18\ \text{m}$$

15. **(1)** Given : Gravitational field,

$$E_G = \frac{Ax}{(x^2 + a^2)^{3/2}},\ V_\infty = 0$$

$$\int_{V_\infty}^{V_x} dV = -\int_{\infty}^{x} \vec{E}_G \cdot \vec{d}_x$$

$$\Rightarrow V_x - V_\infty = -\int_{\infty}^{x} \frac{Ax}{(x^2 + a^2)^{3/2}} dx$$

$$\therefore V_x = \frac{A}{(x^2 + a^2)^{1/2}} - 0 = \frac{A}{(x^2 + a^2)^{1/2}}$$

16. (4) From formula, $\dfrac{dQ}{dt} = kA\dfrac{dT}{dx}$

$$\Rightarrow k = \dfrac{\left(\dfrac{dQ}{dt}\right)}{A\left(\dfrac{dT}{dx}\right)}$$

$$[k] = \dfrac{[ML^2T^{-3}]}{[L^2][KL^{-1}]} = [MLT^{-3}K^{-1}]$$

17. (2) According to the question, all collisions are perfectly inelastic, so after the final collision, all blocks are moving together.

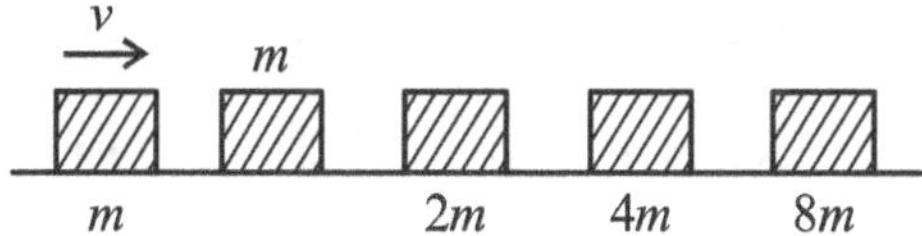

$$m \qquad 2m \qquad 4m \qquad 8m$$

Let the final velocity be v', using momentum conservation

$$mv = 16mv' \Rightarrow v' = \dfrac{v}{16}$$

Now initial energy $E_i = \dfrac{1}{2}mv^2$

Final energy : $E_f = \dfrac{1}{2}\times 16m \times\left(\dfrac{v}{16}\right)^2 = \dfrac{1}{2}\dfrac{mv^2}{16}$

Energy loss : $E_i - E_f = \dfrac{1}{2}mv^2 - \dfrac{1}{2}m\dfrac{v^2}{16}$

$$\Rightarrow \dfrac{1}{2}mv^2\left[1-\dfrac{1}{16}\right] \Rightarrow \dfrac{1}{2}mv^2\left[\dfrac{15}{16}\right]$$

The total energy loss is $P\%$ of the original energy.

$$\therefore \%P = \dfrac{\text{Energy loss}}{\text{Original energy}} \times 100$$

$$= \dfrac{\dfrac{1}{2}mv^2\left[\dfrac{15}{16}\right]}{\dfrac{1}{2}mv^2} \times 100 = 93.75\%$$

Hence, value of P is close to 94.

18. (2) The orderly arrangement of different parts of EM wave in decreasing order of wavelength is as follows:

$$\lambda_{\text{radiowaves}} > \lambda_{\text{microwaves}} > \lambda_{\text{visible}} > \lambda_{\text{X-rays}}$$

19. (1) Graph of V_s and f given at $B\,(5.5, 0)$
Minimum energy for ejection of electron
= Work function (ϕ).

$$\phi - hV \text{ joulc or } \phi = \dfrac{hV}{e} \text{ eV (for } V-0)$$

$$\therefore \phi = \dfrac{6.62\times 10^{-34}\times 5.5\times 10^{14}}{1.6\times 10^{-19}} \text{ eV} = 2.27\,\text{eV}$$

20. (3) Given :
Radius of air bubble = 1 cm,
Upward acceleration of bubble, $a = 9.8$ cm/s^2,
$\rho_{\text{water}} = 1$ g cm^{-3}

$$\text{Volume } V = \dfrac{4\pi}{3}r^3 = \dfrac{4\pi}{3}\times(1)^3 = 4.19\,\text{cm}^3$$

$$F_{\text{buoyant}} - mg = ma \Rightarrow m = \dfrac{F_{\text{buoyant}}}{g+a}$$

$$\therefore m = \dfrac{(V\rho_\omega g)}{g+a} = \dfrac{V\rho_\omega}{1+\dfrac{a}{g}} = \dfrac{(4.19)\times 1}{1+\dfrac{9.8}{980}} = \dfrac{4.19}{1.01} = 4.15\,\text{g}$$

21. (266.67)
Here work done on gas and heat supplied to the gas are zero.
Let T be the final equilibrium temperature of the gas in the vessel.
Total internal energy of gases remain same.

i.e., $u_1 + u_2 = u'_1 + u'_2$

or, $n_1 C_v \Delta T_1 + n_2 C_v \Delta T_2 = (n_1 + n_2)C_v T$

$$\Rightarrow (0.1)C_v(200) + (0.05)C_v(400) = (0.15)C_v T$$

$$\therefore T = \dfrac{800}{3} = 266.67\,\text{K}$$

22. (10553.14)
From Bohr's formula for hydrogen atom,

$$\dfrac{1}{\lambda} = R\left(\dfrac{1}{n_1^2} - \dfrac{1}{n_2^2}\right)$$

$$R = 1.097\times 10^7 \text{ m}^{-1}$$

For Lyman series :

$$\dfrac{1}{\lambda_{\text{min.}}} = R(1) = R \qquad\qquad \because n_2 = \infty \text{ and } n_1 = 1$$

$$\dfrac{1}{\lambda_{\text{max.}}} = R\left\{1-\dfrac{1}{4}\right\} = \dfrac{3R}{4} \qquad \because n_1 = 2,\, n_1 = 1$$

$$\therefore \lambda_{\text{max.}} - \lambda_{\text{min.}} = \dfrac{4}{3R} - \dfrac{1}{R} = \dfrac{1}{3R} = 304 \text{ (Given)}$$

For Paschen series :

$$\lambda'_{\text{min.}} = R\left(\dfrac{1}{9}\right) \text{ and } \lambda'_{\text{max.}} = R\left(\dfrac{1}{9} - \dfrac{1}{16}\right) = \dfrac{7R}{16\times 9}$$

$$\lambda'_{\text{max.}} - \lambda'_{\text{min.}} = \dfrac{16\times 9}{7R} - \dfrac{9}{R} = \dfrac{81}{7R}$$

or, $\lambda'_{\text{max.}} - \lambda'_{\text{min.}} = \dfrac{81}{7R} = \dfrac{81\times 3}{7\times 3R} = \dfrac{81\times 3}{7}\times 304$

$$\left(\because \dfrac{1}{3R} = 304\text{Å}\right)$$

$\therefore$ For Pachen series, $\lambda'_{\text{max.}} - \lambda'_{\text{min.}} = 10553.14$

23. **(4.48)**

According to question, final image i.e., $v_2 = 25$ cm, $f_0 = 1$ cm, magnification, $m = m_1 m_2 = 100$

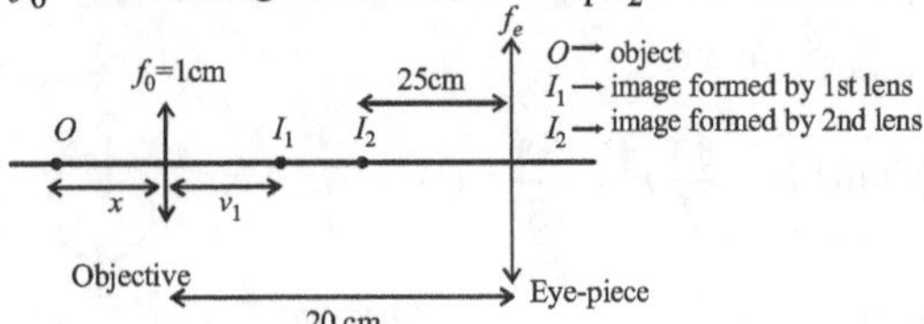

Using lens formula,

For first lens or objective $= \dfrac{1}{v_1} - \dfrac{1}{-x} = \dfrac{1}{1} \Rightarrow v_1 = \dfrac{x}{x-1}$

Also magnification $|m_1| = \left|\dfrac{v_1}{u_1}\right| = \dfrac{1}{x-1}$

For 2nd lens or eye-piece, this is acting as object

$\therefore u_2 = -(20 - v_1) = -\left(20 - \dfrac{x}{x-1}\right)$ and $v_2 = -25$ cm

Angular magnification $|m_A| = \left|\dfrac{D}{u_2}\right| = \dfrac{25}{|u_2|}$

Total magnification $m = m_1 m_A = 100$

$\left(\dfrac{1}{x-1}\right)\left(\dfrac{25}{20 - \dfrac{x}{x-1}}\right) = 100$

$\Rightarrow \dfrac{25}{20(x-1) - x} = 100 \Rightarrow 1 = 80(x-1) - 4x$

$\Rightarrow 76x = 81 \Rightarrow x = \dfrac{81}{76}$

$\Rightarrow u_2 = -\left(20 - \dfrac{\dfrac{81}{76}}{\dfrac{81}{76} - 1}\right) = \dfrac{-19}{5}$

Again using lens formula for eye-piece

$\dfrac{1}{-25} - \dfrac{1}{-\dfrac{19}{5}} = \dfrac{1}{f_e} \Rightarrow f_e = \dfrac{25 \times 19}{106} \approx 4.48 \text{ cm}$

24. **(11)**

Let mass of triangular lamina $= m$, and length of side $= l$, then moment of inertia of lamina about an axis passing through centroid G perpendicular to the plane.

$I_0 \propto ml^2$

$I_0 = kml^2$

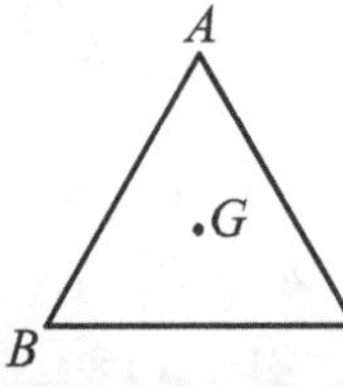

Let moment of inertia of $DEF = I_1$ about G

So, $I_1 \propto \left(\dfrac{m}{4}\right)\left(\dfrac{l}{2}\right)^2 \propto \dfrac{ml^2}{16}$ or $I_1 = \dfrac{I_0}{16}$

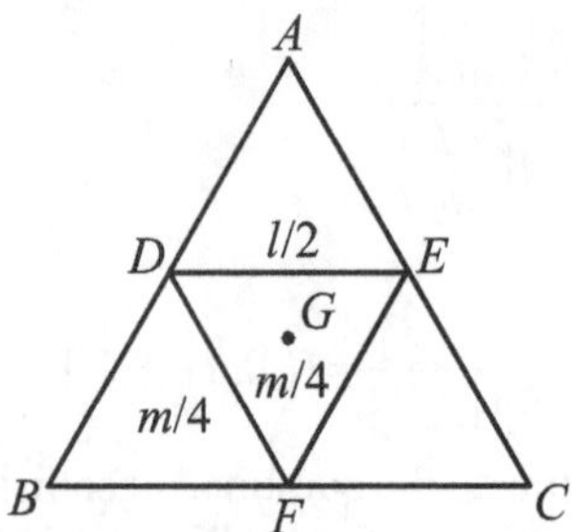

Let $I_{ADE} = I_{BDF} = I_{EFC} = I_2$

$\therefore 3I_2 + I_1 = I_0 \Rightarrow 3I_2 + \dfrac{I_0}{16} = I_0 \Rightarrow I_2 = \dfrac{5I_0}{16}$

Hence, moment of inertia of $DECB$ i.e., after removal part ADE

$= 2I_2 + I_1 = 2\left(\dfrac{5I_0}{16}\right) + \left(\dfrac{I_0}{16}\right) = \dfrac{11I_0}{16} = \dfrac{NI_0}{16}$

Therefore value of $N = 11$.

25. **(20)**

As we know moment of inertia disc, $I_{\text{disc}} = \dfrac{1}{2}MR^2$

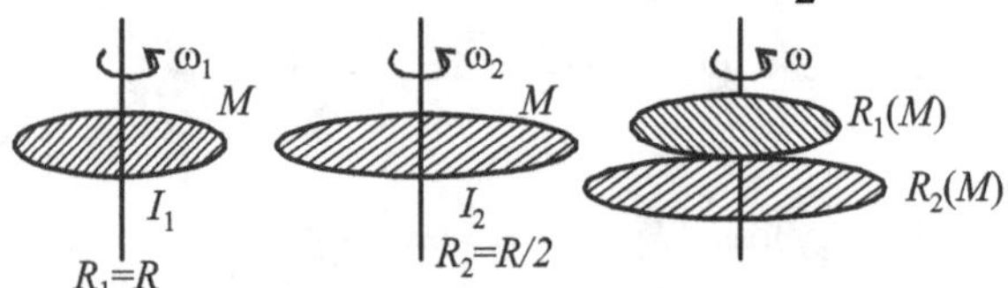

Using angular momentum conservation

$I_1\omega_1 + I_2\omega_2 = (I_1 + I_2) \times \omega_f$

$\dfrac{MR^2}{2} \times \omega + 0 = \left(\dfrac{MR^2}{2} + \dfrac{MR^2}{8}\right)\omega_f \Rightarrow \omega_f = \dfrac{4}{5}\omega$

Initial K.E., $K_i = \dfrac{1}{2}I\omega^2 = \dfrac{1}{2}\left(\dfrac{MR^2}{2}\right)\omega^2 = \dfrac{MR^2\omega^2}{4}$

Final K.E., $K_f = \dfrac{1}{2}\left(\dfrac{MR^2}{2} + \dfrac{MR^2}{8}\right)\dfrac{16}{25}\omega^2 = \dfrac{MR^2\omega^2}{5}$

Percentage loss in kinetic energy % loss

$= \dfrac{\dfrac{MR^2\omega^2}{4} - \dfrac{MR^2\omega^2}{5}}{\dfrac{MR^2\omega^2}{4}} \times 100 = 20\% = P\%$

Hence, value of $P = 20$.

CHEMISTRY

26. **(3)** $_{89}\text{AC} \longrightarrow _{103}\text{Lr}$

Belongs to actinoids series and they all belongs to 3rd group. So atomic no. 101 element is actinoids and atomic number 104 element belongs to 4th group.

27. **(3)** Compounds having $1°$ amine give carbylamine reaction with $CHCl_3$ and alc. KOH.

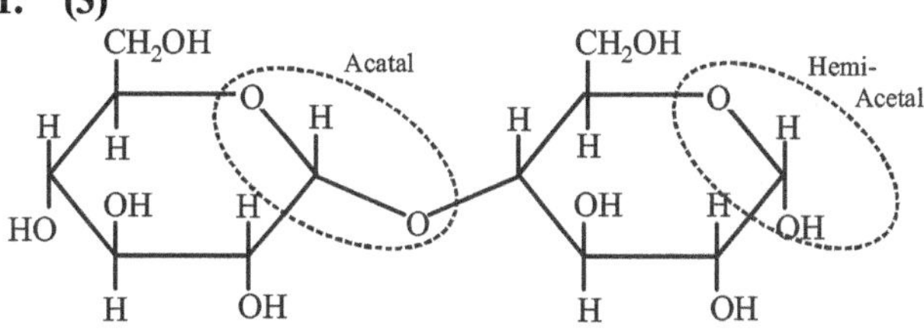

Structures: *Lysine, Proline, Thymine (T), Cytosine (C), Adenine (A)

28. (4) $[Pt(en)(NO_2)_2]$

So, total possible isomers are 3.

29. (1) In hydrogen spectrum maximum lines of Balmer series lies in visible region.

30. (4)
(a) For ideal gas U and H are function of temperature.
(b) Compressibility factor for an ideal gas is 1.
(c) $C_P - C_V = R$
(d) $\Delta U = C_V dT$ for all processes.

31. (3)

One acetal and one hemi acetal group is present in maltose.

32. (2)

4-Bromo-2-methylcyclopentane carboxylic acid

33. (2) On heating in excess air Li form oxide sodium form peroxide while K, Rb, Cs form superoxide.

34. (3) $Pb(NO_3)_2 \xrightarrow{\Delta} PbO + 2NO_2(g)$ (brown gas)
      'A'

$2NO_2(g) \xrightarrow{\text{cooling}} N_2O_4$
 'A'   'B'

$N_2O_4 + NO \longrightarrow \overset{+3}{N_2O_3}$
 'B'   'C'

35. (2) At equilibrium, rate of forward reaction = Rate of backward reaction.

36. (1) All statements are correct.

(a) $CaCO_3 \xrightarrow{\text{500-800 K}} CaO + CO_2$
    Lime stone

(b) In extraction of Ag, it is extracted as an anionic complex $[Ag(CN)_2]^-$.

(c) Ni is purified by Mond's process

$Ni + 4CO \xrightarrow{\text{300 K}} Ni(CO)_4$

$Ni(CO)_4 \xrightarrow{\text{450 K}} Ni + 4CO$

(d) Van Arkel method is used to purify Zr and Ti.

37. (1)

3° Alcohol
(Give Lucas test immediately)

38. (2)

Neopentyl alcohol

85% (Major) Saytzeff alkene

15%

39. (2) $E^o_{cell} = E^o_{Cu^{2+}|Cu} - E^o_{Zn^{2+}|Zn} = 1.1 V$

So, if $E_{ext.} = 1.1$ V no electron will flow

At, $E_{ext.} > 1.1$ V cell act as electrolytic cell and electron will flow from Cu to Zn.

At, $E_{ext.} < 1.1$ V cell act as electrochemical cells so Zn dissolve and Cu deposit.

40. (1)

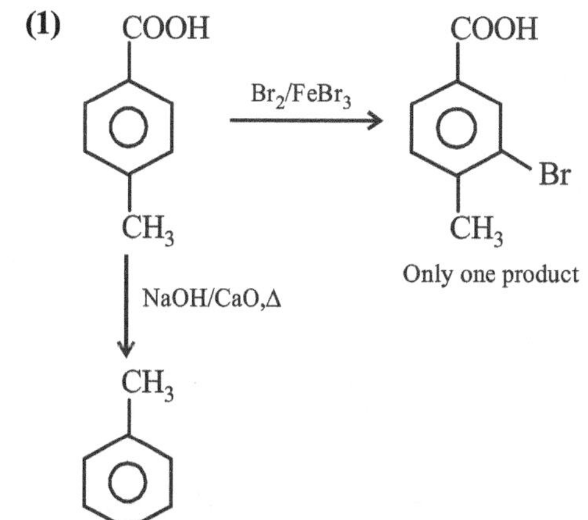

Only one product

41. **(3)**

Type of colloid	Example
Foam	Froth
Gel	Jellies
Aerosol	Smoke
Emulsion	Milk

42. **(1)** $[Cr(H_2O)_6]^{2+} \Rightarrow Cr^{2+} \Rightarrow 3d^4 \Rightarrow t_{2g}^{1,1,1}, e_g^{1,0}$

No. of unpaired e^- : 4

$[Fe(H_2O)_6]^{2+} \Rightarrow Fe^{2+} \Rightarrow 3d^6 \Rightarrow t_{2g}^{2,1,1}, e_g^{1,1}$

No. of unpaired e^- : 4

$[Fe(NH_3)_6]^{2+} \Rightarrow Fe^{2+} \Rightarrow 3d^6 \Rightarrow t_{2g}^{2,1,1}, e_g^{1,1}$

No. of unpaired e^- : 4

$[Co(OH)_4]^{2-} \Rightarrow Co^{2+} \Rightarrow 3d^7 \Rightarrow e^{2,2}, t_2^{1,1,1}$

No. of unpaired e^- : 3

$[CoCl_4]^{2-} \Rightarrow Co^{2+} \Rightarrow 3d^7 \Rightarrow e^{2,2}, t_2^{1,1,1}$

No. of unpaired e^- : 3

$[Mn(H_2O)_6]^{2+} \Rightarrow Mn^{2+} \Rightarrow 3d^5 \Rightarrow t_{2g}^{1,1,1}, e_g^{1,1}$

No. of unpaired e^- : 5

So $[Cr(H_2O)_6]^{2+}$ and $[Fe(H_2O)_6]^{2+}$ have same magnetic moment (spin only).

43. **(4)** A-B bond has highest intermolecular potential energy among the given molecules. Hence, it is strongest bond and has maximum bond enthalpy.

44. **(4)** Given reaction is S_N1 reaction. In S_N1 reaction Rate of reaction $\propto$ Stability of C^+

(A) 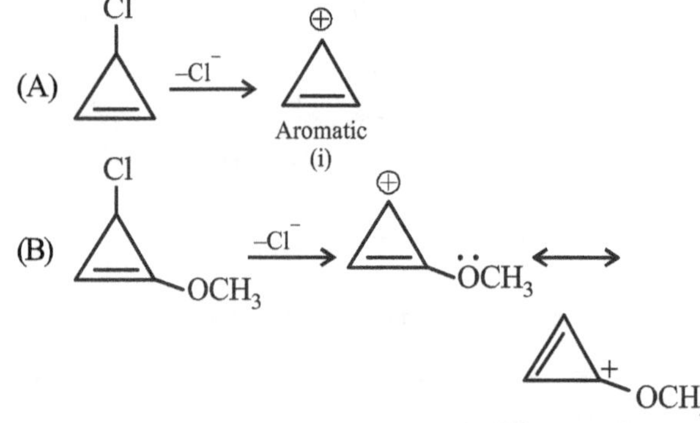

Stability of C^+ : ii > i > iii > iv

Reactivity order : B > A > C > D

45. **(2)**

	O^{2-}	F^-	Na^+	Mg^{2+}
Z	8	9	11	12
No. of e^-	10	10	10	10

In isoelectronic species greater is $Z_{eff.}$ smaller is radius so order is $O^{2-} > F^- > Na^+ > Mg^{2+}$.

46. **(85)**

$$5H_2O_2 + 2MnO_4^- + 6H^+ \longrightarrow 2Mn^{2+} + 5O_2 + 8H_2O$$

Moles of $KMnO_4 = \dfrac{0.316}{158} = 2 \times 10^{-3}$

Equivalents of H_2O_2 = Equivalents of $KMnO_4$

Equivalents of $KMnO_4 = 2 \times 10^{-3} \times 5 = 0.01$

Moles of $H_2O_2 = \dfrac{0.01}{2} = 0.005$

Mass of pere $H_2O_2 = 0.005 \times 34 = 0.170$ g

Percentage purity $= \dfrac{0.17}{0.2} \times 100 = 85\%.$

47. **(4)**

Number of chiral centres, represented as (*) in the product (B) = 4

48. **(3400)**

Mole of $N_2 = \dfrac{2800}{28} = 100$ and Mole of $H_2 = \dfrac{1000}{2} = 500$

$$N_2(g) + 3H_2(g) \rightarrow 2NH_3(g)$$

Initial mole	100	500	
Final mole	0	300	200
	Limiting reagent		

Mass of NH_3 formed $= 200 \times 17 = 3400$ g

49. **(60)**

$$t = \dfrac{2.303}{k} \log\left[\dfrac{100}{100 - x\%}\right]$$

$$t_{75\%} = \dfrac{2.303}{k} \log\left[\dfrac{100}{25}\right] = 90$$

$$t_{60\%} = \dfrac{2.303}{k} \log\left[\dfrac{100}{40}\right]$$

$$\dfrac{t_{75\%}}{t_{60\%}} = \dfrac{2\log 2}{\log 2.5} \Rightarrow \dfrac{90}{t_{60\%}} = \dfrac{2 \times 0.3}{0.4}$$

$$\Rightarrow t_{60\%} = \dfrac{90 \times 4}{6} = 60 \text{ min.}$$

50. **(600)**

$$P_{total} = P^o_{hexane} \cdot X_{hexane} + P^o_{heptane} \cdot X_{heptane}$$

$$550 = [P^o_{hexane}] \times \dfrac{1}{4} + [P^o_{heptane}] \times \dfrac{3}{4}$$

$$\Rightarrow 2200 = P^o_{hexane} + 3P^o_{heptane} \qquad ...(i)$$

$$560 = [P^o_{hexane}] \times \frac{1}{5} + [P^o_{heptane}] \times \frac{4}{5}$$

$$\Rightarrow 2800 = P^o_{hexane} + 4P^o_{heptane} \qquad ...(ii)$$

From equation (i) and (ii),

$$P^o_{heptane} = 600 \text{ mm of Hg}$$

MATHEMATICS

51. (2) The given series is

$$1 + (1 - 2^2 \cdot 1) + (1 - 4^2 \cdot 3) + (1 - 6^2 \cdot 5) + ... (1 - 20^2 \cdot 19)$$

$$S = 1 + \sum_{r=1}^{10} [1 - (2r)^2 (2r-1)]$$

$$= 1 + \sum_{r=1}^{10} (1 - 8r^3 + 4r^2) = 1 + 10 - \sum_{r=1}^{10} (8r^3 - 4r^2)$$

$$= 11 - 8\left(\frac{10 \times 11}{2}\right)^2 + 4 \times \left(\frac{10 \times 11 \times 21}{6}\right)$$

$$= 11 - 2 \times (110)^2 + 4 \times 55 \times 7$$

$$= 11 - 220(110 - 7)$$

$$= 11 - 220 \times 103 = \alpha - 220\beta$$

$$\Rightarrow \alpha = 11, \ \beta = 103$$

$$\therefore (\alpha, \beta) = (11, 103)$$

52. (1) $\dfrac{dy}{dx} - \dfrac{y}{x} = x(x\cos x + \sin x)$

$$\text{I.F.} = e^{-\int \frac{1}{x} dx} = \frac{1}{x}$$

$$\therefore \int d\left(\frac{y}{x}\right) = \int (x\cos x + \sin x)dx$$

$$\Rightarrow \frac{y}{x} = x\sin x + C \qquad \because y(\pi) = \pi \Rightarrow C = 1$$

$$y = x^2 \sin x + x \Rightarrow y\left(\frac{\pi}{2}\right) = \frac{\pi^2}{4} + \frac{\pi}{2}$$

$$y' = 2x\sin x + x^2 \cos x + 1$$

$$y'' = 2\sin x - x^2 \sin x \Rightarrow y''\left(\frac{\pi}{2}\right) = 2 - \frac{\pi^2}{4}$$

$$\therefore y''\left(\frac{\pi}{2}\right) + y\left(\frac{\pi}{2}\right) = 2 - \frac{\pi^2}{4} + \frac{\pi^2}{4} + \frac{\pi}{2} = 2 + \frac{\pi}{2}$$

53. (1) The given series, $\displaystyle\sum_{r=0}^{20} {}^{50-r}C_6$

$$= {}^{50}C_6 + {}^{49}C_6 + {}^{48}C_6 + {}^{47}C_6 + ... + {}^{32}C_6 + {}^{31}C_6 + {}^{30}C_6$$

$$= ({}^{30}C_7 + {}^{30}C_6) + {}^{31}C_6 + {}^{32}C_6 + ... + {}^{49}C_6 + {}^{50}C_6 - {}^{30}C_7$$

$$= ({}^{31}C_7 + {}^{31}C_6) + {}^{32}C_6 + ... + {}^{49}C_6 + {}^{50}C_6 - {}^{30}C_7$$

$$= ({}^{32}C_7 + {}^{32}C_6) + ... + {}^{49}C_6 + {}^{50}C_6 - {}^{30}C_7$$

....

....

....

$$= {}^{51}C_7 - {}^{30}C_7$$

54. (4)

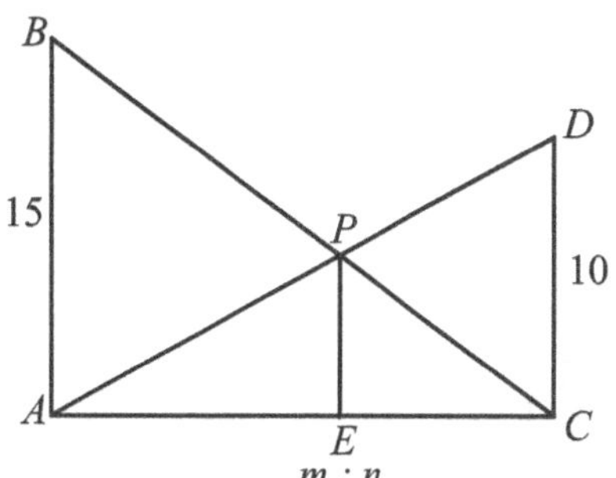

Let $PE \perp AC$ and $\dfrac{AE}{EC} = \dfrac{m}{n}$

$\because \Delta AEP \sim \Delta ACD, \ \dfrac{m}{PE} = \dfrac{m+n}{10}$

$$\Rightarrow PE = \frac{10m}{m+n} \qquad ...(i)$$

$\because \Delta CEP \sim \Delta CAB, \ \dfrac{n}{PE} = \dfrac{m+n}{15}$

$$\Rightarrow PE = \frac{15n}{m+n} \qquad ...(ii)$$

From (i) and (ii),

$$10m = 15n \Rightarrow m = \frac{3}{2}n$$

So, $PE = 6$

55. (2) Let ΔABC be in the first quadrant

Slope of line $AB = -\dfrac{1}{2}$

Slope of line $AC = 2$

Length of $AB = \sqrt{5}$

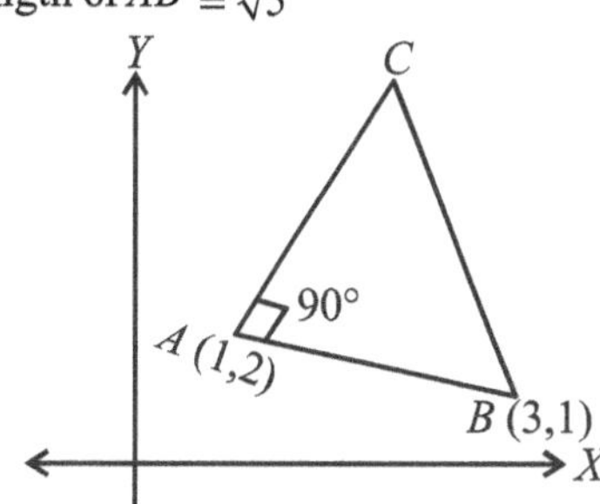

It is given that $\text{ar}(\Delta ABC) = 5\sqrt{5}$

$$\therefore \frac{1}{2} AB \cdot AC = 5\sqrt{5} \Rightarrow AC = 10$$

$\therefore$ Coordinate of vertex $C = (1 + 10\cos\theta, \ 2 + 10\sin\theta)$

$\because \tan\theta = 2 \Rightarrow \cos\theta = \dfrac{1}{\sqrt{5}}, \ \sin\theta = \dfrac{2}{\sqrt{5}}$

$\therefore$ Coordinate of C $= (1 + 2\sqrt{5}, \ 2 + 4\sqrt{5})$

$\therefore$ Abscissa of vertex C is $1 + 2\sqrt{5}$.

56. (4) Let the two remaining observations be x and y.

$$\because \bar{x} = \frac{5+7+10+12+14+15+x+y}{8}$$

$$\Rightarrow 10 = \frac{63+x+y}{8}$$

$$\Rightarrow x+y = 80-63$$

$$\Rightarrow x+y = 17 \qquad \ldots(i)$$

$$\because \operatorname{var}(x) = 13.5$$

$$= \frac{25+49+100+144+196+225+x^2+y^2}{8} - (10)^2$$

$$\Rightarrow x^2+y^2 = 169 \qquad \ldots(ii)$$

From (i) and (ii) we get
$(x, y) = (12, 5)$ or $(5, 12)$
So, $|x-y| = 7$.

57. (4) The given equation

$$[x]^2 + 2[x] + 4 - 7 = 0$$

$$\Rightarrow [x]^2 + 2[x] - 3 = 0$$

$$\Rightarrow [x]^2 + 3[x] - [x] - 3 = 0$$

$$\Rightarrow ([x]+3)([x]-1) = 0 \Rightarrow [x] = 1 \text{ or } -3$$

$$\Rightarrow x \in [-3, -2) \cup [1, 2)$$

$\therefore$ The equation has infinitely many solutions.

58. (1) $\displaystyle \int \frac{x^2}{(x\sin x + \cos x)^2}\,dx$

$$\because \frac{d}{dx}(x\sin x + \cos x) = x\cos x$$

$$= \int \frac{x\cos x}{(x\sin x + \cos x)^2}\left(\frac{x}{\cos x}\right)dx$$

$$= \underset{\text{II}}{\frac{x}{\cos x}}\left[\underset{\text{I}}{\frac{-1}{x\sin x + \cos x}}\right]$$

$$\qquad -\int \frac{x\sin x + \cos x}{\cos^2 x}\left[\frac{-1}{x\sin x + \cos x}\right]dx$$

$$= \frac{x}{\cos x}\left[\frac{-1}{x\sin x + \cos x}\right] + \int \sec^2 x\,dx$$

$$= \frac{-x\sec x}{x\sin x + \cos x} + \tan x + C$$

59. (4) $\because A = \begin{bmatrix} \cos\theta & i\sin\theta \\ i\sin\theta & \cos\theta \end{bmatrix}$

$$\therefore A^n = \begin{bmatrix} \cos n\theta & i\sin n\theta \\ i\sin n\theta & \cos n\theta \end{bmatrix}, \; n \in \mathbf{N}$$

$$\because A^5 = \begin{bmatrix} a & b \\ c & d \end{bmatrix}$$

$$\therefore A^5 = \begin{bmatrix} \cos 5\theta & i\sin 5\theta \\ i\sin 5\theta & \cos 5\theta \end{bmatrix} = \begin{bmatrix} a & b \\ c & d \end{bmatrix}$$

$\therefore a = \cos 5\theta,\ b = i\sin 5\theta = c,\ d = \cos 5\theta$

$$\therefore a^2 - b^2 = \cos^2 5\theta + \sin^2 5\theta = 1$$

$$a^2 - c^2 = \cos^2 5\theta + \sin^2 5\theta = 1$$

$$a^2 - d^2 = \cos^2 5\theta - \cos^2 5\theta = 1$$

$$a^2 + b^2 = \cos^2 5\theta - \sin^2 5\theta = \cos 10\theta = \cos\frac{10\pi}{24}$$

and $0 < \cos\dfrac{5\pi}{12} < 1 \Rightarrow 0 \le a^2 + b^2 \le 1$

$\therefore a^2 - b^2 = \dfrac{1}{2}$ is wrong.

60. (4) It is given that

$$f(x) = \bar{a}\cdot(\bar{b}\times\bar{c}) = \begin{vmatrix} \hat{i} & \hat{j} & \hat{k} \\ x & -2 & 3 \\ -2 & x & -1 \\ 7 & -2 & x \end{vmatrix} = x^3 - 27x + 26$$

$$\Rightarrow f(x) = x^3 - 27x + 26$$

$$\Rightarrow f'(x) = 3x^2 - 27$$

For critical point $f'(x) = 0$

$$\Rightarrow 3x^2 - 27 = 0 \Rightarrow x = -3, 3$$

$$\underset{-3 \quad\quad 3}{+ \quad - \quad +}$$

$$\underset{\text{Max.} \quad \text{Min.}}{}$$

The local maxima of $f(x)$ is, $x_0 = -3$.

Then $\bar{a}\cdot\bar{b} + \bar{b}\cdot\bar{c} + \bar{c}\cdot\bar{a}$

$= -2x - 2x - 3 - 14 - 2x - x + 7x + 4 + 3x = 3x - 13$

So, value at $x = x_0, = \bar{a}\cdot\bar{b} + \bar{b}\cdot\bar{c} + \bar{c}\cdot\bar{a} = 3x - 13$

$$= 3\times(-3) - 13 = -22.$$

61. (3) $(a+\sqrt{2}b\cos x)(a-\sqrt{2}b\cos y) = a^2 - b^2$

Differentiating both sides,

$$(-\sqrt{2}b\sin x)(a-\sqrt{2}b\cos y) + (a+\sqrt{2}b\cos x)$$

$$(\sqrt{2}b\sin y)\frac{dy}{dx} = 0$$

$$\Rightarrow \frac{dy}{dx} = \frac{(\sqrt{2}b\sin x)(a-\sqrt{2}b\cos y)}{(a+\sqrt{2}b\cos x)(\sqrt{2}b\sin y)}$$

$$\therefore \left[\frac{dy}{dx}\right]_{\left(\frac{\pi}{4},\frac{\pi}{4}\right)} = \frac{a-b}{a+b} \Rightarrow \frac{dx}{dy} = \frac{a+b}{a-b}$$

62. (4) The truth table of both the statements is

p	q	~p	~q	q∨p	p↔~q	(S₁)	~p↔q	(S₂)
T	T	F	F	T	F	F	F	F
T	F	F	T	T	T	T	T	T
F	T	T	F	T	T	T	T	F
F	F	T	T	F	F	T	F	F

$\therefore$ S_1 is not tautology and
S_2 is not fallacy.
Hence, both the statements (S_1) and (S_2) are not correct.

63. (1) $f(x) = |x-2| = \begin{cases} 2-x, & x < 2 \\ x-2, & x \ge 2 \end{cases}$

$$g(x) = f(f(x)) = \begin{cases} 2-f(x), & f(x) < 2 \\ f(x)-2, & f(x) \ge 2 \end{cases}$$

$$= \begin{cases} 2-(2-x), & 2-x<2, & x<2 \\ (2-x)-2, & 2-x\ge2, & x<2 \\ 2-(x-2), & x-2<2, & x\ge2 \\ (x-2)-2, & x-2\ge2, & x\ge2 \end{cases}$$

$$= \begin{cases} -x & 0 < x \le 0 \\ x & 0 < x < 2 \\ 4-x & 2 \le x < 4 \\ x-4 & x \ge 4 \end{cases}$$

$$\therefore \int_0^3 [g(x) - f(x)]\,dx$$

$$= \int_0^2 x\,dx + \int_2^3 (4-x)\,dx - \int_0^3 |x-2|\,dx = 1$$

64. **(4)** $u = \dfrac{2(x+iy)+i}{(x+iy)-ki} = \dfrac{2x+i(2y+1)}{x+i(y-k)}$

Real part of $u = \operatorname{Re}(u) = \dfrac{2x^2 + (y-K)(2y+1)}{x^2 + (y-K)^2}$

Imaginary part of u

$= \operatorname{Im}(u) = \dfrac{-2x(y-K) + x(2y+1)}{x^2 + (y-K)^2}$

$\because \operatorname{Re}(u) + \operatorname{Im}(u) = 1$

$\Rightarrow 2x^2 + 2y^2 - 2Ky + y - K - 2xy + 2Kx + 2xy + x$

$= x^2 + y^2 + K^2 - 2Ky$

Since, the curve intersect at y-axis

$\therefore x = 0$

$\Rightarrow y^2 + y - K(K+1) = 0$

Let y_1 and y_2 are roots of equations if $x = 0$

$\because y_1 + y_2 = -1$

$y_1 y_2 = -(K^2 + K)$

$\therefore (y_1 - y_2)^2 = (1 + 4K^2 + 4K)$

Given $PQ = 5 \Rightarrow |y_1 - y_2| = 5$

$\Rightarrow 4K^2 + 4K - 24 = 0 \Rightarrow K = 2 \text{ or } -3$

as $K > 0$, $\therefore K = 2$

65. **(4)** Let $n(U) = 100$, then $n(A) = 63, n(B) = 76$

$n(A \cap B) = x$

Now, $n(A \cup B) = n(A) + n(B) - n(A \cap B) \le 100$

$\qquad = 63 + 76 - x \le 100$

$\Rightarrow x \ge 139 - 100 \Rightarrow x \ge 39$

$\because n(A \cap B) \le n(A)$

$\Rightarrow x \le 63$

$\therefore 39 \le x \le 63$

66. **(2)** Let f be twice differentiable function

$\because f'(x) \ge 1$

$\Rightarrow \dfrac{f(5) - f(2)}{3} \ge 1$

$\Rightarrow f(5) \ge 3 + f(2)$

$\Rightarrow f(5) \ge 3 + 8 \Rightarrow f(5) \ge 11$

and also $f''(x) \ge 4$

$\Rightarrow \dfrac{f'(5) - f'(2)}{5-2} \ge 4 \Rightarrow f'(5) \ge 12 + f'(2)$

$\Rightarrow f'(5) \ge 17$

Hence, $f(5) + f'(5) \ge 28$

67. **(4)** $\displaystyle\int \dfrac{\sqrt{x}}{(1+x)^2}\,dx \ (x > 0)$

Put $x = \tan^2\theta \Rightarrow 2x\,dx = 2\tan\theta\sec^2\theta\,d\theta$

$I = \displaystyle\int \dfrac{2\tan^2\theta \cdot \sec^2\theta}{\sec^4\theta}\,d\theta = \int 2\sin^2\theta\,d\theta$

$= \theta - \dfrac{\sin 2\theta}{2} + C$

$\Rightarrow f(x) = \theta - \dfrac{1}{2} \times \dfrac{2\tan\theta}{1+\tan^2\theta} + C$

$f(x) = \theta - \dfrac{\tan\theta}{1+\tan^2\theta} + C = \tan^{-1}\sqrt{x} - \dfrac{\sqrt{x}}{1+x} + C$

Now $f(3) - f(1) = \tan^{-1}(\sqrt{3}) - \dfrac{\sqrt{3}}{1+3} - \tan^{-1}(1) + \dfrac{1}{2}$

$= \dfrac{\pi}{12} + \dfrac{1}{2} - \dfrac{\sqrt{3}}{4}$

68. **(3)** The given ellipse is

$\dfrac{x^2}{a^2} + \dfrac{y^2}{b^2} = 1, \ (a > b)$

Length of latus rectum $= \dfrac{2b^2}{a}$

$\Rightarrow \dfrac{2b^2}{a} = 10 \Rightarrow b^2 = 5a \qquad \text{...(i)}$

Now $\phi(t) = \dfrac{5}{12} + t - t^2$

$\phi'(t) = 1 - 2t = 0 \Rightarrow t = \dfrac{1}{2}$

$\phi''(t) = -2 < 0 \Rightarrow \text{maximum}$

$\Rightarrow \phi(t)_{\max} = \dfrac{5}{12} + \dfrac{1}{2} - \dfrac{1}{4} = \dfrac{8}{12} = \dfrac{2}{3}$

Since, $\phi(t)_{\max.} = \text{eccentricity}$

$\Rightarrow e = \dfrac{2}{3}$

Now, $b^2 = a^2(1 - e^2)$

$5a = a^2\left(1 - \dfrac{4}{9}\right) \Rightarrow 5a = \dfrac{5a^2}{9} \Rightarrow a^2 - 9a = 0$

$\Rightarrow a = 9 \Rightarrow a^2 = 81 \text{ and } b^2 = 45$

$\therefore a^2 + b^2 = 81 + 45 = 126$

69. **(1)** $\because$ The equation of hyperbola is

$\dfrac{x^2}{a^2} - \dfrac{y^2}{b^2} = 1$

$\because$ Equation of hyperbola passes through $(3, 3)$

$\dfrac{1}{a^2} - \dfrac{1}{b^2} = \dfrac{1}{9} \qquad \text{...(i)}$

Equation of normal at point $(3, 3)$ is :

$\dfrac{x-3}{\dfrac{1}{a^2} \cdot 3} = \dfrac{y-3}{-\dfrac{1}{b^2} \cdot 3}$

$\because$ It passes through $(9, 0)$

$$\dfrac{6}{\dfrac{1}{a^2}} = \dfrac{-3}{-\dfrac{1}{b^2}}$$

$$\therefore \dfrac{1}{b^2} = \dfrac{1}{2a^2} \qquad \text{...(ii)}$$

From equations (i) and (ii),

$$a^2 = \dfrac{9}{2},\ b^2 = 9$$

$\because$ Eccentricity $= e$, then $e^2 = 1 + \dfrac{b^2}{a^2} = 3$

$$\therefore (a^2, e^2) = \left(\dfrac{9}{2}, 3\right)$$

70. **(2)** Let $\alpha,\ \beta,\ \gamma,\ \delta$ be in G.P., then $\alpha\delta = \beta\gamma$

$$\Rightarrow \dfrac{\alpha}{\beta} = \dfrac{\gamma}{\delta} \Rightarrow \left|\dfrac{\alpha-\beta}{\alpha+\beta}\right| = \left|\dfrac{\gamma-\delta}{\gamma+\delta}\right|$$

$$\Rightarrow \dfrac{\sqrt{9-4p}}{3} = \dfrac{\sqrt{36-4q}}{6}$$

$$\Rightarrow 36 - 16p = 36 - 4q \Rightarrow q = 4p$$

$$\therefore \dfrac{2q+p}{2q-p} = \dfrac{8p+p}{8p-p} = \dfrac{9p}{7p} = \dfrac{9}{7}$$

71. **(10.00)**

$$f(x+y) = f(x) + f(y) + xy^2 + x^2 y$$

Differentiate w.r.t. x:

$$f'(x+y) = f'(x) + 0 + y^2 + 2xy$$

Put $y = -x$

$$f'(0) = f'(x) + x^2 - 2x^2 \qquad \text{...(i)}$$

$$\because \lim_{x \to 0} \dfrac{f(x)}{x} = 1 \Rightarrow f(0) = 0$$

$$\therefore f'(0) = 1 \qquad \text{...(ii)}$$

From equations (i) and (ii),

$$f'(x) = (x^2 + 1) \Rightarrow f'(3) = 10.$$

72. **(5.00)**

For infinitely many solutions,

$$\Delta = \Delta_1 = \Delta_2 = \Delta_3 = 0$$

$$\Delta = \begin{vmatrix} 1 & -2 & 3 \\ 2 & 1 & 1 \\ 1 & -7 & a \end{vmatrix} = 0$$

$$\Rightarrow (a+7) - 2(1-2a) + 3(-15) = 0$$

$$\Rightarrow a = 8$$

$$\Delta_3 = \begin{vmatrix} 1 & -2 & 9 \\ 2 & 1 & b \\ 1 & -7 & 24 \end{vmatrix} = 0$$

$$\Rightarrow (24 + 7b) - 2(b - 48) + 9(-15) = 0$$

$$\Rightarrow b = 3$$

$$\therefore a - b = 5.$$

73. **(3.00)**

$$p = \dfrac{1}{10},\ q = \dfrac{9}{10}$$

P (not hitting target in n trials) $= \left(\dfrac{9}{10}\right)^n$

P (at least one hit) $= 1 - \left(\dfrac{9}{10}\right)^n$

$$\because 1 - \left(\dfrac{9}{10}\right)^n > \dfrac{1}{4} \Rightarrow (0.9)^n < 0.75$$

$$\therefore n_{\text{minimum}} = 3.$$

74. **(3.00)**

Equation of plane P is

$$(x + 4y - z + 7) + \lambda(3x + y + 5z - 8) = 0$$

$$\Rightarrow x(1+3\lambda) + y(4+\lambda) + z(-1+5\lambda) + (7-8\lambda) = 0$$

$$\Rightarrow \dfrac{1+3\lambda}{a} = \dfrac{4+\lambda}{b} = \dfrac{5\lambda-1}{6} = \dfrac{7-8\lambda}{-15}$$

From last two ratios, $\lambda = -1$

$$\Rightarrow \dfrac{-2}{a} = \dfrac{3}{b} = -1$$

$$\therefore a = 2,\ b = -3$$

$\therefore$ Equation of plane is, $2x - 3y + 6z - 15 = 0$

$$\text{Distance} = \dfrac{|6 - 6 - 6 - 15|}{7} = \dfrac{21}{7} = 3.$$

75. **(8.00)**

The given expression is $(2x^2 + 3x + 4)^{10} = \displaystyle\sum_{r=0}^{20} a_r x^r$

General term $= \dfrac{10!}{r_1!\,r_2!\,r_3!}(2x^2)^{r_1}(3x)^{r_2}(4)^{r_3}$

Since, $a_7 = $ Coeff. of x^7

$2r_1 + r_2 = 7$ and $r_1 + r_2 + r_3 = 10$

Possibilities are

r_1	r_2	r_3
0	7	3
1	5	4
2	3	5
3	1	6

$$a_7 = \dfrac{10!\,3^7\,4^3}{7!\,3!} + \dfrac{10!(2)(3)^5(4)^4}{5!\,4!}$$
$$+ \dfrac{10!(2)^2(3)^3(4)^5}{2!\,3!\,5!} + \dfrac{10!(2)^3(3)(4)^6}{3!\,6!}$$

$a_{13} = $ Coeff. of x^{13}

$2r_1 + r_2 = 13$ and $r_1 + r_2 + r_3 = 10$

Possibilities are

r_1	r_2	r_3
3	7	0
4	5	1
5	3	2
6	1	3

$$a_{13} = \dfrac{10!(2^3)(3^7)}{3!\,7!} + \dfrac{10!(2^4)(3^5)(4)}{4!\,5!}$$
$$+ \dfrac{10!(2^5)(3^3)(4^2)}{5!\,3!\,2!} + \dfrac{10!(2^6)(3)(4^3)}{6!\,1!\,3!}$$

$$\therefore \dfrac{a_7}{a_{13}} = 2^3 = 8$$

PHYSICS

1. **(3)** Given,

Electric field, $E = E_0(1 - x^2)$

$\therefore$ Force, $F = qE = qE_0(1 - x^2)$

Also, $F = ma = mv\dfrac{dv}{dx}$ $\qquad \left(\because a = v\dfrac{dv}{dx}\right)$

$\therefore mv\dfrac{dv}{dx} = qE_0(1 - x^2)$

$\Rightarrow v\,dv = \dfrac{qE_0(1 - x^2)dx}{m}$

Integrating both sides we get,

$\Rightarrow \displaystyle\int_0^v v\,dv = \int_0^x \dfrac{qE_0(1 - x^2)dx}{m}$

$\Rightarrow \dfrac{v^2}{2} = \dfrac{qE_0}{m}\left(x - \dfrac{9x^3}{3}\right) = 0$

$\Rightarrow x = \sqrt{\dfrac{3}{a}}$

2. **(1)** Potential energy stored in the inductor

$$U = \frac{1}{2}LI^2$$

During growth of current,

$$i = I_{max}\left(1 - e^{-Rt/L}\right)$$

For U to be $\dfrac{U_{max}}{n}$; i has to be $\dfrac{I_{max}}{\sqrt{n}}$

$\therefore \dfrac{I_{max}}{\sqrt{n}} = I_{max}(1 - e^{-Rt/L})$

$\Rightarrow e^{-Rt/L} = 1 - \dfrac{1}{\sqrt{n}} = \dfrac{\sqrt{n} - 1}{\sqrt{n}}$

$\Rightarrow -\dfrac{Rt}{L} = \ln\left(\dfrac{\sqrt{n} - 1}{\sqrt{n}}\right)$

$\Rightarrow t = \dfrac{L}{R}\ln\left(\dfrac{\sqrt{n}}{\sqrt{n} - 1}\right)$

3. **(3)** Let p be the density of the discs and t is the thickness of discs.

Moment of inertia of disc is given by

$$I = \dfrac{MR^2}{2} = \dfrac{[\rho(\pi R^2)t]R^2}{2}$$

$I \propto R^4$ $\qquad$ (As ρ and t are same)

$\dfrac{I_2}{I_1} = \left(\dfrac{R_2}{R_1}\right)^4 \Rightarrow \dfrac{16}{1} = \alpha^4 \Rightarrow \alpha = 2$

4. **(1)** $\vec{E} = E_0(\hat{x} + \hat{y})\sin(kz - \omega t)$

Direction of propagation of em wave $= +\hat{k}$

Unit vector in the direction of electric field, $\hat{E} = \dfrac{\hat{i} + \hat{j}}{\sqrt{2}}$

The direction of electromagnetic wave is perpendicular to both electric and magnetic field.

$\therefore \hat{k} = \hat{E} \times \hat{B}$

$\Rightarrow \hat{k} = \left(\dfrac{\hat{i} + \hat{j}}{\sqrt{2}}\right) \times \hat{B} \Rightarrow \hat{B} = \dfrac{-\hat{i} + \hat{j}}{\sqrt{2}}$

$\therefore \vec{B} = \dfrac{E_0}{c}(-\hat{x} + \hat{y})\sin(kz - \omega t)$

5. **(1)** From the Doppler's effect of sound, frequency appeared at wall

$$f_w = \dfrac{330}{330 - v} \cdot f \qquad \text{...(i)}$$

Here, $v = $ speed of bus,

$f = $ actual frequency of source

Frequency heard after reflection from wall (f') is

$f' = \dfrac{330 + v}{330} \cdot f_w = \dfrac{330 + v}{330 - v} \cdot f$

$\Rightarrow 490 = \dfrac{330 + v}{330 - v} \cdot 420$

$\Rightarrow v = \dfrac{330 \times 7}{91} \approx 25.38 \text{ m/s} = 91 \text{ km/s}$

6. **(4)** Mass defect,

$\Delta m = (50m_p + 70m_n) - (m_{sn})$

$\quad = (50 \times 1.00783 + 70 \times 1.008) - (119.902199)$

$\quad = 1.096$

Binding energy $= (\Delta m)C^2 = (\Delta m) \times 931 = 1020.56$

$\dfrac{\text{Binding energy}}{\text{Nucleon}} = \dfrac{1020.5631}{120} = 8.5 \text{ MeV}$

7. **(3)** When two inputs of NAND gate is shorted, it behaves like a NOT gate so boolen equation will be

$$y = \overline{\overline{A} + \overline{B} + \overline{C}}$$

$$y = A \cdot B \cdot C$$

A	B	C	
0	0	0	0
1	0	0	0
0	1	0	0
0	0	1	0
1	1	0	0
1	0	1	0
0	1	1	0
1	1	1	1

Thus, whole arrangement behaves like a AND gate.

8. **(4)** When two capacitors with capacitance C_1 and C_2 at potential V_1 and V_2 connected to each other by wire, charge begins to flow from higher to lower potential till they acquire common potential. Here, some loss of energy takes place which is given by.

Heat loss, $H = \dfrac{C_1 C_2}{2(C_1 + C_2)}(V_1 - V_2)^2$

In the equation, put $V_2 = 0$, $V_1 = V_0$

$$C_1 = C,\ C_2 = \dfrac{C}{2}$$

Loss of heat $= \dfrac{C \times \dfrac{C}{2}}{2\left(C + \dfrac{C}{2}\right)}(V_0 - 0)^2 = \dfrac{C}{6}V_0^2$

$$H = \dfrac{1}{6}CV_0^2$$

9. **(4)** According to Einstein's photoelectric equation

$$K_{\max} = h\nu - \phi_0$$

$$\Rightarrow eV_s = \dfrac{hc}{\lambda} - \phi_0$$

$$\Rightarrow V_s = \dfrac{hc}{\lambda e} - \dfrac{\phi_0}{e}$$

where $\lambda =$ wavelength of incident light

　$\phi_0 =$ work function

　$V_s =$ stopping potential

Comparing the above equation with $y = mx + c$, we get

slope $= \dfrac{hc}{e}$

Increasing the frequency of incident radiation has no effect on work function and frequency. So, graph will not change.

10. **(1)** Given,

Moment of inertia of circular coil, $I = 0.8\ \text{kg m}^2$

Magnetic moment of circular coil, $M = 20\ \text{Am}^2$

Rotational kinetic energy of circular coil,

$$\text{KE} = \dfrac{1}{2}I\omega^2$$

Here, $\omega =$ angular speed of coil

Potential energy of bar magnet $= -MB\cos\phi$

From energy conservation

$$\dfrac{1}{2}I\omega^2 = U_{\text{in}} - U_f = -MB\cos 60° - (-MB)$$

$$\Rightarrow \dfrac{MB}{2} = \dfrac{1}{2}I\omega^2$$

$$\Rightarrow \dfrac{20 \times 4}{2} = \dfrac{1}{2}(0.8)\omega^2$$

$$\Rightarrow 100 = \omega^2 \Rightarrow \omega = 10\ \text{rad}$$

11. **(4)**

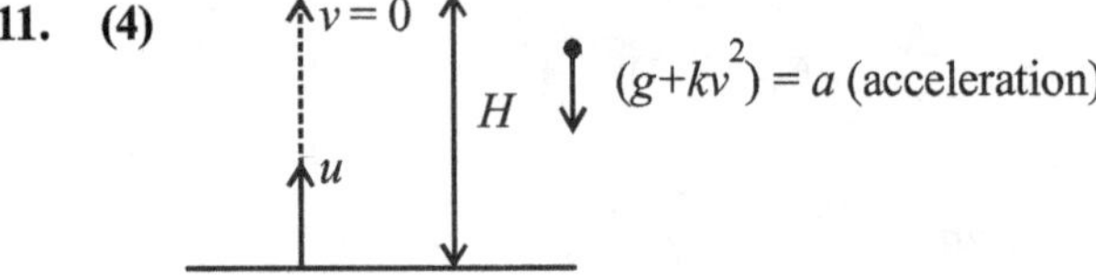

$\vec{F} = mkv^2 - mg$ 　　　　($\because mg$ and mkv^2 act opposite to each other)

$$\vec{a} = \dfrac{\vec{F}}{m} = -[kv^2 + g]$$

$$\Rightarrow v \cdot \dfrac{dv}{dh} = -[kv^2 + g] \qquad \left(\because a = v\dfrac{dv}{dh}\right)$$

$$\Rightarrow \int_u^0 \dfrac{v \cdot dv}{kv^2 + g} = \int_0^h dh$$

$$\Rightarrow \dfrac{1}{2k}\ln\left[kv^2 + g\right]_u^0 = -h$$

$$\Rightarrow \dfrac{1}{2k}\ln\left[\dfrac{ku^2 + g}{g}\right] = h$$

12. **(4)**

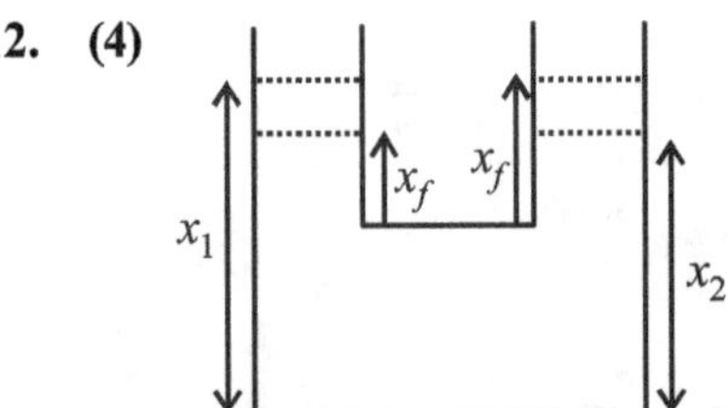

Initial potential energy,

$$U_1 = (\rho S x_1)g \cdot \dfrac{x_1}{2} + (\rho S x_2)g \cdot \dfrac{x_2}{2}$$

Final potential energy,

$$U_f = (\rho S x_f)g \cdot \dfrac{x_f}{2} \times 2$$

By volume conservation,

$$S x_1 + S x_2 = S(2x_f)$$

$$x_f = \dfrac{x_1 + x_2}{2}$$

When valve is opened loss in potentail energy occur till water level become same.

$$\Delta U = U_i - U_f$$

$$\Delta U = \rho S g\left[\left(\frac{x_1^2}{2}+\frac{x_2^2}{2}\right)-x_f^2\right]$$

$$= \rho S g\left[\frac{x_1^2}{2}+\frac{x_2^2}{2}-\left(\frac{x_1+x_2}{2}\right)^2\right]$$

$$= \frac{\rho S g}{2}\left[\frac{x_1^2}{2}+\frac{x_2^2}{2}-x_1 x_2\right] = \frac{\rho S g}{4}(x_1-x_2)^2$$

13. **(1)** Orbital speed of the body when it revolves very close to the surface of planet

$$V_0 = \sqrt{\frac{GM}{R}} \qquad \ldots(i)$$

Here, G = gravitational constant

Escape speed from the surface of planet

$$V_e = \sqrt{\frac{2GM}{R}} \qquad \ldots(ii)$$

Dividing (i) by (ii), we have

$$\frac{V_0}{V_e} = \frac{\sqrt{\dfrac{GM}{R}}}{\sqrt{\dfrac{2GM}{R}}} = \frac{1}{\sqrt{2}}$$

14. **(4)** Bulk modulus, $B = \dfrac{P}{\dfrac{\Delta V}{V}}$

$$\Rightarrow \frac{\Delta V}{V} = \frac{P}{B} \qquad \ldots(i)$$

If the side of cube is L then $V = L^3$

$$\frac{\Delta V}{V} = \frac{3\Delta L}{L} = \frac{P}{B}$$

$$\Rightarrow \frac{\Delta L}{L} = \frac{1}{3}\times\frac{P}{B} = \frac{4\times10^9\,Pa}{3\times8\times10^{10}\,Pa} = \frac{1}{60}$$

$$\Rightarrow \frac{\Delta L}{L}\times100 = \frac{1}{60}\times100 = 1.67\%$$

15. **(3)** Dimension of Force $F = M^1 L^1 T^{-2}$

Dimension of velocity $V = L^1 T^{-1}$

Dimension of work $= M^1 L^2 T^{-2}$

Dimension of length $= L$

Moment of inertia $= ML^2$

$$\therefore x = \frac{IFv^2}{WL^4}$$

$$= \frac{(M^1 L^2)(M^1 L^1 T^{-2})(L^1 T^{-2})^2}{(M^1 L^2 T^{-2})(L^4)}$$

$$= \frac{M^1 L^{-2} T^{-2}}{L^3} = M^1 L^{-1} T^{-2} = \text{Energy density}$$

16. **(2)** Moment of inertia of rectangular sheet about an axis passing through O,

$$I_O = \frac{M}{12}(a^2+b^2) = \frac{M}{12}[(80)^2+(60)^2]$$

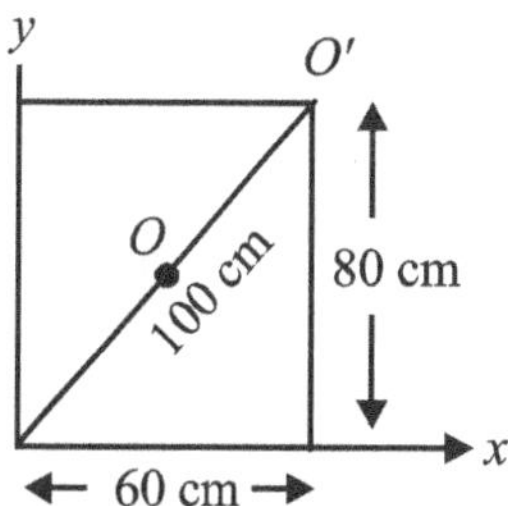

From the parallel axis theorem, moment of inertia about O',

$$I_{O'} = I_O + M(50)^2$$

$$\frac{I_O}{I_{O'}} = \frac{\dfrac{M}{12}(80^2+60^2)}{\dfrac{M}{12}(80^2+60^2)+M(50)^2} = \frac{1}{4}$$

17. **(4)**

(I) **Adiabatic process :** No exchange of heat takes place with surroundings.

$$\Rightarrow \Delta Q = 0$$

(II) **Isothermal process :** Temperature remains constant

$$\therefore \Delta T = 0 \Rightarrow \Delta U = \frac{f}{2}nR\Delta T \Rightarrow \Delta U = 0$$

No change in internal energy $[\Delta U = 0]$.

(III) Isochoric process volume remains constant

$$\Delta V = 0 \Rightarrow W = \int P\cdot dV = 0$$

Hence work done is zero.

(IV) In isobaric process pressure remains constant.

$$W = P\cdot\Delta V \neq 0$$

$$\Delta U = \frac{f}{2}nR\Delta T = \frac{f}{2}[P\Delta V] \neq 0$$

$$\therefore \Delta Q = nC_p\Delta T \neq 0$$

18. **(3)** The equivalent circuit can be drawn as

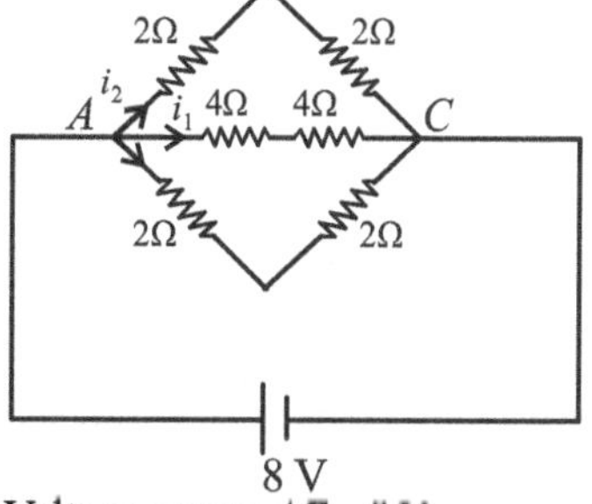

Voltage across $AC = 8$ V

Resistance $R_{AC} = 4+4 = 8\ \Omega$

$$i_1 = \frac{V}{R_{AC}} = \frac{8}{4+4} = 1\ \text{Amp}$$

19. (4) The given situation can be drawn graphically as shown in figure.

Work done = Area under F-x graph

= Area of rectangle $ABCD$ + Area of trapezium $BCFE$

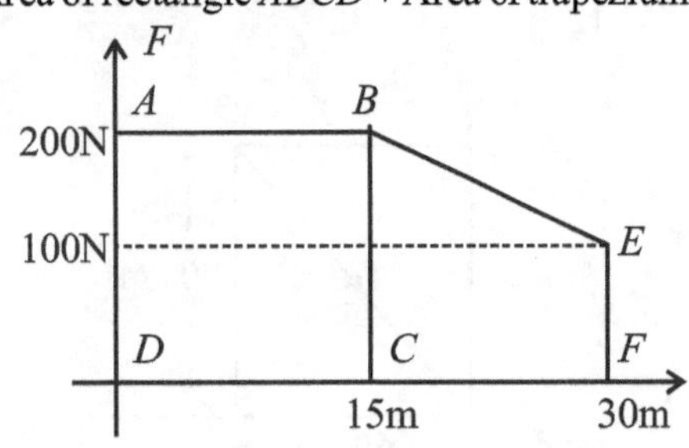

$$W = (200 \times 15) + \frac{1}{2}(100 + 200) \times 15 = 3000 + 2250$$

$$\Rightarrow W = 5250 \text{ J}$$

20. (4) For paramagnetic material. According to curies law

$$\chi \propto \frac{1}{T}$$

For two temperatures T_1 and T_2

$$\chi_1 T_1 = \chi_2 T_2$$

But $\chi = \dfrac{I}{B}$

$$\therefore \frac{I_1}{B_1} T_1 = \frac{I_2}{B_2} T_2$$

$$\Rightarrow \frac{6}{0.4} \times 4 = \frac{I_2}{0.3} \times 24 \Rightarrow I_2 = \frac{0.3}{0.4} = 0.75 \text{ A/m}$$

21. (20)

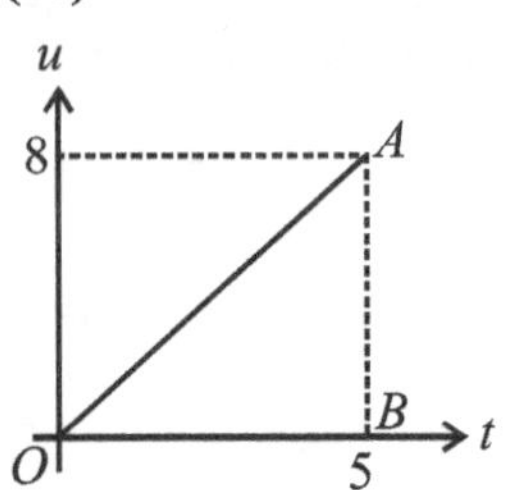

Distance travelled = Area of speed-time graph

$$= \frac{1}{2} \times 5 \times 8 = 20 \text{ m}$$

22. (2)

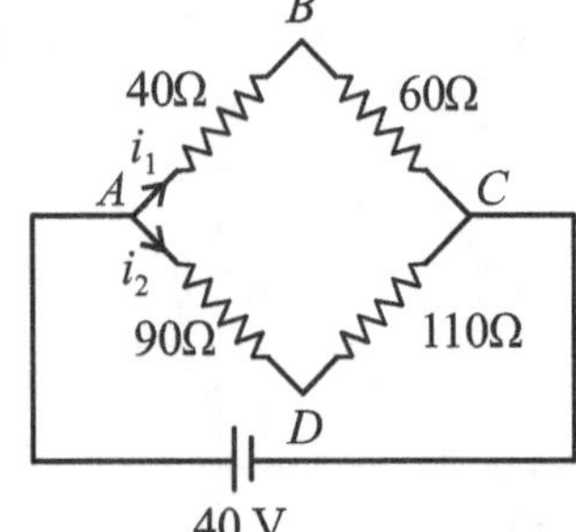

Current through AB, $i_1 = \dfrac{40}{40 + 60} = 0.4$

Current through AD, $i_2 = \dfrac{40}{90 + 110} = \dfrac{1}{5}$

Using KVL in BAD loop

$$V_B + i_1(40) - i_2(90) = V_D$$

$$\Rightarrow V_B - V_D = \frac{1}{5}(90) - \frac{4}{10}(40)$$

$$\Rightarrow V_B - V_D = 18 - 16 = 2 \text{ V}$$

23. (476.19)

Given,

Distance between an object and screen, $D = 100$ cm

Distance between the two position of lens, $d = 40$ cm

Focal length of lens,

$$f = \frac{D^2 - d^2}{4D} = \frac{100^2 - 40^2}{4(100)} = \frac{(100 + 40)(100 - 40)}{4(100)} = 21 \text{ cm}$$

Power, $P = \dfrac{1}{f} = \dfrac{100}{21} = \dfrac{N}{100}$

$$\therefore N = 476.19.$$

24. (150)

In first case,

From ideal gas equation

$$PV = nRT$$

$$P\Delta V + V\Delta P = 0 \qquad \text{(As temperature is constant)}$$

$$\Delta V = -\frac{\Delta P}{P} V \qquad \text{...(i)}$$

In second case, using ideal gas equation again

$$P\Delta V = -nR\Delta T$$

$$\Delta V = -\frac{nR\Delta T}{P} \qquad \text{...(ii)}$$

Equating (i) and (ii), we get

$$\frac{nR\Delta T}{P} = -\frac{\Delta P}{P} V \Rightarrow \Delta T = \Delta P \frac{V}{nR}$$

Comparing the above equation with $|\Delta T| = C|\Delta P|$, we have

$$C = \frac{V}{nR} = \frac{\Delta T}{\Delta P} = \frac{300 \text{ K}}{2 \text{ atm}} = 150 \text{ K/atm}$$

25. (198)

For obtaining secondary minima at a point path difference should be integral multiple of wavelength

$$\therefore d \sin\theta = n\lambda$$

$$\therefore \sin\theta = \frac{n\lambda}{d}$$

For n to be maximum $\sin\theta = 1$

$$n = \frac{d}{\lambda} = \frac{6 \times 10^{-5}}{6 \times 10^{-7}} = 100$$

Total number of minima on one side = 99

Total number of minima = 198.

26. (4)

(a) $\underset{sp^3}{H_3\underline{P}O_2} \xrightarrow{\text{Disproportionation}} \underset{sp^3}{H_3\underline{P}O_4} + \underset{sp^3}{\underline{P}H_3}$

(b) $\underset{sp^3}{H_2\underline{S}O_4} + NaCl \xrightarrow{420K} \underset{sp^3}{Na_2\underline{S}O_4} + 2HCl$

(c) $\underset{sp^3}{\underline{N}H_3} \xrightarrow{H^+} \underset{sp^3}{\underline{N}H_4^+}$

(d) $\underset{sp^3d^2}{\underline{X}eF_4} + SbF_5 \longrightarrow \underset{sp^3d}{[\underline{X}eF_3]^+}[SbF_6]^-$

27. (1) Millimoles of $Au^+ = 0.1 \times 250 = 25$

Mole of $Au^+ = \dfrac{25}{1000} = \dfrac{1}{40} = 0.025$

Similarly, moles of $Ag^+ = 0.025$
Charge passed $= I \times t = 1 \times 15 \times 60 = 900\ C$

Moles of e^- passed $= \dfrac{900}{96500} = 0.0093$ mol.

Species with higher value of SRP will get deposited first at cathode.

$$\underset{0.025}{Au^+\,(aq)} + \underset{0.0093}{e^-} \longrightarrow Au\,(s)$$

So, only Au will get deposited.

28. (4) Solubility of $BeSO_4$ is highest among the given metal sulphates
$BeSO_4 > MgSO_4 > CaSO_4 > SrSO_4 > BaSO_4$
Solubility order for hydroxide is
$Be(OH)_2 < Mg(OH)_2 < Ca(OH)_2 < Sr(OH)_2 < Ba(OH)_2$
Thus $BeSO_4$ is soluble and $Be(OH)_2$ is insoluble.
BeO does not form rock salt like structure.
In the solid state, it adopts the hexagonal neurtzite structure form while in the vapour phase, it is present as discrete diatomic covalent molecules.

29. (3) (i) W(VI) is more stable than Cr(VI) due to smaller size of atoms and also due to lanthanide contraction.
(ii) Permanganate titrations in presence of HCl are unsatisfactory as HCl is oxidised to Cl_2.
(iii) Lanthanoid oxides are used as phosphors.

30. (3) Shortest wavelength $\rightarrow$ Max. energy $(\infty \rightarrow 1)$
For Lyman series of H atom,

$$\dfrac{1}{\lambda_1} = R_H(1)^2\left[\dfrac{1}{1} - 0\right]$$

$$\Rightarrow \dfrac{1}{\lambda_1} = R_H \Rightarrow R_H = \dfrac{1}{\lambda_1}$$

For Balmer series of He^+,

$$\dfrac{1}{\lambda} = R_H(2)^2\left[\dfrac{1}{2^2} - \dfrac{1}{3^2}\right] \Rightarrow \dfrac{1}{\lambda} = R_H(4)\left(\dfrac{9-4}{36}\right)$$

$$\Rightarrow \dfrac{1}{\lambda} = \dfrac{5R_H}{9} \Rightarrow \lambda = \dfrac{9}{5R_H} = \dfrac{9\lambda_1}{5}$$

31. (4) Ease of precipitation of AgBr depends upon the rate of formation of carbocation.

Most stable carbocation due to +R effect of N.

32. (4) $A \rightleftharpoons B + C$ ...(i) $K_{eq}^{(1)}$

$B + C \rightleftharpoons P$ ...(ii) $K_{eq}^{(2)}$

On adding equations (i) and (ii), we get

$A \rightleftharpoons P$

K_{eq} (overall) $= K_{eq}^{(1)} \cdot K_{eq}^{(2)}$

33. (3)

34. (2) $[CoF_3(H_2O)_3] \Rightarrow Co^{3+} \Rightarrow d^6$ or $t_{2g}^4 e_g^2$

$CFSE = -[0.4p + 0.6q]\Delta_0 + n(P)$
$= [-4 \times 0.4 + 2 \times 0.6]\Delta_0 + 0 = -0.4\,\Delta_0.$

35. **(2) Calcination :** Heating of concentrated ore in the absence (or limited supply of air). Mainly used for carbonate ores.

$$\text{Metal carbonate} \xrightarrow{\Delta} \text{Metal oxide} + \underset{\substack{\text{(causes global} \\ \text{warming)}}}{CO_2}$$

Roasting : Heating of concentrated ore in a regular supply of air. Mainly used for sulphide ores.

$$\text{Metal sulphide} + O_2 \longrightarrow \text{Metal oxide} + \underset{\substack{\text{(causes} \\ \text{acid rain)}}}{SO_2}$$

36. **(4)** In expansion against vacuum
$$P_{ext} = 0$$
$$W = -P_{ext}\,\Delta V = 0$$
$$W = 0$$

37. **(3)**

		No. of unpaired electrons
$[Fe(en)(bpy)(NH_3)_2]^{2+}$	: $Fe^{2+} - 3d^6$	0
$[Pd(gly)_2]$	: $Pd^{2+} - 3d^8$	0
$[Co(OX)_2(OH)_2]^-$	: $Co^{5+} - 3d^4$	2
$[Ti(NH_3)_6]^{3+}$	: $Ti^{3+} - 3d^1$	1

Thus, $[Co(OX)_2(OH)_2]^-$ exhibits highest paramagnetic behaviour due to highest number of unpaired electrons.

38. **(1)**

39. **(2)** $Ar(g) + e^- \longrightarrow Ar^-(g)$ (endothermic)

$H(g) + e^- \longrightarrow H^-(g)$ (exothermic)

$Na(g) \longrightarrow Na^+(g) + e^-$ (endothermic)

$O^-(g) + e^- \longrightarrow O^{2-}(g)$ (endothermic)

- Electron gaining enthalpy (EGE) of $H(g)$ is negative while that of $Ar(g)$ is positive due to ns^2np^6 configuration.
- Second EGE is always positive for an atom.
- Ionization potential of an atom is positive.

40. **(4)** Seldane is an *anti*-histamine drug that has inhibitory action on histamine receptor.

41. **(2)**

$$H_3C - CH_2 - \overset{\overset{\displaystyle CH_3}{|}}{CH} - CH_2 - O - CH_2 - CH_3 \xrightarrow[\text{Heat}]{HI}$$

$$CH_3 - CH_2 - \underset{[A]}{\overset{\overset{\displaystyle CH_3}{|}}{CH}} - CH_2 - OH + CH_3CH_2 - I \xrightarrow{H_2SO_4/\Delta}$$

$$\underset{[B]}{CH_3 - CH = \overset{\overset{\displaystyle CH_3}{|}}{C} - CH_3}$$

42. **(1)** Egg white is used to stabilise the prepared colloidal solution of red ink.

43. **(4)** Due to conjugation of lonepair of Cl with π bond, partial double bond character decreases bond length that's why compound (d) has shortest C–Cl bond length.

44. **(1)** (a) $[Ni(CN)_4]^{2-} = dsp^2$
(b) $BrF_5 = sp^3d^2$
(c) $XeF_4 = sp^3d^2$
(d) $[CrF_6]^{3-} = d^2sp^2$

45. **(1)**

$$CH_2 = CH - CHO \xrightarrow{(i)\ NaBH_4} H_2C = CH - CH_2OH$$

$$\downarrow (ii)\ SOCl_2$$

$$\underset{[A]}{H_2C = CH - CH_2 - Cl}$$

$$\underset{[A]}{H_2C = CH - CH_2Cl} \xrightarrow[\text{AlCl}_3]{\text{Anhy}} \underset{[B]}{} \xrightarrow{DBr} \underset{[C]}{} D$$

46. **(167)**

For NaCl : $\pi_1 = iC_1 RT \Rightarrow C_1 = \dfrac{0.10}{2RT}$

For Glucose : $\pi_2 = C_2 RT \Rightarrow C_2 = \dfrac{0.20}{RT}$

When 1 L of NaCl solution and 2 L glucose solution are mixed.

$$\therefore C'_1 = \frac{0.10}{6RT} \text{ and } C'_2 = \frac{0.20 \times 2}{3RT} = \frac{0.40}{3RT}$$

$$\therefore \pi_{Total} = iC'_1 RT + C'_2 RT = \frac{0.10}{3} + \frac{0.40}{3} = \frac{0.50}{3}$$

$$\pi_{Total} = 167 \times 10^{-3} \text{ atm}$$

47. **(2)**

$$\underset{NH_2}{\underset{|}{HOOC - \overset{*}{C}H - \overset{OH}{\overset{|}{C}}H - CH_3}}$$

Threonine
No. of chiral centres = 2

48. (10)

$$\text{Normality} = \frac{\text{No. of equivalents of solute}}{\text{Volume of solution (in L)}}$$

$$0.1 = \frac{1.43}{\dfrac{(106+18x)}{2} \times 0.1} \Rightarrow \frac{106+18x}{2} = 143$$

$$\Rightarrow 18x = 286 - 106 = 180 \Rightarrow x = 10.$$

49. (84297.48)

$$\because k = Ae^{-E_a/RT}$$

$$\ln\frac{k_2}{k_1} = \frac{E_a}{R}\left(\frac{1}{T_1} - \frac{1}{T_2}\right) \Rightarrow \ln 5 = \frac{E_a}{R}\left(\frac{1}{300} - \frac{1}{315}\right)$$

$$\Rightarrow E_a = \frac{1.6094 \times 8.314 \times 300 \times 315}{15} = 84297.48 \text{ J/mol.}$$

50. (19)

$$2Fe^{2+} + H_2O_2 \longrightarrow 2Fe^{3+} + 2OH^-$$

$$2MnO_4^- + 6H^+ + 5H_2O_2 \longrightarrow 2Mn^{2+} + 8H_2O + 5O_2$$

$$\because x = 2,\ y = 2,\ x' = 2,\ y' = 8,\ z' = 5$$

$$\therefore x + y + x' + y' + z' = 19$$

MATHEMATICS

51. (2) We know family of circle be $S_1 + \lambda S_2 = 0$

$$x^2 + y^2 - 6x + \lambda(x^2 + y^2 - 4y) = 0$$

$$\Rightarrow (1+\lambda)x^2 + (1+\lambda)y^2 - 6x - 4\lambda y = 0 \qquad \text{...(i)}$$

Centre $(-g, -f) = \left(\dfrac{3}{1+\lambda}, \dfrac{2\lambda}{\lambda+1}\right)$

Centre lies on $2x - 3y + 12 = 0$, then

$$\frac{6}{\lambda+1} - \frac{6\lambda}{\lambda+1} + 12 = 0 \Rightarrow \lambda = -3$$

Equation of circle (i),

$$-2x^2 - 2y^2 - 6x + 12y = 0$$

$$\Rightarrow x^2 + y^2 + 3x - 6y = 0 \qquad \text{...(ii)}$$

Only $(-3, 6)$ satisfy equation (ii).

52. (4) $\dfrac{a}{e} = 4 \Rightarrow a = 4 \times \dfrac{1}{2} = 2$

Now, $b^2 = a^2(1-e^2)$

$$\Rightarrow b^2 = 4\left(1 - \frac{1}{4}\right) = 4 \times \frac{3}{4} = 3$$

So, equation $\dfrac{x^2}{4} + \dfrac{y^2}{3} = 1$

$$\Rightarrow 3x^2 + 4y^2 = 12 \qquad \text{...(i)}$$

Now, $P(1, \beta)$ lies on it

$$\Rightarrow 3 + 4\beta^2 = 12 \Rightarrow \beta = \frac{3}{2}$$

So, equation of normal at $P\left(1, \dfrac{3}{2}\right)$

$$\Rightarrow \frac{a^2 x}{1} - \frac{b^2 y}{3/2} = a^2 - b^2 \Rightarrow 4x - 2y = 1$$

53. (4) $\dfrac{2^{\sin x} + 2^{\cos x}}{2} \ge (2^{\sin x + \cos x})^{\frac{1}{2}}$ $\qquad (\because \text{AM} \ge \text{GM})$

$$\Rightarrow 2^{\sin x} + 2^{\cos x} \ge 2 \cdot 2^{\frac{\sin x + \cos x}{2}}$$

Since, $-2 \le \sin x + \cos x \le \sqrt{2}$

$$\therefore \text{Minimum value of } 2^{\frac{\sin x + \cos x}{2}} = 2^{-\frac{1}{\sqrt{2}}}$$

$$\Rightarrow 2^{\sin x} + 2^{\cos x} \ge 2^{1 - \frac{1}{\sqrt{2}}}.$$

54. (3)

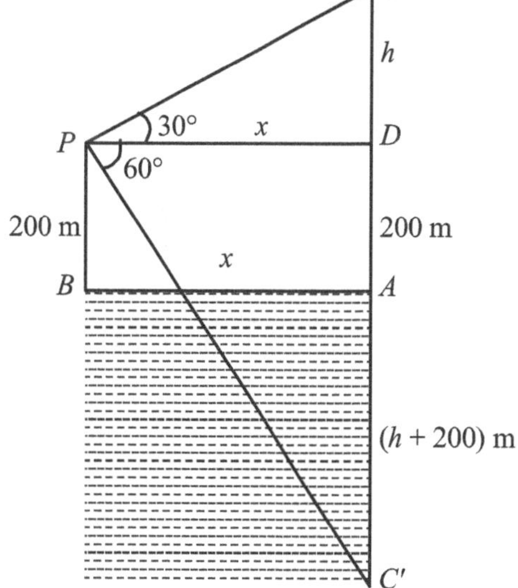

Here in ΔPCD,

$$\sin 30° = \frac{h}{PC} \Rightarrow PC = 2h \qquad \text{...(i)}$$

$$\tan 30° = \frac{h}{x} \Rightarrow \frac{1}{\sqrt{3}} = \frac{h}{x}$$

$$\Rightarrow x = \sqrt{3}h \qquad \text{...(ii)}$$

Now, in right $\Delta PC'D$

$$\tan 60° = \frac{h+400}{x}$$

$$\Rightarrow \sqrt{3}x = h+400 \Rightarrow 3h = h+400 \qquad \text{[From (ii)]}$$

$$\Rightarrow h = 200$$

So, $PC = 400\,\text{m}$ \qquad [From (i)]

55. **(4)** $\begin{vmatrix} 1 & 1 & 1 \\ 2 & 4 & -1 \\ 3 & 2 & \lambda \end{vmatrix} = 0$ \qquad [∵ Equation has many solutions]

$$\Rightarrow -15 + 6 + 2\lambda = 0 \Rightarrow \lambda = \frac{9}{2}$$

$$\therefore D_z = \begin{vmatrix} 1 & 1 & 2 \\ 2 & 4 & 6 \\ 3 & 2 & 2\mu \end{vmatrix} = 0 \Rightarrow \mu = 5$$

$$\therefore 2\lambda + \mu = 14.$$

56. **(4)** Area of rectangle $ABCD$

$$A = 2x\cdot(x^2 - 1) = 2x^3 - 2x$$

$$\therefore \frac{dA}{dx} = 6x^2 - 2$$

For maximum area $\dfrac{dA}{dx} = 0 \Rightarrow x = \pm\dfrac{1}{\sqrt{3}}$

$$\frac{d^2 A}{dx^2} = (12x) \Rightarrow \left(\frac{d^2 A}{dx^2}\right)_{x = \frac{-1}{\sqrt{3}}} = \frac{-12}{\sqrt{3}} < 0$$

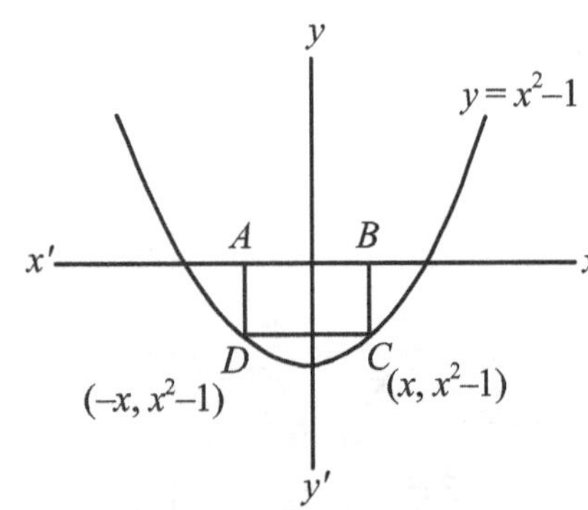

$$\therefore \text{Maximum area} = \left|\frac{2}{3\sqrt{3}} - \frac{2}{\sqrt{3}}\right| = \frac{4}{3\sqrt{3}}$$

57. **(1)** $f(x) = \begin{cases} \dfrac{-x-1}{2}, & x < -1 \\[2mm] \dfrac{\pi}{4} + \tan^{-1}x, & -1 \le x \le 1 \\[2mm] \dfrac{1}{2}(x-1), & x > 1 \end{cases}$

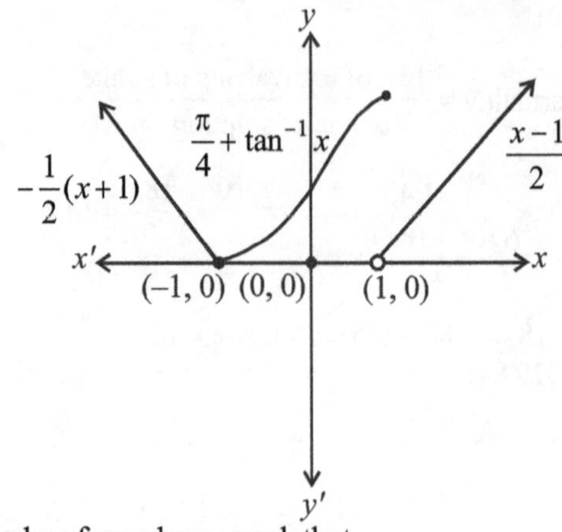

It is clear from above graph that,
$f(x)$ is discontinuous at $x = 1$.
i.e. continuous on $R - \{1\}$
$f(x)$ is non-differentiable at $x = -1, 1$
i.e. differentiable on $R - \{-1, 1\}$.

58. **(1)** Consider the three consecutive coefficients of $(1+x)^{n+5}$ be $^{n+5}C_r$, $^{n+5}C_{r+1}$, $^{n+5}C_{r+2}$

$$\because \frac{^{n+5}C_r}{^{n+5}C_{r+1}} = \frac{1}{2} \qquad \text{(Given)}$$

$$\Rightarrow \frac{r+1}{n+5-r} = \frac{1}{2} \Rightarrow 3r = n+3 \qquad \text{...(i)}$$

and $\dfrac{^{n+5}C_{r+1}}{^{n+5}C_{r+2}} = \dfrac{5}{7}$

$$\Rightarrow \frac{r+2}{n+4-r} = \frac{5}{7} \Rightarrow 12r = 5n+6 \qquad \text{...(ii)}$$

Solving (i) and (ii) we get $r = 4$ and $n = 6$
∴ Largest coefficient in the expansion is $^{11}C_6 = 462$.

59. **(2)** Given that $Ax = b$ has solutions x_1, x_2, x_3 and b is equal to b_1, b_2 and b_3

$$\therefore x_1 + y_1 + z_1 = 1$$

$$\Rightarrow 2y_1 + z_1 = 2 \Rightarrow z_1 = 2$$

Determinant of coefficient matrix

$$|A| = \begin{vmatrix} 1 & 1 & 1 \\ 0 & 2 & 1 \\ 0 & 0 & 1 \end{vmatrix} = 2$$

60. **(2)** Contrapositive statement will be "If a function is not continuous at 'a', then it is not differentiable at 'a'.

61. **(1)** Let $y + 3x = t$

$$\Rightarrow \frac{dy}{dx} + 3 = \frac{dt}{dx}$$

Putting these value in given differential equation

$$\frac{dt}{dx} = \frac{t}{\log_e t}$$

$$\Rightarrow \int \frac{\log_e t}{t} dt = \int dx$$

$$\Rightarrow \frac{(\log_e t)^2}{2} = x - C$$

$$\Rightarrow x - \frac{1}{2}(\ln(y+3x))^2 = C$$

62. **(4)** Probability of sum getting 6, $P(A) = \dfrac{5}{36}$

Probability of sum getting 7, $P(B) = \dfrac{6}{36} = \dfrac{1}{6}$

$P(A \text{ wins}) = P(A) + P(\overline{A})P(\overline{B})P(A)$

$$+P(\overline{A}) \cdot P(\overline{B})P(\overline{A})P(\overline{B})P(A)+.....$$

$$\Rightarrow \frac{5}{36} + \left(\frac{31}{36}\right)\left(\frac{30}{36}\right)\left(\frac{5}{36}\right)+.....\infty$$

$$\Rightarrow \frac{5}{36}\left(1 + \frac{155}{216} + \left(\frac{155}{216}\right)^2 +........\infty\right)$$

$$\Rightarrow \frac{\dfrac{5}{36}}{\dfrac{61}{216}} = \frac{30}{61} \qquad \left(\because S_\infty = \frac{a}{1-r}\right)$$

63. **(2)** Equation of line through point $P(1,-2,3)$ and parallel

to the line $\dfrac{x}{2} = \dfrac{y}{3} = \dfrac{z}{-6}$ is

$$\frac{x-1}{2} = \frac{y+2}{3} = \frac{z-3}{-6} = \lambda$$

So, any point on line $= Q(2\lambda+1, 3\lambda-2, -6\lambda+3)$

Since, this point lies on plane $x - y + 2 = 5$

$$\therefore 2\lambda+1-3\lambda+2-6\lambda+3 = 5 \Rightarrow \lambda = \frac{1}{7}$$

$\therefore$ Point of intersection line and plane, $Q = \left(\dfrac{9}{7}, \dfrac{11}{7}, \dfrac{15}{7}\right)$

$\therefore$ Required distance PQ

$$= \sqrt{\left(\frac{9}{7}-1\right)^2 + \left(-\frac{11}{7}+2\right)^2 + \left(\frac{15}{7}-3\right)^2} = 1$$

64. **(2)** Since α is common root of $x^2 - x + 2\lambda = 0$ and

$3x^2 - 10x + 27\lambda = 0$

$\therefore 3\alpha^2 - 10\alpha + 27\lambda = 0 \qquad ...(i)$

$3\alpha^2 - 3\alpha + 6\lambda = 0 \qquad ...(ii)$

$\therefore$ On subtract, we get $\alpha = 3\lambda$

Now, $\alpha\beta = 2\lambda \Rightarrow 3\lambda \cdot \beta = 2\lambda \Rightarrow \beta = \dfrac{2}{3}$

$$\Rightarrow \alpha + \beta = 1 \Rightarrow 3\lambda + \frac{2}{3} = 1 \Rightarrow \lambda = \frac{1}{9} \text{ and}$$

$\alpha\gamma = 9\lambda \Rightarrow 3\lambda \cdot \gamma = 9\lambda \Rightarrow \gamma = 3$

$$\therefore \frac{\beta\gamma}{\lambda} = 18$$

65. **(3)** $\displaystyle\int_{\pi/6}^{\pi/3}\left[\frac{1}{2}\frac{d(\tan^4 x)}{dx}\cdot\sin^4 3x + \frac{1}{2}\tan^4 x\cdot\frac{d(\sin^4 3x)}{dx}\right]dx$

$$= \frac{1}{2}\int_{\pi/6}^{\pi/3} d(\tan^4 x\cdot\sin^4 3x)dx$$

$$= \left[\frac{\tan^4 x\sin^4 3x}{2}\right]_{\pi/6}^{\pi/3} = \frac{9\cdot 0}{2} - \frac{\dfrac{1}{9}\cdot 1}{2} = \frac{-1}{18}$$

66. **(4)** Given that $a_1 = 1$ and $a_n = 300$ and $d \in \mathbf{Z}$

$\therefore 300 = 1 + (n-1)d$

$$\Rightarrow d = \frac{299}{(n-1)} = \frac{23 \times 13}{(n-1)},$$

$\because d$ is an integer

$\therefore n-1 = 13$ or 23

$\Rightarrow n = 14$ or 24 $\qquad\qquad (\because 15 \le n \le 50)$

$\Rightarrow n = 24$ and $d = 13$

$a_{20} = 1 + 19 \times 13 = 248$

$$s_{20} = \frac{20}{2}(2 + 19 \times 13) = 2490.$$

67. **(1)** Given that, $\alpha = \dfrac{-1+\sqrt{3}i}{2} = \omega$

$\therefore (2+\omega)^4 = a + b\omega \Rightarrow (4 + \omega^2 + 4\omega)^2 = a + b\omega$

$\Rightarrow (\omega^2 + 4(1+\omega))^2 = a + b\omega$

$\Rightarrow (\omega^2 - 4\omega^2)^2 = a + b\omega \qquad [\because 1+\omega = -\omega^2]$

$\Rightarrow (-3\omega^2)^2 = a + b\omega \Rightarrow 9\omega^4 = a + b\omega$

$\Rightarrow 9\omega = a + b\omega \qquad\qquad (\because \omega^3 = 1)$

On comparing, $a = 0$, $b = 9$

$\Rightarrow a + b = 0 + 9 = 9.$

68. **(2)** Mid point of line segment PQ be $\left(\dfrac{k+1}{2}, \dfrac{7}{2}\right)$.

$\therefore$ Slope of perpendicular line passing through

$(0, -4)$ and $\left(\dfrac{k+1}{2}, \dfrac{7}{2}\right) = \dfrac{\dfrac{7}{2}+4}{\dfrac{k+1}{2}-0} = \dfrac{15}{k+1}$

Slope of $PQ = \dfrac{4-3}{1-k} = \dfrac{1}{1-k}$

$\therefore \dfrac{15}{1+k} \times \dfrac{1}{1-k} = -1$

$1 - k^2 = -15 \Rightarrow k = \pm 4.$

69. **(1)** $\lim\limits_{t \to x} \dfrac{t^2 f^2(x) - x^2 f^2(t)}{t-x} = 0$

$\Rightarrow \lim\limits_{t \to x} \dfrac{2t f^2(x) - 2x^2 f(t) \cdot f'(t)}{1} = 0$

Using L'Hospital's rule

$\Rightarrow f(x) = x f'(x)$

$\displaystyle \int \dfrac{f'(x)}{f(x)} dx = \int \dfrac{1}{x} dx$

$\log_e f(x) = \log_e x + \log_e C$

$\Rightarrow f(x) = Cx, \qquad\qquad \because f(1) = e$

$\Rightarrow C = e;\ \text{so} f(x) = ex$

When $f(x) = 1 = ex \Rightarrow x = \dfrac{1}{e}$

70. **(4)** $\displaystyle \bigcup_{i=1}^{50} X_i = \bigcup_{i=1}^{n} Y_i = T$

$\because\ n(X_i) = 10,\ n(Y_i) = 5$

So, $\displaystyle \bigcup_{i=1}^{50} X_i = 500,\ \bigcup_{i=1}^{n} Y_i = 5n$

$\Rightarrow \dfrac{500}{20} = \dfrac{5n}{6} \Rightarrow n = 30$

71. **(135)**

Select any 4 correct questions in $^6C_4$ ways.
Number of ways of answering wrong question = 3

$\therefore$ Required number of ways $= {}^6C_4 (1)^4 \times 3^2 = 135.$

72. **(18)**

$\hat{i} \times (\overline{a} \times \hat{i}) = (\hat{i} \cdot \hat{i})\overline{a} - (\hat{i} \cdot \overline{a})\hat{i} = \hat{j} + 2\hat{k}$

Similarly, $\hat{j} \times (\overline{a} \times \hat{j}) = 2\hat{i} + 2\hat{k},$

$\hat{k} \times (\overline{a} \times \hat{k}) = 2\hat{i} + \hat{j}$

$\therefore |\hat{j} + 2\hat{k}|^2 + |2\hat{i} + 2\hat{k}|^2 + |2\hat{i} + \hat{j}|^2 = 5 + 8 + 5 = 18.$

73. **(21)**

$\displaystyle \int_0^n \{x\}\, dx = n \int_0^1 x \cdot dx = \dfrac{n}{2}$

$\displaystyle \Rightarrow \int_0^n [x]\, dx = \int_0^n (x - \{x\})\, dx = \dfrac{n^2}{2} - \dfrac{n}{2}$

According to the questions,

$\dfrac{n}{2},\ \dfrac{n^2 - n}{2},\ 10(n^2 - n)$ are in GP

$\therefore \left(\dfrac{n^2 - n}{2}\right)^2 = \dfrac{n}{2} \times 10(n^2 - n)$

$\Rightarrow n^2 = 21n \Rightarrow n = 21.$

74. **(4)**

x_i	15	25	35
f_i	2	x	2

$\overline{x} = \dfrac{\Sigma f_i x_i}{\Sigma f_i} = \dfrac{30 + 70 + 25x}{4 + x} = 25$

$\sigma^2 = \dfrac{\Sigma f_i x_i^2}{\Sigma f_i} - (\overline{x})^2$

$\Rightarrow 50 = \dfrac{450 + 625x + 2450}{4 + x} - 625$

$\Rightarrow 675 = \dfrac{2900 + 625x}{4 + x} \Rightarrow 50x = 200$

$\therefore x = 4$

75. **(7)**

Let $P(3\cos\theta,\, 3\sin\theta),\ Q(-3\cos\theta,\, -3\sin\theta)$

$\alpha = \left| \dfrac{3\cos\theta + 3\sin\theta - 2}{\sqrt{2}} \right|,\ \beta = \left| \dfrac{-3\cos\theta - 3\sin\theta - 2}{\sqrt{2}} \right|$

$\alpha\beta = \left| \dfrac{(3\cos\theta + 3\sin\theta)^2 - 4}{2} \right| = \left| \dfrac{5 + 9\sin 2\theta}{2} \right|$

$\alpha\beta$ is max. when $\sin 2\theta = 1$

$\therefore \alpha\beta\big|_{\max} = \dfrac{5 + 9}{2} = 7.$

PHYSICS

1. (a) As we know,

Pressure amplitude, $\Delta P_0 = aKB = S_0 KB = S_0 \times \dfrac{\omega}{V} \times \rho V^2$

$$\left[\because K = \frac{\omega}{V}, V = \sqrt{\frac{B}{\rho}}\right]$$

$\Rightarrow S_0 = \dfrac{\Delta P_0}{\rho V \omega} \approx \dfrac{10}{1 \times 300 \times 1000}\,\text{m} = \dfrac{1}{30}\,\text{mm} \approx \dfrac{3}{100}\,\text{mm}$

2. (c) Since, $R = R_0 e^{-\lambda t}$

$\ln R = \ln R_0 + (-\lambda \ln t)$

$\lambda = \dfrac{\ln 2}{t_{1/2}} = \text{Slope}$

$\lambda_A = \dfrac{6}{10} \Rightarrow T_A = \dfrac{10}{6}\ln 2$

$\lambda_B = \dfrac{6}{5} \Rightarrow T_B = \dfrac{5\ln 2}{6}$

$\lambda_C = \dfrac{2}{5} \Rightarrow T_C = \dfrac{5\ln 2}{6}$

$\therefore T_{\frac{1}{2}A} : T_{\frac{1}{2}B} : T_{\frac{1}{2}C} = \dfrac{10}{6} : \dfrac{5}{6} : \dfrac{15}{6} = 2 : 1 : 3$

3. (d) From figure/ trigonometry,

$\dfrac{h_1}{d} = \tan 45° \qquad \therefore h_1 = d$

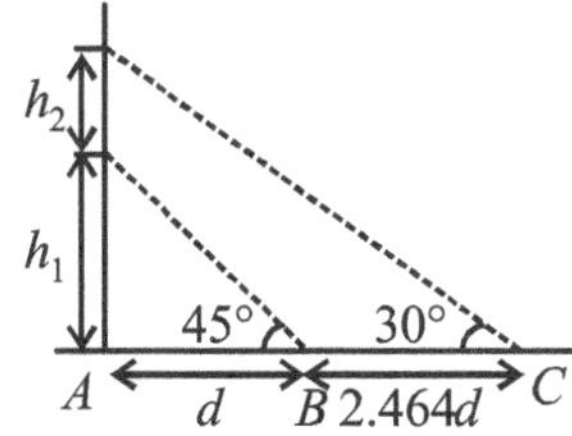

And, $\dfrac{h_1 + h_2}{d + 2.464d} = \tan 30°$

$\Rightarrow (h_1 + h_2) \times \sqrt{3} = 3.46d$

$\Rightarrow (h_1 + h_2) = \dfrac{3.46d}{\sqrt{3}} \Rightarrow d + h_2 = \dfrac{3.46d}{\sqrt{3}}$

$\therefore h_2 = d$

4. (c) In electromagnetic wave, $\dfrac{E_0}{B_0} = C$

$\therefore$ Maximum value of magnetic field, $B_0 = \dfrac{E_0}{C}$

$F_{\max} = qVB_{\max}\sin 90° = \dfrac{qV_0 E_0}{C}$

(Given $V_0 = 0.1$ C and $E_0 = 30$)

$= \dfrac{1.6 \times 10^{-19} \times 0.1 \times 3 \times 10^8 \times 30}{3 \times 10^8} = 4.8 \times 10^{-19}\,\text{N}$

5. (c) For upward motion of helicopter,

$v^2 = u^2 + 2gh \Rightarrow v^2 = 0 + 2gh \Rightarrow v = \sqrt{2gh}$

Now, packet will start moving under gravity.
Let 't' be the time taken by the food packet to reach the ground.

$s = ut + \dfrac{1}{2}at^2$

$\Rightarrow -h = \sqrt{2gh}\,t - \dfrac{1}{2}gt^2 \Rightarrow \dfrac{1}{2}gt^2 - \sqrt{2gh}\,t - h = 0$

or, $t = \dfrac{\sqrt{2gh} \pm \sqrt{2gh + 4 \times \dfrac{g}{2} \times h}}{2 \times \dfrac{g}{2}}$

or, $t = \sqrt{\dfrac{2gh}{g}}(1 + \sqrt{2}) \Rightarrow t = \sqrt{\dfrac{2h}{g}}(1 + \sqrt{2})$

or, $t = 3.4\sqrt{\dfrac{h}{g}}$

6. (d) Galvanometer of resistance (G) converted into a voltmeter of range 0-1 V.

$V = 1 = i_g(G + R_1)$ ...(i)

To increase the range of voltmeter 0-2 V

$2 = i_g(R_1 + R_2 + G)$ ...(ii)

Dividing eq. (i) by (ii),

$$\Rightarrow \frac{1}{2} = \frac{G + R_1}{G + R_1 + R_2}$$

$$\Rightarrow G + R_1 + R_2 = 2G + 2R_1$$

$$\therefore R_2 = G + R_1$$

7. **(b)** When capacitors C and $2C$ capacitance are charged to V and 2V respectively.

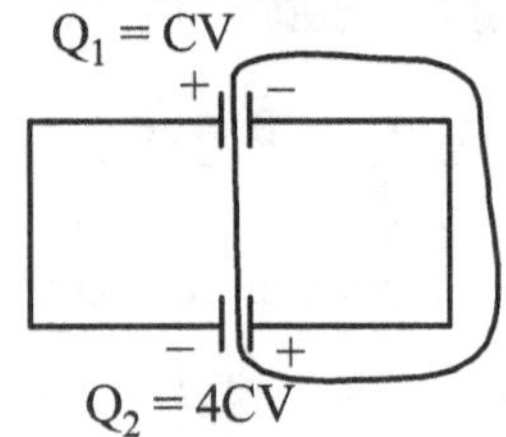

$$Q_1 = CV \quad Q_2 = 2C \times 2V = 4CV$$

When connected in parallel

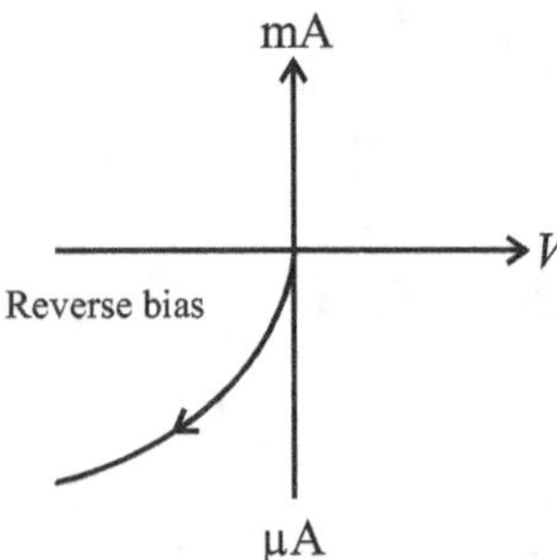

By conservation of charge

$$4CV - CV = (C + 2C)V_{common}$$

$$V_{common} = \frac{3CV}{3C} = V$$

Therefore final energy of this configuration,

$$U_f = \left(\frac{1}{2}CV^2 + \frac{1}{2} \times 2CV^2\right) = \frac{3}{2}CV^2$$

8. **(d)** I-V characteristic of a photodiode is as follows :

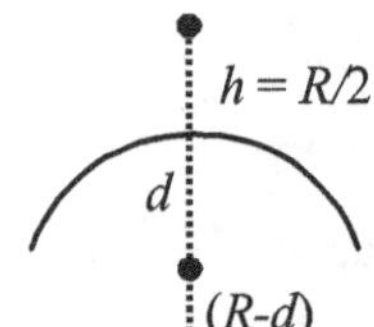

On increasing the biasing voltage of a photodiode, the magnitude of photocurrent first increases and then attains a saturation.

9. **(b)** According to question, $g_h = g_d = g_1$

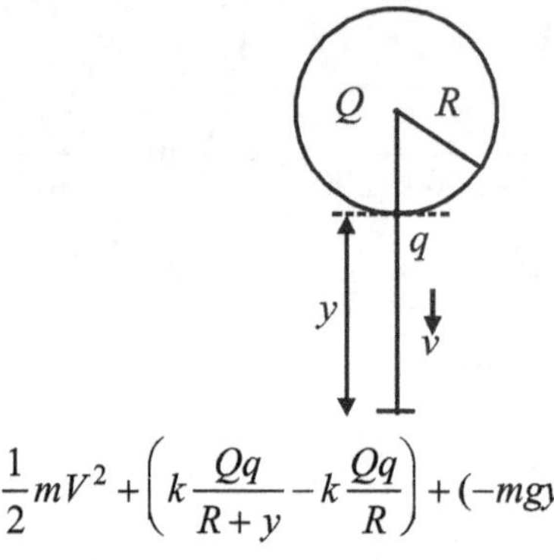

$$g_h = \frac{GM}{\left(R + \dfrac{R}{2}\right)^2} \text{ and } g_d = \frac{GM(R-d)}{R^3}$$

$$\frac{GM}{\left(\dfrac{3R}{2}\right)^2} = \frac{GM(R-d)}{R^3} \Rightarrow \frac{4}{9} = \frac{(R-d)}{R}$$

$$\Rightarrow 4R = 9R - 9d \Rightarrow 5R = 9d$$

$$\therefore \frac{d}{R} = \frac{5}{9}$$

10. **(d)** By using energy conservation,

$$\Delta KE + (\Delta PE)_{Electro} + (\Delta PE)_{gravitational} = 0$$

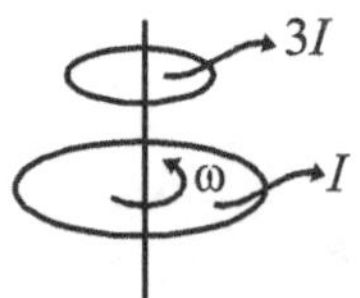

$$\frac{1}{2}mV^2 + \left(k\frac{Qq}{R+y} - k\frac{Qq}{R}\right) + (-mgy) = 0$$

$$\Rightarrow \frac{1}{2}mV^2 = mgy + kQq\left(\frac{1}{R} - \frac{1}{R+y}\right)$$

$$\Rightarrow V^2 = 2gy + \frac{2kQq}{m}\frac{y}{R(R+y)}$$

$$\text{or, } V^2 = 2y\left[\frac{qQ}{4\pi\varepsilon_0 R(R+y)m} + g\right]$$

11. **(d)** By angular momentum conservation, $L_c = L_f$

$$\omega I + 3I \times 0 = 4I\omega' \Rightarrow \omega' = \frac{\omega}{4}$$

$$(KE)_i = \frac{1}{2}I\omega^2$$

$$(KE)_f = \frac{1}{2}(3I + I)\omega'^2$$

$$= \frac{1}{2} \times (4I) \times \left(\frac{\omega}{4}\right)^2 = \frac{I\omega^2}{8}$$

$$\Delta KE = \frac{1}{2}I\omega^2 - \frac{1}{8}I\omega^2 = \frac{3}{8}I\omega^2$$

$$\therefore \text{ Fractional loss in K.E. } = \frac{\Delta KE}{KE_{l_i}} = \frac{\dfrac{3}{8}I\omega^2}{\dfrac{1}{2}I\omega^2} = \frac{3}{4}.$$

12. **(d)** From lens formula,

$$\frac{1}{v} - \frac{1}{u} = \frac{1}{f} \Rightarrow v = \frac{uf}{u+f}$$

Case-I : If $v = u \Rightarrow f + u = f \Rightarrow u = 0$

Case-II : If $u = \infty$ then $v = f$.

Hence, correct u versus v graph, that satisfies this condition is (a).

13. **(b)** Temperature change ΔT is same for all three processes $A \to B$; $A \to C$ and $A \to D$

$$\Delta U = nC_v \Delta T = \text{same}$$

$$E_{AB} = E_{AC} = E_{AD}$$

Work done, $W = P \times \Delta V$

$AB \to$ volume is increasing $\Rightarrow W_{AB} > 0$

$AD \to$ volume is decreasing $\Rightarrow W_{AD} < 0$

$AC \to$ volume is constant $\Rightarrow W_{AC} = 0$

14. **(c)** Given : K.E.$_{\text{mean}} = \frac{3}{2}kT = 4 \times 10^{-14}$

$P = 2$ cm of Hg, $V = 4$ cm^3

$$N = \frac{PV}{KT} = \frac{P\rho g V}{KT} = \frac{2 \times 13.6 \times 980 \times 4}{\frac{8}{3} \times 10^{-14}} \simeq 4 \times 10^{18}$$

15. **(c)** Torque on the loop,

$$\overline{\tau} = \overline{M} \times \overline{B} = MB \sin \theta = MB \sin 90°$$

Magnetic field, $B = \frac{\mu_0 I}{2\pi d}$

$$\therefore \tau = I_1 (2a)^2 \left(\frac{\mu_0 I_2}{2\pi d} \right) \sin 90°$$

$$= \frac{2\mu_0 I_1 I_2}{\pi d} \times a^2 = \frac{2\mu_0 I^2 a^2}{\pi d}$$

16. **(d)** Given : $Z = \dfrac{a^2 b^{2/3}}{\sqrt{c} d^3}$

Percentage error in Z,

$$= \frac{\Delta Z}{Z} = \frac{2\Delta a}{a} + \frac{2}{3}\frac{\Delta b}{b} + \frac{1}{2}\frac{\Delta c}{c} + \frac{3\Delta d}{d}$$

$$= 2 \times 2 + \frac{2}{3} \times 1.5 + \frac{1}{2} \times 4 + 3 \times 2.5 = 14.5\%.$$

17. **(a)** In equilibrium, $mg = F_e$

$F_B = V\rho_0 g$ and mass = volume × density

$$\frac{4}{3}\pi (R^3 - r^3)\rho_0 g = \frac{4}{3}\pi R^3 \rho_w g$$

Given, relative density, $\dfrac{\rho_0}{\rho_w} = \dfrac{27}{8}$

$$\Rightarrow \left[1 - \left(\frac{r}{R} \right)^3 \right] \frac{27}{8} \rho_w = \rho_w$$

$$\Rightarrow 1 - \frac{r^3}{R^3} = \frac{9}{27} \Rightarrow 1 - \frac{1}{3} = \frac{r^3}{R^3} \Rightarrow \frac{2}{3} = \frac{r^3}{R^3}$$

$$\Rightarrow \frac{r}{R} = \left(\frac{2}{3} \right)^{1/3} \Rightarrow 1 - \frac{r^3}{R^3} = \frac{8}{27}$$

$$\Rightarrow \frac{r^3}{R^3} = 1 - \frac{8}{27} = \frac{19}{27}$$

$$\therefore r = 0.89R = \frac{8}{9}R.$$

18. **(a)** Here, $l_1 = 17$ cm and $l_2 = 24.5$ cm, $V = 330$ m/s, $f = ?$

$$\lambda = 2(l_2 - l_1) = 2 \times (24.5 - 17) = 15 \text{ cm}$$

Now, from $v = f\lambda \Rightarrow 330 = \lambda \times 15 \times 10^{-2}$

$$\therefore \lambda = \frac{330}{15} \times 100 = \frac{1100 \times 100}{5} = 2200 \text{ Hz}$$

19. **(b)** Given : Power, $P = 1$ kW $= 1000$ W

$R = 2\Omega$, $V = 220$ V

Current, $I = \dfrac{P}{V} = \dfrac{1000}{220}$

$$P_{\text{loss}} = I^2 R = \left(\frac{1000}{220} \right)^2 \times 2$$

$$\therefore \text{ Efficiency } = \frac{1000}{1000 + P_{\text{loss}}} \times 100 = 96\%.$$

20. **(a)** According to question, one half of its kinetic energy is converted into heat in the wood.

$$\frac{1}{2}mv^2 \times \frac{1}{2} = ms\Delta T$$

$$\Rightarrow \Delta T = \frac{v^2}{4 \times s} = \frac{210 \times 210}{4 \times 4.2 \times 0.3 \times 1000} = 87.5°C$$

21. **(195)**

Given : $\vec{F} = (\hat{i} + 2\hat{j} + 3\hat{k})$ N

And, $\vec{r} = [(4\hat{i} + 3\hat{j} - \hat{k}) - (\hat{i} + 2\hat{j} + \hat{k})] = 3\hat{i} + \hat{j} - 2\hat{k}$

Torque, $\tau = \vec{r} \times \vec{F} = (3\hat{i} + \hat{j} - 2\hat{k}) \times (\hat{i} + 2\hat{j} + 3\hat{k})$

$$\tau = \begin{vmatrix} \hat{i} & \hat{j} & \hat{k} \\ 3 & 1 & -2 \\ 1 & 2 & 3 \end{vmatrix} = 7\hat{i} - 11\hat{j} + 5\hat{k}$$

Magnitude of torque, $|\vec{\tau}| = \sqrt{195}$.

22. (50)

From Bragg's equation $2d\sin\theta = \lambda$ and de-Broglie wavelength, $\lambda = \dfrac{h}{P} = \dfrac{h}{\sqrt{2mE}}$

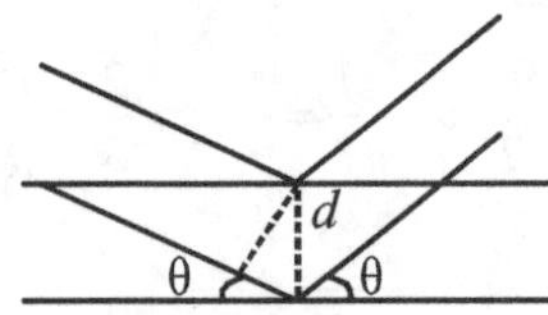

$$2d\sin\theta = \lambda = \frac{h}{\sqrt{2mE}}$$

$$\Rightarrow 2\times10^{-10}\times\frac{\sqrt{3}}{2} = \frac{6.6\times10^{-34}}{\sqrt{2mE}}$$

$[\because \theta = 60° \text{ and } d = 1\mathring{A} = 1\times10^{-10}\text{m}]$

$$\therefore E = \frac{1}{2}\times\frac{6.64^2\times10^{-48}}{9.1\times10^{-31}\times3\times1.6\times10^{-19}} \simeq 50 \text{ eV}$$

23. (51)

Before collision　　　　　　After collision

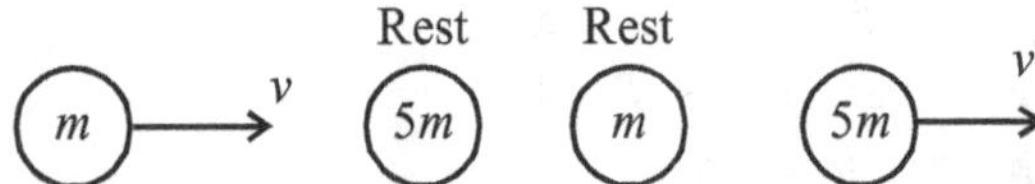

From linear momentum conservation, $L_i = L_f$

$$mV + 0 = 0 + 5mV' \Rightarrow V' = \frac{v}{5}$$

$$\text{Loss of KE} = KE_i - KE_f = \frac{1}{2}mv^2 - \frac{1}{2}(5m)\left(\frac{v}{5}\right)^2$$

$$= \frac{1}{2}mv^2\left(1-\frac{1}{5}\right) = \frac{4}{5}\left(\frac{mv^2}{2}\right)$$

$$= \frac{4}{5}KE_i = 10.2 \text{ eV}$$

$[\because \text{Energy in first excited state of atom} = 10.2 \text{ eV}]$

$$KE_i = 12.75\text{eV} = \frac{N}{4} \Rightarrow N = 51$$

The value of $N = 51$.

24. (50)

Given : Length of compound microscope, $L = 10$ cm

Focal length of objective $f_0 = 1$ cm and of eye-piece, $f_e = 5$ cm

$u_0 = f_e = 5$ cm

Final image formed at infinity (∞), $v_e = \infty$

$v_0 = 10 - 5 = 5$

Using lens formula, $\dfrac{1}{v} - \dfrac{1}{u} = \dfrac{1}{f}$

$$\frac{1}{v_0} - \frac{1}{u_0} = \frac{1}{f_0} \Rightarrow \frac{1}{5} - \frac{1}{u_0} = \frac{1}{1} \Rightarrow u_0 = -\frac{5}{4} \text{ cm}$$

or, $\dfrac{5}{4} = \dfrac{N}{40}$

$$\therefore N = \frac{200}{4} = 50 \text{ cm.}$$

25. (5)

For coil C_1, No. of turns $N_1 = 500$ and radius, $r = 1$ cm.

For coil C_2, No. of turns $N_2 = 200$ and radius, $R = 20$ cm

$$I = (5t^2 - 2t + 3) \Rightarrow \frac{dI}{dt} = (10t - 2)$$

$$\phi_{\text{small}} = BA = \left(\frac{\mu_0 I N_2}{2R}\right)(\pi r^2)$$

Induced emf in small coil,

$$e = \frac{d\phi}{dt} = \left(\frac{\mu_0 N_2}{2r}\right)\pi r^2 N_1 \frac{di}{dt} = \left(\frac{\mu_0 N_1 N_2 \pi r^2}{2R}\right)(10t - 2)$$

At $t = 1$ s

$$e = \left(\frac{\mu_0 N_1 N_2 \pi r^2}{2R}\right)8 = 4\frac{\mu_0 N_1 N_2 \pi r^2}{R}$$

$$= \frac{4(4\pi)10^{-7}\times200}{20}\times500\times\frac{10^{-4}}{10^{-2}}\pi$$

$$= 80\times\pi^2\times10^{-7}\times10\times10^2\times10^{-2}$$

$$= 8\times10^{-4} \text{ volt} = 0.8 \text{ mV} = \frac{4}{x} \Rightarrow x = 5.$$

CHEMISTRY

26. (a) Esters are hydrolysed in basic medium (saponification), so it is unstable in aqueous base.

27. (a) For d^6 configuration, high spin complex.

(i) In case of octahedral field, $t_{2g}^4 e_g^2$

$$\text{CFSE} = [-0.4p + 0.6q]\Delta_0 + n(P)$$
$$= [-0.4\times4 + 0.6\times2]\Delta_0 + 0 = -0.4\Delta_0$$

(ii) In case of tetrahedral field, e^3, t_2^3

$$\text{CFSE} = [-0.6p + 0.4q]\Delta t$$
$$= [-0.6\times3 + 0.4\times3]\Delta t = -0.6\Delta t.$$

28. (c) (i) As reaction is endothermic ($\Delta Hz = +$ve) so on decrease in temperature equilibrium will shift towards reactant side.

(ii) On increase in pressure by adding inert gas (N_2) at same temperature, no shifting will take place. The equilibrium changes only if the added gas is a reactant or product involved in the reaction.

29. **(a)** Acidity $\propto$ stability of conjugate base

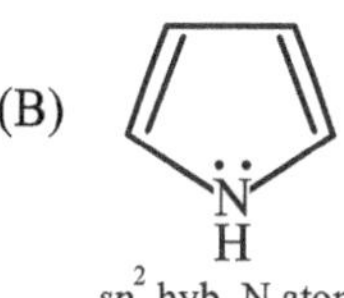

Thus increasing order of acidity is $D < C < A < B$.

30. **(c)** For bcc, $Z = 2$

$$d = \frac{Z \times M}{N_A \times (a)^3}$$

$$\Rightarrow 6.17 = \frac{2 \times M}{6.0 \times 10^{23} \times [3 \times 10^{-8}]^3}$$

$$\Rightarrow 6.17 = \frac{2 \times M}{6.0 \times 2.7} \Rightarrow M = 50$$

No. of mole $= \dfrac{200}{50} = 4$

No. of molecules $= 4\, N_A$.

31. **(b)** When two H-atoms come closer then initially due to attraction P.E. is $-$ve, which decreases more as atoms come closer and after reacting to a minimum value as repulsion starts dominating. So, P.E. increases then.

32. **(a)** In micelle formation, above "CMC" hydrocarbon chains are pointing towards the centre of sphere with COO^- part remaining outward on the surface.

33. **(c)** $r = 0.529 \dfrac{n^2}{Z}$ Å

For Li^{2+},

$$(r_{Li^{2+}})_{n=4} - (r_{Li^{2+}})_{n=3} = \frac{0.529}{3}[4^2 - 3^2] = \Delta R_1$$

For He^+,

$$(r_{He^+})_{n=4} - (r_{He^+})_{n=3} = \frac{0.529}{2}[4^2 - 3^2] = \Delta R_2$$

$$\frac{\Delta R_1}{\Delta R_2} = \frac{2}{3}$$

34. **(a)**

	$6s$	$4f$	$5d$	$6p$
$n + l$	6+0	4+3	5+2	6+1
	$\Downarrow$	$\Downarrow$	$\Downarrow$	$\Downarrow$
	6	7	7	7

Thus, order of orbitals filled are
$6s < 4f < 5d < 6p$.

35. **(c)** $CH_3CH_2 - C \equiv N \xrightarrow{\text{LiAlH}_4} CH_3CH_3 - CH_2 - NH_2$

$NaBH_4$ does not reduce $R{-}CN$.

36. **(b)** If the level of noradrenaline is low, then the person suffers from depression. In such situations, anti-depressant drugs are required.

37. **(a)** Tyrosine is a non-essential amino acid.

38. **(b)** Electronic configuration of

$$_{64}Gd = [Xe]\, 4f^7\, 5d^1\, 6s^2$$

$$_{64}Gd^{3+} = [Xe]\, 4f^7$$

No. of unpaired electron $= 7$

$$\mu = \sqrt{n(n+2)}\,BM = \sqrt{63} = 7.93\ BM$$

39. **(b)**

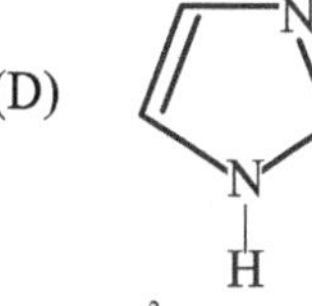

(A) sp^2 hyb. N atom (localised L.P.)

(B) sp^2 hyb. N atom (delocalised L.P.)

(C) sp^3 hyb. N atom (localised L.P.)

(D) sp^2 hyb. N atom (localised L.P. with partial negative ch.)

Thus, increasing order of basicity is
(B) < (A) < (D) < (C).

40. **(b)** $C_t = C_0 e^{-kt}$; $k = \dfrac{\ln 2}{t_{1/2}}$

$$(C_t)_A = (C_0)_A e^{-k_A t}; \ k_A = \frac{\ln 2}{300}$$

$$(C_t)_B = (C_0)_B e^{-k_B t}; \ k_B = \frac{\ln 2}{180}$$

$$\frac{(C_t)_B}{(C_t)_A} = \frac{(C_0)_B}{(C_0)_A} \times e^{(k_B - k_A)t}$$

$$\Rightarrow 4 = e^{(k_B - k_A)t}$$

$$\Rightarrow 2\ln 2 = \left[\frac{\ln 2}{180} - \frac{\ln 2}{300}\right]t$$

$$\Rightarrow 2\ln 2 = \ln 2\left[\frac{1}{180} - \frac{1}{300}\right]t$$

$$\Rightarrow 2 = \left(\frac{120}{180 \times 300}\right)t \Rightarrow t - \frac{2 \times 180 \times 300}{120} = 900\ sec$$

41. **(a)** $2PCl_5\,(s) \longrightarrow [PCl_4]^+\ [PCl_6]^-$
Tetrahedral Octahedral

42. **(b)** Ellingham diagram is the graph of ΔG^0 vs T of any metal/ element oxide. Since

$$\Delta G^\circ = \Delta H^\circ - T\Delta S^\circ$$

For most metal oxide formation.

metal (s) + oxygen (g) $\rightarrow$ metal oxide (s)

$$\Delta H^\circ = -ve; \ \Delta S^\circ = -ve$$

So, graph will be a straight line with –ve intercept and +ve slope.

43. **(b)**

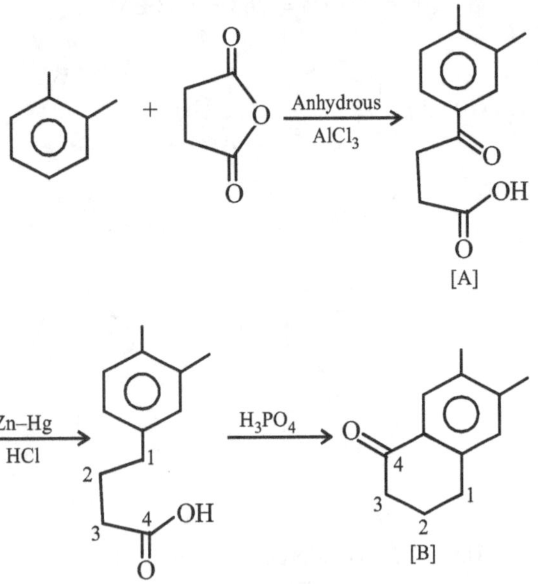

[A]

[B]

44. **(d)** $CO(g) + H_2O(g) \xrightarrow[\text{Catalyst}]{673K} CO_2(g) + H_2(g)$

This reaction is called water gas shift reaction.

45. **(a)** The process in which nutrient enriched water bodies support a dense plant population which kill animal life by depriving it of oxygen results in subsequent loss of biodiversity is known as Eutrophication. So, this condition indicates a polluted environment.

46. **(18)** Complete combustion of hydrocarbons can be represented by the following reaction.

$$C_xH_y + \left(x + \frac{y}{4}\right)O_2 \longrightarrow xCO_2 + \frac{y}{2}H_2O$$

For propane combustion reaction is

$$C_3H_8 + \left(3 + \frac{8}{4}\right)O_2 \longrightarrow 3CO_2 + \frac{8}{2}H_2O$$

$$\therefore C_3H_8 + 5O_2 \longrightarrow 3CO_2 + 4H_2O$$

Similarly, for butane is

$$C_4H_{10} + \left(4 + \frac{10}{4}\right)O_2 \longrightarrow 4CO_2 + \frac{10}{2}H_2O$$

$$\therefore C_4H_{10} + \frac{13}{2}O_2 \longrightarrow 4CO_2 + 5\,{}^2H_2O$$

$\because$ For 1 mol of C_4H_{10} required $O_2 = \dfrac{13}{2}$ mol

$\therefore$ For 2 mol of C_4H_{10} required $O_2 = \dfrac{13}{2} \times 2 = 13$ mol

47. **(6)**

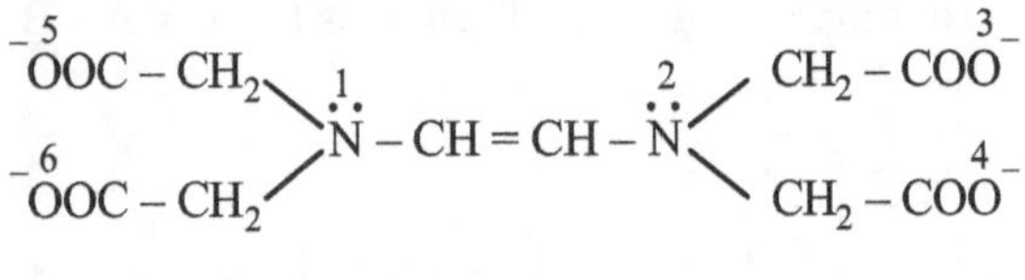

$EDTA^{4-}$ is a hexadentate ligand, since hexa means six and the ligand attaches six times.

48. **(4)**

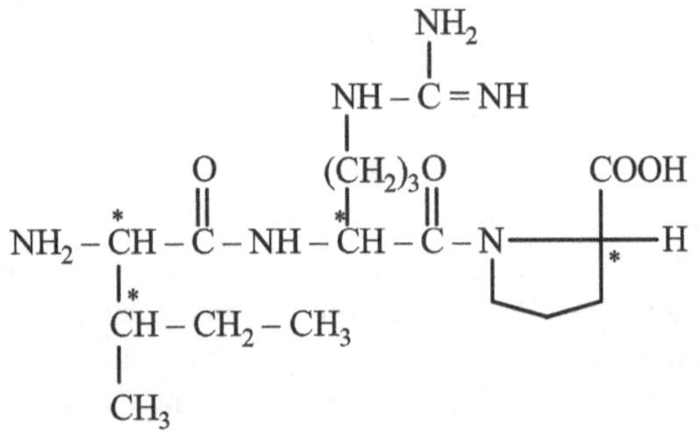

* Represents chiral centre.

49. **(7)** $CO_2 + H_2O \longrightarrow H_2CO_3$

     30 bar .... 1 mol/L

     3 bar .... 0.1 mol/L

$$H_2CO_3 \rightleftharpoons H^+ + HCO_3^-$$

$t=0$ 0.1   0   0

at Equb. $0.1(1-\alpha)$ 0.1α 0.1α

$$4.0 \times 10^{-7} = \frac{0.1\alpha^2}{1-\alpha}$$

$$\Rightarrow (1-\alpha) = 1$$

$$\alpha^2 = 4 \times 10^{-6} \Rightarrow \alpha = 2 \times 10^{-3}$$

$$[H^+] = 2 \times 10^{-4} \ M$$

$$pH = 4 \times \log 2 = 3.7 \approx 37 \times 10^{-1}$$

50. **(– 6)**

$$\Delta G^\circ = -nFE^\circ_{cell}$$

$$17.37 \times 10^3 = -3 \times 96500 \times E^\circ_{cell}$$

$$E^\circ_{cell} = -0.06 \ V \approx -6.0 \times 10^{-2} \ V$$

MATHEMATICS

51. (b) $\dfrac{5+e^x}{2+y}\cdot\dfrac{dy}{dx} = -e^x$

$\displaystyle\int \dfrac{dy}{2+y} = -\int \dfrac{e^x}{5+e^x}\,dx$

$\Rightarrow \log_e|2+y|\cdot\log_e|5+e^x| = \log_e C$

$\Rightarrow |(2+y)(5+e^x)| = C \qquad \because y(0)=1$

$C = 18.$

$\therefore (2+y)\cdot(5+e^x) = 18$

When $x = \log_e 13$ then $(2+y)\cdot 18 = 18$

$\Rightarrow 2+y = \pm 1$

$\therefore y = -1,\, -3$

$\therefore y(\ln 13) = -1$

52. (b) Let $|x| = y$ then

$9y^2 - 18y + 5 = 0$

$\Rightarrow 9y^2 - 15y - 3y + 5 = 0$

$\Rightarrow (3y-1)(3y-5) = 0$

$\Rightarrow y = \dfrac{1}{3} \text{ or } \dfrac{5}{3} \Rightarrow |x| = \dfrac{1}{3} \text{ or } \dfrac{5}{3}$

Roots are $\pm\dfrac{1}{3}$ and $\pm\dfrac{5}{3}$

$\therefore$ Product $= \dfrac{25}{81}$

53. (a) $p : x \leftrightarrow \sim y = (x \to \sim y) \wedge (\sim y \to x)$

$= (\sim x \vee \sim y) \wedge (y \vee x)$

$= \sim(x \wedge y) \wedge (x \vee y) \qquad (\because \sim(x \wedge y) = \sim x \vee \sim y)$

Negation of p is

$\sim p = (x \wedge y) \vee \sim(x \vee y) = (x \wedge y) \vee (\sim x \wedge \sim y)$

54. (c) Let two remaining observations are x_1, x_2.

So, $\bar{x} = \dfrac{2+4+10+12+14+x_1+x_2}{7} = 8$ (given)

$\Rightarrow x_1 + y_1 = 14 \qquad\qquad \text{...(i)}$

Now, $\sigma^2 = \dfrac{\Sigma x_i^2}{N} - \left(\dfrac{\Sigma x_i}{N}\right)^2 = 16$ (given)

$= \dfrac{4+16+100+144+196+x_1^2+x_2^2}{7} - 64 = 16$

$\Rightarrow 460 + x_1^2 + x_2^2 = (16+64)\times 7$

$\Rightarrow x_1^2 + x_2^2 = 100 \qquad\qquad \text{...(ii)}$

$\because (x+y)^2 = x^2+y^2+2xy \Rightarrow xy = 48 \qquad \text{...(iii)}$

$\because (x-y)^2 = (x+y)^2 - 4xy = 196 - 192 = 4$

$\Rightarrow x-y = 2 \Rightarrow |x-y| = 2$

55. (b) Given sequence are in G.P. and common ratio $\dfrac{3}{2}$

$\therefore \dfrac{2^{10}\left(\left(\dfrac{3}{2}\right)^{11} - 1\right)}{\left(\dfrac{3}{2} - 1\right)} = S - 2^{11}$

$\Rightarrow 2^{10}\,\dfrac{\left(\dfrac{3^{11}-2^{11}}{2^{11}}\right)}{\dfrac{1}{2}} = S - 2^{11}$

$\Rightarrow 3^{11} - 2^{11} = S - 2^{11} \Rightarrow S = 3^{11}$

56. (a) Given that $3^{2\sin 2\alpha - 1},\, 14,\, 3^{4-2\sin 2\alpha}$ are in A.P.

So, $3^{2\sin 2\alpha - 1} + 3^{4-2\sin 2\alpha} = 28$

$\Rightarrow \dfrac{3^{2\sin 2\alpha}}{3} + \dfrac{81}{3^{2\sin 2\alpha}} = 28$

Let $3^{2\sin 2\alpha} = x$

$\Rightarrow \dfrac{x}{3} + \dfrac{81}{x} = 28$

$\Rightarrow x^2 - 84x + 243 = 0 \Rightarrow x = 81,\, x = 3$

When $x = 81 \Rightarrow \sin 2\alpha = 2$ (Not possible)

When $x = 3 \Rightarrow \alpha = \dfrac{\pi}{12}$

$\therefore a = 3^0 = 1,\, d = 14 - 1 = 13$

$a_6 = a + 5d = 1 + 65 = 66.$

57. (b) We know that the volume of parallelopiped

$= [\bar{a}\ \ \bar{b}\ \ \bar{c}]$

$\begin{vmatrix} 1 & 1 & n \\ 2 & 4 & -n \\ 1 & n & 3 \end{vmatrix} - 158$

$\Rightarrow (12+n^2) - 1(6+n) + n(2n-4) = 158$

$$\Rightarrow 3n^2 - 5n - 152 = 0$$

$$\Rightarrow 3n^2 - 24n + 19n - 152 = 0$$

$$\Rightarrow 3n(n-8) + 19(n-8) = 0$$

$$\Rightarrow n = 8 \text{ or } n = \frac{-19}{3}$$

$$\Rightarrow n = 8 \qquad (\because n \geq 0)$$

$$\therefore \overline{a} = \hat{i} + \hat{j} + 8\hat{k}, \ \overline{b} = 2\hat{i} + 4\hat{j} - 8\hat{k} \text{ and}$$

$$\overline{c} = \hat{i} + 8\hat{j} + 3\hat{k}$$

$$\overline{a} \cdot \overline{c} = 1 + 8 + 24 = 33$$

$$\overline{b} \cdot \overline{c} = 2 + 32 - 24 = 10$$

58. (a) $S = \tan^{-1}\left(\dfrac{1}{3}\right) + \tan^{-1}\dfrac{1}{7} + \tan^{-1}\dfrac{1}{13} + \ldots$ upto 10 terms

$$= \tan^{-1}\left(\frac{2-1}{1+2\cdot 1}\right) + \tan^{-1}\left(\frac{3-2}{1+3\cdot 2}\right)$$

$$+ \tan^{-1}\left(\frac{4-3}{1+3\cdot 4}\right) + \ldots + \tan^{-1}\left(\frac{11-10}{1+11\cdot 10}\right)$$

$$= (\tan^{-1} 2 - \tan^{-1} 1) + (\tan^{-1} 3 - \tan^{-1} 2) +$$

$$(\tan^{-1} 4 - \tan^{-1} 3) + \ldots + (\tan^{-1} 11 - \tan^{-1} 10)$$

$$= \tan^{-1} 11 - \tan^{-1} 1 = \tan^{-1}\left(\frac{11-1}{1+11\cdot 1}\right) = \tan^{-1}\left(\frac{5}{6}\right)$$

$$\therefore \tan(S) = \frac{5}{6}$$

59. (c)

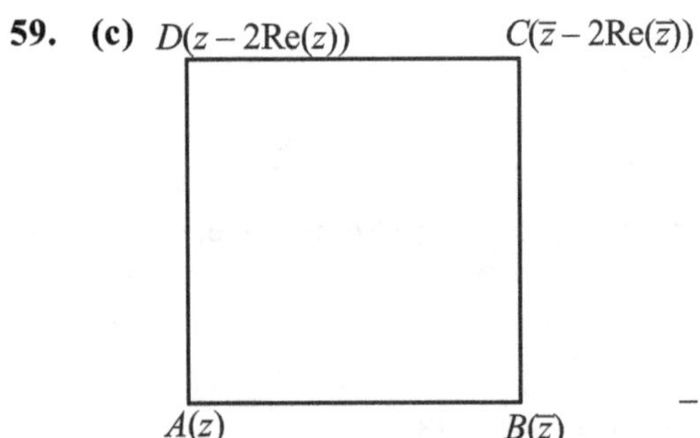

Let $z = x + iy$

$\because$ Length of side of square $= 4$ units

Then, $|z - \overline{z}| = 4 \Rightarrow |2iy| = 4 \Rightarrow |y| = 2$

Also, $|z - (z - 2\text{Re}(z))| = 4$

$$\Rightarrow |2\text{Re}(z)| = 4 \Rightarrow |2x| = 4 \Rightarrow |x| = 2$$

$$\therefore |z| = \sqrt{x^2 + y^2} = \sqrt{4+4} = 2\sqrt{2}$$

60. (b) Given, $n(C) = 73, \ n(T) = 65, \ n(C \cap T) = x$

$$\therefore 65 \geq n(C \cap T) \geq 65 + 73 - 100$$

$$\Rightarrow 65 \geq x \geq 38 \Rightarrow x \neq 36.$$

61. (b) Ellipse : $\dfrac{x^2}{16} + \dfrac{y^2}{9} = 1,$

$$a = 4, \ b = 3, \ c = \sqrt{16-9} = \sqrt{7}$$

$\therefore (\pm\sqrt{7}, 0)$ are the foci of given ellipse. So for any point P on it; $PA + PB = 2a$

$$\Rightarrow PA + PB = 2(4) = 8.$$

62. (a) Ellipse $\equiv \dfrac{x^2}{5} + \dfrac{y^2}{4} = 1$

Let a point on ellipse be $(\sqrt{5}\cos\theta, \ 2\sin\theta)$

$$\therefore PQ^2 = (\sqrt{5}\cos\theta)^2 + (-4 - 2\sin\theta)^2$$

$$= 5\cos^2\theta + 4\sin^2\theta + 16 + 16\sin\theta$$

$$= 21 + 16\sin\theta - \sin^2\theta$$

$$= 21 + 64 - (\sin\theta - 8)^2 = 85 - (\sin\theta - 8)^2$$

PQ^2 to be maximum when $\sin\theta = 1$

$$\therefore PQ^2_{max} = 85 - 49 = 36.$$

63. (a) $\because \begin{vmatrix} 2 & -4 & \lambda \\ 1 & -6 & 1 \\ \lambda & -10 & 4 \end{vmatrix} = 0 \Rightarrow 3\lambda^2 - 7\lambda - 12 = 0$

$$\Rightarrow \lambda = 3 \text{ or } -\frac{2}{3}$$

$$D_1 = \begin{vmatrix} 1 & -4 & \lambda \\ 2 & -6 & 1 \\ 3 & -10 & 4 \end{vmatrix} = 2(3 - \lambda)$$

$$\therefore \text{When } \lambda = -\frac{2}{3}, \ D_1 \neq 0.$$

Hence, equations will be inconsistent when $\lambda = -\dfrac{2}{3}$.

64. (b) Applying $C_2 \rightarrow C_2 - C_1$

$$f(\theta) = \begin{vmatrix} -\sin^2\theta & -1 & 1 \\ -\cos^2\theta & -1 & 1 \\ 12 & -2 & -2 \end{vmatrix}$$

$$= 4(\cos^2\theta - \sin^2\theta)$$

$$= 4\cos 2\theta, \ \theta \in \left(\frac{\pi}{4}, \frac{\pi}{2}\right)$$

Max. $f(\theta) = M = 0$

Min. $f(\theta) = m = -4$

So, $(m, M) = (-4, 0)$

65. (a) $\dfrac{x+1}{2} = \dfrac{y-3}{-2} = \dfrac{z}{-1} = \lambda$

Any point on line $= Q(2\lambda - 1, -2\lambda + 3, -\lambda)$

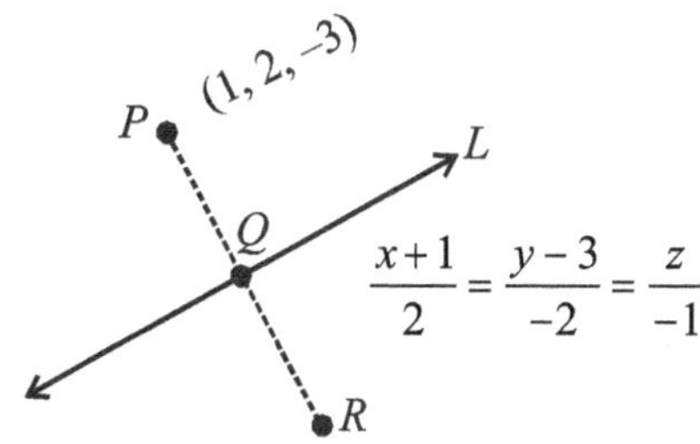

$\therefore$ D.r. of $PQ = [2\lambda - 2, -2\lambda + 1, -\lambda + 3]$

D.r. of given line $= [2, -2, -1]$

$\because$ PQ is perpendicular to line L

$\therefore 2(2\lambda - 2) - 2(-2\lambda + 1) - 1(-\lambda + 3) = 0$

$\Rightarrow 4\lambda - 4 + 4\lambda - 2 + \lambda - 3 = 0$

$\Rightarrow 9\lambda - 9 = 0 \Rightarrow \lambda = 1$

$\because$ Q is mid point of $PR = Q = (1, 1, -1)$

$\therefore$ Coordinate of image $R = (1, 0, 1) = (a, b, c)$

$\therefore a + b + c = 2.$

66. (a) $f(x)$ is differentiable then, $f(x)$ is also continuous.

$\therefore \lim\limits_{x \to \pi^+} f(x) = \lim\limits_{x \to \pi^-} f(x) = f(\pi)$

$\Rightarrow -1 = -K_2 \Rightarrow K_2 = 1$

$\therefore f'(x) = \begin{cases} 2K_1(x - \pi) : & x \le \pi \\ -K_2 \sin x & x > \pi \end{cases}$

Then, $\lim\limits_{x \to \pi^+} f(x) = \lim\limits_{x \to \pi^-} f(x) = 0$

$f''(x) = \begin{cases} 2K_1 & ; \ x \le \pi \\ -K_2 \cos x & ; \ x > \pi \end{cases}$

Then, $\lim\limits_{x \to \pi^+} f(x) = \lim\limits_{x \to \pi^-} f(x)$

$\Rightarrow 2K_1 = K_2 \Rightarrow K_1 = \dfrac{1}{2}$

So, $(K_1, K_2) = \left(\dfrac{1}{2}, 1 \right)$

67. (b) Equation tangent to parabola $y^2 = 4x$ with slope m be:

$$y = mx + \dfrac{1}{m} \qquad \text{...(i)}$$

$\because$ Equation of tangent to $x^2 = 4y$ with slope m be :

$$y = mx - am^2 \qquad \text{...(ii)}$$

From eq. (i) and (ii),

$\dfrac{1}{m} = -m^2 \Rightarrow m = -1$

$\therefore$ Equation tangent : $x + y + 1 = 0$

It is tangent to circle $x^2 + y^2 = c^2$

$\Rightarrow c = \dfrac{1}{\sqrt{2}}$

68. (b) $x^2 - x - 2 = 0 \Rightarrow (x - 2)(x + 1) = 0$

$\Rightarrow x = 2, -1 \Rightarrow \alpha = 2$

$\therefore \lim\limits_{x \to 2^+} \dfrac{\sqrt{1 - \cos(x^2 - x - 2)}}{x - 2}$

$= \lim\limits_{x \to 2^+} \dfrac{\sqrt{2}\left| \sin\left(\dfrac{x^2 - x - 2}{2} \right) \right|}{x - 2}$

$= \lim\limits_{x \to 2^+} \dfrac{\sqrt{2} \sin \dfrac{(x^2 - x - 2)}{2}}{\left(\dfrac{x^2 - x - 2}{2} \right)} \times \dfrac{(x^2 - x - 2)}{2(x - 2)}$

$= \dfrac{1}{\sqrt{2}} \lim\limits_{x \to 2^+} \left(\dfrac{\sin\left(\dfrac{x^2 - x - 2}{2} \right)}{\dfrac{x^2 - x - 2}{2}} \right) \times \lim\limits_{x \to 2^+} \dfrac{(x - 2)(x + 1)}{(x - 2)}$

$= \dfrac{1}{\sqrt{2}} \times 1 \times 3 = \dfrac{3}{\sqrt{2}}$

69. (d) $\displaystyle\int (e^{2x} + 2e^x - e^{-x} - 1) \cdot e^{(e^x + e^{-x})} dx$

$I = \displaystyle\int (e^{2x} + e^x - 1) \cdot e^{(e^x + e^{-x})} dx + \int (e^x - e^{-x}) e^{(e^x + e^{-x})} dx$

$= \displaystyle\int e^x (e^x + 1 - e^{-x}) \cdot e^{(e^x + e^{-x})} dx + e^{(e^x + e^{-x})}$

$= \displaystyle\int (e^x - e^{-x} + 1) e^{(e^x + e^{-x} + x)} dx + e^{(e^x + e^{-x})}$

Let $e^x + e^{-x} + x = t \Rightarrow (e^x + e^{-x} + 1) dx = dt$

$= \displaystyle\int e^t dt + e^{(e^x + e^{-x})} = e^t + e^{(e^x + e^{-x})} + C$

$= e^{(e^x + e^{-x} + x)} + e^{(e^x + e^{-x})} + C$

$= (e^x + 1) . e^{(e^x + e^{-x})} + C$

So, $g(x) = 1 + e^x$ and $g(0) = 2$

70. (c) $I = \displaystyle\int\limits_{-\pi/2}^{\pi/2} \dfrac{1}{1 + e^{\sin x}} dx$

$= \displaystyle\int\limits_{-\pi/2}^{0} \dfrac{1}{1 + e^{\sin x}} dx + \int\limits_{0}^{\pi/2} \dfrac{1}{1 + e^{\sin x}} dx$

$$= \int_0^{\pi/2} \left(\frac{1}{1+e^{\sin x}} + \frac{1}{1+e^{-\sin x}} \right) dx$$

$$= \int_0^{\pi/2} \frac{1+e^{\sin x}}{1+e^{\sin x}} dx = \frac{\pi}{2}$$

71. (8)

We know $[x]$ discontinuous for $x \in Z$

$f(x) = x\left[\dfrac{x}{2}\right]$ may be discontinuous where $\dfrac{x}{2}$ is an

integer.

So, points of discontinuity are,

$x = \pm 2, \pm 4, \pm 6, \pm 8$ and 0

but at $x = 0$

$$\lim_{x \to 0^+} f(x) = 0 = f(0) = \lim_{x \to 0^-} f(x)$$

So, $f(x)$ will be discontinuous at $x = \pm 2, \pm 4, \pm 6$ and ± 8.

72. (30)

$$L_1 : 2x - y + 3 = 0$$

$$L_1 : 4x - 2y + \alpha = 0 \Rightarrow 2x - y + \frac{\alpha}{2} = 0$$

$$L_1 : 6x - 3y + \beta = 0 \Rightarrow 2x - y + \frac{\beta}{3} = 0$$

Distance between L_1 and L_2;

$$\left| \frac{\alpha - 6}{2\sqrt{5}} \right| = \frac{1}{\sqrt{5}} \Rightarrow |\alpha - 6| = 2$$

$$\Rightarrow \alpha = 4, 8$$

Distance between L_1 and L_3 :

$$\left| \frac{\beta - 9}{3\sqrt{5}} \right| = \frac{2}{\sqrt{5}} \Rightarrow |\beta - 9| = 6$$

$$\Rightarrow \beta = 15, 3$$

Sum of all values $= 4 + 8 + 15 + 3 = 30$.

73. (240)

$S \to 2, L \to 2, A, B, Y, U.$

$\therefore$ Required number of ways $= {}^2C_1 \times {}^5C_2 \times \dfrac{4!}{2!} = 240.$

74. (13)

$$T_{r+1} = {}^{22}C_r \cdot (x^m)^{22-r} \cdot \left(\frac{1}{x^2} \right)^r$$

$$T_{r+1} = {}^{22}C_r \cdot x^{22m - mr - 2r}$$

$$\because 22m - mr - 2r = 1$$

$$\Rightarrow r = \frac{22m - 1}{m + 2} \Rightarrow r = 22 - \frac{3 \cdot 3 \cdot 5}{m + 2}$$

So, possible value of $m = 1, 3, 7, 13, 43$

But ${}^{22}C_r = 1540$

$\therefore$ Only possible value of $m = 13$.

75. (11)

Probability of getting at least two 3's or 5's in one trial

$$= {}^4C_2 \left(\frac{2}{6} \right)^2 \left(\frac{4}{6} \right)^2 + {}^4C_3 \left(\frac{2}{6} \right)^3 \left(\frac{4}{6} \right) + {}^4C_4 \left(\frac{2}{6} \right)^4$$

$$= \frac{33}{3^4} = \frac{11}{27}$$

$$E(x) = np = 27 \left(\frac{11}{27} \right) = 11.$$

PHYSICS

1. **(2)** From the Newton's second law,

$$F = \frac{dp}{dt} = \frac{d(mv)}{dt} = v\left(\frac{dm}{dt}\right) \qquad ...(i)$$

We have given, $\dfrac{dM(t)}{dt} = bv^2(t) \qquad ...(ii)$

Thrust on the satellite,

$$F = -v\left(\frac{dm}{dt}\right) = -v(bv^2) = -bv^3 \ [\text{Using (i) and (ii)}]$$

$$\Rightarrow F = M(t)\,a = -bv^3 \Rightarrow a = \frac{-bv^3}{M(t)}$$

2. **(3)** Potential at the centre, $V_C = \dfrac{KQ_{\text{net}}}{R}$

$\because Q_{\text{net}} = 0$

$\therefore V_C = 0$

Let E be electric field produced by each charge at the centre, then resultant electric field will be $E_C = 0$, since equal electric field vectors are acting at equal angle so their resultant is equal to zero.

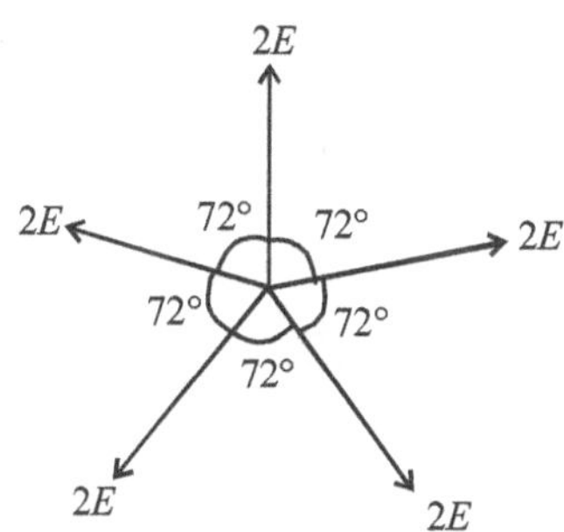

3. **(4)** Magnetic field at a distance r from the wire

$$B = \frac{\mu_0 I}{2\pi r}$$

Magnetic flux for small displacement dr;

$$\phi = B \cdot A = Bldr \qquad [\because A = l\,dr \text{ and } B.A = BA\cos 0°]$$

$$\Rightarrow \phi = \frac{\mu_0 I}{2\pi r} l\,dr$$

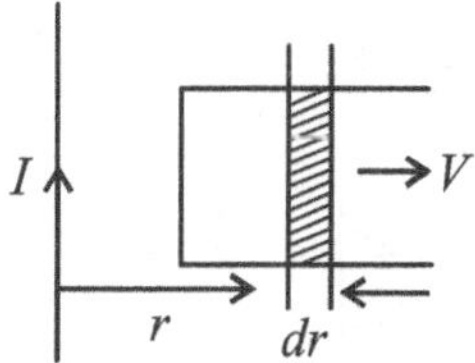

$$\text{Emf, } e = \frac{d\phi}{dt} = \frac{\mu_0 Il}{2\pi r} \cdot \frac{dr}{dt} \Rightarrow e = \frac{\mu_0}{2\pi} \cdot \frac{Ivl}{r}$$

Induce current in the loop, $i = \dfrac{e}{R} = \dfrac{\mu_0}{2\pi} \cdot \dfrac{Ivl}{Rr}$

4. **(1)**

Let q_1 and q_2 be the charge on the capacitors of $2\,\mu$F and $4\,\mu$F. Then charge on capacitor of $5\,\mu$F

$$Q = q_1 + q_2$$

$$\Rightarrow 5V_0 = 2(6 - V_0) + 4(6 - V_0)$$

$$\Rightarrow 5V_0 = 12 - 2V_0 + 24 - 4V_0$$

$$\Rightarrow 11V_0 = 36 \Rightarrow V_0 = \frac{36}{11}V$$

$$\Rightarrow Q = 5V_0 = \frac{180}{11}\mu C$$

5. **(4)** Given,

Current passing through galvanometer, $I = 6\,\text{mA}$

Deflection, $\theta = 2°$

Figure of merit of galvanometer

$$= \frac{I}{\theta} = \frac{6 \times 10^{-3}}{2} = 3 \times 10^{-3} \ \text{A/div}$$

6. **(4)** Energy sequence of radiations is

$$E_{\gamma\text{-Rays}} > E_{\text{X-Rays}} > E_{\text{microwave}} > E_{\text{AM Radiowaves}}$$

$\therefore \lambda_{\gamma\text{-Rays}} < \lambda_{\text{X-Rays}} < \lambda_{\text{microwave}} < \lambda_{\text{AM Radiowaves}}$

From the above sequence, we have

(1) Microwave $\to 10^{-3}$ m (iv)

(2) Gamma Rays $\to 10^{-15}$ m (ii)

(3) AM Radio wave $\to 100$ m (i)

(4) X-Rays $\to 10^{-10}$ m (iii)

7. **(4)** Initially, $S_2 L = 2$ m

$$S_1 L = \sqrt{2^2 + \left(\frac{3}{2}\right)^2} = \frac{5}{2} = 2.5 \text{ m}$$

Path difference, $\Delta x = S_1 L - S_2 L = 0.5 \text{ m} = \dfrac{\lambda}{2}$

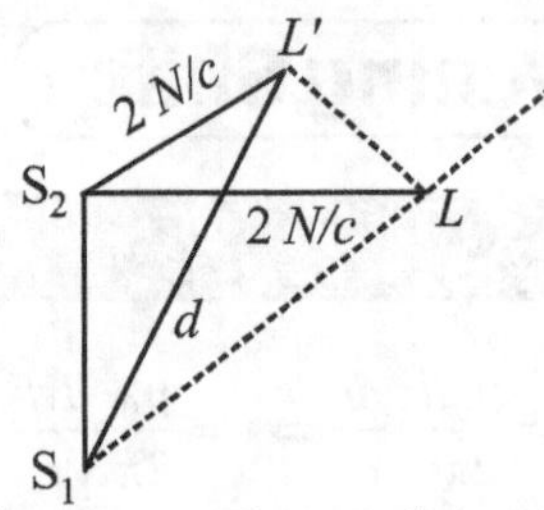

When the listner move from L, first maxima will appear if path difference is integral multiple of wavelength.
For example

$\Delta x = n\lambda = 1\lambda$ ($n = 1$ for first maxima)

$\therefore \ \Delta x = \lambda = S_1L' - S_2L$

$\Rightarrow 1 = d - 2 \Rightarrow d = 3$ m

8. **(1)** Let L'_1 and L'_2 be the lengths of the wire when temperature is changed by $\Delta T°C$.

At $T°C$,

$L_{eq} = L_1 + L_2$

At $T + \Delta°C$

$L'_{eq} = L'_1 + L'_2$

$\therefore \ L_{eq}(1 + \alpha_{eq}\Delta T) = L_1(1 + \alpha_1\Delta T) + L_2(1 + \alpha_2\Delta T)$

$$\left[\because L' = L(1 + \alpha\,\Delta T)\right]$$

$\Rightarrow (L_1 + L_2)(1 + \alpha_{eq}\Delta T) = L_1 + L_2 + L_1\alpha_1\Delta T + L_2\alpha_2\Delta T$

$\Rightarrow \alpha_{eq} = \dfrac{\alpha_1 L_1 + \alpha_2 L_2}{L_1 + L_2}$

9. **(1)**

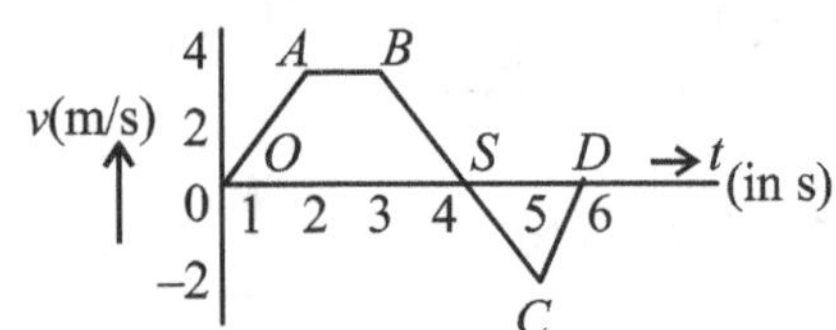

$OS = 4 + \dfrac{1}{3} = \dfrac{13}{3}$

$SD = 2 - \dfrac{1}{3} = \dfrac{5}{3}$

Distance covered by the body = area of v-t graph
= ar $(OABS)$ + ar (SCD)

$= \dfrac{1}{2}\left(\dfrac{13}{3} + 1\right) \times 4 + \dfrac{1}{2} \times \dfrac{5}{3} \times 2$

$= \dfrac{32}{3} + \dfrac{5}{3} = \dfrac{37}{3}$ m

10. **(1)** Using, $v^2 - u^2 = 2gh$

$\Rightarrow v^2 - 0^2 = 2gh \Rightarrow v = \sqrt{2gh}$

Terminal velocity,

$V_T = \dfrac{2}{9} \dfrac{r^2(\rho - \sigma)g}{\eta}$

After falling through h the velocity should be equal to terminal velocity

$\therefore \ \sqrt{2gh} = \dfrac{2}{9}\dfrac{r^2(\rho - \sigma)g}{\eta}$

$\Rightarrow 2gh = \dfrac{4}{81}\dfrac{r^4 g^2(\rho - \sigma)^2}{\eta^2}$

$\Rightarrow h = \dfrac{2r^4 g(\rho - \sigma)^2}{81\eta^2} \Rightarrow h \alpha r^4$

11. **(2)** Capacitance before inserting the slab,

$C_i = \dfrac{\varepsilon_0 A}{d} = \dfrac{\varepsilon_0 lw}{d}$ $(\because A = lw)$

Capacitance after inserting the dielectric slab,

$C_f = \dfrac{K\varepsilon_0 A_1}{d} + \dfrac{\varepsilon_0 A_2}{d}$

$\quad = \dfrac{K\varepsilon_0 Wx}{d} + \dfrac{\varepsilon_0 w(l - x)}{d}$

According to question,
$2 \times$ Initial energy = Final energy

$\Rightarrow \left(\dfrac{1}{2}C_i V^2\right)2 = \dfrac{1}{2}C_f V^2$

$\Rightarrow 2C_i = C_f$

$\Rightarrow 2\left(\dfrac{\varepsilon_0 wl}{d}\right) = \dfrac{\varepsilon_0 Kwx}{d} + \dfrac{\varepsilon_0 w(l - x)}{d}$

$\Rightarrow 2l = kx + (l - x) \Rightarrow x = \dfrac{l}{3}$

12. **(1)** Let f_1 be the frequency heard by wall, $f_1 = \left(\dfrac{v}{v - v_c}\right)f_0$

Here, $v =$ Velocity of sound,
     $v_c =$ Velocity of Car,
     $f_0 =$ actual frequency of car horn
Let f_2 be the frequency heard by driver after reflection from wall.

$f_2 = \left(\dfrac{v + v_c}{v}\right)f_1 = \left(\dfrac{v + v_c}{v - v_c}\right)f_0$

$\Rightarrow 480 = \left[\dfrac{345 + v_c}{345 - v_c}\right]440 \Rightarrow \dfrac{12}{11} = \dfrac{345 + v_c}{345 - v_c}$

$\Rightarrow v_c = 54$ km/hr

13. **(1)** Let I_1 and I_2 be the moment of inertia in first and second case respectively.

$$I_1 = 2MR^2$$

$$I_2 = MR^2 + \frac{MR^2}{2} = \frac{3}{2}MR^2$$

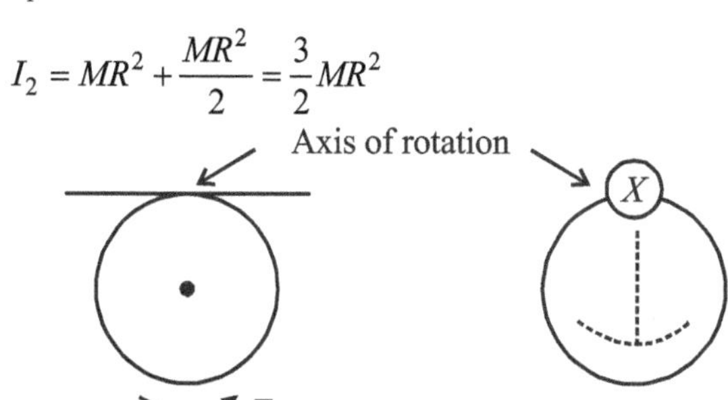

Time period, $T = 2\pi\sqrt{\dfrac{I}{mgd}}$

$$T \propto I$$

$$\therefore \frac{T_1}{T_2} = \sqrt{\frac{I_1}{I_2}} = \sqrt{\frac{2MR^2}{\frac{3}{2}MR^2}} = \frac{2}{\sqrt{3}}$$

14. **(3)** Till input voltage reaches 4 V. No zener is in breakdown region so $V_0 = V_i$. Then now when V_i changes between 4 V to 6 V one zener with 4 V will breakdown and P.D. across this zener will become constant and remaining potential will dorp across resistance in series with 4 V zener.

Now current in circuit increases abruptly and source must have an internal resistance due to which some potential will get drop across the source also so correct graph between V_0 and t will be

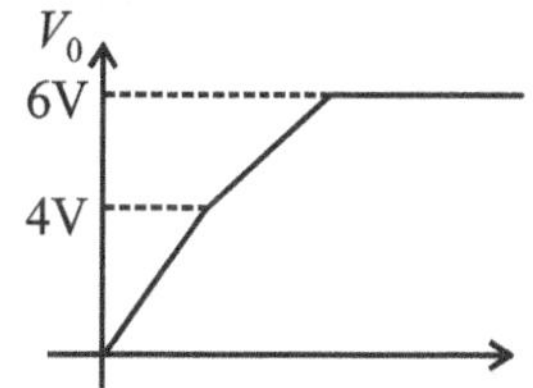

15. **(1)** Let λ_1 and λ_2 be the decay constants of two process. N be the number of nuclei left undecayed after two process. From the law of radioactive decay we have

$$-\frac{dN}{dt} = \lambda_1 N + \lambda_2 N \qquad \left[\because -\frac{dN}{dt} = \lambda N\right]$$

$$\Rightarrow -\frac{dN}{dt} = (\lambda_1 + \lambda_2)N$$

$$\Rightarrow \lambda_{eq.} = (\lambda_1 + \lambda_2)$$

$$\Rightarrow \frac{\ln 2}{T} = \frac{\ln 2}{T_1} + \frac{\ln 2}{T_2} \qquad \left(\because \lambda = \frac{\ln 2}{T}\right)$$

$$\Rightarrow \frac{1}{T} = \frac{1}{T_1} + \frac{1}{T_2}$$

$$\Rightarrow \frac{1}{T} = \frac{1}{10} + \frac{1}{100} = \frac{11}{100} \quad \text{[Given: } T_1 = 10 \text{ s \& } T_2 = 100 \text{ s]}$$

$$\Rightarrow T = \frac{100}{11} = 9 \text{ sec.}$$

16. **(1)** We know that

Speed of light, $c = \dfrac{1}{\sqrt{\mu_0 \varepsilon_0}} = x$

Also, $c = \dfrac{E}{B} = y$

Time constant, $\tau = Rc = t$

$$\therefore z = \frac{l}{Rc} = \frac{l}{t} = \text{Speed}$$

Thus, x, y, z will have the same dimension of speed.

17. **(3)** In adiabatic process

$$PV^\gamma = \text{constant}$$

$$\therefore P\left(\frac{m}{\rho}\right)^\gamma = \text{constant} \qquad \left(\because V = \frac{m}{\rho}\right)$$

As mass is constant

$$\therefore P \propto \rho^\gamma$$

If P_i and P_f be the initial and final pressure of the gas and ρ_i and ρ_f be the initial and final density of the gas. Then

$$\frac{P_f}{P_i} = \left(\frac{\rho_f}{\rho_i}\right)^\gamma = (32)^{7/5}$$

$$\Rightarrow \frac{nP_i}{P_i} = (2^5)^{7/5} = 2^7$$

$$\Rightarrow n = 2^7 = 128.$$

18. **(2)** Value of g at equator, $g_A = g \cdot -R\omega^2$

Value of g at height h above the pole,

$$g_B = g \cdot \left(1 - \frac{2h}{R}\right)$$

As object is weighed equally at the equator and poles, it means g is same at these places.

$$g_A = g_B$$

$$\Rightarrow g - R\omega^2 = g\left(1 - \frac{2h}{R}\right)$$

$$\Rightarrow R\omega^2 = \frac{2gh}{R} \Rightarrow h = \frac{R^2\omega^2}{2g}$$

19. **(4)**

Let us assume the potential at $A = V_A = 0$

Using Kirchoff's junction rule at C, we get

$i_1 + i_3 = i_2$

$1\text{A} + i_3 = 2\text{ A} \Rightarrow i_3 = 2A$

Now using Kirchoff's loop law along $ACDB$

$V_A + 1 + i_3(2) - 2 = V_B$

$\Rightarrow V_A + 1 + i_3(1) - 2 = V_B$

$\Rightarrow V_B - V_A = 3 - 2 = 1$ volt

20. **(2)** Given,

Volume of iron rod, $V = 10^{-3}$ m^3

Relative permeability, $\mu_r = 1000$

Number of turns per unit length, $n = 10$

Magnetic moment of an iron core solenoid,

$M = (\mu_r - 1) \times NiA$

$\Rightarrow M = (\mu_r - 1) \times Ni\dfrac{V}{l} \Rightarrow M = (\mu_r - 1) \times \dfrac{N}{l} iV$

$\Rightarrow M = 999 \times \dfrac{10}{10^{-2}} \times 0.5 \times 10^{-3} = 499.5 \approx 500.$

21. **(18)**

Given, Mass of the body, $m = 2$ kg

Power delivered by engine, $P = 1$ J/s

Time, $t = 9$ seconds

Power, $P = Fv$

$\Rightarrow P = mav$ $[\because F = ma]$

$\Rightarrow m\dfrac{dv}{dt}v = P$ $\left(\because a = \dfrac{dv}{dt}\right)$

$\Rightarrow v\,dv = \dfrac{P}{m}dt$

Integrating both sides we get

$\Rightarrow \displaystyle\int_0^v v\,dv = \dfrac{P}{m}\int_0^t dt$

$\Rightarrow \dfrac{v^2}{2} = \dfrac{Pt}{m} \Rightarrow v = \left(\dfrac{2Pt}{m}\right)^{1/2}$

$\Rightarrow \dfrac{dx}{dt} = \sqrt{\dfrac{2P}{m}}\,t^{1/2}$ $\left(\because v = \dfrac{dx}{dt}\right)$

$\Rightarrow \displaystyle\int_0^x dx = \sqrt{\dfrac{2P}{m}}\int_0^t t^{1/2}\,dt$

$\therefore$ Distance, $x = \sqrt{\dfrac{2P}{m}}\dfrac{t^{3/2}}{3/2} = \sqrt{\dfrac{2P}{m}} \times \dfrac{2}{3}t^{3/2}$

$\Rightarrow x = \sqrt{\dfrac{2 \times 1}{2}} \times \dfrac{2}{3} \times 9^{3/2} = \dfrac{2}{3} \times 27 = 18.$

22. **(41)**

Room mean square speed is given by

$v_{rms} = \sqrt{\dfrac{3RT}{M}}$

Here, $M =$ Molar mass of gas molecule

$T =$ temperature of the gas molecule

We have given $v_{N_2} = v_{H_2}$

$\therefore \sqrt{\dfrac{3RT_{N_2}}{M_{N_2}}} = \sqrt{\dfrac{3RT_{H_2}}{M_{H_2}}}$

$\Rightarrow \dfrac{T_{H_2}}{2} = \dfrac{573}{28} \Rightarrow T_{H_2} = 41$ K

23. **(5)**

Given, Angle of prism, $A = 1°$

Refractive index of prism, $\mu = 1.5$

For a thin prism, minimum angle of deviation is given by

$\delta = (\mu - 1)A$

$\Rightarrow \delta = (1.5 - 1) \times 1° = \dfrac{1}{2} = \dfrac{5}{10}$

$\Rightarrow N = 5.$

24. **2**

From the Einstein's photoelectric equation

Energy of photon

$=$ Kinetic energy of photoelectrons $+$ Work function

$\Rightarrow$ Kinetic energy $=$ Energy of Photon $-$ Work Function

Let ϕ_0 be the work function of metal and v_1 and v_2 be the velocity of photoelectrons. Using Einstein's photoelectric equation we have

$\dfrac{1}{2}mv_1^2 = 4 - \phi_0$ ...(i)

$\dfrac{1}{2}mv_2^2 = 2.5 - \phi_0$ ...(ii)

$\Rightarrow \dfrac{\frac{1}{2}mv_1^2}{\frac{1}{2}mv_2^2} = \dfrac{4 - \phi_0}{2.5 - \phi_0}$

$\Rightarrow (2)^2 = \dfrac{4 - \phi_0}{2.5 - \phi_0} \Rightarrow 10 - 4\phi_0 = 4 - \phi_0$

$\phi_0 = 2eV$

25. **(20)**

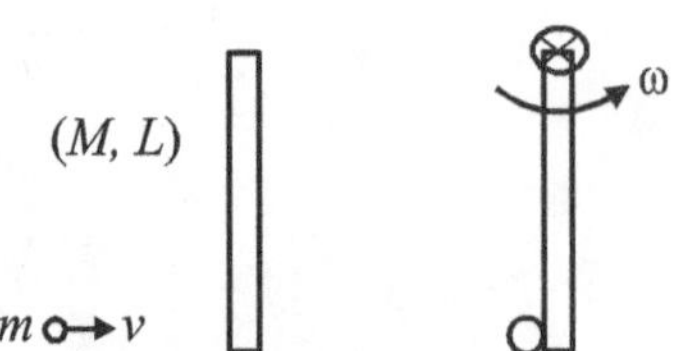

Using principal of conservation of angular momentum we have

$$\vec{L}_i = \vec{L}_f \Rightarrow mvL = I\omega$$

$$\Rightarrow mvL = \left(\frac{ML^2}{3} + mL^2\right)\omega$$

$$\Rightarrow 0.1 \times 80 \times 1 = \left(\frac{0.9 \times 1^2}{3} + 0.1 \times 1^2\right)\omega$$

$$\Rightarrow 8 = \left(\frac{3}{10} + \frac{1}{10}\right)\omega \Rightarrow 8 = \frac{4}{10}\omega$$

$$\Rightarrow \omega = 20 \ \text{rad/sec.}$$

CHEMISTRY

26. (4)

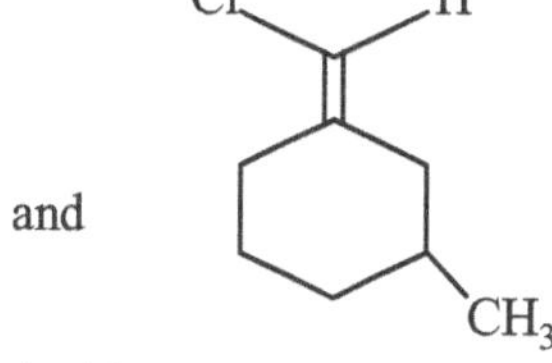

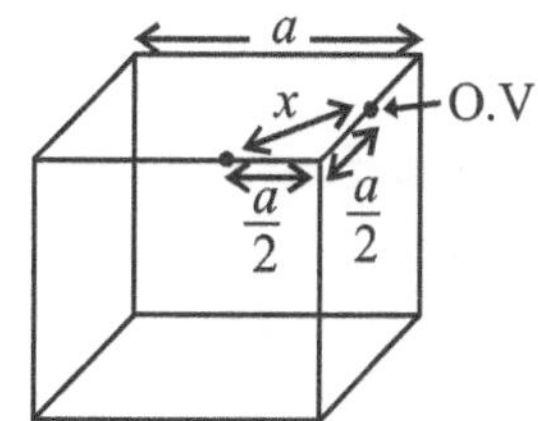

27. (b, c)

Geometrical isomers

Geometrical isomers

28. (1) As adsorption is exothermic process, hence $\dfrac{x}{m}$ decreases with increase of temperature.

29. (1)

Distance between two octahedral voids

$$x = \sqrt{\left(\frac{a}{2}\right)^2 + \left(\frac{a}{2}\right)^2} = \sqrt{\frac{a^2}{4} + \frac{a^2}{4}} = \frac{a}{\sqrt{2}}$$

30. (4) *trans*-$[Co(en)_2Cl_2]^+$ (A) contains a plane of symmetry so (A) cannot be optically active, whereas, (B) *cis* $[Co(en)_2Cl_2]^+$ does not contain any plane of symmetry, so (B) will be optically active.

31. (2) (II) and (III) compounds almost have same boiling point. In the given options, option (b) will be the correct answer.

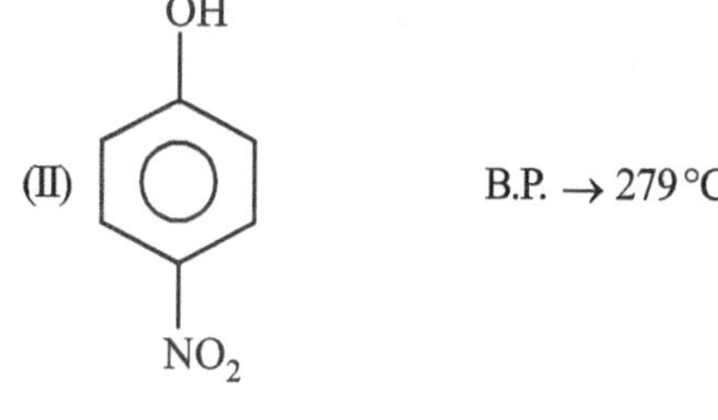

(I) B.P. $\rightarrow$ 202 °C

(II) B.P. $\rightarrow$ 279 °C

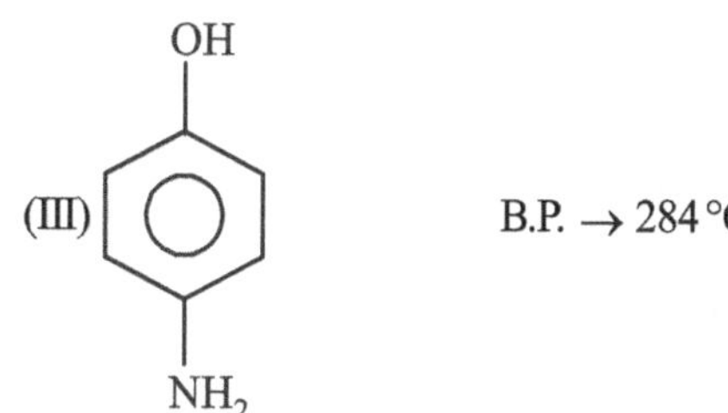

(III) B.P. $\rightarrow$ 284 °C

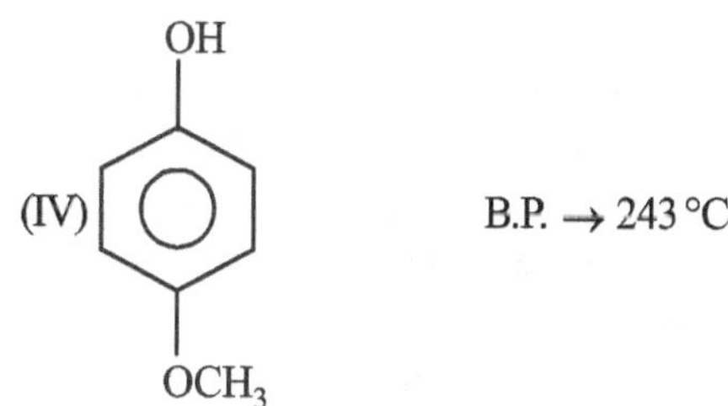

(IV) B.P. $\rightarrow$ 243 °C

32. **(3)** All are isoelectronic species, so more is the Z_{eff} less will be the ionic size.

$\therefore$ Correct order of ionic radii is

$Al^{3+} < Mg^{2+} < Na^{+} < F^{-} < O^{2-} < N^{3-}$

33. **(2)** Buna-N is obtained by addition polymerisation.

$$\underset{\text{1,3-Butadiene}}{nCH_2 = CH - CH = CH_2} + \underset{\text{Acrylonitrile}}{nCH_2 = \overset{\overset{\displaystyle CN}{|}}{CH}} \xrightarrow{\text{Copolymerisation}}$$

$$\underset{\text{Buna-N}}{\left(CH_2 - CH = CH - CH_2 - CH_2 - \overset{\overset{\displaystyle CN}{|}}{CH} \right)_n}$$

Nylon-6, bakelite, nylon-6. 6 are obtained by condensation polymerisation.

34. **(1)**

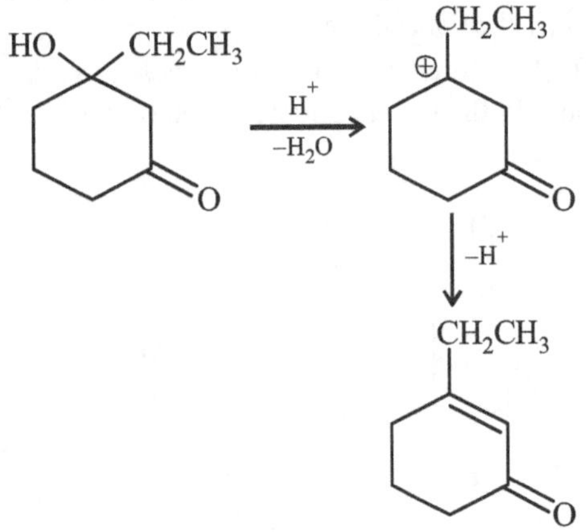

35. **(1)** H_2O_2 has open book like structure, which is non-planar. It is a colourless viscous liquid but in large quantity appears blue in colour.

36. **(4)** Arrhenius equation :

$$k = Ae^{-Ea/RT}$$

$$\ln k = \ln A - \left(\frac{E_a}{R}\right)\frac{1}{T}$$

$$\ln k = \ln A - \left(\frac{E_a}{R \times 10^3}\right) \times \frac{10^3}{T}$$

$$\text{Slope of graph} = \frac{-E_a}{R \times 10^3} = \frac{-10}{5}$$

$$E_a = 2R \times 10^3 \text{ J} = 2R \text{ kJ}$$

37. **(3)** $\Delta_{sol.}H° = \Delta_{lattice}H° + \Delta_{Hyd.}H°$

$4 = 788 + \Delta_{Hyd.}H°$

$\Delta_{Hyd.}H° = -784 \text{ kJmol}^{-1}$

38. **(1)** Clark's method is used to remove temporary hardness, using lime water (or) $Ca(OH)_2$ from water.

39. **(4)** H_2O - 104.5° (sp^3 with 2 lone pair at O)

NH_3 - 107° (sp^3 with 1 lone pair at N)

CH_4 - 109.5° (sp^3)

H_2S - 92° (sp^3 with 2 lone pair at O)

Lone pair-bond pair repulsion in H_2S will increase because 'S' has lower electronegativity than 'O'. So there will be lesser electron density on 'S' and thus H–S–H bond angle will be smaller than H_2O.

40. **(2)** Germanium (Ge), silicon (Si), boron (B), gallium (Ga) and indium (In) can be obtained in pure state by zone refining process.

41. **(3)** Radial node = $n - l - 1$

$\therefore 1s \Rightarrow 0(\psi^2 \neq 0)$

$2s \Rightarrow 1(\psi^2 = 0)$

$2p \Rightarrow 0(\psi^2 \neq 0)$

$3p \Rightarrow 1(\psi^2 = 0)$

Probability density (ψ^2) can be zero for $3p$ orbital other than infinite distance. It has one radial node.

Thus, statement (c) is correct.

42. **(4)** $CH_3CH = CHCH(CH_3)_2 \xrightarrow{H^+}$

$$\underset{\text{2° carbocation}}{CH_3CH_2 - \overset{+}{C}H - \underset{\underset{\displaystyle CH_3}{|}}{C}HCH_3} \xrightarrow{\text{1,2-H}^- \text{ shift}}$$

$$\underset{\text{3° carbocation}}{CH_3CH_2 - CH_2 - \underset{\underset{\displaystyle CH_3}{|}}{\overset{+}{C}}CH_3} \xrightarrow{Br^-} CH_3CH_2 - CH_2 - \underset{\underset{\displaystyle CH_3}{|}}{\overset{\overset{\displaystyle Br}{|}}{C}}CH_3$$

43. **(4)**

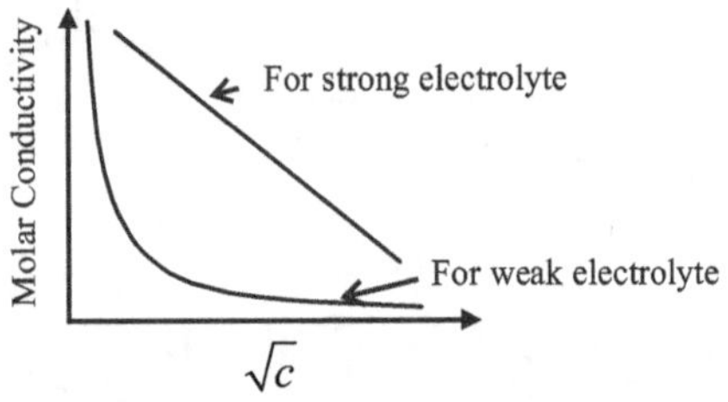

Among given electrolytes, CH_3COOH is weak electrolyte.

44. **(4)** Synthetic drugs, brompheniramine (dimetapp) acts as antihistamines.

45. **(4)** $NH_3 + \underset{\text{(excess)}}{3Cl_2} \longrightarrow NCl_3 + 3HCl$

If NH_3 is used in excess then NH_4Cl is formed instead of NCl_3.

$$\underset{\text{(excess)}}{8NH_3} + 3Cl_2 \longrightarrow 6NH_4Cl + N_2$$

46. **(50)**

M. eq. of $K_2Cr_2O_7$ = M. eq. of FeC_2O_4

$$FeC_2O_4 + Cr_2O_7^{2-} \longrightarrow Fe^{3+} + CO_2 + Cr^{3+}$$

$$V \times 0.02 \times 6 = \frac{0.288}{144} \times 3 \times 1000$$

V = 50 mL

47. **(– 13538)**

From $\Delta H° = \Delta U° + \Delta n_g RT$

$\Delta H° = -20 \times 1000 - 1 \times 8.314\,J/mol.K \times 298\,K$
$\quad = -22477.57\,J$

$\Delta G° = \Delta H° - T\Delta S° = -22477.57 - (298 \times -30)$
$\quad = -13538\,J$

48. **(0.0)**

$Ru^{2+} = 4d^6 = t_{2g}^6 e_g^0$ since $\Delta_0 > P$

No. of unpaired electrons $= 0$

$\therefore$ Magnetic moment $= 0$ B.M.

49. **(16)**

$$\begin{array}{cccc} & X + & Y \rightleftharpoons & 2Z \\ t=0 & 1\text{ mol} & 1.5\text{ mol} & 0.5\text{ mol} \\ t=t_{eq} & 1-a & 1.5-a & 0.5+2a \end{array}$$

$0.5 + 2a = 1;\ a = 0.25$

$$\begin{array}{cccc} X + & Y \rightleftharpoons & 2Z \\ 0.75 & 1.25 & 1 \end{array}$$

$K_{eq} = \dfrac{[Z]^2}{[X][Y]} = \dfrac{1}{0.75 \times [1.25]} = \dfrac{x}{15}$

$\Rightarrow x = \dfrac{15}{(0.75 \times 1.25)} = 16.$

50. **(9)**

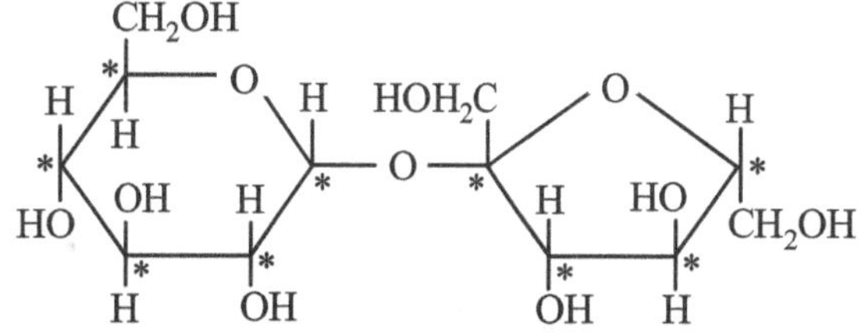

No. of chiral centres $= 9$.

MATHEMATICS

51. **(1)** Since, system of linear equations has non-zero solution

$\therefore \Delta = 0$

$$\Rightarrow \begin{vmatrix} 1 & 1 & 3 \\ 1 & 3 & k^2 \\ 3 & 1 & 3 \end{vmatrix} = 0$$

$\Rightarrow 1(9-k^2) - 1(3-3k^2) + 3(1-9) = 0$

$\Rightarrow 9 - k^2 - 3 + 3k^2 - 24 = 0$

$\Rightarrow 2k^2 = 18 \Rightarrow k^2 = 9,\ k = \pm 3$

So, equations are

$x + y + 3z = 0$ ...(i)

$x + 3y + 9z = 0$ ...(ii)

$3x + y + 3z = 0$ ...(iii)

Now, from equation (i) – (ii),

$-2y - 6z = 0 \Rightarrow y = -3z \Rightarrow \dfrac{y}{z} = -3$ ...(iv)

Now, from equation (i) – (iii),

$-2x = 0 \Rightarrow x = 0$

So, $x + \dfrac{y}{z} = 0 - 3 = -3$

52. **(4)** Let α and β be the roots of the quadratic equation

$7x^2 - 3x - 2 = 0$

$\therefore \alpha + \beta = \dfrac{3}{7},\ \alpha\beta = \dfrac{-2}{7}$

Now, $\dfrac{\alpha}{1-\alpha^2} + \dfrac{\beta}{1-\beta^2}$

$= \dfrac{\alpha - \alpha\beta(\alpha+\beta) + \beta}{1 - (\alpha^2 + \beta^2) + (\alpha\beta)^2}$

$= \dfrac{(\alpha+\beta) - \alpha\beta(\alpha+\beta)}{1 - (\alpha+\beta)^2 + 2\alpha\beta + (\alpha\beta)^2}$

$= \dfrac{\dfrac{3}{7} + \dfrac{2}{7} \times \dfrac{3}{7}}{1 - \dfrac{9}{49} + 2 \times \dfrac{-2}{7} + \dfrac{4}{49}} = \dfrac{27}{16}$

53. **(4)** The given function

$f(x) = (3x^2 + ax - 2 - a)e^x$

$f'(x) = (6x + a)e^x + (3x^2 + ax - 2 - a)e^x$

$f'(x) = [3x^2 + (a+6)x - 2]e^x$

$\because x = 1$ is critical point :

$\therefore f'(1) = 0$

$\Rightarrow (3 + a + 6 - 2) \cdot e = 0$

$\Rightarrow a = -7$ $(\because e > 0)$

$\therefore f'(x) = (3x^2 - x - 2)e^x$

$\quad = (3x+2)(x-1)e^x$

$$\overset{+\qquad\ -\qquad\ +}{\underset{-2/3 \quad\ 1}{\rule{4cm}{0.4pt}}}$$

$\therefore x = -\dfrac{2}{3}$ is point of local maxima.

and $x = 1$ is point of local minima.

54. **(1)** $[x] = 0$ when $x \in [0, 1)$ and $[x] = 1$ when $x \in [1, 2)$

$$y = \begin{cases} 0 & 0 \le x < 1 \\ x - 1 & 1 \le x < 2 \end{cases}$$

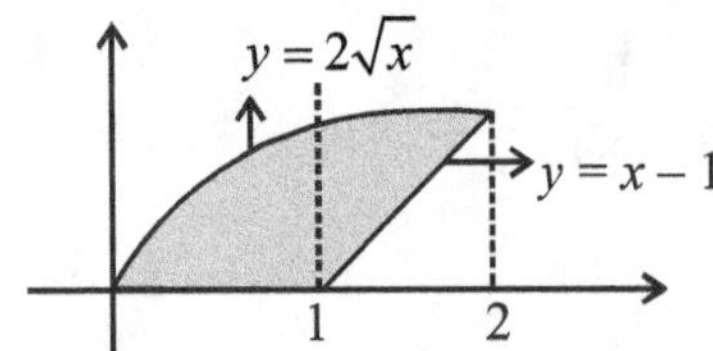

$$\therefore A = \int_0^2 2\sqrt{x}\, dx - \frac{1}{2}(1)(1)$$

$$= \frac{4x^{3/2}}{3}\Big|_0^2 - \frac{1}{2} = \frac{8\sqrt{2}}{3} - \frac{1}{2}$$

55. **(2)** Let the first term be 'a' and common ratio be 'r'.

$$\because ar(1 + r + r^2) = 3 \qquad \qquad ...(1)$$

and $ar^5(1 + r + r^2) = 243 \qquad ...(2)$

From (1) and (2),

$$r^4 = 81 \Rightarrow r = 3 \text{ and } a = \frac{1}{13}$$

$$\therefore S_{50} = \frac{a(r^{50} - 1)}{r - 1} = \frac{3^{50} - 1}{26} \qquad \left[\because S_n = \frac{a(r^n - 1)}{(r - 1)}\right]$$

56. **(3)** $\because -1 + \sqrt{3}i = 2 \cdot e^{\frac{2\pi}{3}i}$ and $1 - i = \sqrt{2} \cdot e^{\frac{-i\pi}{4}}$

$$\therefore \left(\frac{-1 + \sqrt{3}i}{1 - i}\right)^{30} = \left(\sqrt{2}e^{\left(\frac{2\pi}{3} + \frac{\pi}{4}\right)i}\right)^{30}$$

$$= 2^{15} \cdot e^{\frac{-\pi}{2}i} = -2^{15} \cdot i.$$

57. **(4)** $L + M = 1 - 2\sin^2\frac{\pi}{8} = \cos\frac{\pi}{4} = \frac{1}{\sqrt{2}} \qquad ...(i)$

and $L - M = -\cos\frac{\pi}{8} \qquad ...(ii)$

From equation (i) and (ii),

$$L = \frac{1}{2}\left(\frac{1}{\sqrt{2}} - \cos\frac{\pi}{8}\right) = \frac{1}{2\sqrt{2}} - \frac{1}{2}\cos\frac{\pi}{8} \text{ and}$$

$$M = \frac{1}{2}\left(\frac{1}{\sqrt{2}} + \cos\frac{\pi}{8}\right) = \frac{1}{2\sqrt{2}} + \frac{1}{2}\cos\frac{\pi}{8}$$

58. **(2)** Use properties of determinant

$$\begin{vmatrix} x & a+y & x+a \\ y & b+y & y+b \\ z & c+y & z+c \end{vmatrix} = \begin{vmatrix} x & a & x+a \\ y & b & y+b \\ z & c & z+c \end{vmatrix} + y\begin{vmatrix} x & 1 & x+a \\ y & 1 & y+b \\ z & 1 & z+c \end{vmatrix}$$

$$= 0 + y\begin{vmatrix} x & 1 & x+a \\ y-x & 0 & 0 \\ z-x & 0 & -1 \end{vmatrix} \qquad \begin{bmatrix} R_2 \to R_2 - R_1, \\ R_3 \to R_3 - R_1 \end{bmatrix}$$

$$= -y(x - y) = -y(b - a) = y(a - b)$$

59. **(3)** General tangent to hyperbola in slope form is

$$y = mx \pm \sqrt{100m^2 - 64}$$

and the general tangent to the circle in slope form is

$$y = mx \pm 6\sqrt{1 + m^2}$$

For common tangent,

$$36(1 + m^2) = 100m^2 - 64$$

$$\Rightarrow 100 = 64m^2 \Rightarrow m^2 = \frac{100}{64}$$

$$\therefore c^2 = 36\left(1 + \frac{100}{64}\right) = \frac{164 \times 36}{64} = \frac{369}{4}$$

$$\Rightarrow 4c^2 = 369$$

60. **(3)** The given curve is, $x^4 \cdot e^y + 2\sqrt{y + 1} = 3$

Differentiating w.r.t. x, we get

$$(4x^3 + x^4 \cdot y')e^y + \frac{y'}{\sqrt{1 + y}} = 0$$

$$\Rightarrow \left(\frac{dy}{dx}\right) = \frac{-4x^3 e^y}{\left(\dfrac{1}{\sqrt{y + 1}} + e^y x^4\right)}$$

$$\Rightarrow \left(\frac{dy}{dx}\right)_{(1,0)} = -2$$

$\therefore$ Equation of tangent;

$$y - 0 = -2(x - 1) \Rightarrow 2x + y = 2$$

Only point $(-2, 6)$ lies on the tangent.

61. **(4)** The truth table of $(p \to (q \to p)) \to (p \to (p \vee q))$ is

p	q	$p \vee q$	$p \to (p \vee q)$	$q \to p$	$p \to (q \to p)$	$(p \to (q \to p)) \to (p \to (p \vee q))$
T	T	O	T	T	T	T
T	F	T	T	T	T	T
F	T	T	T	F	T	T
F	F	F	T	T	T	T

Hence, the statement is tautology.

62. **(2)** Let $L = \lim_{x \to 0} \dfrac{x\left(e^{\frac{\sqrt{1 + x^2 + x^4} - 1}{x}} - 1\right)}{\sqrt{1 + x^2 + x^4} - 1}$

$$= \lim_{x \to 0} \frac{e^{\frac{\sqrt{1+x^2+x^4}-1}{x}}-1}{\frac{\sqrt{1+x^2+x^4}-1}{x}}$$

Put $\dfrac{\sqrt{1+x^2+x^4}-1}{x}=t$ when $x \to 0 \Rightarrow t \to 0$

$\therefore L = \lim_{t \to 0} \dfrac{e^t-1}{t}=1$

63. **(1)** $S = \log_7 x^2 + \log_7 x^3 + \log_7 x^4 + ...20$ terms

$\because S = 460$

$\Rightarrow \log_7(x^2 \cdot x^3 \cdot x^4 \cdot ......x^{21}) = 460$

$\Rightarrow \log_7 x^{(2+3+4......21)} = 460$

$\Rightarrow (2+3+4+.....+21)\log_7 x = 460$

$\Rightarrow \dfrac{20}{2}(2+21)\log_7 x = 460$

$\Rightarrow \log_7 x = \dfrac{460}{230}=2 \Rightarrow x=7^2=49$

64. **(4)** Let $u = \tan^{-1}\left(\dfrac{\sqrt{1+x^2}-1}{x}\right)$

Put $x = \tan\theta \Rightarrow \theta = \tan^{-1}x$

$\therefore u = \tan^{-1}\left(\dfrac{\sec\theta-1}{\tan\theta}\right)=\tan^{-1}\left(\tan\dfrac{\theta}{2}\right)$

$=\dfrac{\theta}{2}=\dfrac{1}{2}\tan^{-1}x$

$\therefore \dfrac{du}{dx}=\dfrac{1}{2}\times\dfrac{1}{(1+x^2)}$

Let $v = \tan^{-1}\left(\dfrac{2x\sqrt{1-x^2}}{1-2x^2}\right)$

Put $x = \sin\phi \Rightarrow \phi = \sin^{-1}x$

$v = \tan^{-1}\left(\dfrac{2\sin\phi\cos\phi}{\cos 2\phi}\right)=\tan^{-1}(\tan 2\phi)$

$=2\phi = 2\sin^{-1}x$

$\dfrac{dv}{dx}=2\dfrac{1}{\sqrt{1-x^2}}$

$\dfrac{du}{dv}=\dfrac{du/dx}{dv/dx}=\dfrac{\sqrt{1-x^2}}{4(1+x^2)}$

$\therefore \left(\dfrac{du}{dv}\right)_{\left(x=\frac{1}{2}\right)}=\dfrac{\sqrt{3}}{10}$

65. **(4)** Let $\sin\theta = t \Rightarrow \cos\theta\, d\theta = dt$

$$\int \frac{\cos\theta}{5+7\sin\theta-2\cos^2\theta}d\theta = \frac{dt}{5+7t-2+2t^2}$$

$$\Rightarrow \frac{1}{2}\int \frac{dt}{\left(t+\frac{7}{4}\right)^2-\left(\frac{5}{4}\right)^2}=\frac{1}{5}\ln\left|\frac{t+\frac{1}{2}}{t+3}\right|+C$$

$$=\frac{1}{5}\ln\left|\frac{2t+1}{t+3}\right|+C=\frac{1}{5}\ln\left|\frac{2\sin\theta+1}{\sin\theta+3}\right|+C$$

$\therefore B(\theta)=\dfrac{2\sin\theta+1}{2(\sin\theta+3)}$ and $A=\dfrac{1}{5}$

$\Rightarrow \dfrac{B(\theta)}{A}=\dfrac{5(2\sin\theta+1)}{(\sin\theta+3)}$

66. **(3)** $\dfrac{dy}{dx}+2y\tan x = 2\sin x$

I.F. $= e^{\int 2\tan x\,dx}=\sec^2 x$

The solution of the differential equation is

$y \times$ I.F. $= \int$ I.F. $\times 2\sin x\,dx + C$

$\Rightarrow y\cdot\sec^2 x = \int 2\sin x\cdot\sec^2 x\,dx + C$

$\Rightarrow y\sec^2 x = 2\sec x + C$ ...(i)

When $x = \dfrac{\pi}{3}$, $y = 0$; then $C = -4$

$\therefore$ From (i), $y\sec^2 x = 2\sec x - 4$

$\Rightarrow y = \dfrac{2\sec x - 4}{\sec^2 x} \Rightarrow y\left(\dfrac{\pi}{4}\right)=\sqrt{2}-2$

67. **(4)** In right ΔRSQ, $\sin 60° = \dfrac{RS}{r}$

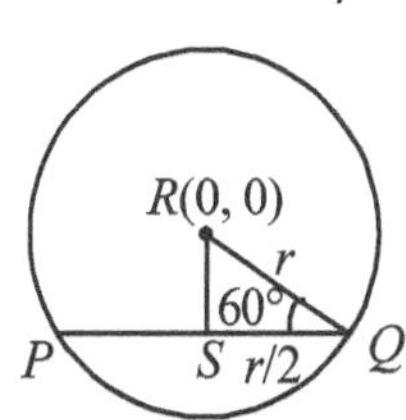

$\Rightarrow RS = r \times \dfrac{\sqrt{3}}{2}=\dfrac{\sqrt{3}r}{2}$

Now equation of PQ is $y - 2x - 3 = 0$

$\therefore \dfrac{\sqrt{3}r}{2}=\dfrac{|0+0-3|}{\sqrt{5}}$

$$\Rightarrow \frac{\sqrt{3}r}{2}=\frac{3}{\sqrt{5}}\Rightarrow r=\frac{2\sqrt{3}}{5}\Rightarrow r^2=\frac{12}{5}$$

68. **(3)** Mean $=\dfrac{3+5+7+a+b}{5}=5\Rightarrow a+b=10$

Variance $=\dfrac{3^2+5^2+7^2+a^2+b^2}{5}-(5)^2=4$

$\Rightarrow a^2+b^2=62$

$\Rightarrow (a+b)^2-2ab=62$

$\Rightarrow ab=19$

Hence, a and b are the roots of the equation,

$x^2-10x+19=0$.

69. **(2)** Since, lince are coplanar

$$\therefore \begin{vmatrix} 1 & 3 & 2 \\ 2 & -1 & 1 \\ \alpha & 5-\alpha & 1 \end{vmatrix}=0$$

$\Rightarrow 1(-1-5+\alpha)-3(2-\alpha)+2(10-2\alpha+\alpha)=0$

$\therefore \alpha=-4$

$\therefore$ Equation of $L_2:\dfrac{x+2}{-4}=\dfrac{y+1}{9}=\dfrac{z+1}{1}$

$\therefore$ Point $(2,-10,-2)$ lies on line L_2.

70. **(4)** Since, each section has 5 questions.

$\therefore$ Total number of selection of 5 questions

$=3\times{}^5C_1\times{}^5C_1\times{}^5C_3+3\times{}^5C_1\times{}^5C_2\times{}^5C_2$

$=3\times5\times5\times10+3\times5\times10\times10$

$=750+1500=2250$.

71. **(120.00)**

Coefficient of x^4 in $\left(\dfrac{1-x^4}{1-x}\right)^6$ = coefficient of x^4 in

$(1-6x^4)(1-x)^{-6}$

$=$ coefficient of x^4 in $(1-6x^4)\left[1+{}^6C_1x+{}^7C_2x^2+....\right]$

$={}^9C_4-6\cdot1=126-6=120$.

72. **(11.00)**

Let 'n' bombs are required, then

$$1-{}^nC_1\cdot\left(\frac{1}{2}\right)^1\left(\frac{1}{2}\right)^{n-1}-{}^nC_0\left(\frac{1}{2}\right)^0\left(\frac{1}{2}\right)^n\geq\frac{99}{100}$$

$\Rightarrow \dfrac{1}{100}\geq\dfrac{n+1}{2^n}\Rightarrow 2^n\geq100(n+1)\Rightarrow n\geq11$

73. **(0.50)**

The given curve $y=(x-1)(x-2)$, intersects the x-axis at $A(1,0)$ and $B(2,0)$.

$\therefore \dfrac{dy}{dx}=2x-3;\left(\dfrac{dy}{dx}\right)_{(x=1)}=-1$ and $\left(\dfrac{dy}{dx}\right)_{(x=2)}=1$

Equation of tangent at $A(1,0)$,

$y=-1(x-1)\Rightarrow x+y=1$

Equation of tangent at $B(2,0)$,

$y=1(x-2)\Rightarrow x-y=2$

So $a=1$ and $b=2$

$\Rightarrow \dfrac{a}{b}=\dfrac{1}{2}=0.5$.

74. **(6.00)**

$\because$ Projection of $\vec{b}$ on $\vec{a}$ = Projection of $\vec{c}$ on $\vec{a}$

$\therefore \vec{a}\cdot\vec{b}=\vec{a}\cdot\vec{c}$

Given, $\vec{b}\cdot\vec{c}=0$

$\because |\vec{a}+\vec{b}-\vec{c}|^2=|\vec{a}|^2+|\vec{b}|^2+|\vec{c}|^2+2\vec{a}\cdot\vec{b}-2\vec{b}\cdot\vec{c}-2\vec{a}\cdot\vec{c}$

$=4+16+16=36$.

$\Rightarrow |\vec{a}+\vec{b}-\vec{c}|^2=6$

75. **(19.00)**

The desired functions will contain either one element or two elements in its codomain of which '2' always belongs to $f(A)$.

$\therefore$ The set B can be $\{2\}$, $\{1,2\}$, $\{2,3\}$, $\{2,4\}$

Total number of functions $=1+(2^3-2)3=19$.

PHYSICS

1. **(2)** Given : No. of division on circular scale of screw gauge $= 50$

Pitch $= 0.5$ mm

Least count of screw gauge

$$= \frac{\text{Pitch}}{\text{No. of division on circular scale}}$$

$$= \frac{0.5}{50} \text{ mm} = 1 \times 10^5 \text{ m} = 10 \ \mu\text{m}$$

And nature of zero error is positive.

2. **(2)** Frequency heard by the observer

$$v_{\text{observed}} = \left(\frac{v_{\text{sound}}}{v_{\text{sound}} - v\cos\theta} \right) v_0$$

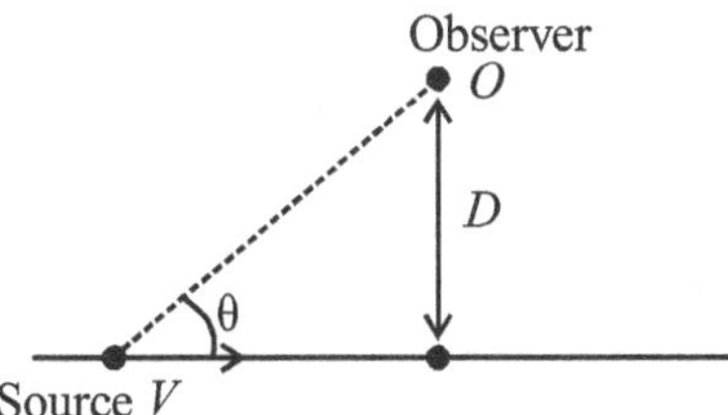

Initially θ will be less so $\cos\theta$ more.

$\therefore v_{\text{observed}}$ more, then it will decrease.

3. **(2)** For (A)

$x_P - x_Q = (d + 2.5) - (d - 2.5) = 5$ m

Phase difference $\Delta\phi$ due to path difference

$$= \frac{2\pi}{\lambda}(\Delta x) = \frac{2\pi}{20}(5) = \frac{\pi}{2}.$$

At A, Q is ahead of P by path, as wave emitted by Q reaches before wave emitted by P.

$\therefore$ Total phase difference at A $\dfrac{\pi}{2} - \dfrac{\pi}{2} = 0$

(due to P being ahead of Q by 90°)

$$I_A = I_1 + I_2 + 2\sqrt{I_1}\sqrt{I_2} \cos\Delta\phi$$

$$= I + I + 2\sqrt{I}\sqrt{I} \cos(0) = 4I$$

For C,

Path difference, $x_Q - x_P = 5$ m

Phase difference $\Delta\phi$ due to path difference

$$= \frac{2\pi}{\lambda}(\Delta x) = \frac{2\pi}{20}(5) = \frac{\pi}{2}$$

Total phase difference at $C = \dfrac{\pi}{2} + \dfrac{\pi}{2} = \pi$

$$I_{\text{net}} = I_1 + I_2 + 2\sqrt{I_1}\sqrt{I_2} \cos(\Delta\phi)$$

$$= I + I + 2\sqrt{I}\sqrt{I} \cos(\pi) = 0$$

For B,

Path difference, $x_P - x_Q = 0$

Phase difference, $\Delta\phi = \dfrac{\pi}{2}$

(due to P being ahead of Q by 90°)

$$I_B = I + I + 2\sqrt{I}\sqrt{I} \cos\frac{\pi}{2} = 2I$$

Therefore intensities of radiation at A, B and C will be in the ratio

$$I_A : I_B : I_C = 4I : 2I : 0 = 2 : 1 : 0.$$

4. **(3)** Given : $U = \dfrac{-A}{r^6} + \dfrac{B}{r^{12}}$

For equilibrium,

$$F = \frac{dU}{dr} = -(A(-6r^{-7})) + B(-12r^{-13}) = 0$$

$$\Rightarrow 0 = \frac{6A}{r^7} - \frac{12B}{r^{13}} \Rightarrow \frac{6A}{12B} = \frac{1}{r^6}$$

$\therefore$ Separation between molecules, $r = \left(\dfrac{2B}{A} \right)^{1/6}$

Potential energy,

$$U\left(r = \left(\frac{2B}{A} \right)^{1/6} \right) = -\frac{A}{2B/A} + \frac{B}{4B^2/A^2}$$

$$= \frac{-A^2}{2B} + \frac{A^2}{4B} = \frac{-A^2}{4B}$$

5. **(1)** Quality factor,

$$Q = \frac{1}{R}\sqrt{\frac{L}{C}} = \frac{1}{100}\sqrt{\frac{80 \times 10^{-3}}{2 \times 10^{-6}}}$$

$$= \frac{1}{100}\sqrt{40 \times 10^3} = \frac{200}{100} = 2$$

6. **(3)** Electric field due charge Q_2, $E_2 = \dfrac{kQ_2}{x_2^2}$

Electric field due charge Q_1, $E_1 = \dfrac{kQ_1}{x_1^2}$

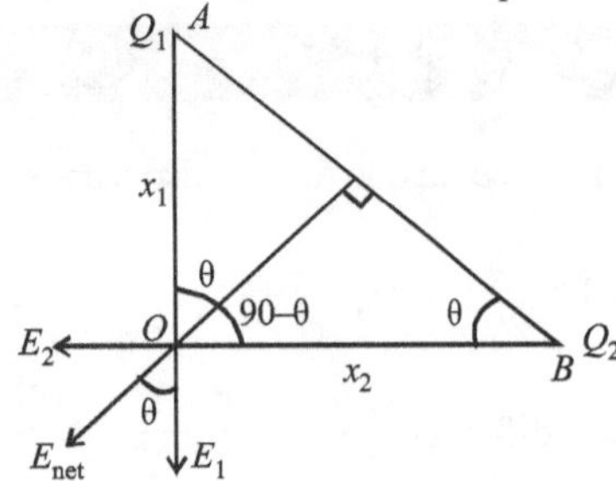

From figure,

$$\tan\theta = \frac{E_2}{E_1} = \frac{x_1}{x_2} \Rightarrow \frac{kQ_2}{x_2^2 \times \dfrac{kQ_1}{x_1^2}} = \frac{x_1}{x_2}$$

$$\Rightarrow \frac{Q_2 x_1^2}{Q_1 x_2^2} = \frac{x_1}{x_2} \Rightarrow \frac{Q_2}{Q_1} = \frac{x_2}{x_1} \text{ or, } \frac{Q_1}{Q_2} = \frac{x_1}{x_2}.$$

7. **(4)** Hollow ice-cream cone can be assume as several parts of discs having different radius, so

$$I = \int dI = \int dm(r^2) \qquad \qquad ...(i)$$

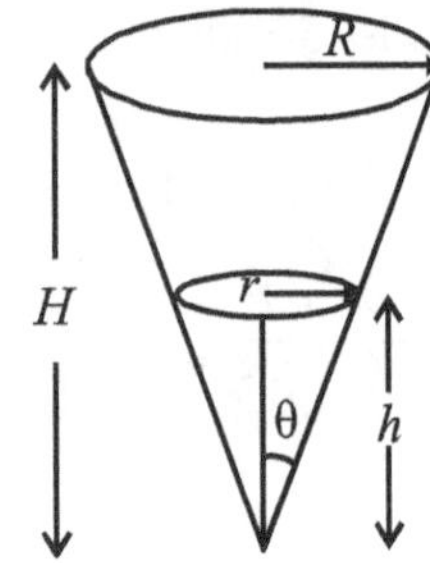

From diagram,

$$\frac{r}{h} = \tan\theta = \frac{R}{H} \text{ or } r = \frac{R}{H}h \qquad ...(ii)$$

Mass of element, $dm = \rho(\pi r^2)dh \qquad ...(iii)$

From eq. (i), (ii) and (iii),

Area of element, $dA = 2\pi r dl = 2\pi r \dfrac{dh}{\cos\theta}$

Mass of element, $dm = \dfrac{2Mh\tan dh}{R\sqrt{R^2 + H^2}\,\cos\theta}$

(here, $r = h\tan\theta$)

$$I = \int dI = \int_0^H dm(r^2) = \int_0^H \rho(\pi r^2)dh\left(\frac{R}{H}\cdot h\right)^2$$

$$= \int_0^H \rho\left(\pi\left(\frac{R}{H}\cdot h\right)^4\right)dh$$

Solving we get, $I = \dfrac{MR^2}{2}$

8. **(3)** Angular momentum, $L = I\omega$

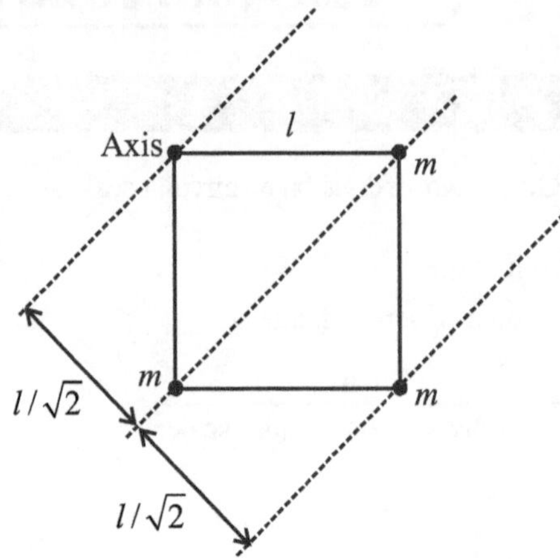

$$I = m(0)^2 + m\left(\frac{l}{\sqrt{2}}\right)^2 \times 2 + m(\sqrt{2}l)^2$$

$$= \frac{2ml^2}{2} + 2ml^2 = 3ml^2$$

Angular momentum $L = I\omega = 3ml^2\omega$

9. **(1)** When first pulse is applied, the potential across capacitor

$$V_0(t) = V_{in}\left(1 - e^{\frac{1}{RC}}\right)$$

At $t = 5\mu s = 5\times 10^{-6}\,s$

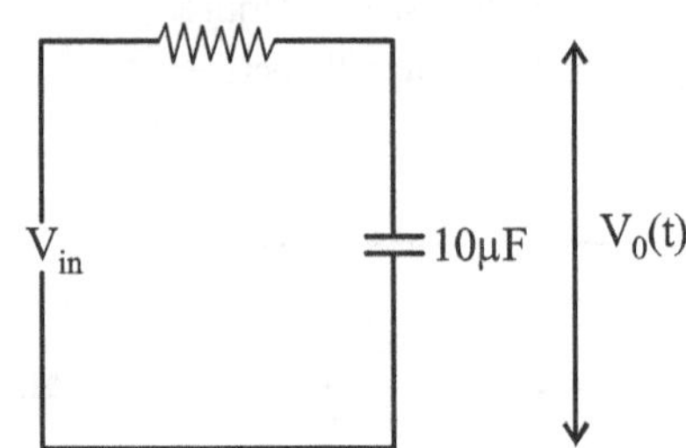

$$V_0(t) = 5\left(1 - e^{\frac{5\times 10^{-6}}{10^3 \times 10\times 10^{-9}}}\right) = 5(1 - e^{-0.5}) = 2V$$

When no pulse is applied, capacitor will discharge. Now, $V_{in} = 0$ means discharging.

$$V_0(t) = 2e^{\frac{1}{RC}} = 2e^{-0.5} = 1.21 \text{ V}$$

Now for next 5 µs

$$V_0(t) = 5 - 3.79e^{\frac{1}{RC}}$$

After 5 µs again, $V_0(t) = 2.79$ Volt ≈ 3 V

Hence, graph (a) correctly depicts.

10. **(3)** In uniform magnetic field particle moves in a circular path, if the radius of the circular path is 'r', particle will not hit the screen.

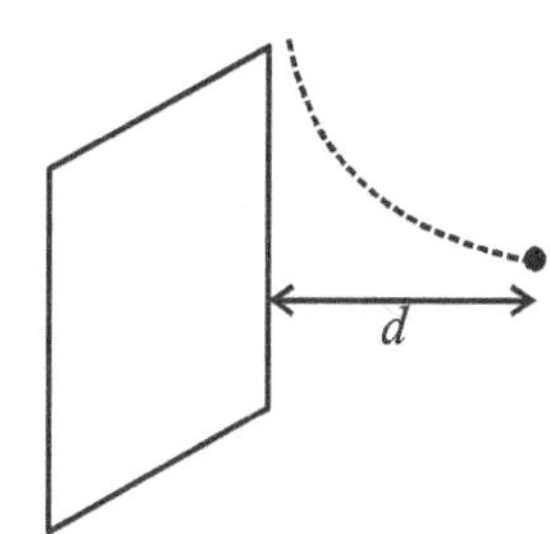

$$r = \frac{mv}{qB_0} \qquad \left[\because \frac{mv^2}{r} = qvB_0\right]$$

Hence, minimum value of v for which the particle will not hit the screen.

$$v = \frac{qB_0 d}{m}$$

11. (1) For balancing, $mg\sin\theta = f = \mu mg\cos\theta$

$$\Rightarrow \tan\theta = \mu = \frac{3}{4} = 0.75$$

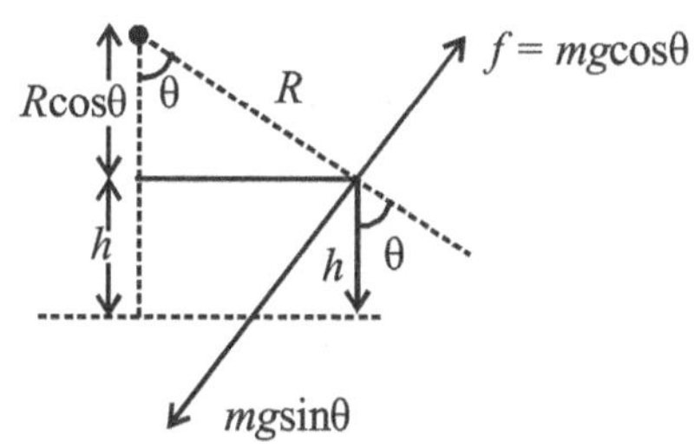

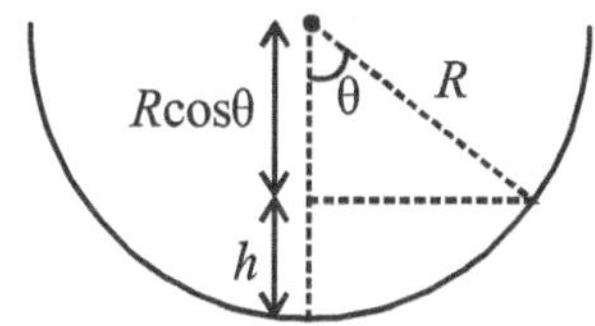

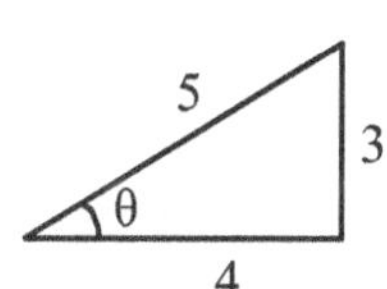

$$h = R - R\cos\theta = R - R\left(\frac{4}{5}\right) = \frac{R}{5}$$

$$\therefore h = \frac{R}{5} = 0.2 \text{ m} \qquad [\because \text{ radius, } R = 1\text{m}]$$

12. (1) By angular momentum conservation

$$r_{\min} v_{\max} = m r_{\max} v_{\min}$$

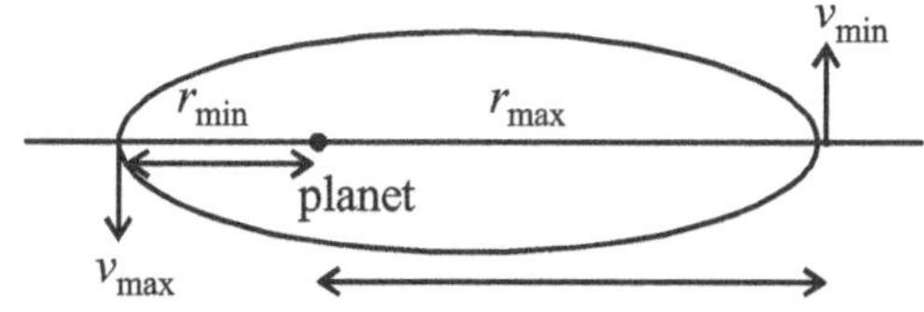

Given, $v_{\min} = \dfrac{v_{\max}}{6}$

$$\therefore \frac{r_{\min}}{r_{\max}} = \frac{v_{\min}}{v_{\max}} = \frac{1}{6}$$

13. (3) de-Broglie wavelength, $\lambda = \dfrac{h}{P} = \dfrac{h}{\sqrt{2m(\text{KE})}}$

$$\therefore \lambda \propto \frac{1}{\sqrt{m}}$$

As $m_{\text{He}^{++}} > m_P > m_e$

$$\lambda_{\text{He}^{++}} > \lambda_P > \lambda_e \text{ or } \lambda_e > \lambda_P > \lambda_{\text{He}^{++}}$$

14. (1) Here, $R = 0.1$ m

$$\omega = \frac{2\pi}{T} = \frac{2\pi}{60} = 0.105 \text{ rad/s}$$

Acceleration of the tip of the clock second's hand,

$$a = \omega^2 R = (0.105)^2 (0.1) = 0.0011 = 1.1 \times 10^{-3} \text{ m/s}^2$$

Hence, average acceleration is of the order of 10^{-3}.

15. (4) $_3^7\text{Li} + _1^1\text{H} \longrightarrow 2\left(_2^4\text{He}\right)$

$$\Delta m \rightarrow [m_{\text{Li}} + m_{\text{H}}] - 2[M_{\text{He}}]$$

Energy released $= \Delta m c^2$

In use of 1 g Li energy released $= \dfrac{\Delta m c^2}{m_{\text{Li}}}$

In use of 20 g energy released $= \dfrac{\Delta m c^2}{m_{\text{Li}}} \times 20$ g

$$= \frac{[(7.016 + 1.0079) - 2 \times 4.0026] u \times c^2}{7.016 \times 1.6 \times 10^{-24}} \times 20 \text{ g}$$

$$= \left(\frac{0.0187 \times 1.6 \times 10^{-19} \times 10^9}{7.016 \times 1.6 \times 10^{-24}} \times 20\right) = 480 \times 10^{10} \text{J}$$

$$\because 1 \text{ J} = 2.778 \times 10^{-7} \text{ kWh}$$

$\therefore$ Energy released $= 480 \times 10^{10} \times 2.778 \times 10^{-7}$
$$= 1.33 \times 10^6 \text{ kWh}$$

16. (4) Focal length of the convex lens, $f = 0.5$ m
Object is at $2f$ so, image (I_1) will also be at $2f$.
Image of I_1 i.e., I_2 will be 1 m behind mirror.
Now I_2 will be object for lens.

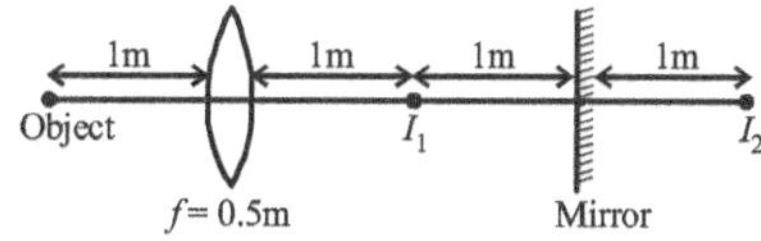

$$\therefore u = (-1) + (-1) + (-1) = -3 \text{ m}$$

Using lens formula, $\dfrac{1}{v} - \dfrac{1}{u} = \dfrac{1}{f}$

$$\frac{1}{v} = \frac{1}{f} + \frac{1}{u} = \frac{1}{+0.5} + \frac{1}{-3} \text{ or } v = \frac{3}{5} = 0.6 \text{ m}$$

Hence, distance of image from mirror
$$= 2 + 0.6 = 2.6 \text{ m and real.}$$

17. **(1)** Boolean expression,

$$y = \overline{\overline{A} \cdot \overline{B}} = \overline{\overline{A}} + \overline{\overline{B}} = A + B$$

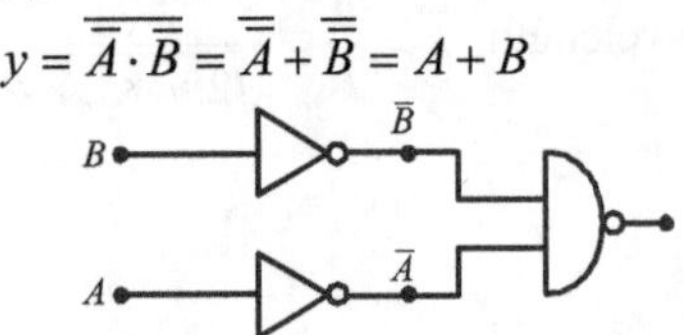

Truth table :

A	B	Y
0	1	1
1	0	1
0	0	0
1	1	1

$$y = A + B$$

18. **(3)** Total degree of freedom $f = 3 + 2 = 5$

Total energy, $U = \dfrac{nfRT}{2} = \dfrac{5RT}{2}$

And $\gamma = \dfrac{C_p}{C_v} = 1 + \dfrac{2}{f} = 1 + \dfrac{2}{5} = \dfrac{7}{5}$

19. **(1)** An elastic wire can be treated as a spring and its spring constant.

$$k = \frac{YA}{L} \qquad \left[\because Y = \frac{F}{A} \bigg/ \frac{\Delta l}{l_0} \right]$$

Frequency of oscillation,

$$f = \frac{1}{2\pi} \sqrt{\frac{k}{m}} = \frac{1}{2\pi} \sqrt{\frac{YA}{mL}}$$

20. **(3)** $\vec{E} = 300\hat{j}$ V/cm $= 3 \times 10^4$ V/m

$$\vec{V} = 6 \times 10^6 \hat{i}$$

$\vec{B}$ must be in $+z$ axis.

$$q\vec{E} + q\vec{V} \times \vec{B} = 0$$
$$E = VB$$

$$\therefore B = \frac{E}{V} = \frac{3 \times 10^4}{6 \times 10^6} = 5 \times 10^{-3}\,T$$

Hence, magnetic field $B = 5 \times 10^{-3}$ T along $+z$ direction.

21. **(1050)**

Density, $\rho = \dfrac{M}{V} = \dfrac{M}{\dfrac{4}{3}\pi\left(\dfrac{D}{2}\right)^3} \Rightarrow \rho = \dfrac{6}{\pi} MD^{-3}$

$$\therefore \% \left(\frac{\Delta\rho}{\rho}\right) = \frac{\Delta m}{m} + 3\left(\frac{\Delta D}{D}\right) = 6 + 3 \times 1.5 = 10.5\%$$

$$\% \left(\frac{\Delta\rho}{\rho}\right) = \frac{1050}{100}\% = \left(\frac{x}{100}\right)\%$$

$$\therefore x = 1050.00$$

22. **(120)**

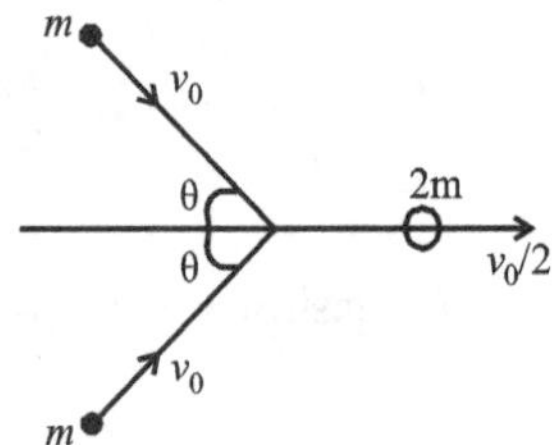

Momentum conservation along x direction,

$$2mv_0 \cos\theta = 2m\frac{v_0}{2} \Rightarrow \cos\theta = \frac{1}{2} \text{ or } \theta = 60°$$

Hence angle between the initial velocities of the two bodies

$$= \theta + \theta = 60° + 60° = 120°.$$

23. **(270)**

Using, intensity, $I = \dfrac{1}{2}C \in_0 E_{rms}^2$

$$\Rightarrow \frac{1}{2}C \in_0 E_{rms}^2 = \frac{315}{\pi}$$

$$E_{rms} = \sqrt{\frac{315 \times 2}{\pi \times 3 \times 10^8 \times 8.86 \times 10^{-12}}}$$

$$= \sqrt{\frac{630}{83.4612 \times 10^{-4}}} = \sqrt{7.5484 \times 10^4}$$

$$= 2.75 \times 10^2 = 275\ \text{V/m}$$

24. **(5)**

Using ideal gas equation, $PV = nRT$

$$\Rightarrow P_1 V_1 = nR \times 250 \qquad [\because T_1 = 250\ \text{K}] \qquad ...(i)$$

$$P_2(2V_1) = \frac{5n}{4}R \times 2000 \qquad [\because T_2 = 2000\ \text{K}] \qquad ...(ii)$$

Dividing eq. (i) by (ii),

$$\frac{P_1}{2P_2} = \frac{4 \times 250}{5 \times 2000} \Rightarrow \frac{P_1}{P_2} = \frac{1}{5}$$

$$\therefore \frac{P_2}{P_1} = 5.$$

25. **(33)**

Here, $L = 50\ \text{mH} = 50 \times 10^{-3}\ \text{H}; I = 1\ \text{A}, R = 2\Omega$

$$V_P - L\frac{dI}{dt} - 30 + RI = V_Q$$

$$\Rightarrow V_P - V_Q = 50 \times 10^{-3} \times 10^2 + 30 - 1 \times 2$$

$$= 5 + 30 - 2 = 33\ \text{V}.$$

CHEMISTRY

26. (4)

(a) N_2 is diamagnetic in nature.

(b) $N_2 + O_2 \underset{2000K}{\rightleftharpoons} NO\,(g)$

(c) Liquid N_2 is used in cryosurgery.

(4) Because of its inertness, it is used where an inert atmosphere is required.

27. (4)

$$\text{(A)} \xrightarrow{\text{Ozonolysis}} \text{(B)} + \text{(C)}$$

(B) $\xrightarrow{I_2 + NaOH}$ $HCOO^- Na^+ + CHI_3$ (Yellow ppt)

$\xrightarrow{Ag_2O}$ $CH_3COO^- + Ag\downarrow$ (Silver mirror)

(C) $\xrightarrow{I_2 + NaOH}$ No yellow ppt

$\xrightarrow{LiAlH_4}$ $C_2H_5 - CH(OH) - C_2H_5$ $\xrightarrow[\text{HCl}]{ZnCl_2}$

Lucas test

$C_2H_5 - CH(Cl) - C_2H_5$

(Turbidity in 5 min.)

28. (1)

29. (3)

	1st component	2nd component
mole	n_1	n_2
m.w	M_1	M_2
mass	n_1M_1	n_2M_2

[$\because$ mass = mole × m.w.]

Mass of solution $= n_1M_1 + n_2M_2$

Mole fraction of the 2nd component $(x_2) = \dfrac{n_2}{n_1 + n_2}$

$\Rightarrow n_1 = \dfrac{n_2(1 - x_2)}{x_2}$

Mass of solution $= n_1M_1 + n_2M_2$

$= \dfrac{n_2M_1(1 - x_2)}{x_2} + n_2M_2$

$= \dfrac{n_2}{x_2}[M_2x_2 - x_2M_1 + M_1]$

Volume of solution $= \dfrac{n_2[M_2x_2 - x_2M_1 + M_1]}{1000dx_2}$

$C_2 = \dfrac{1000n_2dx_2}{n_2[M_2x_2 - x_2M_1 + M_1]}$

$\Rightarrow C_2 = \dfrac{1000dx_2}{M_1 + x_2(M_2 - M_1)}$

30. (4)

(a) Bronze contains 88-96% Cu and 4-12% Sn.

(b) Cast iron is used to make wraught iron.

(c) German silver contains 50% Cu, 30% Zn & 20% Ni.

(d) Brass contains 70% Cu and 30% Zn.

31. (3) High density polythene is formed when addition polymerisation of ethene takes place in the presence of a catalyst (Ziegler Natta catalyst) at a high temp. (333K to 349 K) and under low pressure (6-7 atm).

High density polyethene is hard and chemically inert due to close packing thats why used to make buckets and dustbins.

32. (2)

(A) 0.01 M HCl

$[H^+] = 10^{-2}$, $pH = -\log 10^{-2} = 2$

$pOH = 14 - 2 = 12$

(B) 0.01 M NaOH

$[OH^-] = 10^{-2}$, $pOH = -\log[OH] = 2$

(C) 0.01 M CH_3COONa

$pH = 7 + \dfrac{1}{2}[pK_a + \log 0.01]$

$pH > 7 \Rightarrow pOH < 7$

(D) 0.01 M NaCl, $pH = 7$, $pOH = 7$

Decreasing order of pOH value is,

(A) > (D) > (C) > (B).

33. (3) $BeSO_4$ and $MgSO_4$ are readily soluble in water due to greater hydration enthalpies of Be^{2+} and Mg^{2+} ions, dominate over their lattice enthalpies and therefore their sulphates are highly soluble.

34. (4)

35. (4)

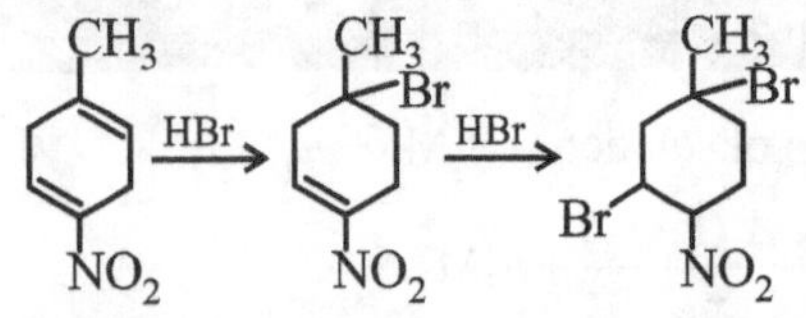

(Reaction scheme: 4-nitrotoluene → addition of HBr → dibromo product, via the intermediate shown with CH₃, Br, NO₂ substituents)

36. (4) Fluoride (F^-) ion conc. upto 1 ppm makes the enamel of teeth much harder by converting

$$[3(Ca_3(PO_4)_2)\cdot Ca(OH)_2] \xrightarrow{\ F^-\ } [3(Ca_3(PO_4)_2)\cdot CaF_2]$$

hydroxyapatite   Fluorapatite (harder)

But above 2 ppm cause brown motting of teeth.

37. (2)

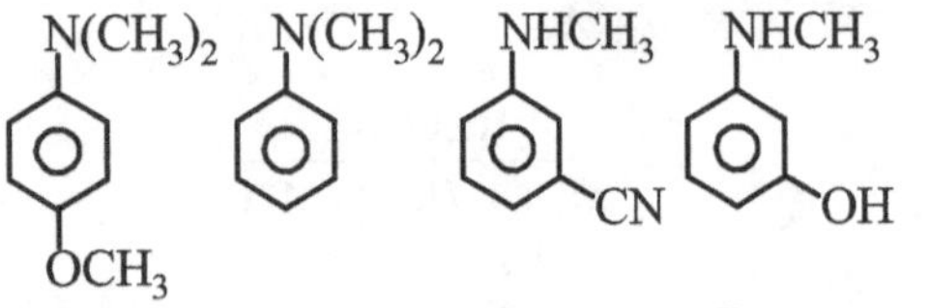

(Four structures: I – $N(CH_3)_2$ with OCH_3; II – $N(CH_3)_2$; III – $NHCH_3$ with CN; IV – $NHCH_3$ with OH)

I   II   III   IV

+R effect   (–I effect   (–I effect
and –I effect   of –CN   of –OH
of –OCH_3 group)   group)

– OCH_3 group increases electron density of ring at *o*- and *p*- position making (I) most basic. (III) is least basic due to –I effect of –CN group at meta position.

Since, –I effect of –CN > –I effect of –OH group.

Hence, correct basic strength will follow the order

$$I > II > IV > III$$

Basic strength $\propto \dfrac{1}{pK_b \text{ value}}$

Order of K_b value is, $I < II < IV < III$.

38. (2)

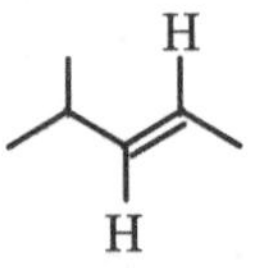

(Structure: 4-Methylpent-2-ene)

4-Methylpent-2-ene

(trans and cis structures)

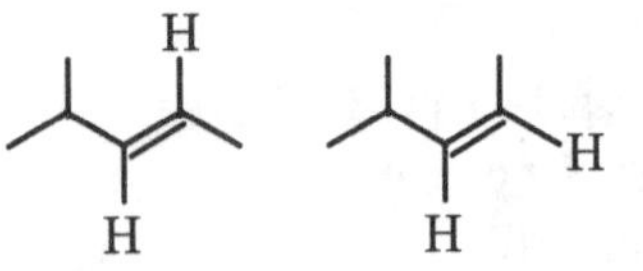

trans   *cis*

Geometrical isomers

39. (2) Elements with atomic number 21, 25, 42 and 72 belongs to transition metals.

40. (3) $\Delta G^\circ = -RT \ln K$, $T_1 = 25^\circ C$, $K_1 = 10$

ΔG° at $T_1 = -8.314 \times 298 \times 2.303 \times \log 10 = -5.71$ kJ/mol

ΔG° at $T_2 = -8.314 \times 298 \times 373 \times 2.303 \times \log(100)$
$= -14.29$ kJ/mol

$\Delta G^\circ = \Delta H^\circ - T\Delta S^\circ$

$\Rightarrow -5.71 = \Delta H^\circ - 298(\Delta S^\circ)$

$\Rightarrow -14.29 = \Delta H^\circ - 373(\Delta S^\circ)$

$\Delta H^\circ = 28.4$ kJ/mol

41. (1) Above Kraft temperature the formation of micelles takes place and the conc. above which micelle formation become appreciable is called critical micelles conc.

42. (3) $K_p = K_C (RT)^{\Delta n_g} = K_C(RT)^{1-3/2} = K_C(RT)^{-1/2}$

$\Rightarrow K_C = K_p (RT)^{1/2}$

43. (4) $[MnBr_4]^{2-} \Rightarrow Mn^{2+} \Rightarrow d^5 (Td)$

[∵ Br is weak field ligand]
$d^5(Td)$ is high spin complex.
So, $\mu = \sqrt{5(5+2)} = 5.91$ B.M.

44. (3) Europium (Eu)
Atomic No. - 63
Electronic configuration - $[Xe]4f^7 6s^2$
It shows only +2 and +3 oxidation state.

45. (4) Rate $= k\,[A]^n$
$\log[\text{Rate}] = \log k + n \log [A]$
Slope $= n$ [n is order of the reaction]
∴ Correct sequence for the order of the reaction is
(iv) > (ii) > (i) > (iii)

46. (50)
Mass of organic compound = 1.6 g
Mass of AgBr = 1.88 g

Moles of Br = Moles of AgBr = $\dfrac{1.88}{188} = 0.01$

Mass of Br = $0.01 \times 80 = 0.80$ g

% of Br = $\dfrac{0.80 \times 100}{1.60} = 50\%$

Alternate Method :

% of Br $= \dfrac{\text{Wt. of AgBr}}{\text{Wt. of O.C.}} \times \dfrac{\text{Molar mass of Br}}{\text{AgBr}} \times 100$

$= \dfrac{1.88}{1.6} \times \dfrac{80}{188} \times 100 = 50\%$

47. (11)

$$6OH^- + Cl^- \longrightarrow ClO_3^- + 3H_2O + 6e^-$$

For synthesis of 1 mole of ClO_3^-, 6F of charge is required.

∵ Current efficiency = 60%

∴ To synthesis 1 mole of ClO_3^-, 10F of charge is required.

To synthesis $\dfrac{10}{122}$ moles of $KClO_3$, charge $= \dfrac{10 \times 10}{122}$ F

$Q = I. t$

$$t = \frac{100 \times 96500}{122 \times 2} = 39549.18 \text{ s}$$

$$= \frac{79098.365}{3600\,\text{s}} = 10.99\,\text{h}$$

$$\therefore t = 11\,\text{h}.$$

48. (3)

The structure of perchloric acid is

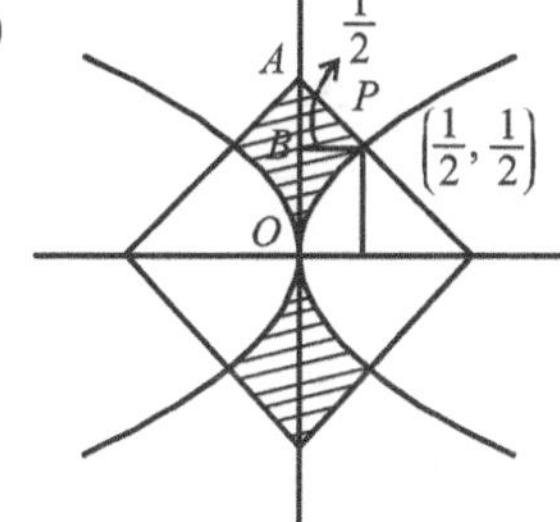

The number $Cl = O$ bond in $HClO_4$ is 3.

49. (5.0)

Molality of $CaCl_2$ solution $= 0.05$ m

$$\Delta T_b = iK_b m = 3 \times K_b \times 0.05 = 0.15\,K_b$$

Molality of $CrCl_3.x NH_3 = 0.10$ m

$$\Delta T_b' = iK_b \times 0.10 \Rightarrow \Delta T_b' = 2\Delta T_b$$

$$iK_b \times 0.10 = 2 \times 0.15\,K_b \Rightarrow i = 3$$

Since, co-ordination number of Cr is 6.

$\therefore$ The complex is $[Cr(NH_3)_5Cl]Cl_2$.

$\therefore x = 5$.

50. (750)

At constant temperature and number of moles

$$P_1 V_1 = P_2 V_2$$

$$P_1 = 48 \times 10^{-3} \text{ bar}; \ V_1 = \frac{4}{3}\pi(3)^3$$

$$V_2 = \frac{4}{3}\pi(12)^3$$

$$P_2 = \frac{P_1 V_1}{V_2} = \frac{48 \times 10^{-3} \times (3)^3}{(12)^3}$$

$$= \frac{48 \times 10^{-3}}{64} = 7.5 \times 10^{-4} = 750 \times 10^{-6} \text{ bar}$$

MATHEMATICS

51. (1) $\because \alpha + \beta = 64, \ \alpha\beta = 256$

$$\frac{\alpha^{3/8}}{\beta^{5/8}} + \frac{\beta^{3/8}}{\alpha^{5/8}} = \frac{\alpha + \beta}{(\alpha\beta)^{5/8}} = \frac{64}{(2^8)^{5/8}} = \frac{64}{32} = 2$$

52. (4)

Required area $= 4\left[\int_0^{\frac{1}{2}} 2y^2\,dy + \frac{1}{2}\text{area}(\Delta PAB)\right]$

$$= 4\left[\frac{2}{3}\left[y^3\right]_0^{\frac{1}{2}} + \frac{1}{2} \times \frac{1}{2} \times \frac{1}{2}\right] = 4\left[\frac{2}{3} \times \frac{1}{8} + \frac{1}{8}\right]$$

$$= 4 \times \frac{5}{24} = \frac{5}{6}.$$

53. (1) $\sqrt{1+x^2} \cdot \sqrt{1+y^2} = -xy\dfrac{dy}{dx}$

$$\int \frac{\sqrt{1+x^2}}{x}dx = -\int \frac{y}{\sqrt{1+y^2}}dy$$

Let $x = \tan\theta \Rightarrow dx = \sec^2\theta\,d\theta$

$$\Rightarrow \int \frac{\sec^3\theta\,d\theta}{\tan\theta} = -\int \frac{2y}{2\sqrt{1+y^2}}dy$$

$$\Rightarrow \int \frac{\sin^2\theta + \cos^2\theta}{\sin\theta \cdot \cos^2\theta}d\theta = -\sqrt{1+y^2}$$

$$\Rightarrow \int (\tan\theta \cdot \sec\theta + \text{cosec}\theta)d\theta = -\sqrt{1+y^2}$$

$$\Rightarrow \sec\theta + \log_e|\text{cosec}\,\theta - \cot\theta| = -\sqrt{1+y^2} + C$$

$$\therefore \sqrt{1+x^2} + \log_e\left|\frac{\sqrt{1+x^2}-1}{x}\right| = -\sqrt{1+y^2} + C$$

$$\Rightarrow \sqrt{1+y^2} + \sqrt{1+x^2} = \frac{1}{2}\ln\left(\frac{\sqrt{1+x^2}+1}{\sqrt{1+x^2}-1}\right) + C$$

54. (1) $L_1 : y = m_1(x+1) + \dfrac{1}{m_1}$ [Tangent to $y^2 = 4(x+1)$]

$L_2 : y = m_2(x+2) + \dfrac{2}{m_2}$ [Tangent to $y^2 = 8(x+2)$]

$$m_1^2(x+1) - ym_1 + 1 = 0 \qquad \text{...(i)}$$

$$m_2^2(x+2) - ym_2 + 2 = 0 \qquad \text{...(ii)}$$

$$\because m_2 = -\frac{1}{m_1} \qquad (\because L_1 \perp L_2)$$

[From (ii)]

$$\Rightarrow 2m_1^2 + ym_1 + (x+2) = 0 \qquad \text{...(iii)}$$

From (i) and (iii),

$$\frac{x+1}{2} = \frac{-y}{y} = \frac{1}{x+2} \Rightarrow x + 3 = 0$$

55. (4) Let $f(1) = k$, then $f(2) = f(1+1) = k^2$

$f(3) = f(2+1) = k^3$

$$\sum_{x=1}^{\infty} f(x) = 2 \Rightarrow k + k^2 + k^3 + \ldots \infty = 2$$

$$\Rightarrow \frac{k}{1-k} = 2 \Rightarrow k = \frac{2}{3}$$

Now, $\dfrac{f(4)}{f(2)} = \dfrac{k^4}{k^2} = k^2 = \dfrac{4}{9}.$

56. (3) $I_2 = \displaystyle\int_0^1 (1-x^{50})^{101}dx = \int_0^1 (1-x^{50})(1-x^{50})^{100}dx$

$$I_2 = \int_0^1 (1-x^{50})^{100}dx - \int_0^1 \underbrace{x \, x^{49}(1-x^{50})^{100}}_{\text{II}} dx$$
$${}^{\text{I}}$$

$$I_2 = I_1 + \left[\frac{x}{5050}(1-x^{50})^{101}\right]_0^1 - \int_0^1 \frac{(1-x^{50})^{101}}{5050}dx$$

$$I_2 = I_1 + 0 - \frac{I_2}{5050}$$

$$\Rightarrow \frac{5051}{5050} I_2 = I_1 \Rightarrow I_2 = \frac{5050}{5051} I_1$$

$$\Rightarrow \alpha = \frac{5050}{5051}$$

57. (3) For an A.P. $2b = a + c$ (even), so both a and c even numbers or odd numbers from given numbers and b number will be fixed automatically.

Required probability $= \dfrac{{}^6C_2 + {}^5C_2}{{}^{11}C_3} = \dfrac{25}{165} = \dfrac{5}{33}$

58. (3)

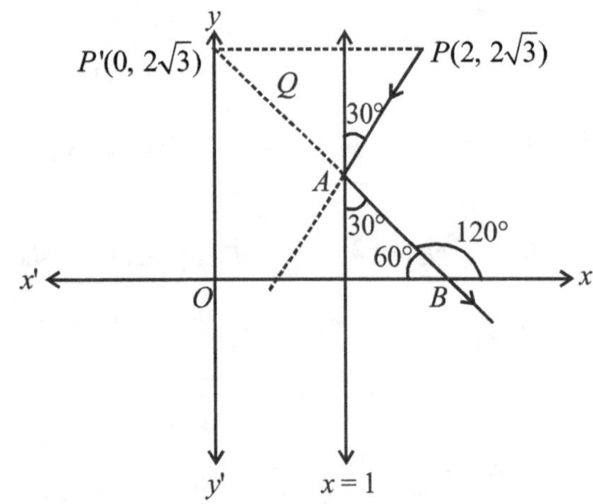

Slope of $AB = \tan 120° = -\sqrt{3}$

$\therefore$ Equation of line AB (i.e. BP'):

$$y - 2\sqrt{3} = -\sqrt{3}(x - 0)$$

$$\Rightarrow \sqrt{3}x + y = 2\sqrt{3}$$

$\therefore$ Point $(3, -\sqrt{3})$ lies on line AB.

59. (3) We know that the locus of the feet of the perpendicular draw from foci to any tangent of the ellipse $\dfrac{x^2}{a^2} + \dfrac{y^2}{b^2} = 1$ is the auxiliary circle $x^2 + y^2 = a^2$

$\therefore$ Auxiliary circle : $x^2 + y^2 = 4$

$\therefore (-1, \sqrt{3})$ satisfies the given equation.

60. (2) $\because |z| - \text{Re}(z) \le 1 \qquad\qquad (\because z = x + iy)$

$$\Rightarrow \sqrt{x^2 + y^2} - x \le 1 \Rightarrow \sqrt{x^2 + y^2} \le 1 + x$$

$$\Rightarrow x^2 + y^2 \le 1 + x^2 + 2x$$

$$\Rightarrow y^2 \le 1 + 2x \Rightarrow y^2 \le 2\left(x + \frac{1}{2}\right)$$

61. (3) Average speed $= f'(t) = \dfrac{f(t_2) - f(t_1)}{t_2 - t_1}$

$$2at + b = a(t_1 + t_2) + b \Rightarrow t = \frac{t_1 + t_2}{2}$$

62. (Bonus)

$$\lim_{x \to 1} \frac{\frac{1}{2}\sin(x-1)^4}{(x-1)\sin(x-1)}$$

Let $x - 1 = h$ when $x \to 1$ then $h \to 0$

$$\lim_{h \to 0} \frac{\sin h^4}{h^4} \times \frac{h}{\sin h} \times h^2 = 1 \times 1 \times 0 = 0$$

(No any option is correct)

63. (4) Standard deviation

$$= \sqrt{\frac{\displaystyle\sum_{i=1}^{n}(x_i - a)^2}{n} - \left(\frac{\displaystyle\sum_{i=1}^{n}(x_i - a)}{n}\right)^2} \qquad [\because n, a > 1]$$

$$= \sqrt{\frac{na}{n} - \left(\frac{n}{n}\right)^2} = \sqrt{a - 1}$$

64. (4) $\dfrac{3^{200}}{8} = \dfrac{1}{8}(9^{100})$

$$= \frac{1}{8}(1+8)^{100} = \frac{1}{8}\left[1 + n \cdot 8 + \frac{n(n+1)}{2} \cdot 8^2 + \ldots\right]$$

$$= \frac{1}{8} + \text{Integer}$$

$$\therefore \left\{\frac{3^{200}}{8}\right\} = \left\{\frac{1}{8} + \text{integer}\right\} = \frac{1}{8}$$

65. **(2)** For line of intersection of planes $x + y + z + 1 = 0$ and $2x - y + z + 3 = 0$:

$$\vec{b}_2 = \begin{vmatrix} \hat{i} & \hat{j} & \hat{k} \\ 1 & 1 & 1 \\ 2 & -1 & 1 \end{vmatrix} = 2\hat{i} + \hat{j} - 3\hat{k}$$

Put $y = 0$, we get $x = -2$ and $z = 1$

$L_2 : \vec{r} = (-2\hat{i} + \hat{k}) + \lambda(2\hat{i} + \hat{j} - 3\hat{k})$ and

$L_1 : \vec{r} = (\hat{i} - \hat{j}) + \mu(-\hat{j} + \hat{k})$ (Given)

Now, $\vec{b}_1 \times \vec{b}_2 = -2[\hat{i} + \hat{j} + \hat{k}]$ and $\vec{a}_2 - \vec{a}_1 = -3\hat{i} + \hat{j} + \hat{k}$

$\therefore$ Shortest distance $= \dfrac{1}{\sqrt{3}}$

66. **(2)** Negation of given statement $= \sim (p \vee (\sim p \wedge q))$

$= \sim p \wedge \sim (\sim p \wedge q) = \sim p \wedge (p \vee \sim q)$

$= (\sim p \wedge q) \vee (\sim p \wedge \sim q)$

$= F \vee (\sim p \wedge \sim q) = \sim p \wedge \sim q$

67. **(2)** Number of arrangement

$= (3! \times 3! \times 4!) \times 3! = (3!)^3 \, 4!$

68. **(2)** $C_1 \to C_1 + C_2$

Let $f(x) = \begin{vmatrix} 2 & 1 + \sin^2 x & \sin 2x \\ 2 & \sin^2 x & \sin 2x \\ 1 & \sin^2 x & 1 + \sin 2x \end{vmatrix}$

$R_1 \to R_1 - 2R_3; \ R_2 \to R_2 - 2R_3$

$= \begin{vmatrix} 0 & \cos^2 \theta & -(2 + \sin 2x) \\ 0 & -\sin^2 x & -(2 + \sin 2x) \\ 1 & \sin^2 x & 1 + \sin 2x \end{vmatrix} = -2 - 2\sin 2x$

$f'(x) = -2\cos 2x = 0$

$\Rightarrow \cos 2x = 0 \Rightarrow x = \dfrac{\pi}{4}, \dfrac{3\pi}{4}$

$f''(x) = 4\sin 2x$

So, $f''\left(\dfrac{\pi}{4}\right) = 4 > 0$ (minima)

$m = f\left(\dfrac{\pi}{4}\right) = -2 - 1 = -3$

$f''\left(\dfrac{3\pi}{4}\right) = -4 < 0$ (maxima)

$M = f\left(\dfrac{3\pi}{4}\right) = -2 + 1 = -1$

So, $(m, M) = (-3, -1)$

69. **(3)** Rearrange given equation, we get

$(a^2 p^2 - 2abp + b^2) + (b^2 p^2 - 2bcp + c^2)$

$$+ (c^2 p^2 - 2cdp + d^2) = 0$$

$\Rightarrow (ap - b)^2 + (bp - c)^2 + (cp - d)^2 = 0$

$\therefore ap - b = bp - c = cp - d = 0$

$\Rightarrow \dfrac{b}{a} = \dfrac{c}{b} = \dfrac{d}{c}$ $\therefore a, b, c, d$ are in G.P.

70. **(3)** $D = \begin{vmatrix} 1 & 1 & 1 \\ 1 & 2 & 3 \\ 1 & 3 & \lambda \end{vmatrix} = 0 \Rightarrow \lambda = 5$

$D_x = \begin{vmatrix} 2 & 1 & 1 \\ 5 & 2 & 3 \\ \mu & 3 & 5 \end{vmatrix} = 0 \Rightarrow \mu = 8$

71. **(28)**

$2^m = 112 + 2^n \Rightarrow 2^m - 2^n = 112$

$\Rightarrow 2^n (2^{m-n} - 1) = 2^4 (2^3 - 1)$

$\therefore m = 7, \ n = 4 \Rightarrow mn = 28$

72. **(5)**

$$f'(x) = \begin{cases} 5x^4 \cdot \sin\left(\dfrac{1}{x}\right) - x^3 \cos\left(\dfrac{1}{x}\right) + 10x, & x < 0 \\ 0, & x = 0 \\ 5x^4 \cos\left(\dfrac{1}{x}\right) + x^3 \sin\left(\dfrac{1}{x}\right) + 2\lambda x, & x > 0 \end{cases}$$

$$f''(x) = \begin{cases} (20x^3 - x)\sin\left(\dfrac{1}{x}\right) - 8x^2 \cos\left(\dfrac{1}{x}\right) + 10, & x < 0 \\ 0, & x = 0 \\ (20x^3 - x)\cos\left(\dfrac{1}{x}\right) + 8x^2 \sin\left(\dfrac{1}{x}\right) + 2\lambda, & x > 0 \end{cases}$$

Now, $f''(0^+) = f''(0^-) \Rightarrow 2\lambda = 10 \Rightarrow \lambda = 5$

73. **(4)**

Let angle between $\vec{a}$ and $\vec{b}$ be θ.

$|\vec{a} + \vec{b}| = \sqrt{1 + 1 + 2\cos\theta} = 2\left|\cos\dfrac{\theta}{2}\right|$ $[\because |a| = |b| = 1]$

Similarly, $|\vec{a} - \vec{b}| = 2\left|\sin\dfrac{\theta}{2}\right|$

So, $\sqrt{3}\,|\vec{a} + \vec{b}| + |\vec{a} - \vec{b}| = 2\left[\sqrt{3}\left|\cos\dfrac{\theta}{2}\right| + \left|\sin\dfrac{\theta}{2}\right|\right]$

$\because$ Maximum value of $(a\cos\theta + b\sin\theta) = \sqrt{a^2 + b^2}$

$\therefore$ Maximum value $= 2\sqrt{(\sqrt{3})^2 + (1)^2} = 4.$

74. **(5)**

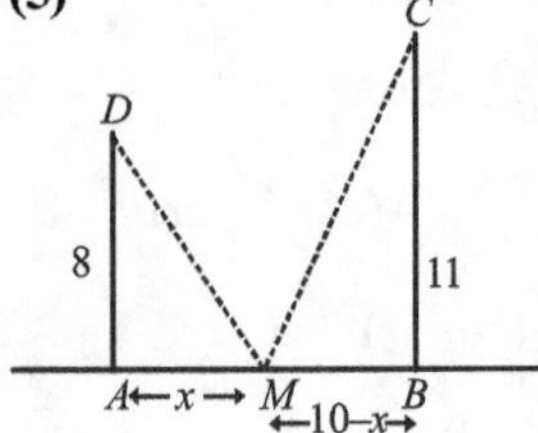

Let $AM = x$ m

$\therefore (MD)^2 + (MC)^2 = 64 + x^2 + 121 + (10-x)^2 = f(x)$

                                            (say)

$f'(x) = 2x - 2(10-x) = 0$

$\Rightarrow 4x = 20 \Rightarrow x = 5$

$f''(x) = 2 - 2(-1) > 0$

$\therefore f(x)$ is minimum at $x = 5$ m.

75. **(80)**

Let height $(AB) = h$ m, $CD = x$ m and $ED = y$ m

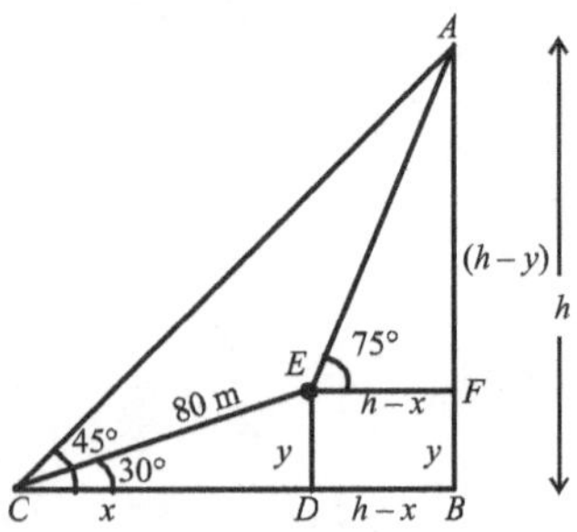

In rt. ΔCDE,

$\sin 30° = \dfrac{y}{80} \Rightarrow y = 40$

$\cos 30° = \dfrac{x}{80} \Rightarrow x = 40\sqrt{3}$

Now, in ΔAEF,

$\tan 75° = \dfrac{h-y}{h-x}$

$\Rightarrow (2+\sqrt{3}) = \dfrac{h-40}{h-40\sqrt{3}}$

$\Rightarrow (2+\sqrt{3})(h-40\sqrt{3}) = h-40$

$\Rightarrow 2h - 80\sqrt{3} + \sqrt{3}h - 120 = h - 40$

$\Rightarrow h + \sqrt{3}h = 80 + 80\sqrt{3}$

$\Rightarrow (\sqrt{3}+1)h = 80(\sqrt{3}+1)$

$\therefore h = 80$ m

PHYSICS

1. **(3)**

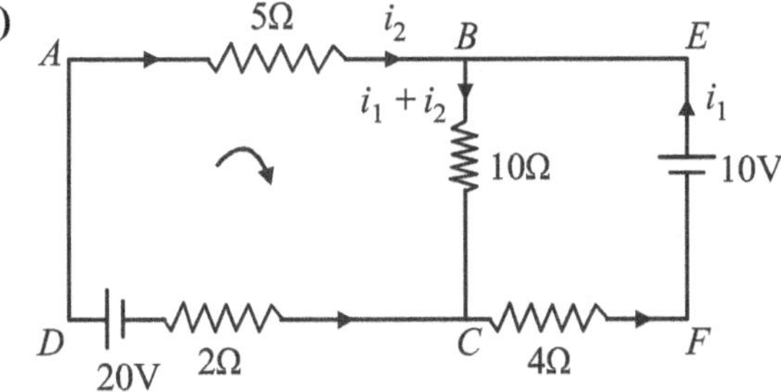

Using Kirchoff's loop law in loop $ABCD$

$-5i_2 - 10(i_1 + i_2) - 2i_2 + 20 = 0$

$\Rightarrow -10i_1 - 17i_2 + 20 = 0$ ...(i)

Using Kirchoff's loop law in loop $BEFC$

$\Rightarrow -10 + 4i_1 + 10(i_1 + i_2) = 0$

$\Rightarrow 14i_1 + 10i_2 + 10 = 0$ ...(ii)

Multiplying equation (i) by 10, we have

$(10i_1 + 17i_2 = 20) \times 10$

$\Rightarrow 100i_1 - 170i_2 = 200$ ...(iii)

Multiplying equation (ii) by 17, we have

$(14i_1 + 10i_2 = 10) \times 17$

$\Rightarrow 238i_1 - 170i_2 = 170$ ...(iv)

On solving equations (iii) and (iv), we get

$-138i_1 = 30 \Rightarrow i_1 = -\dfrac{30}{138} = -0.217$

i_1 is negative it means current flows from positive to negative terminal.

2. **(4)**

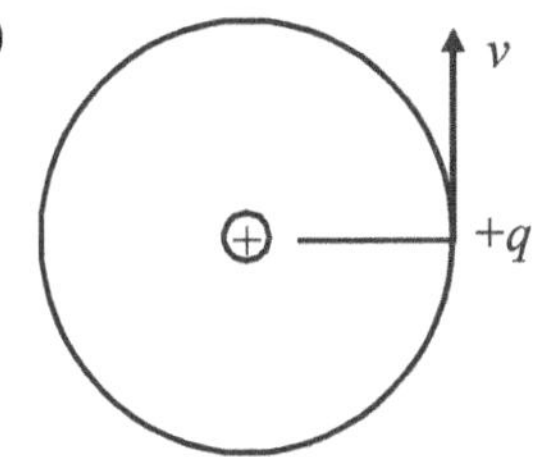

Length of the circular path, $l = 2\pi r$

Current, $i = \dfrac{q}{T} = \dfrac{qv}{2\pi r}$

Magnetic moment $M =$ Current $\times$ Area

$\qquad = i \times \pi r^2 = \dfrac{qv}{2\pi r} \times \pi r^2$

$M = \dfrac{1}{2} q \cdot v \cdot r$

Radius of circular path in magnetic field, $r = \dfrac{mv}{qB}$

$\therefore M = \dfrac{1}{2} qv \times \dfrac{mv}{qB} \Rightarrow M = \dfrac{mv^2}{2B}$

Direction of $\vec{M}$ is opposite of $\vec{B}$ therefore

$\vec{M} = \dfrac{-mv^2 \vec{B}}{2B^2}$

(By multiplying both numerator and denominator by B).

3. **(1)** As the rods are identical, so they have same length (l) and area of cross-section (A). They are connected in series. So, heat current will be same for all rods.

Heat current $= \left(\dfrac{\Delta Q}{\Delta t}\right)_{AB} = \left(\dfrac{\Delta Q}{\Delta t}\right)_{BC} = \left(\dfrac{\Delta Q}{\Delta t}\right)_{CD}$

$\Rightarrow \dfrac{(100-70)K_1 A}{l} = \dfrac{(70-20)K_2 A}{l} = \dfrac{(20-0)K_3 A}{l}$

$\Rightarrow K_1(100-70) = K_2(70-20) = K_3(20-0)$

$\Rightarrow K_1(30) = K_2(50) = K_3(20)$

$\Rightarrow \dfrac{K_1}{10} = \dfrac{K_2}{6} = \dfrac{K_3}{15} \Rightarrow K_1 : K_2 : K_3 = 10 : 6 : 15$

$\Rightarrow K_1 : K_3 = 2 : 3$.

4. **(2)** Let v be the speed of dipole.

Using energy conservation

$K_i + U_i = K_f + U_f$

$\Rightarrow 0 - \dfrac{2k \cdot p_1}{r^3} p_2 \cos(180°) = \dfrac{1}{2} mv^2 + \dfrac{1}{2} mv^2 + 0$

$\left(\begin{array}{l} \because \text{ Potential energy of interaction between dipole} \\ \qquad\qquad\qquad\qquad\qquad = \dfrac{-2p_1 p_2 \cos\theta}{4\pi \in_0 r^3} \end{array} \right)$

$\Rightarrow mv^2 = \dfrac{2kp_1 p_2}{r^3} \Rightarrow v = \sqrt{\dfrac{2kp_1 p_2}{mr^3}}$

When $p_1 = p_2 = p$ and $r = a$

$v = \dfrac{p}{a} \sqrt{\dfrac{1}{2\pi \in_0 ma}}$

5. **(1)** Relation between electric field E_0 and magnetic field B_0 of an electromagnetic wave is given by

$c = \dfrac{E_0}{B_0}$ \qquad (Here, $c =$ Speed of light)

$\Rightarrow E_0 = B_0 \times c = 1.2 \times 10^{-7} \times 3 \times 10^8 = 36$

As the wave is propagating along x-direction, magnetic field is along z-direction

and $(\hat{E} \times \hat{B}) \parallel \hat{C}$

$\therefore \vec{E}$ should be along y-direction.

So, electric field $\vec{E} = E_0 \sin \vec{E} \cdot (x, t)$

$$= [-36 \sin (0.5 \times 10^3 x + 1.5 \times 10^{11} t)\hat{j}]\frac{V}{m}$$

6. (4)

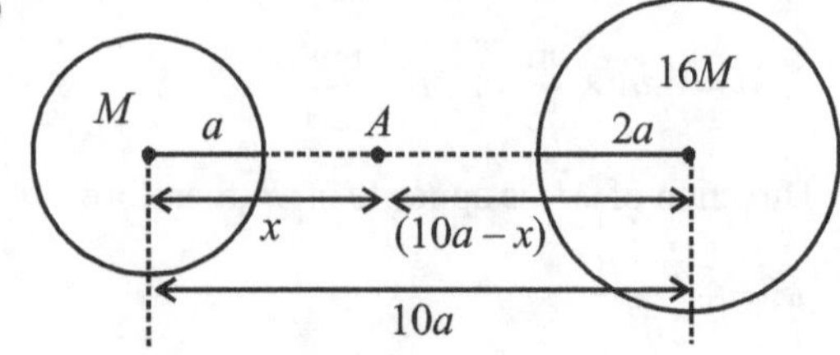

Let A be the point where gravitation field of both planets cancel each other i.e. zero.

$$\frac{GM}{x^2} = \frac{G(16M)}{(10a - x)^2}$$

$$\Rightarrow \frac{1}{x} = \frac{4}{(10a - x)} \Rightarrow 4x = 10a - x \Rightarrow x = 2a \qquad ...(i)$$

Using conservation of energy, we have

$$-\frac{GMm}{8a} - \frac{G(16M)m}{2a} + KE = -\frac{GMm}{2a} - \frac{G(16M)m}{8a}$$

$$KE = GMm\left[\frac{1}{8a} + \frac{16}{2a} - \frac{1}{2a} - \frac{16}{8a}\right]$$

$$\Rightarrow KE = GMm\left[\frac{1 + 64 - 4 - 16}{8a}\right]$$

$$\Rightarrow \frac{1}{2}mv^2 = GMm\left[\frac{45}{8a}\right] \Rightarrow v = \sqrt{\frac{90GM}{8a}}$$

$$\Rightarrow v = \frac{3}{2}\sqrt{\frac{5GM}{a}}$$

7. (1) Given, $\vec{F} = k(v_y\hat{i} + v_x\hat{j})$

$\therefore F_x = kv_y\hat{i}$, $F_y = kv_x\hat{j}$

$$\frac{mdv_x}{dt} = kv_y \Rightarrow \frac{dv_x}{dt} = \frac{k}{m}v_y$$

Similarly, $\dfrac{dv_y}{dt} = \dfrac{k}{m}v_x$

$$\frac{dv_y}{dv_x} = \frac{v_x}{v_y} \Rightarrow \int v_y dv_y = \int v_x dv_x$$

$$v_y^2 = v_x^2 + C$$

$$v_y^2 - v_x^2 = \text{constant}$$

$$\vec{v} \times \vec{a} = (v_x\hat{i} + v_y\hat{j}) \times \frac{k}{m}(v_y\hat{i} + v_x\hat{j})$$

$$= (v_x^2\hat{k} - v_y^2\hat{k})\frac{k}{m} = (v_x^2 - v_y^2)\frac{k}{m}\hat{k} = \text{constant}$$

8. (4) Before collision,

Velocity of particle A, $u_1 = (\sqrt{3}\hat{i} + \hat{j})$ m/s

Velocity of particle B, $u_2 = 0$

After collision,

Velocity of particle A, $v_1 = (\hat{i} + \sqrt{3}\hat{j})$

Velocity of particle B, $v_2 = 0$

Using principal of conservation of angular momentum

$$m_1\vec{u}_1 + m_2\vec{u}_2 = m_1\vec{v}_1 + m_2\vec{v}_2$$

$$\Rightarrow 2m_2(\sqrt{3}\hat{i} + \hat{j}) + m_2 \times 0 = 2m_2(\hat{i} + \sqrt{3}\hat{j}) + m_2 \times \vec{v}_2$$

$$\Rightarrow 2\sqrt{3}\hat{i} + 2\hat{j} = 2\hat{i} + 2\sqrt{3}\hat{j} + \vec{v}_2$$

$$\Rightarrow \vec{v}_2 = (\sqrt{3} - 1)\hat{i} - (\sqrt{3} - 1)\hat{j} \Rightarrow \vec{v}_1 = \hat{i} + \sqrt{3}\hat{j}$$

For angle between $\vec{v}_1$ and $\vec{v}_2$,

$$\cos\theta = \frac{\vec{v}_1 \cdot \vec{v}_2}{\vec{v}_1\vec{v}_2} = \frac{2(\sqrt{3} - 1)(1 - \sqrt{3})}{2 \times 2\sqrt{2}(\sqrt{3} - 1)} = \frac{1 - \sqrt{3}}{2\sqrt{2}}$$

$$\Rightarrow \theta = 105°$$

Angle between $\vec{v}_1$ and $\vec{v}_2$ is $105°$

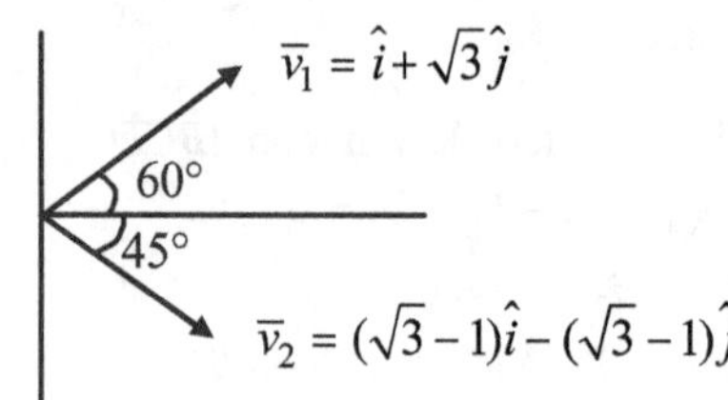

9. (4) The given situation is shown in the diagram. Here v_r be the velocity of rain drop.

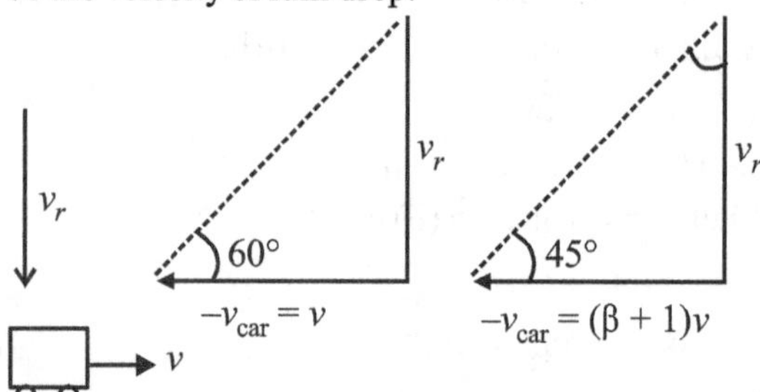

When car is moving with speed v,

$$\tan 60° = \frac{v_r}{v} \qquad ...(i)$$

When car is moving with speed $(1 + \beta)v$,

$$\tan 45° = \frac{v_r}{(\beta + 1)v} \qquad ...(ii)$$

Dividing (i) by (ii) we get,

$$\sqrt{3}v = (\beta + 1)v \Rightarrow \beta = \sqrt{3} - 1 = 0.732.$$

10. (3) For the momentum and energy conservation, mass defect (Δm) should be positive. Since some energy is lost in every process.

$$(m_p + m_n) > m_d$$

11. (4) Ammeter : In series connection, the same current flows through all the components. It aims at measuring the current flowing through the circuit and hence, it is connected in series.

Voltmeter : A voltmeter measures voltage change between two points in a circuit. So we have to place the voltmeter in parallel with the cicuit component.

12. (3) For spherical shell

$$E = \frac{1}{4\pi\varepsilon_0}\frac{Q}{r^2} \qquad (\text{if } r \geq R)$$

$$= 0 \qquad (\text{if } r < R)$$

Force on charge in electried field, $F = qE$

$\therefore F = 0$ (For $r < R$)

$F = \dfrac{1}{4\pi\varepsilon_0}\dfrac{Qq}{r^2}$ (For $r > R$)

13. **(4)** Average diameter, $d_{av} = 5.5375$ mm

Deviation of data, $\Delta d = 0.07395$ mm

As the measured data are upto two digits after decimal, therefore answer should be in two digits after decimal.

$\therefore d = (5.54 \pm 0.07)$ mm

14. **(4)** Given, using lens maker's formula

$\dfrac{1}{f} = (k-1)\left(\dfrac{1}{R_1} - \dfrac{1}{R_2}\right)$

Here, $R_1 = R_2 = R$ (For double convex lens)

$\therefore \dfrac{1}{f} = (\mu-1)\left(\dfrac{1}{R} - \dfrac{1}{-R}\right)$

$\Rightarrow P = \dfrac{1}{f} = (\mu-1)\dfrac{2}{R}$ ...(i)

For plano convex lens,

$R_1 = R',\ R_2 = \infty$

Using lens maker's formula again, we have

$1.5P = (\mu-1)\left(\dfrac{1}{R'} - \dfrac{1}{\infty}\right)$ ...(ii)

$\Rightarrow \dfrac{3}{2}P = \dfrac{\mu-1}{R'}$

From (i) and (ii),

$\dfrac{3}{2} = \dfrac{R'}{2R} \Rightarrow R' = \dfrac{R}{3}$

15. **(2)**

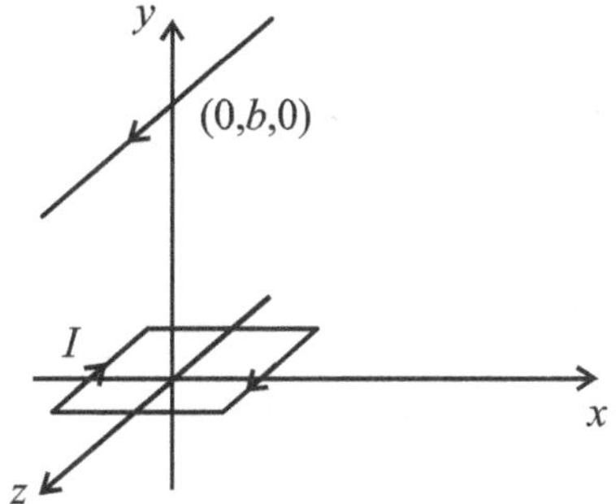

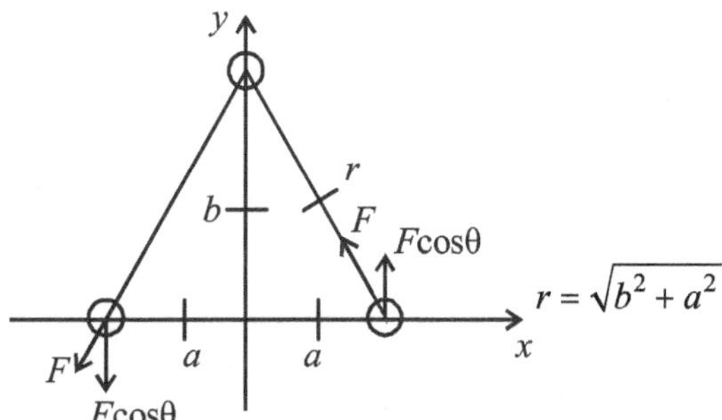

Force, $F = BI2a = \dfrac{\mu_0 I}{2\pi r} I \times 2a$

Force, $F = \dfrac{\mu_0 I^2 a}{\pi\sqrt{b^2 + a^2}}$

Torque, $\tau = F_1 \times$ Perpendicular distance $= F\cos\theta \times 2a$

$= \dfrac{\mu_0 I^2 a}{\pi\sqrt{b^2 + a^2}} \times \dfrac{b}{\sqrt{b^2 + a^2}} \times 2a$

$\Rightarrow \tau = \dfrac{2\mu_0 I^2 a^2 b}{\pi(a^2 + b^2)}$

If $b \gg a$ then $\tau = \dfrac{2\mu_0 I^2 a^2}{\pi b}$

16. **(4)** Using Bernoulli's equation

$P_1 + \dfrac{1}{2}\rho\upsilon_1^2 + \rho g h_1 = P_2 + \dfrac{1}{2}\rho\upsilon_2^2 + \rho g h_2$

For horizontal pipe, $h_1 = 0$ and $h_2 = 0$ and taking

$P_1 = P, P_2 = \dfrac{P}{2}$, we get

$\Rightarrow P + \dfrac{1}{2}\rho\upsilon^2 = \dfrac{P}{2} + \dfrac{1}{2}\rho V^2$

$\Rightarrow \dfrac{P}{2} + \dfrac{1}{2}\rho\upsilon^2 = \dfrac{1}{2}\rho V^2 \Rightarrow V = \sqrt{\upsilon^2 + \dfrac{P}{\rho}}$

17. **(3)** $y = y_0 \sin^2 \omega t$

$\Rightarrow y = \dfrac{y_0}{2}(1 - \cos 2\omega t)$ $\left(\because \sin^2 \omega t = \dfrac{1 - \cos 2\omega t}{2}\right)$

$\Rightarrow y - \dfrac{y_0}{2} = \dfrac{-y_0}{2}\cos 2\omega t$

$\Rightarrow y = A\cos 2\omega t$

$\therefore$ Amplitude $= \dfrac{y_0}{2}$

Angular velocity $= 2\omega$

For equilibrium of mass, $\dfrac{ky_0}{2} = mg \Rightarrow \dfrac{k}{m} = \dfrac{2g}{y_0}$

Also, spring constant $k = m(2\omega)^2$

$\Rightarrow 2\omega = \sqrt{\dfrac{k}{m}} = \sqrt{\dfrac{2g}{y_0}} \Rightarrow \omega = \dfrac{1}{2}\sqrt{\dfrac{2g}{y_0}} = \sqrt{\dfrac{g}{2y_0}}$

18. **(2)** Mean free path, $\lambda = \dfrac{1}{\sqrt{2}\pi n d^2}$

where, $d =$ diameter of the molecule

$n =$ number of molecules per unit volume

But, mean time of collision, $\tau = \dfrac{\lambda}{v_{rms}}$

But $v_{rms} = \sqrt{\dfrac{3kT}{R}}$

$\therefore \tau = \dfrac{\lambda}{\sqrt{\dfrac{3kT}{m}}} \Rightarrow t \propto \dfrac{1}{\sqrt{T}}$

19. **(1)** Rms speed of gas molecule, $V_{rms} = \sqrt{\dfrac{3kT}{m}}$

de Broglie wavelength, $\lambda = \dfrac{h}{p} = \dfrac{h}{\sqrt{2mk}}$

$$\therefore \lambda = \frac{h}{\sqrt{2m \times \frac{1}{2}mV_{rms}^2}} = \frac{h}{\sqrt{m \times \frac{3}{2}kT}} = \frac{h}{\sqrt{3mkT}}$$

Substituting the respective values we get

$$\lambda = \frac{6.63 \times 10^{-34}}{\sqrt{3 \times 4.64 \times 10^{-26} \times 1.38 \times 10^{-13} \times 400}} = 0.24\text{Å}$$

20. (2)

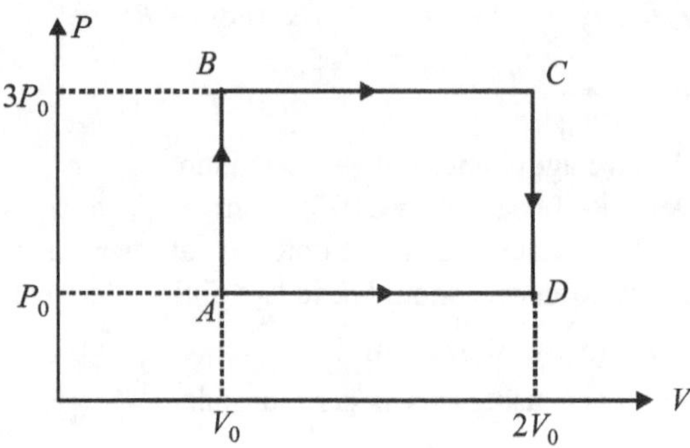

Mass of the small element of the rod

$dm = \lambda \cdot dx$

Moment of inertia of small element,

$$dI = dm \cdot x^2 = \lambda_0 \left(1 + \frac{x}{L}\right) \cdot x^2 \, dx$$

Moment of inertia of the complete rod can be obtained by integration

$$I = \lambda_0 \int_0^L \left(x^2 + \frac{x^3}{L}\right) dx$$

$$= \lambda_0 \left|\frac{x^3}{3} + \frac{x^4}{4L}\right|_0^L = \lambda_0 \left[\frac{L^3}{3} + \frac{L^3}{4}\right]$$

$$\Rightarrow I = \frac{7\lambda_0 L^3}{12} \qquad \text{...(i)}$$

Mass of the thin rod,

$$M = \int_0^L \lambda \, dx = \int_0^L \lambda_0 \left(1 + \frac{x}{L}\right) dx = \frac{3\lambda_0 L}{2}$$

$$\therefore \lambda_0 = \frac{2M}{3L}$$

$$\therefore I = \frac{7}{12}\left(\frac{2M}{3L}\right)L^3 \Rightarrow I = \frac{7}{18}ML^2$$

21. (150)

At $V_{CE} = 10$ V and $I_C = 4$ mA

Change in base current, $\Delta I_B = (30 - 20) = 10$ μA

Change in collector current, $\Delta I_C = (4.5 - 3) = 1.5$ mA

$$\beta = \left(\frac{\Delta I_C}{\Delta I_B}\right) = \frac{1.5 \ mA}{10\mu A} = 150$$

22. (3)

Centre of mass of solid hemisphere of radius R lies at a

distance $\dfrac{3R}{8}$ above the centre of flat side of hemisphere.

$$\therefore h_{cm} = \frac{3R}{8} = \frac{3 \times 8}{8} = 3 \text{ cm}$$

23. (19)

From the figure,

Work, $W = 2P_0 V_0$

Heat given, $Q_{in} = W_{AB} + W_{BC} = n \cdot C_V \Delta T_{AB} + nC_P \Delta T_{BC}$

$$= n\frac{3R}{2}(T_B - T_A) + \frac{n5R}{2}(T_C - T_B)$$

$$\left(\because C_v = \frac{3R}{2} \text{ and } C_P = \frac{5R}{2}\right)$$

$$= \frac{3}{2}(P_B V_B - P_A V_A) + \frac{5}{2}(P_C V_C - P_B V_B)$$

$$= \frac{3}{2} \times [3P_0 V_0 - P_0 V_0] + \frac{5}{2}[6P_0 V_0 - 3P_0 V_0]$$

$$= 3P_0 V_0 + \frac{15}{2}P_0 V_0 = \frac{21}{2}P_0 V_0$$

Efficiency, $\eta = \dfrac{W}{Q_{in}} = \dfrac{2P_0 V_0}{\dfrac{21}{2}P_0 V_0} = \dfrac{4}{21}$

$$\eta\% = \frac{400}{21} \approx 19.$$

24. (9)

In young's double slit experiment, intensity at a point is given by

$$I = I_0 \cos^2 \frac{\phi}{2} \qquad \text{...(i)}$$

where, $\phi = $ phase difference,

Using phase difference, $\phi = \dfrac{2\pi}{\lambda} \times$ path difference

For path difference λ, phase difference $\phi_1 = 2\pi$

For path difference, $\dfrac{\lambda}{6}$, phase difference $\phi_2 = \dfrac{\pi}{3}$

Using equation (i),

$$\frac{I_1}{I_2} = \frac{\cos^2\left(\dfrac{\phi_1}{2}\right)}{\cos^2\left(\dfrac{\phi_2}{2}\right)} = \frac{\cos^2\left(\dfrac{2\pi}{2}\right)}{\cos^2\left(\dfrac{\pi}{3}\right)}$$

$$\Rightarrow \frac{K}{I_2} = \frac{1}{\dfrac{3}{4}} = \frac{4}{3} \Rightarrow I_2 = \frac{3K}{4} = \frac{9K}{12}$$

$\therefore n = 9.$

25. (400)

Given: Power $P = 400$ W, Voltage $V = 250$ V

$$P = V_m \cdot I_{rms} \cdot \cos\phi$$

$$\Rightarrow 400 = 250 \times I_{\text{rms}} \times 0.8 \Rightarrow I_{\text{rms}} = 2\,\text{A}$$

Using $P = I_{\text{rms}}^2 R$

$$(I_{\text{rms}})^2 \cdot R = P \Rightarrow 4 \times R = 400$$

$$\Rightarrow R = 100\,\Omega$$

Power factor is, $\cos\phi = \dfrac{R}{\sqrt{R^2 + X_L^2}}$

$$\Rightarrow 0.8 = \dfrac{100}{\sqrt{100^2 + X_L^2}} \Rightarrow 100^2 + X_L^2 = \left(\dfrac{100}{0.8}\right)^2$$

$$\Rightarrow X_L = \sqrt{-100^2 + \left(\dfrac{100}{0.8}\right)^2} \Rightarrow X_L = 75\,\Omega$$

When power factor is unity,

$$X_C = X_L = 75 \Rightarrow \dfrac{1}{\omega C} = 75$$

$$\Rightarrow C = \dfrac{1}{75 \times 2\pi \times 50} = \dfrac{1}{7500\pi}\,F$$

$$= \left(\dfrac{10^6}{2500} \times \dfrac{1}{3\pi}\right)\mu F = \dfrac{400}{3\pi}\,\mu F$$

$N = 400$

CHEMISTRY

26. (2)

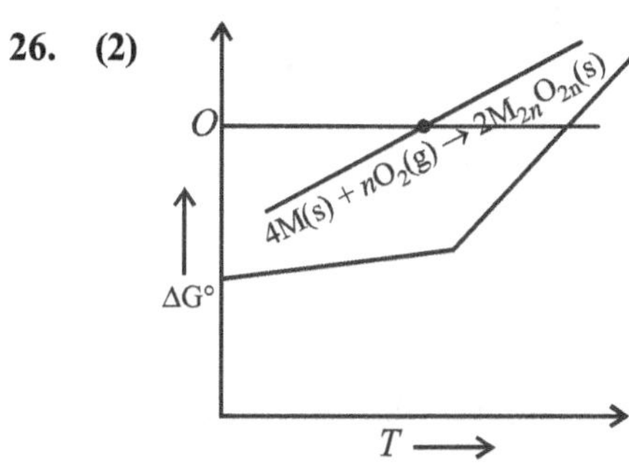

Ellingham Diagram

From graph it is evident that the temperature below which the oxide is stable, is the point at which free energy change shows a change from negative to positive.

27. (2)

	^{35}Cl	^{37}Cl
Molar ratio	x	$(1-x)$

$M_{\text{avg.}} = 35 \times x + 37\,(1-x) = 35.5$
$\qquad = 35x + 37\,(1-x) = 35.5$

$$\Rightarrow 2x = 1.5$$

$$x = \dfrac{3}{4}$$

So, ratio of $^{35}\text{Cl} : {}^{37}\text{Cl} = \dfrac{3}{4}\Big/\dfrac{1}{4} = 3:1.$

28. (1) Lactose contains β-glycosidic linkage between C_1 of galactose and C_4 of glucose.

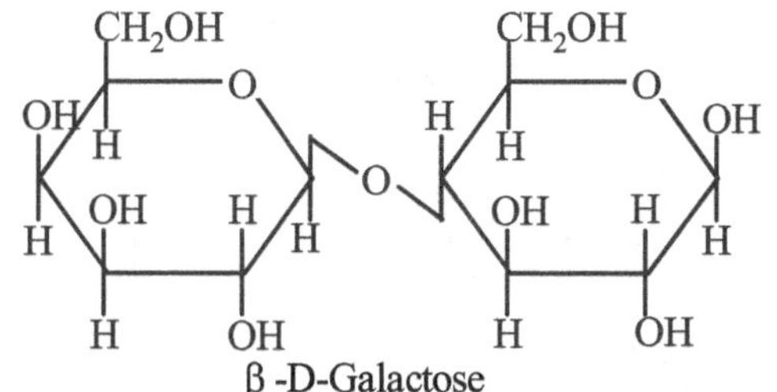

β-D-Galactose

29. (4) $N_2(g) + 3H_2(g) \rightleftharpoons 2NH_3(g)$; K_c

$2NH_3(g) \rightleftharpoons N_2(g) + 3H_2(g)$; $\dfrac{1}{K_c}$
For

$NH_3(g) \rightleftharpoons \dfrac{1}{2}N_2(g) + \dfrac{3}{2}H_2(g)$; $\dfrac{1}{K_c^{1/2}}$

$$\dfrac{1}{K_c^{1/2}} = \dfrac{1}{(64)^{1/2}} = \dfrac{1}{8}$$

30. (4) Dihydrogen of high purity ($> 99.95\%$) is obtained by the electrolysis of $Ba(OH)_2$ using Ni electrodes.

31. (3) $2NO + N_2O_4 \xrightarrow{\ 250\,K\ } 2N_2O_3$

32. (3) (I) benzene $\xrightarrow[\text{AlCl}_3]{\text{CO, HCl}}$ benzaldehyde (CHO)
(Gatterman Koch Reaction)

(II) benzonitrile ($C\equiv N$) $\xrightarrow[\text{HCl}]{\text{SnCl}_2 + H_3O^+}$ benzaldehyde (CHO)
(Stephen's Reduction)

(III) benzoyl chloride ($\overset{O}{\overset{\|}{C}}-Cl$) $\xrightarrow[\text{Quinoline, S}]{H_2,\ Pd\text{-}BaSO_4}$ benzaldehyde (CHO)
(Rosenmund Reduction)

33. (1)

	M_1	M_2	O
	50%	12.5%	ccp
	octahedral void	tetrahedral void	
	$\dfrac{50}{100} \times 4$	$\dfrac{12.5}{100} \times 8$	4
	2	1	4
Charge	$2x$	$1y$	4×2

So, $2x + y = 8$
$x = 2;\ y = 4$

34. **(2)** Zn, Cd and Hg are purified by fractional distillation process.

35. **(1)** If $\Delta_0 > P$ then fot $d^4 \Rightarrow t_{2g}^4 e_g^0$

If $\Delta_0 < P$ then for $d^4 \Rightarrow t_{2g}^3 e_g^1$

36. **(3)** (I) Lucas reagent - Conc. $HCl/ZnCl_2$
(II) Dumas method - CuO/CO_2
(III) Kjeldahl's method - H_2SO_4
(IV) Hinsberg test - $C_6H_5SO_2Cl/$aq. KOH

37. **(2)** (I) $Ca(OH)_2$ is used in white wash.
(II) NaCl is used in preparation of washing soda (Na_2CO_3).

(III) $CaSO_4 \cdot \dfrac{1}{2}H_2O$ is used for making casts of statues.

(IV) $CaCO_3$ is used as an antacid.

38. **(3)**

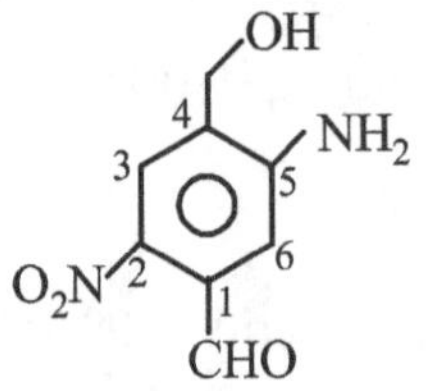

5-Amino-4-hydroxymethyl-2-nitrobenzaldehyde

39. **(1)** Gabriel phthalimide synthesis gives $1°$ amine in good yield.

40. **(3)** Relative lowering in vapour pressure (RLVP)

$$= \frac{P - P_s}{P} = \frac{n}{n + N}$$

$n \rightarrow$ moles of solute

$N \rightarrow$ moles of solvent

$$n_A = \frac{10}{100}, \; n_B = \frac{10}{200}, \; n_C = \frac{10}{10000}$$

Moles of solvent $(H_2O) = \dfrac{180}{18} = 10$ mol

$$RLVP_A = \frac{0.1}{10.1} = \frac{1}{101}$$

$$RLVP_B = \frac{0.05}{10.05} = \frac{1}{201}$$

$$RLVP_C = \frac{10^{-3}}{10} = 10^{-4}$$

From the above relation
$RLVP(A) > RLVP(B) > RLVP(C)$

41. **(4)** For the concentration cell, $E_{cell}^{\circ} = 0$

Anode : $Cu(s) \longrightarrow Cu^{2+} (aq)_A$

Cathode : $Cu^{2+}(aq)_e \longrightarrow Cu(s)$

Overall : $Cu^{2+}(aq)_C \longrightarrow Cu^{2+}(aq)_A$
$\qquad\qquad\quad (C_2M) \qquad\qquad\quad (C_1M)$

As $\Delta G = -nFE$

If $\Delta G = -ve$, then E_{cell} is $+ve$.

$$E_{cell} = E_{cell}^{\circ} - \frac{RT}{2F} \ln \frac{C_1}{C_2}$$

$$E_{cell} = 0 - \frac{RT}{2F} \ln \frac{C_1}{C_2}$$

$$E_{cell} = \frac{RT}{2F} \ln \frac{C_2}{C_1}$$

So, $C_2 > C_1$.

Thus, $C_2 = \sqrt{2}C_1$ relation is correct.

42. **(3)** $X = Na_2SO_3$

$$\underset{(X)}{SO_3^{2-}} + H_2SO_4 \rightarrow [H_2SO_3] \rightarrow H_2O + \underset{(Y)}{SO_2}$$

$$SO_2 + 2NaOH \rightarrow \underset{(X)}{Na_2SO_3} + H_2O$$

$$\underset{(X)}{Na_2SO_3} + \underset{(Y)}{SO_2} + H_2O \rightarrow \underset{(Z)}{2NaHSO_3}$$

43. **(1)**

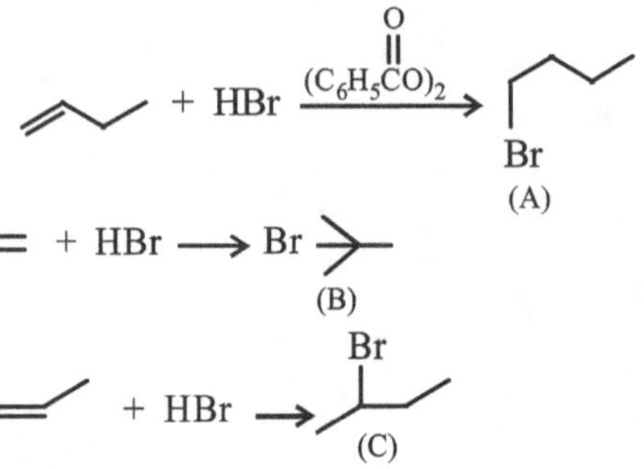

The boiling points of isomeric haloalkanes decrease with increase in branching.
So order of B.P. is $A > C > B$.

44. **(1)** Mischmetal is an alloy consisting mainly of lanthanoid metals.
Alloy $\Rightarrow$

Lan. metal $\Rightarrow \approx 95\%$

Iron $\Rightarrow \approx 5\%$

S, C, Ca, Al $\Rightarrow$ traces

45. **(3)** (A) Natural rubber - Polymer of isoprene
(B) Neoprene - Polymer of chloroprene
(C) Buna N - Polymer of 1,3-butadiene and acrylonitrile
(D) Buna S - Polymer of 1,3-butadiene and styrene

46. **(2.0)**

$$\underset{s}{AB_2} \rightleftharpoons \underset{}{A^{2+}}(aq) + \underset{2s}{2B^-}(aq)$$

$$K_{sp} = 4s^3 = 3.2 \times 10^{-11}$$

$$\Rightarrow s^3 = 8 \times 10^{-12} \quad \Rightarrow s = 2 \times 10^{-4}$$

47. **(48)** Freundlich adsorption isotherm :

$$\frac{x}{m} = k_p^{1/n}$$

$$\Rightarrow \log \frac{x}{m} = \log k + \frac{1}{n} \log p$$

Slope $\left(\dfrac{1}{n}\right) = 2$

Intercept $= \log k = 0.4771$, so $k = $ Antilog $(0.4771) = 3$

So, $\left(\dfrac{x}{m}\right) = k(p)^{1/n}$

$$\frac{x}{m} = 3 \cdot p^2 \quad (p = 0.04 \text{ atm}) = 3 \times (0.04)^2 = 48 \times 10^{-4}$$

48. (69)

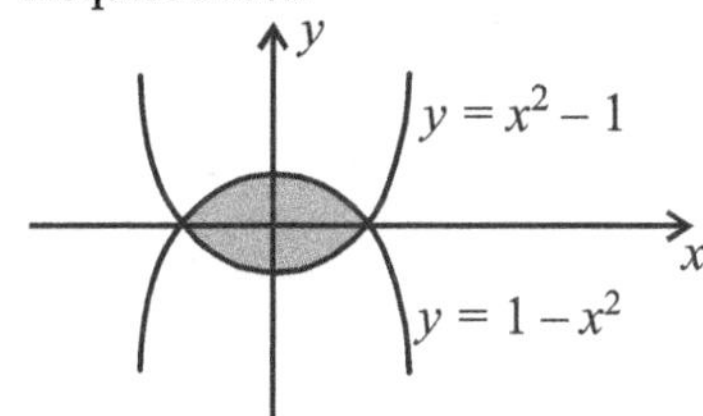

Molecular formula of product 'P' $= C_7H_6O_2$

So, mass % of C in 'P' $= \dfrac{12 \times 7}{84 + 6 + 32} \times 100 = 68.85\% \approx 69\%$

49. (101)

$$\boxed{\text{Un}} \quad \boxed{\text{nil}} \quad \boxed{\text{un}} \quad \text{ium}$$
$$\downarrow \qquad \downarrow \qquad \downarrow$$
$$1 \qquad 0 \qquad 1$$

IUPAC symbol = Unu

Atomic no. (Z) = 101

50. (100) The Arrhenices equation is

$$k = Ae^{\frac{E_a}{RT}}$$

Assuming A and E_a to be independent of temperature

$$\ln \frac{k_2}{k_1} = \frac{E_a}{R}\left(\frac{1}{T_1} - \frac{1}{T_2}\right)$$

$$\ln 3.555 = \frac{E_a}{8.314}\left(\frac{1}{303} - \frac{1}{313}\right)$$

$$\Rightarrow E_a = \frac{1.268 \times 8.314 \times 303 \times 313}{10}$$

$$= 99980.7 = 99.98 \text{ kJ/mol}$$

MATHEMATICS

51. (1) $I = \displaystyle\int_1^2 e^x x^x (2 + \log_e x)\, dx$

$$I = \int_1^2 e^x x^x [1 + (1 + \log_e x)]\, dx$$

$$= \int_1^2 e^x [x^x + x^x (1 + \log_e x)]\, dx$$

$$\because \int e^x (f(x) + f'(x))\, dx = e^x f(x) + c$$

$$\therefore I = \left[e^x x^x \right]_1^2 = e^2 \times 4 - e \times 1 = 4e^2 - e = e(4e - 1)$$

52. (2) Required area

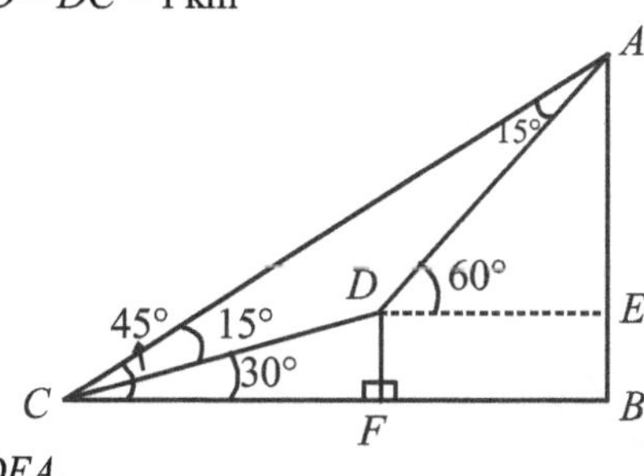

$$\text{Area} = 2\int_0^1 \left((1 - x^2) - (x^2 - 1)\right) dx = 4\int_0^1 (1 - x^2)\, dx$$

$$= 4\left(x - \frac{x^3}{3}\right)\Bigg|_0^1 = 4\left(1 - \frac{1}{3}\right) = 4 \cdot \frac{2}{3} = \frac{8}{3} \text{ sq. units}$$

53. (3) $\because \angle DCA = \angle DAC = 30°$

$\therefore AD = DC = 1 \text{ km}$

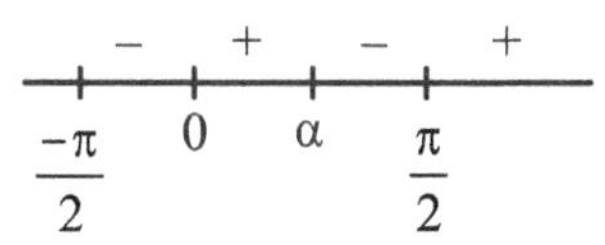

In $\triangle DEA$,

$$\frac{AE}{AD} = \sin 60° \Rightarrow AE = \frac{\sqrt{3}}{2} \text{ km}$$

In $\triangle CDF$, $\sin 30° = \dfrac{DF}{CD} \Rightarrow DF = \dfrac{1}{2} \text{ km}$

$$\therefore EB = DF = \frac{1}{2} \text{ km}$$

$\therefore$ Height of mountain $= AE + EB$

$$= \left(\frac{\sqrt{3}}{2} + \frac{1}{2}\right) = \left(\frac{\sqrt{3} + 1}{2}\right) \text{ km} = \frac{1}{\sqrt{3} - 1} \text{ km}$$

54. (4) $f(x) = (1 - \cos^2 x)(\lambda + \sin x) = \sin^2 x(\lambda + \sin x)$

$$\Rightarrow f(x) = \lambda \sin^2 x + \sin^3 x \quad \text{...(i)}$$

$$\Rightarrow f'(x) = \sin x \cos x [2\lambda + 3\sin x] = 0$$

$$\Rightarrow \sin x = 0 \text{ and } \sin x = -\frac{2\lambda}{3} \Rightarrow x = \alpha \text{ (let)}$$

So, $f(x)$ will change its sign at $x = 0$, α because there is

exactly one maxima and one minima in $\left(\dfrac{-\pi}{2}, \dfrac{\pi}{2}\right)$

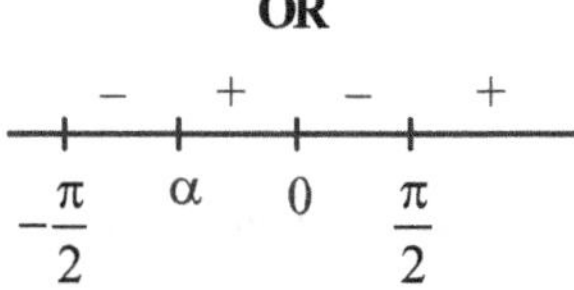

OR

Now, $\sin x = -\dfrac{2\lambda}{3}$

$$\Rightarrow -1 \le -\frac{2\lambda}{3} \le 1 \Rightarrow -\frac{3}{2} \le \lambda \le \frac{3}{2} - \{0\}$$

$\because$ If $\lambda = 0 \Rightarrow f(x) = \sin^3 x$ (from (i))

Which is monotonic, then no maxima/minima

So, $\lambda \in \left(-\dfrac{3}{2}, \dfrac{3}{2}\right) - \{0\}$

55. **(2)** Let α and β be the roots of the given quadratic equation,

$$2x^2 + 2x - 1 = 0 \qquad \text{...(i)}$$

Then, $\alpha + \beta = -\dfrac{1}{2} \Rightarrow -1 = 2\alpha + 2\beta$

and $4\alpha^2 + 2\alpha - 1 = 0 \qquad [\because \alpha \text{ is root of eq. (i)}]$

$\Rightarrow 4\alpha^2 + 2\alpha + 2\alpha + 2\beta = 0 \Rightarrow \beta = -2\alpha(\alpha + 1)$

56. **(2)** Let $f : R \to R$, with $f(0) = f(1) = 0$ and $f'(0) = 0$

$\because f(x)$ is differentiable and continuous and $f(0) = f(1) = 0$.

Then by Rolle's theorem, $f'(c) = 0$, $c \in (0, 1)$

Now again

$\because f'(c) = 0$, $f'(0) = 0$

Then, again by Rolle's theorem,

$f''(x) = 0$ for some $x \in (0, 1)$

57. **(1)** $\because y = \left(\dfrac{2}{\pi}x - 1\right) \operatorname{cosec} x$

$\dfrac{dy}{dx} = \dfrac{2}{\pi} \operatorname{cosec} x - \left(\dfrac{2}{\pi}x - 1\right) \operatorname{cosec} x \cdot \cot x$

$= \operatorname{cosec} x \left[\dfrac{2}{\pi} - \left(\dfrac{2}{\pi}x - 1\right) \cot x\right]$

$\Rightarrow \dfrac{dy}{dx} - \dfrac{2}{\pi} \operatorname{cosec} x = y \cot x \qquad \text{...(i)}$

It is given that,

$\Rightarrow \dfrac{dy}{dx} - \dfrac{2}{\pi} \operatorname{cosec} x = -yp(x) \qquad \text{...(ii)}$

By comparision of (i) and (ii), we get

$p(x) = \cot x$

58. **(1)** The line in xy-plane is,

$\dfrac{x}{3} + y = 1 \Rightarrow x + 3y - 3 = 0$

Let image of the point $(-1, -4)$ be (α, β), then

$\dfrac{\alpha + 1}{1} = \dfrac{\beta + y}{3} = -\dfrac{2(-1 - 12 - 3)}{10}$

$\Rightarrow \alpha + 1 = \dfrac{\beta + 4}{3} = \dfrac{16}{5} \Rightarrow \alpha = \dfrac{11}{5}, \beta = \dfrac{28}{5}$

59. **(2)** The given tangent to the curve is,

$$y = x \log_e x \qquad (x > 0)$$

$\Rightarrow \dfrac{dy}{dx} = 1 + \log_e x$

$\Rightarrow \dfrac{dy}{dx}\Big]_{x=c} = 1 + \log_e c \qquad \text{(slope)}$

$\because$ The tangent is parallel to line joining $(1, 0), (e, e)$

$\therefore 1 + \log_e c = \dfrac{e - 0}{e - 1}$

$\Rightarrow \log_e c = \dfrac{e}{e - 1} - 1 \Rightarrow \log_e c = \dfrac{1}{e - 1} \Rightarrow c = e^{\frac{1}{e-1}}$

60. **(a)**

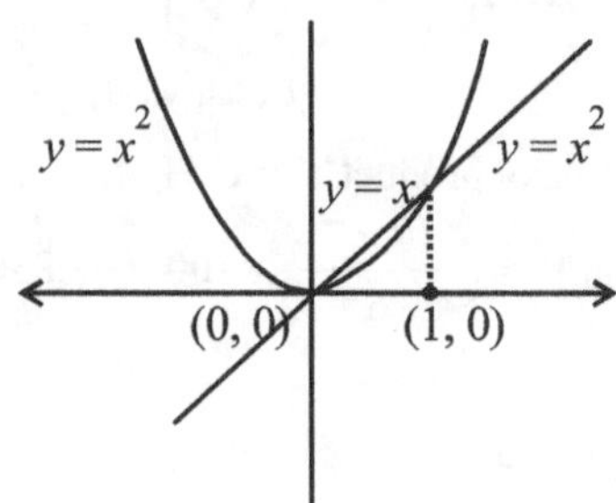

$f(x) = \max.\left\{x, x^2\right\}$

$\Rightarrow f(x) = \begin{cases} x^2, & x < 0 \\ x, & 0 \le x < 1 \\ x^2, & x \ge 1 \end{cases}$

$\therefore f(x)$ is not differentiable at $x = 0, 1$

61. **(d)** $\because A = \begin{bmatrix} \cos\theta & \sin\theta \\ -\sin\theta & \cos\theta \end{bmatrix}$

$\therefore A^n = \begin{bmatrix} \cos n\theta & \sin n\theta \\ -\sin n\theta & \cos n\theta \end{bmatrix}, \ n \in N$

$\therefore B = A + A^4$

$= \begin{bmatrix} \cos\theta & \sin\theta \\ -\sin\theta & \cos\theta \end{bmatrix} + \begin{bmatrix} \cos 4\theta & \sin 4\theta \\ -\sin 4\theta & \cos 4\theta \end{bmatrix}$

$\therefore B = \begin{bmatrix} \cos\dfrac{\pi}{5} + \cos\dfrac{4\pi}{5} & \sin\dfrac{\pi}{5} + \sin\dfrac{4\pi}{5} \\ -\sin\dfrac{\pi}{5} - \sin\dfrac{4\pi}{5} & \cos\dfrac{\pi}{5} + \cos\dfrac{4\pi}{5} \end{bmatrix}$

Then, $\det(B) = 2\sin\left(\dfrac{\pi}{5}\right) \cdot \begin{vmatrix} 0 & 1 \\ -1 & 0 \end{vmatrix}$

$= \dfrac{\sqrt{10 - 2\sqrt{5}}}{2} \approx \dfrac{2.35}{2} \approx 1.175$

$\therefore \det B \in (1, 2)$

62. **(c)**

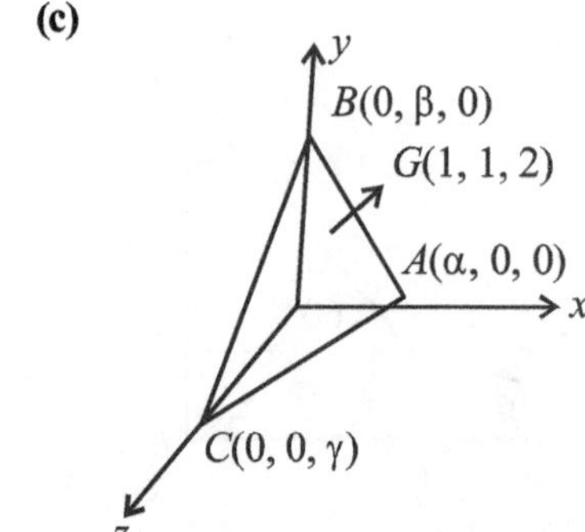

$\therefore \alpha = 3, \beta = 3$ and $\gamma = 6$ as G is centroid.

$\therefore$ The equation of plane is

$$\frac{x}{\alpha} + \frac{y}{\beta} + \frac{z}{\gamma} = 1$$

$$\Rightarrow \frac{x}{3} + \frac{y}{3} + \frac{z}{6} = 1 \Rightarrow 2x + 2y + z = 6$$

$\therefore$ The required line is, $\dfrac{x-1}{2} = \dfrac{y-1}{2} = \dfrac{z-2}{1}$

63. **(c)** Let common difference of series

$a_1, a_2, a_3, ..., a_n$ be d.

$\because a_{40} = a_1 + 39d = -159$ ...(i)

and $a_{100} = a_1 + 99d = -399$ ...(ii)

From equations (i) and (ii),

$d = -4$ and $a_1 = -3$

Since, the common difference of $b_1, b_2, ..., b_n$ is 2 more than common difference of $a_1, a_2, ..., a_n$.

$\therefore$ Common difference of $b_1, b_2, b_3, ...$ is (-2).

$\because b_{100} = a_{70}$

$\Rightarrow b_1 + 99(-2) = (-3) + 69(-4)$

$\Rightarrow b_1 = 198 - 279 \Rightarrow b_1 = -81$

64. **(c)** Normal to the ellipse $\dfrac{x^2}{a^2} + \dfrac{y^2}{b^2} = 1$ at $\left(ae, \dfrac{b^2}{a} \right)$ is

$$\frac{a^2 x}{ae} - \frac{b^2 y}{b^2/a} = a^2 - b^2$$

$$\Rightarrow x - ey = \frac{e(a^2 - b^2)}{a} \qquad ...(i)$$

$\because (0, -b)$ lies on equation (i), then

$$be = \frac{e(a^2 - b^2)}{a}$$

$$\Rightarrow ab = a^2 e^2 \Rightarrow b = ae^2 \Rightarrow \frac{b^2}{a^2} = e^4$$

$$\therefore 1 - e^2 = e^4 \Rightarrow e^4 + e^2 - 1 = 0$$

65. **(d)** $f(f(x)) = \dfrac{a - \left(\dfrac{a-x}{a+x} \right)}{a + \left(\dfrac{a-x}{a+x} \right)} = x$

$$\Rightarrow \frac{a - ax}{1 + x} = f(x) \Rightarrow \frac{a(1-x)}{1+x} = \frac{a-x}{a+x} \Rightarrow a = 1$$

$$\therefore f(x) = \frac{1-x}{1+x} \Rightarrow f\left(-\frac{1}{2}\right) = 3$$

66. **(c)** General term $= T_{r+1} = {}^{10}C_r (\sqrt{x})^{10-r} \cdot \left(-\dfrac{k}{x^2} \right)^r$

$$= {}^{10}C_r (-k)^r \cdot x^{\frac{10-r}{2} - 2r} = {}^{10}C_r (-k)^r \cdot x^{\frac{10-5r}{2}}$$

Since, it is constant term, then

$$\frac{10-5r}{2} = 0 \Rightarrow r = 2$$

$\therefore {}^{10}C_2 (-k)^2 = 405$

$$\Rightarrow k^2 = \frac{405 \times 2}{10 \times 9} = \frac{81}{9} = 9$$

$\therefore |k| = 3$

67. **(d)** Circle passes through $A(0, 1)$ and $B(2, 4)$. So its centre is the point of intersection of perpendicular bisector of AB and normal to the parabola at $(2, 4)$.

Perpendicular bisector of AB;

$$y - \frac{5}{2} = -\frac{2}{3}(x-1) \Rightarrow 4x + 6y = 19 \qquad ...(i)$$

Equation of normal to the parabola at $(2, 4)$ is,

$$y - 4 = -\frac{1}{4}(x-2) \Rightarrow x + 4y = 18 \qquad ...(ii)$$

$\therefore$ From (i) and (ii), $x = -\dfrac{16}{5}, y = \dfrac{53}{10}$

$\therefore$ Centre of the circle is $\left(-\dfrac{16}{5}, \dfrac{53}{10} \right)$

68. **(c)** Let $z = x + iy$

$\because z^2 = i|z|^2$

$\therefore x^2 - y^2 + 2ixy = i(x^2 + y^2)$

$\Rightarrow x^2 - y^2 = 0$ and $2xy = x^2 + y^2$

$\Rightarrow (x-y)(x+y) = 0$ and $(x-y)^2 = 0$

$\Rightarrow x = y$

69. **(a)** Contrapositive statement will be

"For an integer n, if n is not odd then $n^3 - 1$ is not even".

or

"For an integer n, if n is even then $n^3 - 1$ is odd".

70. **(b)** $\because P(A \cap B) = P(A) + P(B) - P(A \cup B)$

$$= 1 - 0.8 = 0.2$$

Now, $\because P(A \cup B \cup C) = P(A) + P(B) + P(C) - P(A \cap B)$

$$- P(B \cap C) - P(C \cap A) + P(A \cap B \cap C)$$

$\Rightarrow \alpha = 0.6 + 0.4 + 0.5 - 0.2 - \beta - 0.3 + 0.2$

$\Rightarrow \beta = 1.2 - \alpha$

$\because \alpha \in [0.85, 0.95]$ then $\beta \in [0.25, 0.35]$

71. **(5.00)**

$\because f(x+y) = f(x) \cdot f(y) \qquad \forall x \in R$ and $f(1) = 3$

$\Rightarrow f(x) = 3^x \Rightarrow f(i) = 3^i$

$$\Rightarrow \sum_{i=1}^{n} f(i) = 363 \Rightarrow 3 + 3^2 + 3^3 + ... + 3^n = 363$$

$$\Rightarrow \frac{3(3^n - 1)}{3 - 1} = 363 \qquad \left[\because S_n = \frac{a(r^n - 1)}{(r-1)} \right]$$

$$\Rightarrow 3^n - 1 = \frac{363 \times 2}{3} = 242$$

$$\Rightarrow 3^n = 243 = 3^5 \Rightarrow n = 5$$

72. (3.00)

For non-zero solution, $\Delta = 0$

$$\Rightarrow \begin{vmatrix} \lambda-1 & 3\lambda+1 & 2\lambda \\ \lambda-1 & 4\lambda-2 & \lambda+3 \\ 2 & 3\lambda+1 & 3(\lambda-1) \end{vmatrix} = 0$$

$$\Rightarrow 6\lambda^3 - 36\lambda^2 + 54\lambda = 0 \Rightarrow 6\lambda[\lambda^2 - 6\lambda + 9] = 0$$

$$\Rightarrow \lambda = 0,\ \lambda = 3 \qquad \text{[Distinct values]}$$

Then, the sum of distinct values of $\lambda = 0 + 3 = 3$.

73. (1.00)

$$\because |\vec{x} + \vec{y}| = |\vec{x}|$$

Squaring both sides we get

$$|\vec{x}|^2 + 2\vec{x}.\vec{y} + |\vec{y}|^2 = |\vec{x}|^2$$

$$\Rightarrow 2\vec{x}.\vec{y} + \vec{y}\cdot\vec{y} = 0 \qquad \text{...(i)}$$

Also $2\vec{x} + \lambda\vec{y}$ and $\vec{y}$ are perpendicular

$$\therefore 2\vec{x}\cdot\vec{y} + \lambda\vec{y}\cdot\vec{y} = 0 \qquad \text{...(ii)}$$

Comparing (i) and (ii), $\lambda = 1$

74. (6.00)

$$\text{Mean} = \frac{\Sigma x_i f_i}{\Sigma f_i}$$

$$= \frac{0 \cdot {}^nC_0 + 2 \cdot {}^nC_1 + 2^2 \cdot {}^nC_2 + ... + 2^n \cdot {}^nC_n}{{}^nC_0 + {}^nC_1 + ... + {}^nC_n}$$

To find sum of numerator consider

$$(1+x)^n = {}^nC_0 + {}^nC_1 x + {}^nC_2 x^2 + ... + {}^nC_n x^n \qquad \text{...(i)}$$

Put $x = 2 \Rightarrow 3^n - 1 = 2 \cdot {}^nC_1 + 2^2 \cdot {}^nC_2 + ... + 2^n \cdot {}^nC_n$

To find sum of denominator, put $x = 1$ in (i), we get

$$2^n = {}^nC_0 + {}^nC_1 + ... + {}^nC_n$$

$$\therefore \frac{3^n - 1}{2^n} = \frac{728}{2^n} \Rightarrow 3^n = 729 \Rightarrow n = 6$$

75. (120.00)

For vowels not together

Number of ways to arrange L, T, T, R $= \dfrac{4!}{2!}$

Then put both E in 5 gaps formed in ${}^5C_2$ ways.

$$\therefore \text{No. of ways} = \frac{4!}{2!} \cdot {}^5C_2 = 120$$